THE DECISIVE BATTLES OF THE WESTERN WORLD

The Decisive Battle

Major-General J.F.C. Fuller C.B., C.B.E., D.S.O.

of the Western World

and their influence upon history

Volume One

edited by John Terraine

Paladin

Granada Publishing Limited
Published in 1970 by Paladin
Frogmore, St Albans, Herts AL2 2NF
Reprinted 1972 (twice), 1975

First published in Great Britain by
Eyre & Spottiswoode (Publishers) Ltd
1954, in the complete edition
Complete edition copyright ©
J. F. C. Fuller 1954
This specially abridged and
revised edition copyright ©
Granada Publishing Limited 1970
Made and printed in Great Britain by
Compton Printing Ltd
Aylesbury, Bucks
Set in Monotype Baskerville

To Francis Neilson

Contents

Maps and Diagrams

Editor's Preface

Major-General J. F. C. Fuller, C.B., C.B.E., D.S.O. – "Boney" Fuller to all who knew him – died in 1966 at the age of 87, by which time he had become probably the most prolific soldier-writer in our language. He published his autobiography, *Memoirs Of An Unconventional Soldier,* in 1936; that was his twenty-fifth book. The final score was over forty. Much of this output was, of course, strictly professional. Fuller was a preacher; he applied his highly active mind to his soldiering; a stream of ideas poured forth, and as they did so Fuller promptly nailed them into books and articles. Inevitably, since he wrote with excitement to expound his doctrines, sparing none, much of what he wrote provoked deep opposition, particularly in military "establishment" circles. As Liddell Hart once wrote to him, "they now suffer a sort of prickly affection of the skin whenever a book of yours appears in sight."

Fuller's writing falls into two categories: professional-polemical, and historical. His reputation as a writer was first founded on the polemics – the very sharp polemics which surrounded the beginnings of armoured, mechanized warfare. He joined the newly formed Headquarters of the Tank Corps – then known as the Heavy Branch of the Machine Gun Corps – on December 26th 1916; as he wrote later, "though I did not realise it at the time, only now was my career as an unconventional soldier to begin." Repelled, like many others, by the costly static warfare of the Western Front – what he called the war of "cattle-wire and spade" – he was quick to see and develop the potentialities of the new Arm. He was able to look beyond the very limited mobility conferred by the Tanks of 1916-1918[1] to a future of fast-moving mechanized war which, he believed, would produce its results more quickly and at less human cost than the war of massed artillery and infantry masses. It is ironical that the war which, in due course, came closest to the fulfilment of Fuller's vision proved, in fact, to be much longer and vastly more destructive of human life than the one which so appalled him.

Having received his vision, Fuller evolved his message and advocated it with all the considerable power of his tongue and pen. This brought him into conflict with all in the Army that was hidebound and somnolent, and also with vested interests – the horse cavalry faction above all. For the military teacher, as for the commander, the study of past wars is a valuable exercise, but for both it can be dangerous. Fuller began by using history to fortify his arguments and illustrate his ideas. This is where the danger lies: in the case of the war in which he himself had taken part, and in which the Tanks had struggled, at times painfully, to find their role, Fuller's judgment was not at first entirely to be accepted. He made a bogy of the High Command, unnecessarily; he was never able to understand that his beloved Tanks had no stauncher supporter in that war than the Commander-in-Chief himself, Field-Marshal Sir Douglas Haig. But Fuller's analytical brain was too good to go on missing main points; if he never was able to bring himself to write kindly about Haig, Haig's strategic principles found handsome vindication in one of Fuller's profoundest treatises, *The Conduct Of War 1789-1961*, published in 1961.

Fuller's army career ended in 1933, on a sour note. He felt strongly the frustration of his attempts to instil what he considered to be the correct principles of mechanized warfare; he thought himself insulted by the offer of command of the Bombay District, and sent in his papers. His friends and brother officers who shared his forward-looking ideas deeply regretted this act, but later generations will take another view. It meant that he was able to free himself more and more for the writing of history, and more and more history itself took possession of him, rather than being a tool which he found convenient for other purposes. Few will dispute that the most magnificent flowering of this pursuit of history is *The Decisive Battles Of The Western World*. This great work, in three volumes, began to appear in 1954; Volume II emerged in 1955, and Volume III in 1956. All three went to a third impression. The complete book has now for fourteen years been a standard work of reference for military historians. It will go on being so, and nothing would be more desirable than for it to become a work of reference for historians in other fields as well. The full title is *The Decisive Battles Of The Western World And Their Influence Upon History*. It is precisely in tracing that influence that Fuller is at his most stimulating and revealing.

It has been my task here to edit Fuller's three volumes down to a more manageable two; this was not easy, because his approach to his subject was consecutive and compendious. It was difficult simply to omit sections without damaging the argument of the whole. I had to make a hard decision – to concentrate on Europe and cut out Fuller's narrative of campaigns outside Europe; no matter how important these might be (e.g. the war against Japan, 1941-1945). But in order to preserve the essential continuity, and to illustrate developments in society and war which would be essential for the understanding of later passages (e.g. the American Civil War) I have had to substitute for Fuller's detailed analyses much shorter statements of my own, in which I have at all times tried to preserve the flavour and penetration of Fuller's own material. I hope that I have succeeded; one thing I know, that merely to attempt such a task is to enlarge one's own knowledge and understanding. But Fuller always was a bracing teacher.

John Terraine

---

[1] In my book *The Western Front* I wrote:

... useful as the 1916-1918 tanks were for breaking into enemy positions and saving infantry lives, they were not weapons of exploitation such as we saw in World War 2. Their 'mobility' over rough ground was often reduced to 1 or 1½ miles per hour: the maximum speed of a Mark 4 (1917) was 3.7 m.p.h., of a Mark 5 (1918) 5 m.p.h., and of a 'Whippet' 7 m.p.h.. Partly because of this, but for other reasons too, they were extremely vulnerable....

Preface

Whether war is a necessary factor in the evolution of mankind may be disputed, but a fact which cannot be questioned is that, from the earliest records of man to the present age, war has been his dominant preoccupation. There has never been a period in human history altogether free from war, and seldom one of more than a generation which has not witnessed a major conflict: great wars flow and ebb almost as regularly as the tides.

This becomes more noticeable when a civilization ages and begins to decay, as seemingly is happening to our world-wide industrial civilization. Whereas but a generation or two back war was accepted as an instrument of policy, it has now become policy itself. Today we live in a state of "wardom" – a condition in which war dominates all other human activities. How long this tension will last, whether there is a definite answer to it, or whether it is destined blindly to work out its own end, no man can say; yet one thing is certain, and it is that the more we study the history of war, the more we shall be able to understand war itself, and, seeing that it is now the dominant factor, until we do understand it, how can we hope to regulate human affairs?

It was shortly after the first World War that I began to consider this problem, and when, in 1923, I became an instructor at the Camberley Staff College, I found that, beyond the reading up of a campaign or two, the study of the history of war was sadly neglected by the very people who should be most interested in it. As one reason for this was that there was no single book in English covering the whole subject, I decided to supply its want. In order to condense so vast a task, the method I elected was to concentrate on what I believed to be the decisive battles fought between Western peoples; next, to weave round them the wars and campaigns in which they were fought, and lastly to deduce from them their influence on history. Further, in order that the story of war might be as continuous as possible, I decided to preface each Battle Chapter with a Chronicle of preceding events, describing in it how the wars, campaigns and battles arose and how they were shaped by their political origins. Taken as a whole, the book I had in mind may be compared with the surface of a wind-swept sea: the Battle Chapters are the crests of the waves and the Chronicles the dips between them, the one linked to the other in the flow and ebb of 3,500 years of warfare.

From 1923 on I set out to collect data, and this led in 1939-40 to the publication of two volumes on Decisive Battles. But as I was far from satisfied with the book as it then stood, when shortly after the second volume appeared the whole stock was destroyed by enemy action, in no way did I regret its loss, because it presented me with the opportunity to rewrite the work. Since then I have devoted ten years to the task; have extended the book from two to three volumes; have rewritten twenty-eight of the original twenty-nine chapters; omitted one and added twenty-three new ones. Further, all the Chronicles are new, as also is the Introductory Chapter. The book is, therefore, not a revised edition, but a new work.

In the selection of my battles I have relied on my own judgement. Nevertheless, I am well aware that others could be added; but of not a few so little has been recorded as to make an extended study of them impossible, and others I have been compelled to omit if only because of linguistic difficulties.

A more complex problem has been the selection of sources. Whenever possible I have relied upon the accounts given by participants, eyewitnesses, and contemporary historians, checking them with the works of recognized modern authors. But at times I have found that war—that "impassioned drama" as Jomini calls it—is more fully and understandingly dealt with by historians of past ages, now long superseded, than by those of the present day. I think the reason for this is that, whereas in past times historians looked upon war as a natural process, today some are apt to regard it as an infernal nuisance, and therefore of secondary interest. However, my main difficulty has been to discover reliable sources for the most recent war of all—World War II—for since it ended there has been such an outpouring of undigested history larded with war propaganda, such a want of political veracity, and in certain cases, more particularly in that of Russia, such a lack of reliable information, that it is still impossible to obtain anything like a clear picture of several of the great battles fought.

Two small points remain to be mentioned. The first is that of numerical strengths of fighting forces and their battle losses. Seldom are they reliably reported, and as often as not they are twisted to fit some propaganda motive. This holds as good today as it did 3,000 years ago. Therefore I cannot vouch for the accuracy of many of the figures in this book. The other point is, that all foreign and ancient money values, when converted into pounds sterling, refer to the value of the sovereign in 1913.

Finally, my thanks are due to all those who have assisted me with advice and criticism. Among those to whom I am especially indebted are Professor David Douglas, M.A., F.B.A., Professor of History, University of Bristol; Mr. J. P. V. D. Balsdon, M.A., Fellow of Exeter College, Oxford; Professor Edouard Perroy, Professor of Mediaeval History at the Sorbonne; Mr. G. Stephenson, B.A., Oxford; The Rev. R. Trevor Davies, M.A., Lecturer in Modern History, Oxford, and my friend and publisher Mr. Douglas Jerrold, who has given me unstinting assistance over many years and whose advice has been invaluable to me. In addition, I wish to tend my grateful thanks to Mr. Anthony S. F. Rippon, who spent infinite trouble in preparing the typescript for the press. While it would be difficult to exaggerate the value of the assistance I have received from all those I have mentioned, I am alone responsible for the text as it stands and for such errors as it may contain.

Crowborough,   J. F. C. FULLER.
    September, 1953.

THE DECISIVE BATTLES OF THE
WESTERN WORLD

The rise of imperialism

The wars discussed in this book may be divided into three geographical groups: those which from the earliest times to the battle of Lepanto, in 1571, were mostly fought in the Mediterranean lands and south-western Asia; those which from then on to the battle of Waterloo were for the most part fought in the lands bordering or dependent upon the Atlantic, and those which since 1815, because of the progress of industry, science, and locomotion, have claimed increasingly the whole world for their stage.

In the first group, the supreme political event was the emergence of the Roman Empire; in the second, of the British Empire, and in the third it has still to appear. That it will run true to precedent and assume the form of yet another imperialism would seem probable. And because to-day the only two great war-powers left in the world are the United States and Russia, should, in the conflicts of to-morrow, one or the other gain supremacy, then the next empire is likely to be global. Kant suggests this in his treatise on *Perpetual Peace* (*Zum Ewigen Frieden*): wars, according to him, tend in the long run to unite the human race, because grouping lessens their incidence. It would appear that though Nature's goal is concord, her driving force is discord. Thus, the tribe, by striving to remain a tribe, through inter-tribal warfare becomes a multi-tribal community or people. Similarly, a people, striving to remain a closed community, through inter-community wars becomes a nation, and a nation, striving to remain a nation, through international wars grows into an empire. So it comes about that the unit, at any particular time, through striving to remain single, inevitably is duplicated through absorption until ultimately the biological and economic frontiers of the globe are reached.

Though warfare is primeval, as the disappearance of Mousterian man after the arrival of Aurignacian man suggests, organized warfare would seem to have been unknown before the advent of civilization, which sprang from two roots: the discovery that certain grass seeds could be cultivated and that certain grass-feeding animals could be domesticated. From these roots sprouted two very differently organized human communities, the agricultural and the pastoral. The former first arose in the Nile valley and in the "Fertile Crescent" linking Palestine to the upper Euphrates and then followed that river to the Persian Gulf; the latter is thought by some to have been located mainly in the Eurasian steppelands of the Caspian region.

In the one case the first step taken towards civilization was the appearance of the village, a fenced area protecting the tillers of the soil and their stores of food; and in the other the domestication of the horse and the invention of the wheel and wagon. Thus arose two ways of life, the settled and the wandering, and throughout history they have been in opposition.

In time, and frequently to gain security from the attacks of the wagon folk, villages grew into walled cities, each becoming a small world of its own. The wall challenged the wagon, and defence becoming the stronger form of war, the civilization of the city men soon outstripped that of the wagon folk. Not only did the wall protect the growth of civilization, but also it forced a differentiation between weapons of war and the instruments of the hunt and the field. In their turn, weapons dictated the form military organization should take, the most primitive being that of the citizen phalanx. One such, a line of men six ranks deep, is to be seen depicted on the fragment of a Sumerian monument of 2900 B.C. Each hoplite is armed with bow and spear, wears a leathern helmet, and carries a square shield which covers his entire body.

In both civilizations the fundamental causes of war were biological and economic. The more prolific the herds and flocks, the more frequently had new grass-lands to be sought for: at any moment a drought might precipitate an invasion. Similarly, the more prolific the city population, the more food was needed and the more land was necessary for its cultivation. War, accordingly, was constant in both civilizations; for stomachs, whether animal or human, dictated its necessity and *Lebensraum* (living space) became and has since remained the one great problem in the struggle for existence.[1]

Plato discusses the city's problem in his *Republic*. In a conversa-

---

[1] *Cf.* Hobbes's remark, "And when all the world is overcharged with inhabitants, then the last remedy is Warre; which provideth for every man, by Victory, or Death" (*Leviathan*, pt. II, chap. 30).

tion between Socrates and Glaucon he shows that war is endemic in civilization. Starting with the city in its simplest form, he points out that as civilization advances the call for man-power becomes greater, and that the lands which were sufficient to sustain a primitive civilization are insufficient to support an advancing one. The gist of his argument is contained in the following extract:

Socrates: "Then we must enlarge our borders; for the original healthy State is no longer sufficient . . . and there will be animals of many other kinds, if the people eat them."

Glaucon: "Certainly."

Socrates: "And the country which was enough to support the original inhabitants will be too small now, and not enough."

Glaucon: "Quite true."

Socrates: "Then a slice of our neighbour's land will be wanted by us for pasture and tillage, and they will want a slice of ours, if, like ourselves, they exceed the limit of necessity, and give themselves up to the unlimited accumulation of wealth?"

Glaucon: "That, Socrates, will be inevitable."

Socrates: "And so we shall go to war, Glaucon. Shall we not?"

Glaucon: "Most certainly. . . ."

Socrates: "Then, without determining as yet whether war does good or harm, thus much we may affirm, that now we have discovered war to be derived from causes which are also the causes of almost all the evils in States, private as well as public."

Glaucon: "Undoubtedly."[1]

The first great clash known to us between the pastoral and agricultural civilizations occurred during the third millennium B.C. From the northern grasslands of the Caspian region came a vast outpouring of a warrior people, known as the Indo-Europeans, which continued for centuries. Horde after horde moved eastward, south-eastward, westward and southward. What set these migrations in motion is not known exactly. It may have been a change of climate resulting in periods of drought, or, as some historians have suggested, the adoption of a superior breed of horse combined with the invention of the sword.

In the West, many of the nomadic bands had crossed the Danube before the year 2000 B.C. to become the ancestors of the Greeks, Romans, and other European peoples; others, called Aryans, broke into two groups about 1800 B.C., one moving south-

[1] *The Republic of Plato*, trans. B. Jowett (1888), pp. 54–55.

eastward into India and the other south-westward into the mountainous lands to the north of the "Fertile Crescent." The latter group became known as the Iranian, and its two most powerful tribes were the Medes and the Persians.

About the same time as these incursions a people, probably of Semitic origin, known as the Hyksos (princes of the desert), appeared in western Asia and overran Upper Egypt. They brought with them the horse, until then unknown to the Egyptians. Their success mainly would seem to have been due to their horse-drawn chariots and superior weapons. The first may have been adopted from the Babylonians, into whose lands the horse had been introduced from the north in about 2100 B.C.

Though Upper Egypt put up a stout resistance to the Hyksos, it was from Thebes (Karnak and Luxor) in Lower Egypt that a national revolt against them began, to end in their final expulsion by Ahmose I (1580–1557 B.C.), founder of the XVIIIth Egyptian Dynasty. The old Egyptian militia was transformed during these wars into a well-organized army of two grand divisions, one garrisoned in the delta and the other in the upper country. The soldiers were armed with bows and spears and carried shields, but wore no armour. The quiver was introduced from Asia and "fire" was by volleys. Though cavalry was not yet employed, the chariot was adopted. Thousands of horses were bred in Pharaoh's State stables and chariot-making became an art.

Ahmose died in 1541 B.C. He was succeeded by Amenhotep I, and then by Thutmose I, both warrior kings who carried war into Syria, as far north as the Euphrates; but neither attempted to organize his conquests. On the death of the latter, his elder son, also named Thutmose, reigned for a few years, and was succeeded by his half-sister Hatsheput, the first great woman in history, who would appear to have married his younger brother–yet another Thutmose–in 1501 B.C. He remained no more than her consort until her death in about 1481 B.C. Her rule was so peaceful and unmilitary that when he succeeded her as Thutmose III,[1] the king of Kadesh headed a revolt of all the city kings of Syria and Palestine against him. In answer, on about April 19, 1479, B.C., after he had assembled his army at Tharu (Kantara), Thutmose marched by way of Gaza to Yehem (Yemma), a town on the southern slopes of the Carmel range, and arrived there on May 10.

Meanwhile the forces of the city kings, under the command

[1] He dated his reign from his marriage day and not from the death of his wife.

of the king of Kadesh, had occupied the fortress of Megiddo (Armageddon) which lay on the northern slope of the Carmel

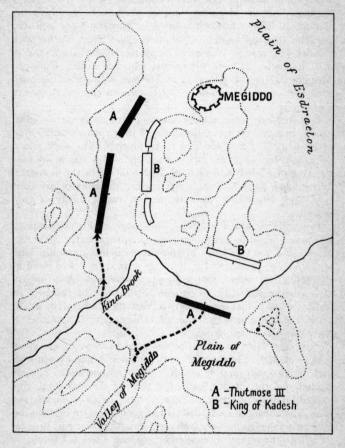

I. BATTLE OF MEGIDDO, 1479 B.C.

ridge and which blocked the main road from Egypt to the Euphrates. Moving along this road on Megiddo, on May 14 Thutmose led his army through the pass traversed by Lord Allenby

3,397 years later. He debouched on the Plain of Megiddo, south of the fortress, and the next day he advanced with his army in battle order against the king of Kadesh, whose forces were encamped outside Megiddo. With the southern horn of his army resting on a hill south of the brook of Kina, and the northern pointing toward Megiddo, Thutmose, "like Horus armed with talons", in a shining chariot of electrum, led the attack, and in one charge he scattered his enemy, who fled headlong toward Megiddo "as if terrified by spirits". The men of Kadesh abandoned their chariots of gold and silver and, finding the city gates closed to them, were hauled up its walls by the citizens.[1]

Unfortunately for Thutmose, instead of assaulting the city when all was in confusion his soldiers pillaged their enemy's camps and, in consequence, Megiddo had to be invested. The siege was a short one; but when the city was surrendered it was found that the king of Kadesh had escaped. The spoil taken was immense. It included 924 chariots, 2,238 horses, 200 suits of armour,[2] the king's household furniture, and a vast quantity of gold and silver.

Immediately after the victory, unlike any of his predecessors, Thutmose began to reorganize the reconquered territories. First, he replaced the city kings by those of their leading nobles who were likely to prove loyal to him. He gave them a free hand in governing their cities as long as they promptly paid tribute to him. Secondly, he sent their eldest sons to Egypt to be educated in loyalty to him so that when they succeeded their fathers they would prove reliable rulers. He returned to Thebes in October when these things had been done.

Two years later he set out on his second campaign. In all he undertook fifteen. In the fifth, so that he might land an army on the Syrian coast and establish a base of operations against Kadesh and the interior, he built a fleet. In the sixth he disembarked his army at Simyra, a little north of Tripoli on the Syrian coast, and advanced on Kadesh, a fortress of great strength on the left bank of the Orontes, not far from Homs. After a lengthy siege he took it. In the seventh campaign he subdued a series of revolts to his rear, and in the eighth he invaded the country of the Mitanni,

---

[1] *A History of Egypt*, W. M. Flinders Petrie (1896), vol. ii, pp. 107–109.

[2] "One excellent suit of bronze armour" and a "bronze suit of armour of the chief of Maketa [Megiddo]" are also mentioned (*ibid.*, vol. ii, p. 110). These were coats of scale armour. Soon after they were adopted by the Egyptian kings and nobles (*ibid.*, p. 146).

an Aryan people who had occupied the region within the great bend of the Euphrates. Also he took Aleppo.

His fame by now had so spread that most of the local princes brought him tribute and even distant Babylon sent him gifts, as did the great Hittite Empire, which now for the first time is mentioned in history. What is even more remarkable was that his fleet was so feared that he was able to establish naval command over the eastern Mediterranean as far as the Aegean Islands, bringing Crete and Cyprus under his sway.

In his last campaign he destroyed Kadesh, which city had once again raised a coalition against him, and with its end the last vestige of Hyksos power disappeared. Sixteen years later, in the spring of 1447 B.C. and in the fifty-fourth year of his reign, he died. He was buried in the Valley of the Kings, and his body still survives in the museum at Cairo.

Breasted writes of him:

"He was the first to build an empire in any real sense; he was the first world-hero. He made, not only a world-wide impression upon his age, but an impression of a new order. His commanding figure, towering over the trivial plots and schemes of the petty Syrian dynasts, must have clarified the atmosphere of oriental politics as a strong wind drives away miasmic vapours. The inevitable chastisement of his strong arm was held in awed remembrance by the men of Naharin [the Mitanni] for three generations. His name was one to conjure with, and centuries after his empire had crumbled to pieces it was placed on amulets as a word of power. And to-day two of this king's greatest monuments, his Heliopolitan obelisks, now rise on opposite shores of the western ocean, memorials of the world's first empire-builder."[1]

By 1400 B.C., under Amenhotep III, Egypt reached the height of her imperial power, and Pharaoh having by then become an international ruler for the first time in history the conception of a single universal world god arose. He was called Aton, and his worship was established by Amenhotep IV, who succeeded Amenhotep III in 1375 B.C.

[1] *The Cambridge Ancient History*, vol. II, p. 87. The obelisks are in London and New York. In his *A History of Israel* (vol. I, p. 4, 1945) Theodore H. Robinson said of his reign: "Modern history properly begins with the year 1479 B.C., and treats of that epoch in the story of our race which we may call territorial imperialism. For thirty-four centuries, all political ambition, whether of the individual or of the race, has aimed at geographical extension, and at the subjugation of neighbouring tribes and peoples."

Amenhotep IV hated Amon, the god of Thebes, and all the other ancient gods. He changed his name to Ikhnaton ("He-in-whom-Aton-is-satisfied"), closed the old temples, and turned out their priests.

This religious revolution shook the empire to its foundations, and in the confusion Egyptian hold of the Asiatic dominions became little more than nominal.

Ikhnaton died about 1360 B.C. and was succeeded by his son-in-law, Tutenkhaton, who, as soon as he had ascended the throne, was forced by the old priesthood to reinstate the worship of Amon and to change his name to Tutenkhamon ("Living-image-of-Amon"). On his death, probably in 1354 B.C., anarchy followed, until, in about 1350 B.C., an Egyptian named Harmhab made himself Pharaoh and the old order was restored completely. During these disturbances Palestine was overrun by nomadic tribes of the eastern desert, among which were the Hebrews, and Syria was occupied by the Hittites.

In 1315 B.C., Harmhab was succeeded by Ramses I with his son Seti I as co-partner. Thus was the XIXth Dynasty founded.

Seti reorganized the army and reconquered Palestine, but was unable to shake the power of the Hittites in Syria; Kadesh on the Orontes and all Syria north of Palestine remaining in their hands. His son, Ramses II, succeeded him in 1292 B.C. and set out to regain Kadesh. He might have equalled the exploits of Thutmose III had not two things been against him. The first was that the old national Egyptian army had given way to a mercenary one, consisting largely of Nubians and men drawn from the northern Mediterranean lands. The second was that the Hittites were armed, in part at least, with weapons of iron, whereas his soldiers were still armed with those of bronze.

In the spring of 1288 B.C. Ramses advanced on Kadesh; fell into a trap; was surrounded; cut his way out; and, while the Hittites were plundering his camp, turned the tables upon them and won a Pyrrhic victory, for Kadesh remained in their hands. This battle was the last won by the Egyptian Empire.

In his old age – he lived to be over ninety, reigning sixty-seven years – Ramses became senile, and before his death in 1225 B.C. the Libyans and their allies invaded the western Egyptian desert and extended their settlements to the walls of Memphis (12 miles south of Cairo). With him the empire ended, and until the rise of Assyria, three centuries later, Egypt was hard put to it to protect her frontiers, north, south, and west.

Though the Assyrians first appear in 3000 B.C., when as a wandering Semitic tribe they settled at Assur on the upper Tigris and there founded a small city kingdom, it was not until the tenth century B.C. that their star began to rise in the western Asiatic firmament. A century later, under Ashur-nasirpal II (884–859 B.C.), they set out on their imperial way and created a vast empire which, in the days of Shalmaneser V (727–722 B.C.) and Sargon II (722–705 B.C.), reached the border of Egypt.

The Assyrians were essentially a warrior people, for their army was the State. It was a highly disciplined and organized force, and for its age superbly armed. Already, in the tenth century B.C., it is known to have employed powerful battering rams, an essential in city warfare. These instruments were mounted in wooden towers, roofed and shielded in front with metal plates, and moved on six wheels. Under the roof was a platform for archers to pick off the defenders on the walls. Through contact with the Hittites iron weapons had been introduced.[1]

The army was composed of archers supported by spearmen and shield bearers, and the mobile arm was the chariot. But its main weapon was "terror". Cities were stormed, sacked and systematically demolished, and prisoners were often impaled or flayed alive.

Under Sennacherib (705–681 B.C.), Tarsus was plundered and Babylon obliterated; and his successor, Esarhaddon (681–669 B.C.), conquered Egypt from the delta to Thebes, sacking and burning its cities in 671 B.C. This conquest, when added to the lands already won, made the Assyrian Empire the most extensive yet seen in the world. But in her effort to establish universal dominion Assyria overreached herself. Her destructive wars obliterated the wealth of the countries she won and led to their constant revolt, so making necessary an immense network of garrisons. In the end her imperial commitments exceeded her power to hold them.

Meanwhile the nomads were on the move again. Aramean hordes drifted in from the desert; from the head of the Persian Gulf came the Kaldi, or Chaldeans, and from the northern moun-

[1] "The Assyrian forces", writes Breasted, "were . . . *the first large armies equipped with weapons of iron*. A single arsenal room of Sargon's palace was found to contain two hundred tons of iron implements. To a certain extent the rise and power of the Assyrian Empire were among the results of the incoming of iron" (*The Conquest of Civilization*, 1926, p. 173).

tains hordes of Indo-European peoples, led by Medes and Persians, swept down on the Assyrian homelands.

Egypt was then abandoned, but Pharaoh Psamalik I (Psammetichus), who feared an invasion by the northern barbarians, came to terms with Assyria and sent out an army to support her tottering empire. Its fall was imminent. In 614 B.C. the Medes, under Cyaxares, took Assur, and the Chaldeans, under Nabopolasser (625–604 B.C.), having conquered the Babylonians, linked up with them, and in 612 B.C. the two together stormed Nineveh and utterly destroyed it.

"Thy shepherds slumber, O King of Assyria; thy nobles shall dwell in the dust; thy people is scattered upon the mountains, and no man gathereth them.

There is no healing of thy bruise; thy wound is grievous; all that hear the bruit of thee shall clap the hands over thee; for upon whom hath not thy wickedness passed continually?"[1]

Seven years later, the Chaldeans, under Nabopolasser's son, Nebuchadrezzar II (604–562 B.C.), who had rebuilt Babylon, met the army of Necho, King of Egypt, at Carchemish on the Euphrates, and routed it.

"They did cry there, Pharaoh king of Egypt is but a noise; he had passed the time appointed."[2]

Later, Nebuchadrezzar, the greatest of the Chaldean kings, overran Judea. In 586 B.C. he stormed Jerusalem, carried the Jews into captivity, and then advanced to the threshold of Egypt.

Though the fall of Assyria was swift and dramatic, once again the rule of a single sovereign had been enforced on a great group of peoples. In spite of Assyrian destructiveness, this gave increasing strength to the idea of a universal monarchy and no sooner had the empire of Assyria vanished than another people was ready to take up the task; this time neither African nor Semitic, but Indo-European—the Persians.

It is now necessary to leave Asia for Europe to trace events in the south-eastern corner of that continent during the centuries which followed the arrival of the Indo-Europeans; for it was their descendants who were destined to halt and to ruin the third attempt to create a universal empire.

At what date the first Greek tribes percolated into Greece is unknown. Professor Bury suggests that by 2000 B.C. "Zeus, the great Indo-European lord of Heaven, was probably invoked

---

[1] Nahum iii. 18, 19.   [2] Jeremiah xlvi. 17.

throughout the length and breadth of the land".[1] Gradually their van, a people known as the Achaeans,[2] moved southwards into the Peloponnese, to overwhelm and mingle with its highly civilized Aegean dwellers. Later came a second wave of people, called the Dorians, who reached the Peloponnese by 1500 B.C. and subdued the Achaeans. Next, the Dorians took to the sea and conquered Crete and the Aegean Islands, and by 1325 B.C. we find Eteokles, who called himself an Aeolian, so firmly established on the western coast of Asia Minor that he entered into friendly relations with the Hittite Emperor, whose chief city was Hatti (Boghaz Keui) to the east of the river Halys (Kizil Irmak). Two generations later these relations were broken by yet another series of migrations of Indo-European peoples, the Phrygians from Thessaly and the Armenians from the region of Lake Van, who overwhelmed the Hittite Empire which, by 1200 B.C., disappears. A band of Phrygians also occupied the ancient mound of Hissarlik on the eastern side of the Dardanelles, and there built Troy, which in 1184 B.C., after a nine-year siege, fell to the Achaeans under Agamemnon, king of Argos. By the year 1000 B.C. the Greeks had gained possession of the entire Greek peninsula and of the whole of the Aegean coast of Asia Minor; the Dorians occupying the south, the Ionians the centre, and the Aeolians the north.

Between 1200 and 1000 B.C. the whole western world was in turmoil. Hordes, tribes, and peoples were moving in all directions to conquer or to escape conquest. Waves of fleeing Aegeans broke on the Syrian coast and swamped the Egyptian delta. Some, called Philistines, established themselves in Palestine, giving to that country their name. This period of chaos coincided with the introduction of iron weapons, and possibly also of the horse as a cavalry charger and not merely as a draught animal.

Those who settled in the conquered lands built villages in the form of groups of family hutments, which grew into cities. The peculiar topography of Greece, a small country split by numerous mountain ranges and possessing few land communications, led to the creation of separate city states, each becoming the only nation the Greeks ever knew. Each was a sovereign power, having its own king, its own laws, gods, and field lands. Within the city amity was the governing principle; without its walls, it was enmity.

[1] *A History of Greece*, J. B. Bury (1916), p. 6. In the 1951 edition, revised by Russell Meiggs, is substituted: "At some time near 2000 B.C. there are signs of a new people entering Greece. A new style of pottery . . . is introduced. . . ." (!)
[2] The common designation for Greeks in Hittite and Egyptian texts and in Homer.

Thus in Greece itself and along the coast and in the islands of the Aegean, hundreds of city states arose: self-interested communities and jealous of each other, they were constantly at war. Frequently, when the cities became overcrowded, they threw off colonies, and it was the shortage of good agricultural land more than the desire to conquer and plunder that made of the Greeks the greatest colonizing people in classical history.

In 750 B.C. the first Greek colonies appeared in the central Mediterranean, where the Phoenicians were already established. There were three main groups: the Euboean in Sicily and Italy; the Achaean in southern Italy, which was called "Great Greece"; and the Dorian in Sicily, of which the most important was Syracuse. Others were established in Cyprus, Lydia, southern Gaul, and eastern Spain, and soon the coasts of the Black Sea were girdled with them. This extraordinary expansion, which lasted until the middle of the sixth century B.C., would have made Greece the first great maritime empire in the world had the Greeks been a united nation under a single ruler. As it was, their colonies, well over a hundred in all, were no more than duplications of their city states, the existence of which depended on their military strength.

In the early days of the city kings, battles were little more than duels between selected heroes, as depicted by Homer, in which valour was the supreme virtue, valour and virtue being expressed by the same word. It is out of valour that European history rises; the spear and sword, and not, as in Asia, the bow and arrow, are its symbols. The bravest and not the most crafty are the leaders of men, and it is their example rather than their skill which dominates battle. Fighting is a contest between man and man more than between brain and brain. The spearman Achilles, and not Paris the archer, is the typical hero. Psychologically the *arme blanche* dominates the missile.

Later, as had happened in Egypt and Asia, the phalanx appeared, Sparta being the first fully to develop it. With its appearance, largely due to the progress in working metals and the consequent fall in the cost of armour, the nobles, hitherto the warriors of the city, gradually were ousted by the people. With armour at a reasonable price, each well-to-do citizen could provide himself with a complete panoply, comprising a metal helmet, breast-plate, greaves and thigh-pieces, a round shield, spear, and heavy two-edged sword – the bow was seldom carried. This transformation was both levelling and democratic because it placed the noble and the ordinary citizen on a footing of equality in the field. "It is significant", writes Bury, "that in Thessaly, where the system of hoplites was not introduced and cavalry was always the kernel of the army, democratic ideas never made way. . . ."[1] Wherever they did, the development was one which was to become normal throughout history.

Incapable of ruling themselves, the people became easy prey to those who were capable of leading them and it frequently came about that a leader of an aristocratic faction would place himself at the head of the dissatisfied citizens, and having expelled his rivals by their aid would make himself sole ruler of the city. Such rulers were called "tyrants", a "tyranny" being an office and not a term of abuse.

By 650 B.C. tyrants began to appear in Greece and soon became so numerous that the following hundred and fifty years has been called the "Age of the Tyrants". They flourished in the Ionian cities and islands, in Corinth, Sicily, Euboea and Athens, but not in Sparta, where, to avert a tyranny, a dual monarchy was established, one king acting as a check to the other. The Spartans feared the growth of the tyrannies, and in the last half of the sixth century B.C. they established the Peloponnesian League. It was a loose alliance of the Peloponnesian states under the leadership of Sparta, coupled with the autonomy and territorial integrity of the members of the league: a kind of Monroe Doctrine. Although the members were free to fight each other, should anyone be attacked by a non-member all were bound to coalesce against him. By the end of the sixth century B.C. the league included the whole of the Peloponnese, except Argos and Achaea. Of all organizations it was the most permanent in Greek politics.

When the Peloponnesian League was being formed, an event occurred in Asia which in the years to come was destined to endow the league with a significance of overwhelming importance. The prelude to this event was as follows:

When Nebuchadrezzar was conquering Judea, Cyaxares, king of Media (634–594 B.C.), his recent ally, overran the lands east of the Halys. This conquest brought Media into contact with Lydia, and a war between the two countries followed. It was an inconclusive affair and ended in a peace cemented by the marriage of the daughter of Alyattes, king of Lydia (617–560 B.C.), and Astyages, the son of Cyaxares.

[1] *A History of Greece*, J. B. Bury (1951 edit.), p. 129.

Alyattes's eastern frontier was now secure and he determined to push his western frontier to the Aegean. To do this he set out to conquer Miletus (Palatia), the most important city of the Ionian Confederacy. A long indecisive war followed which was only brought to a successful issue by his son Croesus (560–546 B.C.), who reduced all the Ionian and Aeolian cities and compelled the Dorian cities to become subject to him. Next Croesus conceived the idea of raising a fleet to conquer the Aegean Islands. Then the above-mentioned event occurred—his brother-in-law, Astyages (594–549 B.C.), was hurled suddenly from his throne by an obscure Persian prince called Kurush, the Cyrus of the Greeks.

Cyrus was Prince of Anshan, a country subject to Media. About 552 B.C. he revolted against Medish rule. His soldiers were hardy peasants and expert archers, and it would appear that he was the first great captain to possess a body of really efficient cavalry. Within three years of the start of his revolt the whole of Media was his; a success largely due to the troops of Astyages changing sides.

This event alarmed Croesus. Because he feared that Cyrus would next cross the Halys he abandoned his Aegean project and went into alliance with Egypt, Babylonia (Chaldea), and the Spartans, to check the new conqueror. He crossed the Halys in 547 B.C., near Pteria (site unknown), and fought an indecisive battle with the Persians; after which, as winter was near, he retired to his capital, Sardes (Sart), and sent envoys to his allies to ask them to be prepared to carry out a combined advance against the Persians the following spring.

No sooner had Croesus retired than Cyrus, bent upon making the most of his interior position, advanced across the Halys and defeated the Lydian army in a great battle outside Sardes. Next, he took Sardes and made Croesus his prisoner. Leaving his general, Harpagus, to reduce the Greek coastal cities, which, because of their disunity, he did easily, Cyrus established himself in Lydia, then, in 540 B.C., marched eastward and defeated the Babylonian army under Belshazzar at Opis (near Ctesiphon). Two years later he took Babylon, the fall of which is poetically referred to by the prophet Daniel in his fifth chapter.

The surrender of Babylon brought with it the submission of all the countries from northern Syria to the borders of Egypt. Cyrus left his son Cambyses to prepare an invasion of Egypt, and organized his conquests, taking the title of "King of Babel, Sumer and Akkad, and the four quarters of the world." Thus he claimed dominion over all the lands of the East—Hyrcania, Parthia, Bactriana and Sogdiana—which had formed part of the Median Empire. Of the campaigns which followed in these countries and beyond them nothing is known, except that in his last one Cyrus was warring against the Massagetae, a Scythian people in the region of Lake Aral. During this campaign he was either killed in battle or died in 528 B.C. His body was taken to Pasargadae (Murghab) and buried there.

Three years after his death, Cambyses (528–522 B.C.) invaded Egypt, and won so decisive a victory at Pelusium (at the eastern mouth of the Nile) that Egyptian resistance virtually collapsed. Next, he set out up the Nile to conquer Ethiopia, but because of the difficulty of supplying his army, he abandoned the project. Meanwhile the Greek colony of Cyrene submitted to him, and he was declared king of Egypt.

When he died in 522 B.C., the Persian Empire stretched from the borders of India to the Aegean, from the Black Sea to Nubia, and from the Caspian Sea to the Indian Ocean. Four great kingdoms had disappeared—Media, Babylonia (Chaldea), Lydia and Egypt. Such were the fruits of thirty warring years.

The heir to this vast and as yet undigested conglomeration of kingdoms was Hystaspes, satrap of Parthia, but as he made no attempt to secure the succession the throne was seized by a pretender who posed as the dead brother of Cambyses. His reign was a brief one: soon after his usurpation, Darius (521–483 B.C.), son of Hystaspes, killed him and assumed the sovereignty.

The first years of his reign were spent in quelling widespread rebellion, and once order was reinstated he began organizing his empire. First, he divided the whole realm into twenty satrapies, placing over each a governor, who was a true civil servant and not, as hitherto, a mere tax collector. Next, he raised a powerful Phoenician fleet to command the eastern Mediterranean and built a network of roads linking the satrapies with his capital Susa (Suster, Biblical Shushan). Posting-stations and inns were established every four parasangs (about 14 miles), making possible so rapid a postal service that a royal messenger took less than a week to travel by relays from Sardes to Susa, a distance of some 1,600 miles. Also he reopened the Suez Canal, which existed in the days of Seti I, and explored the Indian Ocean.

Darius placed the army on a divisional basis. Each division was

10,000 men strong and consisted of ten battalions of ten companies each, and each company of ten sections. His royal bodyguard, known as the "Immortals", also 10,000 strong, was exclusively Persian, as was his cavalry. Nearly all superior officers and garrison commanders were either Persians or Medes. His army in this way closely resembled the recent British Indian Army. Taken as a whole, Breasted speaks of Darius's imperial organization as "one of the most remarkable achievements in the history of the ancient Orient, if not of the world",[1] and Robinson states that "it proved to be the model for all latter empires",[2] and in particular the Roman.

With his empire secure from internal disturbances, Darius's next problem was to secure it against dangers from without–that is, to provide it with secure frontiers. Of these, the two more important lay in diametrically opposite directions–in the east and in the west. To establish the first, in a series of campaigns he pushed the eastern frontier beyond the Indus, so that that great river and the mountains to the west of it together would form a moated wall against invasion. The second problem was more complex. With the exception of the gap between the Caspian and the Hindu Kush, the weakest section of the Persian frontiers lay along the shores of the Aegean and the Propontis (Sea of Marmara). The reason for this was that the peoples on each side of these narrow seas were of kindred race, and in times of trouble were always liable to support each other. The only practical solution was to establish an ethnic frontier by pushing the western frontier westward until it included all the Greeks. This idea, it would seem, led him to the Danube in or about 512 B.C.

He assembled a fleet of possibly 200 to 300 ships and an army 70,000 strong,[3] bridged the Bosphorus in the vicinity of Chalcedon (Kadikoy), and having crossed his army over reached the Danube while his fleet, sailing up the mouth of that river, threw a bridge of boats over it near Galatz or Braila. Next, he pushed on north of the Danube, possibly to reconnoitre the country and to impress the Scythians with his power. How far he advanced is not known; but the Scythians, wasting the land, compelled him to turn back, and as he did so they attacked his rearguard and captured his baggage train.

[1] *The Conquest of Civilization*, p. 199.
[2] *A History of Israel*, vol. i, p. 5.
[3] These are the figures given in *The Cambridge Ancient History*, vol. iv, p. 212. Those of Herodotus are 600 and 700,000–800,000 respectively.

The Asiatic Greek detachment he had left behind to guard the boat bridge was incited by Miltiades, tyrant of the Thracian Chersonese (Gallipoli peninsula), to break it and thereby to cut off Darius from his base; but Histiaeus, tyrant of Miletus, persuaded the Greeks not to do so, for should Darius meet with a catastrophe the chances were that the Ionian cities would revolt, expel their tyrants, and become democracies. Darius crossed the bridge and withdrew to Sardes, leaving behind him his lieutenant, Megabazus, and a powerful army to reduce Thrace. This Megabazus successfully did from the sea of Marmara to the river Strymon (Struma), and though he failed to reduce Macedonia, Alexander, its king, acknowledged allegiance to Darius.

Thus opened the two hundred years' struggle between Greece and Persia, and though it was between two Aryan peoples it is the first recorded contest between Europe and Asia—the West and the East—a struggle which stands apart from the innumerable internal wars between European peoples and nations and which from that day to this has constituted the major war problem of Europe as a whole.

While the above events were taking place, equally important ones were perplexing the Greeks. In the year in which Cyrus died in distant Sogdiana, in Athens, Peisistratus, tyrant of that city, also died and was succeeded by his two sons, Hippias and Hipparchus. The latter was murdered in 514 B.C., and four years later the former made himself so unpopular that the people, helped by a body of troops under Cleomenes (540–491 B.C.) king of Sparta, expelled him and he fled to the court of Darius to seek assistance. To pay Sparta for their deliverance the Athenians were compelled to enter the Peloponnesian League and Sparta so acquired a certain right to interfere in Athenian affairs.

Freed of their tyrants, the Athenians, under Cleisthenes, a noble friendly to the people, established a democracy; but no sooner had Cleisthenes gained power than Isagoras, another noble and his rival, appealed to Cleomenes to eject him. Again the Spartan king entered Athens; but the people rose against him and he and his small army, and Isagoras, were blockaded in the Acropolis and forced to capitulate—a disgrace no king of Sparta had suffered hitherto.

Again in power, Cleisthenes set about reforming the Athenian state, and one of the first laws he introduced was that of ostracism, by which any prominent citizen considered dangerous to the state could by popular vote be banished for ten years. Next, he re-organized the army, basing it on the ten artificial Athenian tribes he had created. Each tribe was called upon to raise a *taxis*, or regiment, of hoplites, and a squadron of cavalry. Each *taxis* was commanded by a *strategos* (later a *taxiarch*) or general, and the whole was commanded by a titular commander-in-chief, the *pole-march*.

Because he feared that Cleomenes would again invade Attica to wipe out his disgrace, Cleisthenes appealed to Darius for aid; but when Cleomenes's first coalition against Athens foundered he changed his mind. A year or two later Cleomenes formed another coalition to crush Attica, but again quarrels between his allies brought it to nought. At length, realizing that to accomplish his end it was as useless to depend on allies as it was to attempt to extend Spartan hegemony to Greece north of the Isthmus of Corinth so long as he was not master of the Peloponnese, he de-cided that the first step must be the destruction of the power of Argos, the most powerful Peloponnesian state not yet in the League. The upshot was that in about 494 B.C. he invaded Argos and at Sepeia (near the hill of Tiryns) routed the Argive army. Though this decisive victory opened Argos to assault he refrained from taking the city, probably because the destruction of Argos would have been detrimental morally to Sparta's ascendancy in the eyes of the Greeks. The effects of the victory were immediate; opposition to Sparta within the Peloponnesian League ceased, and soon after Athens virtually conceded to Sparta political leadership in the Greek world.

Five years before this momentous victory was won, a conflict of nations began which went further than any other classical war to determine the history of Europe: it was the Ionic Revolt, the origins of which were as follows:

In 499 B.C. Miletus was governed by Aristagoras, son-in-law of Darius, whose ambition was to bring the Cyclades under his sway. Because he did not possess a strong enough fleet he applied to Artaphernes, Satrap of Sardes and brother-in-law of Darius, for assistance. Artaphernes obtained the king's authority and sent him 200 ships under the command of Megabates. Soon after their arrival Megabates and Aristagoras quarrelled, and the former, to score off the latter, informed the Naxians of their approaching danger. The result was that the expedition failed. Aristagoras, fearing disgrace, and knowing that the Ionian cities were eager to throw out their tyrants, resolved to retrieve his fortunes by precipitating a general rebellion.

First he went to Greece to seek aid from Sparta; but as the Spartans refused he went to Athens and Eretria (Aletria), obtaining twenty ships from the former and five from the latter. Had support been more generous the revolt might have succeeded and the whole course of history changed.

With these paltry reinforcements, which were to lead to prodigious consequences, Aristagoras returned to Miletus, and in the spring of 498 B.C. he marched on Sardes which, except for the citadel, he occupied. This success was short-lived, for soon after he was routed by a Persian army in the vicinity of Ephesus and the Athenian and Eretrian contingents returned home.

The capture of Sardes was followed by a general rising of the cities, the rebellion rapidly sweeping southward to Caria and Cyprus and northward to the Propontis. City after city threw off the Persian yoke; then, one by one, they were retaken and subdued. Aristagoras lost heart and fled to Thrace where he met his death.

The main event of the war was the siege of Miletus, headquarters of the rebellion. The Persians invested it on its landward side and blockaded it with 600 ships. The Greeks, who had 353 ships, sallied forth to break the blockade and off the island of Lade were beaten decisively. This disaster sealed the fate of Miletus and with it that of the rebellion.

Immediately after this disaster the Phoenician fleet entered the Hellespont and retook all the towns on the Thracian coast to as far north as Byzantium (Constantinople). Miltiades, tyrant of the Chersonese, then fled from Cardia to Athens, where his arrival precipitated a political crisis. By birth an Athenian, and violently hostile to Persia and the Peisistratids—who had put his father Cimon to death—he was the very man the aristocratic anti-Persian opposition needed to lead them against the democrats under Cleisthenes who, as we have seen, was one of the first to medize. The outcome was that Miltiades was chosen general of his tribe.

Now that the Hellespont was again in Persian hands, Hippias, the banished Athenian tyrant, who was still at the Persian court, urged Darius to move on Athens and to reinstate him. His appeal was heard because now that the Ionian revolt had collapsed it would appear that Darius was as eager as ever to establish his ethnic western frontier, and in Hippias he saw a tool which would help him to do so. He determined, directly he had reorganized Asiatic Greece, to reconquer Thrace and Macedonia, which had been lost during the rebellion, and to restore Hippias to his tyranny as his vassal, after which Sparta and the rest of Greece could be swallowed piecemeal. His goal then was the occupation of Athens, which, when occupied, would isolate Sparta.

In 492 B.C., Mardonius, the king's son-in-law, was sent with an army to Thrace. He reduced Thrace, compelled Alexander, king of Macedonia, again to submit to Persia, and was on the point of advancing into Greece when most of his fleet was wrecked in a storm off Mount Athos and he was compelled to return to Asia. This set-back in no way affected Darius's decision, for at once he ordered another expedition, this time to proceed across the Aegean, but not by the land route, and as Mardonius had been disabled by a wound its command was given to Artaphernes, son of the satrap of Sardes, and Datis, a Median admiral. What its strength was is not known; perhaps 25,000 infantry and 1,000 cavalry.[1] As the entire force was moved by sea, it could not have been much larger.

What was the Persian plan of campaign? Here we must rely on conjecture, based on what happened and not on what was proposed, because the account set down by Herodotus is devoid of any clear strategical idea. Following Munro's speculations,[2] which in part are adopted by Grundy,[3] it was as follows, and it in no way contradicts what Herodotus says:

Through Hippias, Darius learnt that the Alcemaeonidae[4] in Athens were violently opposed to Miltiades, and were now willing to reinstate him. Further, to obtain a pardon for the part Athens had played in the Ionian revolt, they were prepared to toe the Persian line. In other words, there existed in Athens what to-day would be called a powerful "fifth column" which favoured Persia. If the Athenian army could be lured away from Athens, and simultaneously a Persian force landed at Phalerum (Phaleron) to support the Alcemaeonidae, Athens could be carried by revolt instead of by battle. How to reinforce the morale of the con-

---

[1] *The Cambridge Ancient History*, vol. IV, p. 234.
[2] "The Campaign of Marathon", J. Arthur R. Munro, *The Journal of Hellenic Studies*, vol. XIX (1899), pp. 185–197.
[3] *The Great Persian War*, G. B. Grundy (1901), pp. 171–172.
[4] A noble Athenian family which played a leading part in Attic politics in the seventh, sixth, and fifth centuries B.C.

spirators in Athens, and how to entice from Athens the Athenian army, which kept them in check, were the two main problems the plan had to solve.

The solution of the former was sought in first subduing Eretria – which could offer little resistance–because its reduction would strike terror into the Athenians and drive them into the con-spirators' arms. The solution of the latter problem was to land an army in the Bay of Marathon–25 miles north-east of Athens–and by threatening a land advance on Athens to draw the Athenian army out of the city.

In late August or early September, 491 B.C.,[1] all was ready to carry out this astute plan, and the Persian transports under escort of the fleet sailed from Samos to Naxos, and after operating in the Cyclides, reached Carystus (Karysto) on the south coast of Euboea (Negropont). From there the expedition sailed up the Euboean channel to Eretria, when the Persian aim became apparent to the Greeks. Determined to resist attack, the Eretrians sent an urgent message to Athens for help. Agreeing, but also realizing that single-handed they were not strong enough, the Athenians immediately sent a courier, Pheilippides, to solicit the support of the Spartans, and presumably, another messenger to the Plataeans. Pheilippides covered a hundred and fifty miles in forty-eight hours and arrived at Sparta on September 9. As Athens was a member of the League the Spartans at once promised aid, but pointed out that as the Carneian festival forbade them going to war until after the full moon on the night of September 19-20, they could not move until then.

Artaphernes, with part of the Persian army, laid siege to Eretria, and Datis, with the remainder, crossed the Euboean channel and landed in the bay of Marathon. Simultaneously the Athenian army, 9,000 to 10,000 strong, marched north from Athens under the command of Callimachus, the *polemarch*, accompanied by his ten tribal generals, among whom was Miltiades. They had not gone far when, hearing that the Persians had landed in the Bay of Marathon (Marathona), Callimachus wheeled to the right and gained the valley of Avlona where he encamped the army at the shrine of Heracles. There he was joined by 1,000 Plataeans.

When the Athenians arrived at the shrine of Heracles–some-where to the north of Vrana–presumably the Persian fleet was

---

[1] The traditional date is 490. The date 491 was maintained by J. A. R. Munro. The argument for the correction is strong, but has not been universally accepted.

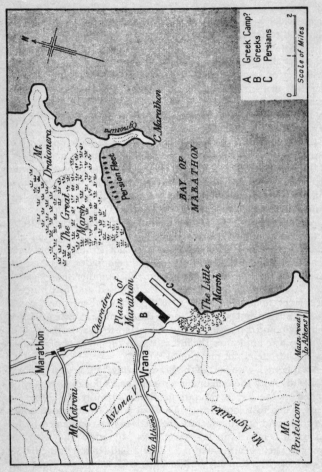

2. BATTLE OF MARATHON, 491 B.C.

Greek Camp?
Greeks
Persians

A
B
C

Scale of Miles
0   1   2

Mt. Drakonera

C. Marathon

The Great Marsh

Persian Fleet

BAY OF MARATHON

Plain of Marathon

Charadra

The Little Marsh

Marathon

Mt. Kotroni

Vrana

Avlona V.

To Athens

Main road to Athens

Mt. Agrieliki

Mt. Pentelicon

at anchor on the western side of the promontory of Cynosura, and the army[1] was ashore, encamped under cover of the Great Marsh which flanked this section of the coast. To the south of it lay the Plain of Marathon, cut into two by a small river, Charadra,[2] and south of the plain was a stretch of swampy ground, known as the Little Marsh, lying between the coast and the foothills of Mount Agrieliki.

The position the Athenians had occupied was virtually un-attackable, and it must have been clear to them that because the Persians had not seized the passes leading from the plain towards Athens—namely, by way of the Little Marsh and the valleys of the Charadra and Avlona—they did not intend to make an overland advance on Athens. Their sole risk in not attacking the Persians was that while Athens lay undefended, treachery might work its will within the city. Otherwise there was every reason for them to delay an attack until the Spartans arrived after the full moon. The issue was that for eight days the opposing armies peacefully confronted each other, and it was not until the ninth day, when the fall of Eretria through treachery became known to the Athenians, that it was imperative for Callimachus and his generals to arrive at a decision. Clearly the reason was that as Artaphernes was now free to move, and were he to do so under cover of Datis's holding operation, he might slip round by sea to Athens. A council of war was assembled at which Miltiades pressed for an immediate attack. Because five generals were against him and four for him, he appealed to Callimachus, who gave him his vote and settled the question: attack it was to be. But no action was taken until it became known that Artaphernes was embarking his troops, and as it happened, the receipt of this information coincided with Miltiades's turn to assume tactical command of the army.[3]

It was probably on September 21 that Miltiades, the general of the day, drew up the Athenian army in order of battle, and it would seem that he must have marched his 10,000 or 11,000 men in two parallel columns, each about half a mile in length, and

[1] Possibly 15,000 strong (*The Cambridge Ancient History*, vol. IV, p. 243).
[2] The word means "torrent" or "stream".
[3] The whole question of command is obscure. The *polemarch* was titular commander-in-chief and the ten generals were his council. Tactics in the fifth century B.C. consisted in little more than drawing up the order of battle. From Herodotus it would appear that each general had the honour of doing so in turn. This in no way infringed the authority of the *polemarch* because it was no more than a question of drill which any general could carry out. It was as if to-day a colonel had ten sergeant-majors and employed them in rotation.

then, on entering the plain of Marathon, to have wheeled them outwards into line. The Persians, seeing this, immediately deployed their army between the right bank of the Charadra and the Little Marsh so that their front must have been parallel to the shore. The interval between the two armies is stated to have been less than eight stades, or slightly less than a mile.[1] Next, to prevent the Persian front overlapping the Greek, Callimachus, or Miltiades, reduced the Greek centre to possibly four ranks, maintaining eight on the flanks.[2] The right wing of the Greeks – the post of honour – was led by Callimachus; the Plataeans were on the left, and Miltiades, presumably, was at the head of his tribal regiment. Among those present was Aeschylus, the tragic poet.

Tactically Callimachus and Miltiades were faced by a difficult problem. It was that the bulk of the Persian infantry consisted of archers. At close quarters, the two generals could rely on their armoured hoplites breaking the Persian front; but the assault would have to be rapid directly arrow range was reached. Once the "beaten zone" was entered – that is, 200 yards in front of the Persian archers – the assault would have to be carried out at the double. For a mile long phalanx to maintain its dressing at this pace was impossible; disorder had to be risked.

As soon as battle order was formed and the sacrifices proved propitious, the advance in slow time began, to be followed by the double as the "beaten zone" was approached. Though what now happened is conjectural, it is common sense. It would be normal in the advance of a long line under frontal fire for the wings to sweep forward faster than the centre. This must have happened, with the result that the Greek front became concave, and as the centre was, presumably, four ranks deep, and the wings in eight ranks, gaps began to appear in the former through which the Persians broke, driving the centre back in rout. The Greek retreat in the centre, besides drawing the Persian front into a convex line, drew the Greek wings inwards and thereby reduced the original length of the front. This reduction automatically led to an inward wheel of the Greek wings against the flanks of the Persian line. The result was a double envelopment, very similar to that intentionally effected by Hannibal three hundred years later at Cannae, and the battle ended when the whole Persian army, crowded into confusion, in panic broke back to the ships and was pursued by the Greeks. A fight then took place on the

[1] *History of Herodotus*, trans. George Rawlinson (1880), VI, 112.   [2] *Ibid.*, VI, 102.

shore, but Datis, at a loss of seven ships and 6,400 killed,[1] escaped.

Only 192 Athenians fell, we are told. These included the gallant *polemarch*, Callimachus, one other general, and Cynegirus, the brother of Aeschylus. The losses of the Plataeans are not recorded. The dead were buried under a mound which still marks the site of the battlefield.

When Datis hastily embarked the remnants of his army, Artaphernes must have been at sea, and his van may well have been passing the headland of Cynosura. At this juncture, a signal was flashed from a shield by someone on Mount Pentelicon.[2] Who held the shield and what the signal conveyed are unknown; but the later day explanation is that it was an invitation to the Persians to sail straight for Athens to support the conspirators.[3]

For the Greeks there was not a moment to lose. As soon as Datis had put to sea they marched for Athens, arriving there in time to prevent Artaphernes securing a footing at Phalerum. Artaphernes saw that his chance had gone, set about his fleet, and steered for Asia. That same evening the Spartan van entered Attica, and learning that the battle had been fought and won, marched on to Marathon to view the Persian dead.

Marathon was a remarkable battle, both from the point of view of Persian strategy, which was admirable, and of Grecian tactics, which were no less so. Though it wrecked Darius's punitive expedition it was in no sense a decisive victory. It did not end the contest for supremacy between Greek and Persian; rather it prepared the way for the conflict which was to do so. "It was", Munro writes, "a brilliant prologue to a grand drama."[4] For the first time in their history the Greeks had beaten the Persians on their own element, the land, and Marathon endowed the victors with a faith in their destiny which was to endure for three centuries, during which western culture was born. Marathon was the birth cry of Europe.

---

[1] Herodotus, VI, 117.　　　　　　　　　　[2] *Ibid.*, VI, 121 and 124.
[3] Regarding this signal, it would seem in all probability that the intention was to give it when the *coup d'état* was on the point of being carried out, but for some reason the uprising was delayed, and when the conspirators learnt that the Spartans were approaching they sent it out in desperation, for were the Spartans to go straight to Athens the revolt would at once be quashed.
[4] *The Cambridge Ancient History*, vol. IV, p. 252.

CHAPTER I

The Battles of Salamis, 480 B.C., and Plataea, 479 B.C.

"Now there was at Athens", writes Herodotus, "a man who had lately made his way into the first rank of citizens: his true name was Themistocles; but he was known more generally as the son of Neocles."[1] More clairvoyant than most of his contemporaries, he saw that Marathon was no more than the beginning of the war with Persia and not its ending as many supposed. He also saw that unless Athens built a strong enough fleet to win the command of the Aegean her doom was virtually sealed.

When great men appear, and Themistocles is among the greatest, it frequently happens that events play into their hands. This was so in his case. Firstly, a war between Athens and Aegina showed clearly the need for a stronger Athenian navy. Secondly, though Darius was more determined than ever to prosecute the war against Greece, he was diverted from his purpose by a revolt in Egypt. Thirdly, a rich bed of silver was discovered at Maroneia in the mining district of Laurion, and though at first it was proposed to divide the bullion among the citizens of Athens, in the end Themistocles persuaded the Assembly to spend it on the building of one hundred triremes. Lastly, before Darius could suppress the rebellion in Egypt, he died, and was succeeded by his son Xerxes (485–465 B.C.). This gave Greece yet further breathing space; for not only had Xerxes to end the revolt, but at the same time he had to establish himself securely on the throne.

Once order had been re-established in Egypt, as it was in 484 B.C., Xerxes began preparing for the now long delayed invasion of Greece, and in spite of Herodotus's exaggerations the four years spent in preparing it prove that the expedition was a formidable one. Each satrapy was called upon to provide its quota of fighting men. "For was there a nation in all Asia", writes Herodotus, "which Xerxes did not bring against Greece?"[2] Sir

[1] *History of Herodotus*, trans. George Rawlinson (1880), VII 143.
[2] *Ibid.*, VII, 21.

Frederick Maurice estimates the strength of the levy at 150,500[1] and Munro at 180,000 combatants,[2] which are small figures compared with Herodotus's 2,641,610. Whatever the actual figure, it was far too large to allow of another approach by sea; the land route had to be followed, and this time the crossing into Europe was to be made at the Hellespont instead of the Bosphorus. To avert a disaster such as Mardonius had suffered in 492 B.C., Xerxes ordered the cutting of a canal through the narrow isthmus which connects Mount Athos with the mainland of Chalcidice. Also he ordered the river Strymon to be bridged and depôts to be established along the coastal road the army was to follow.

The bridging of the Hellespont between Abydus and Sestus was for its day a phenomenal undertaking; even to-day it would be no mean task. The first attempt failed, but the second, directed by the Greek engineer Harpalus, was successful. Two boat-bridges formed of triremes and penteconters (fifty-oared galleys) were built. They were linked by six long cables, two of flax and four of papyrus, and over the vessels was constructed a wooden roadway. In all 314 ships were used for the western bridge and 360 for the eastern.

By the winter of 481 B.C. the preparations ended. Xerxes established his headquarters at Sardes and sent heralds to all the Greek states, except Athens and Sparta, to demand earth and water—the symbols of submission. In the spring the advance began and the army set out for Abydus, where, according to Herodotus, 1,207 warships and 3,000 transports were assembled already. At Abydus Xerxes reviewed his army, after which it crossed over to Sestus, marched up the Thracian Chersonese, rounded the bay of Melas, and so reached Doriscus, where it was joined by the fleet, which later passed through the Mount Athos canal. Xerxes reviewed the fleet, then left for Therma (Salonica) where the expedition rested, the king going ahead by ship to explore the pass of Tempe, which lies south of Mount Olympus and north of Mount Ossa.

Before the events which followed are described, it is as well briefly to consider the art of war in Greece at this period, and, to complete the subject, to carry its development to the end of the fifth century.

By now the phalangial organization had reached its highest

[1] "The Size of the Army of Xerxes", *Journal of Hellenic Studies* (1930), pp. 210–235.
[2] *The Cambridge Ancient History*, vol. IV, p. 273.

perfection in Sparta, where by law the citizen soldier was required "to conquer or die." To him war was a festival and battle a competition of courage. Each Spartan soldier was accompanied by a shield-bearer, for his equipment weighed some seventy-two pounds. At the battle of Plataea, in 479 B.C., the hoplite had seven helots, or serfs, who formed the rear ranks, making the depth of the phalanx eight in all. These men clubbed to death the enemy wounded and attended to their masters should they be injured. To maintain line of battle the hoplites kept step to the music of flute-players.

In these ceremonial battles, tactics were limited to push of pikes, and remained so until light troops were added to the phalanx. Had it not been for the religion of valour there can be little doubt that this would have been done from the start. Yet, even so late as the Peloponnesian War (431–404 B.C.), except among the northern semi-Greek tribes, light troops were held in disdain. Nevertheless, in 426 B.C., the Athenians under Demosthenes were severely defeated by Aetolian javelin-men who, refusing to close, destroyed the phalanx from a distance. Through force of circumstances, this change was imminent, for early in the fourth century B.C. the Athenian general Iphicrates raised a body of true light infantry, called peltasts, who were trained for rapid movements. They wore a quilted or leathern jerkin and carried shields, javelins, and swords. In 390 B.C. he proved their worth by annihilating a Spartan *mora* (battalion).

It is strange that the Athenians, an intelligent people, should have been so slow in creating this essential arm, because for long past they had maintained a highly efficient body of naval bowmen, recruited from the second richest class, those not wealthy enough to keep a horse. During the Peloponnesian War these archers were so successfully employed in sea raids on Sparta that, according to Thucydides, the Spartans took the unusual step of raising four hundred horse and a body of bowmen to meet them.

At the time of the Persian invasions the sole true cavalry soldiers in Greece were the Thessalians, but they played no part in the defence of Greece for they were completely outclassed by the Persian cavalry. In spite of the mountainous nature of their country, it is strange that the Greeks should have been so backward in this arm; for twenty years earlier, in 511 B.C., the Spartans had experienced its value and to their cost, for they had been defeated by Thessalian horsemen not far from Athens. According to Delbrück, the whole course of the Persian Wars was determined by the Greek fear of Persian horseman.

The point to note in this brief summary of Greek warfare is that changes in armament were due solely to compulsion, because, throughout, valour disdained inventiveness. Only in siege operations do we find play given to imagination. At the siege of Plataea, in 429 B.C., the Plataeans would seem to have used fire arrows to burn the besiegers' engines; at the siege of Delium an attack with burning sulphur and pitch was made; and, in 413 B.C., it would appear that the Syracusans defended their walls with liquid fire.

Long before Xerxes arrived at Therma, many Greek cities had sent delegates to a Panhellenic Congress to discuss his advance. It met at the Isthmus of Corinth under the presidency of Sparta. Many states were absent, the more important being Thessaly and most of the Boeotian cities.

The scheme of defence discussed was first of all governed by the fact that, as the Peloponnese was held by its states to be the "citadel of Greek independence", the defence of the Isthmus of Corinth was for them imperative. The second consideration was that were the isthmus alone held, all northern and central Greece would be abandoned, and once occupied by the enemy the isthmus defences could be turned by sea; therefore, to avert this risk it was also imperative to hold the enemy as far north of the isthmus as possible. The army and navy, because of their numerical inferiority, could only hope to do so, the one in the narrow passes and the other in the narrow seas. Except for the isthmus itself, the vale of Tempe and the pass of Thermopylae offered such localities for the army, and except for the strait of Salamis, the Euripus, or Euboean Channel, offered an equally good one for the fleet. Further, because the last mentioned narrow stretch of water flanked all practical landing places on the east coast of Greece between Tempe and Thermopylae, a fleet operating in it could cooperate with an army holding either Tempe or Thermopylae. Nor need the army be large; only strong enough to hold up the Persian land advance sufficiently long to induce the Persians to outflank the position held by means of their fleet and thereby to bring on a naval engagement in the Euboean Channel, where their numerical superiority would be at a discount. Were the Persians to be decisively beaten in these waters, then the isthmus would be secured against an outflanking sea attack.

When the above strategy was being discussed and Xerxes was

still at Abydus, the Thessalians appealed to the Greek Congress to block the vale of Tempe. This resulted in a Greek fleet carrying 10,000 hoplites in two divisions, one a Spartan, under Evaenetus, and the other an Athenian, under Themistocles, being sent through the Euripus to Halus in Achaea Phthiotis. From Halus, Evaenetus, who was general-in-chief, marched to Tempe, but when there he found that there were several passes and that he had not sufficient men to hold them all, so he returned to the isthmus. This retreat on the threshold of the war greatly discouraged the northern Greeks; also it reinforced the opinions of those members of the Congress who were for holding the isthmus only.

The situation was further complicated by the Oracle at Delphi. Impressed by the vastness of the Persian preparations, which Xerxes in no way attempted to conceal, it prophesied evil of the Hellenic cause: "Wretches why sit you here? Fly, fly to the ends of creation. Quitting your homes, and the crags which your city crowns with her circlet."[1]

This advice was given to the Athenians alone, apparently because the Oracle thought that Athens was the sole object of the expedition, and that, were she punished, the other states would be spared so long as they did not support her.

The Athenians were so depressed by these gloomy words that they consulted the Oracle for a second time,[2] when they received another utterance, ending with the famous lines:

Safe shall the wooden wall continue for thee and thy children.
Wait not the tramp of the horse, nor the footmen mightily moving
Over the land, but turn your back to the foe, and retire ye.
Yet shall a day arrive when ye shall meet him in battle.
Holy Salamis, thou shalt destroy the offspring of women,
Where men scatter the seed, or where they gather the harvest.[3]

Were these words ever uttered? If so, then it would seem that the Oracle had fairly accurately gauged the probability that a decision must be sought on the sea and not on the land. Be this as it may, soon after Evaenetus returned, the Congress appealed for help to the then greatest power in the Greek world: to Gelo, tyrant of Syracuse, whose fleet in size equalled the Athenian.

Though, according to Herodotus, Gelo would have been

---

[1] Herodotus, VII, 140.
[2] See *A History of the Delphic Oracle*, H. W. Parke (1939), chap. IX.
[3] Herodotus, VII, 141.

pleased to help, he was unable to do so, for he was threatened by an impending Carthaginian invasion of Sicily on a vast scale.

Here an interesting question intrudes. Were the Persian and Carthaginian invasions parts of one combined operation aimed at wrecking not only Greece, but the entire Greek world?

According to Diodorus, Xerxes, "desiring to drive all the Greeks from their homes, sent an embassy to the Carthaginians to urge them to join him in the undertaking and closed an agreement with them to the effect that he would wage war upon the Greeks who lived in Greece, while the Carthaginians should at the same time gather great armaments and subdue those Greeks who lived in Sicily and Italy".[1] Grundy considers that this is probable; firstly, because the Phoenicians were both subjects of Persia and blood relations of the Carthaginians, and secondly, because each invasion would clearly assist the other.

The Tempe fiasco, coupled with the failure to obtain Gelo's help, compelled the Greek Congress to decide on one of two courses of action: whether to seek a naval battle in the Euboean Channel, which carried with it the holding of Thermopylae; or whether to stand at the isthmus and await a naval battle in the strait of Salamis. The Spartans urged the latter and the Athenians the former; but in the end the Spartans had to give way, for were Attica abandoned the Athenians might prefer to medize than see their country wasted, and were they to do so their fleet would pass into Persian hands and without it the isthmus would lose its defensive value.

So it came about that the Congress sent the allied fleet to Artemisium (Potaki?) which lay on the north-western coast of Euboea, and an army under Leonidas, the Agiad king of Sparta, to Thermopylae. The latter consisted of some 7,000 to 8,000 hoplites and light armed troops, and included the royal bodyguard of 300 Spartans. The former consisted of 324 triremes and nine penteconters, of which the Athenian contingent was 180 ships under Themistocles, and though the Spartan contingent, commanded by Eurybiades, numbered only ten ships, because he represented the leading member of the League he was given supreme command.

Although the disproportion between the sea and land forces indicates that the primary object was a naval battle, the holding

[1] *Diodorus Siculus*, trans. C. H. Oldfather (1946), xi, 2.

of Thermopylae was of equal importance, because the halting of the Persian army was the most likely operation to compel the Persian fleet to fight. As we shall see, the weakness in the Greek plan was that Leonidas–like Evaenetus before him–had not sufficient troops to carry out his task. This was because the

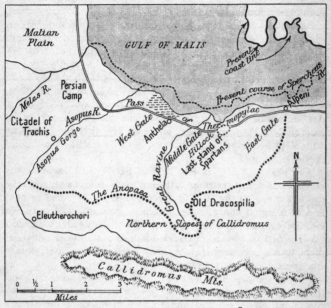

3. DEFENCE OF THERMOPYLAE, 480 B.C.

Spartans insisted that the garrison of the isthmus could not be too strong.

The Persian plan was that the army and the main fleet were to arrive simultaneously before Thermopylae and the northern entrance of the Euboean Channel, the latter engaging the Greek fleet. At the same time, the Phoenician squadron of 200 ships was to sail round the east and south coasts of Euboea and to block the southern entrance of the channel: thus the Greek fleet would be bottled up.

On the twelfth day after the Persian army marched south from Therma, the main Persian fleet and the Phoenician squadron put to sea. Eurybiades heard of the squadron's movement and sent fifty-three Attic ships to Chalcis to hold the waist of the Channel. Meanwhile the fleet sailed down the east coast of the Magnesian Peninsula, and before the roadstead of Aphetae could be reached it was caught in a south-easterly gale—the *Hellespontias*—and, according to Herodotus, 400 warships were wrecked and provision craft "beyond count".[1]

Eurybiades assembled a council of war to discuss the disaster, during which—following Diodorus—all the commanders except Themistocles favoured the defensive; nevertheless he persuaded them to take a contrary course, pointing out that that party ever had the advantage who, in good order, made the first onset upon an enemy in disorder.[2] An obstinate and indecisive fight followed, and the day afterwards news from Chalcis was received at Artemisium that the Phoenician squadron had been caught in the gale and for the greater part wrecked, and that the fifty-three Attic ships were returning. Probably they were back at Artemisium on the evening of the day of the battle.

The next day it was the Persian fleet which assumed the offensive. The Greeks ranged their ships in a crescent, with the cusps pointing to the land to prevent their flanks being turned, and at a signal charged the oncoming Persians. The battle at once developed into a close quarter mêlée; but again no decision was reached. A council of Greek admirals met after the engagement to consider a retreat. As they were arguing, a triaconter (thirty-oar galley) arrived from Thermopylae with the portentous news that the pass had been lost, that Leonidas had fallen, and that the Persians were marching towards Athens.[3] This left no choice but to retire, and under cover of darkness the Greeks sailed south for Salamis.

Before outlining the events which led up to this disaster, it is essential briefly to describe the pass. In 480 B.C. it skirted the southern shore of the Malian Gulf and was divided into three "gates", the West, Middle, and East. The first lay a little east of the mouth of the Asopus river; the third on the western side of the town of Alpeni, and the Middle half way between the two. To the south lay Mount Callidromus, over the northern slopes of which a track, called the Anopaea, ran from near the East Gate to close by a place in the mountains called Dracospilia and thence westwards to the Asopus gorge in the vicinity of the citadel of Trachis.

[1] Herodotus, VII, 190–191.   [2] Diodorus, XI, 13.   [3] Herodotus, VIII, 21.

By way of this track the coastal road running through the three gates could be turned either from the west or east.[1]

On his arrival at Thermopylae Leonidas occupied the Middle Gate, and to secure his left flank he posted 1,000 Phocians on the Anopaea, not far from Dracospilia.[2] Soon after he had done so Xerxes entered the Malian plain and encamped his army west of the West Gate and the Asopus. There he remained for four days, expecting, so Herodotus says, that the vastness of his army would frighten the Greeks away; but it seems more probable that he was waiting to give his fleet time to win a naval battle and then to turn the Greek position.

On the fifth day he launched his first assault against the Middle Gate; but only to find that his unarmoured men were no match for armoured. The next day the assault was repeated, and again it was beaten back. The Persian king's position was now becoming critical. Neither his army nor his fleet could force a passage, and we may assume that the supply of the former was running short. At this juncture, had the Greeks numbered 16,000 men instead of 8,000 the probabilities are that Xerxes would have been forced to retreat, and had he done so it is more than likely that the Greek fleet would have attacked all out.

Xerxes was at a loss what to do when a man of Malis, Ephialtes, told him "of the pathway which led across the mountains of Thermopylae".[3] Xerxes saw the possibility of turning the Middle Gate by moving along this path and sent Hydarnes and the Immortals at "about the time of the lighting of the lamps"[4] to make the attempt. They marched all night and at daybreak surprised the Phocian detachment near Dracospilia and drove it into the mountains; after which Hydarnes pushed on. Some time later, scouts–presumably Phocians–reached Leonidas and told him of the disaster. What next happened is obscure. Grundy's reconstruction is that Leonidas divided his army into two divisions. Keeping the Spartans, Thebans, and Thespians at the Middle Gate, he sent the rest back "to seize the forest path before the Persians had time to debouch from it in any strength"[5] so that his line of communications might be kept open. What occurred after this is unknown, but it would seem that either the rear half of the army arrived too late to stop the Persians or took panic and re-

---

[1] This track has been discussed by nearly every historian of the campaign and few agree on its location.

[2] The *Cambridge Ancient History* (vol. IV, p. 296) suggests at Eleutherochori.

[3] Herodotus VII, 213.   [4] *Ibid.*, VII, 215.   [5] *The Great Persian War*, p. 309.

treated through the East Gate to Elataea. Whatever happened, Leonidas was soon after attacked in front and rear, and, scorning surrender, fell fighting. Thus the pass was cleared for the Persians and the road to Athens was opened.

At once Xerxes struck south to impose his will on the Athenians and Spartans and to end the war in triumph. His universal kingship demanded nothing less, and nothing now seemed to stand in his way to prevent him adding the whole Grecian peninsula to his empire.

In Athens consternation reigned. Its citizens expected to see their Peloponnesian allies march into Boeotia and there halt the barbarian descent. Instead, they heard that they were still busily fortifying the isthmus. Rather than surrender, they made the most heroic decision in their history. They stockaded and garrisoned the Acropolis, evacuated Athens and Attica, and transported their families to Aegina, Salamis, and Troezen.

In spite of the confusion that this migration must have caused, and in spite of Spartan self-interest, Themistocles still held the ace of trumps—the Athenian fleet. If the defence of Thermopylae had depended on the fleet, doubly now did the defence of the isthmus so depend. But how should the fleet act? At Artemisium, and more particularly in the second naval battle, the error had been to engage a numerically superior enemy in open water. As he was bent on not repeating this mistake, Themistocles's thoughts now fixed on the strait of Salamis. But, as Grundy points out: ". . . if the Persians chose to ignore the Greek fleet at Salamis, and to sail straight to the Isthmus, the situation would be dangerous to the last degree."[1] Therefore, how to induce the Persians to attack at his chosen point became the heart of Themistocles's problem.

The island of Salamis lies to the south of the bay of Eleusis, which is approached from the west and east by two narrow channels: the one between Salamis and Megara and the other between the promontory of Cynosura and the mouth of the Piraeus. The latter is separated by the island of Psyttaleia into two sub-channels, the western being half a mile in width and the eastern a little more than three-quarters of a mile.

To persuade the Persians to carry out the same manœuvre they attempted at Artemisium—namely, to bottle up the Greek fleet and to capture rather than to destroy it—Themistocles took the tremendous risk of leaving the channel between Salamis and

[1] Herodotus, p. 352.

Megara unguarded. For the defence of the two eastern sub-channels he could rely on 366 triremes and seven penteconters.[1]

For a moment we will look at this great man through the eyes of Thucydides. He says:

"... Themistocles was a man who exhibited the most indubitable signs of genius; indeed, in this particular he has a claim in our

4. CAMPAIGNS OF SALAMIS AND PLATAEA, 480-479 B.C.

admiration quite extraordinary and unparalleled. By his own native capacity, alike unformed and unsupplemented by study, he was at once the best judge in those sudden crises which admit of little or of no deliberation, and the best prophet of the future, even to its most distant possibilities. An able theoretical expositor of all that came within the sphere of his practice, he was not

[1] Herodotus, p. 354.

without the power of passing an adequate judgement in matters in which he had no experience. He could also excellently divine the good and evil which lay hid in the unseen future. In fine, whether we consider the extent of his natural powers, or the slightness of his application, this extraordinary man must be allowed to have surpassed all others in the faculty of intuitively meeting an emergency."[1]

While Themistocles planned, Xerxes marched. He reached Athens, lay siege to the Acropolis, took it after a severe fight, and slaughtered its defenders. This seemingly unexpected disaster threw the crews of the Greek fleet into a panic which precipitated a council of war. But the alarm was so great that some of the captains "did not even wait for the council to come to a vote, but embarked hastily on board their vessels, and hoisted sail as though they would take flight immediately".[2] Themistocles heard of this and persuaded Eurybiades to "quit his ship and again collect the captains to council".[3] Then Themistocles spoke as follows:

" With thee it rests, O Eurybiades! to save Greece, if thou wilt only hearken unto me, and give the enemy battle here, rather than yield to the advice of those among us, who would have the fleet withdraw to the Isthmus. Hear now, I beseech thee, and judge between the two courses. At the Isthmus thou wilt fight in the open sea, which is greatly to our disadvantage. . . . The land and sea force of the Persians will advance together, and thy retreat will but draw them towards the Peloponnese, and so bring all Greece into peril. If, on the other hand, thou doest as I advise, these are the advantages which thou wilt so secure: in the first place, as we shall fight in a narrow sea with a few ships against many, if the war follows the common course, we shall gain a great victory; for to fight in a narrow space is favourable to us—in an open sea, to them. . . . Nay, that very point by which ye set most store, is secured as much by this course as by the other; for whether we fight here or at the Isthmus, we shall equally give battle in defence of the Peloponnese. . . . When men counsel reasonably, reasonable success ensues; but when in their counsels they reject reason, God does not choose to follow the wanderings of human fancies."

He was opposed by Adeimantus the Corinthian, who called on

---

[1] *The History of the Peloponnesian War by Thucydides*, trans. Richard Crawley (1874), I, 138.
[2] Herodotus, VIII, 56.　　　　　　　　　　[3] *Ibid.*, VIII, 58.

Eurybiades to reject Themistocles's plan. Turning to Eurybiades, Themistocles then played his ace of trumps:

" 'If thou wilt stay here and behave like a brave man', he said, 'all will be well. . . . If not, we will take our families on board and go, just as we are, to Siris (? Torre di Senna), in Italy, which is ours from of old. . . . You then, when you have lost allies like us, will hereafter call to mind what I have now said.'

"At these words. . . . Eurybiades changed his determination . . . because he feared that if he withdrew the fleet to the Isthmus, the Athenians would sail away, and knew that without the Athenians the rest of their ships could be no match for the fleet of the enemy. He therefore decided to remain, and give battle at Salamis."[1]

The next day, September 22, 480 B.C., the eve of the battle, Aeschylus, who was present at it, relates that a message came to Xerxes from the Greek fleet. In Lewis Campbell's translation it reads:

> Let but the shades of gloomy Night come o'er
> The Hellenes will not bide, but, each his way,
> Manning the benches with a rush, will seek
> By covert flight to save themselves alive.[2]

When he received the message—probably during the early afternoon—Xerxes, who had already ordered his fleet to put to sea, cancelled the order and postponed the movement until nightfall. Who sent the message and why? The story, as given by Herodotus, is as follows:

There was so much dissatisfaction with Eurybiades's decision to fight at Salamis that a third council of war assembled on the morning of September 22 at which the same old subject was again discussed. But "Themistocles, when he saw that the Peloponnesians would carry the votes against him, went out secretly from the council, and, instructing a certain man what he should say, sent him on board a merchant ship to the fleet of the Medes". And this is what the messenger said to Xerxes:

"The Athenian commander has sent me to you privily, without the knowledge of the other Greeks. He is a well-wisher to the king's cause, and would rather success should attend on you than on his countrymen; wherefore he bids me tell you that fear has seized the Greeks and they are meditating a hasty flight. Now then it is open to you to achieve the best work that ever ye wrought, if only ye will hinder their escaping. They no longer agree among them-

[1] Herodotus, VIII, 60–62.   [2] Aeschylus (1890), "The Persians", p. 63.

selves, so that they will not now make any resistance—nay, 'tis likely ye may see a fight already begun between such as favour and such as oppose your cause."[1]

That Xerxes fell into the trap is understandable; for all along he must have heard from his spies of the dissensions in his enemy's camp. As has been mentioned, he immediately modified his plan, now deciding secretly and simultaneously to block the western and eastern straits of Salamis and so to bottle up the Greek fleet. According to Aeschylus, these operations were to be put into force at nightfall.[2]

The Egyptians' contingent of 200 ships was instructed to sail round Salamis to block the western passage, while the remainder of the fleet formed a triple line from south of the promontory of Cynosura to the Piraeus. The island of Psyttaleia was to be occupied by Persian troops. These movements, so it would seem, were completed shortly before daybreak on September 23.

While they were under way, oblivious of what was happening, the Greek captains were still arguing when they were suddenly cut short by the appearance of Aristeides, the rival of Themistocles. He had just come from Aegina, and calling Themistocles apart, he told him that "however much the Corinthians and Eurybiades may wish it, they cannot now retreat; for we are all enclosed on every side by the enemy".[3] Then Themistocles asked him to speak to the Council. This he did, but the Spartans refused to believe him and it was not until the arrival of a Tenian trireme, which had deserted from the Persians, confirmed what Aristeides had told them that they realized that their problem was solved and without their assistance.

Compelled now to fight, the Greek admirals hastily prepared for battle. First, it may be assumed, the Corinthian squadron was sent to hold the western channel against the Egyptians. Next, they drew their ships in line of battle across the channel between the town of Salamis and the shore under the Heracleion on the southern slope of Mount Aegaleos. It was in the following order: on the right, Eurybiades and sixteen ships; on the left, the Athenians with more than half the ships present; and in the centre the remainder of the allies.

As yet hidden from view, the Persian fleet lay in three lines. Soon it began to break into columns of ships in order to pass

[1] Herodotus, VIII, 75.   [2] Aeschylus. "The Persians", line 364.
[3] Herodotux, VIII, 79.

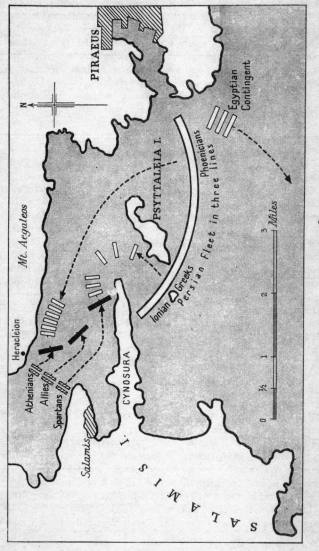

PIRAEUS

N

Mt. Aegaleos

Heracleion

Athenians
Allies
Spartans

Salamis

CYNOSURA

SALAMIS I.

PSYTTALEIA I.

Egyptian Contingent

Phoenicians

Ionian Greeks

Persian Fleet in three lines

0   ½   1   2   3
Miles

5. BATTLE OF SALAMIS, 480 B.C.

Psyttaleia, the Phoenicians on the right and the Ionian Greeks on the left. As soon as this manœuvre began, then either because of the number of the ships, the ineptness of their crews, or the roughness of the sea–possibly all three combined–the columns were thrown into confusion and were still in disorder when the Greeks rowed upon them and a mêlée began in which the heaviest and not the fastest ships held the advantage. Soon the leading Persian ships were forced back on those in the rear, doubling the confusion, while the Athenian ships, more strongly built, shaved close past their enemy's vessels, sheering away their oars on one side to render them unmanageable, and then hauled round to ram them amidships. On each Athenian trireme there was a boarding party of eighteen marines–fourteen hoplites and four bowmen.

The decisive action was fought on the Greek left. There the Athenians and Aeginetans, rowing close to the shore, and in full view of Xerxes–who had taken up his position on a hill north of the Piraeus to watch the surrender of the Greek fleet–turned the Phoenician right and drove it back towards the Persian centre, where the fighting was as yet more even, while the Greek right, having advanced too rapidly, like the Phoenician had been attacked in flank. Gradually the wave of victory advanced from the left to the right of the Greek line until the encirclement of the Persian centre by the Athenians and Aeginetans threatened a rear attack on the Persian left. The Ionian Greeks then began to fall back and their withdrawal brought the battle to an end after a hotly contested fight of some seven to eight hours.

There would appear to have been little or no pursuit; probably the Greeks had had enough. Psyttaleia was cleared of its defenders by Aristeides; the defeated Persians returned to Phalerum and the victorious Greeks to Salamis. There is no reliable account of losses. According to Diodorus,[1] the Greeks lost forty ships and the Persians 200, not counting those captured.

Tactically, Salamis was not a superlatively great victory, but strategically it was shattering. It knocked the bottom out of the Persian plan, which, for success, depended on the closest co-operation of fleet and army. It was not the loss of ships which was so serious for Xerxes, it was the loss of prestige. The one could be replaced, the other could not be in a conglomerate empire held together by the autocracy of its universal monarch. It was a loss

[1] Diodorus, XI, 19.

which heralded revolt in the rear and more especially among the Ionian Greeks.

Up to the date of Salamis, Persian naval power had been supreme in the Aegean because of the number of ships the Persians could muster and because, since the failure of the Ionian revolt, the Persian naval bases along its eastern shore had been secure. Now they were no longer so; for the Greek triremes at Salamis not only shattered the Persian fleet but simultaneously shivered the loyalty of the Ionians to Persia. Though at the time it was not appreciated by both sides, Salamis spelt the end of Persian naval command of the Aegean, and without it the Persians were unable to maintain a great army in so poor a country as Greece. The vast forces they had carried there, as Grundy states, had now to be reduced to a point which enabled the Greeks successfully to challenge them in the field. As he says, "Salamis was the turning-point of the war. Plataea was the consummation of Salamis."[1]

The battle ended, Xerxes's all-mastering anxiety was for the security of the bridges over the Hellespont. He had lost his nerve and he magnified the danger: were they destroyed either by the victorious Greeks or by the Ionians, it appeared to him that his whole army must perish. So he at once sent his fleet back to Asia to hold the eastern coast of the Aegean, and a few days after he set out northward with his army.

Meanwhile the Greeks, seeing the Persian army in position, supposed that the Persian navy was still at Phalerum, and it would appear that not until the army began to withdraw did they set out to make certain. They found that the fleet had gone, and failing to catch up with any Persian ships, they proceeded no farther than the island of Andros, where they disembarked and held a council of war. Themistocles proposed that they should sail on to the Hellespont and destroy the bridges. But this suggestion was opposed by Eurybiades, for were it carried out the Persian army would be cut off from Asia, and, in consequence, if only to live, it would waste all Greece. As the majority declared itself of the same mind the project was abandoned.

When he found that the Greek navy was inactive, it would seem that Xerxes regained his nerve. He now realized that to withdraw the whole army from Greece would be nearly as calamitous as were it to perish there—for it would be an acknowledgement of so overwhelming a defeat that the very foundations of his empire

The Great Persian War, p. 407.

would be upheaved—and decided to hold on to Greece. He left Mardonius and Artabazus, the one in Thessaly and the other in Thrace and Macedonia, with one part of the army, for in those countries supplies had been accumulated and the lines of communication with Asia were short, and with the other part he withdrew over the Hellespont to be in a position to suppress any rebellion that might break out.

According to Herodotus, 300,000 of the best troops in the Persian army were left with Mardonius, and though this is an exaggerated number,[1] whatever the actual figure was it was sufficient to enable Mardonius to renew the offensive whenever he chose. But as the Persian fleet had been withdrawn this did not solve the problem of the isthmus. That this was apparent to him is clear; for instead of advancing on it he attempted to turn the never ceasing discussions within and between the Greek city states to his advantage.

In Athens the year 479 B.C. opened with a new board of generals. Themistocles—we do not know for what reason—had not been re-elected, but two of his political opponents, Aristeides and Xanthippus, had been. This was fortunate for Mardonius because their past suggested that they would prefer a reconciliation with the Persians to an alliance with Sparta. Could he but win them over, the problem of the isthmus would be solved.

In the early summer of 479 B.C. he sent Alexander of Macedonia to the Athenians with an offer of a free pardon for the past and an alliance with Persia on equal terms. This became known to the Spartans, who at once took alarm, and the Athenians agreed to reject the offer on the understanding that the Spartans would join them in an offensive against the common enemy.

Mardonius then began stirring up trouble within the Peloponnese. Knowing that the Argives were hostile to the Spartans, he intrigued with them to attack the latter so that when the two were engaged he might suddenly march down from the north and carry the isthmus by a *coup de main*. The plot miscarried.

Mardonius then returned to a modified edition of his first plan. This time it was to bring the Spartans into the open by putting pressure on the Athenians. On his way down from Thessaly, he changed his direction accordingly and marched on Athens, at the same time sending an envoy to Salamis to reopen negotiations with the Athenians in the hope of alarming the Spartans. It succeeded

Munro, in *The Cambridge Ancient History* (vol. IV, p. 317), suggests 120,000.

in doing so; Aristeides at once sent representatives to Sparta urging immediate action should the Spartans wish to retain the loyalty of the Athenians. The result of the threat was that after considerable delay a field army of 5,000 Spartan hoplites and 35,000 armed helots was sent to the isthmus under the command of Pausanias, regent for Pleistarchus, the young Spartan king. Mardonius, who had thus far refrained from damaging Athens, then fired the city and withdrew to Boeotia to draw the Spartans and their allies into country more suitable for his cavalry to operate in.

When he arrived at the isthmus, probably in July, Pausanias first assembled the Peloponnesian contingents there, and then passed over to Eleusis, where Aristeides joined him with 8,000 hoplites and a considerable body of archers. From Eleusis he marched to Erythrae (site uncertain) where from the northern foot-hills of Cithaeron, he could view Mardonius's stockaded camp on the river Asopus.

Though the Greek position was unsuited for cavalry to operate against, the ground being hilly and broken, Mardonius, eager to attack his enemy before he could be reinforced, launched the whole of his cavalry, under Masistius, against the Greeks, and with disastrous results. Masistius was unhorsed by an Athenian arrow and then killed. A fierce fight for his body followed in which the Persians were worsted, and then withdrew.

Though the action was little more than a big skirmish it had important tactical results. The Persians were taught the lesson that on broken hilly ground it does not pay cavalry to chance a fight at close quarters with close-ordered heavy infantry. But the Greeks were so elated by their success that they made the error of assuming that they could defeat cavalry on any ground. As we shall see, the results were that in the next operation the Persians were over-cautious and the Greeks over-bold.

The success against the Persian cavalry, the lack of an adequate supply of water at Erythrae, and, seemingly, the difficulty of assuming an offensive against the Persian right wing, which if turned would lay bare Mardonius's communications with his base at Thebes, persuaded Pausanias, under cover of the hills and so out of view of the Persians, to move out of his good defensive position into the Plataean plain between Plataea and the Asopus. There he drew up his army, the Spartans on the right, the Athenians on the left, and the remainder of the allies—nineteen contingents – between the two:[1] in all, according to Herodotus, his army numbered 108,200.[2]

From his new position, so long as he struck before his enemy could conform with his move, Pausanias was well placed to manœuvre against the Persian right flank. So it is surprising to learn that once the position was occupied he did not attack at once. Whatever the reason may have been, Mardonius soon discovered his opponents' change of position, drew his army out of its stockaded camp, and brought it into parallel order on the opposite (northern) bank of the Asopus – directly facing the Greeks. On the left were the Persians proper, opposite the Spartans; the Asiatic contingents were in the centre, and the Boeotians and other medized Greeks on the right, facing the Athenians, Plataeans, and Megarians.

For eight days, so Herodotus states, the two armies faced each other inactively, and the question "why" has been asked.[3] There are two probable reasons: (1) that the Persian cavalry had been so roughly handled at Erythrae by close-ordered heavy infantry that Mardonius was waiting for his enemy to move over the Asopus which, even if half-dry, would have disordered the Greek ranks before he attacked, and (2) that as Pausanias was now unable to turn the Persian right flank, and as he had won his last success when in a stationary position and so in perfect battle order, he was waiting for his enemy to move first.

At length, on the eighth day, a Theban, Timagenidas, advised Mardonius to keep a watch on the passes of Cithaeron, telling him how supplies of men kept coming in day after day, and assuring him that he might cut off large numbers. These were the passes through which Pausanias's supply columns moved, the most important being that of Dryoscephalae ("oaks-heads"). The advice was accepted and a cavalry raid was made on Dryoscephalae with immediate success: a Greek provision train of 500 pack animals was caught in the pass and destroyed, not a man or beast being spared.

What the raid actually showed was that Pausanias's position was untenable; possessing no cavalry, he could only protect his line of communication by falling back on the passes. Further, it

[1] For the complete order of battle see Herodotus, IX, 28.
[2] Ibid., IX, 30. Munro's estimate is about 80,000, of whom about two-fifths were hoplites (The Cambridge Ancient History, vol. IV, p. 324).
[3] See The Cambridge Ancient History, vol. IV, p. 331. Is it however a coincidence that an eight-day pause also occurred at Marathon?

66

woke up the Persians, for during the next two days much skirmishing between the armies took place, and to the disadvantage of the Greeks, whose bowmen were vastly outnumbered by those of their enemy.

Impatient now to take advantage of his enemy's intolerable position, and probably also because the supply of his army—particularly of his cavalry—was becoming increasingly difficult, Mardonius contemplated a full-out offensive in spite of Artabazus's suggestion that he should withdraw to Thebes and bribe the Greek commanders. Having more faith in his army than in his colleague, Mardonius decided on a cavalry attack; but this time at long range with missiles, and not at close quarters.

At the time, the Greeks were in line south of the Asopus, the Athenians on the left and the allies in the centre. Both depended for their water on the river, whereas on the right the Spartans drew theirs from the spring of Gargaphia. The river supply was a precarious one, because the Asopus flowed between the Greeks and Persians; but the spring was secure enough, for it lay in rear of the Spartan wing. When the Persian cavalry advanced, so formidable a missile attack was opened on the Athenians and allies that both were cut off from the Asopus and were compelled to draw their water from Gargaphia. Next, the Spartans must have been driven back, though this is not actually stated, and before they could advance again the Persians "choked up and spoiled" the spring, with the result that when it was retaken it was found to be useless.[1]

The position of the Greeks, which, since their communications had been raided, had become critical, with the loss of their water supply became impossible, and on the morning of the second day of the attack a council of war was held at which it was decided to move by night back to a position called the "Island", a tract of ground about one mile east of the ruins of Plataea and lying between two head streams of the Oëröe river to the south of Gargaphia. "It was agreed likewise", writes Herodotus, "that after they had reached the place . . . they should dispatch, the very same night, one half of their army . . . to relieve those whom they had sent to procure provisions, and who were now blocked up in that region."[2]

From this and what actually happened, it would appear that the withdrawal was planned as follows: The whole army to with-

[1] Herodotus, IX 49.　　[2] Ibid., IX, 51.

draw to Mount Cithaeron, where it would cover the three passes:
Plataea–Megara Pass; Plataea–Athens Pass, and Athens–Thebes
Pass (Dryoscephalae). It was complicated by three factors. The
first was that the provision parties were still besieged and had to
be relieved *at the earliest moment*. The second, that the movement
had to be carried out by night and so would be slow, too slow for
the left and centre of the army to reach Mount Cithaeron and to

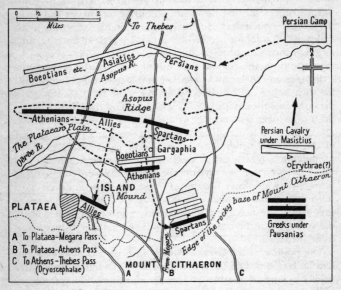

6. BATTLE OF PLATAEA, 479 B.C.

form line before daylight. Because of this it was decided to send
back the right wing (Spartans)–the closest to the passes–to
relieve the besieged provision parties, and at the same time to take
up an intermediate position on the Island with the centre and
left wing. Tactically this position must have stretched from the
Citadel of Plataea to the Megara–Thebes road, a distance of two
miles–about one mile each side of the mound which marks the
centre of the Island. Now enters the third factor. Clearly the
simplest thing to do was to withdraw the centre (lesser allies) to
the east of the mound and the left wing (Athenians) to the west of

it; but this would have violated military etiquette, so the lesser allies were ordered to the new left and the Athenians to the new right. This meant that the Athenians could not withdraw until the lesser allies and Spartans had cleared their rear; they had to move last.

At the second watch of the night the withdrawal began. The Greek centre fell back to its position between Plataea and the mound and would seem to have accomplished its task in spite of Herodotus's strictures.[1] When he heard that the centre was in movement Pausanias ordered his right wing to withdraw, when one of his divisional commanders, Amompharetus–a typically stupid Spartan–holding that a retreat in face of the enemy was disgraceful, refused to budge. The upshot was that the best part of the night was spent in the customary Greek wrangling and it was not until day was breaking that Pausanias, leaving Amompharetus behind, got under way. Meanwhile the Athenians, who had been waiting for the centre to clear their rear, were further delayed by having to wait for Pausanias to do the same.

Soon after Pausanias had begun to withdraw, Amompharetus–the source of all these delays–found himself abandoned and set off after the right wing just in the nick of time, for as he caught up with it the Persian cavalry attacked. Unfortunately for the Spartans, the delay had prevented them gaining the hilly ground and they were caught on a gentle open slope in every way favourable for the Persian horse, whose aim evidently was to pin the Spartans down before they could gain the rocky slopes of Cithaeron and to hold them until the Persian infantry came up.

Leaving his right wing to move against the Athenians–still far behind–Mardonius ordered up his Persian infantry to support his cavalry, and behind them he set in motion the whole of his Asiatic centre. Pausanias saw that most of the enemy's army was moving directly against him and sent an urgent message to the Athenians to come to his aid. They were unable to do so because the Persian right wing was marching on them. Thus it came about that Pausanias and his men were left to face the bulk of the Persian army.

The Persian cavalry by adhering to missile tactics soon placed the Spartans in an intolerable position; and when the fight was in progress the Persian infantry came up, took over from the cavalry, and built up a "rampart of wicker shields, and shot from

[1] Herodotus, IX, 53.

behind them such clouds of arrows, that the Spartans were sorely distressed".[1] Now Mardonius made the crucial blunder, which was to cost him the battle and his life. Instead of leaving plenty of room in rear of his bowmen to give them space to withdraw and advance in again and thus to maintain an elastic tactical front, he jammed behind them the mass of his Asiatic troops and so rendered the bow-front rigid.

At length the omens proving propitious, or, in other words, when Pausanias saw that with the closing up of the Asiatics the decisive moment had come, he launched his counter-attack. His hoplites scattered the rampart of shields and drove the bowmen back on the Asiatics. A fierce contest followed. "The barbarians," writes Herodotus, "many times seized hold of the Greek spears and brake them; for in boldness and warlike spirit the Persians were not a whit inferior to the Greeks; but they were without bucklers, untrained, and far below the enemy in respect of skill in arms. Sometimes singly, sometimes in bodies of ten, now fewer and now more in number, they dashed forward upon the Spartan ranks, and so perished." Herodotus continues:

"The fight went most against the Greeks, where Mardonius, mounted upon a white horse, and surrounded by the bravest of all the Persians, the thousand picked men, fought in person. So long as Mardonius was alive, this body resisted all attacks, and, while they defended their own lives, struck down no small number of Spartans, but after Mardonius fell, and the troops with him, which were the main strength of his army, perished, the remainder yielded to the Lacedaemonians, and took to flight. Their light clothing, and want of bucklers, were of the greatest hurt to them: for they had to contend against men heavily armed, while they themselves were without any such defence."[2]

Thus "did Pausanias, the son of Cleombrotus . . . win a victory exceeding in glory all those of which our knowledge extends".[3] The day of his victory was in all probability August 27, 479 B.C.

Meanwhile, what of the Athenians? When they received Pausanias's urgent message they at once changed direction and started out for where the Spartan wing then was. But no sooner had they done so than the Boeotians and other medized Greeks swept down on their left flank and compelled them to form front against them. A stiff fight followed, which ended in the Boeotians being routed and driven in disorder towards Thebes. At the same time the

---

[1] Herodotus, IX, 61.   [2] Ibid., IX, 62-63.   [3] Ibid., IX, 64.

Greek centre, which had been holding the left flank of the Island position and which so far had been unengaged, seeing the enemy in flight, moved forward in two columns, and in the plain below, the left column was routed by Theban cavalry, losing 600 men killed. It was the only disaster the Greeks suffered in this extraordinary battle.

Of the casualties little is known. Herodotus says, "of the 300,000 men who composed the [Persian] army . . . no more than 3,000 outlived the battle", and that the Spartans lost 91 killed, the Tegeans 16, and the Athenians 52.[1] In his life of Aristeides, Plutarch says that in all the Greeks lost 1,360 men killed.[2]

Ten days after the victory the Greeks invested Thebes, and on the twentieth day of the siege Mardonius's base surrendered to them on terms.

On the day Thermopylae was being fought, according to Diodorus,[3] Gelo of Syracuse decisively defeated Hamilcar at Himera (near Termini), a victory which gained for Sicily immunity from Carthage for seventy years. Also the Greek fleet, which we last heard of at Andros, was not idle. Some time in the summer of 479 B.C., when an appeal was received from Samos that if the Ionian Greeks were supported they would again revolt, the fleet was ordered to carry war into the enemy's waters.

It was at Delos at the time under the command of the Spartan king, Leotychidas. When he sailed to Samos the Persian fleet retired to Mycale, where Xerxes had posted a considerable army under Tigranes to watch the Ionian cities. At Mycale the ships were beached and fortifications were built to protect them. Leotychidas rowed past the enemy fleet, disembarked his marines and hoplites some twenty miles from Mycale, marched upon the position and carried it by assault, the Ionian Greeks helping him by turning on the Persians. Leotychidas then burnt the Persian fleet—or found it burnt—and returned to Samos.

Next, it was decided to sail to the Hellespont to impound the bridging cables and to take Sestus, the key to the Thracian Chersonese and the Persian *tête-du-pont* in Europe. But as it was strongly fortified and the Spartans disliked sieges, Leotychidas returned home, leaving it to the Athenians under Xanthippus to besiege it. Though the siege was begun in the autumn it took the

[1] Herodotus, ix, 70, a worthless estimate.
[2] *Plutarch's Lives*, trans. Bernadotte Perrin (1914), xix.
[3] Diordorus, xi, 24; Herodotus, vii, 166, says on the day Salamis was fought.

Athenians most of the winter to reduce the fortress through starvation. Artabazus, instead of coming to its relief, withdrew to Byzantium and crossed the Bosphorus into Asia.

Thus ended the first great struggle between Asia and Europe of which a full record has been preserved. And so far as war is concerned, the first thing which strikes us is that in the fifth century B.C., in all its essentials the art of war was almost as highly developed as it is to-day. Secondly, that the mistakes made during war are as common now as they were then.

To create a diversion in the central Mediterranean by stirring up the Carthaginians against the Sicilian Greeks shows that the Persians were fully aware of the meaning of grand strategy, and the Greek appeal to Gelo goes to prove that the Persians knew exactly what they were doing. Even should this diversion be set aside as uncertain, the combination of fleet and army leaves no doubt whatsoever that the relationship between sea and land power was as clearly understood as it is to-day, and not only by the Persians but by the Greeks also. Further, the administration of the fighting forces of both sides must have been of a remarkably high order; even should the army Xerxes brought to Europe have numbered no more than 100,000 men, that it was able to operate in a roadless country 800 miles from its Asiatic base is proof positive that its system of supply must have been superbly organized. And for Pausanias, in a mountainous country, to have maintained in the field an army of 80,000 strong—or even considerably less—was in itself no mean feat of administration.

In tactics, the mistakes made were those which have since pursued the soldier over many a battlefield, notably reliance on masses of semi-trained men, expecting that quantity can make good a deficit in quality, and a lack of appreciation of weapon power as well as the misapplication of weapons to ground and the tactical conditions of the moment. But above all, the whole war shows that the psychological factor, loss or gain of morale by the soldier and loss or gain of prestige by the supreme command was, as it still remains, the determining factor in war.

It was loss of prestige which not only checked the expansion, but undermined the foundations of the Persian Empire, and, like most empires before or since, led to its eventual ruin. Also it was the prestige won by the Greeks at Salamis and Plataea which started them on their astonishing course, for as Professor Bury writes: "Men seemed to rise at once to the sense of the high historical importance of their experience. The great poets of the day wrought it into their song; the great plastic artists alluded to it in their sculptures. . . . The idea was afloat in the air that the Trojan war was an earlier act in the same drama, – that the warriors of Salamis and Plataea were fighting in the same' cause as the heroes who had striven with Hector on the plain of Troy."[1]

With these battles we stand on the threshold of the western world to be, in which Greek intellect was to conquer and to lay the foundations of centuries to come. No two battles in history are, therefore, more portentous than Salamis and Plataea; they stand like the pillars of the temple of the ages supporting the architecture of western history.

[1] *A History of Greece*, J. B. Bury (1951 edit.), pp. 284–285.

VICTORY in war was the begetter of astonishing glories in peace. The 5th Century B.C. was the great age of Greece. Five years[1] before the Battle of Marathon it is thought that Sophocles was born. Four years before the Battle of Salamis Herodotus came into the world; in the year of that battle, Euripides; ten years later, Socrates. During the remainder of the century the talents of these men, and others as various as Thucydides, Aeschylus, Aristophanes, the sculptor Pheidias and the young Plato, produced the supreme flowering of Hellenic culture.

Yet victory itself is full of deceit; the decades during which the Greek cities celebrated immunity from the threat of foreign conquest, and bore sons who have been citizens of the Western world ever since, were decades of constant internecine struggle, ending in a fall as resounding as the defeat of the Persian king. The second half of the century was the period of the Peloponnesian Wars, during which the rivalries of the city-states polarised around the antagonism of Sparta and Athens. In effect, this was a contest between a land-power (Sparta) and a sea-power (Athens). The sea-power, enriched by the trade which naval supremacy guarantees, turned itself into an empire, thus arousing many resentments and jealousies. Significantly, that empire was overthrown when, but not until, its naval strength was broken.

Inevitably, because of the nature of the records left to us, we tend to see the Peloponnesian Wars from the Athenian point of view. The rise and fall of Athens do, indeed, provide a tragic drama in history as compelling as those with which the Athenian dramatists were simultaneously exciting the admiration of all Greece. Athens reached a zenith of power, says Fuller, under the leadership of Pericles in 457, when victory abroad attended her arms, and the city itself was made practically impregnable by the

---

[1] See note on p. 27

completion of the famous Long Walls connecting it with the port of the Piraeus. The decline began almost immediately afterwards; its first indication was a shattering defeat in Egypt in 454.

From 432 onwards, when the Second Peloponnesian War began, the decline gathered momentum. Natural catastrophe played its part: Pericles was among the many victims of the great plague of 430-429. "Irreplaceable," says Fuller, "for he was indispensable in his particular system of government, the destiny of Athens passed into the hands of Cleon, a man of the people who made the fatal mistake of converting what in essence was a defensive war into a war of aggression." After the death of Cleon in 423, the devious figure of Alcibiades made its first appearance, luring Athens to ultimate ruin with complex ambitions. The turbulent, anonymous Athenian "democracy" swung from one leader to another, steadfast only in its obstinate determination to cling to empire in the face of all disasters – and these were not few.

The greatest disaster was, without doubt, the utter failure of the Syracuse Expedition (415-413). Out of some 45,000 Athenian and allied troops employed, only 7,000 survived, mostly to die miserably in the quarries of Syracuse, or to be sold into slavery. In the words of Thucydides:[1]

This was the greatest Hellenic action that took place during this war, and, in my opinion, the greatest action that we know of in Hellenic history – to the victors the most brilliant of successes, to the vanquished the most calamitous of defeats; for they were utterly and entirely defeated; their sufferings were on an enormous scale; their losses were, as they say, total; army, navy, everything was destroyed, and, out of many, only few returned."

Fuller comments:

Absolute as the disaster was, its cause was not faulty strategical conception, but inept tactical execution. When the pretexts of war are set aside, the former appears brilliant: it was to make good the lack of Athenian man-power, which prohibited Athens from gaining supremacy over her enemies on land, by depriving the enemy's superior man-power of its means o subsistance – its corn, oil and trade . . . [Victory] would have

---

[1] Fuller uses Richard Crawley's translation of 1874; I have given here the version provided by Rex Warner for Penguin Books in 1954, which seems clearer. Thucydides, *The Peloponnesian War*, Bk. VII, Ch. 7.

resulted in so complete a strangulation of Peloponnesian food supplies that, faced by the returned and triumphant Athenian army, Sparta and Corinth would have been unable to maintain sufficient men in the field to wage a successful war against Athens. Athens would, consequently, and in spite of her inferior man-power, have been able to impose her will on both without resorting to battle.

If one accepts this argument, then the origins of the disaster are directly traceable to Alcibiades who . . . [substituted] a political war for a tactical operation.

Athens never recovered from the Syracuse débâcle; it was to her what the retreat from Moscow was to Napoleon. No later success, no matter how outwardly brilliant, could retrieve her spent fortune. Indeed, it is a matter for wonder that she was able to hold out for ten years longer – but in those distant days events moved more slowly to their climaxes. In this case the climax was the "battle" of Aegospotami – in fact not a battle at all, but the virtual annihilation of the last fleet of Athens, while the ships were beached and the crews dispersed, by the Spartan general Lysander. That was in 405; one year later Athens surrendered, the Long Walls were thrown down, and Spartan soldiers quartered in the Acropolis. Fuller sums up:

Thus ended the first attempt at empire building in Europe; an empire built on force and destroyed not by force or by internal decay, but by crowd psychology. After the disaster in Sicily, the most the Athenians could do was to stave off defeat; therefore they should have sought peace at the first opportune moment. But the demos would not have this, and incapable of judging events, they proved themselves incapable of holding fast to their empire. Not only did they lose it, but what was more catastrophic, by losing it the cultural and political leadership of Hellas were divorced.

The rise of Macedonia

Though, in the Peloponnesian wars, Sparta's avowed aim was the liberation of the states Athens had subjected, no sooner did the Athenian Confederacy collapse than the Spartans resolved to bring the states they had freed under their own dominion. For the age-old policy of isolation was substituted a policy of aggrandizement beyond the confines of the Peloponnese.

The first step taken was to repress the Athenian democracies and establish oligarchies in their stead, and the next was to banish their political opponents and confiscate their estates. Added to these exiles, many of whom sought refuge in Persia, were many soldiers; for during the long struggle, through constant service in the field, the old city militias had grown into standing armies, and with the coming of peace the professional soldiers were thrown out of work.

Among these mercenaries, who sold their services to the highest bidder, was Xenophon, an Athenian knight and friend of Socrates, who, with the Spartan general Clearchus, entered the service of Cyrus, satrap of Asia Minor, who was then planning to oust his elder brother Artaxerxes from the throne of Persia. Cyrus instigated the Ionian cities to revolt against their satrap, Tissaphernes, collected together an army of some 30,000 Oriental troops and 13,000 Greek mercenaries, 10,600 of whom were hoplites commanded by Clearchus, and in 401 B.C. set out from Sardes. After a march of some fifteen hundred miles he reached Cunaxa, sixty miles north of Babylon, and there came face to face with Artaxerxes and his army. In the battle which followed the initial onslaught of the Greeks carried everything before it. Cyrus thought the battle won—which it virtually was—and accompanied by a small body of horsemen, and over-eager to slay his brother with his own hand, recklessly galloped forward and was killed. His Asiatic troops were then seized with panic and fled. Nevertheless, the Greek mercenaries, though soon surrounded, refused to surrender, and Artaxerxes, fearing to attack them, yet wishing to be quit of them, agreed to provide them with guides and an escort, under Tissaphernes, to lead them back to Greece.

On the way home, by means of a ruse, the crafty satrap separated the Greek generals from their men, seized the former and sent them to Artaxerxes, who put them to death. Because he expected that the now leaderless Greeks would surrender and he still feared to attack them, Tissaphernes held back; but they, largely because of the exertions and exhortations of Xenophon, rapidly recovered from their dismay, appointed new generals, and set out on what to history is known as the "Retreat of the Ten Thousand", so fully described in Xenophon's *Anabasis*. Early in 400 B.C., and after one of the most famous retreats in history, they reached the coast of the Black Sea at Trapezus (Trebizond).

This remarkable feat electrified every Greek city. Never before had a Greek army marched to the centre of the Persian Empire, fought a great battle, and in face of hostile multitudes marched safely home again. These things clearly showed that no Oriental forces could hope to withstand an army of well-trained Greek soldiers. As Professor Bury writes of this campaign: "It is an epilogue to the invasion of Xerxes and a prologue to the conquest of Alexander."

Its consequences were immediate. The Greek Asiatic cities, fearing the return of Tissaphernes, appealed to Sparta for protection, and a Spartan army under King Agesilaus was sent to their aid. They carried war into Phrygia and Lydia with considerable success and were dreaming of marching on Babylon and dethroning Artaxerxes, when, in 394 B.C. the Spartans were rudely awakened by the reappearance of Conon, the Athenian admiral who had escaped at the battle of Aegospotami. Now in command of the Persian navy, in August Conon decisively defeated Agesilaus's fleet, commanded by Peisander, in the battle of Cnidus (Kirio-Burnu) and thereby destroyed Sparta's maritime power.

Meanwhile war had broken out in Greece between Sparta and her allies. Exasperated by Spartan exactions and supported by Persia, Thebes revolted and was joined by Athens, Corinth, and Argos, and a battle was fought near Corinth, in July, 394 B.C., in which the Spartans were victorious. Thus opened an eight-year struggle known as the Corinthian War, in which, soon after the above battle, though the Spartans under Agesilaus – now back from Asia – beat the Confederates again at Coronea (S.E. of Lake Kopias), they were compelled to abandon Boeotia and to withdraw to the Peloponnese, where they were blockaded.

The Spartans ascribed the success of their enemies to the support given them by Persia, and in 392 B.C. they sent Antalcidas to the Persian commander, Tiribazus, to propose that for Persian support they were willing to recognize the Great King's rights over all the Greek cities in Asia. Nothing definite came of this proposal until 386 B.C., when Persia's fears that Athens might rise again in the ascendant compelled her to accept the shameful "King's Peace", dictated to the Greek states by Artaxerxes. Under its terms, the Asiatic Greek cities and Cyprus were abandoned to Persia; the leadership of Sparta within Greece was acknowledged; and any state which did not accept the peace was to be compelled by Persia to do so. Thus the Great King became the arbiter of Greece with the right of perpetual interference.

Supported by Persia and now freed from her complications in Asia, Sparta returned to her despotic policy. In 378 B.C. this led Thebes again to revolt and to enter into an alliance with Athens, who meanwhile had begun to build up a second naval league on the Delian lines. War with Sparta followed, in which the Thebans successfully defended themselves and Athens gained considerable advantages at sea. In 371 B.C. a mutual agreement was arrived at between the contending parties to discuss peace; but because Sparta refused to allow Thebes to represent the whole of Boeotia, the latter decided to carry on the war single-handed, and in the eyes of all the Greeks her doom appeared sealed.

Had it not been for the Theban commander, Epaminondas, there can be little doubt that Thebes would have succumbed. But he realized that the Spartans would never change their traditional shock tactics, the success of which depended on an advance in perfect order, all spears of the phalanx striking the enemy's front simultaneously, and devised a tactics which would prevent this and throw the phalanx into confusion. Instead of drawing his troops up in parallel lines to the Spartan army, he formed them into oblique order to it, with his left leading and his right drawn back. At the same time he massed on his left wing a column of troops fifty ranks deep. Its object was to meet shock by super-shock and simultaneously to have enough reserve force in hand to lap round the enemy's right wing. In July, 371 B.C., he met King Cleombrotus and the Spartan army at Leuctra (near Domvrena) in southern Boeotia, and by means of these tactics decisively defeated him, Cleombrotus being killed. This battle not only broke the charm of Spartan prestige, but brought the short-lived Spartan hegemony to its end.

Thebes now rose in the ascendant, and between 369 and 362 B.C. had the chance of accomplishing what both Athens and Sparta had failed to do–namely, to weld the Greek states into a nation. She built a fleet and weakened Athens at sea, and under Epaminondas and Pelopidas gained the leadership of Greece. But her supremacy hung on the mortal life of one man–Epaminondas–who, in the summer of 362 B.C., at Mantinea in Arcadia, with the same tactics he had employed at Leuctra, again defeated the Spartans. Nevertheless, it was the death blow to the supremacy of Thebes, for in the pursuit Epaminondas was killed, and the light which had guided the Thebans since 379 B.C. was extinguished–her power by land and sea collapsed. Thus three great states, Athens, Sparta, and Thebes, each in turn had failed to establish a federated Hellenic world, and Hellas was ready to fall before a conqueror from the outside. His name was Philip of Macedon.

Born in 382 B.C., Philip, the third son of Amyntas III, on the death of his brother Perdiccas III, in 359 B.C., seized the throne of Macedonia, and from then to his death in 336 B.C. by sheer force of personality he dominated events. Restless and energetic, far-seeing and crafty, according to Polyaenus he won the land "by wiles rather than arms", and Hogarth, his best biographer, says of him: "Fraud before force, but force at the last" was his principle of empire.

In 367 B.C. he had been a hostage in Thebes, and during his three years there he had learnt much of war from Pelopidas and Epaminondas. This knowledge he put to good account once he had established his authority over the turbulent Macedonian clans. Next, he did something no ruler had yet done: out of his feudal bands he created a professional army endowed with a national spirit. He evolved, as Hogarth says, "the first European Power in the modern sense of the word–an armed nation with a common national ideal".

The wars he fought fall roughly into four groups: those to the west, north, and east of Macedonia, to establish his base of operations; those to the south of Macedonia, to gain control of Thessaly; those to establish his dominion over Thrace and to win the command of the Bosphorus; and those fought to impose his authority over the whole of Greece south of Thermopylae.

In 358 B.C. he warred against the Illyrian tribes, and in 357 occupied the former Athenian colony of Amphipolis on the river

Strymon and the gold mines of Pangaeus, which were of the utmost value to him. About this time he married Olympias, daughter of the Epirote king, and, in 356 B.C., she bore to him his son Alexander. Four years later he invaded Thrace and Thessaly, which led Lycophron, tyrant of Pherae (W. of Volo), to call to his help a body of Phocian mercenaries who had profaned Delphi. Philip was checked by them and retired; but he returned in the following year and proclaiming himself the champion of the outraged Apollo, he routed them in a battle fought near Volo. Other campaigns followed, when in 346 B.C., bent on gaining the command of the land route leading into Greece, he marched on Thermopylae and bribed the Phocian commander to surrender the famous pass to him. Sensing which way the wind was blowing, the Delphic Amphictyony[1] received him into the innermost circle of the Hellenes, and under his presidency the Pythian games of 346 B.C. were celebrated at Delphi in honour of its deliverance. For Philip, this was a political victory of the first order.

Of the next six years little is known, other than that Philip marched into the Peloponnese, warred on the Adriatic coast, and led his army to and beyond the Danube. During these years his final ambition took shape, "for it was coming to be his desire", writes Diodorus, "to be designated Captain-General of Hellas and to wage war against the Persian".

This grand project was in the air; for others besides Philip saw in Persia the standing danger to a divided Greece. It was almost forty years since Isocrates first urged the Greeks to bury their differences and unite as a nation. In an inspiring address given at the Olympic Games, he had said: "Anyone coming from abroad and observing the present situation of Greece would regard us as great fools struggling among ourselves about trifles and destroying our own land, when without danger we might conquer Asia."

Before he finally established his dominion over Greece, Philip determined to gain control of the Hellespontine corn route; once this was in his hands he would possess a powerful economic weapon with which to coerce the Greeks. Further, he would gain the key to the Asiatic door. He carried war into the Propontis and met with a signal failure; in 340 B.C. he failed to take by siege both Perinthus (Eregli) and Byzantium. This setback was

---

[1] The Delphic Amphictyony was originally a league of twelve ancient Greek tribes inhabiting the country round Thermopylae, which assumed the protection of the temple and worship of Apollo at Delphi and the direction of the Pythian games.

short-lived; early in 338 B.C. a herald came to him at Pella (near Janitza) from the Synod of the Amphictyons with a request that he should coerce Amphissa, a town near Delphi. Philip at once agreed, and some have credited him with having invented the invitation to efface the memory of Perinthus and Byzantium. Thebes and Athens went into alliance to oppose his advance and took the field against him. Philip then crossed into Boeotia and, late in August or early in September, 338 B.C., met them at Chaeronea (E. of Mt. Parnassus). He had with him 30,000 infantry and 3,000 cavalry, and probably his opponents were not inferior to him in numbers. But theirs was a mixed force of mercenaries and civic militias under a dual command, whereas Philip's army was a highly trained national one under his single direction.

Though little is known of the battle which followed, it would appear that the first onslaught was stubborn, and that Philip's aim was to wear down his enemies' resistance before he delivered the decisive blow. When it came, it was dealt by his son Alexander, in command of the Macedonian cavalry who shattered the Theban flank. The whole of the Theban-Athenian line then gave way and a general rout, including Philip's implacable enemy Demosthenes, the Athenian orator, followed.

Chaeronea made Philip lord of the Hellenes *de facto*, and to become so *de jure*, he first secured Corinth and next he invited all the Greek states within Thermopylae to send delegates to a Congress at the isthmus; all sent delegates except Sparta, which refused. He spoke at length at the congress of his resolution to make war on Persia and to liberate the Greek cities in Asia. The Confederacy elected him Captain-General with supreme powers, and Parmenio, Amyntas, and Attalus, with a strong force, were sent to hold the Hellespont and to win a footing in the Troad and Bithynia, while the main Panhellenic army of invasion was being assembled.

In the autumn of 336 B.C., immediately before he intended to set out to join Parmenio, he was assassinated while attending in Pella the marriage of his daughter. Thus the great project became the inheritance of his son, whose work – the expansion of the Macedonian hegemony into one of world-wide empire – is the most authentic testimony of his father's genius.

CHAPTER 2

The Battle of Gaugamela or Arbela, 331 B.C.

Imperialism was an essentially eastern conception and foreign to Hellenism. In idea it was theocratic and not aristocratic or democratic. Nor was it purely autocratic, as were the Greek tyrannies; instead it was mystical, because in eastern eyes the king was more than an absolute monarch, above all he was the vicar, or son of the gods, and their priests were his ministers. He ruled his empire, not so much by the right of the sword as by the will of the gods, and when many lands were concerned, as an instrument of government it became clearly convenient that there should be one god who gave to their common ruler power and authority over all men irrespective of race. Further, should this expansion of divinity be carried a step farther, so that it embraced the whole of the known world, then it followed that the right to conquer the lands of a neighbouring god could be expanded into the right or even duty to establish a world-wide empire, the secular domain of the one and only god. Aton, as we have seen, was probably the earliest example of this divine evolution.

This idea was totally foreign to Philip, for the Corinthian League he created, like all the Greek leagues which had preceded it, was no more than a confederation of city states under his military leadership. We may, therefore, conclude that, had Philip lived, though he might have avenged Greece upon Persia, because he neither believed himself to be, nor was accepted as a vicar of the gods, he could never have carried the idea of a world ruler into his conquests, and thereby have leavened them into a world empire – that is, an empire extending over the known world of its day.

This supreme idea of divine conquest was left to his son, and though Dr. Tarn is probably right when he says that Alexander never contemplated becoming a world ruler,[1] the fact remains, which will be discussed later, that he conceived the idea of a divine world ruler, out of which the conception of a universal world empire took shape. It was because he discerned a new relationship between God and man, the aim of which, as we shall see, was

[1] *Alexander the Great* W. W. Tarn (1948), vol. II, Appendix 24.

to establish harmony between man and man—undermining the principle of enmity which separated city from city and people from people, and exalting the principle of amity which united them into a single city and a common brotherhood—that it was possible for Droysen to open his history of him by saying: "The name of Alexander betokens the end of one world epoch and the beginning of another." Equally it made possible what one of his latest biographers, Wilcken, has written: "The whole subsequent course of history, the political, economic and cultural life of after times, cannot be understood apart from the career of Alexander."[1]

More than a world-conqueror, he established a world idea which ever since has reverberated down the ages, and because of this, no man in history approaches him in the span of his fame. In Rome he was glorified by the early Caesars; in Jewish folk-lore he was acclaimed the precursor of the Messiah; and in Turkestan and Badakhshan chieftains of note still seek in him their ancestor. The "Romance"[2] which emanated from his life swept from Iceland to the Yellow Sea; it transformed him into the son of the last Pharaoh, Nectanebo; a scion of the Achaemenid house; a fervent Moslem; a Christian saint; and an all-powerful magician. Fabulous though these legends are, each contains a grain of truth, that Alexander was a prodigy among men.

Born in 356 B.C., probably in the month of October, though it was his father, whose legendary ancestor was Heracles, who impregnated him with the idea of vengeance against Persia, it was from his mother, Olympias, that he inherited the passion which fructified it. A remarkable woman, savage, mystical and domineering, she was the daughter of Neoptolemus of Epirus, who traced his descent from Achilles. At Dodona (Dramisos) in her native land, she had worshipped at the most ancient oracle of Zeus,[3] and was aware that the more mysterious oracle of Amon was situated at the oasis of Siwa. Besides Heracles and Achilles, Dionysus, son of Zeus and Semele, a daughter of Cadmus king of Thebes, was also one of Alexander's legendary ancestors, and in Macedonia a day was set apart for his worship.[4] He was a man-god who,

---

[1] *Alexander the Great*, Ulrich Wilcken (1932), p. 265.

[2] *The Romance of Alexander*, attributed to "Pseudo-Callisthenes" (Aisopos) is the work of many hands. There are several versions of it, the original appearing in Egypt in the second century A.D. The Ethiopic Version has been translated by Sir Ernest W. Budge under the title *The Alexander Book in Ethiopia* (1933).

[3] Its greatest influence was during the heroic age; later on it was supplanted by the oracle of Delphi.

[4] *Arrian's Anabasis Alexandri*, trans. E. Iliff Robson (1929), IV, VIII.

tradition affirmed, had journeyed through Lydia and Egypt to India, spreading the mystical cult of the vine and conquering the nations as he went. These myths, which were spiritual realities in the age in which Olympias lived, had a profound influence upon her and through her upon her son.

Next to the influence of his father and mother came that of Aristotle, whom Philip engaged as his tutor when his son was thirteen years old, and with whom he remained in the little village of Mieza for three years. Under him he became inspired with love of Greek culture and a deep veneration for Homer, a copy of whose works, annotated by Aristotle, it is said he carried with him throughout his campaigns. While under his tutorship there can be little doubt that Aristotle instilled into him hatred of the Persians, for they had murdered Aristotle's friend and relative, Hermeias tyrant of Atarneus.

With such parents and such a tutor, coupled with his native genius and inexhaustible energy, it is not to be wondered at that everything Alexander did took upon itself the superlative mood. He was incredibly brave and yet profoundly cautious. Both as realist and idealist, a doer and a foreseer, he stood out above all his fellows, whether as a man of action or man of thought. He was both mystical and practical, and to all who came into contact with him infinitely magnetic. Though imaginative in the extreme, his imagination seldom ran away with his reason, and he was as meticulous in detail as he was expansive in general ideas. In his eulogy of Alexander, Arrian says it seemed to him that a hero so totally unlike any other human being could not have been born "without some divine influence".[1]

We are told that Alexander was of medium height and of fair complexion; he had, says Plutarch, a habit of inclining his head "a little to one side towards his left shoulder". A swift runner, he despised professional athletes, and on his campaigns, when he was free from employment, "he would spend the day in hunting, or administering justice, or arranging his military affairs, or reading. . . . Often too, for diversion he would hunt foxes or birds. . . ."[2] "He was also by nature", Plutarch further relates, "a lover of learning and a lover of reading . . . and when he could find no other books [except the *Iliad*] in the interior of Asia, he ordered Harpalus to send him some. So Harpalus sent him the books of

---

[1] *Arrian's Anabasis Alexandri*, VII, XXX.
[2] *Plutarch's Lives*, trans. Bernadotte Perrin (1919), "Alexander", XXIII.

Philistus", and "a great many of the tragedies of Euripides, Sophocles and Aeschylus. . . ."[1]

But it was his moral outlook which, above all his qualities, distinguished him from his contemporaries. He could, in an age in which compassion was considered to be unmanly, show compassion to others and pity to those in misfortune. At Ephesus he stopped the Ephesians slaughtering the oligarchs, for he knew if the people were not checked, they "would put to death, together with the guilty, certain others, some from hatred, and some for plunder of their goods".[2] At the siege of Miletus, when some of the besieged had sought refuge on an island, Alexander, seeing that they "were going to fight to the death, he felt compassion for them; as noble and loyal soldiers, and made terms with them that they should join his forces".[3] After the battle of Issus he showed compassion to the Theban ambassadors, partly out of pity for Thebes[4] which he regretted having destroyed. And when on his return from India, during the march through the desert of Gedrosia (Makran), some of the famishing soldiers placed on guard over the magazines of corn, pilfered from them, Alexander, "on learning of the grave necessity pardoned the offenders".[5]

But it was in his outlook upon women—in nearly all ages considered the legitimate spoil of the soldier—that Alexander stood in a totally different moral world compared with the one inhabited by his contemporaries. Not only did he treat the captive wife and daughters of Darius with a royal respect, but he held in abhorrence rape and violence, which in his day were the universal concomitants of war. On one occasion, "when he heard that two Macedonians of Parmenio's regiment had outraged the wives of some of the mercenary soldiers, he wrote to Parmenio ordering him, in case the men were convicted to punish them and put them to death as wild beasts born for the destruction of mankind".[6] On another occasion, when Atropates, viceroy of Media, presented him with a hundred girls equipped and armed like horsemen, "Alexander sent them from the army, lest they should meet any roughness from the Macedonians or foreign troops. . . ."[7] And at the sack of Persepolis he issued the amazing order that the women were not to be touched. Yet, in spite of this extraordinary respect for womanhood, his highest moral virtue is to be discovered in one of the final remarks Arrian makes in *The Anabasis*. In his

[1] Arrian, VIII.   [2] *Ibid.*, I, XVII.   [3] *Ibid.*, I, XIX.   [4] *Ibid.*, II, XV.
[5] *Ibid.*, VI, XXIII.   [6] Plutarch's "Alexander", XXII.   [7] Arrian, VII, XIII.

apology for Alexander's errors he writes: "But I do know that to Alexander alone of the kings of old did repentance for his faults come by reason of his noble nature."[1]

Of his generalship much has been written; but of all the summaries Arrian's is probably the most true, because the main source of *The Anabasis* was the lost history of Alexander's general, Ptolemy, written after he had become king of Egypt. It runs as follows:

He was "of much shrewdness, most courageous, most zealous for honour and danger, and most careful of religion . . . most brilliant to seize on the right course of action, even where all was obscure; and where all was clear, most happy in his conjectures of likelihood; most masterly in marshalling an army and in arming and equipping it; and in uplifting his soldiers' spirits and filling them with good hopes, and brushing away anything fearful in dangers by his own want of fear—in all this most noble. And all that had to be done in uncertainty he did with the utmost daring; he was most skilled in swift anticipation and gripping of his enemy before anyone had time to fear the event. . . ."[2]

On his accession Alexander found himself menaced on all sides and acted with startling rapidity. First he advanced into Thessaly and by turning the flank of the Thessalian garrison at Tempe he won so decisive a bloodless victory that he was at once elected head of the Thessalian League. Next, he descended on Thermopylae and was recognized by the Amphictyony as Philip's successor. So rapid was his southward advance that Athens, then preparing to break away from Macedonia, at once submitted to him and the Congress of the Corinthian Confederacy elected him Captain-General in his father's place. Thus, within a few weeks of Philip's death, he had so firmly established his position within Greece that he was able to set out and secure the northern and western frontiers of his realm by imposing his will on the wild tribes bordering upon them. In two astonishing campaigns, the one on the Danube and the other in Illyria, he established his authority, and, immediately he had done so, set out southward at top speed, for again trouble was brewing within Greece, this time fostered by Persia.

In 338 B.C. Artaxerxes III, son of Artaxerxes II, the victor of Cunaxa, was assassinated and succeeded by Codomannus, a distant relative, who, adopting the name Darius, became Darius III. He feared the rise of Macedonia, and when Alexander was en-

---

[1] Arrian, VII. XXIX.
[2] *Ibid.*, VII, XXVIII.

gaged in the north seized the opportunity to send 300 talents to Athens as a bribe. Though the Athenians refused it, it was accepted by Demosthenes, and about the same time rumours came in that Alexander and his army had perished in the wilds of Illyria. The Thebans did not wait to verify these reports and laid siege to the Macedonian garrison holding the Cadmea, the Athenians supporting the former with a contingent. Then, suddenly, the Thebans learnt that instead of being dead Alexander was at Onchestus, a town some fifteen miles north-west of Thebes. He had marched there with such speed that his coming fell like a thunderbolt on the Thebans. The next day he was before the walls of their city, and seizing one of its gates in a surprise attack, 6,000 Thebans were slaughtered; after which the city was levelled with the ground and its lands divided up among the members of the Confederacy. Terrified by this catastrophe, the Athenians at once submitted and were treated with great leniency, not only because Alexander recognized Athens to be the cultural centre of Greece, but because he did not want the powerful Athenian fleet to go over to the Persians. Thus, in little more than twelve months he had securely established a base of operations in Europe from which he could launch his attack against Persia.

Alexander left Antipater with some 9,000 foot and a small body of horse to hold Greece and to watch Sparta and assembled his fleet of 160 triremes at Lake Cercinitis–the lower waters of the Strymon river. Late in 335 B.C., or early in the following year, he set out from Pella with his army for Sestus. While it was being ferried over to Abydus, he sailed down the Hellespont and visited Troy, so that he might lay a wreath on the tomb of Achilles and propitiate the genius of the most human of his traditional ancestors. At Arisbe, a few miles east of Abydus, he rejoined his army, which now numbered 30,000 foot and 5,000 horse,[1] and, to clear his left flank before marching into central Persia, he advanced on the river Granicus (Bigha Tschai), where lay an army of 20,000 Asiatic horse and 20,000 Greek mercenaries under Memnon of Rhodes.[2] On the Granicus, in May or June, 334 B.C., he won the first of his four major battles. It was followed by the submission of the whole of Hellespontine Phrygia. Turning south, he marched on Sardes, which capitulated; next to Ephesus, which submitted; and

[1] Arrian, I, XI.
[2] Ibid., I, XIV. Tarn (Alexander the Great, vol. I, p. 16) says the cavalry must have been considerably less.

then to Miletus, which refusing to do so was besieged and occupied in July. There he made his first great decision since the campaign had opened. It was to wrest the command of the sea from the Persians, not by destroying their fleet, for he had not the means to do so, but by occupying all its ports and bases on the shores of the eastern Mediterranean. This formidable task took him two years to accomplish.

The first of these bases was Halicarnassus (Bodrum). When he found that its reduction would be a long task, Alexander left 3,000 foot and 200 horse under Ptolemy to besiege it while he pressed on to Gordium (Bela-Hissar), in two columns, one under Parmenio moving through Lydia, and the other, under himself following the Lycian coast. From Gordium he marched by way of Ancyra to Tarsus, and thence to where Alexandretta now stands, arriving there in October, 333 B.C.

Meanwhile Darius had assembled an army at Sochoi, to the east of the Amanus Mountains, and learning that Alexander was advancing southward along the coast, he abandoned the plain lands, crossed the Amanus range, came down on Issus, at the northern extremity of the Gulf of Alexandretta, and cut the Macedonian line of communications and supply. Immediately this became known to Alexander he doubled back and fought the second of his major battles—the Battle of Issus—on the banks of the river Pinarus (Deli Tschai). There the Persians were routed and Darius put to flight.

Alexander held fast to his aim—the occupation of the Persian naval bases—and instead of pushing inland after his beaten enemy he continued his advance down the Syrian coast. Aradus (near Tripoli), Byblus (Jebeil), and Sidon opened their gates to him, and Tyre would have done likewise had not he demanded the right of sacrificing to the Tyrian god Melkarth, whom the Greeks called the Heracles of Tyre. The request was refused, the island city was besieged, and after one of the most famous and extraordinary sieges in history, which lasted from January to August, 332 B.C., it was stormed. Thus, not only did all the Persian naval bases, but also all the Phoenician city fleets, including that of Cyprus, pass into Alexander's hands. Together, they gave him absolute command of the eastern Mediterranean and made Macedonia the greatest naval power in the world.

He moved on through what to-day is Palestine, and Gaza, after a two-month siege, was stormed and Egypt cut off from any possible Persian assistance. Alexander sent his fleet to Pelusium, marched on to Memphis, and entered the capital of the Pharaohs where, according to the "Romance", he was placed on a throne in the temple of Ptah, and invested as King of Egypt. From Memphis he sailed down the Nile to Canopus, and close by Rhacotis he chose the site of Alexandria, the most famous of the many cities which bore his name.

Early in 331 B.C. he marched two hundred and twenty miles over the desert to visit the oracle of Amon at Siwa, which legend affirmed had been conquered by his ancestors Perseus[1] and Heracles. According to Plutarch (though modern scholarship disputes the story), as he approached the shrine in the oasis he was met by a priest who, wishing to give him a friendly greeting in the Greek language, said, "O my son", but being a foreigner, mispronounced the words so as to say "Son of Zeus", a mistake which pleased Alexander and as a story caused men to say that the god himself had addressed him as "O son of Zeus".[2] Together they went to the god; but what was revealed to Alexander is unknown, except that it was so great a secret he dared not even communicate it to his mother in writing.[3]

Whatever it was, it would seem to be more than a coincidence that, immediately after the priest addressed Alexander as "Son of Zeus", Plutarch relates the following incident: That while in Egypt, he attended the lectures of the philosopher Psammon, and was especially pleased when he pointed out that God is King over all men, "since in every case that which gets the mastery and rules is divine. Still more philosophical, however, was his own opinion and utterance on this head, namely that although God was indeed common father of all mankind, still He made peculiarly His own the noblest and best of them."[4]

---

[1] Perseus was the grandfather of Alcmena, the mother of Heracles.

[2] Plutarch's "Alexander", XXVII. Alexander never claimed to be son of Zeus, though he acquiesced in people calling him so. But in Egypt, having been crowned Pharaoh, he automatically became son of his divine father Amon-Re as well as of his actual father Philip.

[3] In all probability it was that Amon declared Alexander to be his beloved son, on whom he bestowed "the immortality of Ra, and the royalty of Horus, victory over all his enemies, and the dominion of the world," etc., etc. In this the important point is that this declaration "was the only formula known by which the priests could declare him *de jure* King of Egypt, as he already was *de facto*" (*A History of Egypt under the Ptolemaic Dynasty*, J. P. Mahaffy, 1899, p. 16).

[4] *Ibid.*, XXVII. ". . . what he had in mind was presumably his own adoption by Ammon, for his whole career illustrates his conviction that Ammon had made him 'peculiarly his own'" (*Alexander the Great and the Unity of Mankind* W. W. Tarn, 1933, p. 25).

From this we may hazard that, whatever the priest or god actually said to him, he came away from the shrine with the idea in his mind that, because the sun-god Amon-Re shines upon all men, good and evil, alike, the conception of *Homonoia* – "unity in concord" or "being of one mind together" – without which there could be no true peace within a city state, should be expanded to include the whole world as the City of God, and, therefore, to all human beings irrespective of race. According to Dr. Tarn, this was an advance far beyond the idea of *Homonoia* held by either Plato, Aristotle, or Isocrates.[1] Professor Wright holds the same opinion. He says: "To Aristotle he owed much, but he went far beyond his master when, casting aside the distinction between Hellene and barbarian, he boldly proclaimed the universal brotherhood of man."[2] On this question, possibly the most important intellectual event in the history of the world, Tarn writes:

"What Eratosthenes says amounts to this. Aristotle told Alexander to treat Greeks as friends, but barbarians like animals; but Alexander knew better, and preferred to divide men into good and bad without regard to their race, and thus carried out Aristotle's real intention. For Alexander believed that he had a mission from the deity to harmonize men generally and be the reconciler of the world, mixing men's lives and customs as in a loving cup, and treating the good as his kin, the bad as strangers; for he thought that the good man was the real Greek and the bad man the real barbarian. "

Commenting on this, he continues:

"It is obvious that, wherever all this comes from, we are dealing with a great revolution in thought. It amounts to this, that there is a natural brotherhood of all men, though bad men do not share in it; that *Homonoia* is no longer to be confined to the relations between Greek and Greek, but is to unite Greek and barbarian; and that Alexander's aim was to substitute peace for war, and reconcile the enmities of mankind by bringing them all – all that is whom his arm could reach, the peoples of his empire – to be of one mind together; as men were one in blood, so they should become one in heart and spirit."[3]

Xenophon, in his *Cyropaedia*, had in Cyrus presented Alexander with the picture of the ideal world ruler. Plato had written of the

[1] *Alexander the Great and the Unity of Mankind*, pp. 4–5.
[2] *Alexander the Great*, F. A. Wright (1934), p. 2.
[3] *Alexander the Great and the Unity of Mankind*, p. 7.

philosopher-king, and, as Henri Berr has pointed out: "Being accustomed to leave the circle of facts to soar into the sphere of ideas, he [Alexander] rose to the principle that there must be one single ruler for men, just as there is only one sun to light the earth."[1] Thus, in his mystical metamorphosis at Siwa, the philosopher-taught king became the god-king. So it came about that through Alexander the West received from the East the ideas of the theocratic empire and king worship, the one to find its blossoming in the Roman Empire and its successor, the Empire of Christendom, and the other to be transmuted into the divine right of kings.

This extended interpretation of *Homonoia*—"one of the supreme revolutions in the world's outlook"[2]—afterwards became the goal of all his conquests, and it lead him from Siwa towards the ends of the world, as they seemed to be in his day.

When he returned to Memphis and found reinforcements from Greece awaiting him, Alexander hastened to organize his control over Egypt. He appointed his garrison commanders and ordered them to allow the governors to rule their respective districts according to ancient custom; but to collect from them the tribute due to him.[3] His method throughout his reign was invariably the same: he separated civil administration from military control. The former he handed over to the representatives of the conquered people, and the latter he placed in the hands of one of his chosen Macedonians.

In the spring of 331 B.C., he bridged the Nile and marched back to Tyre, where he found his fleet had already arrived. From there he sent a strong squadron to the Peloponnese to counteract the intrigues of the Spartans, and thence, by way of the valley of the Orontes, he marched towards Antioch. Turning eastward he debouched on the Euphrates at Thapsacus (the ford of El-Hamman), and in its vicinity founded the city of Nicephorium (Rakkah) as a strong point and depot on his line of communications. At first he intended to cross the Tigris near Nineveh, at the spot where Mosul now stands; but when he learnt that Darius was in this region with a large army he decided to cross the river north-west of the old Assyrian capital and to march down its left bank towards Arbela (Erbil).

The army which was now destined to win what was to be the

---

[1] In Foreword to *Macedonian Imperialism and the Hellenization of the East*, Pierre Jouguet (1928), pp. xiii-xiv.
[2] *Alexander the Great and the Unity of Mankind*, p. 28.   [3] Arrian, III, v.

most epoch-making of all the decisive battles of the western world was the creation of Philip, and as a military organizer his greatness springs from his appreciation that mobility is the governing tactical element in army organization. Up to his day battles had been looked upon as competitions of endurance, in which victory went to the side which won the battlefield and erected a trophy upon it. In any case, because of its rigidity, the phalanx could not pursue without breaking its order, when it became easy prey to light-armed and mounted troops. What Philip saw was that the tussle on the battlefield was only a means to an end, the tactical end being the annihilation of the enemy in the pursuit. He organized his army with this aim in view and combined all classes of fighters in one tactical instrument. While his infantry clinched with the enemy and held him, his cavalry manœuvred and struck the decisive blow: the first was the bow from which the arrow was shot.

Long before his day the Macedonian cavalry had consisted of nobles called *Hetairoi*, or the King's Companions. It was a very ancient title, dating back to the *Iliad*, in which the 2,500 Myrmidons of Achilles are called by the same name. In Philip's day the infantry was already in the process of being transformed from a mere gathering of armed peasants into organized regular infantry called *Pezhetairoi*, or Foot Companions. Philip divided the cavalry into regiments (*Ilae*), each from 1,500 to 1,800 strong, one of which was constituted the *Agema* of the Companions, or the Royal Horse Guard. The Companion (heavy) cavalry were armed with the sword and wore helmets and corselets, but their chief weapon was the lance. Because stirrups were not introduced until the sixth century A.D., the lance was used as a thrusting weapon and was not couched for shock as in the Middle Ages. For the old hoplite Philip substituted a soldier who was a cross between the hoplite and the light armed *peltast*, armed with a long pike and small round shield (*pelta*), introduced by the Athenian general Iphicrates in 392 B.C. The new hoplite was armed with a fourteen-foot spear, the *sarissa*,[1] and a light shield carried on the right arm; he wore greaves and a metal protected jerkin of leather. Philip organized the infantry of the phalanx in regiments (*taxeis*) each normally containing 1,536 men divided into battalions and companies. The smallest unit was the file of sixteen men, but by Alexander normally it was reduced to eight men.

[1] See Tarn's *Alexander the Great*, vol. II, pp. 170–171.

Besides the phalangites, Philip raised three battalions of light-armed infantry, the Hypaspists, each 1,000 strong, to act as a link between the faster moving cavalry of the right wing and the slower moving phalanx. The three together may be compared to a slow moving wall on the left, a fast moving door on the right, with a hinge in between. The hinge, or flexible link – Hypaspists – was essential to an advance in oblique order, for without it contact between the cavalry and phalanx would almost certainly be lost, and in all ancient fighting the maintenance of an unbroken front was always the aim. One battalion of the Hypaspists was known as the *Agema*, or Royal Foot Guard.

In addition to the above, which were wholly Macedonian, Philip raised a considerable body of light allied cavalry, mainly Thessalian. And in addition to the Macedonian infantry, Alexander had a large force of Confederate infantry and also a force of mercenaries.

Up to Philip's time, sieges in Greece had depended upon starving out the besieged garrisons. To speed this slow process, Philip introduced siege engines from Sicily, where for long they had been used by Greek and Carthaginian engineers.

Of Alexander's artillery and engineers[1] we know next to nothing, and nothing whatever of his baggage and supply trains. The artillery was provided with two types of catapults, one which threw stone shot and the other javelins, and the engineers were provided with the necessary tools and materials for building battering-rams, siege-towers, ramps, bridges, and encampments. All these arms and services were commanded by Alexander, who was helped by an organized staff, comprising a Secretariat; the Keepers of the Diary; Keepers of the King's Plans; Surveyors; the Official Historian; and many specialists and scientific research workers. As a whole, the army, unlike any which had preceded it, was not solely an army of conquest, but above all an army of occupation, organized for scientific exploration as well as for fighting.

Darius recruited another army after his defeat at Issus, and since we are told that he armed certain of his divisions with swords

[1] Tarn (*Alexander the Great*, vol. II, pp. 39–40) gives the names of the following engineers on the headquarters staff: Diades of Thessaly, Charias and Poseidonius, siege engineers; Gorgos, water and mining engineer; Deinocrates, town planning expert; Aristobolus, architect and engineer; Baeton, Diognetos and Philonides, bematists (steppers), who dealt with routes and camps and kept geographical records. Besides these, Nearchus and Onesicritus were naval experts, and Eumenes head of the Secretariat.

and longer spears, the better to cope with the *sarissa*, it is apparent that he was not beyond learning a lesson. He marched northward from Babylon, crossed to the left bank of the Tigris, and proceeded to Arbela, the "city of the four gods", where he established his magazines and harem. From there he moved forward to Gaugamela (Mound of Tel Gomel) on the river Bumodos (Khajir), a tributary of the Greater Zab; which place is about eighteen miles north-east of Mosul and thirty-five west of Arbela. The reason why he selected this locality was that it consisted of an extensive plain (near Keramlais), and, therefore, favoured his large forces of cavalry.

Alexander crossed the Tigris while this was being done and, on September 20, when resting his army on its eastern bank, a partial eclipse of the moon occurred, so he sacrificed to Selene, Helios, and Ge (Moon, Sun, and Earth).[1]

A few days later, after his scouts had informed him that the Persians were approaching, he at once prepared for battle, and at the head of a picked force of cavalry marched with all speed towards his enemy, having ordered the rest of his army to follow at walking pace.[2] From captured prisoners he learnt that the Persian king was at Gaugamela at the head of 40,000 cavalry, 1,000,000 infantry,[3] 200 scythe-bearing chariots[4] and a few war elephants.[5] Meanwhile Darius, by levelling the land and removing obstacles, converted the plain of Gaugamela into an immense parade ground, on which he drew up his army in the following order of battle:

"The left wing the Bactrian cavalry held, and with them the Dahans [a Scythian tribe] and the Arachotians; next to them were arrayed the Persians, cavalry and infantry mixed, and after the Persians Susians, and after the Susians Cadusians. This was the

[1] Arrian, III, VII. As Alexander selected these gods, it may be concluded that he understood the cause of a lunar eclipse.

[2] *Ibid.*, III, VIII.

[3] These figures are Arrian's and clearly are exaggerated. What the actual strength was is unknown. Justin gives 400,000 foot and 100,000 horse; Curtius 45,000 cavalry and 200,000 infantry; and Diodorus and Plutarch 1,000,000 all told.

[4] Chariots at times could be very effective, see Xenophon's *Hellenica*, IV, I, 18. Lucretius (*On the Nature of Things*, III, 660–662) gives a dramatic description of their use: "Reeking with indiscriminate slaughter, they lop off limbs so instantaneously that what has been cut away is seen to quiver on the ground before any pain is felt. One man perceives not that the wheels and devouring scythes have carried off among the horses' feet his left arm, shield and all; another while he presses forward sees not that his right arm has dropped from him; a third tries to get up after he has lost a leg, while the dying foot quivers with its toes on the ground close by."

[5] The first recorded instance outside India of the employment of elephants in battle.

disposition of the left wing up to the centre of the entire phalanx. On the right were marshalled the troops from Lowland Syria and Mesopotamia; and next on the right were Medes, and with them the Parthyaeans and Sacians, then Tapurians and Hyrcanians, and then Albanians and Sacesinians, right up to the centre of the entire phalanx. In the centre, where was King Darius, were posted the king's kinsmen, the Persians whose spears are fitted with golden apples, Indians, the 'transplanted' Carians, as they were called, and the Mardian bowmen. The Uxians, Babylonians, Red Sea tribes, and Sitacenians were in deep formation behind them. Then, in advance, on the left wing, facing Alexander's right, were the Scythian cavalry, some thousand Bactrians, and a hundred scythe-chariots. The elephants were posted ahead of Darius's royal squadron and fifty chariots. In front of the right wing were posted the Armenian and Cappadocian cavalry and fifty scythe-chariots. The Greek mercenaries, close by Darius, and his Persian troops, on either side were stationed exactly opposite the Macedonian phalanx as being the only troops able to meet the phalanx."[1]

From this discription it is not possible to make out how the various bodies of men were actually marshalled. The accompanying diagrams show what Colonel Dodge[2] considered to be the probable distribution. According to Tarn, the whole of the first line was composed of cavalry "with a second line of infantry behind them".[3] The right wing was commanded by Mazaeus and the left by Bessus.[4]

After he had ascertained the dispositions of his enemy, Alexander spent four days in resting his army and in strengthening his camp with a ditch and a stockade. About the second watch of the fourth night after crossing the Tigris he broke camp and marched towards Darius, "so as to meet the enemy at dawn".[5] When some three and a half miles distant from the Persians, he halted and assembled his generals. Parmenio, his second in command, suggested that they should encamp where they were and reconnoitre the ground and the enemy. Alexander agreed to this, and while the camp was being fortified he "took the light infantry and the Cavalry Companions and rode all round surveying the ground which was to be the battlefield".[6]

[1] Arrian, III, XI.   [2] *Alexander*, Theodore Ayrault Dodge (1890), vol. II, p. 371.
[3] *Alexander the Great*, vol. II, p. 183.
[4] *Quintus Curtius*, trans. John C. Rolfe (1946), IV, XVI, and IV, XV, 2.
[5] Arrian, III, IX.   [6] *Ibid.*, III, IX.

He again called together a conference on his return at which he discussed what he had seen and urged upon his generals the importance of the immediate execution of orders.

On September 30, the night before the battle, when Darius was holding a kind of midnight tattoo, Alexander's army rested. Parmenio came to the king's tent to suggest a night attack, but

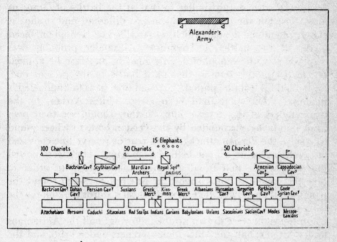

7. DARIUS'S ORDER OF BATTLE AT ARBELA, 331 B.C.

(See footnote 3, page 100.)

Alexander refused to consider it.[1] In the forthcoming battle he had planned to deliver a decisive blow, and he realized well the difficulties coincident with night operations. Alexander drew up his army as follows:

The right wing was held by the Companions, the Hypaspists, and presumably, three *taxeis* of the phalanx. Thus, to the right front stood the Royal Squadron of Clitus; slightly to his left the squadrons of Glaucias, Aristo, Sopolis, Heraclides, Demetrius, Meleager, and Hegelochus. The whole of the cavalry was under the command of Philotas, son of Parmenio. Next came the *Agema*, and then the Hypaspists under Nicanor. The phalanx was marshalled as follows: the brigade of Coenus on the right, then

[1] Arrian, III, x.

those of Perdiccas, Meleager, Polysperchon, Simmias, and Craterus; Craterus, as usual, commanded the infantry of the left wing. On the left came the Greek cavalry under Erigyius, then the Thessalian cavalry under Philip. The whole of the left wing was under the command of Parmenio, around whose person were ranged the Pharsalian horsemen.[1]

So far there was nothing unusual in this order of battle. The array was normal and similar to that at the battles of Granicus and Issus; but the tactical problem was different, and in idea it closely resembled the one which, as described by Xenophon, faced Cyrus at the battle of Thymbra.[2] Alexander probably was acquainted with Xenophon's *Cyropaedia*; in any case he applied the tactics of this semi-mythological battle to the present one, for behind his front he posted "a second line, so as to duplicate his phalanx".[3] Directions had been given, writes Arrian, to the commanders of this reserve line, "if they should see their own front line being surrounded by the Persian host, to wheel round to receive the Persian attack".[4] This rear or reserve line consisted of two flying columns, one behind each wing. They were posted "angular wise"—that is, at an angle to the front—in order to take the enemy in flank should he attempt to sweep round the wings; or, if he did not, they were to wheel inwards to reinforce the front of the army.

On the right were drawn up the following: half the Agrianians under Attalus; half the Macedonian archers under Briso, and the Veteran Mercenaries (infantry) under Cleander. In front of the first two were posted the light cavalry under Aretes and the Paeonians under Ariosto, and to their front the Grecian mercenary cavalry under Menidas. The rest of the Agrianians, archers and javelin-men of Balacrus, was drawn up in front of the Companion cavalry to oppose the charge of the Persian scythe-bearing chariots. Instructions had been given to Menidas and the troops under him to wheel round and attack the enemy in flank if they should ride round their wing.[5] The left column was similarly marshalled at an angle to the front. First the Thracians under Sitalces, then the cavalry of the Greek allies under Coeranus, next the Odrysian cavalry under Agatho. In front of these were drawn up the Greek mercenaries under Andromachus. The baggage guard consisted

[1] Arrian, III, XI.   [2] *Cyropaedia*, VII, I.
[3] Arrian, III, XII. See Arrian's *Tactics*, 29, for this arrangement.
[4] *Ibid.*, III, XII.   [5] *Ibid.*, III, XII.

of Thracian infantry. In all, Alexander's army numbered 7,000 cavalry and 40,000 infantry.

Of Alexander's grand tactical formation Colonel Dodge writes: "This disposition has been called a grand hollow square, but it

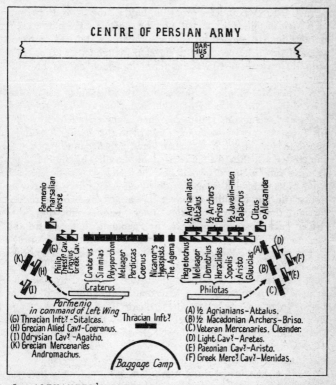

8. ALEXANDER'S ORDER OF BATTLE AT ARBELA, 331 B.C.

was more than that. The arrangements were such as to ensure greater mobility than a square is capable of possessing. For the flying columns were so organised and disposed that they could face in any direction, and were prepared to meet attacks from front, flank or rear. Indeed, the left flying column met an attack from within, and beat it off. 'In fine', says Curtius, 'he had so disposed his army that it fronted every way'—he should have said could front every way—'and was ready to engage on all sides, if attempted to be encompassed; thus the front was not better secured than the flanks, nor the flanks better provided than the rear!"[1]

Such was Alexander's order of battle, and it is important to bear it in mind; for, as will now be shown, in the battle itself, because he had gauged his enemy's intentions and had prepared to meet them, he was able to develop his tactics in accordance with his own idea. It was his foresight which gained him the victory.

As the Macedonians approached the Persians, Alexander, instead of moving directly upon them, inclined towards their left wing, and seeing this Darius marched along parallel with him,[2] his Scythian cavalry galloping forward to the attack. Alexander continued his oblique approach and gradually began to get beyond the ground which had been cleared and levelled by the Persians.[3] Fearing that his chariots would become useless, Darius ordered the front units of his left wing to ride round Alexander's right wing and compel it to halt. To meet this attack, Alexander moved forward the Greek mercenaries under Menidas, but they were driven back in confusion. Next, the Paeonians under Aristo and Cleander's mercenaries were ordered forward; and, in reply, Bessus sent in the Bactrian and Scythian horsemen. These broke the ranks of the Companions and heavy losses resulted, the Scythians and their horses being "better protected by defensive armour".[4] In spite of this, Macedonian discipline and valour began to tell as squadron after squadron charged home, and Bessus's attack was driven back. Apparently to take advantage of the confusion into which the Companions had been thrown, Darius launched his chariots to throw the phalanx into disorder; but, as soon as they approached, they were met by showers of arrows and javelins from the Agrianians and the men of Balacrus who had been drawn up in front of the Companion cavalry. Thus ended the first phase of the battle on the Macedonian right wing.

The second opened by an order to Aretes to attack those who were riding round the Macedonian right wing. Next, placing himself at the head of the Companion cavalry, Alexander wheeled it round, formed it into a wedge, and with the four right *taxeis* of

[1] *Alexander*, vol. II, p. 372.
[2] Arrian, III, XIII.
[3] *Ibid* III, XIII.
[4] *Ibid.*, III, XIII.

the phalanx, led his horse towards a gap formed in the Persian front by the advance of their own cavalry. Lastly, he galloped forward making straight for Darius—the decisive point. The

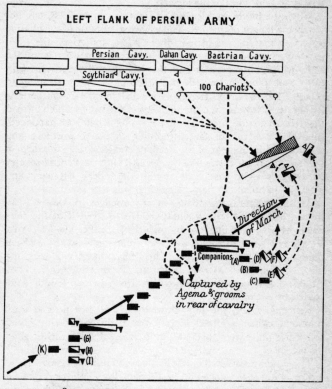

9 . BATTLE OF ARBELA, FIRST PHASE

charge, closely supported on its left by the dense array of bristling pikes of the phalanx, smote such terror into the Persian king that he fled the field. Meanwhile the enemy cavalry on Alexander's original right, finding their rear threatened by Aretes, took to flight, and the Macedonians followed and slaughtered them. The scene must have been an extraordinary one, for both Curtius and Diodorus say: "That so thick a cloud of dust was raised by the mighty mass of fugitives, that nothing could be clearly distinguished, and that thus the Macedonians lost the track of Darius. The noise of the shouting and the cracking of whips served as guides to the pursuers."[1]

When the battle on Alexander's right was in progress, another was being fought on the left. The left wing, because of the oblique approach march, was in rear of the right, and Alexander's impetuous advance appears to have created a gap between it and the right wing. Through this gap the Indian and Persian cavalry burst and galloped towards the Macedonian baggage camp to rescue Darius's family. Here, as Arrian states, the action became desperate. "However the commanders of the troops which formed the reserve to the first phalanx, learning what had happened, smartly turned about face, according to previous orders, and so appeared in the rear of the Persians and slew large numbers of them. . . ."[2] While this action was being fought the Persian cavalry on Darius's right wing rode round Alexander's left wing and attacked Parmenio in flank. Parmenio was now surrounded.

At this juncture, Parmenio sent a messenger to Alexander to inform him of his critical situation. He received it at the time when he was pursuing the fragments of the Persian left wing. At once he wheeled round with the Companion cavalry and led them against the Persian right. The Persian cavalry, now falling back, finding their retreat menaced, fought stubbornly. They struck and were struck without quarter, and at length were routed by Alexander.

Parmenio freed, the pursuit was renewed and pressed until midnight, when a forced march was made on Arbela. About thirty-five miles were covered, but in vain, for Darius made good his escape.

The casualties suffered in this battle are impossible even to guess. Arrian states that 300,000 of the Persians were slain, and that far more prisoners were taken.[3] Alexander's losses are given as 100 killed and 1,000 horses lost. Curtius says that 40,000 Persians were killed and 300 Macedonians, and Diodorus 90,000 and 500 respectively.[4]

Instead of pursuing Darius farther Alexander marched on Babylon, which was not defensible as its walls for long had been

---

[1] Diodorus, XVII, 5, and Curtius, IV, XV, 33.　　　　[2] Arrian, II, XIV.
[3] Ibid., III, XV.　　　　[4] Curtius, IV, XVI, 26, and Diodorus, XVII, 61.

destroyed. When he entered it he ordered the restoration of the temple of Marduk (the Semitic Bel). Thence he advanced on Susa where he seized 50,000 talents in bullion (£12,000,000 at £3 17s. 10½d. the fine ounce); next to Pasargadae where he seized 120,000 talents (£29,000,000), and from there to Persepolis

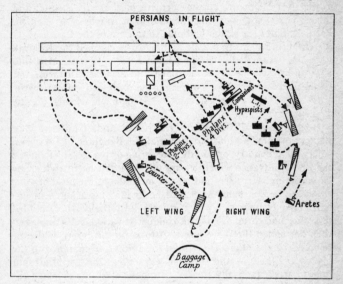

10. BATTLE OF ARBELA, SECOND PHASE

where, as an act of ritualistic vengeance, the palace of Xerxes was burnt. It was at Persepolis that Alexander heard from Antipater that in a great battle before Megalopolis he had defeated and slain Agis, king of Sparta, and that the Peloponnesian League had been dissolved and Sparta compelled to enter the Corinthian League.

Alexander left Persepolis during the winter of 330 B.C., and set out for Ecbatana (Hamadan) where he seized 180,000 talents (£43,785,000). But once again Darius eluded him. At length, covering 390 miles in eleven days, he caught up with Darius, only to find that he had been murdered by Bessus. With his death, Alexander's political object was attained, by right of the sword he had become King of Kings. As such it was imperative that he should impose his will on his empire by establishing his authority over its eastern satrapies and, if possible, by providing them with secure frontiers.

He subdued the Caspian region and then marched eastward to Herat, where he founded Alexandria in Aria; next southward to the river Helmand, on the northern borders of Gedrosia; and thence north-east, founding Alexandria in Arachosia at Ghazni. From Kabul, near which he built Alexandria of the Caucasus, in the early spring of 329 B.C. he and his army climbed the Khawak Pass and scrambled over the Hindu-Kush. He descended into Bactria, crossed the Oxus, marched into Scythia (Tartary), and established a chain of forts as his northern protective frontier, the most important being Alexandria Eschate (Khojend) on the Jaxartes (Syr Daria).

He formed an alliance with the Scythians and, in order to bind Bactria to him, he married Roxana, the daughter of Oxyartes, chief of that country, and in the late spring of 327 B.C., he followed the line of advance which legend affirmed had been trodden by Dionysus and Heracles, and set out for India at the head of some 27,000 to 30,000 men. At Kabul he divided his army, sent one half under Hephaestion and Perdiccas down the Khyber, and led the other half through Chitral, conquered various hill tribes, and then descended through Swat to Attock, on the Indus, where he rejoined Hephaestion. He crossed the Indus and marched to the Hydaspes (Jhelum) and there, in 326 B.C., in the last of his four major battles, tactically the most brilliant of all, he defeated the Indian king Porus. He reinstated him for his bravery, reduced Sangala (near Lahore), crossed the river Acesines (Chenab), and led his army towards the Hydraotis (Ravee) and then on to the Hyphasis (Sutlej), his intention being to reach the Ganges and to move down to the sea, which he supposed, and rightly so, would provide him with his eastern frontier.[1] Here it was that his army,

[1] Though it may be true, as Tarn points out, that the Ganges was unknown to the Greek world before Megasthenes—that is, until the close of the fourth century B.C. (*Alexander*, vol. II, Appendix 14), it is incredible that Alexander did not know of its existence; for it was only 150 miles from the Sutlej, and then as now it was the most sacred river in India. That he considered the "Eastern Sea" (Bay of Bengal) far closer than it actually was is probably true, and that he minimized the distance to encourage his men is also possible. Though his projects of future conquests, as related by Arrian (v, xxvi), have been shown by Tarn to be later interpolations (*Alexander*, vol. II, pp. 287–290), their strategical aim—namely, to establish an unattackable empire—is common sense, and is one which must have occurred to Alexander, more especially so as it is alleged that he said: "But if you flinch now, there will be many warlike races left behind on the far side of the Hyphasis up to the Eastern Sea, and many too stretching from these to the Hyrcanian Sea towards the north wind, and

having marched some seventeen thousand miles and having gained the eastern border of Darius's empire, refused to go farther. Most reluctantly he halted and prepared for the homeward journey. Before turning westward he built twelve altars on the bank of the river Hyphasis "as thank offerings to the gods" and "as memorials of his labours".[1] While they were being erected, there was with him in his camp an exiled Indian chief named Sandrocottus (Chandragupta), who a few years later, in emulation of Alexander, founded the great Mauryan empire with its capital at Palibotha (Patna), on the Ganges.

As he was unable to secure his eastern frontier by the ocean, it must have been apparent to him that the next best line of defence was the Indus, and more particularly so were it possible by sea to link its mouth with that of the Euphrates; for then the deserts of Persia and the western mountains of India would be circumvented.

Alexander began his return journey, and on the Jhelum built a fleet. When, in November 326 B.C., it was ready, he poured out libations to his forefather Heracles, to Amon, and other gods,[2] and then set out. On his way southward he fought a campaign against the Malli (Mahlavas), in which he nearly lost his life, and eventually arrived at the delta of the Indus. After he had explored the mouth of the river down to the sea, he built a naval station at Patala (? Haiderabad) and next decided that his admiral Nearchus, with a fleet of perhaps 100 to 150 ships, should sail westward in search of the Persian Gulf. He divided his army into two divisions and ordered Craterus with the larger of the two to return by way of the Bolan Pass and Kandahar to Persepolis, while he and the smaller, 8,000 to 10,000 men, marched homeward through the coastal region of the desert of Gedrosia in order to establish depôts of food on the shore of the Arabian Sea for the provisioning of Nearchus's fleet. He lost most of his baggage and many of the non-combatants during the march, but extricated his forces without great loss. All three expeditions ended happily, and the sea route to India was established.

In the spring of 324 B.C. he was back in Susa, where, in

---

not far from these, again, the Scythian tribes, so that there is reason to fear that if we turn back now, such territory as we now hold, being yet unconsolidated, may be stirred to revolt by such as we do not yet hold. Then in very truth there will be no profit from our many labours; or we shall need once more, from the very beginning, more dangers and more labours" (Arrian, v, xxvi). In the circumstances, this seems exactly what Alexander should have said.

[1] Arrian, v, xxix.   [2] *Ibid.*, vi, iii.

celebration of his conquests, he held a great feast during which he and many of his officers, as well as 10,000 of his men, married Persian women.[1] Soon after this symbolic act of fusion of victors and vanquished, and to remove a danger that ever since the days of Xenophon had threatened Greece—the floating mass of homeless Greeks who were ever ready to sell their services as mercenaries—he ordered the cities of the League of Corinth to readmit their exiles and their families. Because this order exceeded his rights as Captain-General, Tarn has suggested that to correct the anomaly he sent instructions to the cities of the League to recognize him as a god, for as such he would not be bound by the League's rules. They did so and the exiles returned.

Soon afterwards he determined to send back to Greece all veterans past service. This common-sense decision was taken at Opis and was strongly resented by the Macedonians, who suspected that his aim was to oust them in favour of the Persians and to transfer his seat of government from Macedonia to Asia. Soon discontent led to the mutiny of the whole army, except the *Agema* of the Hypaspists. The soldiers demanded to go home and told Alexander to prosecute the war in company with his father Amon.[2] Alexander arrested the ringleaders and took the mutineers at their word. He dismissed the whole army from his service and began forming a Persian one. This drastic action broke the back of the mutiny, which was followed by a remarkable reconciliation. A vast banquet was held to which 9,000 guests were invited, the feast being symbolic of the peace he intended to establish in his empire. Macedonians and Persians—the two great antagonists in the war—sat at his own table, and every race of the empire was represented. Arrian informs us that Alexander "and his comrades drank from the same bowl and poured the same libations, while the Greek seers and the Magians began the ceremony".[3] During this banquet, writes Tarn, Alexander "prayed for peace, and that Macedonians and Persians and all the peoples of his Empire might be alike partners in the commonwealth (*i.e.* not merely subjects), and that the peoples of the world he knew might live together in harmony and in unity of heart and mind—that *Homonoia* which for centuries the world was to long for but never to reach. He had previously said that all men

---

[1] Arrian, VII, IV.   [2] *Ibid.*, VII, VIII.
[3] *Ibid.*, VII, XI, and Plutarch's *Moralia*, trans. Frank Cole Babbit (1926), vol. IV "on the Fortune and Virtue of Alexander", pp. 327–330.

were sons of one Father and his prayer was the expression of his recorded belief that he had a mission from God to be the Reconciler of the World. Though none present could foresee it, that prayer was to be the crown of his career. . . ."[1]

In the spring of 323 B.C. he returned to Babylon, which he selected as his capital, and there was met "by embassies from the Libyans, who congratulated him and offered him a crown on his becoming King of Asia [the Persian Empire]. From Italy also Bruttians and Lucanians and Tyrrhenians [Etruscans] sent envoys for a like purpose."[2] Other envoys are also mentioned by Arrian, but are discounted by Tarn as later additions.[3]

At Babylon he busied himself with the planning of a number of expeditions. One was to explore the Hyrcanian (Caspian) Sea, to discover whether it was a lake or a gulf of the ocean; others were to explore the Persian Gulf. For the latter expedition he built a great harbour at Babylon, from which ships could set out to colonize the eastern coast of the gulf; to explore the sea-route between Babylon and Egypt and so link the latter to India by the way Nearchus had discovered; and also to circumnavigate Arabia, an expedition he intended to lead in person. While the fleet was being built, he remodelled the phalanx by incorporating Persian light armed troops with the Macedonian hoplites.

None of these projects was destined to see fruition, for while the preparations were under way, on June 2 he was taken ill with malaria. He grew steadily worse and was carried into the palace of Nebuchadrezzar. There, on June 12, his veterans filed past him in silence as he lay speechless, "yet he greeted one and all, raising his head, though with difficulty and signing to them, with his eyes".[4] The following day, June 13, 323 B.C., towards evening, he died in his thirty-third year, after a reign of twelve years and eight months. He was buried in Alexandria.

Though under his successors, the Diadochi,[5] the empire he founded split into fractions, four great monarchies arising in its stead—Egypt under the Ptolomies, Asia under the Seleucids, Macedonia under the Antigonids, and in India the empire of Chandragupts[6]—his idea of world unity as the brotherood of man

---

[1] *Alexander the Great*, vol. I, pp. 116–117.   [2] Arrian, VII, XV.
[3] *Alexander the Great*, vol. II, Appendix 23.   [4] Arrian, VII, XXVI.
[5] More especially Antigonus, Ptolemy, Seleucus and Lysimachus.
[6] ". . . Chandragupta saw him and deduced the possibility of realizing in actual fact the conception, handed down from Vedic times, of a comprehensive monarchy in India; hence Alexander indirectly created Asoka's empire and enabled the spread of Buddhism" (*Alexander the Great*, W. W. Tarn, vol. I, p. 143).

was never extinguished. The fusing of races, which on his return to Susa from India he had symbolized by mass-weddings between Macedonians and Persians, became a daily occurrence in the great cosmopolitan cities he had founded. In these the various races mingled and out of their mingling arose a common culture—the Hellenistic.

Soon after his death, Alexandria, the greatest of these cities, became the power-house of the new culture. It was "the meeting place of the world". There, writes Reinach, an indefatigable curiosity "drove men's minds to multiply inquiries and information in every direction. They wanted to know everything, to explain everything. They interrogated old texts. . . . They travelled over the inhabited earth. . . . They carried to a very high pitch the study of the sciences properly so-called, which tended to become definitely separated from philosophy. . . . What is all this, if it is not the very principle of the scientific spirit?"[1] There steam-power was discovered, mathematics extended, mechanics developed, and new faiths and cults compounded, to flow east and west.

The process of fusion was much accelerated by the financial system Alexander introduced. Before he set out on his great adventure he most certainly must have realized that his father's strength was derived largely from his gold mines in Thrace. Further, when in Egypt, he must have realized that gold was looked upon as a divine substance which gave immortality to its kings, masking them in their tombs. He seized the hoarded wealth of Persia and de-sterilized it by minting it into coin. When Alexander carried off the treasures of Asia, writes Athenaeus, "the sun of 'wealth, with far-flung might', as Pindar has it, verily rose".[2] Not only did he issue coin, but he unified the financial system by introducing a uniform standard. After his death the Ptolomies monopolized the whole of the banking business in Egypt, and through "their central bank at Alexandria they . . . transacted business in money with foreign countries".[3] Wilcken further writes:

" In Alexander's wars, the previous barriers between East and West were removed, and in the next generation thousands of Greek traders and artisans entered the new world, to seek their

[1] *L'Hellénisation du Monde Antique*, A. J. Reinach (1914), p. 270.
[2] *Athenaeus*, trans. Charles Burton Gulick (1929), vol. III, "Deipnosophistae," VI, 231, e.
[3] *Alexander the Great*, Ulrich Wilcken, p. 292.

fortunes in the new Greek cities, which shot up out of the ground like mushrooms. In this way the two previously detached circles came more and more to coincide and form a single economic circle; and when the Western Mediterranean was attracted into the orbit of the great revolution that occurred in the East, there was finally created a world commerce, which embraced the whole inhabited world, and extended from Spain to India, and beyond through Central Asia to China. This development was completed only under the Roman Empire, but its basis was the conquest of Asia by Alexander."[1]

In the great monarchies which arose after his death not only was an aristocracy of wealth created, but the divine right of kingship became the corner-stone of the state. "Hardly was he dead", writes Professor Tarn, "when legend became busy with his terrible name. . . . Around him the whole dream-world of the East took shape and substance; of him every story of a divine world-conqueror was told afresh. . . . He lifted the civilized world out of one groove and set it in another; he started a new epoch; nothing could again be as it had been."[2] As we shall see in succeeding chapters, the effects of his work were to reach far and wide. In the middle of the third century B.C., immediately after the ending of the First Punic War, Greek culture began to influence Roman society, and during and after the Second Punic War it expanded steadily under the Scipios. Wilcken says: "It was the Romans who first gave Alexander the title of 'The Great' (Magnus)", and that "it was left to Greek historians to draw a parallel between Alexander and the great Scipio Africanus, the conqueror of Hannibal, and the founder of the Roman world-empire; they made Scipio the son of Jupiter Capitolinus, and transferred to him the legend about Alexander that he was the offspring of a sacred snake. . . ."[3]

Later, when Augustus, a fervent admirer of Alexander, and under whom the worship of the emperor as the divine world-ruler was established, placed his effigy upon the imperial signet, Alexander's dream, in part at least, came true; for under the *Pax Romana* the western world tasted for the first time the blessings of a prolonged peace. It was but a step from this idea—Alexander as god-king—coupled with what Plutarch attributed to him as

---

[1] *Alexander the Great*, Ulrich Wilcken, p. 284.
[2] *The Cambridge Ancient History*, vol. VI, pp. 435-436, and *Alexander the Great*, W. W. Tarn, vol. I, p. 145.
[3] *Alexander the Great*, Ulrich Wilcken, p. 277.

saying: "God is the common father of all men, but he makes the best ones peculiarly his own", to the establishment of Christianity and later to the transference of the temporal rule of the Roman emperors to the spiritual rule of the medieval Popes. Further, strange as it may seem, Islam, the great opponent of Christendom, was only rendered possible by the contact of Arabianism with Hellenism in Egypt, Syria, and Asia Minor.

The rise of Rome and her conflict with Carthage

During the great migratory movements which took place between the years 1200 and 1000 B.C., two peoples of Asiatic stock appeared in the central Mediterranean. They were the Phoenicians of Tyre who, about 1100 B.C., established the first of their North African colonies at Utica and founded Carthage (Kart-hadasht or "New Town") in the second half of the ninth century B.C., and the Etruscans, who settled in Italy, north of the Tiber, before 1000 B.C. South of the Tiber lay Latium, a small gathering of villages inhabited by the Latins, tribes of Indo-European stock grouped about Alba Longa, who, about 753 B.C.– the traditional date of the founding of Rome by Romulus—were overrun by the Etruscans. Under the latter the villages in the neighbourhood of the Palatine Hill gradually merged into the city state of Rome.

Two hundred and fifty years later–that is, about 500 B.C.– while the Etruscans were busily engaged with the Gauls in the north, the Latin tribes drove their Etruscan kings out of Rome and invaded Etruria. Eventually the Gauls overran Etruria, crossed the lower Tiber, and about 390 B.C., Rome, as yet un-walled, was occupied by them and burnt. Only the citadel on the Capitoline Hill held out, and soon weary of besieging it, they accepted a ransom in gold and departed northward.

At this early period the Roman military unit was the legion, levy, or "gathering of the clans". It was recruited from the burgesses of Rome, those who belonged to one of the original tribes, who alone had the right to bear arms. They formed the "spear-armed body of warriors upon whom the blessing of Mars was invoked", and because service in war was the sole road to civic honours it was these men of hereditary valour who shaped the character of the Roman people.

Originally the legion was a phalanx armed in the old Doric style. At an early date it consisted of 3,000 to 4,000 men in eight ranks. The first six were hoplites and the last two *velites*–the light armed. Like the Greek phalanx its tactical principle was shock; it had no reserves, and as it was supported by a mere handful of cavalry, pursuit was difficult.

According to tradition, immediately after the burning of Rome this primitive military organization was completely transformed by Marcus Furius Camillus, the most celebrated Roman general of the Gallic Wars. For arrangement by census he substituted arrangement by age, in order to make the most of individual capacity and experience. The heavy infantry, which were the real legionary troops, were organized in three bodies, *hastati, principes,* and *triarii*: the first comprising the youngest men and the third the oldest. The *velites* were maintained, but continued to be recruited on the census.

Next, to gain the necessary elasticity to meet the highly mobile Gauls, the phalangial legion was divided into three divisions ordered in depth: the *hastati* in front, the *principes* in rear of them, and behind the latter the *triarii*–veterans. Each of these divisions was organized into ten companies (*manipuli*), the first two of 120 men each and the third of 60. A cohort consisted of one maniple of each class and 120 *velites* and a squadron (*turma*) of cavalry 30 strong: in all 450 soldiers. Ten cohorts made a legion. In battle order the maniples were drawn up chequer-wise, so that those of the second division covered the intervals in the front of the first, and the third those of the second. The cavalry, ten *turmae*, formed a wing (*ala*).

The growth of this new organization probably was gradual. The armament is fully described by Polybius in sections 19-42 of his Sixth Book.[1] The *velites* carried a sword, spear, and a target (*parma*) three feet in diameter. The spear was for throwing and had so slender a point that, once cast, it bent and became useless in the hands of the enemy. The *hastati* carried a large shield (*scutum*), semi-cylindrical in shape. It was two feet six inches wide and four feet long, and was made of two layers of wood glued together, covered with hide and bound with iron. They were armed with a short thrusting sword (*gladius*) and two javelins (*pila*) and wore a brass helmet and greaves and a brass plate on their breasts (*pectorale*), or, if they could afford it, a cuirass (*lorica*). The *principes* and *triarii* were armed and armoured in like manner, except that instead of *pila* they carried long spears (*hastae*).

[1] For a full account of the developments of Roman armament see *Les Armes Romaines*, Paul Couissin (1926).

The cavalry, it would seem, was completely neglected, for even at the opening of the Punic Wars cavalrymen had no armour; their shields were of leather and their swords and lances indifferent. Normally, they preferred to fight on foot.

Collective fighting was discouraged in favour of single combats. The one great shock of the phalanx gave way to a series of shocks in rapid succession. The entrenching of camps was also introduced, even when a halt was made for a single night. The old discipline, always severe, was unaltered, and drill and training were prolonged. Tactically, these changes were radical. Close and distant fighting were combined; a reserve came into being, and the offensive and defensive were closely knit together. Mommsen writes of the manipular legion:

"The Roman combination of the heavy javelin with the sword produced results similar . . . to those attained in modern warfare by the introduction of bayonet muskets; the volley of javelins prepared the way for the sword encounter, exactly in the same way as a volley of musketry now precedes a charge with the bayonet. Lastly, the thorough system of encampment allowed the Romans to combine the advantages of defensive and offensive war, and to decline or give battle according to circumstances, and in the latter case to fight under the ramparts of their camp just as under the walls of a fortress."

After the Gallic invasion Rome was turned into a walled city and the Romans, who now had a secure base from which to operate, set out on their path of conquest. In 325 B.C. their expansion brought them into conflict with the Samnites to the south of them, and a series of wars followed which, in 295 B.C., was ended by the decisive battle of Sentinum (near Fabriano), in which the combined forces of the Samnites, Etruscans, and Gauls were routed by the Romans. This victory made Rome the leading power from the river Arnus to the Gulf of Salerno and, as Breasted says, "decided the future of Italy for over two thousand years". Within Italy, Rome's only potential enemies were, in the north the Gauls, and in the south the Lucanians, and, if they opposed her, the Greek city states on the coast.

Tarentum (Taranto) was the foremost of these cities, and the Tarentines, thoroughly alarmed by the rapid expansion of Rome, called to their assistance Pyrrhus, King of Epirus and kinsman of Alexander the Great, a leading soldier of his day. He landed in Italy in 280 B.C. and defeated the Romans in two battles, at

Heraclea on the Gulf of Taranto, and near Asculum, east of present-day Venosa. His losses in these battles were so great that when the Syracusans asked him to help them against the Carthaginians he transferred his army to Sicily. From there, after several brilliant campaigns and because of the normal dissension between the Greek cities, he returned to Italy in 276 B.C., and was so badly beaten by the Romans at Beneventum (Benevento) that he withdrew to Epirus, exclaiming: "What a battlefield I am leaving for Carthage and Rome." A true prediction, for as soon as he had left, one by one the Greek cities surrendered to the Romans, and with the occupation of Rhegium, the two great powers were left to face each other over the Strait of Messina.

Between 310 and 289 B.C. most of Sicily had been subdued by Agathocles, tyrant and king of Syracuse: a remarkable soldier and the first European to carry war into Carthaginian Africa. The prolonged disorders after his death, which were used by Carthage to her advantage, were the reason why Syracuse had sought the assistance of Pyrrhus, who had married a daughter of Agathocles. When Pyrrhus left Sicily, Hiero II, then king of Syracuse, became involved in a war with a body of Agathocles's former mercenaries, called Mamertines after Marmar the Oscan Mars, which had seized Messana (Messina). Hard pressed by him, the Mamertines appealed to Carthage and Rome for assistance at the same time. Both answered the call and a clash followed which, in 264 B.C., detonated the First Punic War.

When they found that without a fleet they could not prevent the Carthaginians from sending over reinforcements from Africa, in 261 B.C. the Romans decided to build one and become a naval power: a singularly daring resolution, since they had little knowledge of the sea and at the time Carthage was the leading naval power in the Mediterranean. After they had built ships and manned them with partially trained crews, in 260 B.C. they attempted to seize Messana and were defeated. In no way discouraged by the reverse, and realizing that they could not hope to equal the Carthaginians at sea as long as they themselves adhered to the conventional tactics of the day, they set about devising an altogether new tactics which would enable the superiority of their soldiers in hand-to-hand fighting to have full scope. To effect this they fitted their galleys with wooden boarding-bridges called *corvi* ("crows"), each provided with a spike under its fore-end. By means of a pole fixed in the prow of each ships the bridge could be raised vertically, swung to right or left, and dropped on the deck of an enemy ship and the ship firmly grappled. The boarding party would pass over the bridge.

They put to sea again and met the Carthaginian fleet off Mylae (Cape Milazzo), when the Carthaginians steered straight for them. "But the engines", writes Polybius, "swung round to meet them in every direction, and dropped down upon them so infallibly, that no ship could come to close quarters without being grappled. Eventually the Carthaginians turned and fled, bewildered at the novelty of the occurrence, and with it a loss of fifty ships."

The victory of Mylae made Rome a naval power, and its immediate results were the evacuation of Corsica by the Carthaginians and the invasion of Sardinia by the Romans.

The Romans now, like Agathocles, resolved to transfer the war to Africa. Their fleet consisted of 330 ships, and though the Carthaginians assembled a considerably larger fleet at Heraclea Minoa, west of Agrigentum (Agrigento), in order to take the Roman advance on Africa in flank, when the two fleets met the *corvi* once again proved decisive and the Carthaginians lost ninety-four ships to the Romans' twenty-four. The battle of Heraclea won for the Romans the command of the central Mediterranean.

The Romans refitted their ships and the fleet steered straight for Hermaeum (Cape Bon), where the army, under M. Atilius Regulus, was landed. First he occupied Tunes (Tunis) to establish a base of operations against Carthage. But while he was doing so a force of Greek mercenaries, under a Spartan named Xanthippus, reinforced the Carthaginians. Xanthippus was an able soldier. Polybius says of him: "For it was one man, one brain, that defeated the numbers which were believed to be invincible and able to accomplish anything; and restored to confidence a whole city that was unmistakably and utterly ruined, and the spirits of its army which had sunk to the lowest depths of despair." He selected a battleground on which the superior Carthaginian cavalry would have full scope and defeated and captured Regulus. The Romans abandoned the invasion and returned to Sicily. In July, 255 B.C., they met with a terrible disaster. In a storm they lost 284 ships out of 364. Through this mischance the Carthaginians regained command of the sea and at once reinforced Lilybaeum (Marsala). In 249 B.C. another storm virtually annihilated the Roman fleet, and so discouraged were the Romans by its loss that they abandoned the idea of fighting at sea. Two years later the Carthaginians sent Hamilcar Barca, the father of Hannibal, to Sicily.

When they had recovered their nerve, in 242 B.C. the Romans once again set to work and built another fleet, and in the following year, when they had 250 quinqueremes ready, they surprised the Carthaginian seaports of Lilybaeum and Drepana (Trapani). This caused high alarm in Carthage because they were the nearest of the Sicilian ports to Cape Bon. They at once put to sea to regain them, and the two fleets met at the Aegates (Egadi) islands. The Roman fleet was victorious, seventy Carthaginian ships were captured and fifty sunk. Carthage was now exhausted and so was Rome, and in 241 B.C. peace between the two was re-established on condition that Carthage evacuated Sicily. Sicily thus became the first province of the Roman Empire.

For the Carthaginians the cessation of war was immediately followed by general unrest and widespread mutinies among their mercenaries. In Sardinia, they revolted from Carthage, and on being expelled by the Sardinians they appealed to Rome to re-establish order. The Romans agreed, and in 238 B.C. they intervened; Carthage abandoned Sardinia and the island passed into Roman hands.

When the Romans were reducing the wild tribes in Sardinia, which took many years, they were also engaged in a grim frontier war with the Gauls in northern Italy, and between 229-219 B.C. in a series of punitive operations against the Illyrian pirates in the Adriatic. In 225 B.C. the Gauls were brought to a temporary halt in a great battle in which 40,000 are said to have been killed and 10,000 captured. After this victory, Roman colonies were established at Cremona and Placentia (Piacenza), and to reinforce these and other northern garrisons the Via Flaminia was made fit for the passage of troops as far as Arimini (Rimini). The Illyrian war, which for the first time brought the Romans into diplomatic contact with Greece, roused the fears of Philip V of Macedonia, who from then on took up a position of hostility to Rome.

Meanwhile Carthage, to make good her losses in the central Mediterranean, sent Hamilcar Barca to Spain to extend her dominion over that country. In 229 B.C. he died, and was succeeded in command by his son-in-law Hasdrubal who, in 228 B.C., founded Nova Carthago (Cartagena). Apparently in answer to this extension of Carthaginian power, Rome made an alliance with the wealthy Greek city of Saguntum (Sagunto), and being fully occupied with the Gauls, and so for the time being not desiring another war with Carthage, a treaty was agreed upon between the Romans and Hasdrubal by the terms of which the Iberus (Ebro) river was fixed as the boundary between the Carthaginian and Roman spheres of interest in Spain. In 221 B.C. Hasdrubal was assassinated, and was succeeded by his brother-in-law Hannibal, son of Hamilcar Barca.

CHAPTER 3

The Battles of the Metaurus, 207 B.C., and Zama, 202 B.C.

Rome all but accomplished what Alexander attempted, for Rome, as we shall see, absorbed his idea. But this was not done in a purposeful way, because history grows by force of circumstances. The imperial urge was now in the bones of Rome, and rightly Livy says: "No great state can long be in peace. If it lacks an enemy abroad it finds one at home, just as powerful bodies seem protected against infection from without, but are of themselves weighed down by their very strength."[1] Thus it comes about that in the life history of every virile nation two events control its destiny, inner and outer conflicts, which are called revolutions and wars. Not until nations grow old is peacefulness established, and what ages them the more rapidly is the feeling of security. In no way was this true of Rome, for when the Second Punic War broke out she was in her early youth and confronted by two great powers—Macedonia in the east and Carthage in the south. Before security could be gained, these powers had to be eliminated, for the goal of a virile nation is the establishment of unattackable frontiers—the Alexandrian drive.

In Spain such a frontier did not exist, for the Ebro was little more than a geographical expression, and once the Gaulish war was ended, Rome, with an eye on the Spanish silver mines and markets, brought into power a party within Saguntum which attacked the Torboletae, who were subjects of Carthage. Hannibal took action and was warned by the Romans to leave the Saguntines alone. He refused to do so, and in 219 B.C. attacked their city and after an eight-month siege took it by storm. Though the Romans had made no effort to help the Saguntines, in March the following year they sent envoys to Carthage demanding the surrender of Hannibal and his assessors. The ultimatum was rejected and a formal declaration of war followed.

That Hannibal had every right to retaliate seems clear; yet there can be little doubt that, when he laid siege to Saguntum, he

[1] *Livy* (trans. Frank Gardner Moore, 1949), xxx, 44.

did so in full knowledge of the probable consequences. That his idea was to revenge himself on Rome may be true; though not in the sense of fulfilling the "Wrath of the house of Barca", but rather to cancel out the results of the First Punic War and thereby to reinstate the supremacy of Carthage. He possessed a high political instinct and realized that Rome was as yet no more than a patchwork power. She had won her supremacy by force and not by persuasion; the Gauls were permanently antagonistic to her, and during the incursion of Pyrrhus several of her allies had deserted her cause. Strategically the moment seemed propitious, and tactically Hannibal was in a strong position; for so far the revolution in the art of war created by Alexander's use of cavalry, which he understood, was little appreciated by the Romans.

The situation was also clear to the Roman Senate and the moment seemed equally propitious. In northern Italy the Gauls had been defeated and Latin colonies had been established to control them; Tarentum and other southern ports had been garrisoned, no danger threatened across the Adriatic and the command of the seas was in Roman hands. Not only were Roman sea communications with Spain safe, but from Sicily a direct attack could be launched against Carthage. But war is always a game of chance and the plaything of the unexpected. The senators calculated all things correctly enough except one imponderable factor. They could measure up the Carthaginians, but the genius of Hannibal was hidden from them. They could not see, as Dodge says, that from beginning to end Hannibal was to be the pivot around which all things were to revolve;[1] and that before them lay a war of over sixteen years, during which one man was to fight Rome and to teach her how to conquer the world. What manner of man was he?

Little is known of Hannibal, except for what may be learnt from his campaigns, and none of these is described by a friendly pen. He was born in 249 B.C., and at the age of nine left Carthage with his father for Spain. There he remained until his great adventure began, and though he must have accompanied Hamilcar on many of his campaigns, in which he was schooled in the art of war, his education was in no way neglected. We are told that he could speak Greek fluently as well as read and write it, and that he was deeply versed in the history of Hellenistic warfare. He was lightly yet firmly built, an excellent runner and fencer and

[1] *Hannibal*, Theodore Ayrault Dodge (1891), vol. II, p. 638.

a fearless rider. Possessed of an iron constitution, he could support hardship, and endowed with a quick and calculating brain he was able to sum up situations. In his living he was simple and little addicted to wine or women. "To his reckless courage in encountering dangers", says Livy, "he united the greatest judgement when in the midst of them", nevertheless, he attributes to him inhuman cruelty, more than Punic perfidy, "no regard for truth, and none for sanctity, no fear of the gods, no reverence for an oath, no religious scruple".[1] Also Polybius says that he was "extraordinarily cruel" and "exceedingly grasping for money".[2] These vices, we think, may be largely discounted; as we shall see, his "perfidy" was no greater than that of his great adversary Scipio, and his cruelty in no way abnormal in his age.

When, in the spring of 218 B.C., he set out from Nova Carthago for the Ebro, his object was clear. It was not to conquer Italy, but instead to break up the Italian Confederacy and to force Rome to make peace as once Agathocles had forced Carthage to do. After his victory at Lake Trasimene he said: "I am not come to fight against Italians, but on behalf of Italians against Rome."[3] He moved forward not as a conqueror, but as a liberator. With this idea as the linchpin of his strategy he advanced on modern Perpignan at the head of 90,000 foot, 12,000 cavalry and 37 elephants.[4] The reason why he took the land route in preference to the sea route was not only because the Romans held command of the sea, but because it was essential for him to rouse the Gauls against them and to establish a supply base and recruiting ground as close to Cisalpine Gaul as he could; for his line of communications with Spain could readily be cut.

From the Pyrenees he moved to a little north of Avignon without opposition, because the Roman Senate had failed completely to fathom his intentions. When they had assembled one army under Tiberius Sempronius in Sicily for an expedition against Carthage, the Senate ordered another under Publius Cornelius Scipio to march by way of Massilia (Marseilles) to the Ebro. When Scipio got to Massilia he learnt that Hannibal was fifty

---

[1] *Livy*, trans. B. O. Foster (1929), XXI, 4.
[2] *The Histories of Polybius*, trans. Evelyn S. Shuckburgh (1889), IX, 22. This translation is quoted throughout and as regards the "fragments" does not follow the rearrangement by Büttner-Wobst in his Teubner edition of 1914.
[3] *Ibid.*, I, III, 85.
[4] *Ibid.*, I, III, 35. These numbers would appear to be exaggerated, for Polybius says: "The army was not so much numerous as highly efficient, and in an extraordinary state of physical training. . . ."

miles to the north of him and so out of his reach, and instead of bringing his army back to Italy by the coast road he sent it on under his brother Gnaeus to Spain to attack Hannibal's base, while he himself returned with a few men to Pisa.

Directly the whereabouts of Hannibal became known, word was sent to Sempronius to transfer his army to the north. Meanwhile Hannibal, by a manœuvre very similar to Alexander's on the Hydaspes, forded the Rhône and headed his army for the Maritime Alps. Where he crossed them is unknown, though it was somewhere between the little St. Bernard and Mt. Genèvre. His main difficulty was not the mountains,[1] but the hostility of the Allobroges, who constantly attacked his rearguard. His losses from these affrays were so considerable that, though he crossed the Rhône with 50,000 foot and 9,000 horse,[2] he entered the plains of Cisalpine Gaul with no more than 20,000 and 6,000 respectively; that is almost exactly one quarter of the strength accredited to him by Livy on leaving New Carthage.

Whether this heavy loss of men was due to faulty generalship it is not possible to say; but it certainly does not point to a high state of discipline in his army, and this, in its turn, throws into relief the amazing series of victories he was to win with it during the next few years.

In December, 218 B.C., on the banks of the Trebia, he lured Sempronius into battle.[3] He bewildered him, held him in front, and with half his cavalry outflanked him and fell upon his rear, when Sempronius was utterly routed. In April the following year, on the northern shore of Lake Trasimene, by deliberately placing himself between the armies of Servilius and Flaminius he surprised the latter and all but annihilated his army.[4]

Hannibal then moved south towards the Adriatic coast and captured a Roman supply depôt at Cannae on the river Aufidus (Ofanto). But it would seem that his main reason for going there was to gain suitable country for his cavalry. At the time there were four double legions at Gerunium (to the south of Termoli), under command of the Consuls Aemilius Paullus and C. Terentius Varro.

---

[1] Napoleon says: "Les éléphants seuls ont pu lui donner de l'embarras" (*Commentaires*, VI, p. 163).

[2] The difference between this and the original strength was due mainly to Hannibal leaving behind him in Catalonia 22,000 men. To account for the remaining 21,000 points to considerable desertions.

[3] Polybius gives the strength of the opposing forces as – Carthagians, 28,000 infantry and 10,000 cavalry; Romans 36,000 infantry and 4,000 cavalry (*The Histories*, III, 72).

[4] *Ibid.*, III, 84. The Roman losses were 15,000 killed and 15,000 prisoners.

When Hannibal's whereabouts were known, they marched to the Aufidus and camped on its right bank three miles above Hannibal.

Because of the superiority of the Carthaginian cavalry, Aemilius was against giving battle, but Varro thought differently, and because the two consuls were in chief command on alternate days, and the day after their arrival it was Varro's turn to command, he ordered an immediate advance. An indecisive skirmish followed; but on the next day, August 2, 216 B.C., Aemilius could no longer draw off his army as he wished and, probably realizing this, Hannibal drew out his in a crescent formation. In the centre he marshalled his Spaniards and Gauls, with his Africans on their flanks. On each wing of the infantry line he posted a powerful force of cavalry. Faced by the Romans drawn up in parallel order, he first routed the Roman cavalry, and next awaited the advance of the Roman infantry. They pressed the Carthaginian crescent back until it became concave. Then, suddenly, Hannibal advanced his two divisions of African infantry, wheeled them inwards, and closed on the flanks of the Romans engaged in the pocket. Lastly, the Carthaginian cavalry returned from the pursuit and fell upon the Roman rear. The Roman army was swallowed up as if by an earthquake.[1]

When the battles of the Trebia, Lake Trasimene, and Cannae are examined, there is not the slightest doubt that victory was won by the tactical genius of Hannibal and that his genius was able to achieve what it did because of the Roman outlook upon war. It was purely mechanical and depended solely upon valour, discipline, and drill. Of generalship there was next to none, a general still being looked upon as a drill-master, a man who could successfully carry out a number of parade evolutions with little reference to ground or to tactical requirements. Because they had won innumerable battles against undisciplined and poorly drilled barbarians through discipline and drill, and because they had learnt nothing from the wars of Alexander and his successors, the Romans invariably were surprised, as much by their ignorance and tactical blunders as by Hannibal's insight, foresight, and imagination. Nor was it the fault of the generals themselves, who

[1] Polybius (iii, 107) gives the Roman strength at 80,000 infantry and 9,600 cavalry. In *The Cambridge Ancient History* doubt is thrown on this (see vol. VIII, p. 53), and the Roman strength is calculated at 48,000. According to Polybius (iii, 117) the Roman casualties were the whole of their cavalry less 370, 10,000 infantry captured (who were not actually engaged in the battle) and 70,000 killed; the Carthaginian casualties were 5,700 in all.

seldom lacked courage, but of the Roman military system. Each citizen was considered fit to be a general, because each citizen was supposed to know his drill. As Mommsen says: "It was simply impossible that the question as to the leadership of the armies of the city in such a war should be left year after year to be decided by the Pandora's box of the balloting-urn."[1] This was largely because of party politics, arising out of rivalries between the great families. Livy, perhaps with some exaggeration, tells us that "All the tribes voted for Publius Scipio. In spite of that, the consuls cast losts for Africa as a province, for so the Senate had decreed."[2] The result was the creation of a stolid, static army, in which the generals were elected, not because of their experience or ability, but because of their devotion to party interests.

In contrast, Hannibal was a general who could adapt himself to every circumstance except one–siege warfare–and who, by an act of will, could pass from the unequalled boldness shown during the campaigns of his first three years in Italy to the obstinate and closely circumscribed defensive he adopted during the thirteen which followed. It was his ability to adapt his actions to changing circumstances which justifies the remark of Polybius: "Of all that befell the Roman and Carthaginians, good or bad, the cause was one man and one mind, Hannibal. . . . So great and wonderful is the influence of a Man, and a mind duly fitted by original constitution for any undertaking within the reach of human powers."[3] He further says of him: "For sixteen continuous years Hannibal maintained the war with Rome in Italy, without once releasing his army from service in the field, but keeping those vast numbers under control, like a good pilot, without any sign of disaffection towards himself or towards each other, though he had troops in his service who, so far from being of the same tribe, were not even of the same race. . . . Yet the skill of the commander was such, that these differences, so manifold and so wide, did not disturb the obedience to one word of command and to a single will."[4]

To quote a modern historian, Mommsen says: "He was peculiarly marked by that inventive craftiness, which forms one of the leading traits of the Phoenician character; he was fond

---

[1] *The History of Rome*, Theodor Mommsen (1921), vol. II, p. 126.
[2] *Livy*, XXX, 27. On this question see *Roman Politics 200–150 B.C.*, H. H. Scullard (1951), pp. 79-80. Behind it was the divided strategical aims of Fabius and Scipio. The former wanted to drive Hannibal out of Italy and end the war; the latter to force Hannibal out of Italy by attacking Carthage, and winning peace in Africa (*ibid.*, pp. 75-76).
[3] Polybius, IX, 22.   [4] *Ibid.*, XI, 19.

of taking singular and unexpected routes, ambushes and strata-gems of all sorts were familiar to him; and he studied the character of his antagonists with unprecedented care. By an unrivalled system of espionage—he had regular spies even in Rome—he kept himself informed of the projects of the enemy; he himself was frequently seen wearing disguises and false hair in order to procure information on some point or other. Every page of the history of the period attests his genius as a general; and his gifts as a statesman . . . He was a great man; wherever he went, he riveted the eyes of all."[1]

What could the Roman military system accomplish against such a man? Nothing; yet in the end it was the Roman character which won through. After Cannae, what do we see? A general disruption of the Republic as Hannibal had hoped for? No—not a single Latin city revolted; all held fast to Rome paralysed though she was, and had Hannibal been Alexander Rome would have fallen. Realizing, as he must have done by now, the strength of the Roman Confederacy, it was Rome or nothing. Maharbal, his cavalry general, urged him to advance on the capital—but he would not. Then Maharbal cried: "In very truth the gods bestow not on the same man all their gifts. You know how to gain a victory, Hannibal; you know not how to use one." As Livy comments: "That day's delay is generally believed to have saved the City and the Empire."[2]

Why did not Hannibal advance on Rome? Mr. Hallward's answer is, because he conceived a new strategy: "The whole strength of Carthage was to be employed in extending the war to new areas to produce the encirclement of Italy." While he was detaching city after city, the home government was to prepare the way for peace "by pushing the Romans out of Spain, by regaining Sardinia and above all by re-establishing themselves in Sicily".[3] To that end, in 215 B.C., Hannibal had already received and accepted an offer of alliance and cooperation from Philip V of Macedonia.[4] Yet was this the more speedy way of gaining his end?

[1] *History of Rome*, vol. II, p. 88.   [2] *Livy*, XXII, 51.
[3] *The Cambridge Ancient History*, vol. VIII, p. 61.
[4] On learning of Hannibal's victory at Lake Trasimene, Philip V of Macedonia set about to prepare to attack Italy, and after the battle of Cannae entered into alliance with Hannibal. This led to the Roman Senate, supported by Attalus, King of Pergamum, engaging in war with him in 214 B.C., which became known as the First Macedonian War. In 211 B.C. a treaty was concluded between the Romans and the Aetolian League, and in 205 B.C. the war was brought to an end by the Peace of Phoenice, according to which Philip agreed not to molest the states in alliance with Rome.

Had Rome capitulated or been stormed, all Spain, Sardinia and Sicily would have fallen with her into his lap. It was not because the "new strategy" was best, but because it was forced upon Hannibal by his lack of a siege train. He knew he could not storm Rome, therefore he was compelled to abandon the offensive and, like his opponent, Q. Fabius Cunctator, to assume the defensive and henceforth rely upon attrition.

Why had no city revolted? Not only because each was loyal to Rome, but because all were walled and connected by roads. They were not only safe against Hannibal's field army, but they could readily be supplied. It was the walled cities which now formed the pivots of the Roman strategy, and it is strange that Hannibal did not realize this. Had he done so when, in 215 B.C., he established himself at Capua and the greater part of southern Italy became his, surely he would have organized a siege train to knock the props out of his enemy's tactics. For four years onwards the war became a matter of marches, counter-marches, threats and withdrawals, and in 211 B.C., when Fulvius besieged and took Capua, all Hannibal could do was to advance across the Anio, approach the walls of Rome, and wave his sword outside the Colline Gate: an heroic gesture, but five years too late.

While this dual defensive was being waged in Italy, largely because of Hannibal's diplomacy the war was vigorously conducted in other quarters. In Spain Hannibal's brothers, Hasdrubal and Mago, as well as Hasdrubal, son of Gisgo, were fighting the two Scipios—Publius and Gnaeus. In 215 B.C. an insurrection broke out in Sardinia, and the following year the Consul, M. Claudius Marcellus, went to Sicily, where Syracuse had gone into alliance with Carthage, and his siege of that city became for the time being the dominant event in the war. As a military episode it is of marked interest, for then was displayed the inventive genius of Archimedes, of whom Polybius says: "In certain circumstances, the genius of one man is more effective than any numbers whatever."[1] Syracuse held out until 211 B.C., when by treachery it was delivered to the Romans, after which all resistance in Sicily was stamped out.

Though success crowned Marcellus in Sicily, disaster shrouded the Scipios in Spain; for this year, their Celtiberian troops deserted them and both were defeated and killed. Again Rome lay paralysed, and once again the selection of a commander was left

[1] Polybius VIII, 5.

to the popular vote. Since no man of mark, such as had been consuls or praetors, came forward, at length a youth of twenty-four, who had held the minor offices of military tribune and aedile, presented himself for election, and because of the clamour of the people was somewhat reluctantly accepted by the Senate. He bore the same name as his father–Publius Cornelius Scipio–and later became known to history as Scipio Africanus, conqueror of Hannibal.

Born in 235 B.C., he is first heard of during the Trebia campaign, when, though still a boy, he saved his father's life;[1] and next, at Cannae, as a military tribune. He escaped from the slaughter and, learning that Metellus and a number of young nobles intended to fly from Italy, he went to the lodgings of that officer and standing over him with a drawn sword made him swear that he and his followers would never desert Rome. Though a man of remarkable courage, his character is not an easy one to gauge. Mommsen's estimate of him is as follows:

"He was not one of the few who by their energy and iron will constrain the world to adopt and to move in new paths for centuries. . . . Yet a special charm lingers around the form of that graceful hero; it is surrounded, as with a dazzling halo, by the atmosphere of serene and confident inspiration, in which Scipio with mingled credulity and adroitness always moved. With quite enough of enthusiasm to warm men's hearts, and enough of calculation to follow in every case the dictates of intelligence, while not leaving out of account the vulgar; not naïve enough to share the belief of the multitude in the divine inspirations, nor straightforward enough to set it aside, and yet in secret thoroughly persuaded that he was a man specially favoured of the gods–in a word, a genuine prophetic nature; raised above the people, and not less aloof from them; a man steadfast to his word and kingly in his bearing, who thought that he would humble himself by adopting the ordinary title of a king, but could never understand how the constitution of the republic should in his case be binding; so confident in his own greatness that he knew nothing of envy or of hatred, courteously acknowledged other men's merits, and compassionately forgave other men's faults; an excellent officer and a refined diplomatist without presenting offensively the special stamp of either calling, uniting Hellenic culture with the fullest national feeling of a Roman, an accomplished speaker and of

[1] Polybius, x. 3

graceful manners – Publius Scipio won the hearts of soldiers and of women, of his countrymen and of the Spaniards, of his rivals in the Senate and of his greater Carthaginian antagonist.''[1]

His record of unbroken successes from the day he was appointed to command the forces in Spain until the final act of the war was due to his Hellenic open-mindedness. Whereas other generals learned little from the Roman defeats, he learned far more from them than from his own successes. Hannibal, though his enemy, was simultaneously his master, who taught him not only the art of war, but the art of leading and governing men. His most remarkable gift was his insight into crowd psychology. When in Spain his men mutinied, he commented on this mishap as follows: ". . . a crowd is ever easily misled and easily induced to any error. Therefore it is that crowds are like the sea, which in its own nature is safe and quiet; but, when the winds fall violently upon it, assumes the character of the blasts which lash it into fury; thus a multitude is ever found to be what its leaders and counsellors are.''[2]

Scipio sailed from the Tiber and landed at Emporium (Ampurias) late in 210 B.C. The situation which faced him on his arrival was far from an encouraging one. He found that, except for the fortified cities of Castulo (Cazlona) and Saguntum, hold had been lost on all the country south of the Ebro. This situation merely stimulated his generalship. His first move was one of the most daring and dramatic in the history of the war, and it was only possible because of his command of the sea. It was, while the forces of the two Hasdrubals and Mago were divided, to seize New Carthage by a *coup de main* and so to establish himself on the eastern flank of his enemies and to attack them in rear as well as to threaten their sea communications.[3] He did this, displaying high tactical skill in the storming of that city. Once it was in his hands he established a terror by sacking the town, and then behaving kindly to the Spanish hostages he found impounded there, he released them and loaded them with presents, "the girls with ear-rings and bracelets, the young men with daggers and swords'',[4] which had a marked influence in winning the good will of the people.

Once New Carthage was his and his fleet and army had been refitted, he marched into Andalusia and, in 208 B.C., defeated but

---

[1] *History of Rome*, vol. II, pp. 148–149   [2] Polybius, XI, 29.
[3] See Polybius, X, 8.   [4] *Ibid.*, X, 18.

by no means annihilated Hasdrubal's army at Baecula (? Bailen); for that skilful soldier withdrew towards San Sebastian, crossed into France, and eventually passed into Italy. Though several historians have blamed Scipio for allowing him to escape, there is no justification for their criticism, because to have plunged after Hasdrubal through an unknown and most difficult country, leaving behind him the forces of Mago and Hasdrubal, son of Gisgo, intact, would have been an act of tactical folly.

Next, he concentrated his army at Castulo and advanced on Hasdrubal, son of Gisgo, and Mago at Ilipa (near Seville), and by remarkable tactics,[1] which resembled in part those used by Hannibal at Cannae, he decisively defeated them, Hasdrubal fleeing to Mauritania (Morocco) and Mago to the Balearic Isles, where he set about recruiting a new army to help Hannibal. The battle decided the fate of Carthage in Spain; by the autumn of 206 B.C. the whole country had submitted to Rome.

Meanwhile, in the spring of 207 B.C., Hasdrubal had crossed the Alps, followed the same road taken by his brother eleven years earlier, and debouched into the valley of the Po, where, after he had recruited 10,000 Gauls,[2] he laid siege to Placentia. He failed to take the town and pushed on to Fanum Fortunae (Fano), a small port on the Adriatic at which the Via Flaminia strikes the coast. There he came into contact with the outposts of the combined armies of the praetor L. Porcius and the consul M. Livius, which were encamped at Sena Gallica (Senigallia) a few miles south of Fanum Fortunae. Hannibal was still in winter quarters in southern Italy at the time, watched by 40,000 Roman infantry and 2,500 horse, under the consul C. Claudius Nero and Q. Fulvius Flaccus. His intention was to effect a junction with his brother's army in central Italy; but because he had also to keep an eye on his bases in Bruttium (the toe of Italy), he did not want to move north until he was certain where Hasdrubal was. According to Livy, he did not expect him to cross the Alps as rapidly as he did, and when he heard that he had laid siege to Placentia, and knowing how long sieges generally take, he moved no further north than Canusium (Canosa) and awaited a message from his brother.

While there, one of those incalculable incidents occurred which

---

[1] Polybius, XI, 20-22.

[2] What the strength of his army was is uncertain. B. H. Hallward in *The Cambridge Ancient History* (vol. VIII, p. 93) suggests 30,000.

in war have so frequently decided the fate of nations. When he raised the siege of Placentia, Hasdrubal sent four Gallic and two Numidian horsemen with a letter to Hannibal. These men traversed the whole of Italy, but unaware that Hannibal had moved to Canusium they sought him near Tarentum, missed their way and were captured by a party of Roman foragers. Claudius Nero learnt from them that Hasdrubal proposed to cross the Apennines to meet his brother in Umbria, and, as Livy writes, he "judged that the situation of the state was not such that they should carry on the war by routine methods, each consul within the bounds of his own province, operating with his own armies against the enemy prescribed by the Senate. Rather must he venture to improvise something unforeseen, unexpected, something which in the beginning would cause no less alarm among citizens than among enemies, but if accomplished, would convert great fear into great rejoicing."[1] He therefore sent Hasdrubal's letter to Rome and informed the conscript fathers that while Hannibal remained in doubt, he, at the head of 6,000 picked infantry and 1,000 cavalry, would move north to reinforce Porcius and Livius, leaving Quintius Catius in command of his army to watch Hannibal. He suggested also that the legion at Capua should be moved to Rome and that the troops in Rome should move to Narnia (Narni). He sent messengers in advance through the territories he intended to traverse with orders that "they should carry from the farms and the cities provisions, ready for the soldiers to eat, down to the road, and should bring out horses and mules as well, that the weary might have no lack of vehicles."[2] He knew that there was not a moment to be lost and did not wait for a reply but set out northward.

This unprecedented step threw the senators into high alarm. They saw Hannibal again unleashed, and "The earlier disasters in that war, the deaths of two consuls in the preceding year, were still terrifying. And they said that all those misfortunes had befallen them when the enemy had but a single general, a single army, in Italy. At present it had become two Punic wars, two mighty armies, two Hannibals, so to speak, in Italy. . . ."[3]

Nero and his 7,000 set out at top speed, marched day and night, and when they approached Sena Gallica messengers were sent forward to Livius to tell him of their approach and that they would enter his camp secretly by night. So that their arrival

[1] Livy, xxvii, 43.   [2] Ibid., xxvii, 43.   [3] Ibid., xxvii, 44.

should not become known to Hasdrubal by an enlargement of Livius's camp, each of Nero's officers and soldiers doubled-up with one of Livius's and together shared the same tent.

Immediately after Nero's arrival a council of war was assembled, and though many wanted to defer the engagement until Nero's weary men were thoroughly rested, Nero urged an immediate attack while Hasdrubal was unaware of his arrival and Hannibal of his departure. On his proposal being accepted, the signal for battle was displayed and the troops marshalled.

In spite of the precautions taken to assure secrecy, through a foolish mistake on the part of the Romans, Hasdrubal learnt that Livius had been reinforced. A reconnoitring patrol reported on its return that though the signal had sounded once in the praetor's camp, it had sounded twice in the consul's. Hasdrubal judged from this that there must be two consuls in Livius's camp, suspected that Livius had been reinforced and decided to refuse battle. That night he slipped away up the valley of the Metaurus (Metauro) river to gain the Via Flaminia; but in the darkness his guides deserted him and he lost so much time in striking the road that the Romans, who discovered his withdrawal, caught up with him and forced him to accept battle.

Hasdrubal drew up his army as follows: In the centre he deployed the Ligurians covered by his elephants, with his Spanish troops on their right and his Gauls on their left. The Gauls occupied a hill overlooking a ravine – possibly that of San Angelo – and would appear to have been separated from the Ligurian left by a considerable distance. Opposite the Gauls, on a height overlooking the ravine, Nero took up his position, with Livius also separated from him and well away on his left, facing the Spaniards, who were under the direct command of Hasdrubal. We are told by Livy that Hasdrubal's line was "rather long than deep" and that the Roman right wing extended beyond the line of battle.

The battle was opened by the Spaniards. "There both [Roman] generals were engaged, there the greater part of the Roman infantry and cavalry, there the Spanish troops, the old soldiers, acquainted also with the Roman mode of fighting, and the Ligurians, a hardy race of warriors. To the same place came the elephants, which had thrown the front lines into confusion by their first charge and had by this time forced the standards back. Then as the conflict and the shouting increased, they were no longer under control and roamed about between the two battle-

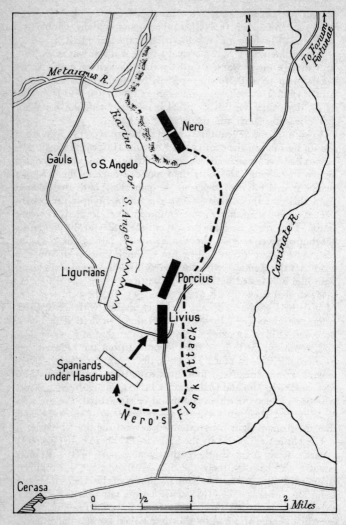

II. BATTLE OF THE METAURUS, 207 B.C.

The "Ravine of S. Angelo" is, of course, a modern name, but as, according to Hallward, "the evidence does not permit any reasonably certain certification of the precise site of the battlefield" it has been used, although out of historical context, as a guide.

lines, as though uncertain to whom they belonged, not unlike ships drifting without their steering-oars."[1] Eventually, many had to be killed by their mahouts, who were equipped with a long knife and mallet for that purpose, the latter used to drive the former into the elephant's spinal cord.

Meanwhile, on Hasdrubal's left, the formation of the ground prevented an engagement and Nero, who saw that a furious battle was being fought away to his left, decided to take part in it. He left a force to demonstrate against the Gauls and led "several cohorts" out of sight of his enemy and round the rear of Livius's army, much as centuries later Marlborough did at Ramillies. To the surprise of Hasdrubal he charged the right flank of the Spaniards and then fell upon their rear, pushing them on to the Ligurians.

When he saw that the battle was lost, Hasdrubal spurred his horse and "rushed upon a Roman cohort, where he fell fighting, as was worthy of the son of Hamilcar and the brother of Hannibal".[2] Of this incident Polybius remarks that "as long as there was any hope of being able to accomplish anything worthy of his former achievements", Hasdrubal "regarded his personal safety in this battle as of the highest consequence; but when Fortune deprived him of all hopes for the future, and reduced him to the last extremities, though neglecting nothing either in his preparations or on the field that might secure him the victory, nevertheless considered how, in case of total overthrow, he might face his fate and suffer nothing unworthy of his past career".[3]

The casualties, as given by Polybius, were "not less than 10,000 in killed for the Carthaginians, including the Celts, and about 2,000 for the Romans".[4]

On the night after the battle Nero set out on his return, and marching even more rapidly than when he came, he arrived at his camp before (Hannibal) on the sixth day.[5] Meanwhile a vague report of his victory reached Rome. At first the people "rather heard than credited the news"; but when it was confirmed, the whole city was swept by a wild joy—for the victory was the greatest yet won against their deadly enemy.

When he heard of his brother's defeat and death, Hannibal retired to Bruttium. Still the Romans did not dare to attack him, so great was the terror of his name. Yet it must have been apparent

[1] Livy, XXVII, 48.   [2] Ibid., XXVII, 49.   [3] Polybius, XI, 2.
[4] Ibid., XI, 3.   [5] Livy, XXVII, 50.

to them that their victory was in every way a decisive one. It ended Hannibal's last desperate hope of breaking the Roman hold on Italy; it restored confidence to the Roman soldiers, and it assured the loyalty of Rome's allies and subject peoples. Hence onwards the initiative passed into Roman hands.

If it be a fact that, after his victory of Cannae, Hannibal abandoned his advance on Rome because he believed that the encirclement of Italy would prove more profitable, after his brother's defeat on the Metaurus he must have realized his mistake; instead it was he who was encircled. By 205 B.C. he was isolated in the toe of Italy; Sicily had been lost and so had Spain, and peace had been agreed between Rome and Philip V of Macedonia.[1] So it came about that because Hannibal was reduced to a passive defensive, the initiative passed into the hands of the Romans. Their intention was slowly to strangle him; but Scipio thought differently, and, it would seem, had done so from the moment he took over command in Spain. His idea was to carry the war into Africa with Spain his stepping-stone. Polybius tells us that, after he had driven the Carthaginians out of Spain, he was advised "to take some rest and ease". He answered that, instead, he was "more than ever revolving in his mind how to begin the war with Carthage".[2] All along, it would appear, he had the campaign of Agathocles in his head, a man whose boldness he greatly admired.[3] So convinced was he of the necessity of carrying the war into Africa that, shortly after the battle of Ilipa, he had risked his life to visit Mauritania in order to win over Syphax, king of the Masaesylli, and to obtain from Masinissa, king of Numidia, a body of cavalry.[4]

After this mission, in 205 B.C., he returned to Italy, where he was acclaimed by the people and opposed by the elder generals who, because of his youth, were jealous of his success. He was chosen consul and Sicily was assigned to him as his province, more to get rid of him than to make use of his services. There he found himself in command of two legions formed from the

---

[1] The Roman operations in Illyria have not been examined because they were but a by-product of the war, and inglorious on both sides. Their importance lies in the future, namely the intervention of Rome in Greece and the declaration of the Second Macedonian War in 200 B.C. For the First Macedonian War see F. W. Walbank's *Philip V of Macedon* (1940), chap. III.

[2] Polybius, XI, 24.　　　　　　　　　　　　　　　[3] *Ibid.*, XV, 35.

[4] Mommsen (*History of Rome*, vol. II, p. 152) calls this "a foolhardy venture", and Captain B. H. Liddell Hart (*A Greater than Napoleon*, 1927, pp. 64–66) " a mission of diplomatic importance". Masinissa's capital was at Cirta (Constantine) and Syphax's at Siga (west of Oran).

remnants of the army of Cannae, and was refused all further help; yet, instead of being dejected, he set to work to recruit, organize, and train the army of the great revenge.

He sent his lieutenant, C. Laelius, over to Africa during 205 B.C., and in the spring of the following year he embarked his army at Lilybaeum, landed it at Cape Farina, near Utica, and was at once joined by Masinissa, who had been driven from his territories by Syphax. Scipio's expeditionary force consisted of his two legions and such volunteers he had been able to recruit, about 25,000 men in all, 40 warships and 400 transports. Meanwhile, since his return to Africa, Hasdrubal, son of Gisgo, had raised a Carthaginian army of 20,000 foot, 6,000 cavalry and 140 elephants, and was expecting the arrival of a corps of Celtiberian mercenaries. Syphax also was engaged in raising a large body of horsemen in his support.

Because Scipio's first need was to secure a base of operations, he laid siege to Utica, but on the approach of Hasdrubal and Syphax he was compelled to raise the siege and to retire to a rocky promontory some two miles distant, which he called Castra Cornelia; there he wintered. Syphax thought him cornered, which he very nearly was, and offered terms of peace. Scipio, with a cunning surpassing anything as yet done by a Carthaginian, prolonged the negotiations so that he might reconnoitre the enemy's camps which were but six miles distant from his own; his intention was suddenly to attack them under cover of night.

This craftiness has rightly been condemned by many as sheer treachery; yet, in mitigation, it should be remembered that Scipio's situation was a critical one, more particularly so because his enemy's numerous cavalry seriously restricted his foraging. But whatever view is taken, the fact remains that what Scipio was about to do was so decisive that, had he not done it, the probability is that his final victory would have been impossible. By "appearing excessively eager for peace" he lured his two opponents, Syphax and Hasdrubal, into a false sense of security, suddenly concluded the truce, and further to mislead them he began preparing to reopen the siege of Utica. He then hastily marshalled his two legions, set out at sunset, and ordered Laelius and Masinissa to fall upon Syphax's camp "and throw fire upon it", while he went to Hasdrubal's to do the same.

The Carthaginian outposts seemingly were negligent or asleep when suddenly flames shot up into the night and pandemonium followed. The accounts given by both Livy and Polybius are dramatic in the extreme. The latter writes: "It is . . . impossible for the imagination to exaggerate the dreadful scene, so completely did it surpass in horror everything hitherto recorded"; and the former informs us that 40,000 men were slain or destroyed by the flames and 5,000 were captured as well as 2,700 Numidian horses and six elephants. In short, if Livy's figures are not a gross exaggeration, though Hasdrubal and Syphax escaped, their combined armies were all but annihilated.[1]

Utica still held out, and instead of marching on Carthage, which would have been a risky operation, Scipio returned to Utica and pressed the siege. Meanwhile Hasdrubal and Syphax, now joined by 4,000 Celtiberian mercenaries, began to organize a new army. Scipio realized the danger of the probable withdrawal of Hannibal to Africa and the urgent need to smash Hasdrubal before he could arrive, and with one legion and the whole of his cavalry, now much strengthened, again took the field. On the great plains of the Bagradas (Mejerda) river he met Hasdrubal and Syphax, and by a tactical manœuvre similar to the one he had made use of at Ilipa, for the first time in Roman history the enemy was defeated by cavalry charges alone. Hasdrubal was overwhelmed, and Syphax, who broke away with a remnant of his horse, was pursued by Masinissa to Cirta and taken prisoner. For Scipio this action was of the utmost value, not only because it enabled him to reinstate Masinissa, but because it simultaneously deprived Carthage of its most valuable cavalry recruiting ground and won it for himself.

The result of the battle was panic in Carthage; peace was once again proposed, and Mago, then operating in the valley of the Po, and lastly Hannibal, in Bruttium, were recalled. Scipio thus gained his first objective, the evacuation of Italy by Hannibal, and, by offering a generous peace settlement, he hoped to gain his second, the victorious termination of the war.

Mago slipped away, while peace was being debated, but though his army gained the African shore he died of a wound during the voyage.

Hannibal was at Croton (Cotrone) when he received his orders to withdraw. He first killed his horses, then on June 23, 203 B.C.,

---

[1] For full accounts of the burning of these camps see Livy, xxx, 4–7, and Polybius, xiv, 1–6. Though it would seem to go unnoticed, there is little doubt that this ruse was inspired by Scipio's readings of the campaigns of Agathocles, during which a very similar incident occurred. (See Diodorus, xx, 64–66; also xx 18.)

under protection of the armistice, he embarked his army, some 15,000 to 20,000 men, and landed it at Leptis Minor (Lemta). Thence he moved to Hadrumentum (Susa) to collect such cavalry as he could, which action so encouraged the patriot party in Carthage that its adherents refused to ratify the peace and seized the Roman envoys. Indignant at this treachery, early in 202 B.C., Scipio struck his camp at Tunes and marched up the valley of the Bagradas, burning the villages as he went to terrorize the people and to cut off the food stocks upon which Carthage largely depended. This struck such fear into that city that its inhabitants urged Hannibal to act without further delay. So it came about that a few days later he struck camp at Hadrumentum and marched inland to Zama (Zowareen), which lies five days' march south-west of Carthage. There he was received with foreboding news that Masinissa, at the head of 6,000 infantry and 4,000 cavalry, had joined Scipio.

He realized that with so great a preponderance of cavalry against him his chances of victory were slight and he sought an interview with his adversary. It was granted, and on the following day "both commanders advanced from their camps attended by a few horsemen. Presently they left their escorts and met in the intervening space by themselves, each accompanied by an interpreter."[1] Hannibal pointed out how fickle in war fortune could be and urged that a settlement should be agreed whereby Sicily, Sardinia, and Spain should be retained by Rome, the Carthaginians engaging never to go to war for these territories. Scipio, who realized full well his military superiority, brushed these proposals aside and said that because of the breaking of the recent truce he could no longer trust the Carthaginian word. The conference ended, both returned to their camps, and at dawn the following day they drew out their respective armies in order of battle.

In quality and training Hannibal's army was vastly inferior to his opponent's, and the order in which he marshalled it shows that he understood this. He had three divisions of infantry: his own army, Mago's, and a body of Carthaginian and African troops hastily raised by the Carthaginian Senate. The first and second he could rely upon, the third he could not; therefore he drew up the second, composed of Ligurian and Gallic auxiliaries, in front, presumably in open order of units, for he intermixed with it Balearic slingers and Moorish light infantry. The third, consisting

[1]Polybius, xv, 6.

of Carthaginian and African troops, he formed in second line immediately in rear of the first. The first he held in reserve some 200 yards in rear of the second line; it consisted mainly of Bruttians. In front of his first line he drew up in extended order eighty elephants; lastly he posted on the wings of his army his 2,000 cavalry, the Carthaginian on the right and the Numidian on the left. Because the weakness of his cavalry prohibited him from turning his enemy's flanks, as he had done at Cannae, his idea was to break the Roman front, a gamble which depended on the behaviour of his elephants. Were they to behave themselves well, the Roman front would undoubtedly be thrown into disorder, and this would not only facilitate the assault of his first line, but also encourage his second line, the hastily raised Africans. Lastly, with his veteran third line, he hoped to deliver the knock-out blow.

Scipio maintained the normal legionary organization, but adapted it to the tactical situation as it faced him. Instead of drawing up the maniples of the three lines chequer-wise, so that those of the second covered the intervals in the first–the usual formation–the maniples of the second line were marshalled immediately behind those of the first to create lanes for the Carthaginian elephants to pass along. Further, the *triarii* were held back well in rear, so they would not be thrown into confusion should the elephants break through, and the *velites* were posted in the lanes with orders to fall back should they be unable "to stand the charge of the elephants". On the left flank he posted Laelius with the Italian cavalry, and on the right Masinissa with the Numidian.

The battle may be divided into four phases: (1) The charge of Hannibal's elephants and the rout of his cavalry; (2) the fight between Hannibal's first two lines and Scipio's *hastati* supported by his *principes*; (3) the fight between the opposing reserves; and (4) Masinissa'a rear attack on Hannibal's veterans.

According to Polybius's account, though Livy's is the more dramatic,[1] the battle opened with a skirmish between the opposing forces of Numidian cavalry, during which Hannibal ordered his elephants to charge. But as they approached their enemy, the noise of the Roman horns and trumpets so terrified them that those on the left wing rushed backwards and threw Hannibal's Numidian horse into confusion. Masinissa seized the oppor-

[1] Polybius, xv, 12–14; Livy, xxx, 33–35.

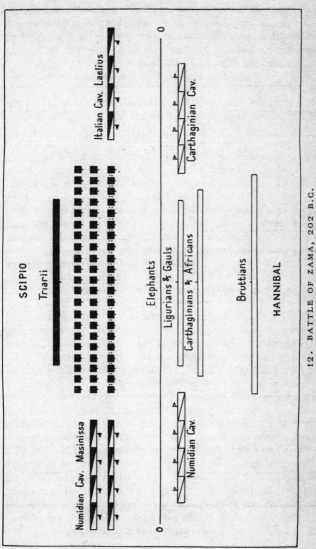

SCIPIO

Triarii

Numidian Cav. Masinissa

Italian Cav. Laelius

Elephants

Ligurians & Gauls

Carthaginians & Africans

Carthaginian Cav.

Numidian Cav.

Bruttians

HANNIBAL

12. BATTLE OF ZAMA, 202 B.C.

tunity, charged home, and drove the Numidians from the field. In the centre the elephants drove the *velites* down the lanes and punished them severely. Next came Laelius's opportunity, and he seized it; for while the elephants were surging towards the Roman rear, he charged Hannibal's Carthaginian cavalry and drove it back in rout, and, emulating Masinissa, he set out on a vigorous pursuit.

Not until the cavalry of both sides were off the field did the infantry action begin, and it proved to be, as Polybius says, "a trial of strength between man and man at close quarters". At first it would appear that the advantage was with Hannibal; but because his second line failed to support the first, the latter was slowly forced back until it felt that it had been abandoned, broke to the rear, and not being allowed to pass through the second line, its panic-stricken men tried to hack their way through it. A general mêlée followed in which the first and second lines, pressed by the *hastati* who had been reinforced by the *principes*, fell back on Hannibal's third lines, and being refused admittance its men disappeared in rout round its flanks.

The third phase then opened. It is a grim picture, for the ground was now encumbered with the dead, the wounded "lying piled up in bloody heaps". Scipio ordered the wounded to be carried to the rear to clear the ground for his final assault, withdrew his *hastati* to the flanks, and between them he advanced the *principes* and *triarii* in close order. And "when they had surmounted the obstacles [the corpses] and got into line with the *hastati*, the two lines charged each other with the greatest fire and fury. Being nearly equal in numbers, spirit, courage and arms, the battle was for a long time undecided, the men in their obstinate valour falling dead without giving way a step."[1]

Had the action now remained solely an infantry one, it is possible that Hannibal might have won it; but most fortunate for Scipio, "in the very nick or time" Masinissa and Laelius returned, and "charging Hannibal's rear, the greater part of his men were cut down in their ranks; while of those who attempted to fly very few escaped with their life. . . ." This led to a total defeat of the Carthaginian forces. "On the Roman side there fell over fifteen hundred, on the Carthaginian over twenty thousand, while the prisoners taken were almost as numerous."[2] Hannibal, accompanied by a few horsemen, escaped to Hadrumentum.

[1] Polybius, xv, 14.　　　　[2] *Ibid.*, xv, 14.

Scipio did not march upon Carthage after the battle because, as Livy informs us, he thought that were he to lay siege to it and be recalled before it finished, his successor would come in for the glory of finishing the war,[1] and Polybius says that the dignity of Rome demanded lenity and magnanimous behaviour.[2] Both these reasons are suspect because undoubtedly the true reason is that Scipio was in no way prepared to carry out a prolonged siege. Like Hannibal, though a master of fieldcraft, his siegecraft was indifferent. Besides, the war had now lasted for sixteen years and Rome was weary and exhausted. In any case a siege was likely to absorb much time, for Carthage was superlatively well fortified.[3] Peace with Carthage rather than its occupation was, therefore, essential, and so it came about that the peace terms offered by Scipio were both generous and wise. The main clauses agreed upon were:

(1) The handing over of all ships of war and all elephants.

(2) Agreement to carry on no future war without the consent of Rome.

(3) The reinstatement of Masinissa in his former kingdom.

(4) The payment of 10,000 talents of silver (£2,970,000) spread over fifty years.

These terms were accepted by the Roman Senate and people. "Thus", writes Mr. Scullard, "the conqueror of Hannibal having vindicated his military strategy, triumphed also in the political field; he negotiated a wise peace such as could never have been made if Hannibal had been defeated in Italy. . . . His success owed much to the enthusiastic and loyal support of the People of Rome."[4] Mommsen remarks: "It is . . . probable that the two great generals, on whom the decision of the political question . . . devolved, offered and accepted peace on such terms in order to set just and reasonable limits on the one hand to the furious vengeance of the victors, on the other to the obstinacy and imprudence of the vanquished. The noble-mindedness and statesmanlike gifts of the great antagonists are no less apparent in the

---

[1] Livy, xxx, 36.　　　　　　　　　　　　[2] Polybius, xv, 17.

[3] The citadel or Byrsa of Carthage was built on a hill near the extremity of a peninsula connected with the mainland by an isthmus about three miles broad, defended by a triple line of fortifications, the outer wall of which was forty-five feet high with towers at intervals of 200 feet. The whole peninsula thus enclosed was about thirty miles in circuit. Carthage was in fact a vast and immensely strong entrenched camp stored with all the necessaries for sustaining a siege.

[4] *Roman Politics 220–150 B.C.*, p. 81.

magnanimous submission of Hannibal to what was inevitable, than in the wise abstinence of Scipio from an extravagant and insulting use of victory."[1]

Though, at the time, no doubt, neither of the two great men fully realized the supreme importance of the event, in part at least the words which Livy and Polybius wrote in later years must have found an echo in Scipio's heart. Livy, when about to describe the battle of Zama, writes that, "before nightfall they would know whether Rome or Carthage should give laws to the nations. . . . For not Africa . . . or Italy, but the whole world would be the reward of victory."[2] And Polybius says: "To the Carthaginians it was a struggle for their own lives and the sovereignty of Libya; to the Romans for universal dominion and supremacy."[3]

These words are true, for Zama, by deciding who should rule supreme in the western Mediterranean, decided the coming struggle for supremacy in its eastern half. Even during the war the alliance between Carthage and Macedonia had compelled the Romans to glance eastward; but now that they were freed of Carthage they could, and of necessity were compelled to, stare in that direction.

"The immediate results of the war out of Italy were, the conversion of Spain into two Roman provinces—which, however, were in perpetual insurrection; the union of the hitherto dependent kingdom of Syracuse with the Roman province of Sicily; the establishment of a Roman instead of a Carthaginian protectorate over the most important Numidian chiefs; and lastly the conversion of Carthage from a powerful commercial state into a defenceless mercantile town. In other words, it established the uncontested hegemony of Rome over the western region of the Mediterranean."[4] The battle of Zama constitutes one of the great turning points in history; it led the Roman people across the threshold of a united Italy to the high-road of world dominion.

---

[1] *History of Rome*, vol. II, pp. 175–176. [2] Livy, xxx, 32.
[3] Polybius, xv, 9. Appian writes, "Hannibal said that the battle would decide the fate of Carthage and all Africa", and Scipio "that there was no safe refuge for his men if they were vanquished" (*The Punic War*, VIII, 42).
[4] *History of Rome*, vol. II, p. 176–177.

The 170 years which followed the Battle of Zama were the years of Rome's rise to power and fall from grace; her armies prospered in the three known continents, carving out an empire; the Roman Republic slowly died of success. Above all, these seventeen decades were times of war – ceaseless, often seemingly senseless war, since the imperial idea took a while to harden out, and imperial adventures lacked meaning until it did so. But war had always been accepted as the normal condition of man, and Fuller tells us why this was particularly so in the case of rising Rome:

> . . . the devastation of the farms had driven large numbers of free labourers into the cities and the enrolment of freemen in the legions, by further depleting the farm workers, had led to an ever-increasing demand for cheap slave labour. Abroad, the opening up of vast wheat regions in Africa, Sicily, and Sardinia brought with it a further need for slaves, and the slave markets could be supplied by war. War thus became a necessity of Roman civilization.

Pressure on Rome from the north and north-east never stopped. In northern Italy the Gauls were always a danger; behind them, tribal movements, impelled by constant stirrings in the Euro-Asian hinterland, brought the molten condition of Central Europe to periodical boiling-points. Nevertheless, as Fuller says, despite these recurring alarms, having defeated the great enemy in the west, it was to the eastern Mediterranean that Rome next turned.

After the death of Alexander the Macedonian Empire disintegrated into warring components (Macedonia itself, Syria and Egypt chief among them) and Rome was drawn into their struggles. Hannibal, in exile, lent his ability and prestige to whatever cause might damage his old enemies. However, two major campaigns at the opening of the 2nd Century B.C. demonstrated again the superiority of the Roman legion, if properly led. "These two wars," says Fuller,

> the first with Macedonia and the second with Syria, were struggles in the first place for security, though they led the way to wealth and power. They did not add a square foot to Roman territory; for with constant war in northern Italy and Spain, Rome had not the men to hold the conquered lands. Their main influence was that they further stimulated the rising monied nobility and corrupted both the people and the army.

The effects of this corruption were soon apparent; Macedonia remained a challenge to Roman power, prolonged by military incompetence at both the Command and executive levels. The Macedonians were not finally defeated until the arrival of Lucius Aemilius Paullus, and his victory over King Perseus at Pydna in 168. This battle, says Fuller, made Rome "a world power and an empire all but in name". He continues:

> Yet, this vast extension of power was not planned. It was the outcome of the growth of a virile people in the conditions which prevailed in an age in which the balance of power was unknown. In such an age each nation, once it has attained internal unity, is for self-preservation compelled either to subdue its neighbours or emasculate them. The Hellenic states attempted the first course, Rome the second; but it was only a slower process toward the same end, because abject weakness whets the appetite of conquest. Thus it came about, as Mommsen says: '. . . all the other richly endowed and highly developed nations of antiquity had to perish in order to enrich a single people, as if the ultimate object of their existence had simply been to contribute to the greatness of Italy and to the decay involved in that greatness.' [1]
>
> Nevertheless, once this ruthlessness ended, the result was not the decay of Greece, but the victory of Hellenism; for the Greeks were the Chinese of the ancient world and always conquered their conquerors. What they needed, in order to exorcise the excessive individualism which had kept them fractionized and mutually antagonistic, was the authority of a strong and stable world government. And what Rome needed,

[1] Mommsen, *History of Rome*, Vol. II, p. 294.

in order to become a civilizing world power, was the culture of the Hellenistic world. These two things and not plunder and tribute were the true booty of Pydna and the Third Macedonian War.

The complete subjection of Greece, and its reduction to the status of a Roman province did not, in fact, take place until twenty-two years after the Battle of Pydna. In 146 B.C. Rome celebrated a double triumph: rebellious Corinth was captured looted and razed to the ground; in the same year Carthage, forced into war, suffered a like fate, so complete that "a plough could be drawn over its site". Not even Ypres, after four and a half years of bombardment, nor Hiroshima, after an atomic bomb was so utterly wiped out. "The obliteration of cities," says Fuller,

> had now become the seal of Roman power. Yet, as Polybius remarks: 'To destroy that for which a war is undertaken seems an act of madness, and madness of a very violent kind.' Corinth, Carthage, and later Numantia (Guarray, near Soria) in Spain (133 B.C.) were destroyed to show the might of Rome and also to sate her greed for plunder. Also, the sale of their citizens as slaves was profitable, and many of these rebellions and so-called wars were little more than slave hunts.

For the next hundred years, as with the Greeks after the "crowning mercy" of Salamis, victory over foreign foes brought in its train internal strife – the struggles for power within Rome which transformed her from a more or less viable republic into an empire. As the middle of the 1st Century B.C. approached, these struggles focussed around the personalities of two remarkable generals, Cn. Pompeius (Pompey) and Caius Julius Caesar. Pompey's period of glory was 67-61, when he crushed the Mediterranean pirates, marched up the Euphrates to the Caspian Sea, entered Jerusalem and brought the Jews under Roman rule. In 60 B.C. Caesar returned to Rome from successes in Spain, and in the following year the government of the city was divided among the triumvirate: Pompey, the banker M. Licinius Crassus, and Caesar. To Caesar were assigned the provinces of Cisalpine and Transalpine Gaul, now to become the scene of one of the greatest military achievements in history. The conquest of Gaul was not completed until 52, when the chief Vercingetorix was defeated at Alesia. Fuller's summary:

It had been an amazing task, for all in all, as Plutarch writes, Caesar 'took by storm more than eight hundred cities, subdued three hundred nations, and fought pitched battles at different times with three million men, of whom he slew one million in hand to hand fighting and took as many more prisoners.'[1] It was his amazing energy which had accomplished this, and not only did it give Rome Gaul, but its conquest made Caesar both the hero of the people and master of the most powerful Roman army. Pompey entered his eclipse.

During this period of perpetual war, the Roman army changed markedly in character; what had begun as a well-organized assembly in arms of full Roman citizens now became an army of professional mercenaries drawn from all classes, including criminals and frequently also foreigners. "Where in former days," says Fuller, "the soldier swore allegiance to the Republic, he now swore to serve his general. Such an army demanded highly educated and skilful generals, and when these were forthcoming success was assured. When they were not, discipline was apt rapidly to break down."

Professionalism expressed itself in other ways, too: technology played its part in Rome's victories. Artillery and the science of military engineering made considerable strides. The Romans developed a "field gun" (Catapulta) which was more accurate than the flintlock musket of the 18th Century A.D. and could shoot up to five hundred yards (long musket range), a "heavy gun" (Ballista) which could throw stones weighing up to fifty or sixty lb., and a useful "howitzer" (Onager).[2] Fuller continues:

Hand in hand with increasing missile power went progress in fortification and siege work, and in these branches of the art of war Caesar is without a rival. In 52 B.C., at the siege of Alesia (Auxois), it has been calculated that his men shifted 2,000,000 cubic metres of earth from the trenches they dug. Four years later, at the siege of Dyrrhachium, much the same must have been done, and at the siege of Massilia in 49 B.C., all manner of engines were employed.

It was in the year 49 that Caesar crossed the Rubicon to march

[1] Fuller's note: "These figures are obviously exaggerated."

[2] See Fuller, *Julius Caesar, Man, Soldier, and Tyrant,* Eyre & Spottiswoode, 1965; pp. 92-6.

on Rome and begin the last short phase of his contest with Pompey. During all this time the Greek peninsula provided a "cockpit" of the ancient world as the Low Countries did for Western Europe at the end of the Middle Ages. The scene of Caesar's struggle with Pompey was first Dyrrhachium (Durazzo, in what is now Albania) and then Thessaly in Greece. There, at the Battle of Pharsalus on 9 August, 48, Pompey was utterly defeated. He fled to Egypt, where Caesar followed him, only to learn that his rival had been assassinated; Caesar remained long enough to fight a small war on behalf of Queen Cleopatra, and make her pregnant, before carrying out his mopping-up operations against the Pompeians. These took him to Syria, North Africa and Spain, so that he did not return to Rome until 45. On 15 March, 44, he was assassinated at the foot of Pompey's statue in the Senate. Fuller describes the components of his greatness:

As a leader of men Caesar was not only the brain but the soul of his army; in this respect he equals Alexander and Hannibal. The well-being of his soldiers was his constant concern, and though, when on service, he enforced the strictest discipline, when not, he relaxed it as occasion demanded; for he knew that vice as well as virtue is a component of human contentedness. Suetonius tells us that "he valued his soldiers neither for their personal character nor their fortune, but solely for their prowess", and, as Mommsen says, he treated his soldiers "as men who are entitled to demand and were able to endure the truth". He so fully won their respect and fidelity that, when present among them, defeat seemed to them to be impossible.

As a commander of armies he excelled in three main respects: Firstly, with Alexander and Hannibal he possessed the skill to fashion an instrument of war which fitted his own genius. He was a marvellous organiser and his faith in his genius was unshakable. Secondly, he grasped the nature of war in his age. It was national: not merely the contending of armies, but the struggle of an entire people yearning for something new. In such wars grand strategy – the utilization of all means towards the end – predominates: men, money, trade, political reactions and propaganda must all be canalized and lead to the one goal. Lastly, his amazing boldness and seeming rashness were founded on his grasping of the secret that in war, as in peace, most difficulties are self-suggested – that, generally speaking, because opponents are equally fearful of each other, he who first brushes the terrors of the moment aside is the first to set his foot on the high road to victory. Caesar, like Alexander, possessed that spirit of audacity which raises general-ship to its highest level. He divined his enemy's intentions and he set aside his own fears.

Gifts such as these could not fail to fashion him into a statesman of outstanding ability. He understood what the conditions of the Republic were and in what direction they tended. He read the inner meaning of the times as clearly as he fathomed the heart of Pompey. He saw that they demanded a monarchical democracy: freedom under discipline and not licence under greed; in short, what the Duke of Wellington once called a *démocratie royale*. Keeping his mind on this goal he became, as Warde Fowler has so truly said, "a great schoolmaster of mankind".

Though in his short reign he could do no more than sow the seed of the autocratic empire, much of which was trampled into the mire by his successors, he changed Rome from a municipality into a world-kingdom, and extended it in idea until the hub was swallowed by the circumference. He breathed into the Republic a new life, and thereby not only gave life to the *démo-cratie royale* of Augustus, the first true world ruler, but blazed the trail for a still higher conception, that of unity in concord, which became the ideal of the universal Church.

The final struggle for power after Caesar's death, and the demise of the Republic, occupied another thirteen years. The first stage, however, was brief: in his will Caesar designated his grand-nephew Caius Octavius (Octavian) as his heir; in uneasy alliance with Marcus Antonius (Mark Antony), Caesar's lieuten-ant, Octavian set about the destruction of the great man's assassins. Once more Macedonia was the chief seat of war (though every part of Rome's large domain was affected). The leading conspirators, Brutus and Cassius, took up their positions at Philippi in Thrace, and there, in two battles in 42 B.C. they were defeated and met their deaths.

Octavian and Antony manage to co-exist until 33, when the latter in turn fell under the spell of Cleopatra. He married her, and proclaimed her son by Julius Caesar – Caesarion – "King of Kings". Antony was a bold and inspiring leader, Egypt a country of great wealth; the combination was formidable. Indeed, it was too formidable; the Romans were frightened into believing that Antony intended to supplant Rome by Alexandria as the seat of power. They may well have been right; but in any case, their reaction was to rally to Octavian against Antony in the spirit of a crusade. Yet again the decisive encounter was in Greece – this time a naval battle, Actium, in 31 B.C. (in the Gulf of Amvrakia, facing Catanzaro). Octavian's victory was complete, and in the following year he landed in Egypt. First Antony, then Cleopatra committed suicide, and Octavian became the master of the known world. Fuller writes:

Though Philippi – ironically won for him by Antony – was the copestone of Octavian's power, his defeat of Antony at Actium was the cornerstone of the world empire which had been struggling to come into being since the days of the Diadochi. The one was the climax of a political struggle within a democracy to decide whether autocracy or democracy was to prevail. The other was the climax reached between the contending halves of a divided autocracy to decide whether the split was to be permanent or which half was to dominate the whole. Had Brutus and Cassius won at Philippi, the fruits of their victory could never have matured, because the political roots of the Roman Republic were withering away. Even had Antony and Cleopatra success-fully defended Egypt, by preventing Octavian acquiring the treasure of the Ptolemies, without which he could not have paid the rewards he had promised his supporters and soldiers, the division between the East and the West of the Empire might have become permanent, as in a later age it did. But had Antony and Cleopatra won at Actium, there can be little doubt that they would have transferred the capital of the Empire from Rome to Alexandria, which both strategically and commercially was a better site, and that in the stead of the national Roman *Imperium*, established by their conqueror, there would have arisen a cosmo-politan world empire as dreamt of by Alexander. It is because of this probability that Actium was one of the most decisive battles ever fought: it prevented Europe changing its cultural axis.

Its first fruits were plucked immediately. When Octavian had fulfilled Cleopatra's last wish, to be buried beside Antony, he annexed Egypt in the name of the Roman people. He realized the importance of its corn as an instrument of government and took special precautions to bring the country under his personal control; to establish his prestige in the East he assumed the divine honours and titles of its Ptolemaic kings. A little over three years later, on January 17, 27 B.C., outwardly he restored the Republic and was given by the Senate the semi-divine name of

Augustus—the Consecrated.

But he never forgot that his adoptive father had perished by, as well as conquered by, the sword, and throughout his reign he sought to disguise the power the sword had won him by introducing new forms under old titles. He grasped at real power and surrendered to the Senate and the people the outward show in which that power was wrapped. According to the letter of his theory of government, sovereignty was vested in the Senate and people; in fact authority over both was vested in himself. Because continuous tenure of the consulship would have been too open a break with tradition, after 23 B.C. he ceased to hold this magistracy, and directly from Rome, through *legati* appointed by himself, governed the provinces where legions were stationed. Elsewhere in the empire, when necessity arose, he could enjoy an authority superior to that of all provincial governors through the *maius imperium* which he was granted. At home he relied on tribunician power, already granted to him for life, and in 23 B.C. strengthened to make good what he had lost when he gave up the consulship. Though he assumed *Imperator* as a first name, *Princeps*—First Citizen—was the title by which, at his wish, men spoke of him. For it was by *auctoritas*—personal prestige—that he governed, as well as in virtue of his cleverly devised constitutional powers.

Augustus realized, as did Thomas Hobbes centuries later, that "Covenants, without the Sword, are but Words, and of no strength to secure a man at all", and he based his rule on military power. Because, in normal times, the legions were quartered in the provinces and not in Italy, when, in 27 B.C., he nominally restored the Senate, he kept all frontier provinces, except that of Africa, under his personal charge; hence all the legions, except one, were under his command.

Under the Republic, in theory at least, the armies had been enrolled for each campaign and disbanded on its conclusion. But during the Civil War this system of raising emergency forces largely had given way to the establishment of professional armies, the main allegiance of which was to their paymasters. One of his first reforms was to abolish this system and to create a standing army on an imperial footing; its men swore fealty to himself alone. He reduced the legions to twenty-eight, and divided the army into two grand divisions—legions and *auxilia*. The former were recruited from Roman citizens; the latter from Roman non-citizen subjects. Service in the legions was for twenty years, recruiting was voluntary, and on discharge each legionary received a bounty or an award of land. In the *auxilia*, service was also voluntary though frequently longer, and on discharge a bounty was paid to the soldier and the Roman franchise granted to him, his wife, and his children. Besides providing many cohorts of foot, the *auxilia* supplied all the archers and nearly all of the cavalry.

Because Augustus's policy was based on security and not on conquest, the legions and the *auxilia* were distributed in groups to hold the frontiers, each groupd based on a defended military centre called a *castellum*, which was linked to the frontier posts by road. This policy of containment, in contradistinction to expansion, had a profound, moral effect on the legions. As their purpose was now to maintain peace and not to make war, their valour, which formerly had been stimulated by patriotism or plunder, gradually deteriorated. First, the growth of pacifism, through loss of fear, led to the recruitment of fewer and fewer citizens and of more and more barbarians in order to keep the legions up to establishment. Secondly, a most pernicious form of militarism crept in – the dependence of the Emperor's political status on the will of the army.

This latter defect was stimulated by yet another reform. Besides the above two bodies of troops, Augustus organized what to-day would be called a "private army" of his own – the Praetorian Guards. During the last year of the Republic many commanders had raised for their personal protection special bodyguards, *cohortes praetoriae*, so named because the general's camp headquarters was called the *praetorium*. When Augustus restored the Republic, he kept these guards in Italy, organized them into nine cohorts, each of 1,000 men, and placed them under two *praefecti* who commanded them in his name. They were an ever-present sanction of his authority and the symbol of what his government really was, a judiciously organized military tyranny. As we shall see, the danger inherent in this reform was that, because the Praetorians were the instrument of the Imperial authority, in the final issue its existence depended upon their loyalty.

This government, so profoundly undemocratic in practice, was accepted by all Roman citizens and subject peoples because, after a hundred years of civil turmoil and strife, the army of Augustus re-established order and maintained the public peace. For two centuries it secured the Empire against invasion, and for two centuries more it held its own against the Teutonic barbarians in spite of occasional defeat. It was the army which maintained the *Pax Romana*, during which western Europe was latinized and the Christian religion struck root. And it was the battles of Philippi and Actium which enabled Augustus to create it.

The establishment of the Imperial frontiers

The empire which Octavian won at Actium stretched from the Atlantic to the Euphrates and from the North Sea to the Sahara Desert, including within it all the states which fringed the Mediterranean, now a Roman lake. It had grown by chance and not by design, and to consolidate it and transform its diverse peoples into a single Roman nation demanded two things: first, internal pacification, and secondly, the establishment of secure frontiers. These were the major problems which occupied Augustus during his long reign of forty-one years, and though Suetonius tells us that "the temple of Janus Quirinus, which had been shut twice only, from the era of the building of the city to his own time", Augustus "closed thrice in a much shorter period, having established universal peace both by sea and land", his entire Principate was, nevertheless, one long record of military operations, for the most part conducted by others than himself. These, by the date of his death, had added to the Empire an area even greater than that conquered by his adoptive father, Julius Caesar.

Of the two major problems, the more pressing was the first, which included the pacification of Spain and Africa as well as the reorganization of the provinces generally. Augustus began with the West, set out for Spain in the summer of 27 B.C., and after a series of successful campaigns returned to Rome in 24 B.C. War immediately broke out again, and it was not until 19 B.C. that Agrippa finally broke the spirit of the Cantabrians by a wholesale massacre. This same year witnessed the final subjection of the province of Africa, by Cornelius Balbus.

On his return from Spain, Augustus set out to tackle the problem of the eastern frontier. Six years before, after his occupation of Alexandria and when the whole Orient lay at his feet, popular opinion in Rome had urged the subjection of the East as far as India, and had he been Caesar, undoubtedly he would have set out to conquer Parthia. But he was a diplomatist and not a soldier, and though, in order to restore the prestige of Rome lost by Crassus and Antony in their Parthian campaigns, he understood that action of a kind was necessary, he also realized that, because the Empire was based on the Mediterranean, its proper limits were the Mediterranean lands, and that any considerable extension eastward would result in weakness, not in increased strength. He had made Syria the pivot of the eastern defences and had returned to Rome firmly resolved that Roman interests could better be secured by diplomacy than by war. Now he returned to the problem with this idea in mind. It was a threefold one, for it included the frontiers of Egypt in the south, Syria in the centre, and Asia Minor in the north.

In Egypt he established a line of fortified posts across Upper Egypt, and probably one on the Egyptian north-western frontier, toward Cyrene, though this is not known definitely. These defences proved so successful that no violation of the Egyptian frontiers occurred until the middle of the third century A.D. At the same time he sent an exploratory expedition under Aelius Gallus down · the eastern coast of Arabia Felix to Mariaba (Marib), the capital city of the Sabaeans in Yemen (Land of Sheba), to gain control of the Indian trade; but it accomplished nothing.

While Egypt was being secured, he annexed Galatia and extended Roman control over Pontus and Cappadocia, and in 19 B.C. he sent Agrippa to the East to superintend the government of the provinces. Among his tasks was the regulation of affairs in the Bosporan Kingdom, a state north of the Black Sea between the rivers Dniester and Dnieper, inhabited by a Graeco-Iranian people. Its importance was considerable, because it was the main source of wheat for the cities of Asia Minor and the Aegean, and when Roman troops were operating in the northern section of the eastern front their provisioning depended chiefly on south Russia. Later, this kingdom was brought under Roman vassalage.

As he decided on the upper Euphrates and the Syrian desert to the south of it as the natural defensive line to cover the central Mediterranean sector, it would have been as well had Augustus abandoned all claims to Armenia. Not only would its retention establish a salient both difficult to hold and reinforce, but it would create a perpetual source of quarrel with Parthia, which, if left alone, was no great menace; as a feudal country it possessed no standing army, and though its levies of horse archers could win battles, they were so badly supplied that they could not for long be kept together in the field. But prestige was at stake, and, in consequence, Augustus fell back on the old Roman half-measure; instead of annexing Armenia or abandoning it, he decided to convert it into a client state. As this solution annoyed Phraates, king of Parthia, in 23 B.C. he refused to comply with a request to return the Carrhae standards, and in the following year Augustus went to Syria and at the same time instructed his stepson Tiberius to bring a large legionary force out to Armenia. It had the desired effect; on May 12, 20 B.C., Phraates restored the standards lost by Crassus and Antony as well as all surviving prisoners. It was a notable diplomatic success, which Augustus ranked higher than a victory in the field, and Tiberius entered Armenia and placed Tigranes, the Roman monarchial candidate, on the throne. But the settlement was far from a satisfactory one, and toward the end of Augustus's reign Armenia passed out of Roman control.

The northern frontier, as Augustus found it, ran from the mouth of the Rhine and along that river to Bâle, thence over the western slopes of the Jura mountains southward between the Rhône and the Maritime Alps, where it formed a narrow appendix of land west of Cisalpine Gaul with its southern extremity all but touching the Mediterranean. From there it swung northward along the Maritime Alps and thence eastward over the southern slopes of the Alps to north of Aquileia (Aquilega), from where it ran south-eastward to end on the Hellespont.

From a defensive point of view, it was a thoroughly defective frontier, because it did not prevent northern Italy and Macedonia from being raided by the wild tribesmen of the Alps and Danube basin, nor did it allow adequate communications to be established between Italy and Gaul and between Italy and Macedonia. The sole road linking Italy to the former ran along the Mediterranean coast, because the passes of the Little and Great St. Bernard had not yet been secured; and between Italy and Macedonia there was no road at all, all communications with the eastern half of the Empire being by way of the Adriatic and *Via Egnatia*. This, as Augustus had learnt during the Civil War, was a fundamental weakness, because in the age under review storms at sea were incomparably more fatal to the transport of troops and their supply and maintenance in the field than they are to-day. The lack of a road linking Italy with Macedonia had, as we have seen, been the main difficulty Caesar had had to overcome in his 48 B.C. campaign against Pompey. Even in his own Actium campaign, when the command of the sea was his, a sudden storm might have wrecked it at the start.

In 25 B.C. Augustus set out to rectify these strategic defects. He started in Gaul and instructed Terentius Varro and Marcus Vinicius to secure the passes of the Little and Great St. Bernard by reducing the appendix of still unconquered land. This was done successfully by establishing two new lines of approach, one leading by the Little St. Bernard into central Gaul, and the other by the Great St. Bernard toward the upper Rhine. Next, in 17 or 16 B.C., P. Silius Nerva reduced the tribes east of Lake Garda and probably also those in the upper Adige (Val Venosta). Because this advance opened up a road towards the valley of the Inn, in 15 B.C. Augustus decided on a more far-reaching campaign, the aim of which was to bring under Roman subjection the great block of mountainous country which now includes Tirol, eastern Switzerland, western Austria, and southern Bavaria, and to carry the central section of the northern frontier northward to the upper Danube.

This important campaign Augustus entrusted to his two step-sons, Tiberius and Drusus, sons of Tiberius Claudius Nero and Livia, Augustus's second wife. Tiberius was to march eastward from Gaul toward Lake Constance, and Drusus northward from Italy by way of the Val Venosta and over the pass of Resia (the Reschen-scheideck) to the valley of the Inn, and thence into Bavaria where he was to meet his brother. The campaign was a signal triumph, Noricum (Styria, Carinthia and southern Bavaria) was annexed, and Roman control extended down the Danube as far as Vienna. The strategical gain was enormous. Italy no longer required the protection of the army in Illyricum, which could now be set free to win a land route to Macedonia.

Except for the valley of the Save there is no route; therefore Augustus decided to advance from Aquileia to Emona (Ljubljana) and thence down the valley of the Save to Siscia (Sisak), Sirmium (Mitrovitz) and Singidunum (Belgrade), whence the road could be continued eastward by way of Naissus (Nish) and Serdice (near Sophia) to Byzantium. Even to-day this is the only road by which, with some measure of rapidity and comfort, Yugoslavia can be traversed from end to end. Besides this road there was another route down the valley of the Drave to Sirmium by way of Mursa (Osijek). To win these two roads meant carrying the northern frontier of Illyricum to the Danube from Vienna to Belgrade. And when this was done, because of the occupation of Noricum by Tiberius and Drusus, a continuous route could be established from Bâle to Byzantium, which would enable troops to be moved rapidly east and west of the Empire independently of the sea.

In 13 B.C., what the Romans called the *Bellum Pannonicum* was launched by Agrippa and Vinicius against the Pannonian tribes on the Save and Drave. When Agrippa died in the following year, Tiberius took his place, and by 9 B.C., when he had occupied Siscia and Sirmium, he advanced to the Danube, and the extensive area conquered was incorporated into the province of Illyricum. Meanwhile his brother Drusus was warring successfully in Germany.

CHAPTER 4

The Battle of the Teutoburger Wald, A.D. 9

The Germans, an Indo-European people, first appear in Roman history towards the close of the second century B.C., and, after they had thrown Rome into a panic as great as previously had the Gauls, were, as we have seen, finally defeated by Marius and Catulus in the great battle of Vercellae in 101 B.C. Some thirty years later the Sequani, a Gaulish tribe inhabiting the country between the Jura and the Vosges, appealed to Ariovistus, the leader of a German host beyond the Rhine, to help them against a neighbouring tribe, the Aedui, west of the river Saône. Ariovistus accepted the invitation, defeated the Aedui, in the battle of Magetobriga and, as a reward, he and his people were allowed to occupy upper Alsace. This battle, writes Mr. C. Hignett, was probably ". . . the decisive factor which produced a chain of consequences leading ultimately to Caesar's intervention in Central Gaul".[1]

Some ten years later, in 59 B.C., two events occurred which brought the north-eastern frontier problem o Gaul into prominence. The first was that Ariovistus formally was recognized by the Senate as "king" and "friend of the Roman people". Friendship was short-lived, for no sooner was he recognized as king than he set out to persuade fresh bands of Germans to cross the Rhine, who, in their turn, demanded fresh grants of land. The second event was that the province of Transalpine Gaul was conferred upon Caesar, and once he had settled with the Helvetii, then moving westward into Gaul to escape hordes of Germans which had entered their country (roughly co-extensive with modern Switzerland), he turned his attention to Ariovistus. In his Commentaries on the Gallic War he writes:

"Next he could see that the Germans were becoming gradually accustomed to cross over the Rhine, and that the arrival of a great host of them in Gaul was dangerous for the Roman people. Nor did he suppose that barbarians so fierce would stop short after seizing the whole of Gaul; but rather, like the Cimbri and Teutoni before them, they would break forth into the Province,

[1] *The Cambridge Ancient History*, vol. IX, p. 546.

and push on thence into Italy. . . . All this, he felt, must be faced without a moment's delay."[1]

In 58 B.C., Caesar ordered Ariovistus to put a stop to further immigration of Germans, and when the order was ignored, he set out by forced marches to Vesontio (Besançon) to enforce it. From there he advanced on the Belfort Gap, where Ariovistus and his army lay encamped awaiting a Swabian horde which was then gathering on the eastern bank of the Rhine, preliminary to crossing. In the middle of September he brought Ariovistus to battle, and after a critical fight routed him. Though Ariovistus himself escaped the slaughter, soon after his crushing defeat he died.

As he realized that, were he now to withdraw, the German migrations would inevitably begin again, Caesar decided to make the Rhine the eastern frontier of central and northern Gaul, and, to establish it as an effective barrier, he next set out to conquer the Belgic tribes, most of which were of German origin.[2] They inhabited the region which is approximately that of present-day Belgium. In 57 B.C. he led eight legions northward from Vesontio and by defeating the Nervii he gained effective control over the left bank of the Rhine below Cologne. Two years later he advanced toward Xanten, and by means of a discreditable trick he inveigled the Germanic chieftains into his power, then he fell upon their leaderless followers and butchered them.[3] When he had thus secured the whole length of the Rhine from Xanten to Belfort, he decided to cross the river, for he writes: ". . . as he saw the Germans so easily induced to enter Gaul, he wished to make them fearful in turn for their own fortunes, by showing them that a Roman army could and durst cross the Rhine," which he now established as the final "limit of the Roman empire".[4] He bridged the Rhine south of Coblenz, carried out a demonstration in force on its eastern bank, and after ravaging the territory of the Sugambri withdrew into Gaul.

Here it is as well, so far as it is possible, to look at the Germans through Roman eyes. Writing of them, Caesar says:

"Their whole life is composed of hunting expeditions and military pursuits; from early boyhood they are zealous for toil and hardship. Those who remain longest in chastity win greatest praise among their kindred. . . .

[1] *Caesar, The Gallic War*, trans. H. J. Edwards (1922), I, 33.
[2] *Ibid.*, II, 4.   [3] *Ibid.*, IV, 13–15.   [4] *Ibid.*, IV, 16.

"For agriculture they have no zeal, and the greater part of their food consists of milk, cheese, and flesh. No man has a definite quantity of land or estate of his own; the magistrates and chiefs every year assign to tribes and clans . . . as much land and in such place as seems good to them, and compel the tenants after a year to pass on elsewhere. They adduce many reasons for that practice–the fear that they may be tempted by continuous association to substitute agriculture for their warrior zeal . . . that some passion for money may arise to be the parent of parties and of quarrels. It is their aim to keep common people in contentment, where each man sees that his own wealth is equal to that of the most powerful.

"Their states account it the highest praise by devastating their borders to have areas of wilderness as wide as possible around them. They think it the true sign of valour when the neighbours are driven to retire from their lands and no man dares to settle near, and at the same time they believe they will be safer thereby, having removed all fear of a sudden inroad. When a state makes or resists aggressive war, officers are chosen to direct the same, with the power of life and death. In time of peace there is no general officer of state, but the chiefs of districts and cantons do justice among their followers and settle disputes. . . . They do not think it right to outrage a guest; men who have come to them for any cause they protect from mischief and regard as sacred; to them the houses of all are open, with them is food shared."[1]

From this full description, it may be gathered that the Germans were a semi-nomadic people, belonging to what in the introduction of this book has been called "wagon-folk'. Though Caesar does not mention that they possessed horses or ox-drawn vehicles, without them they could not have moved in the numbers they did. The Helvetii, we know, did possess carts, for Caesar mentions them; further he informs us that they constructed "ramparts of carts"–that is, wagon laagers–to fight from.[2] It was the restlessness of the German way of life and not over-population which was the urge that moved them.

[1] Caesar, VI, 22–23.
[2] *Ibid.*, I, 24 and 26. Of the German peoples, Strabo writes: "All these nations easily change their abode, on account of the scantiness of provisions, and because they neither cultivate the lands nor accumulate wealth, but dwell in miserable huts, and satisfy their wants from day to day, the most part of their food being supplied by the herd, as amongst the nomad races, and in imitation of them they transfer their households in waggons, wandering with their cattle to any place which may appear most advantageous" (VII, i, 4).

Tacitus[1] describes them as being large of body, blue eyed and fair haired, "powerful only spasmodically and impatient at the same time of labour and hard work".[2] Though fierce fighters, their military organization was of the crudest, consisting of squadrons and battalions fortuitously collected by families and clans. "Few have swords or the longer kind of lance: they carry short spears, in their language frameae, with a narrow and small iron head, so sharp and so handy in use that they fight with the same weapon, as circumstances demand, both at close quarters and at a distance. The mounted man is cõntent with a shield and framea: the infantry launch showers of missiles in addition, each man a volley, and hurl these to great distances, for they wear no outer clothing, or at most a light cloak. There is no bravery of apparel among them: their shields only are picked out with choice colours. Few have breast-plates: scarcely one or two at most have metal or hide helmets. The horses are conspicuous neither for beauty nor speed; but then neither are they trained like our horses to run in shifting circles; they ride them forwards only or to the right, but with one turn from the straight, dressing the line so closely as they wheel that no one is left behind. On a broad view there is more strength in their infantry, and accordingly cavalry and infantry fight in one body,[3] the swift-footed infantry-man, whom they pick out of the whole body of warriors and place in front of the line. . . . The battle-line itself is arranged in wedges: to retire, provided you press on again, they treat as a question of tactics, not of cowardice."[4] To this account Strabo adds: "Against these people mistrust was the surest defence; for those who were trusted effected the most mischief."[5]

Their leaders were selected for their valour, and commanded less through force of authority, than by example. Further, Tacitus tells us: "On the field of battle, it is disgraceful for a chief's companions not to equal him, and that to aid, to protect him, and by their own gallant actions add to his glory, were their most sacred engagements." On the other hand, "each companion requires from his chief, the warlike steed, the murderous and conquering

---

[1] Born c. A.D. 55 and lived until after A.D. 117.
[2] *Tacitus*, trans. Maurice Hutton (1925), "Germania", 4. The evidence of the *Germania* of Tacitus should not be treated as if it were a modern survey. To praise the German as a "noble savage" was a means of reflecting on what Tacitus considered to be the failings of contemporary civilization in Rome.
[3] See Caesar, *The Gallic War*, I, 48, and VIII, 13.
[4] Tacitus, *Germania*, 6.
[5] *The Geography of Strabo*, trans. W. Falconer (1912), VII, i, 4.

spear and in place of salary, he expects to be supplied with fare homely and plentiful. The cost of which must be met by war and foray."[1]

Such were the people, as known to the Romans, who inhabited the vast unknown area of mountains, forests, and marshes east of the Rhine and north of the Danube, which together had by 12 B.C. become the northern frontier of the Empire.

Strategically it was far from a perfect boundary, because the two rivers formed an extensive salient with its apex at Bâle. Within this the German tribes could work on interior lines, but without the Roman legions were compelled to operate on exterior ones. The former, should they wish to, could attack either the Rhenish or Danubian sectors; but the latter had to defend both, and to reinforce the one from the other meant moving round two sides of a triangle. Further, the Rhine, like the Aegean Sea in the days of Darius I, was not an ethnic frontier. West of it large numbers of the inhabitants were of German stock, and in times of trouble the Germans east of the river were likely to sympathize with them, as the Greeks in Europe sympathized with the Greeks in Ionia. Already in 17 B.C. the Sugambri and other tribes had raided west of the river and had taken Marcus Lollius off his guard.[2] Besides these weaknesses, Augustus looked upon Gaul as the Egypt of the West and, therefore, of vital importance for supplies, especially for the great armies on the Rhine, and though the Rhine was a formidable barrier for barbarians unacquainted with the art of bridging, was it wise, as Gaul was not as yet fully pacified, to leave room in central Europe for the growth of a power hostile to Rome?

Though there was no one solution of these several problems, it was clear to Augustus, now that his legions in Illyricum were freed from conquest, that could the Rhine frontier be pushed first to the Weser and then to the Elbe–eastward of which he did not intend to go[3]–the following improvements in the northern frontier would accrue: The salient would be eliminated and replaced by an approximately straight river frontier running from Hamburg to Vienna; a lateral line of communications could

---

[1] Tacitus, *Germania*, 14.
[2] See Velleius Paterculus, trans. Frederick W. Shipley (1924), II, XCVII, and Dio Cassius, LIV, 20. Suetonius (*Caesar Augustus*, XXIII) says: "In all his wars, Augustus never received any signal or ignominious defeat except twice in Germany, under his lieutenants Lollius and Varus. Of these the former was more humiliating than serious."
[3] Strabo, VII, i, 4.

be built from Hamburg by way of Leipzig and Prague to Vienna to supplement the line Cologne–Bâle–Vienna; and though the accretion of territory necessary to effect this would not establish an ethnic frontier, by pushing the existing frontier 200 to 250 miles eastward Gaul would be incomparably better secured against German attack. In fact, what Augustus appears to have had in his mind was not very different from what Napoleon had when, in 1806, he created the Confederation of the Rhine as a buffer state between France and her potential enemies Austria and Prussia– a problem which is still agitating the French.

In 15 and 14 B.C., as we have seen, Drusus was warring with his brother Tiberius in southern Bavaria, after which he was made *legatus* of the Three Gauls. Born in 38 B.C. and cast in the heroic mould, he was a man of immense activity and ambition. He lived for great deeds and vast conquests,[1] and when it was decided that Germany should be invaded, the project he had in mind was not merely to punish the Sugambri for their victory over Lollius, but to cut off the salient between the Rhine and the Danube and so to shorten the line of communications between the armies in Gaul and Illyricum. In this ambitious plan the first step was to reach the upper Elbe and to subdue the tribes *en route*.

First, Drusus established a line of winter camps on the Rhine; the two principal ones were Vetera (? Wesel) facing the valley of the Lippe, and Moguntiacum (Mainz) facing the valley of the Main. Next, in 12 B.C., after he had ravaged Westphalia, he assembled a large flotilla on Lacus Flevo (Zuyder Zee, then a lake); sailed to the mouth of the river Ems; won a considerable naval victory; went on to the mouth of the Weser, and there cemented an alliance with the Frisians. The sea-coast won; next, in 11 B.C., he began his invasion of Germany proper. He marched up the Lippe valley through the territory of the Sugambri, gained the middle Weser, halted there, and then returned to the Rhine. The following year, he left Mainz, invaded the lands of the Chatti (Nassau) and advanced through the Hercynian forest (Harz) from the Main to the Weser, striking at the Marcomanni in Thuringia. Then moving northward he traversed the land of the Cherusci (Brunswick) and reached the Elbe, probably at Magdeburg. On his return journey from there in 9 B.C. he was thrown by his horse and died of his injuries. He was succeeded by his brother Tiberius, six years his senior, and under him the cam-

[1] See *Histoire de la Gaule*, Camille Jullian (1914), vol. IV, pp. 106–113.

paign was brought to a successful issue. On its conclusion, in 7 B.C., Tiberius left Germany to take up an appointment in the East.

Drusus's conquests had been made too rapidly to prove lasting, with the result that in 1 B.C. the Cherusci broke into revolt, and by A.D. 4 the general situation in Germany had grown so serious that Tiberius returned to restore the authority of Augustus.

In his first campaign he marched to the Weser and received the submission of the tribes as far as the shore of the North Sea. He wintered in the valley of the Lippe, and in A.D. 5 he carried out the most distant and extraordinary expedition that had hitherto been undertaken against the northern Germans. He marshalled two armies on the Rhine, embarked one in a large fleet which sailed to the sea, skirted the Frisian coast and entered the mouth of the Elbe. The other army marched eastward from the Rhine, and after defeating the Langobardi (Lombards) united with the seaborne expedition which had meanwhile explored the coast of Jutland as far north as the Skagerrak. When he had subdued the northern tribes, he made ready to turn south and conquer Maroboduus, king of the Marcomanni, who in 9 B.C. had migrated with his tribe from Thuringia to Bohemia.

The plan he decided upon for his A.D. 6 campaign was to pinch out Maroboduus by a simultaneous advance eastward by the army of the Rhine under Saturninus, advancing from the Main toward Nuremberg or Eger, and by the army of Illyricum under his personal command, advancing northward from Carnuntum (near Hainburg) on the Danube. In all, twelve legions were mustered and the campaign which followed has been acclaimed "a masterpiece of organization and deserves a proud place in the annals of the military art".[1] But when the two armies were but a few miles distant from their final goal in the centre of Bohemia, news was received of a critical rising in Illyricum. At once Tiberius came to terms with Maroboduus and turned his columns southward.

What had happened was this: the Dalmatians, exasperated by the requisitioning of supplies and men, had revolted, and as the garrisons had been withdrawn, all restraint had been removed. Rapidly the revolt spread until the whole of Illyricum and Pannonia was ablaze; the rebels numbered 200,000 infantry and 9,000 horsemen. Rome was thrown into a frenzy of terror, for no reserves existed; recruits were impossible to find, and in consequence new legions could not be raised. Nevertheless, in spite

[1] *The Cambridge Ancient History*, vol. x, p. 368.

of the extent of the revolt, Tiberius handled it in a masterly way. Instead of seeking pitched battles, he split his army into columns, occupied all points of importance, and by devastating the country methodically reconquered it by famine. In A.D. 8 Pannonia capitulated, followed the next year by Dalmatia. Tiberius left Germanicus[1] to reinstate the reconquered territories and returned to Italy, when five days after the collapse of the revolt a report was received in Rome of a terrible calamity in Germany.

When, in A.D. 6, Tiberius left Germany for his campaign against Maroboduus, Saturninus was succeeded by Publius Quintilius Varus, who had been governor of Syria, where he is reputed to have made a great fortune,[2] in which there is certainly nothing exceptional in this age. He "was a man of mild character and of a quiet disposition, somewhat slow in mind as he was in body, and more accustomed to the leisure of the camp than to actual service in war".[3] He had married the grand-niece of Augustus, in fact he was a "court appointment"; yet because a state of peacefulness had settled on the Rhine frontier, for "the barbarians were adapting themselves to Roman ways, were becoming accustomed to hold markets, and were meeting in peaceful assemblages",[4] there is in this little to find fault, a point which is sometimes overlooked. Gaul was now pacified, and fortunately for Roman rule the German tribes were without a head. Therefore, as so often happens on a quiet frontier, the garrisons had grown soft and indolent.

That Varus should have corrected this is true; but though his faults were many, and were heaped upon him after his defeat, stupidity rather than oppression would seem to have been his main defect. Apparently he was too unimaginative to grasp the difference between virile Germans and effete Syrians. Dio Cassius tells us that "Besides issuing orders to them as if they were actually slaves of the Romans, he exacted money as he would from subject nations".[5] Velleius Paterculus, a hostile critic, says that: "When placed in charge of the army in Germany, he entertained a notion that the Germans were a people who were men only in limbs and voice, and that they, who could not be subdued by the sword, could be soothed by the law."[6] It would appear that he was more

---

[1] The son of Nero Claudius Drusus and Antonia (daughter of Mark Antony and Octavia), born 15 B.C. and adopted by his uncle Tiberius.
[2] Velleius Paterculus, II, CXVII.
[3] *Ibid.*, II, CXVII.
[4] *Dio's Roman History*, trans. E. Cary (1916), LVI, 18.
[5] *Ibid.*, LVI, 18.
[6] Velleius Paterculus, II, CXVII.

of a bureaucrat than a soldier, and his rule was weak rather than calculatedly oppressive.

The real trouble seems to have arisen over the payment of tribute in gold and silver. In the West, as in the East, gold was exacted in payment of taxes; but whereas in the East it returned through the purchase of luxuries, in the West it did not, because few luxuries were produced. The result was a continuous drain of precious metals, which among the Germans were mainly used in the manufacture of ornaments. This caused much discontent among the tribal nobles, for gold was exceedingly scarce.[1]

In all, Varus had under his command five legions, two of which were stationed at Mogontiacum and three, during the winter, at Vetera or at Aliso (? Haltern) on the upper Lippe, and during the summer in the neighbourhood of Minden on the Weser.[2] Because of the prevailing peacefulness, the legions were not kept together, but were engaged upon felling trees, building roads, and bridging. Also, as was usual, the garrisons included many women and children.

The summer of A.D. 9 passed by in profound quiet, when, in September, as Varus was about to move from summer to winter quarters, news was received of a neighbouring tribal rising. He resolved, instead of returning direct to Aliso, to pass through the refractory area, to settle the dispute and then to march back to his winter camp. Before setting out he should have sent the women and children back to Aliso; but possibly he looked upon the rising as a mere local brawl, and therefore did not consider this precaution worth while. As he moved off, little did he dream that what lay in store for him was to be one of the decisive battles in the history of the world.

The revolt of which he had received news was the bait of a skilfully laid plan devised by a young Cheruscan, Arminius, who, under Tiberius, had served with a contingent of Cheruscan troops during the revolt in Pannonia and Illyricum, and who, no doubt, had watched the Romans closely during that campaign. He was son of Sigimer, chief of the Cherusci, had been granted Roman citizenship and held equestrian rank. He was not quite twenty-six years old when he was posted to Varus's headquarters. In character he was impetuous. Tacitus calls him "a frantic spirit" and "the incendiary of Germany". Further, he was

---

[1] See *The Greatness and Decline of Rome*, Guglielmo Ferrero (1909), vol. v, pp. 124–126.
[2] This distribution is uncertain.

possessed by an inborn hatred for the Romans. Apparently he hoped to effect what the rebellion in the south had failed to accomplish. Also, it would appear, he itched to avenge himself on his uncle, Segestes, a loyal supporter of Varus, who had refused him his daughter, Thusnelda, in marriage, but with whom he had eloped. Lastly, he had the highest contempt for Varus, for he looked upon him as a city praetor and not as a general, and in this he was probably right.

His plot was laid carefully. He made use of Varus's negligence "as an opportunity for treachery, sagaciously seeing that no one could be more quickly overpowered than the man who feared nothing, and that the most common beginning of disaster was a sense of security".[1] When Varus was about to return to Aliso, Arminius engineered the uprising in order to draw him through what appeared to be friendly though difficult country, so that he might be put off his guard, and after he had led him into the depths of the forests he intended to annihilate him.

To keep secret so elaborate a plot was scarcely possible, and Segestes heard of it and informed Varus, whom he advised to place the conspirators in chains. Varus refused to do so, possibly because he considered the accusation of treason an attempt on the part of Segestes to square his quarrel with his nephew. So it came about that, some time in September or October, A.D. 9, at the head of the XVIIth, XVIIIth, and XIXth Legions, some 20,000 men in all, Varus set out followed by a long baggage train and the soldiers' families.

Exactly what happened during the opening stages of the march we do not know, and though several modern writers have given a full description of the disaster, the information provided by the two most reliable authorities—Velleius Paterculus and Dio Cassius—does not warrant it. But what we do know is that Arminius accompanied Varus, his men escorted the column, and that he remained with him until the evening before the insurrection was planned to begin. Again Segestes warned Varus, and again he was brushed aside. Next, as the legions were winding their way through the swamps and forests, Arminius and his followers disappeared, and the first intimation of the revolt was a report that outlying detachments of soldiers had been slaughtered. Then, so it would appear, Varus turned and headed for the road which ran by way of the Dören Pass to Aliso.

[1] Velleius Paterculus, ii, cxviii.

Though, because of his baggage train and followers, his situation was not an enviable one, it was by no means worse than many Julius Caesar or Drusus had faced on former occasions; but then, they were leaders of men and Varus was but a camp attorney. Where the battle proper began is not known; Tacitus mentions the forest of Teutoburgium; it was there, so he relates, that Germanicus discovered the bones of Varus and his legions.[1] The forest lay between the Ems and the Weser, and, in the year A.D. 9, must have covered a vast area. Some authorities place the actual battlefield near Detmold; others, near Münster. Possibly the action began near the former and ended in the vicinity of the latter; because if Minden was Varus's summer camp, in his retirement he would almost certainly make for the Dören Pass, and then, finding Aliso besieged, as it was, his best line of retreat would appear to be along the lower Ems toward Münster. But there is no agreement at all between the experts concerning where the disaster happened.

Once in the forest, Dio tells us that, while the Romans were cutting a track, a violent storm of rain made the ground slippery and walking "very treacherous"; the "tops of the trees kept breaking off and falling down, causing much confusion".[2] It was then, when "the Romans were not proceeding in any regular order, but were mixed in helter-skelter with the wagons and the unarmed",[3] that Arminius suddenly attacked and hurled volleys of javelins into the disordered masses of men. Nevertheless, a halt was made, and a camp fortified.

Next morning, after they had burnt most of their wagons, "in a little better order" the Romans fought their way into open country; then once again they "plunged into the woods" and "suffered their heaviest losses". That night they halted, and when they advanced again on the following morning were caught by a heavy downpour of rain which prevented them "from going forward and even from standing securely, and moreover deprived them of the use of their weapons. For they could not handle their bows or their javelins with any success, nor for that matter, their shields, which were thoroughly soaked."[4] Now came Arminius's opportunity. He closed on his disorganized enemy and broke through his ranks; Vala Numonius, in charge of the cavalry, fled,[5]

---

[1] Tacitus, *Histories and Annals*, trans. C. H. Moore and J. Jackson, I, 60.
[2] *Dio's Roman History*, LVI, 20.   [3] *Ibid.*, LVI, 20.
[4] *Ibid.*, LVI, 21.   [5] Velleius Paterculus, II, CXIX.

and Varus and "all his more prominent officers, fearing that they should either be captured alive or be killed by their bitterest foes (for they had already been wounded), made bold to do a thing that was terrible yet unavoidable; they took their

13. THE TEUTOBURGER WALD CAMPAIGN, A.D. 9

own lives".[1] At length, Velleius tells us, "Hemmed in by forests and marshes and ambuscades", the Roman army was "exterminated almost to a man by the very enemy whom it had always slaughtered like cattle".[2]

Those who were captured were crucified, buried alive, or offered up as sacrifices to the gods. When, a few years later, Germanicus visited the battlefield, he found whitening bones,

[1] *Dio's Roman History*, LVI, 21.   [2] Velleius Paterculus, II, CXIX.

fragments of javelins, limbs of horses, and skulls fixed upon the trunks of trees; a grim picture, grimly described by Tacitus.[1]

In spite of this overwhelming defeat, Lucius Caedicius held firmly to Aliso, and by means of his archers beat back every attack made on the camp. Later, when blockaded, he broke out on a dark night, and with the remnants of the army, encumbered with numerous women and children, reached Vetera, where he was met by Lucius Nonius Asprenas and two legions, and Arminius and his hordes then retired. It was a fine ending to a fearful failure.

The extent of the disaster is clearly reflected in the portents of doom which went whispering through the Empire. Dio informs us that the temple of Mars was struck by lightning, that the Alps seemed to collapse upon one another, and that "a statue of Victory that was in the province of Germany and faced the enemy's territory turned about to face Italy".[2] Rationally incredible, morally these portents were true; Roman prestige had received a mortal blow and henceforth the barbarians knew that the legions were not invincible, and that what Arminius had accomplished could be repeated. Further, and worse still, Rome also knew it. This is why "Augustus, when he learned of the disaster . . . rent his garments . . . and mourned greatly . . . because he expected that the enemy would march against Italy and against Rome itself. For there were no citizens of military age left worth mentioning."[3] Nevertheless, he set to work; "and when no men of military age showed a willingness to be enrolled, he made them draw lots, depriving of his property and disfranchising every fifth man of those still under thirty-five and every tenth man amongst those who had passed that age. Finally, as a great many paid no heed to him even then, he put some to death."[4] Yet these drastic punishments effected little; during his lifetime the lost legions were never replaced. This was the most terrifying portent of all. So it came about that "he let the hair of his head and beard grow for several months", and would sometimes thump his head against the door-posts, crying out, "Quintilius Varus, give me back my legions!"[5]

Even should all this be untrue, the fact remains that the three legions were never re-raised, not because Varus had lost them, but because Rome was losing her vigour. It is true that after the

---

[1] *The Annals*, Tacitus, I, 61.   [2] *Dio's Roman History*, LVI, 24.
[3] *Ibid.*, LVI, 23. Concerning this, it should be remembered that Dio is not a very reliable historian.
[4] *Ibid.*, LVI, 23.   [5] Suetonius, "Caesar Augustus," XXIII.

disaster Tiberius again took over the German command, and that in A.D. 13, Germanicus, who succeeded him, in a series of campaigns reached the Elbe and more than once defeated the Germans. Nevertheless, that river was to be the Roman Hyphasis; all these campaigns were little more than an apology for a final retreat to the Rhine, which henceforth was to remain the north-eastern frontier of Latin civilization.

Yet there was a deeper reason still, deeper than the loss of Roman vigour; it must be sought in the character of Augustus himself. In spite of the glamour of his age, he was a splendid rather than an heroic figure. Though not lacking in courage or pertinacity, as a leader of men he cannot compare with Julius Caesar. He was a tolerant opportunist who, by means of his policy of *divide et impera*, became the managing director rather than the monarch of his Empire. He believed in Rome as a great business, a vast monopoly, and looked upon states and frontiers as bonds and securities. He lacked that power to electrify men and to compel them to accomplish the seemingly impossible which distinguishes the man of genius from the merely great. In two words, he was supremely a "bourgeois emperor". So it came about that though his conquests were many, in spirit they were defensive investments, and as the frontiers were closed, simultaneously were closed down with them all intellectual and moral endeavour: adventures of the mind and soul ceased with the cessation of the adventures of the body.

In the end this loss of moral stimulus compelled him to leave the north-eastern frontier where his predecessor had established it, and what were the historical results? In attempting to fathom so hypothetical a question, we must beware of the "might-have-beens"; yet certain and not altogether improbable speculations are permissible. Though Germany was not Gaul, for the Germans were more barbaric than the Gauls, as the Empire was destined to last for another four hundred years, it is not illogical to suppose that, had the north-eastern frontier rested on the Elbe, instead of on the Rhine, the next chapter in this book could not have been written, and because of it every other chapter would have been different. Creasy quite rightly points out that, had the Elbe been held, "This island" of ours "would never have borne the name of England".[1] More important still: we should never have become English. The whole course of our history would have been

[1] *The Fifteen Decisive Battles of the World*, Sir Edward S. Creasy (edit. 1931) p. 119.

different. Again, had Germany west of the Elbe been for four centuries Romanized and roaded, one culture and not two in unending conflict would have dominated the western world. There would have been no Franco-German problem, or at least a totally different one. There would have been no Charlemagne, no Louis XIV, no Napoleon, no Kaiser William II, and no Hitler.

Though we are told that, when at Alexandria, Augustus ordered the sarcophagus of Alexander the Great to be opened so that he might place a golden crown upon his head and scatter flowers on his corpse,[1] and though on his ring he had the head of the mighty Macedonian engraved,[2] he set a seal on the limits of his "Great Idea"; for in the mind of Alexander there was no boundary but that of the Great Ocean. Thus, though under succeeding emperors the Empire was still further to expand physically, spiritually it was to stand still, passing from an empire into a limited liability company. This was the "Great Idea" Augustus bequeathed to the Empire when, on August 29, A.D. 14, at the age of seventy-six, he died at Nola and was succeeded by Tiberius.

[1] Suetonius, "Caesar Augustus," XVIII.   [2] *Ibid.*, L.

The weakness of the Roman imperial system lay in the question of succession. The celebrated Pax Romana was the condition which (sometimes) accompanied the long reign of a strong man; its antithesis may be found in, say, the anarchy of A.D. 69 – the "year of the four emperors". The imperial succession depended almost always on the will of the army – in particular the Praetorian Guard, which attended the person of the Emperor. Never a healthy state of affairs, this inevitably produced its worst results when the army (including the Guard) came to be more and more recruited from the barbarian tribes beyond the frontiers.

Fuller places the zenith of the Empire during the period of Hadrian (117-138) "in whose reign Rome became the most magnificent city in the world" and the early years of Marcus Aurelius, who succeeded in 161.

By now there had grown up a Mediterranean nation, and, as fore-shadowed by Augustus, Italy had dropped to the level of a province. Of the factors which led to this, the first was the establishment, largely under Stoic influence, of a common law which, as J. H. Robinson writes, 'conceived mankind, not as a group of nations or tribes, each with its own lands, but as one people included in one great empire and subject to a single system of law based on fairness and reason'. Other factors were the wonderful system of roads, which linked the Empire culturally, commercially, and strategically; a common currency and common weights and measures; the establishment of banks and bank drafts; the freeing of the seas from pirates, and the expansion of trade as far as India and China. West of Sicily the language of civilized intercourse was Latin, east of that island it was Greek. Lastly, the whole Empire was circled by legions from the borders of Scotland to the Euphrates and the Province of Africa 'like a dike restraining the stormy sea of barbarians outside.'

Internal economic factors, as well as external dangers, steadily eroded the strength of Rome. The decline of farming was perhaps the most serious of these, due partly to the continuous swallowing up of small farms into large estates, partly to other reasons –

A further cause in the decline of farming was the progressive exhaustion of the soil. The amount of land under cultivation continually decreased, until the Empire could no longer feed its teeming millions. As the economic dry rot spread, all who could drifted to the cities, which became the tombs of the race; for the countryside favoured procreation, the cities recreation. The growing city proletariat became an ever-increasing financial burden. Producing next to nothing, it had to be fed, and when the country communities became too poor to purchase the manufactures of the cities, the dole-fed rabble was multiplied when the city industrial workers were thrown out of work. Lack of agriculture led to the decline of industry.

As the four centuries of the Roman Empire passed by, there were further changes in the army. To pay the vast forces required to hold the imperial frontiers, assignments of land were made to the soldiers in lieu of money. Those who received these were called *limitanei* ("frontiersmen"); they became, says Fuller, "little more than a peasant militia, a totally inadequate substitute for the magnificent legionaries of Trajan and Hadrian. With the increasing recruitment of barbarian limitanei, the legional organization disappeared, and with its disappearance the power of Rome over the barbarians vanished and the barbarian soldiery became the highest power in the state."

To overcome this defect, the Emperor Diocletian (234-305) created a new field army, independent of the frontier garrisons. The strength of this force *(comitatenses)* has been estimated at 150,000 foot and 46,000 horse, which, as Fuller remarks, seems excessive. What is interesting is the new relationship of cavalry to infantry. Rome had always depended on her legions of foot-soldiers; now the cavalry, organized in units called *vexillationes*, were becoming increasingly numerous and important. The organization itself told a significant story; under Diocletian the legion of 4,000-6,000 men was reduced to what we would call a battalion of about 1,000 while the *vexillum* contained 500 horsemen about the strength of a cavalry regiment at the turn of the 20th Century.

Profound change came to the whole Roman Empire in the 4th Century. The inevitable struggle for power after the death of Diocletian ended in 324 with the victory of Constantine the Great, who changed the very axis of the Empire.

He selected Byzantium for his capital and renamed it Constantinople. This change in the imperial seat of government definitely meant the separation of the eastern from the western half of the Empire as soon as Constantine's strong hand was removed. Meanwhile the Christian Church had gained vastly in power. Already in 311, the Emperor Galerius, who realized the dangers threatening Rome from without, and the futility of the struggle against the Christians within, had placed the Church on a footing of equality with the worship of the gods. Though not baptized until on his death-bed, Constantine maintained this decree, and in 325, under his direction, the first great council of the churches of the Empire assembled at Nicaea (Iznik). There 'sitting amongst the Christian bishops', writes Mr N. H. Baynes in the *Cambridge Ancient History*, he 'is in his own person the beginning of Europe's Middle Ages'.

Constantine died in May 337, and, says Fuller, "like a burnt-down candle the flame of Empire began to flicker blue". In the reign of the brothers Valentinian and Valens (co-emperors, 364-75) the Goths, who had been allies of Rome for a hundred years, began to stir again under the pressure of the Huns in the East. "The strength of the Goths," says Fuller,

> lay not only in their numbers and the terror they instilled, but also because thousands of their warriors had served as Roman mercenaries and were far better armed than their ancestors had been in the days of Tacitus. 'The rank and file bore iron-bound bucklers, pikes, the short stabbing sword *(sacramasax)*, as well as the long cutting sword *(spatha)*, and among some races the deadly *francisca*, or battle-axe, which, whether thrown or wielded, would penetrate Roman armour and split the Roman shield.'[1] Their method of fighting, like that of the Huns, and later of Zisca in the 15th Century and the Boers in the 19th, was founded on their wagon-forts, or laagers. Ammianus says that they would form up in circles *(masses)* with their wagons for a rampart, 'as if enclosed in a space between city-walls'. From these slow-moving fortresses

[1] Sir Charles Oman, *The Art of War in the Middle Ages*, Vol. I, p. 12.

by a pre-concerted signal the predatory bands dispersed for plunder, and on orders from their leaders, 'like fire-darts, returned with winged speed to their wagon city (as they themselves called it)'. Equally important, the plundering raids were carried out mainly by mounted men; which meant that the Goths had at their disposal a formidable body of cavalry. Their one great tactical weakness lay in their inability to storm walled cities and towns.

Whatever their weaknesses, the Goths were Rome's most deadly enemies yet; in 378 they achieved the utter destruction of the Emperor Valens and his army at the Battle of Adrianople.

On several occasions in her history Rome had suffered as overwhelming a disaster, yet never so decisive a one; for the battle of Adrianople, like that of Gaugamela, was an epoch-making conflict. It was far more than a second Cannae. 'The Empire rocked to its foundations,' writes Professor Martin Bang. 'Sheer panic fell upon all that bore the name of Rome. The power and glory of the Empire seemed stamped into the dust by the barbarian hordes. The struggle between Rome and the Teutons which we have followed through five centuries was drawing to a close. The battle of Adrianople introduces the last act of the great drama, the most pregnant with consequences which the history of the world has ever seen.'[1]

After Adrianople the pressure of the barbarians – not only Goths, but also Vandals, Alans, Alemanni, Quadi and others – became irresistible. In 406 a vast mixed horde crossed the frozen Rhine and overran Gaul. In 408 the Visigoths (West Goths) under Alaric attacked Rome herself and had to be bought off with tribute. In 410 they returned and sacked the "eternal city".

Thus, in the unheroic and simple words of Orosius, the dream of Alexander faded away into the twilight of the Dark Ages: *Adest Alaricus, trepidam Romam obsidet, turbat, irrumpit* ('Alaric appeared before trembling Rome, laid siege, spread confusion and broke into the city'). Of what happened little has been recorded other than that, before he entered the city, Alaric gave orders that all Christian edifices should be left

[1] *Cambridge Medieval History*, Vol. I, p. 217.

uninjured, and that right of asylum in the basilicas of St Peter and St Paul should be respected. These orders would appear to have been obeyed. At the time, St Jerome was in his cell at Bethlehem, when 'a terrible rumour from the west was brought to him', and as he heard it he exclaimed: 'To quote a common proverb, I well nigh forgot my own name.' Also, at this time, St Augustine was at Hippo (Bona) in Numidia, and the news of the fall stimulated him to write his greatest work, for he says in his 'Retractations': 'Rome, meanwhile, by the invasion of the Goths, under their King Alaric, was overthrown with the crash of a mighty slaughter . . . Wherefore, I, inflamed with zeal for the Lord's house, determined to write a treatise on The City of God.'

The wandering of the nations

The Wandering of the Nations, or what the Germans call the *Völkerwanderung*, began, as we have seen, with the crossing of the Danube by the Goths in 376, an incursion definitely caused by the westerly advance of the Huns from the region of the Volga. But whether the Huns were also responsible for setting in motion the second wave of Teutonic peoples which swept over the Rhine in 406, though not known, seems highly probable. Yet even had they nothing to do with it, it was an inevitable event, for since the days of Tacitus the Germans had not only increased in numbers, but the small tribes, which had existed in his day, had been replaced by large groupings of tribes under recognized leaders. Added to this "the Roman population", writes Sir Ernest Barker, "had decayed for century after century, and the land had gone steadily out of cultivation, until nature herself seemed to have created the vacuum into which, in time, she inevitably attracted the Germans", and ". . . when the barrier finally broke, the flood came as no cataclysm but as something which was almost in the nature of things". Further, the invaders did not come as actual enemies, but, nominally, as *foederati* to defend the Empire against their like, and, once enlisted as such they were able to establish a legal claim to remain within the Empire. Next, when they had been armed and equipped, they gained the power to elect their own puppet emperors, and, lastly, to establish kingdoms of their own.

Thus it came about that in the hundred years of the Wandering (376–476) the Western Empire was digested into a number of independent kingdoms. It did not so much collapse as vanish in them, bit by bit as each was established. Why the Eastern Empire did not suffer a similar transformation was because its emperors discovered in the virile and warlike Isaurians a substitute for barbaric auxiliaries. Thanks to these people, who inhabited the country north of the Taurus, between Pisidia and Cilicia, the existence of the Eastern Empire was prolonged for centuries after the Western had disappeared.

In 407, Constantine, a common soldier in Britain, was proclaimed emperor and crossed to Gaul. Two years later Gerontius, his general in Spain, revolted against him, and, in order to strengthen himself against Constantine, he invited the Vandals and their allies to cross the Pyrenees. Shortly after they had entered Spain, yet another wave of barbarians, this time of Franks, Alemanni, and Burgundians, occupied the region west of the Rhine. The Franks were divided into two groups, the Salians who seized the lands between the Scheldt and Meuse, and the Ripuarians between the Moselle and Rhine.

At the time of this third incursion, Constantius, the new Master of the Troops, arrived in Gaul to defend the cause of Honorius. In 411 he overwhelmed both Constantine and Gerontius, after which he turned against the Franks, Alemanni, and Burgundians, who meanwhile had elected a puppet emperor named Jovinus to give legal colour to their position in Gaul. But no sooner had Constantius done so, than he learnt that Ataulf (Adolphus), who had succeeded Alaric in 410, had left Italy for Gaul and had carried away with him Placidia, the sister of Honorius. Infuriated at this, for his intention long had been to marry Placidia so that he might secure the succession on the death of Honorius, who was childless, he set out after Ataulf, who had seized Toulouse and occupied Narbonne. When he failed to take Marseilles, which was held by Boniface (the future Count of Africa), Ataulf withdrew and in 414 married Placidia. In retaliation Constantius blockaded the Gallic ports with his fleet to bring Ataulf to submission by cutting off his African supplies. To escape starvation, Ataulf crossed into Spain, and at Barcelona Placidia gave birth to a son, who was named Theodosius. Soon after the child died, and in 415 Ataulf was assassinated and succeeded by a chieftain called Wallia.

In order to feed his men, Wallia decided to cross to Africa; but when it put to sea his fleet was wrecked in a storm, his people were reduced to starvation, and in 416 he was compelled to seek peace with Constantius. The terms were agreed: for 600,000 measures of corn he surrendered Placidia, became Rome's ally and promised to recover Spain from the Vandals, Alans, and Sueves.

In 417 Constantius at length achieved his aim, and, much against her will, married Placidia, and was raised to the status of an Augustus. She bore to him two children, Honoria and Valentinian. Meanwhile Wallia defeated the Vandals and their allies and drove them into the north-west corner of Spain, the present-day Galicia. For this he was rewarded by permission to establish his people in Aquitania and to occupy Toulouse. This was the first time the Imperial Government, of its own accord, gave a settlement to a Teutonic people within the Empire under their own king.

In 421 Constantius died and was succeeded by Castinus as Master of the Troops. Soon after, Honorius and Placidia quarrelled and two parties were formed in Italy, one under Boniface which supported Placidia and the barbarians, and the other under Castinus which favoured Honorius and the Romans.

This year or in the following, Theodoric I, who had succeeded Wallia in 418, fulfilled the agreement he had made with Constantius to send a contingent to the Roman army which was operating under Castinus against the Vandals. But in the middle of the battle which followed it suddenly changed sides, fell upon the Roman rear and routed the Romans. About the same time, Boniface, who was now in Africa, revolted from Honorius and Placidia and her two children were banished to the court of Theodosius II (408–450), at Constantinople, and were there when, in 423, Honorius died. As her son was then only four years old, she became virtual regent. She returned with him to Italy in 424, and in the following year the boy was proclaimed emperor and became Valentinian III (425–455).

The death of Honorius gave rise to a new personality, Aetius, who was to dominate events during the next thirty years. He was a Roman from Silistria, born about 390, and had been a hostage once with Alaric and once with the Huns, who by 423 formed the bulk of the armies of the Empire, for the German recruiting grounds were now largely closed. On Valentinian's accession he was made *comes* (count) and given the command of Gaul. In 425 he marched against Theodoric, who was then besieging Arles, the key city of the Rhône valley. He forced him to raise the siege, made peace with him, and granted him full sovereignty over the provinces originally assigned to Wallia.

Three years later the Vandals, under Gaiseric, born about 400 and one of the most famous figures in the Wandering of the Nations, began to move from Spain to Africa; the immediate occasion was furnished by a revolt of the Moors. In May, 429, the main body, some 80,000 people, crossed from Julia Traducta, now Tarifa, to find the final home of their wandering.

Because this new invasion threatened the main Italian corn

supply, the Romans came to terms with Count Boniface; yet in spite of the resistance he put up against the Vandals, he was beaten back and in 437 Hippo was occupied by them. Again defeated, Boniface was summoned to Italy by Placidia to act as a counterpoise to Aetius, who meanwhile had recovered Gaul from the Franks and had become, like Caesar before him, the leading man in the West.

At once a struggle began between the two, in which Aetius was defeated near Ravenna, now the Imperial capital of the West. He sought refuge with his old friends the Huns and was well received by their king Rua or Rugila. Shortly after his victory Boniface died and his son-in-law Sebastian took his place.

Boniface now out of the way, in 433 Aetius returned with an army of Huns and compelled Placidia to dismiss Sebastian and to admit himself to the dignity of *Patricius* (Patrician), a title introduced by Constantine the Great.[1] Hence onward until his death in 454 he ruled the West. His first action was to come to terms with the Vandals by ceding Mauretania and part of Numidia to Gaiseric; his second was to march against the Burgundians, who were attacking the lands round Metz and Trèves; and his third, to repress a jacquerie of revolted peasants and slaves (the Baguadae) which then raged in many districts, and to drive back the Visigoths who were attacking Narbonne. In all three operations he was successful, and ended his campaign in 442 by making peace with the Goths and planting a colony of Alans near Orléans in order to guard the valley of the Loire against them.

In spite of the peace, the Vandals paid little attention to it and continued their piratical operations in the western and central Mediterranean. On October 19, 439, they unexpectedly captured Carthage, which they at once adopted as their main naval base. Next, in 440, they ravaged Sicily, and Theodosius sent a fleet against them. As he did not wish to be involved with the Eastern Empire while raiding the Western, Gaiseric, the outstanding diplomatist of his age, fell back on his now considerable wealth and by its judicious use induced the Huns on the Danube to attack the Eastern Empire. Once threatened in the north, Theodosius recalled his fleet. At this juncture the state of the Western Empire was as follows.

---

[1] At first, the holder ranked next after the emperor and the consul. Later the title became synonymous with "vice-regent", and in the days of Ammianus Marcellinus, a *patricius* was regarded as "father of the emperor" or "paternal guardian of the state" (XXIX, ii, 2).

Gaul had been recovered, but was sown with barbaric settlements: the Franks in the north; the Visigoths in the south-west; the Burgundians in Savoy; the Alemanni on the upper Rhine; the Alans at Valence and Orléans; and the Bretons in the north-west. Africa had been lost completely and so had Britain which, since the great raid of 406 and 407 across the Rhine, virtually had been severed from the Empire. Lastly, in Spain the Sueves had found a leader in a chieftain called Rechiar, who in 439 took Merida and in 441 Seville, and then conquered the provinces of Baetica (Andalusia) and Cartagena. All that was left to the Romans in Spain was its north-eastern corner, the present Catalonia. Besides these many losses, the diocese of Illyricum had been partly ceded to the Eastern Empire and partly occupied by the Huns.

CHAPTER 5

The Battle of Châlons or of the Mauriac Plain, 451

The Huns with whom, in or about the year 440, Gaiseric opened negotiations, were a nomadic people of Turanian stock, and in their conflicts with the Romans and German tribes is again introduced the clash between the wagon folk and the city dwellers. Though, so far as war is concerned, the Huns at first carried all before them, in the end they were overwhelmed, not so much by the arms of the western peoples as by their lack of civilization. In at least one respect their story is that of the Hyksos over again, for in both incursions—as in centuries to come was to be repeated in the Arab, Seljuk, and Mongol invasions—the dominant factor which led to their initial successes was the horse.

Who the Huns were and where they originated have not yet been determined. In the middle of the eighteenth century M. Deguignes,[1] a French Chinese scholar, conceived that they might be identified with the Hiong-nu (or Hsiung-nu),[2] who at the time of their supremacy inhabited the region between the Altai, Kuen-lun and Khingan mountains, and to limit whose depredations, in 258 B.C., the Emperor Hwang-te built the Great Wall of China. But whether this is so is of little consequence here, for what matters in this chapter is their coming and its influence on western history. Further, what caused their westerly advance against the Alans, another people of Turanian stock, which precipitated the Gothic invasions of 376, is also unknown. Some think that it may have been due to the epoch of increasing aridity which set in in central Asia during the first few centuries of the Christian era and which culminated in about A.D. 500.[3] Others believe that it was caused by the destruction of irrigation canals by nomadic raiders, for as Mr. T. Peisker points out: In order to make a whole oasis liable to tribute "they need only seize the

---

[1] In his *Histoire Générale des Huns, des Turcs, des Mongols, et des autres Tartares Occitentaux, avant et depuis Jésus Christ jusqu'à present* (1756–8), 4 vols. See also appendix 6 of Bury's edition of Gibbon's *Decline and Fall*.
[2] The word means "common slaves".
[3] See *The Pulse of Asia*, E. Huntington (1907), p. 359.

main canal; and the nomads often blindly plundered and destroyed everything. A single raid was enough to transform hundred of oases into ashes and desert. The nomads moreover not only ruined countless cities and villages of Central Asia, but also denuded the steppe land itself, and promoted drift-sand by senseless uprooting of trees and bushes for the sake of firewood."[1] Judging from subsequent nomadic inundations, this second reason would seem the more probable. Gibbon thinks likewise, and when considering the violence of the Mongols, he writes: ". . . from the Caspian to the Indus they ruined a tract of many hundred miles which was adorned with the habitations and labour of mankind, and five centuries have not been sufficient to repair the ravages of four years."[2] As we shall see, when the Huns came into contact with Latin civilization, because they could give it nothing, they could only take from it, and, in fact, *had* to in order to survive alongside it. Had this process of a lower civilization living on a higher endured long enough, the latter would have perished utterly, and Roman Europe would have become a second Khorasan.

Like all wagon folk the Huns were wanderers, and in consequence civilization was all but unknown to them. For unnumbered generations they had driven their herds and flocks—cattle, horses, goats, and sheep—over the steppes of central and southern Siberia; yet so primitive were their handicrafts that it would appear they were unable to weave, and, therefore, make woollen garments. Ammianus Marcellinus, who lived and wrote in the days of the Emperor Valens, has left us the following contemporary description of them:

"They all have compact, strong limbs and thick necks and are so monstrously ugly and misshapen, that one might take them for two-legged beasts or for the stumps, rough-hewn into images, that are used in putting sides [adorning] to bridges. . . . Roaming at large amid the mountains and woods, they learn from the cradle to endure cold, hunger and thirst. . . . They dress in linen cloth or in the skins of field-mice sewn together. . . . They are not at all adapted to battles on foot, but they are almost glued to their horses, which are hardy, it is true, but ugly. . . . They are all without fixed abode, without hearth, or law, or settled mode of life, and keep roaming from place to place, like fugitives, accompanied

---

[1] *The Cambridge Medieval History*, vol. I, p. 327.
[2] *The Decline and Fall of the Roman Empire*, vol. VII, p. 10.

by the wagons in which they live. . . . In truces they are faithless and unreliable, strongly inclined to sway to the motion of every breeze of new hope that presents itself, and sacrificing every feeling to the mad impulse of the moment. Like unreasoning beasts, they are utterly ignorant of the difference between right and wrong."[1]

Like all true nomads, agriculture was unknown to the Huns; therefore the linen garments, mentioned by Marcellinus, must, like many other things they possessed, have been obtained through barter. Of internal trade there can have been practically none, because the standard of living was so low that each family group could supply its own needs. Their external trade consisted in bartering horses, meat, furs, and slaves for the produce, arms, and manufactures of the settled agricultural peoples with whom they came into contact.

In order to subsist, it is clearly impossible that they can have wandered about in enormous hordes, if only because as they had to live upon their herds and flocks, these demanded extensive grazing grounds. Probably, like many other nomadic people, they were split into patriarchal groups of from fifty to a hundred persons, each group moving over a comparatively wide front from grazing ground to grazing ground. Their society was communistic and, according to Marcellinus, though the groups were under paternal leaders, whom he calls "important men", the whole had no king.[2] The high figures, so frequently quoted by classical and ecclesiastical historians, were undoubtedly exaggerated by the rapidity with which the Huns moved and the terror their uncouthness and lack of resemblance to Europeans instilled. According to Jordanes, the Goths believed that the Huns were the offspring of sorceresses and "the unclean spirits, who beheld them as they wandered through the wilderness, bestowing their embraces upon them and begat this savage race, which dwelt at first in the swamps, a stunted, foul and puny tribe, scarcely human and having no language save one which bore but slight resemblance to human speech". He adds:

"For by the terror of their features they inspired great fear in those whom perhaps they did not really surpass in war. They made their foes flee in horror because their swarthy aspect was fearful, and they had, if I may call it so, a sort of shapeless lump, not a head, with pin-holes rather than eyes. Their hardihood is

---

[1] Ammianus Marcellinus, XXXI, ii, 2–11.　　　[2] *Ibid.*, XXXI, ii, 7.

evident in their wild appearance, and they are beings who are cruel to their children on the very day they are born. For they cut the cheeks of the males with a sword, so that before they receive the nourishment of milk they must learn to endure wounds. Hence they grow old beardless and their young men are without comeliness, because a face furrowed by the sword spoils by its scars the natural beauty of a beard. They are short in stature, quick in bodily movement, alert horsemen, broad shouldered, ready in the use of bow and arrow, and their firm-set necks are ever erect in pride. Though they live in the form of men, they have the cruelty of wild beasts."[1]

Two generations after their first appearance, though the terror they instilled continued to paralyse the Romans, the ease with which they were able to extract tribute from their neighbours brought them to a standstill in the Danubian lands; when their social order rapidly began to change. In or about 430 they were no longer an amorphous mass of family groups, but instead a confederacy under a single ruler, Rua–the friend and protector of Aetius–who was sufficiently powerful to force a treaty on the Eastern Romans, by the terms of which Theodosius II (408–450) undertook to pay him a yearly tribute of 350 pounds of gold. When he died in 433, Rua was succeeded by his two nephews Attila and Bleda. Of the latter nothing is known other than that, in 445, he was murdered by his brother, of whom Jordanes and Priscus have left the following vivid description. He was of short stature, his eyes were small and bead-like, his nose snub and his skin swarthy. His head was large, his beard scanty, and his hair was already sprinkled with white. He was covetous, vain, superstitious, cunning, excessively arrogant, and cruel. Yet in his way of living he was markedly simple. As Priscus informs us, while "the guests drank from cups of gold and silver, Attila had only a wooden cup; his clothes . . . were only distinguished from the other barbarians because they were of one colour, and were without ornaments; his sword, the cords of his shoes, the reins of his horse, were not like those of the other Scythians, decorated with plates of gold or precious stones".[2]

---

[1] *The Gothic History of Jordanes*, trans. Charles Christopher Mierow (1915), XXIV, pp. 85–87. Jordanes wrote his history about 100 years after the events recorded in this chapter and many of his statements are epic tales.

[2] "Priscus' Narrative of the Embassy sent in 449 to Attila, by Theodosius the Younger, Emperor of the East", quoted from *The History of Civilization* by F. Guizot (1856), vol. II, p. 430. See also J. B. Bury, *History of the Later Roman Empire* (1923), vol. I, pp. 279–288.

Attila's rule over the Confederacy he inherited was absolute, and though when he appeared among his people they received him with shouts of applause, their respect for him was based solely upon fear, for all stood in terror of him. "He realized more clearly than any of his predecessors", writes Mr. Thompson, "that if all the tribes could be united under an unquestioned and absolute leader, the Huns would form an unparalleled instrument for the exploitation of the peoples of central Europe. . . . Instead of relying on the unruly and divided tribal chiefs, he based his power on vassals . . . who were bound to him personally by an inviolable allegiance without the handicap of tribal obligations."[1]

When, in 499, Theodosius sent his famous embassy under Priscus to Attila, the Huns had ceased to be a wholly nomadic people and had become "a parasitic community of marauders. . . . Instead of herding cattle they had now learned the more profitable business of herding men. Sharp differences of wealth have appeared among them, though not perhaps differences of class. Their society could only be maintained as long as Attila was able to supply the mass of his men with the necessities of life and a few luxuries. . . ."[2] This change may be gathered from Priscus's narrative, for he informs us that Attila no longer lived in a tent or a wagon, but in a log-hut of considerable size, surrounded by a palisade. In this hut he received the Roman ambassador Maximin, and welcomed him with the appellation of "shameless beast". A feast next followed which is minutely described. Further, Priscus tells us that Attila married his daughter Esca – "the laws of the Scythians allow this" – and that when the embassy put up at a certain village "one of the wives of Bleda, sent us nourishment and beautiful women. This among the Scythians is looked upon as an honour." In fact, the Hunnish customs were not far removed from those which are still to be met with in certain regions of central Asia.

As a soldier, Attila was no more than a plunderer. Hodgkin says of him: "He made war on civilization and on human nature, not on religion, for he did not understand it enough to hate it."[3] Of constructive genius he shows none, in spite of the fact that Priscus tells us that he believed himself destined to be lord of the whole world. The extent of his empire is but vaguely known. Its

---

[1] *A History of Attila and the Huns*, E. A. Thompson (1948), pp. 208–209.
[2] *Ibid.*, p. 177.
[3] *Italy and Her Invaders*, Thomas Hodgkin (1880), vol. II, p. 130.

central grazing ground appears to have covered modern Hungary and Transylvania, and the rest stretched from Gaul eastward into the unknown.

Though the mode of life of the nomad was primitive in the extreme, as Ellis H. Minns points out, it possessed certain military advantages over that of the village or city dweller, and so fitted him better for war. "His life is laborious and dangerous", writes Minns; "it requires skill, courage, endurance, but he is exempt from that continuous back-breaking toil which bends the hoeman to mother earth. He has change of scene, wide spaces, and a sense of freedom. His leaders are used to problems of transport and the management of large bodies of men. The whole people is a ready-made army, easily marshalled, self-supporting, capable of sudden attacks, of long-distance raids. In the steppe the nomad is always on a war footing, prepared to extend his pastures at another tribe's expense, or to defend his own. . . . But whether for attack or defence the tribe must be well led; and the leader must have absolute authority."[1]

The Huns' conquests were not due to superiority of numbers, but to the high mobility of small bands of horse-archers who could concentrate rapidly at any given point, quickly disperse and re-concentrate at another. Though, on their first appearance, their ponies were no match for the Roman horses, they soon acquired the latter and the disadvantage rapidly disappeared.

When on the war path, the bands of mounted men, moving on a wide front, were followed by their families and wagons–travelling fortresses–which could quickly be drawn up into a defensive laager. Though the bands were extremely mobile, the wagon columns were slow-moving and frequently must have been immobile, especially in the hilly and wooded country of western Europe. Therefore it must often have happened that the fighting horde–the bands in total–was separated from its base, and when this occurred the horde had to keep moving in order to live, and as movement depended on forage, not only had the horde to split into groups, but campaigning during the winter months was normally not attempted. It was for this reason that Emperor Leo the Wise laid it down that Scythians and Huns should be attacked during February and March, when their horses are weakened by the hardships of winter.

[1] "The Art of the Northern Nomads", Ellis H. Minns, *Proceedings of the British Academy*, 1942, pp. 51–52.

To overcome the difficulties of rationing, the Huns, like the Mongols in the twelfth and thirteenth centuries, lived on their horses. In Genghis Khan's army, Marco Polo informs us that each Mongol was obliged to take with him eighteen horses and mares, so that he might have mare's milk and horse's blood for food and drink.[1] Their steeds were not only mounts and remounts, but self-replenishing canned food.[2] With this may be compared a remark made by T. E. Lawrence on operations in Arabia: "Our cards were speed and time, not hitting power. The invention of bully-beef had profited us more than the invention of gunpowder, but gave us strategical rather than tactical strength. . . ."[3]

From this self-supplying base a cyclonic strategy was developed; operations took the form of whirlwind advances and retirements. Whole districts were laid waste and entire populations annihilated, not only in order to establish a heat of terror which would evaporate opposition, but also to leave the rear clear of all hostile man-power and so to facilitate withdrawals. The tactics adopted may be defined as "ferocity under authority". Fury, surprise, elusiveness, cunning and mobility, and not planning, method, drill and discipline were its elements. "Try twice, turn back the third time" is as much a Hunnish as a Turkoman proverb; and as Amédée Thierry points out: "The nomads, unlike ourselves, do not consider flight a dishonour. Considering booty of more worth than glory, they fight only when they are certain of success. When they find their enemy in force they evade him to return when the occasion is more opportune." Their master weapon was the bow, mainly made of horn as the steppes were treeless. Its value largely lay in the noiselessness of the arrows, which were tipped with bone. But in close-quarter fighting they relied on the sword "regardless of their own lives; and while the enemy are guarding against wounds from the sabre-thrusts, they throw strips of cloth plaited into nooses [lassos] over their opponents and so entangle

---

[1] See the *Book of Ser Marco Polo*, trans. Colonel Sir Henry Yule (3rd edit., 1903), vol. I, p. 254.

[2] "The principal food consists of milk-products—not of the fresh milk itself, which is only taken by children and the sick. A special Turko-Tartar food is *yogurt*, prepared with leaven from curdled milk. The Mongols also ate butter—the more rancid the more palatable—dripping with dirt, and carried without wrapping in their heavy greasy coat-pockets. From mare's milk, which yields no cream, *kumiz* (Kirghiz), *tshegan* (Mongolish) is fermented, an extremely nutritious drink which is good for consumption, and from which by itself life can be sustained" (*The Cambridge Medieval History*, vol. I, p. 339).

[3] *Seven Pillars of Wisdom*, T. E. Lawrence (1935), p. 196.

them that they fetter their limbs and take from them the power of riding or walking".[1]

The weakness in their tactics lay in that they could seldom halt in any one place for long, because forage was rapidly exhausted. This and their inability to storm fortresses and walled cities rendered their occupation of any given area impermanent. At Asemus (Osma), twenty miles south of Sistova, in 443, Attila was easily repulsed, and when he started plundering the neighbouring country sallies against him were made from that fortress. In brief, the Hunnish method of fighting, though admirably suited for the steppes of Asia, in the end failed in more civilized and topographically difficult Europe.

The first great incursion of the Huns came in 395. They crossed the frozen Danube and their hordes devasted Dalmatia and Thrace, but their greatest effort was made far away to the east. They passed through the defiles of the Caucasus overran Armenia, devastated Cappadocia and parts of Syria and Cicilia, and laid siege to Antioch and many other cities on the Halys, Cyndus, Orontes, and Euphrates. The terror caused by this extensive raid is vividly described by St. Jerome. "Lo," he writes, "suddenly messengers ran to and fro and the whole East trembled, for swarms of Huns had broken forth from the far distant Maeotis (Sea of Azov) between the icy Tanais (Don) and the monstrous peoples of the Massagetae, where the Gates of Alexander pen in the wild nations behind the rocks of Caucasus. They filled the whole earth with slaughter and panic alike as they flitted hither and thither on their swift horses. . . . They were at hand everywhere before they were expected: by their speed they outstripped rumour, and they took pity neither upon religion nor rank nor age nor wailing childhood."[2]

The next incursion of importance came in 441, immediately after Gaiseric's negotiations with Attila. Again the Huns crossed the Danube and destroyed Viminacium (Kostolacz),[3] Margus, at the mouth of the Morava, Singidunum (Belgrade), Sirmium (Mitrovitz), and many lesser places. This lightning campaign compelled Theodosius to recall his fleet from Sicily and to abandon his projected attack on Gaiseric.

[1] Ammianus Marcellinus, xxxi, ii, 9. See also Sozomen's *Ecclesiastical History*, trans. E. Walford (1855), vii, 26, 8.

[2] Quoted from *A History of Attila and the Huns*, p. 27.

[3] In recent times 100,000 coins, buried at the time of this raid, have been dug out of the site of this city (*ibid.*, p. 80).

In 442 a truce was agreed upon, but as Theodosius refused to hand over to Attila the fugitives demanded by him, in the following year the war was renewed. By occupying Ratiaria (Anzar Palanka), capital of the province of Dacia Ripensis and the base of the Roman fleet on the Danube, Attila secured his rear and then advanced up the valley of the Margus (Morava) and destroyed Naissus. Next he moved up the river Nischava and razed Sardica (Sofia) and Philippopolis to the ground. By-passing Adrianople and Heraclea because they were too strong for him to storm, in the neighbourhood of Constantinople he defeated Theodosius's army under Aspar, an Alan, in a series of battles, and finally exterminated it on the shores of the Dardanelles. These defeats compelled Theodosius to seek peace, which was granted by Attila. The main terms were that all fugitives should be handed over to him, that arrears of tribute, calculated at 6,000 lb. of gold (£280,000), should be paid, and that the annual tribute should be fixed at 2,100 lb. This peace was agreed upon in August, 443.

In 447 Attila again invaded the Eastern Empire, but on what pretext is unknown. When he was about to advance, a series of terrible earthquakes threw down the walls of many Greek cities, and did such extensive damage to the fortifications of Constantinople that at first it appeared that the city was doomed. To protect it, the army of Theodosius advanced to the river Utus (Vid), and though it met with defeat, it would seem to have inflicted such heavy losses on the Huns that, after they had plundered and devastated the land as far south as Thermopylae, Attila thought it better to withdraw.

His rear secured by these incursions, Italy and Gaul lay at his mercy; but as Gaiseric looked upon the former as his private preserves, some time before the spring of 450 he pointed out to Attila how profitable it would be for him to raid the lands of the Visigoths. This suggestion, it would seem, decided the question Attila had for some time been turning over in his mind – namely, how best to attack Gaul? He fell in with Gaiseric's idea, and as he knew that the Visigoths were the inveterate enemies of the Romans, he decided to march against them in the guise of Valentinian's ally, hoping thereby to neutralize Roman opposition. Further, Theodoric and Gaiseric were at loggerheads because Hunneric, Gaiseric's son, had recently repudiated his wife, Theodoric's daughter, and had returned her to her father minus her nose and ears. Therefore, with the Romans neutralized and Gaiseric hostile, Theodoric would be completely isolated.

While this scheming was in progress, on July 26, 450, Theodosius was thrown by his horse, and two days later died of his injuries. He was succeeded by Marcian (450–457) who had married Theodosius's sister Pulcheria, and one of the first acts of the new emperor was to stop paying tribute to the Huns. Enraged by this, Attila sent two embassies, one to Constantinople to demand the resumption of tribute, which was emphatically refused, and the other to Ravenna to make a request relative to an incident which had occurred sixteen years earlier.

In 434, Honoria, Valentinian's sister, when in her seventeenth year, had been seduced by one of her chamberlains and was sent by her mother Placidia in disgrace to Constantinople. She bitterly resented this and in a passion sent a ring to Attila begging him to accept her as his wife. Now that she had returned to Ravenna, the mission of the second embassy was not only to claim her as Attila's bride, but also to demand half the Western Empire as her dowry. No sooner was this demand refused than an event occurred which further widened the breach between Attila and Valentinian. The king of the Ripuarian Franks died and a succession quarrel broke out between his two sons; the elder appealed to Attila for aid and the younger to Aetius. As the latter was well received and adopted by Aetius as his son, it must have become apparent to Attila that he could no longer rely on Aetius's former friendship to maintain Roman neutrality during his projected attack on Gaul; therefore that, before he could deal with Marcian, he must first settle his account with the Western Empire, where he had many supporters among the Bagaudae–again in revolt–where the Visigoths were still hostile to the Romans and Vandals, and where the Ripuarian Franks were in the throes of a civil war. To Attila, Ravenna seemed impotent; but, as so often happens, the unexpected lurked round the corner. Again a single man was destined to change the course of the apparently inevitable: this man was Aetius, called "The last of the Romans".

Renatus Frigeridus has left us the following brief description of him:

"Of middle height, he was manly in appearance and well made, neither too frail nor too heavy; he was quick of wit and agile of limb, a very practised horseman and skilful archer; he was indefatigable with the spear. A born warrior, he was renowned for the arts of peace, without avarice and little swayed by desire, endowed with gifts of the mind, not swerving from his purpose for any kind of evil instigation. He bore wrongs with the utmost patience, and loved labour. Undaunted in danger, he was excelled by none in the endurance of hunger, thirst, and vigil. From his early youth he seemed forewarned of the great power to which he was destined by the fates."[1]

Early in 451, when war between Attila and Aetius became certain, the problem the latter had to consider was: would the kingdoms and tribes of Gaul set aside their quarrels and unite against the invader? Above all, would Theodoric, the most powerful of the kings, join hands with him—his old and persistent enemy? Attila's aim clearly was to prevent this, and being "a subtle man", and one who "fought with craft before he made war",[2] he sent an embassy to both Valentinian and Theodoric. To the former he proclaimed that his invasion was but a continuation of the former campaign of Roman and Hun against the Visigoths, and to the latter he pointed out the danger of an alliance with Rome. Valentinian guessed what Attila had in mind and sent ambassadors to Theodoric to warn him against Attila. Among other things these ambassadors said: "Since you are mighty in arms, give heed to your own dangers and join hands with us in common. Bear aid also to the Empire, of which you hold a part. If you would learn how such an alliance should be sought and welcomed by us, look into the plans of the foe."[3]

While Theodoric hesitated, Attila struck, and, early in 451, he set out from beyond the Rhine and marched westward. His army is reputed to have numbered 500,000 men, a figure obviously exaggerated by panic. It was a conglomerate force, for besides the Huns there were in it Ostrogoths and Gepids, who formed its kernel, as well as Sciri from Riga, Rugi from Pomerania, Franks from the Neckar, Thuringi from Bavaria, and Burgundians from east of the Rhine. His first objective was probably the lands of the Ripuarian Franks, and his next Orléans, for located as it is at the apex of the great bend in the river Loire, once in his hands he could sweep into Gothia (Aquitania).[4]

His army poured through Belgic Gaul in three columns of fighting groups and advanced on a wide front, its right moving

---

[1] *The History of the Franks*, by Gregory of Tours, trans. O. M. Dalton (1927), II, 7 (8), vol. II, pp. 48–49.
[2] Jordanes, XXXVI, p. 103.   [3] *Ibid.*, XXXVI, p. 104.   [4] See map on p. 343.

on Nemetacum (Arras), its left up the Moselle to Mettis (Metz) and its centre on Lutetia Parisiorum (Paris) and Aureliani (Orléans). The devastation was appalling; fire, smoke, murder and rapine swept through the lands. Rheims, Metz, Cambrai, Trèves, Arras, Tongres, Tournai, Thérouanne, Cologne, Amiens, Beauvais, Worms, Mainz and Strasbourg were sacked and burnt. Paris, then but a small town built on an island in the Seine, was saved, so the story goes, by a young girl of the neighbouring village of Nanterre, Genovefa by name, better known to posterity as Saint Geneviève. When its inhabitants in panic were about to flee, she urged them to place their trust in God, and through her simple prayers held them to the city walls.

Meanwhile Valentinian's embassy had failed to win Theodoric over, and the vital question remained—could a coalescence of the tribes be effected? As usual, there was no reserve army in Italy, which the year before had been devastated by a terrible famine. For twenty-five years Aetius had relied upon the Huns to fill his ranks; now they were his enemy, and nothing but blank files met his anxious gaze. He hurried to Gaul and collected together such *feoderati* as were to be found there; apparently checked the impulse of the Alans at Valence to open the gates of that city to Attila; and then went to Arverni (Clermont in Auvergne) and sent to the Gothic court at Tolosa (Toulouse) a Roman Senator named Avitus (the future Emperor of the West, 454–456), who won Theodoric's support.

Meanwhile the hordes of Huns swarmed toward Orléans, in the neighbourhood of which Sangiban, king of the Alans, who had been settled there by Aetius in 442, promised to betray the city to Attila. When a report of this came to the ears of Aetius and Theodoric they set out at top speed to occupy the city before Attila could seize it, but the Huns arrived first and at once besieged the city. According to Gregory of Tours, it was saved through the intercessions of the blessed bishop Anianus (St. Aignan).[1] In the *Vita Aniani*, as quoted by Amédée Thierry, the story is as follows: He visited Aetius and impressed upon him the fact that Orléans could not hold out beyond June 14. Early in May, Attila appeared and for five weeks pounded at the walls with his rams and poured an unceasing hail of arrows into the city. As the walls crumbled, the worthy bishop restored them by perambulating certain holy relics round and round the battle-

[1] Gregory of Tours, II, 5 (6), vol. II, p. 46.

ments. Toward the middle of June all seemed lost, when one morning a soldier ascended the highest turret and spied in the distance a tiny cloud of dust—it hid Aetius and Theodoric. As it grew bigger, out of it gleamed the eagles of the legions and the embroidered banners of the Goths. Lastly, the armies met in a fierce fight in the suburbs. "Driven from street to street, beaten down by the stones hurled at them by the inhabitants from the roofs of the houses, the Huns no longer knew what was to become of them, when Attila sounded the retreat. The patrician, Aetius, had not failed in his word; it was the 14th of June. Such was that famous day which in the West saved civilization from total destruction."[1]

Whatever happened, it would appear that Attila experienced a disastrous defeat; for instead of pressing the attack, he and his horde slipped away during the night, passed by Sens and made for the valleys of the Seine and the Aube where the country was open and called "Campania"—Champagne. On the former river, probably in the vicinity of, or at Méry-sur-Seine, he established his rearguard, a horde of Gepids, and retired his main body a little east of it on to "the Catalaunian Plains, which are also called Mauriacian".[2] Against the rearguard Aetius launched a night attack, which must have crushed it out of existence, for, according to Jordanes,[3] his enemy lost in killed and wounded 15,000 men, which though an impossible number, suggests heavy fighting.

Presumably on the next day, June 20,[4] the battle opened.

It would appear from Jordanes that Attila was in no way confident of success, and to shorten the engagement so that he might

---

[1] *Histoire d'Attila*, Amédée Thierry (1856), vol. i, p. 178.

[2] Jordanes, xxxvi, p. 105. I have adopted the locality as given by Hodgkin (vol. ii, pp. 160–162). Professor Bury (*History of the Later Roman Empire*, vol. i, p. 293) places the battlefield near Troyes, 20 miles south of Méry-sur-Seine, and *The Cambridge Medieval History*, vol. i, pp. 280 and 416, says a few miles "in front" (i.e. west) of that city. That the battle was fought in the vicinity of Troyes is quite possible, because from Sens the topographical line of retreat would be up the Vanne valley and then presumably north on Arcis-sur-Aube. But that the battle was fought west of Troyes is unlikely, for Attila would scarcely have halted with his back to the Seine. Really all that can be said is that the battle was fought in the triangle Troyes–Méry–Arcis, because the Mauriac Plain, according to Jordanes, was "in length one hundred *leuva*, as the Gauls express it, and seventy in width". As the *leuva* measured a distance of 1,500 paces, the Mauriac Plain is a district and not a locality, and because Jordanes also calls it the Catalaunian Plain, this has led to the battle being known as "The Battle of Châlons".

[3] Jordanes, xli, p. 112.

[4] This date is a conjecture. (See Bury, vol. i, pp. 292–293.) As Troyes or Méry-sur-Seine is a little over 100 miles from Orléans, if Attila's retreat was a rapid one, it is possible that the battle was fought on this day. Hodgkin (vol. ii, p. 139) says "early in July", and Clinton (*Fasti Romani*, vol. i, p. 642) on September 27.

continue his retreat under cover of night, he did not issue out of his wagon laager until the early afternoon, when he formed up his horde in the following order. He took command of the centre with his bravest troops, with Walamir and the Ostrogoths on the left and Ardaric and the Gepids, etc., on the right. Apparently his idea was to charge his enemy's centre, to drive it back in confusion and then to withdraw to his camp and await nightfall. In his turn Aetius, who presumably realized what was in his opponent's mind, decided upon two outflanking attacks, the aim of which was to cut off the Huns from their laager. He drew up his most unreliable troops, the Alans, under Sangiban, in the centre; placed Theodoric and his Visigoths on his right to oppose the Ostrogoths; and himself took command of the left wing with his Romans.

When the armies were being marshalled, a skirmish for a rising piece of ground took place in which Thorismund, son of Theodoric, threw the Huns' advanced guard back in confusion. Disconcerted by this attack, Attila, according to Jordanes, addressed his troops. He pointed to the Alans and said: "Seek swift victory in that spot. . . . For when the sinews are cut the limbs soon relax, nor can a body stand when you have taken away the bones. . . . No spear shall harm those who are seen to live; and those who are sure to die Fate overtakes even in peace."[1] Their hearts being warmed by these words, "they all dashed into battle".

Next Jordanes writes: "Hand to hand they clashed in battle, and the fight grew fierce, confused, monstrous, unrelenting – a fight whose like no ancient time has ever recorded. There such deeds were done that a brave man who missed this marvellous spectacle could not hope to see anything so wonderful all his life long." A terrific struggle took place along a brook: "Here King Theodorid [Theodoric], while riding by to encourage his army, was thrown from his horse and trampled under foot by his own men, thus ending his days at a ripe old age. . . . Then the Visigoths, separating from the Alani, fell upon the horde of the Huns and nearly slew Attila. But he prudently took flight and strait way shut himself and his companions within the barriers of the camp, which he had fortified with wagons."[2]

Darkness now set in, and with it complete confusion; for Thorismund, we are told, lost his way in the blind night, and thinking that he was rejoining his own men came upon the

[1] Jordanes, xxxix, p. 108. [2] Ibid., xl, p. 109.

wagons of the enemy; while "Aetius also became separated from his men in the confusion of night and wandered about in the midst of the enemy. Fearing disaster had happened, he went about in search of the Goths. At last he reached the camp of his allies and passed the remainder of the night in the protection of their shields."[1]

"At dawn on the following day, when the Romans saw the fields were piled high with bodies and that the Huns did not venture forth, they thought the victory was theirs, but knew that Attila would not flee from the battle unless overwhelmed by a great disaster. Yet he did nothing cowardly, like one that is overcome, but with clash of arms sounded the trumpets and threatened an attack. He was like a lion pierced by hunting spears, who paces to and fro before the mouth of his den and dares not spring, but ceases not to terrify the neighbourhood by his roaring. Even so this warlike king at bay terrified his conquerors. Therefore the Goths and Romans assembled and considered what to do with the vanquished Attila. They determined to wear him out by a siege, because he had no supply of provisions and was hindered from approaching by a shower of arrows from the bowmen placed within the confines of the Roman camp."[2]

In spite of his roarings and ravings, Attila's situation was a desperate one, and further still he knew it, for in the semi-legendary history of Jordanes, we are told that he considered his position so critical that he constructed a funeral pyre of horses' saddles in the flames of which he determined to hurl himself should the enemy break through. Curious as it may seem, Aetius's situation was almost as perturbing; for shortly after the sun rose Theodoric's body was found and Thorismund was proclaimed king of the Goths.[3]

Apparently it was only then Aetius decided that though he had Attila cornered, it would be wiser to let him escape. Seemingly he did not trust Thorismund, and he feared that, were Attila and his horde annihilated, the Visigoths would at once replace the Huns as the enemies of Rome. This is Jordanes's opinion, for he says:

"But Aetius feared that if the Huns were totally destroyed by the Goths, the Roman Empire would be overwhelmed, and

---

[1] Jordanes, XL, p. 110.   [2] *Ibid.*, XL, p. 110.
[3] In 1842 near the village of Pouan, on the south bank of the Aube and about ten miles from Méry-sur-Seine, the grave of a Gothic warrior was discovered, and from the ornaments found in it M. Peigne Délacourt considered it to be that of Theodoric. See *Italy and Her Invaders*, Thomas Hodgkin, vol. II, 155-159.

urgently advised him (Thorismund) to return to his own do-minions to take up the rule which his father had left him. Other-wise his brothers might seize their father's possessions and obtain the power over the Visigoths."[1] Further, the conditions at Ravenna were such that Aetius could feel safe only as long as he was indispensable, and to remain so it was necessary that Attila should not be crushed completely.[2]

The upshot was that, once Thorismund had marched away, Attila noticed his empty bivouac, harnessed his wagons and trekked back to beyond the Rhine. What his losses were is not known. Jordanes says that 165,000 men were slain on both sides, not including the 15,000 killed and wounded in the night before the battle. Idatius puts the number of killed at 300,000. All these figures are fantastic.

No sooner had Attila returned to his timber palace than again he claimed Honoria as his bride, and, in the spring of 452, he set out to invade Italy. He crossed the Julian Alps–from which the garrisons had been withdrawn–descended upon Aquileia, and after a long and desperate siege stormed the city and so annihilated it that even a century later scarcely the vestiges of it remained. Next he marched into Venetia and he wiped out Julia Concordia, the luxurious Altinum and Patavium (Padua). As he marched on, Vicenza, Verona, Brescia, Bergamo, Milan, and Pavia, struck by the terror of Aquileia, opened their gates, and though their buildings were not destroyed their inhabitants were either mas-sacred or carried away into captivity. At length, Attila halted on the Mincio.

Aetius had been caught so completely unaware by this bold campaign that, unhinged by the prevailing panic, his first thought was to take Valentinian with him and to abandon Italy. Then, when he recovered his nerve, he decided to beg peace of Attila. Once this decision was agreed upon, an embassy consisting of Pope Leo, Trygetius, an ex-prefect, and Gennadius Avienus, consul for 450, was sent to the Mincio, and, according to ecclesi-astical legend, the dreaded king of kings was vanquished "before the unarmed successor of St. Peter. . . . The awe of Rome was

---

[1] Jordanes, XLI, p. 111.

[2] The whole story of Attila's escape is so strange that it may be that Aetius never lost his way on the night of June 20–21; but instead paid a secret visit to Attila and arranged the whole incident with him. Otherwise, why did not Attila attack him after Thorismund left: or why did not Aetius follow up Attila's retirement and cut off his foragers?

upon him . . . and he was forced incessantly to ponder the question 'What if I conquer like Alaric, to die like him?' "[1] But as Bury points out: "It is unreasonable to suppose that this heathen king would have cared for the thunders or persuasions of the Church."[2]

The true reasons are probably those given by Thompson:[3] that Italy was still suffering from the famine of the previous year, which meant its inseparable companion, pestilence. Further, when Attila entered Italy, Marcian seized the opportunity to send an army under a general, also named Aetius, over the Danube. His enterprise was successful, for he routed the Huns left behind by Attila to protect his base. It was this bold counter-stroke, coupled with lack of supplies and the dread of pestilence, which in all probability compelled Attila to come to terms. His losses at Châlons had been so heavy that he dared not risk a further loss of men.

The next year he took to himself another wife, a girl Ildico (Hilda); drank copiously at the wedding feast and retired to his marriage bed. During the night he was attacked by a violent fit of bleeding at the nose, and lay on his back when the blood poured down his throat and drowned him.

Attila dead, his empire flew to pieces. As soon as he was secretly buried his tribe of sons divided his realm between them, then quarrelled over the divisions and fought each other. While thus engaged, the Ostrogoths, who had been herded by Attila into the valley of the Theiss (Tisza), revolted. A general rising of the German tribes followed, and finding a leader in Ardaric, king of the Gepids, in 454, on the unknown river Nedao, in Pannonia, they routed the Huns so completely that within two or three generations they virtually disappeared.

The sequel to these events—Attila's death and the collapse of his empire—is a strange one. Two daughters and no son had been born to Valentinian and the empress Eudoxia, daughter of Theodosius II, and Aetius, to secure the succession for his own family, in 454 sought to gain the hand of one of the daughters for his son. In a passion Valentinian stabbed Aetius to death, and in

[1] *Italy and Her Invaders*, Thomas Hodgkin, vol. II, pp 174–179. The whole story is dramatic in the extreme. Regarding it, see also Milman's *History of Latin Christianity*, vol. I, pp. 200–203; Bury's *History of the Later Roman Empire*, vol. I, pp. 295–296, and Gibbon's *The Decline and Fall of the Roman Empire*, vol. III, pp. 500–501.

[2] *Later Roman Empire*, vol. I, p. 295.

[3] *A History of Attila and the Huns*, pp. 147–148.

the following year was himself assassinated and succeeded by Petronius Maximus. He forced Eudoxia to marry him, and it is said that in revenge she appealed to Gaiseric to aid her. In June, 455, he sailed up the Tiber, was met by Eudoxia, whom he stripped of her robes and jewels, and for fourteen days sacked Rome, but the lives of its inhabitants were spared by the intercession of Pope Leo. Before the looting Maximus was assassinated, and when Gaiseric withdrew, power passed into the hands of Ricimer, the barbarian Master of the Troops and grandson of Wallia the Visigoth. In rapid succession emperor followed emperor until 475, when Orestes, a Roman who had served as secretary to Attila, won the support of the barbarian mercenaries, had his young son Romulus, surnamed Augustulus, proclaimed emperor at Ravenna, and marched on Rome. But no sooner had he set out than his troops demanded one-third of Italy as their reward, and because this preposterous claim was refused, on August 23, 476, they raised their leader, Odovacar–who appears to have been the son of one of Attila's lieutenants, the Hun Edeco[1] –upon a shield and proclaimed him king of Italy. From then until Christmas Day of the year 800, when Pope Leo III crowned Charlemagne in St. Peter's and inaugurated what was to become the Holy Roman Empire, there was no Emperor of the West. Romulus opened the great cycle in the legendary year 753 B.C., and twelve hundred and twenty-nine years later his effete namesake closed it. Henceforth for long centuries the twilight of legend returned in the West.

It will be seen from these events that the victory Aetius and Theodoric won at Châlons in no way saved the Western Empire from obliteration. Also it will be seen that, even had they suffered defeat, Attila's empire would have collapsed on his death; it had no political bottom–it was built wholly on terror and was devoid of creative force. Nevertheless, when we look back on the making rather than the winning of the Battle of Châlons, its importance becomes apparent.

It was not a Roman victory or a Teutonic victory, but a victory of both peoples combined over Asiatics, as Salamis had been a victory of both Athenians and Spartans over Persians. Once again West and East–Europe and Asia–were in clinch, and once again Europeans set aside their private quarrels in order to face a common foe.

[1] Edeco was probably king of the Scirs.

More important still, the ecclesiastical organization in the Frankish territories remained unbroken, with the result that the Church became the chief international authority during the Middle Ages, and the only authority which could trace unbroken descent from Roman times. Frankland was, therefore, more fortunate than England, where ecclesiastical organization was destroyed completely by the Saxons, with the result that its inhabitants had to be reconverted by missionaries from Ireland and Rome. Had the same happened in what to-day is France, the whole course of medieval history would have been changed.

Further, the prestige of the papacy was vastly enhanced, for though the probability is that, when Pope Leo met Attila on the Mincio, he came as a humble suppliant, the sudden death of the ferocious Hun following so closely on the meeting appeared to a superstitious age to be the judgement of God. The devil had been subdued by God's vicar, and the legend which sprouted from this victory of righteousness over evil went far to set the papal chair firmly on the floor of the miraculous, and as Thomas Hodgkin writes: ". . . thus it is no paradox to say that indirectly the King of the Huns contributed more perhaps than any other historical personage, towards the creation of that mighty factor in the politics of medieval Italy, the Pope-King of Rome."[1] What Attila began Gaiseric added to. "From now on", writes Dean Milman, "Rome ceased altogether to be a pagan city."[2] And as the old Roman nobility went down, the papal power went up; yet the horror of these invasions lived on and the very features of Attila were transmogrified into the countenance of Satan – the Black Magician. Even to-day, when we seek to insult our enemies, we call them Huns.

As religious outlook changed, so did the outlook on war, which so often is the physical expression of mystical beliefs. Horror was so complete, impotence so deep-founded, and fear so universal that the miraculous alone could be relied upon. Though the generals created hell on earth, the priests could at least promise heaven in the world to come. Had not a girl saved Paris by her prayers? Had not 11,000 virgins been martyred in Cologne, and did not their dusty bones stir forth miracles? Was it not a bishop who had saved Orléans? Had not Heraclea in Macedonia been defended by a saint? Therefore, would not the innumerable cities

---

[1] *Italy and Her Invaders*, Thomas Hodgkin, vol. II, p. 189.
[2] *History of Latin Christianity*, Henry Hart Milman (1857), vol. I, p. 204.

wasted by the Huns have beaten back their onslaught had there been more saints, even if less soldiers? Thus it came about that relics became spiritual ammunition and papal authority the engine which detonated their power.

As the greatness of Alexander may be judged from his legend, so may the horror of Attila be translated from his. He was the *Flagellum Dei*, the Grandson of Nimrod, the Anti-Christ of the Scriptures, and the Etzel of the Nibelungenlied. It was he who married Kriemhild (Ildico); the Nibelungs visited him in Hunland, and "reaping the due of hoarded vengeance" Kriemhild murders him for love of her girlhood husband Siegfried. The great epic sprouts out of the blood-soaked fields of Europe, cropping forth a common heritage. It is found in Byzantium, in Germany, France, Italy, Scandinavia, and Iceland; it is one of the great legends of the western world. Taken together, these things made the Battle of Châlons one of the decisive moments in western history.

It is indicative of the durability of the Roman Empire, both as an institution and as an idea fixed in men's minds, that there continued to be emperors in the West for over sixty years after the sack of Rome, and all through the ravages of the Huns. But although the Western Empire thus remained formally in existence, the true Roman power was now definitely located in the East. Italy, during the 5th Century, became a Gothic kingdom, and under the rule of Theodoric (474-526) there was a distinct chance, says Fuller, "of a true revival of the West through the fusion of barbaric vigour with what remained of Roman civilization". This opportunity, however, evaporated into the limbo of lost dreams when the Eastern and Western Empires came into conflict.

The origin of the conflict was religion – the proscription of Arianism by the Eastern Emperor Justin I; this was the debut of Christianity as a militant (and therefore military) force. The Goths being Arians, Justin's act put an end to the possibilities of fruitful cooperation between the two parts of the Roman world, and brought instead bitter war. Like all religious wars, it was intensely destructive, and Fuller compares its results with those of the Thirty Years' War in Germany in the 17th Century.

It was Justin's successor, Justinian "the Great" (527-65) who waged the struggle. Beginning in 533, it was this, more than any other factor, that made the Dark Ages of Europe so long and bleak. Justinian did not take the field himself; he acted through his generals, Belisarius and Narses. Belisarius has left a name of military genius which is still applauded – his achievements in several campaigns with very small resources are indeed a matter of wonder, especially when the unsatisfactory raw material of his armies is taken into account. Yet it was the more subtle Narses who clinched the exploits of Belisarius by his own victory at Taginae in 552. Outwardly, Justinian's success was impressive:

By annihilating the Vandals in Africa and the Ostrogoths in

Italy, he extirpated Arianism within the bounds of the greater part of the old Western Empire, and brought under his dominion the whole of North Africa, Dalmatia, Italy, southern Spain, Sicily, Sardinia, Corsica and the Balearic Islands. Except for the Visigoths in Spain and Septimania (the region between the eastern Pyrenees and the Rhône) and the Franks in Provence, the Mediterranean was again a Roman lake.

Such was Justinian's achievement; but Fuller asks, "what did it cost and what were its repercussions on history?"

Like Africa, Italy emerged out of twenty years of war ruined by long sieges, famines, massacres, devastations, plunderings, and pestilences. "The largest towns, such as Naples, Milan, and specially Rome", writes Professor Charles Diehl, "were almost devoid of inhabitants, the depopulated country was uncultivated and the large Italian proprietors were repaid for their devotion to Byzantium and their hostility to Totila by total ruin."

Gibbon is even more scathing. He writes: "But the wars, the conquests, and the triumphs of Justinian are the feeble, and pernicious efforts of old age, which exhaust the remains of strength, and accelerate the decay of the power of life. He exulted in the glorious act of restoring Africa and Italy to the republic; but the calamities which followed . . . betrayed the impotence of the conqueror and accomplished the ruin of those unfortunate countries." And again: "The triple scourge of war, pestilence, and famine, afflicted the subjects of Justinian, and his reign is disgraced by a visible decrease of the human species, which has never been repaired in some of the fairest countries of the globe."

And what was the outcome of Justinian's victories? From the Euphrates to the Pillars of Hercules, war, fiscal oppression[1] and religious persecutions prepared ". . . the provinces of the East, pale, emaciated, and miserable, for the advent of the Moslem conquerors, who", within a century of Justinian's death, "were to win the fairest of them and were to hold them even to our own day". Africa under the Moors, who had been kept in check by the Vandals, returned to her primitive barbarism, and in con-

[1] "The imperial *logothetae* applied the burdensome system of Roman taxes to the ruined countries without making any allowance for the prevailing distress. They mercilessly demanded arrears dating from the time of the Goths, falsified the registers in order to increase the returns, and enriched themselves at the expense of the taxpayer to such an extent that, according to a contemporary writer, 'nothing remained for the inhabitants but to die, since they were bereft of all necessities of life' " (*The Cambridge Medieval History*, vol. II, p. 23).

sequence could in no way withstand the Saracens of the following century. And Italy, once the Goths had been exterminated and the *logothetes* under Narses had for twelve years sucked dry whatever wealth was left from war, was in 568 invaded by the ferocious Lombards under Alboin, the last of the German peoples to establish themselves within the bounds of the former Western Empire. They rapidly occupied the region north of the Po—still called Lombardy—more gradually extended southward, pillaging and massacring as they went, and eventually, except for Ravenna and Rome, overran the northern two-thirds of the peninsula. In 589, under Zotto, they stormed and destroyed St. Benedict's monastery on Monte Cassino, and in 774 were conquered by Charles the Great and absorbed into his empire.

Had Italy never been invaded; had the battle of Taginae never been fought; and had the Ostrogoths continued to rule in Italy, medieval history would have been different. Instead of reduction to a ruined, second-rate city of no political importance, Rome would have remained the active centre of western culture and civilization, and the blending of Gothic vigour with Latin culture would have gone far to dispel the gloom which since the battle of Adrianople had steadily crept over the West. Although for Justinian, Taginae was his greatest victory, for the Christian world of his day and for many years to come it was an immeasurable disaster.

The rise and expansion of Islam

Justinian was the last of the great Roman emperors, for under his successor, Justin II (565–578), the Eastern Empire ceased to be Roman even in theory, and became wholly Byzantine. From then on all thought of reconquering the West was set aside, imperial policy became purely defensive, and threatened on the lower Danube by the Avars and Slavs, and on the upper Euphrates by the Persians, Justin was faced by the impossible strategical problem of holding two widely separated defensive fronts with forces inadequate to hold one securely. The outcome was an unceasing shuttling of armies from one front to the other, a condition his enemies were not slow to exploit.

The first shift of forces came in 572, when war again broke out with Persia, and by 591, when Maurice (582–602) was emperor, the garrisons in Europe had been so heavily drawn upon that peace was patched up with Chosröes II (590–628), in order to repel the Avars and Slavs. The former were a Tartar people who had been pushed westward by the Turks,[1] and the latter a non-German group of Indo-European peoples who in 577 began to sow the seeds of the future Slav kingdoms in the Balkans. In 591 the Avars swarmed southward, plundering and ravaging until in 604 they were bought off by the emperor Phocas (602–610) in order that he might meet Chosröes, who had broken the peace.

In 610, Phocas–"a hideous nightmare brooding over an exhausted and weary realm"–was hewn to pieces by Heraclius (610–642), who succeeded him. The war continued, and in 613 the Persians invaded Syria and took Damascus and Jerusalem. With the latter was lost "The Wood", as the True Cross, discovered by Helena the mother of Constantine the Great, was called; a loss which seemed to portend the ruin of the Empire. Next, in 617, when the Slavs raged at will over the European provinces and the Avars surged up to the Golden Gate, Chalcedon (Kadikeui) on the Propontis was lost, and two years later Egypt was invaded

---

[1] The name Turk (Tou-Kiue) is first mentioned in Chinese history in 545. Between 546 and 582 the Turks established themselves as a great power between China and Persia, and in 565 sent a mission to Justin to open up the silk trade and to seek his cooperation against the Persians.

and its corn supply cut off; meanwhile Armenia was overrun and the Empire deprived of its main recruiting ground. These disasters so overwhelmed Heraclius that he resolved to transfer the capital to Carthage, and was only prevented from doing so by the patriarch, who exacted from him an oath that he would never abandon Constantinople. The relief caused by this was so great that a sudden outburst of religious enthusiasm seized the people and a crusade was preached to rescue the Holy City and the Holy Cross.

Thus it came about that in 623 Heraclius took the field to fight six campaigns, during the fifth of which, in 626, hordes of Avars, Slavs, Bulgars, and Gepids, acting in concert with the Persian forces at Chalcedon, laid siege to Constantinople. Because of Byzantine command of the sea the city was saved. The following year Heraclius invaded Persia by way of Azerbaijan, marched southward, and on December 1 reached the Great Zab; eleven days later he decisively defeated the Persians in the neighbourhood of Nineveh. He then marched on Ctesiphon, but was compelled to retire before he reached the Persian capital. But no further campaign was necessary, for in the spring of 628 Chosröes was assassinated and peace followed. Its terms are unknown, except that they included the restoration of the Cross and the evacuation of the Empire's territory by the armies of Persia.

Thus, at the very moment when a new invader mobilized in the south, the two great empires in the East lay exhausted; their territories ravaged, their man-power wasted, their wealth gone; they were vacuums ready to be filled by the followers of the Prophet.

A few months after the True Cross had been restored to the Holy City on March 21, 630, a struggle began which, with scarcely an intermission, was to last for a thousand years. In the autumn of that year Mahomet who, at the important battle of Bahr, in 624, had finally established his authority over the Arabs, sent northward a raiding force, which at Muta, east of the Dead Sea, clashed with a Byzantine outpost and was defeated. Three years later, on June 7, he died, and as he left no son a minority of his followers recognized Abu Bakr (632–634) as Caliph ("Successor"). Because many Arabs objected to paying tribute to Medina, which since the year of the *hegira* (622) had become the centre of the Islamic faith, a rebellion, known as the *Ridda*, followed, which was finally suppressed by Khalid ibn al-Walid in his victory over the Meccans at Akraba. After this battle, to keep his victorious troops employed, Abu Bakr sent Khalid and 500 men to raid Irak, and three small forces to help the Christian Arabs of the border districts of Syria who, because the yearly subsidies paid to them by the Byzantines had been suspended, had sought his aid.

At the time these raiders set out, Heraclius was at Emesa (Homs), and because he trusted the Christian Arabs of the desert to prove a sufficient barrier against a Moslem advance, he had made no preparation to oppose one. But when he heard that southern Palestine had been raided, he assembled a considerable army south of Damascus under his brother Theodorus and ordered him to repel the invaders. When Khalid heard this, with lightning speed he passed from Hirah on the Euphrates through Palmyra and suddenly appeared before the walls of Damascus. From there, with great difficulty, he joined the three raiding columns, met Theodorus at Ajnadain, between Jerusalem and Gaza, and on July 30, 634, won a brilliant victory.

Soon afterward Abu Bakr died and was succeeded by Omar (634–644), and as he decided not merely to raid but to conquer Syria, an inundation of Moslem tribes under Khalid moved north. Damascus was betrayed to him, and toward the end of 635 he occupied Emesa.

In the spring of 636, Heraclius sent a new army, about 50,000 strong, under Theodorus Trithurius to oppose Khalid. At once the latter fell back, and relinquishing Damascus concentrated his forces, 25,000 in all, south-east of the Yarmuk valley, where, after much manœuvring and several engagements, on August 20, 636, he cut Trithurius's communications and annihilated his army. The battle was decisive; for so hated was Byzantine rule that everywhere in Syria the Moslems were welcomed as deliverers: the whole country fell to them, and in the north for centuries to come the Amanus range became the northern boundary of the Caliph's dominions.

The collapse of Persia was as swift and complete as that of Syria, and the main reason for it was the same; for, like the Syrians, the Aramaic peasants greeted their conquerors as deliverers. In the autumn of 635, Mutanna, a local chieftain, helped by troops from Medina, defeated a Persian army at Buwaib (south of Kufa) and in June, 637, Rustam, at the head of a numerically superior Persian army, was routed and slain by Sad ibn Wakkas at Khadisiya (west of Buwaib). The king of Persia and his court then fled before Sad's advance up the Tigris to the Iranian mountains. Next, Ctesiphon opened its gates, and lastly the whole of Irak passed into Arab hands. From now on, Islam ceased to be dependent on Medina, and instead represented the Arabs as a common empire. In consequence systematic conquest took the place of desultory raids, and during it whole tribes usually participated. Syria and Irak were linked by the conquest of Mesopotamia; Ecbatana fell in 641; the Persian Gulf passed under Arab dominion; and by 652 Khorasan was overrun.

Astonishing as it may seem, the conquest of Egypt falls in the same period, and again this can only be explained by reaction to Byzantine rule, which had imposed extortionary taxes on the Egyptians and had prohibited the Coptic faith.

The conqueror of Egypt was Amr ibn al-As. In January, 640, he took Pelusium and in July defeated the Byzantines at Heliopolis. Babylon, near modern Cairo, was occupied in April 641, and Alexandria surrendered on terms on September 17, 642. Next, to cover his western flank, Amr overran Cyrenaica.

This last advance was followed by decades of plundering raids, and though the Moslems penetrated to Kairouan in present-day Tunisia, and more than once held the town, it was not until they substituted a policy of occupation for that of plunder and gained naval command of the Mediterranean that they were able to seize and hold the Byzantine coastal towns, which were the keys to the hinterland. When, at the close of the century, this was done, Hassan ibn an Numan, basing himself on Kairouan, took Carthage in 695, and in a remarkably short time Latin civilization was extinguished in northern Africa.

Throughout the expansion, the conquest of Constantinople remained the ultimate Moslem goal, and the first attempt to attain it was made by the Caliph Othman (644–656) as early as 655. That year he sent out a naval expedition to effect it; but though the Byzantine fleet was decisively defeated, the assassination of Othman in the following year and the succession war which immediately broke out between Muawiya (660–680) and Ali, the son-in-law of the Prophet, forced its abandonment. In 659, occupied with Ali, Muawiya made peace with Byzantium. He was the founder of the Omayad line of Caliphs, with his capital at Damascus.

When he had consolidated his position, Muawiya returned to the project in 668. That year he sent an expedition into Asia

Minor–called by the Byzantines "Romania"–which occupied Chalcedon, from where, in the spring of 669, it crossed into Thrace and attacked Constantinople, though no serious siege was undertaken. In 672 Muawiya followed up this expedition by sending a fleet to win command of the Bosphorus, and from then until 677 Constantinople was attacked intermittently, each attack being frustrated by the fleet of Emperor Constantine IV (668–685). Loss of men and ships compelled the Moslems to withdraw, and during their return most of their fleet was lost in a storm and its remnants destroyed by the Byzantines. This disaster caused Muawiya for a second time to make peace.

On Muawiya's death, in 680, another war of succession occupied the greater part of the stormy reign of the Caliph Abd-al-Malik (685–705), and under his successor Walid (705–715) the Arabian Empire attained its greatest expansion. In the west the Atlantic coast was reached in 710, and Spain was overrun the following year. In the east the Arabs penetrated into the Punjab, and in central Asia reached the borders of China. In the last years of his reign Walid returned to the project of capturing Constantinople, and on his death in 715 it became an inheritance of his successor, the Caliph Suleiman.

CHAPTER 6

The siege of Constantinople, 717–718, and the Battle of Tours, 732

When, in 711, the Emperor Justinian II, who succeeded Constantine IV in 685, died, the Empire sank to the lowest level of impotence it had yet reached. Distracted, depopulated, plundered by Bulgars and Slavs in Europe and ravaged by the Saracens in Asia Minor, its army and fleet in constant mutiny, it appeared that its last days were at hand, when suddenly, in 717, out of the débris of twenty years of anarchy, a man created a new empire which was destined to become the bulwark of Europe against Asia for 700 years. A soldier by profession, this man is known to history as Leo the Isaurian.

Of his origin we know next to nothing. Probably he was a Syrian and not an Isaurian,[1] for he was born about the year 687 at Germanicea (Marash) in the province of Commagene, the north-easterly district of Syria. His true name was Conon, and we first hear of him and his family in 705 in Thrace, when his father made a gift of 500 sheep to Justinian, who in return made his son Leo a *spatharius* or aide-de-camp. Later, apparently to get rid of him, the Emperor sent him on a mission to Alania, a country north of the Caucasian mountains, and, after his return, the Emperor Anastasius (713–716), who was seeking out able soldiers, gave him command of the Anatolic theme. When in 716 Anastasius was deposed, all eyes were fixed upon Leo as the man best qualified to succeed him.

Meanwhile the Caliph Suleiman (715–717), as a first step toward carrying out Walid's projected expedition against Constantinople, sent two armies from Taurus into Romania, one under his brother Maslama and the other under a general named Suleiman. The latter advanced through the Anatolic theme and approached Amorium, which lay to the north of Lake Aksehir. Though it had no garrison, he was forced to blockade the city, and as he thought Leo destined to be the next emperor, he resorted to a ruse in order to capture him. In this he was unsuccessful, and

[1] Isauria, a district of Asia Minor on the north side of the Taurus, modern Konia.

when the siege of Amorium was raised, Leo, after having removed its women and children, garrisoned the city with 800 soldiers. Next, Maslama, who was advancing through Cappadocia, set out to trap Leo; but, like Suleiman, he was outwitted by the crafty Isaurian.

While this strange campaign of wits was being fought, Theodosius III (716–717) invested his son with the purple and posted him on the Asiatic side of the Sea of Marmara. First Leo assured himself that Maslama had evacuated Romania, then he advanced to Nicomedia (Ismid) and routed the young prince, whose name is unknown; after which he probably wintered at Nicaea or Nicomedia, and early in 717 crossed to Constantinople. This persuaded Theodosius to exchange the throne for a monastery, and on March 25 Leo was crowned by the Patriarch in St. Sophia and became Leo III (717–740).

Leo had not a moment to lose. The granaries and arsenals of Constantinople were replenished, its walls repaired and numerous engines of war mounted upon them. Strategically the city was immensely strong, virtually impregnable, as long as its sea communications were kept open. It was built on a promontory flanked on the north by the Golden Horn and on the south by the Sea of Marmara. On its western or landward side ran an inner and an outer wall; the former built by Constantine the Great and the latter by Theodosius II, which was some four miles in length. At this period the normal population numbered about half a million, but it must now have been swollen considerably with refugees. If strongly held, to take the city by storm was not, until the invention of gunpowder, a practical operation of war; therefore the only certain method was blockade. This meant closing the Bosphorus as well as the Dardanelles, and to close the former was difficult, because the city flanked its approach from the south. Therefore, for Leo, everything depended on his fleet, which numerically was vastly inferior to his enemy's.

Maslama's plan was a twofold one: to advance by land and sea and to surround the city. The army, some 80,000 strong, he kept under his own command, and the fleet he handed over to Suleiman the General; it is said to have numbered 1,800 vessels and to have had on board 80,000 infantry. Besides these, other forces were in preparation: 800 ships, probably mostly supply vessels, were being made ready in the ports of Africa and Egypt, and at Tarsus a reserve army was being formed under the Caliph.[1]

[1] All these figures are probably much exaggerated.

First, Maslama marched to Pergamum, and once he had taken it he next advanced to the Hellespont, crossed it at Abydus, probably in July, and appeared before the outer, landward wall of Constantinople on August 15, 717. There he entrenched his army and sent a detachment to watch Adrianople and Tervel, king of the Bulgars, with whom Leo was in communication.

A land attack was at once attempted; but when it was beaten back by the engines and the skill of the Byzantine engineers, Maslama surrounded his camp with a deep ditch and decided to reduce the city by blockade. To do this, he instructed Suleiman the General to divide his fleet into two squadrons, one to be stationed at Eutropius (Mundi Burnou) and Anthemius on the Asiatic coast, to cut off supplies from the Aegean, and the other to move through the Bosphorus to above Galata and to cut off the city from the Black Sea and, more particularly, from the cities of Cherson (near Sevastopool) and Trebizond.

The second squadron arrived on September 1, and on September 3 got under way to sail north of the Golden Horn, where Leo lay with his fleet. The entrance to the harbour was protected by a great chain suspended between two towers, from which it could be raised or lowered.

While the blockading squadron approached, the strong current which sweeps round Seraglio Point threw its advanced ships into confusion. At once Leo ordered the chain to be lowered, stood out with his galleys, and before his enemy could form a line of battle, poured Greek fire[1] upon his ships, destroyed twenty and captured others. Immediately after, when he saw the main body of Suleiman's fleet approaching, he returned to the inner waters of the Golden Horn.

This rapid and well-directed attack was so successful and terrifying that though, in order to entice his enemy on, Leo kept the boom lowered throughout the rest of that day and the following night, no further attempt was made to force the strait. A victory

---

[1] An inflammable composition. According to the *Chronography of Theophanes*, during the reign of Constantine Pogonatus (684–685) an architect named Callinicus, who fled from Heliopolis in Syria to Constantinople, prepared a "wet fire" which was projected by means of siphons. Lieut.-Colonel Hime (see his *Gunpowder and Ammunition, their Origin and Progress*, 1904) considers that it was composed of sulphur, naphtha and quicklime which took fire spontaneously when wetted, and that portions of it were "projected and at the same time ignited by applying the hose of a water engine to the breech of the siphon". Somewhat similar substances had long been in use, see Thucydides II, 77, and IV, 100: Siege of Delium, 424 B.C. Vegetius (c. A.D. 350) gives as a receipt naphtha or petroleum. (See also Gibbon's *The Decline and Fall of the Roman Empire*, vol. VI, pp. 9–12.)

had been won at practically no loss, so complete that Leo was able to pour supplies into Constantinople and prevent its reduction through famine. To add to Maslama's difficulties, his brother the Caliph, who was then on his way to reinforce him, suddenly died of indigestion.[1] He was succeeded by Omar II (717–730), a religious bigot and no soldier.

A partial investment had now to be resorted to, and during it winter set in with unwonted severity. For a hundred days snow lay on the ground, and unaccustomed to the rigours of a European winter, thousands of Moslems died, among them Suleiman the General. In spring the following year the Egyptian squadron from Alexandria, 400 ships in all, commanded by Sofiam, arrived, passed Constantinople under cover of darkness, took station at Kalos Argos (Buyuk-Deré), and closed the passage of the Bosphorus. Shortly after it was followed by the African squadron, 360 ships under Yezid, which cast anchor on the Bithynian shore. Finally, the reserve army, now under Merdasan, arrived to reinforce the garrisons of the trenches, which were so decimated by famine that many men were reduced to feed upon human flesh.

Though the closing of the Bosphorus would in time have compelled capitulation, fortunately for Leo large numbers of the Egyptian crews were impressed Christians, and many of these men deserted and provided him with exact information concerning the Moslems. He lowered the boom, again put to sea, fell upon his enemy and caught him completely unprepared. It was a rout rather than a battle; for the Christian crews deserted by thousands, and their unmanned vessels were rammed or burned with Greek fire. This decisive naval victory was, astonishing as it may seem, followed by a land pursuit; for immediately after Leo had destroyed the African squadron, he ferried over to the Asiatic shore a considerable force of soldiers, which trapped Merdasan in an ambush, cut many of his men to pieces and routed the rest.

Meanwhile, through his diplomacy, Leo had persuaded Tervel and his Bulgars to march against Maslama and they won a battle somewhere south of Adrianople in which 22,000 Moslems are said to have been killed. To add to the terror the Moslems now

---

[1] According to Gibbon (*The Decline and Fall of the Roman Empire*, vol. VI, p. 7), "The Caliph had emptied two baskets of eggs and figs, which he swallowed alternately, and the repast was concluded with marrow and sugar." In one of his pilgrimages to Mecca, Suleiman ate, at a single meal, seventy pomegranates, a kid, six fowls, and a huge quantity of the grapes of Tayeff . . . (Abulfeda, *Annal. Moslem*, p. 126, quoted by Gibbon).

were in, "A report was dexterously scattered that Franks, the unknown nations of the Latin world, were arming by sea and land in the defence of the Christian cause, and their formidable aid was expected. . . ."[1]

This last disaster persuaded the Caliph to recall Maslama, and on August 15, 718, he raised the siege, which had now lasted exactly twelve months. He embarked the remnants of his army and landed them at Cyzicus (Bal-Kis) on the Asiatic coast of the Sea of Marmara. His fleet stood out for the Hellespont and was lost in a storm. We are told that only five galleys of the 2,560 vessels employed in the siege returned to Syria and Alexandria. Of the land forces, which, according to Arab reckoning, must have totalled well over 200,000 men, no more than 30,000 regained Tarsus.

Thus Leo's victory was decisive, and further added to by his defeat of the Arabs at Acroinon (Afyon Karahisar) in Phrygia in 739, which compelled them to withdraw from western Asia Minor. It was his generalship which had won it, and every historian of his reign has dwelt upon its importance. Vasiliev writes: "It is justly claimed that by his successful resistance Leo saved not only the Byzantine Empire and the eastern Christian world, but also all of Western European civilization";[2] Bury calls 718 "an ecumenical date";[3] Foord considers that it was "the greatest success in Roman history";[4] Finlay, "that it was one of the most brilliant exploits of a warlike age";[5] and Gibbon calls the Moslem defeat an "almost incredible disaster".[6] This was not because of the ships lost and the men who perished, both of which could be replaced; but because the fall of Constantinople would have remodelled the entire history of the East, as seven centuries later it did. Beyond question, the Moslem repulse was one of the great decisive events in western history, for it saved Europe from invasion at the moment when a new power within its as yet un-defined frontiers was struggling into being. This power was the Frankish kingdom, which was now about to take the first step toward creating a new universal empire.

In 710—possibly a few years earlier—the Arab invasion of

---

[1] *The Decline and Fall of the Roman Empire*, vol. VI, p. 9.
[2] *History of the Byzantine Empire* (1928), vol. I, p. 289.
[3] *History of the Later Roman Empire* (1889), vol. II, p. 405.
[4] *The Byzantine Empire* (1911), p. 171.
[5] *History of Greece from its Conquest to Present Times* (1877), vol. II, p. 18.
[6] *The Decline and Fall of the Roman Empire*, vol. VI, p. 9.

Africa, as mentioned in Chronicle 11, had reached the shores of the Atlantic. It was only made possible because the Berbers or Moors – the Numidians of Hannibal's day – were able to supply the necessary men. Plunderers by nature, once the western sea was reached, in order to keep them employed, Musa ibn Nusair, governor of northern Africa, turned his gaze toward Spain. To conquer that country does not seem to have been his intention, instead, merely to raid it, and as he had no ships he approached a certain Julian,[1] the Byzantine governor of Ceuta. This man readily agreed to assist him, for he bore a grudge against Roderic, the Visigothic king in Toledo, who had dishonoured his daughter. Promised four vessels by Julian, Musa sought permission of the Caliph, then established at Damascus, to invade Spain. Grudgingly he agreed, for he replied: Do not for the present expose a large army to the dangers of an expedition beyond the seas. The issue was that, during the summer of 710, Abu Zora Tarif and 400 men crossed the strait, pillaged the neighbourhood of Algeciras and returned with plunder.

Encouraged by this reconnaissance, and having heard that Roderic was engaged in a war with the Franks and Vascons in the north of Spain, in 711 Musa decided upon an extensive expedition, and in batches of 400 men at the time, for he still had no more than Julian's four ships, he sent over 7,000 under Tarik ibn Ziyad. Tarik landed at Gibraltar, did not wait for Musa and the main body, but pushed westward along the coast, met Roderic in the Valley of the Wadi Bekka (Salado), between Lake Janda and the town of Medina Sidonia, and thanks to treachery in Roderic's army, on July 19 he routed him. Tarik won another battle at Ecija and occupied Toledo, the Visigothic capital. Next year Musa took over the supreme command, and by showing leniency to all who submitted and by using violence against all who opposed him,[2] he conquered nearly the whole of Spain before the close of the year, when he was recalled by the Caliph.

No sooner was Spain overrun than the Moorish-Moslem horde flowed over the Pyrenees into Aquitaine, then ruled by Duke Eudo; according to M. Mercier, this invasion began in 712.[3] In 717-718, Musa's successor, Hurr, set out on a full-scale plundering expedition, which in idea seems to have become more and more

---

[1] Also called Urban and Olban, probably a Christian Berber.
[2] See *Invasions des Sarrazins en France*, Reinaud (1836), p. 8.
[3] *Revue Historique* (May, 1878), "La Bataille de Poitiers", E. Mercier, p. 3. Part of the Visigothic kingdom lay north of the Pyrenees.

an invasion of conquest as the siege of Constantinople lagged and ultimately failed; for we are told that the Moslem intention was to push through France and to return to Damascus by way of Germany, taking Constantinople on the way, and thus to make the Mediterranean a Moslem sea.[1] In 719 Narbonne was occupied, and two years later, when Samḥ laid siege to Toulouse, he was defeated by Eudo and routed. In spite of this defeat, the Moslem flood returned; in 725 Carcassonne and Nîmes were occupied and, the following year, Anbaca advanced up the Rhône valley, ravaged Burgundy and penetrated as far north as the Vosges.[2]

When this incursion took place, the future conqueror of the Moors was warring on the Danube; he was Charles, son of Pepin II, and the sworn enemy of Eudo of Aquitania.

To appreciate the relationship between these two men, who soon were to act in unison, it is necessary to go back into history. At the battle of Châlons legend affirms that the Salian Frankish *feoderati* who joined Aetius were led by a chieftain called Merovech (Merovaeus) who founded the Merovingian dynasty, which in power reached its zenith under Clovis his grandson, who by his victory at Vouillé, in 507, finally drove the Visigoths out of France into Spain. But since 639 this dynasty had fallen into decay and had produced a succession of *rois fainéants*.[3] Under these effete kings all power passed into the hands of the Mayor of the Palace,[4] the old Master of the Trooops, of whom the most able came from Austrasia, the region roughly lying between the Meuse and the Main. Of this line, Pepin II established himself as mayor in 687, and made himself master of Austrasia, Neustria (between the Loire and Meuse) and Aquitania (between the Garonne and Loire). When in 714 he died, his natural son Charles was in prison accused of the murder of Pepin's legitimate son Grimoald and the mayoralty passed to his son, a minor. In the circumstances, as was all but inevitable, anarchy swept Gaul, and in the turmoil Charles escaped from prison and Eudo proclaimed his independence. Charles collected a band of adherents, first established himself in Austrasia, and next, in 719, he marched against Eudo,

---

[1] See *Invasions des Sarrazins*, Reinaud, p. 9, and *Cambridge Medieval History*, vol. II, p. 373.

[2] *Revue Historique* (May 1878), "La Bataille de Poitiers", E. Mercier, p. 4.

[3] "It was a dynasty of children; they died at the age of 23, 24 or 25, worn out by precocious debauchery. They were fathers at sixteen, fifteen and even fourteen years, and their children were miserable weaklings" (*Cambridge Medieval History*, vol. II, 125–126).

[4] For his functions see *Histoire de France*, edit. Ernest Lavisse, vol. II, pt. I, pp. 176–177.

defeated him near Soissons and subdued Neustria. With Eudo brought to terms, he set out to war against the Germans, Saxons, and Swabians, in order to secure his north-eastern frontier before he subjected Aquitania, and in 725 he was warring on the Danube when he learnt of Anbaca's advance up the Rhône.

Meanwhile Eudo, though he knew nothing of Charles's intention to establish his authority over the whole of Gaul, nevertheless realized the precariousness of his position, wedged between the Franks in Neustria and the Moslems in Spain. Therefore, to secure his southern frontiers, he entered into relations with a Berber potentate named Othman ben abi Neza, whose realm lay on the northern side of the Pyrenees, and cemented an alliance with him by marrying his daughter Lampagie, a girl of remarkable beauty. Realizing that Eudo could not at the same time defend both his southern and northern frontiers, Abd-ar-Rahman, Governor of Spain, set out to punish the rebellious Othman, and in 731 he chased him into the mountains, when, to escape capture, the latter leapt over a precipice, and Lampagie, because of her beauty, was sent to Damascus to adorn the Caliph's harem.

Eudo's Moslem ally overcome, Abd-ar-Rahman decided to invade Aquitaine. His object was undoubtedly plunder and not the conquest of France; yet again it would seem that in his head there lurked the possibility of "uniting Italy, Germany and the empire of the Greeks to the already vast domains of the champions of the Koran".[1] He concentrated his main army along the upper reaches of the Ebro, took the road to Pamplona, crossed the Bidassoa at Irun and advanced into Gascony. His army cannot have been large, because we are told that it marched in a single column, and when it was moving north an independent force was detached to strike at Arles, in order to distract the enemy and spread terror throughout Aquitaine.

Directing his course on Bordeaux, Eudo met him there and was defeated decisively, and the city was stormed, plundered and burnt. The valley of the Garonne left behind him, Abd-ar-Rahman moved north and crossed the Dordogne, pillaging and massacring as he advanced. In order to plunder more freely, he split his army into several columns and moved on Tours; for he had heard that its abbey possessed untold treasures. At Poitiers, some sixty miles south of Tours, he found its gates closed to him, invested the city, and then continued his advance.

[1] *Invasions des Sarrazins en France*, Reinaud, p. 35.

Meanwhile Charles, his Saxon and Danubean conquests finished, had arrived in Neustria, from where, in 731, he crossed the Loire and ravaged Berri. Placed thus between two fronts,

14. HUNNISH AND MOSLEM INVASIONS OF FRANCE,
451 AND 732

Eudo had no option but to turn to Charles, hurried to Paris and won his support on the condition that he submitted to Frankish control. Then, at the head of a horde of fighting men, Charles

235

crossed the Loire, probably at Orléans. Abd-ar-Rahman, whose army was now loaded with loot, then fell back upon Poitiers.

Of Abd-ar-Rahman's military organization little is known, except that the bulk of his men were Moors and that most of them were mounted. The bow seems to have been little used by them, instead the lance and sword, and armour was seldom worn. It is known that many mules followed the fighting troops; but it would seem that these animals were used mainly for carrying plunder and not supplies. The army lived on the country, was followed by a rabble of cut-throats, and its tactics were wasteful of men, for they consisted entirely in wild, headlong charges.

Of the Frankish army we have a more detailed account. Unlike the Gothic, the infantry arm solely was relied upon. It was divided into two classes of men, the General's private host, which had to be constantly employed, for plunder was the only remuneration it received, and local levies, a militia of ill-armed men. The host had been trained in many wars, and the levies were little more than foragers. The whole organization was primitive in the extreme and could only be kept together as long as food was obtainable. When it was not, it dissolved.[1] Of discipline there was virtually none; things were much the same as they had been in the days of Gregory of Tours when he wrote: "What were we to do? no one fears his king, no one fears his duke, no one respects his count; and if perchance any of us tries to improve his state of affairs, and to assert his authority, forthwith sedition breaks out in the army, and mutiny swells up."[2]

It would seem that in the Frankish army horses were seldom used, except by the nobles, and then only on the line of march. Armour rapidly was coming into vogue again; for, in 574, we find Bishop Saggettarius blamed for going to war "armed not with the sign of the heavenly cross, but with the secular cuirass and helmet", and, in 585, Gundovald Ballomer was saved by his body armour from a javelin.[3] The shield was universal, and arms consisted of swords, daggers, javelins, and two kinds of axes, one for wielding and the other for throwing—the *francisca*.

Though tactics were crude, Charles, a good general, understood his enemy's weakness. According to Gibbon, he wrote to Eudo: "If you follow my advice you will not interrupt their

[1] For further particulars see *Histoire de France*, edit. Ernest Lavisse, vol. II, pt. I, pp. 191–194.
[2] *Gregory of Tours*, IX, 31.   [3] *Ibid.*, IV, 18, and VII, 38.

march nor precipitate your attack. They are like a torrent, which it is dangerous to stem in its career. The thirst of riches and the consciousness of success, redouble their valour, and valour is of more avail than arm or numbers. Be patient till they have loaded themselves with the encumbrance of wealth. The possession of wealth will divide their counsels and assure your victory."[1]

The sudden appearance of Charles caused consternation among the Moslems, for by now they were so weighed down with loot that they had lost all mobility; so encumbered that Abd-ar-Rahman contemplated abandoning his plunder, but did not do so, possibly because his men would have refused to obey him, and possibly also because Charles did not press him; for we are told that the two armies faced each other for seven days. What occurred during this pause is obvious: Abd-ar-Rahman withdrew his plunder southward, and Charles awaited the arrival of his levies.

Of the battle itself we have few details, nor do we even know where it was actually fought, but the date given is October, 732. Probably the armies came into contact somewhere near Tours and skirmished for a while. Next, that Abd-ar-Rahman fell back towards Poitiers,[2] and when he found that his loot had got no farther south, decided to accept battle in order to cover its withdrawal.

As the Moslems were solely an offensive force and lacked defensive power, this meant that, whatever the circumstances, Abd-ar-Rahman was forced to attack. Clearly realizing this, Charles drew up his army in solid phalanx, the kernel of which consisted of his Frankish followers. Isidore de Béja calls it an army of Europeans (*Europenses*) because it was composed of men speaking many languages.

As was usual with the Moslems, the battle was opened with a furious cavalry charge, which was repeated again and again; nevertheless, the Frankish phalanx remained unshaken. "The men of the North", says one chronicler, "stood as motionless as a wall; they were like a belt of ice frozen together, and not to be dissolved, as they slew the Arab with the sword. The Austrasians, vast of limb, and iron of hand, hewed on bravely in the thick of the

---

[1] *The Decline and Fall of the Roman Empire*, Edward Gibbon, vol. VI, p. 15, and *Histoire de la Gaule Méridionale*, etc., Fauriel, vol. III, p. 127.

[2] In all there were three famous battles fought at or near Poitiers: the first in 507, that of Clovis and his Franks against the Visigoths, in which he slew Alaric II with his own hand and added Aquitaine to his dominions; the second, the one here described; and the third fought by the Black Prince on September 19, 1356.

fight; it was they who found and cut down the Saracen King."[1]
Seemingly, toward evening Eudo and his Aquitanians turned
one of the Moslem flanks, and launched an attack on Abd-ar-
Rahman's camp, in which the bulk of his loot was still stacked.
Upon this the Moslems fell back, and only then discovered that
Abd-ar-Rahman had been killed. Night set in and the battle
ended.

On the following morning, Charles again drew up his army to
meet a second attack, when his scouts reported to him that the
Moslem camp had been abandoned. Apparently, seized by
panic at the loss of their leader, the Moslems and Moors had fled
south and left the bulk of their plunder behind them.

There was no pursuit and the reasons for this are apparent.
First, Charles could not pursue a retiring mounted force; secondly,
the capture of the plunder prohibited such an operation; and
thirdly, it was not Charles's policy entirely to relieve Eudo of
Moslem pressure; for it was solely the threat from the south which
enabled the Franks to keep some hold over Aquitaine. So he
collected the loot and recrossed the Loire, to become known
to posterity as Charles Martel – "The Hammer". "*Comme le
martiaus debrise et froisse le fer et l'acier, et tous les autres metaux,
aussi froissait-il et brisait-il par la bataille tous ses ennemis et toutes
autres nations.*"[2]

Of the casualties, fantastic figures are given, mounting to
360,000 Moslems killed; and Charles's losses are stated to have
been 1,500. Probably the forces engaged were not large, and for
the simple reason that, as neither side possessed a supply train, it
would have been impossible for hundreds of thousands of men to
face each other for even seven days without starving. Of the
results of this famous battle Gibbon writes:

"A victorious line of march had been prolonged above a thousand
miles from the rock of Gibraltar to the banks of the Loire; the
repetition of an equal space would have carried the Saracens to
the confines of Poland and the Highlands of Scotland: The Rhine
is not more impassable than the Nile or Euphrates, and the Arabian
fleet might have sailed without a naval combat into the mouth of
the Thames. Perhaps the interpetation of the Koran would now
be taught in the schools of Oxford, and her pupils might demon-

[1] Quoted from Oman's *The Art of War in the Middle Ages*, vol. I, p. 58; also *L'art
militaire et les armées au moyen age*, Ferdinand Lot (1946), vol. I, p. 113.
[2] "Chronicle of Saint-Denis", quoted in *Recueil des Historiens des Gaules*, Bouquet,
vol. III, p. 310 (compiled *c.* 1270).

strate to a circumcised people the sanctity and truth of the revelation of Mahomet."[1]

This apocalyptic picture has long been discounted; yet, as frequently happens, the pendulum of criticism has swung too far in the opposite direction. Though, in effect, Charles's victory cannot be compared with Leo's, it was nevertheless one of the decisive victories in the history of Europe, if only because it was the epilogue of Leo's masterpiece. Had Constantinople fallen in 717, there can be little doubt that Moslem pressure in the east would have stimulated Moslem conquest in the west; and, if this probability is accepted, then it follows that it was Leo as much as Charles Martel who saved France. Nevertheless the immediate factor which halted further Moslem expansion in the west was the Berber revolt in Morocco, the cause of which briefly was as follows:

About the time of the battle of Tours, internal dissensions broke out within the Arabian Empire, for though the Arabs were united by the bond of Islam they continued to maintain their tribal institutions and with them their old feuds and factions. Of the latter the two most important were the Maadites and the Yemenites, the one representing the original northern tribes and the other the original southern tribes of Arabia. The Meccans belonged to the former and the Medinians to the latter. When the Maadites gained the upper hand, the Berbers in Africa refused to obey them, rose in revolt and the whole territory of what now is Morocco seceded. The final result was that out of the turmoil most of Spain became an independent Moorish state, the Christian kingdoms of Leon, Castile, and Navarre, as well as the County of Barcelona took form, and in Africa a series of independent states was gradually precipitated. But the important point to note is that, because of the revolt immediately after Abd-ar-Rahman's defeat at Tours, the Arab leaders in Spain were cut off from the Caliph in Damascus, and because of the revolution in Morocco they were no longer able to recruit their Berber armies. Added to this, it is highly probably that, because plunder was the main incentive which kept the Berbers in the field, Charles's victory added much to the general confusion.

But the real importance of the battle of Tours lies in quite another direction. It was not that Charles's victory saved western Europe from Arab rule, and, therefore, prevented the Koran

[1] *The Decline and Fall of the Roman Empire*, vol. VI, p. 15.

from being taught at Oxford, but that it made Charles supreme in Gaul and enabled him to establish his dynasty. As H. Pirenne writes: "Without Islam the Frankish Empire would probably never have existed and Charlemagne, without Mahomet, would be inconceivable."[1]

In 735 Eudo died at the age of sixty-six, and Charles overran Aquitaine and compelled his two sons to do homage to him, after which for four years he undertook several campaigns against the Moslems in the Rhône valley, and so completely undermined their power that a few years later they withdrew south of the Pyrenees for good.

Throughout these many wars his supreme difficulty was always the payment of his army. Money was scarce, and as the Roman system of taxation had vanished in the general chaos, two alternatives remained: plunder or the sequestration of lands and estates. Because many of the latter were in the hands of the Church, frequently it happened that Charles seized them in order to reward his turbulent vassals. This brought him into conflict with the Papacy, and how violently may be judged by the stories which accumulated round his name. After his death in 741 Gibbon writes: "His merits were forgotten", and "His sacrilege alone was remembered".[2] Thus it came about that as the years passed, not a few of his successes were credited by ecclesiastical writers to his grandson, Charles the Great–Charlemagne.

Six years before the battle of Poitiers was fought and for many years after it, a still more violent dispute had arisen between the Papacy and Leo III; a quarrel which caused Pope Gregory III, in 739, to appeal to Charles and to offer him the significant, yet undefined title of Roman consul. This quarrel was the first fruit of the siege of Constantinople.

The siege had vastly increased Leo's prestige, and he at once began to invest it in a series of reforms, out of which a new Eastern Empire emerged. Not only was he the ablest general of his age, but also its greatest statesman; for besides knowing how to win a war, he knew how to win the peace ensuing. The reforms which he introduced fall under three main headings: military, civil, and religious; they were all-embracing. The army was overhauled and a police force created; the judicial system was entirely reformed, and order and justice were established; the whole of the financial

---

[1] "Mahomet et Charlemagne", in *Revue belge de philologie et d'histoire* (1922), I, p. 86.
[2] *The Decline and Fall*, vol. VI, p. 18.

system was reorganized, and industry, agriculture and trade encouraged. He realized that it would be impossible to enforce these reforms in his Italian provinces and he decided to let Italy fend for itself. The effect of this was threefold: it opened Rome to the incursions of the Lombards; it eased his path in carrying out his religious reforms; and the two together brought upon his head the anathemas of the Papacy and widened the gap between the Eastern (Orthodox) Church and the Western (Catholic).[1]

Strange as it may seem, it was his contact with Islam which precipitated and shaped his religious reforms. A man of inquiring mind who was not beneath learning from his enemies, he saw that the Moslem successes were founded upon a high morality, a firm discipline, and above all a fanatical belief in the unity of God, a God who had no rivals or collaborators. Yet, when he looked at his own people, what did he see? As Iorga says, that "What was lacking in a society for long accustomed to an autocratic government was the autocrat himself".[2] This deficiency he determined to make good by reducing the immense powers and privileges of the Church, and the means he decided to employ were, by prohibiting the worship of images, icons, and relics, to liberate the people from the thralls of the clergy and monks who relied on image-worship as their strongest tool in securing the allegiance of the masses and in extracting money from them.

Thus opened the great inconoclastic controversy, an extremely complex problem, for its political implications were as involved as its theological. To appreciate this, it is only necessary to realize that at this date the monasteries and their vast estates were exempt from taxation; that education was in their hands; that the number of their monks has been estimated at 100,000,[3] and that this vast segregation of unproductive man-power seriously influenced industry and agriculture, and deprived the army of thousands of recruits. Further, the Asiatic provinces of the Empire were strongly iconoclastic, and in consequence religious friction with the European was endemic.

The first edict against image-worship was not promulgated until the year 726, and if it did not accomplish its end, it came as a

[1] Though final separation did not come until 1054 when Pope Leo IX smote Michael Cerularius and the whole of the Eastern Church with an excommunication; from the middle of the eighth century onward separation was nominal if not actual, and was inevitable from the day Constantine the Great transferred his capital to Byzantium.
[2] Histoire de la vie Byzantine (1934), vol. II, p. 17.
[3] History of the Byzantine Empire, A. A. Vasiliev, vol. I, p. 314.

salutary shock to the sorcery which was replacing religion. At once the Papacy thundered forth its disapproval, and the result was that, by the time Leo died, on June 18, 740, in the orthodox histories he was represented as little better than a Saracen. Nevertheless the influences of this quarrel, both on peace and war, were profound. A new life was breathed into the Byzantine Empire, which kept it virile for over three hundred years, and during them it became the reservoir of culture, which in time was destined to be drawn upon by western Europe.

Leo and Charles were, therefore, the parents of vital historical changes which would not have occurred had the one lost Constantinople or·had the other been defeated at Tours. Separated by fifteen hundred miles of barbaric ignorance, their influences upon history were as complementary as their lives. Both emerged out of chaos; both won great victories over a common enemy; the one saved the East and the other heralded a new imperialism in the West.

The rebirth of imperialism in western Europe

In the year 751, Pepin the Short, who ten years before had succeeded his father Charles Martel as Mayor of the Palace, with the sanction of Pope Zacharias set aside the effete Childeric III and was crowned by St. Boniface "*Gratia Dei Rex Francorum*". Soon after he was re-crowned by Pope Stephen II and the title "Patrician of the Romans" was conferred upon him. Thus the Merovingian dynasty gave way to the Carolingian, and out of gratitude for the extraordinary powers granted him, Pepin marched against the Lombards, wrested the exarchate of Ravenna from them, and presented it to the Pope, and thereby created the Papal States, which endured until 1870.

Pepin died on September 24, 768, and was succeeded by his two sons, Charles and Carloman. On the death of the latter, in 771, the former was left sole ruler of Frankland, and was to become known to history as Charlemagne, or Charles the Great.

Great both in body and mind, his master idea was to bring all western peoples into one vast Christian empire, and in the realization of this mission, by the end of his reign he had established his rule from the Baltic to the Tiber and from the Elbe and Böhmerwald to the Atlantic and the Pyrenees.

In order to maintain his authority over the turbulent peoples of this vast area, Charles made systematic use of fortified posts. Each district was, so to say, picketed by a number of palisaded "burgs", which could be used as pivots of manœuvre by his mobile forces. The emphasis was on quality rather than quantity, and as these forces consisted mainly of armoured cavalry, the poorer classes were relieved from the burden of war. Such foot soldiers that he raised were not as they had been hitherto, a rabble carrying clubs and agricultural implements, but a well-equipped force armed with sword, spear, and bow. Further, each count was compelled to provide his horsemen with shield, lance, sword, bow, and dagger. Charles realized that no army could be really mobile as long as it relied on foraging and was unable to storm walled cities, and he organized two separate trains, one for siege and the other for supply.

In these changes we see the first blossoming of a new military order, the feudal, which provided the security necessary for Christendom to take root and to grow. But as the Church was the ministry of the eternal, and the feudal state represented no more than the temporal, it followed that complete religious dominance could only become possible when war, as much as peace, was conducted according to the rulings of the Church. Out of this struggle for dominance emerged the medieval conception of war as a trial by battle, in which the Church refereed for God. War was not prohibited, nor were attempts made to abolish it, because it was recognized as part of man's very nature, the fruit of original sin, which was the fulcrum of the Church's power. Therefore, war could only be restricted and mitigated by Christianizing – ennobling – the warrior and by limiting its duration.

As war teaches men how to die bravely, war is the school of heroism: such was the pagan ideal. But as death is the portal of the life eternal, war must also be the school of righteousness, or death can lead only to eternal damnation: such is the Christian outlook. Thus the classical soldier is transformed into the idealized Christian knight of chivalry, "uniting", as Lecky writes, "all the force and fire of the ancient warrior with something of the tenderness and humility of the Christian saint . . . and although this ideal, like all others, was a creation of the imagination not often perfectly realized in life, yet it remained the type and model of warlike excellence to which many generations aspired".

The fighter ennobled, the next task was to restrict his activities by sanctions and rules. The first step taken toward this end was the establishment of "The Peace of God" (*Pax Dei*), which is first heard of in the year 990. Its aim was to protect ecclesiastical buildings, clerics, pilgrims, women and peasants from the ravages of war; also cattle and agricultural instruments. The means to enforce this peace were religious sanctions – excommunication and nterdict – and though the results were meagre, these sanctions did effect something, for in the eyes of Christendom they branded the aggressor the culprit.

The ennoblement of war carried with it two further restrictions. The first was, that as only men of wealth and position could afford armour, war was placed on an aristocratic footing. And as the wearing of armour led to in-fighting, missile warfare was restricted, and in consequence, casualties were reduced. Many of the battles of this period were no more than shock skirmishes between small bodies of armoured knights, in which individual combats were sought, rather to prove the worth of the fighter than his destructive capabilities. The object was to unhorse his opponent rather than to slay him, and then to put him to ransom. In brief, battles were frequent little more than sharp-weapon tourneys in which ransom was the prize.

The second was an attempt by the Church to limit the use of missile weapons which were likely to proletarianize war, such as the arbalest or crossbow. Though the origins of this weapon are unknown, it would appear to have come into use at the beginning of the eleventh century. It was the most deadly missile thrower before the introduction of the longbow. In 1139 the Second Lateran Council forbade its use–except against infidels–under penalty of anathema "as a weapon hateful to God and unfit for Christians". Yet, in spite of this, its adoption was fairly general, except in England.

It is important to bear these restrictions in mind when we consider the warcraft of this period, for though, as Sir Charles Oman points out, the accession of Charles the Great marks the birth of a new epoch in the art of war, that epoch was essentially romantic. "The hero of the imagination of Europe", as Lecky remarks, "was no longer a hermit, but a King, a warrior, a knight. . . ." The age of the ascetic and of martyrdom was fast withering and the age of chivalry blossoming.

This romanticism was thrilled into life by Charles's conquests, which had raised him above the narrow limits of a national king, and his self-imposed mission to convert the entire German world into a Christian empire demanded that his authority should assume a theocratic and universal form. "If the Christian teaching", points out Professor G. L. Burr, "was to conquer the world, political power must be aimed at along with the spread of the faith." Therefore two forces were required–a spiritual and a secular. The one existed, the other had to be created, and as frequently happens when times demand a radical change, an accident brought it about.

In April, 799, Pope Leo III, accused of adultery and perjury, fled to Charles's court at Paderborn, and was sent back by Charles to Rome and reinstated. As this annoyed the anti-papal party, in the autumn of 800 Charles went to Italy and settled the dispute. On Christmas Day, clothed in the robe of a patrician, he entered St. Peter's, kneeled before the altar, and Leo took from it a crown and placed it upon his head. Then the multitude shouted: "Hail to Charles the Augustus, crowned of God, the great and peace-bringing Emperor of the Romans." After this cry of homage, Leo offered him the adoration due to the Byzantine Emperors and proclaimed him Emperor and Augustus. Thus the birthday of Christ was the birthday of the new Western Roman Empire.[1]

This sudden crowning took Charles completely by surprise, and though the Frankish Annals give no reason for it, it may be conjectured that it was Leo's reward for the services Charles had rendered him. Be this as it may, it raised Charles from the position of a Frankish king to that of the consecrated lord of Christendom, and since for long past the faith represented by the Pope had been one, from now onward the temporal authority over the realm of that faith became one also in the Emperor. The consequences of the coronation were vast: it was, as Bryce says, "the central event of the Middle Ages".

Charles's empire did not survive his death, and its disintegration and eventual resurrection were vastly influenced by two great ethnic upheavals: the coming of the Vikings[2] in the ninth century and of the Magyars in the tenth. The latter were a Ural-Altaic people who in 895 occupied the region of the upper Theiss, and by doing so divided the northern from the southern and the western from the eastern Slavs, and in consequence altered the course of European history. Between 907 and 955 they were the scourge and terror of central Europe.

The anarchy following these incursions, coupled with that created by the Vikings and Slavs, resulted in West Frankland reverting to its tribal divisions of Saxony, Bavaria, Franconia, Swabia, and Thuringia, each under its own duke. Although these duchies tended toward becoming separate kingdoms, they could not altogether afford to dispense with a central government. Nevertheless, anarchy continued until 918, when Conrad I (911–918)–then nominal King of Germany–offered the crown to Henry the Fowler (919–936), son of Otto the Illustrious, Duke

[1] Since in 800 the theory still held that there was but one Roman Empire, not until 812, when the Byzantine Emperor Michael I Rangabé (811–813) saluted Charles as Emperor Basileus, was his imperial election legalized. Thence, theoretically, two emperors ruled the single empire, as they had done in the days of Honorius and Arcadius, the Byzantine Empire becoming the eastern half and the Frankish the western.

[2] A generic term for the Scandinavian sea rovers of the ninth and tenth centuries; called also Northmen or Norsemen, Danes and Varangians, according to the localities of their operations. The word is derived from "vik", an inlet, creek, or bay, and as "wick" is to be found in many English place-names.

of Saxony, as the only man able to cope with the prevailing disorder.

A born soldier and able statesman, Henry subdued Swabia and Bavaria, annexed Lorraine, drove back the Slavs and Magyars, and finally reunited all Germany. On his death in 936, he was succeeded by his son Otto I (936–973), known as the Great, a brother-in-law of King Athelstan of England. He overthrew the Magyars at Lechfeld, near Augsburg, in 955, and next forced the Bohemians, then the strongest Slav state, to pay tribute to him. In 961 he was called to Rome by Pope John XII, who needed his aid. There, on February 2, 962, he was crowned by John, and after the customary courtesies and promises had been exchanged between them, John owned himself his subject, and the citizens of Rome swore that in the future no pontiff would be elected without the Emperor's consent. Thus, by vesting the sovereignty of Germany and Italy in a German prince, the Holy Roman Empire, as it was known in later centuries, came into being. It was a prolongation of the empire of Charles, and as Bryce says, "not a mere successor after an interregnum, but rather a second foundation of the imperial throne of the West".

Before these changes, the Vikings – the wagon-folk of the seas – had swept up the creeks and rivers of western Europe, and though the first of their raids came early in the reign of Charles the Great, it was not until after his death that they grew more and more formidable. In 850 the whole manhood of Scandinavia took to the sea, and the half-century which followed was one of the darkest in European history.

These incursions, which were carried as far as Novgorod, Sicily, Iceland, Greenland, and America, vastly stimulated the military organization initiated by Charles. As ill-armed levies were useless, professional soldiers became essential, and because mounted men alone could keep pace with the raiders, more and more did military power pass into the hands of the nobility. Thus, out of these troubled times, emerged a completely feudalized society based on the stronghold and the mounted knight. In England alone were other means adopted by King Alfred (871–900); for although he also relied on fortifications, instead of raising cavalry he built a fleet and beat the Vikings on their own element. This led to the English continuing to rely upon infantry, while on the Continent cavalry became the dominant arm.

Of these many incursions, the two most pregnant with future

events were those made against England and northern France. Both began with plundering raids, were succeeded by settlements and finally developed into conquests. The former, which began at the end of the ninth century, ended when England was annexed to Denmark under King Cnut (995–1035) to become part of his Scandinavian empire. The latter dates from 896, when a Viking named Rollo or Rolf came to France. For a time he struggled against Charles the Simple (893–929), and in 911, Charles, unable to overcome him, by the treaty of Saint Clair-sur-Epte, agreed to cede to him and his followers the region of the lower Seine on condition that they were baptized, and he himself did homage to him for his lands. Thus was created the Duchy of Normandy, which by 933 extended to the Breton border. Thus also was the stage set for the struggle between Normandy and England.

In brief, the events which led to this climax were as follows:

In the year 1002, as some historians suppose, in order to deny the harbours of Normandy as refuges to the Danish invaders, Aethelred II, the Unraed (of No-Counsel) or Unready, married Emma, sister of Rollo's great-grandson, Richard II of Normandy. Next, in 1013, during the invasion of England by Swein Forkbeard, King of Denmark, Aethelred, his wife and two sons, Alfred and Edward, fled to Normandy and were kindly received by Richard. A few weeks later Swein died, and when Aethelred returned to England, Cnut, the younger of Swein's two sons, found himself unready to meet him and carried the Danish fleet back to Denmark to recruit fresh forces. In 1015 he returned and within four months of his landing established himself firmly in Wessex. On Aethelred's death, in the following year, the war against the Danes was continued by Edmund Ironside, son of Aethelred by his first wife Aelfgifu. After fighting six battles, in 1016 Edmund was defeated decisively at Ashingdon (Assandun), and came to an agreement with Cnut. By its terms Edmund was to keep Wessex, and the whole of England north of the Thames was to go to Cnut. This settlement was short-lived, for on November 30 Edmund died, and in order to avert a renewal of the war, the West Saxons accepted Cnut as king of all England. Edmund's two young sons, Edmund and Edward, were then banished by Cnut, and to avert assassination they sought refuge in Hungary. The next year, to forestall any action by Richard of Normandy on behalf of his nephews–Aethelred's and Emma's two sons–Cnut entered into treaty with Richard and married Emma.

Cnut's empire included the kingdoms of England, Denmark, and Norway, and on his death in 1035, like Charles the Great's, it was divided between his three sons. Swein took Norway, Harthacnut Denmark, and Harold, surnamed Harefoot, claimed England. The first and third were Cnut's alleged sons by Aelfgifu of Northampton, and the second his legitimate son by Emma; therefore, so far as succession was concerned Harthacnut had a better claim than Harold to the English throne. But there were other candidates in the field who had as good, if not a better claim than either — namely, the sons of Edmund Ironside and those of Aethelred and Emma. The former were out of reach in Hungary, and the latter were no longer under the care of the friendly Robert I who had succeeded Richard II in 1028 and who had died in 1035. He had left his duchy in the hands of his son William, later to become known as the Conqueror, but as he was not yet eight years of age, and his duchy was distracted, he was not capable of intervening on behalf of the Aetheling Alfred and his brother.

In order to settle the question of succession, a national Witanagemot was convened at Oxford, and there, after much contention, Harold was elected but not crowned. Taking advantage of the broil, the Aetheling Alfred, supported by Baldwin V of Flanders, landed in England, and when on his way to London was met by Godwine, Earl of Wessex, who had been Cnut's chief lieutenant. Godwine greeted him in a friendly way and trapped him and his party during the night. He seized the Aetheling and sent him to London, and Harold had him blinded in so brutal a way that shortly after he died. Harold was then re-elected and acknowledged king, and Emma was expelled and found refuge with Baldwin of Flanders.

In 1040 Harold died, and the Witan, with general approval, elected Harthacnut, who so far had not pressed his claim to the English throne because Denmark was threatened by Magnus the Good of Norway, who had succeeded Swein in 1036. Not until a treaty between the two was arranged which provided that should either die without heir, his kingdom would pass to the survivor, was Harthacnut free to turn his attention to England. He landed at Sandwich about June 17, 1040, and was well received and hallowed king.

Because Harthacnut was childless and unmarried, in 1041 he invited his half-brother Edward, still in Normandy, to return to England, a request which implied a tacit recognition of Edward as heir presumptive to the throne. A year later, on June 8, Harthacnut died, and, according to the *Anglo-Saxon Chronicle*, "before he was buried all the people chose Edward as king in London"; yet it was not until Easter Sunday, April 3, 1043, that at Winchester he was consecrated king by Archbishop Eadsige.

Edward, later surnamed the Confessor, was not only half Norman by blood but fully Norman by upbringing, for he had resided in the duchy since 1013. His following was Norman and he was surrounded by Norman priests and clergy. The upshot was that England was soon divided between two parties, a pro-English, led by Godwine of Wessex, and a pro-Norman, supported by Leofric of Mercia and Siward of Northumbria, and to strengthen his position Godwine married his third son, Tostig, to Judith, sister of Baldwin V of Flanders. In 1051 a crisis was reached, and Godwine and his sons Swein, Harold, Tostig, Leofwine, and Gyrth were outlawed and fled oversea.

No sooner had the dominance of the Norman party been established than an event occurred which was destined to change the axis of English history. Duke William of Normandy, Edward's cousin, now about twenty-four years old, came to England, and all we are told of his visit is that he arrived with a great force of Frenchmen, that Edward received him, loaded him with presents and sent him home. Yet, considering the situation in England at the time, and that Edward was childless and vowed to perpetual chastity, it is all but inconceivable that the visit was a mere act of courtesy. Far more probable is it that the question of succession was discussed, and that William left for home with a claim of some sort to the English crown in his pocket.

Be this as it may, in the following year the entire situation was reversed. Godwine returned, was supported by the people, and Edward was compelled to restore to him his earldom. Further, we are told that "all the Frenchmen who had promoted injustices and passed unjust judgments and given bad counsel in the country" were outlawed. It was a complete triumph for the English party, and again the question of succession arose; but Godwine was fated not to take part in the answer, for in 1053 he died, and the earldom of Wessex went to his son Harold, as that of Northumbria had gone to Tostig two years before.

There was only one claimant who fitted the policy and aspirations of the English party, the Aetheling Edward, son of Edmund Ironside, as his elder brother was now dead. In 1054 his recall to England was resolved upon, and Bishop Ealdred of Winchester was sent to the Emperor Henry III to effect it. Delays followed, and it was not until 1057 that the Aetheling landed with his wife and infant son Edgar in England. Thus it must have appeared to all that the succession was now secured; but fate decided against it. Within a few days of his landing, and before he could be presented to the king, the Aetheling died, and "to the misfortune of this poor realm", as the Chronicle records.

CHAPTER 7

The Battle of Hastings, 1066

William, named the Bastard, and later the Conqueror and the Great, was the natural son of Robert I of Normandy by Arlette,[1] the daughter of a tanner of Falaise. Born, probably, in September, 1027, when he was seven years old his father went on a pilgrimage to the Holy Land, and on his way back died at Nicaea in July, 1035. From then on William's youth was surrounded by dangers, but when he attained manhood he rapidly showed his worth. When twenty, with the help of King Henry I of France, he defeated his rebel barons at Val-ès-Dunes, near Caen. He then demolished their castles and until 1064 was at constant war with either Anjou, the Bretons, his vassals, or the King of France.

That he was ever able to establish his authority was due to his masterful character, his indomitable will, and his unalterable purpose. A man of steel, he could be brutal or lenient as it paid him to be so, but never merciful when it did not. He would tolerate no opposition; his will was law, and he would not be thwarted, whether by overlord, vassal, or pope. He was a great administrator and an able soldier, who based his strategy on striking at the towns and castles of his enemy and on winning possession of them by intimidation rather than by assault. In his hands devastation was the decisive weapon, and he used it with annihilative effect; he showed no feeling for the wretched peasantry he exterminated.

In the *Anglo-Saxon Chronicle* we read that "He was gentle to the good men who loved God, and stern beyond measure to those people who resisted his will. . . . Also, he was a very stern and violent man, so that no one dared to do anything contrary to his will. He expelled bishops from their sees, and abbots from their abbacies, and put thegns in prison, and finally did not spare his own brother [Odo]. . . . Amongst other things the good security he made in this country is not to be forgotten—so that any honest man could travel over his Kingdom without injury

---

[1] After Robert's death she married Herlouin Viscount of Conteville and bore him William's half-brothers Odo Bishop of Bayeux and Robert Count of Mortain.

with his bosom full of gold: and no one dared strike another, however much wrong he had done him."[1]

Another contemporary account of him reads:

"This king excelled in wisdom all the princes of his generation, and among them all he was outstanding in the largeness of his soul. He never allowed himself to be deterred from prosecuting any enterprise because of the labour it entailed, and he was ever undaunted by danger. So skilled was he in his appraisal of the true significance of any event, that he was able to cope with adversity, and to take full advantage in prosperous times of the false promises of fortune."[2]

In order to strengthen his position, he determined on an alliance with Baldwin V of Flanders, and in 1048 proposed for the hand of his daughter Matilda. Although in the following year the marriage was objected to by Pope Leo IX on the ground of affinity–which remains obscure–in spite of this prohibition, in 1053 he married her, and six years later a formal recognition of the marriage was granted by Pope Nicholas II on the understanding that he and Matilda built two monasteries at Caen, which they agreed to do and did.

The year after this recognition, William's strategic position was greatly strengthened by the death of Henry I, who was succeeded by his infant son Philip I, under the guardianship of Baldwin of Flanders. This most fortunate event raised William to the position of potential master of France, with her king in the pocket of his father-in-law.

In 1064, shortly after William had ruthlessly devastated Maine and annexed that county to Normandy, an unlooked for event occurred which was to furnish him with his strongest claim to the crown of England. It was a visit to France from Harold Earl of Wessex, now Edward the Confessor's chief lieutenant. There are two main versions of this strange episode, the one given by William of Poitiers and the other by William of Malmesbury. The first reads:

Edward, "who loved William as a brother or a son", feeling "the hour of his death approaching", in order to establish William "as his heir with a stronger pledge than ever before . . . dispatched Harold to William in order that he might confirm his promise

---

[1] "The Anglo-Saxon Chronicle (1042–1154) E", in *English Historical Documents* edit. by David Douglas (1953), vol. II, pp. 163–164.

[2] "An account of the death and character of William the Conqueror written by a monk of Caen", in *English Historical Documents*, edit. by David Douglas, vol. II, p. 280.

[? of 1051] by an oath". On his way across the Channel Harold ran into a storm and was forced to land on the coast of Ponthieu, where he fell into the hands of Count Guy, who cast him into prison. When he learnt of his misfortune, William brought about his release, and at Bonneville Harold "swore fealty to the duke employing the sacred ritual recognized among Christian men". He swore: "firstly that he would be the representative (*Vicarius*) of Duke William at the court of his lord, King Edward, as long as the king lived; secondly that he would employ all his influence and wealth to ensure that after the death of King Edward the kingdom of England should be confirmed in the possession of the duke; thirdly that he would place a garrison of the duke's knights in the castle of Dover and maintain these at his own care and cost; fourthly that in other parts of England at the pleasure of the duke he would maintain garrisons in other castles and make complete provision for their sustenance."[1]

William of Malmesbury's version is as follows:

From Bosham, then an important seaport in Wessex, Harold went on a fishing cruise, and caught in a storm was driven on to the coast of Ponthieu. There he was at once seized "and bound hand and foot". To effect his release he persuaded "a person, whom he had allured by very great promises", to go to William and inform him of his predicament, and "that he had been sent into Normandy by the king, for the purpose of expressly confirming, in person, the message which had been imperfectly delivered by people of less authority". William at once compelled Guy – his vassal – to release Harold, and William took Harold with him on an expedition against Brittany. Next we read: "There, Harold, well proved both in ability and courage, won the heart of the Norman; and, still more to ingratiate himself, he of his own accord, confirmed to him by oath the castle of Dover, which was under his jurisdiction, and the Kingdom of England, after the death of Edward. Wherefore, he was honoured both by having his daughter, then a child, betrothed to him, and by the confirmation of his ample patrimony. . . ."[2]

Both accounts are suspect. Regarding the former, would Harold,

---

[1] "William of Poitiers: 'The Deeds of William, duke of the Normans and king of the English' ", in *English Historical Documents*, edit. by David Douglas, vol. II, pp. 217–218. William of Poitiers was William the Conqueror's chaplain.

[2] *William of Malmesbury's Chronicle of the Kings of England*, trans. J. A. Giles (1904), pp. 254–255. At the time William's daughter Adela or Agatha was about eleven years old.

who at the time was virtually under-king of England, have agreed to carry out such a mission? Further, as Sir James Ramsay points out, even if he did, surely on so important an embassy he would have travelled under safe-conduct, which would have made it unlawful for Guy to arrest him.[1] And for the latter it would appear far more probable that when he learnt of Harold's misfortune, William looked upon it as an act of God, and once he had Harold in his power, he refused to release him unless he did homage to him and swore that on his return to England he would recognize William's claim to the English throne.

Be this as it may, there can be no doubt that the oath was taken. Not only does the episode figure conspicuously in the Bayeux Tapestry, but, as we shall see, when William presented his claim to the pope, the Emperor, and the world in general, Harold did nothing to refute it, and the most probable reason why he did not is that he could not because the evidence against him was overwhelming.

Soon after Harold's return to England he was faced by a national crisis, which was to prove as detrimental to him as his oath. The appointment of his brother Tostig to the earldom of Northumbria had never been popular, and when, in early October, 1065, Tostig was absent with the King at Brentford, the thegns of Yorkshire rose against him, deposed him and offered his earldom to Morcar, grandson of Leofric and brother of Edwin Earl of Mercia. Morcar accepted the offer and marched on Northampton, where he was joined by Edwin. At Oxford, Harold met the rebels, and when he failed to establish concord between them and Tostig, much against his will Edward was compelled to outlaw Tostig and to accept Morcar. Tostig and his wife sought refuge with her brother, Baldwin of Flanders.

This was a grievous blow for Harold; it split the house of Godwine and exalted that of its rival Leofric, and it drove Tostig into the arms of William's father-in-law and ally.

The exertions which Edward underwent during the rebellion would appear to have hastened his end. In December, he held his usual Christmas court in London, but on the 28th was too ill to attend the consecration of his new abbey at Westminster. On January 5th, 1066, just before he died, he held out his hand to Harold and commended to his care his wife, his foreign retainers, and all his kingdom. The next day he was buried hastily in his

[1] *The Foundations of England* (1898), vol. 1, pp. 496–497.

abbey, and immediately afterward the members of the Witan[1] present in London held a council to consider his successor. Although nothing is known of their deliberations, their decision was to elect[2] Harold. The times demanded a strong king, for the kingdom was beset with dangers: by Normandy, under William; by Norway, now ruled by Harold Hardrada, who had succeeded Swein; by Tostig in Flanders; and by Malcolm Canmore of Scotland, his sworn brother. If the council ever considered the Aetheling Edgar, grandson of Ironside, its members must immediately have banished him from their minds, for he was still a minor, and Harold was a man of mature age who in the recent wars against the Welsh had proved himself an able general. When to this is added Edward's commendation, there was really no choice other than Harold.[3] The decision made, Harold was taken to Westminster Abbey and crowned by Ealdred, Archbishop of York.

The news of Edward's death and Harold's election was rapidly conveyed to William at Rouen, and at once, as William of Poitiers informs us, he "resolved to avenge the insult by force of arms and to regain his inheritance by war".[4] But before doing so, to justify a declaration of war in the eyes of the world, he sent an embassy to Harold formally demanding the fulfilment of his oath.[5] It is as well here to assess the strategical positions of the contending parties.

William was well placed, as he deserved to be, for ever since his victory at Val-ès-Dunes, his policy consistently had been to strengthen his duchy internally and to secure it externally, and in this, as we have seen, he had been greatly assisted by good fortune. From the Scheldt to the Loire every harbour was either in his hands or those of an ally.

In the east he was secured by his alliance with Flanders; in the west by his subjugation of Brittany; and in the south by his occupation of Maine, a friendly regency in Paris, and by another stroke of good fortune. In 1060 – the year Henry I died – William's most formidable enemy, Geoffrey Martel of Anjou, also died, and since

---

[1] The Witanagemot was partly an assembly of Notables (earls, bishops, abbots and nominated thegns) and partly a royal Privy Council. It had a voice in all public matters of importance and also performed the duties of a Supreme Court of Justice.

[2] For the "elective" and "hereditary" principles in the Anglo-Saxon monarchy see F. M. Stenton's *Anglo-Saxon England* (1947), p. 544, and *William the Conqueror and the Rule of the Normans* (1908), pp. 149–152.

[3] The Witan, had it knowledge of it, was in no way bound by Harold's oath, for not being of royal blood, it was not in his power, even morally, to pledge the English crown.

[4] William of Poitiers, p. 218.   [5] William of Malmesbury, p. 271.

his death his county had been distracted by a civil war between his two nephews. This meant that William had nothing to fear from Anjou during his projected conquest of England. Lastly, his position internationally was considerably strengthened by Harold's accession, for the Continent in general looked upon Harold as a usurper and on William as the aggrieved party.

Compared with William, Harold could hardly have been in a worse position. England was disunited, and Harold, not of royal blood, could not even evoke its mystical support. The two great northern earls, Edwin and Morcar, could not possibly have welcomed his accession. Indeed, the latter refused to recognize it, and while William mobilized his forces, Harold was compelled to journey to York to win over Morcar. This he did in a nominal way by marrying his sister Ealdgyth. On his return to London at Easter, April 16, Harold was acknowledged king of all England.

Tactically, his position was almost as bad, as a comparison between the English and Norman military systems will show. The former consisted of two forces, the fyrd, or national militia, and the housecarles. Apparently, the former was recruited on the basis of one man from each five hides—a hide being 120 acres—"each hide giving the soldier four shillings for pay and rations for two months, or twenty shillings in all".[1] The latter, originally the personal body-guards of king, earls, and thegns, in Harold's time had developed into a small force or forces of paid, professional men-at-arms, whose main purpose in war was to stiffen the ranks of the fyrd. Though in numerical strength the two forces were sufficient to meet normal emergencies, because the fyrd was scattered all over England it was difficult to concentrate it at short notice, and once its two months' pay and rations were exhausted, it would seem that no system of maintenance other than a fresh levy of money (Danegeld) existed, and this was highly unpopular. Though the housecarles and most of the fyrd were mounted, fighting was on foot. The one recorded instance of a mounted action, in Norman fashion, made by Ralph, Earl of Hereford in 1055, ended disastrously,[2] and, it seems, was not repeated. Of weapons, the more important were the spear, javelin,

---

[1] *The Foundations of England*, Sir James H. Ramsay, vol. I, p. 520.
[2] Of it we read: "But before any spear had been thrown the English army fled because they were on horseback" (*Anglo-Saxon Chronicle C*, p. 133). This should be substantiated by the fact that Ralph's mounted men were received by such volleys of missiles from the Welsh javelin and bowmen that they experienced a foretaste of Crécy. Cavalry, unsupported by archers, could not face archers: it took nearly 300 years to learn this lesson.

two-edged sword, and cumbersome long-handled Danish axe—clearly, in origin, a boarding weapon. Archery, though practised as a sport, was little used in war. Shields were both round and kite-shaped, and the helmet and coat of mail (*byrne*) were worn by all who could afford them.

A further difficulty Harold had to face was that Edward had disbanded the small fleet he inherited, and in consequence there was neither a fleet in being, nor the means of raising one in 1066, other than by requisitioning commercial and fishing craft and impressing their crews. As Professor Stenton points out, the mobilization of such a fleet was a slow business, "and the period for which it could remain at sea was narrowed by the absence of any organization for the replacement of the provisions with which it had sailed".[1] On the other hand, at the opening of 1066, William would appear to have had no ships suitable for carrying horses, and therefore had to build them. The only serious difficulty he had to face—a really terrifying one—was the crossing of the Channel.

The Norman military system was very different. Each baron or bishop held his land from the duke on the understanding that he maintained and equipped for his immediate service a number of mounted knights determined on by the duke. It was on this armoured and mounted cavalry that Norman military power was based, and during William's numerous wars it had become highly skilled and disciplined. The main arms were lance, sword, and mace, and its armour, as may be judged from the Bayeux Tapestry, was similar to that of the English. Of the Normans in general William of Malmesbury says: "They are a race inured to war, and can hardly live without it, fierce in rushing against the enemy, and when strength fails of success, ready to use stratagem, or to corrupt by bribery . . . they are faithful to their lords, though slight offence renders them perfidious."[2]

The Norman infantry consisted of men-at-arms and archers, the latter armed with either the short Norman bow or the crossbow. William was a highly skilled general, familiar with every device of continental war, and knew not only how to enforce discipline but how to supply his army in the field.

The English made practically no use of castles[3] for internal

---

[1] *Anglo-Saxon England*, p. 574.   [2] William of Malmesbury, p. 280.
[3] Most castles in the eleventh century were stockades built on mounds. Not until after the conquest of England did stone castles appear in numbers.

defence, but William held his dukedom and his subjugated lands by means of them. This enabled him to hold extensive areas with a minimum of troops, and, comparatively speaking, to concentrate large forces in the field. Nevertheless, in his day, two to three thousand men would be a considerable army.

Once he decided to challenge Harold, William recognized that his project was no feudal affair of overlord against vassal or vassal against overlord, but an international undertaking, and that, in consequence, it had to be placed on an international footing. And because in his day the two great international authorities were the Pope and the Emperor, it was essential to gain their sanction and, if possible, their support. His first step was, therefore, to open negotiations with both, as well as to send envoys to the principal courts of Europe, to set forth his claim to the English crown. Through the diplomatic skill of his confidant and adviser, the learned Lanfranc, Prior of Bec, he won the support of Archdeacon Hildebrand (later Pope Gregory VII), who in his turn persuaded Pope Alexander II to bless the Norman cause and to send William a consecrated banner. From the Emperor Henry IV William obtained a promise of German help, should he need it, and Swein Estrithson, king of the Danes, also pledged his support, but did not keep his word.[1] Though Harold must have heard of these many negotiations, he nevertheless allowed William's case before the papal court to go against him by default.

William realized that the army he would need could not be recruited from Normandy alone, and as by feudal law he did not possess the power to call out his vassals for service oversea, William assembled a great council of his barons at Lillebonne to ascertain their sentiments on his venture and "to prepare shipping in proportion to the extent of their possessions".[2] Later, he appointed Matilda regent during his absence, and supported her with a council presided over by Roger of Beaumont.

With the papal sanction behind it, William's cause attracted many followers, for the conquest of so extensive and wealthy a country as England offered all but unlimited plunder and estates to soldiers of fortune and land-hungry younger sons of the nobility. From every quarter of France and from places beyond its borders volunteers flocked to William's standard: from Brittany, Maine, Flanders, central France, Poitou, Burgundy, Aquitaine, and southern Italy. Among the men of his own allegiance, the more

[1] William of Poitiers, pp. 219–220.   [2] William of Malmesbury, p. 273.

N

important were his two half-brothers, Odo Bishop of Bayeux and Robert Count of Mortain. Others were: Geoffrey Bishop of Coutances; Ivo, son of Guy of Ponthieu; William, son of Richard Count of Evreux; Geoffrey, son of Robert Count of Mortagne; Robert of Meulan, son of Roger of Beaumont; Roger of Poitou, son of Roger of Montgomery; William fitz Osbern; Walter Giffard; Ralph of Tosny; Hugh of Grantmesnil; William of Warenne; Hugh of Montfort; William Malet; and Humphrey of Tilleul. And from those who came from beyond his domains, the most noted were: Eustace of Boulogne; Alan of Brittany; Gilbert of Ghent; Walter of Flanders; Gerbod, son of Matilda by her first husband; Amaury Viscount of Thouars; and Geoffrey of Chaumont. Such a gathering of notables had never been seen before, and it presaged the approaching days of the crusades.

About the time when the Norman barons were assembled at Lillebonne, Tostig, who had nothing to gain from Harold's election, left Flanders for Normandy, and, according to Ordericus Vitalis, obtained William's permission "to return to England".[1] What is actually meant by this is not clear, because the duke's preparations were only in their initial stage, and not until they were well advanced could Tostig effect anything of predictable importance. What seems more probable is that Tostig was unable to pay his followers, and as he had estates in the Isle of Wight he decided on his own to go there to collect what money he could. In May he sailed from the Continent with sixty ships, landed in the Isle of Wight, obtained money and provisions,[2] and then set out to harry the coast of Sussex and Kent. At Sandwich he impressed a number of men, but he heard there that Harold was marching from London against him and rapidly re-embarked his force and sailed for the Humber. There he landed and, it seems, was caught unawares while ravaging by the northern fyrd, under Edwin, and so heavily defeated that he was left with only twelve small ships. In them he effected his escape to Scotland, where he sought refuge with Malcolm Canmore.[3]

Unsuspected by either William or Harold, this fiasco would appear to have had an important bearing on the approaching Hastings campaign; for it would seem to have persuaded Harold to assume that William's invasion was imminent. The result was

[1] *The Ecclesiastical History of England and Normandy*, trans. Thomas Forester (1853), vol. I, p. 463.
[2] *Anglo-Saxon Chronicle C*, p. 142.
[3] *The Chronicle of Florence of Worcester*, trans. Thomas Forester (1854), p. 168.

that Harold prematurely ordered the mobilization of his sea and land forces, for we are told that when he heard that Tostig was at Sandwich, "he assembled a naval force and a land force larger than had ever been assembled before".[1] In other words, he ordered a general and not a partial mobilization,[2] and on its completion, which must have taken a considerable time, he posted the fyrd along the coast of Sussex and Kent and assembled his fleet off the Isle of Wight. Thus things stood until about September 8 when the legal term of service expired and the provisions and money were exhausted, and he was compelled to disband the fyrd and order the fleet to London to be dispersed.[3] Thus, as we shall see, at the very moment when William was ready to embark, the Channel was opened to him. It may, therefore, be asked, had it not been for Tostig's raid, would Harold have called out a general mobilization when he did? Also, it may be asked, had he delayed doing so for, say, a month, would England have been conquered? Again fortune favoured William.

No sooner had demobilization begun than Harold received the startling news that Harold Hardrada (1015–1066), King of Norway,[4] accompanied by Tostig, had invaded the North. Apparently what had happened was that Tostig, soon after he had sought refuge in Scotland, had visited Norway and urged Hardrada to invade England and to claim its crown on the strength of the treaty between Harthacnut and Magnus.[5] Yet it would seem even more probable that William's threat to England was itself sufficient reason for Hardrada to go on a plundering expedition while the going was good.

Hardrada sailed from the Sogne Fiord, near Bergen, with 300 ships[6] to the Shetlands and the Orkneys, and next, turning south, he picked up Tostig and his followers off the Tyne. He plundered and burnt Scarborough, rounded Spurn Head, entered the Humber, and thence rowed up the Ouse to Riccall, ten miles south of York. There he disembarked his army, set out for York, and at Gate Fulford, two miles from the city, met the Yorkshire fyrd, under Edwin and Morcar. On September 20 a fierce battle

---

[1] *Anglo-Saxon Chronicle C*, p. 142.

[2] Seeing that the fyrd could only be called out for 40 days, the sole possible way to keep a force in the field for longer was to call it out in relays.

[3] Florence of Worcester, p. 169, and *Anglo-Saxon Chronicle C*, p. 144.

[4] One of the most noted soldiers of his day, who had served in the Eastern Roman Empire and visited Jerusalem.

[5] See *The Heimskringla Saga*, trans. Samuel Laing (1889), vol. IV, pp. 31–32.

[6] *Anglo-Saxon Chronicle E*, p. 142.

was fought, which is poetically described in the saga.[1] Its outcome was the rout of the two northern earls. The Chronicle mentions "heavy casualties and many of the English host were killed and drowned",[2] and the saga informs us that so many English were slain that "they paved a way across the fen for the brave Norsemen".[3]

When he learnt of Harold Hardrada's invasion, Harold took his housecarles and such men of the fyrd who had not yet been disbanded – almost certainly a mounted force[4] – and "went northwards day and night".[5] On the 24th he rode into Tadcaster, and on the following day, when Hardrada was negotiating over hostages with the two earls, he surprised the invaders, forced a passage over the Derwent, and after a prolonged and desperate struggle at Stamfordbridge all but annihilated them. Not only did Hardrada and Tostig perish in the fray, but when the battle was over, we are told that no more than twenty shiploads of the enemy were left. These Harold allowed Olaf, Hardrada's son, to take back with him to Norway.[6] That Harold's losses were heavy is recorded in the Chronicle, and Ordericus Vitalis, writing between 1123 and 1141, informs us that in his day great heaps of bones still lay on the battlefield, "memorials to the prodigious number which fell on both sides".[7]

The importance of these two actions cannot be overestimated, coming as they did less than a month before the Battle of Hastings, for they seriously reduced the strength of Harold's army. In Professor Stenton's opinion, the losses suffered by Edwin and Morcar were so severe that they "deprived them of any chance of effective action during the critical weeks of early October". Further, he writes of the two earls:

"They have often been regarded as unpatriotic because they held aloof from the campaign of Hastings. It can at least be urged on their behalf that they had recently stood for the defence of the realm against the greatest northern warrior of the age, and that the battle of Hastings had been fought long before either of them could have replaced the men whom he had lost at Fulford."[8] This may be true, yet against it may be urged: Was it for the defence of the realm that they faced up to Harold of Norway; was not

---

[1] See *Heimskringla Saga*, vol. IV, pp. 37–38.
[2] *Anglo-Saxon Chronicle C*, p. 144.
[3] *Heimskringla Saga*, vol. IV, p. 39.
[4] See *ibid.*, vol. IV, pp. 40 and 41.
[5] *Anglo-Saxon Chronicle C*, p. 144.
[6] See *ibid.*, pp. 145–146; *Heimskringla Saga*, vol. IV, pp. 40–50, and Florence of Worcester, p. 169.
[7] Vol. I, p. 480.
[8] *Anglo-Saxon England*, p. 582.

it rather for the defence of their earldoms? After all, Tostig was Harold Hardrada's ally and also their bitterest enemy, and his brother Harold was no *persona grata* of theirs.

What seems more important than either their loyalty or treachery is that Harold's housecarles almost certainly were mounted, and that probably most of Edwin's and Morcar's fyrd-men were not, and that when Harold heard of William's landing, as we shall see, he moved south with such speed that it was quite impossible for an unmounted force to keep pace with him along the Ermine Street, which probably had not been repaired for 600 years. Though rather obscurely, this is corroborated by William of Malmesbury who says: "Edwin and Morcar, by Harold's command, then [*i.e.* after the battle of Stamfordbridge] conveyed the spoils of war to London, for he himself was *proceeding rapidly* to the battle of Hastings; where, falsely presaging, he looked upon the victory as already gained."[1] Therefore, what would appear to be more important than Edwin's and Morcar's losses at Fulford, are the losses suffered by Harold's housecarles – his *élite* troops – at Stamfordbridge.

When Tostig was sheltering in Scotland and Hardrada was preparing his invasion, William was busily engaged upon building a fleet and recruiting an army, and such was his energy that towards the middle of August everything was ready, most of the armament having by then been gathered together along the banks and in the mouth of the river Dives. What it actually consisted in is impossible to determine with any exactness. William of Poitiers states that the army numbered 50,000 men, and William of Jumièges that the ships built totalled 3,000. These are impossible figures, and Sir James Ramsay suggests that they should be divided by ten.[2]

The only reliable standard of measurement we have, is that we are told that both the embarkation at St. Valéry and the disembarkation at Pevensey occupied one day – that is, about twelve hours.[3] From this it follows that William's army could not have

---

[1] William of Malmesbury, p. 285. Italics ours.

[2] *The Foundations of England*, vol. ii, p. 17. Other estimates are: J. H. Round, *Feudal England* (1895), pp. 289–293, 5,000; *The Cambridge Medieval History*, vol. v, p. 498, 5,000; Ferdinand Lot, *L'Art Militaire et les Armées au Moyen Age* (1946), vol. i, p. 285, below rather than above 7,000; and Wilhelm Spatz, *Die Schlacht von Hastings* (1896), p. 30, not more than 6,000 to 7,000.

[3] Sir James Ramsay points out that "At Harfleur, in 1415, three August days were required for the landing of Henry's 8,000-10,000 men" (*The Foundations of England*, vol. ii, p. 17).

much exceeded 5,000 men, though when boatmen and non-combatants are added, the grand total may have been between 7,000 and 8,000. Accepting Mr. Corbett's estimate of 2,000 knights and 3,000 foot, and that of the former, 1,200 came from Normandy,[1] even then, how the knights in so short a time embarked and disembarked their horses from the type of boat depicted in the Bayeux Tapestry is a puzzle, unless portable ramps were carried, and none is shown in the one example of horses disembarking.[2]

Concerning the number of boats required for these conjectural figures, we know that the average crew of the Viking ships of this period was forty men. Also, if it can in any way be relied upon, the Bayeux Tapestry shows in one case ten horses in a single boat. Assuming, then, that each boat had a crew of five men, and accepting that thirty-five soldiers or ten horses was a boat-load, the number of boats required for the combatants would be 343. If to these we add, say, 100 for food, wine, munitions, tools, possibly also some tents, extra horses and non-combatants, we obtain a grand total of nearly 450. This figure is probably not far out, for William of Malmesbury informs us that, in 1142, Robert Earl of Gloucester embarked "more than three, but less than four hundred horsemen [say 350 knights and horses] on board fifty-two vessels".[3]

For a whole month from August 12 bad weather and a northerly wind detained the fleet in the Dives. On September 12, the wind veered west. William took advantage of the change and promptly moved his ships to St. Valéry in the estuary of the Somme, from where the crossing of the Channel would be shorter. But the wind changed north, and a further delay followed, which caused so much discontent that William was hard put to it to maintain discipline.[4]

At last, on September 27, the wind changed to the south. William embarked his army, and so energetically was the task carried out that everything was on board by nightfall. He instructed each boat to bear a light and on the mast of his own ship, the *Mora*, presented to him by Matilda, he had a great lantern lashed, which the fleet was ordered to follow. About midnight the expedition sailed, and at nine o'clock on the following day—Thursday, September 28, 1066—the duke set foot on the English shore at

---

[1] *The Cambridge Medieval History*, vol. v, p. 498. For the 1,200 knights see pp. 488–489.
[2] Inscribed "EXEVNT CABALLI DENAVIBUS".
[3] P. 533.
[4] See William of Poitiers, p. 221.

Pevensey, the Anderida of the Romans. There the army disembarked, and on the next day William marched it to Hastings, the coastal terminus of the great north road to London. At Hastings he pitched his camp, built a timber castle to secure his base, and set about ravaging the country-side and gathering supplies.

When William landed, Harold was at York, resting his men and celebrating his victory. There, on October 1, he received the unwelcome news, and even if he forthwith issued summons for the reassembly of the fyrd, he must have realized that, unless the country south of London was to be abandoned, it would be possible only for the men of the shires along his march southward to reach London in time to join him in a campaign in Sussex.

Presumably, he set out on October 2 to cover the 200 miles to London, and pushing on at top speed he reached the capital on October 5 or 6. There he remained until the 11th, collecting such forces as came in. According to William of Poitiers, he planned a surprise or night attack on his enemy, and to prevent his escape, he "sent out a fleet of seven hundred armed vessels to block their passage home".[1] Ordericus Vitalis sensibly reduces this number to seventy.[2]

Probably Harold's best course would have been – and had William been in his shoes he would most certainly have taken it – to remain in London until his whole army had been assembled, and meanwhile to harry the country to the south, in order to starve William out. But in temperament Harold was too impatient and impulsive to pause. Besides, the bulk of his supporters inhabited the south, and to have begun devastating part of his own estates would most certainly not have added to their loyalty. Further, it would seem that he held his enemy in contempt.

He assembled his army in London. Its core consisted of his own housecarles, now considerably depleted, and those of his brothers Gyrth and Leofwine. The remainder was composed of such men of the fyrd – mounted and unmounted thegns and their retainers – who were able to reach London during his five or six days' halt. It was, therefore, a quality army, and the stories that at Hastings Harold's fyrd-men were a rabble of ill-armed peasantry is quite untrue. What the strength of his army was is unknown. W. Spatz suggests 6,000–7,000 men,[3] but when one considers the losses suffered at Stamfordbridge, the absence of Edwin and Morcar,

[1] P. 224. [2] P. 483. [3] *Die Schlacht von Hastings* (1896), pp. 33–34.

and the shortness of the period of mobilization, this seems a high figure. It may be wiser to reduce it to 5,000, or even 4,000. Florence of Worcester says that when Harold led his army out of London "he was very sensible that some of the bravest men in England had fallen in the two battles [Fulford and Stamford-bridge], and that one half of his troops was not yet assembled". Further, that at Hastings he met William "before a third of his army was in fighting order",[1] which suggests that the rapidity of his advance had been too much for many of his unmounted men. Also, William of Malmesbury says that he went to Hastings "accompanied by very few forces",[2] yet even 4,000 men was a large army in the eleventh century.

On October 11, Harold set out from London to cover the sixty miles to Hastings, and on the night of October 13–14 he arrived at the site of the present town of Battle, and encamped his men on or near a rise in the downs marked by a "hoary apple-tree".[3] William of Poitiers says, "they [the English] took up their position on . . . a hill abutting the forest [of Anderid] through which they had come. There, at once dismounting from their horses . . ."[4] And William of Jumièges writes: "after riding all night, he [Harold] appeared on the field of battle early in the morning."[5] If surprise was Harold's aim, then, in all probability he encamped in the forest, and only occupied the "hoary apple-tree" position early on the following day.

According to Malmesbury and Wace, Harold's men passed the night of October 13–14 in drinking and singing and the Normans in confessing their sins and receiving the sacrament.[6] Though, no doubt, after a forced march the English were thirsty, and before an impending battle many Normans offered up fervent prayers, common sense dictates that Harold's men–certainly his foot–slept like logs, and that, as William had learnt through his scouts of his enemy's approach,[7] his men spent most of the night in preparing for battle.

---

[1] P. 170. It is a point of interest to note that in his march from York to London (October 2–6) Harold averaged 40 miles a day, and in his march from London to Battle (October 11–13) only 19 miles. This points to his having been encumbered with unmounted men on the latter. Had he left them behind, he could have reached Hastings on the 12th, and, possibly, have surprised William, but whether he would have been numerically strong enough to defeat him is another question.

[2] P. 274.   [3] *Anglo-Saxon Chronicle D*, p. 144.   [4] P. 225.

[5] William of Jumièges: description of the invasion of England by William the Conqueror", in *English Historical Documents*, edit. by David Douglas, vol. II, p. 216.

[6] P. 276 and *Roman de Rou* (edit. Pluquet, 1827), p. 184.

[7] William of Poitiers, p. 224.

What was Harold's plan? Was it to surprise William, as has already been mentioned, or was it to assume a passive defensive—that is, to block the London Road and await attack? That Harold did fight a purely defensive battle is true, but he may have been compelled to do so because he had not reached the Battle position as early as he had hoped. To have pushed on the remaining seven miles to Hastings after dark, and then to have attempted a night attack, unpreceded by a daylight reconnaissance, would have been madness. In the circumstances, the only chance to surprise William was to attack him at dawn, which would have demanded an advance soon after midnight. Even if considered, the weariness of Harold's men must have prohibited this. That surprise based on speed was in his mind is supported by his previous generalship. In his Welsh campaign of 1063[1] and in his Stamfordbridge campaign he had moved like lightning in order to surprise; therefore, probably Mr. Round is right in surmising that this was also his intention in the present campaign.[2] Simply to hold the "hoary apple-tree" position was not sufficient to rid England of her invaders, because it did not prevent William from re-embarking his army under the cover of his archers and moving it to some other spot along the coast. Therefore, its occupation did not pin William down, nor did it compel him to attack Harold. Yet, as we shall see, William did attack, and he moved so rapidly against his enemy that it was Harold and not he who was surprised. This is supported by the Chronicle, which states that "William came against him by surprise before his army was drawn up in battle array".[3] In other words, Harold and his men would appear to have overslept themselves.

Harold's position must next be considered.

The high ground (Wealden Hills) north of Battle is connected with a rise or ridge—now in part occupied by the abbey buildings—by a neck or isthmus along which the present High Street of Battle runs. The highest point on this ridge is the site of the Abbey House, and from it the ground falls gently east and west. On its southern side the slope drops about a hundred feet in 400 yards to the head of the Asten brook, now dammed to form a series of fishponds. From the Asten it rolls southward, gradually rising to Telham Hill one and a half miles south-east of the abbey. To the

---

[1] See Florence of Worcester, p. 164.
[2] *Revue Historique*, September, 1897, vol. LXV, p. 61 *et seq.*
[3] *Anglo-Saxon Chronicle D*, p. 144.

north of the ridge the flanks of the isthmus are sufficiently steep to form serious military obstacles, and, in 1066, the drainage from the high ground had cut them into ravines, which were covered with brushwood. Further, on the northern side of the ridge, and in each case 300 yards from the Abbey House–on the western along a little brook, and on the eastern at the junction of the Hastings and Sedlescombe roads–the ridge drops so sharply that its slope forms an effective obstacle to cavalry.

In all probability, it was on the summit of the ridge that Harold first planted his two standards, the Dragon of Wessex and his personal banner, the Fighting Man, which at the close of the battle fell at a spot seventy yards to the east of the Abbey House, and marked later by the high altar of the Abbey Church. Rightly, Harold drew up his housecarles on their flanks, because–assuming he occupied the crest of the ridge–his centre was more open to cavalry assault than his wings, which must have been composed mainly of fyrd-men. Although we have few details of Harold's formation, the normal Saxon one was that of the shield-wall–a phalanx: "shield to shield and shoulder to shoulder" as Asser describes it at Ashdown in 871. It was an admirable formation against infantry armed with sword, spear and axe, and an essential one for infantry against cavalry relying on shock.

Tactically, Harold's problem was both to maintain an unbroken front and to prevent the flanks of his shield-wall from being overlapped; therefore, as Mr. Baring suggests, it is highly probable that he occupied the 600 yards between the little brook west of the Abbey House and the junction of the Hastings and Sedlescombe roads in order that his flanks might rest on the two steep depressions.[1] If Harold drew up his army in a phalanx of ten ranks deep, allowing two feet frontage for each man in the first rank–the shield-wall–and three feet frontage for those in the nine rear ranks, then, on a 600 yards front, his total strength would be 6,300 men, and, if in twelve ranks–7,500. These figures tally closely with those suggested by Spatz–6,000 to 7,000.[2]

Because we are told that the battle of Hastings opened at nine o'clock on the morning of October 14, William must have set out at an early hour. He had nearly six miles to cover before reaching Telham Hill, somewhere north of which he deployed.

[1] See his *Domesday Tables for the Counties of Surrey, etc.* (1909), appendix B, pp. 217–232. There is an excellent plan of the battle in this book showing contours at ten feet intervals.

[2] *Die Schlacht von Hastings*, p. 33.

Therefore, after reckoning the time taken for assembly, march and deployment, he must have started at between 4.30 a.m. and 5 a.m. His order of battle was in three divisions, left, centre, and right. The left consisted mainly of Bretons, under Count Alan of Brittany; the right of William's French and other mercenaries, under Eustace of Boulogne; and the centre of Normans, under

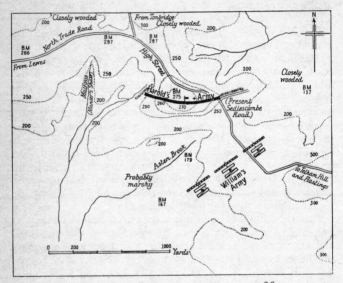

15. THE BATTLE OF HASTINGS, 1066

his personal command: before him was carried the papal banner. Each division was divided into three *échelons* or lines: the first, archers and crossbow men in front; the next, the more heavily armed infantry; and lastly the mounted knights.[1] Therefore, tactically, the order of battle closely resembled that of the early Roman legion, the *triarii* now being mounted.

At nine o'clock, to the blast of trumpets, the battle opened when the Normans slowly advanced up the rise toward the wall of English shields crowning its crest. The lay of the ground suggests that, when William's central division, which must have advanced on the western side of the Hastings Road, moved directly on

William of Poitiers, p. 225.

Harold's standards, the right and left divisions moved outwardly in order to prolong his front. Further, that the left wing, before mounting the slope on the English right, must have crossed the Asten brook, which runs into a stream coming from the ravines on the western side of the isthmus.

As William's centre closed on Harold's, the Norman archers began to discharge their arrows, but as they had to shoot uphill, most of them must either have struck their enemies' shields or passed over their heads. Following William of Poitiers' description of the battle,[1] the English resisted valiantly and met the assault with showers of "spears and javelins and weapons of all kinds together with axes and stones fastened to pieces of wood". Then "the shouts both of the Normans and of the barbarians were drowned in the clash of arms and by the cries of the dying, and for a long time the battle raged with the utmost fury".

Harold's men had the advantage of ground, and, as William of Poitiers points out, "profited by remaining within their position in close order", and maintained an impregnable front. Further, he informs us that the attackers suffered severely because of "the easy passage" of the defenders' weapons through their shields and armour, which does not speak much for them. The English, he continues, "bravely withstood and successfully repulsed those who were engaging them at close quarters, and inflicted loss upon the men who were shooting missiles at them from a distance" – namely, the Norman archers. Should this be correct, it points to a failure on the part of the Norman archers and infantry to make any real impression on the shield-wall.

The next recorded event supports this contention, for without further introduction William of Poitiers tells us that "the foot-soldiers and the Breton knights, panic-stricken by the violence of the assault, broke in flight before the English", and that soon "the whole army of the duke was in danger of retreat". This suggests that when it mounted the slope the Norman left wing got into difficulties, and that the English right, or part of it, suddenly counter-attacked, and swept the Breton archers and infantry down the slope so that they carried away with them in their flight the knights in rear. Next, William's central division found its left flank uncovered and began to fall back, as did his right division.

Now was Harold's chance, and he failed to seize it. He has often

[1] Pp. 226–229.

been blamed for not having rigidly maintained his shield-wall throughout the battle. Though to have done so might have saved him from defeat, it could not have gained a victory. Had he now seized his chance, he would have ordered a general advance, and pouring down the slope on both sides of the Hastings road would, almost certainly, have annihilated the Norman archers and infantry. True, the Norman cavalry would have got away, but bereft of their infantry, in all probability they would not have drawn rein until they had found security behind their stockade at Hastings. The victory would have been Harold's, and it might well have been decisive enough to have compelled William to re-embark and abandon the campaign.

As it happened, as soon as the panic on the Norman left wing began to affect the morale of the centre, a fortuitous event occurred which would have gone far to crown a general counter-attack on Harold's part with success.

During the initial attack William was in rear and, it seems, when the front of his central division broke back, in the resulting confusion he was unhorsed, and a cry went up that he had fallen. For him, this must have been the most critical moment in the battle; for in classical and medieval warfare the loss of the general-in-chief, which carried with it the loss of the entire command, as often as not led to immediate defeat. It was as if in a modern battle the whole of an army's general staff were suddenly eliminated. In the present case, the danger though critical was momentary, for William mounted another horse, pushed back his helmet so that he might be recognized by all, and stayed the panic in the centre by shouting out: "Look at me well. I am still alive and by the grace of God I shall yet prove victor." Meanwhile, on the left, presumably around the Asten brook, the English counter-attackers had got into difficulty, and when the Norman centre turned about a general rally followed, and some of the pursuers were cut off and slaughtered. William of Poitiers mentions "several thousands", but immediately qualifies this estimate by informing us that, even after this loss, the English "scarcely seemed diminished in number".

As soon as the Normans had re-formed their ranks, the attack was renewed, but this time under William's personal leadership, which means that the knights were brought forward and the infantry withdrawn from the immediate front. From now on for several hours the struggle raged along the whole line, individual bodies of knights riding forward at the charge to hurl or thrust their spears at the shield-wall. Nevertheless, all attempts to force a gap proved ineffectual.

Unable to break the shield-wall, William now made use of a *ruse de guerre* common in Byzantine and Oriental warfare. He determined to lure his enemy down from the hoary apple-tree hill by means of a feint retreat.

The most suitable part of the field for this somewhat risky operation, for we may assume that the Normans were not exercised in it, was probably on the right, for there a withdrawal would bring William's men down to the valley and next up to high ground where they could face about as their pursuers moved uphill. Also a withdrawal in this direction would enable his centre to take the pursuers in flank. Clearly this was a purely cavalry operation; therefore we may assume that, while the fighting was in progress, the Norman infantry was withdrawn out of harm's way.

All this is, of course, conjecture, for all William of Poitiers tells us is the following:

"Realizing that they could not without severe loss overcome an army massed so strongly in close formation, the Normans and their allies feigned flight and simulated a retreat, for they recalled that only a short while ago their flight had given them an advantage. The barbarians thinking victory within their grasp shouted with triumph, and heaping insults upon our men, threatened utterly to destroy them. Several thousand of them, as before, gave rapid pursuit to those whom they thought to be in flight; but the Normans suddenly wheeling their horses surrounded them and cut down their pursuers so that not one was left alive. Twice was this ruse employed with the utmost success."

Harold has been blamed for falling into the trap, but probably the discipline of his troops was such that they acted on their own initiative, and wrongly, because the tactical situation was very different from the one which led to the initial counter-attack.[1] Then they were faced by foot, but now by horse, therefore they could not possibly hope to outpace them.

Though, after the second feigned flight and slaughter of the pursuers, William of Poitiers tells us that Harold's army "was

---

[1] With reference to these advances, it should not be overlooked that in all early warfare in which javelins and arrows were the missiles, the normal way of replenishing their stock was to drive the enemy back and gather them from the ground he abandoned.

still formidable and very difficult to overwhelm", it is certain that its left wing must have been seriously weakened, and it may have been now, in order to strengthen it morally, that Harold moved his standards from the summit of the hill nearer to his left. Also it may have been at this time that to prepare the way for what was to be the final assault, William instructed his archers to use high-angle fire[1]–that is, to shoot their arrows into the air so that they would pass over the heads of his knights and, falling vertically on the enemy, induce the men of the shield-wall to raise their shields.

Night was closing in when the final phase of the battle opened, and by then we may assume that the English missiles had been spent and that Harold's men were exhausted. What happened is largely conjectural, but the most probable sequence of events would appear to be as follows: When twilight was setting in, Harold was hit in the eye by an arrow,[2] and a moment after was cut down.[3] As his brothers Gyrth and Leofwine had already fallen there was no one to replace him. Next, the weakened English left gave way before Eustace of Boulogne. The whole shield-wall then began to disintegrate, and Harold's men, some on horseback and some on foot, fled the field to the west and north-west to escape from Eustace, who would appear to have led the pursuit. Nevertheless, in spite of the panic, a number of Harold's men–probably housecarles–remained unaffected, fell back on the isthmus, and showed so bold a front that Eustace signalled his men to fall back. A moment later, William came up, counter-ordered the signal and urged his men forward. They scattered the housecarles, and a group, in the twilight, following the fugitives through the undergrowth, fell headlong into a ravine on the west of the isthmus, at a spot to become known as the Malfosse–probably the present Manser's Shaw.[4]

It must have been nearly dark when William returned to the main battlefield, to find Harold's body stripped and so hacked that it was barely recognizable. He had it brought to his camp, and later it was buried by the seashore.

Of William, William of Poitiers writes: "He dominated this battle, checking his own men in flight, strengthening their spirit,

---

[1] This incident is mentioned by Henry of Huntingdon, see *The Chronicle of Henry of Huntingdon*, trans. Thomas Forester (1853), p. 212.

[2] Florence of Worcester (p. 170) says that Harold fell at twilight.

[3] For both see the Bayeux Tapestry.

[4] See *Domesday Tables, etc.*, p. 229. Mr. Baring writes: "The original name being Malfosset, corruption was easy to Manfussé (? Manfsey), Mansey and finally Manser's."

and sharing their dangers. He bade them come with him, more often than he ordered them to go in front of him. Thus it may be understood how he led them by his valour and gave them courage. . . . Thrice his horse fell under him." Unfortunately, no friendly pen has depicted the part played by his valiant antagonist.

Two days after the battle William returned to Hastings, and five days later he occupied Dover. When he had strengthened its castle, he set out for Canterbury. Thence, following Mr. Baring's account,[1] he advanced by way of Lenham, Seal, and Westerham to Godstone, where he gained the London–Hastings road. From Godstone he sent a party of horsemen north, who burnt Southwark, while the main body marched on westward through Guildford and Micheldever to Basing. From Alresford he appears to have been reinforced from either Chichester or Portsmouth, where his fleet had moved at some time after the battle. Next, he swept northward by way of Lambourn to Wallingford, where his army crossed the Thames, circled round the Chilterns and came southward to Little Berkhampstead. There William was met by the magnates of London, who tended to him the submission of the city and offered to him the crown.

From the ravagings deduced from Domesday Book, Baring's conclusion is that William's army cannot have been more than from 8,000 to 10,000 strong. "Nor", he writes, "can he have had much time for mere devastation; he could hardly have covered some 350 miles between Canterbury and Little Berkhampstead within seven weeks, if he had allowed his troops to be scattered for wide-spread ravage. . . . Outside the line of march the immediate effect of the conquest on the value of land in the south-east seems to have been very slight."[2]

When he was offered the crown, William at first feigned hesitation, then he accepted it, sent forward a picked body of men to build what was to become the Tower of London, and on Christmas Day, 1066, he was crowned by Ealdred of York in Westminster Abbey. Thus his claim to England was vindicated.

The next three years were spent by William in putting down rebellions, more particularly in Northumbria, and in each case he did so by methodical devastation, until, in 1069, a third of his

---

[1] Who traces the march by the ravages deduced from Domesday Book. See *ibid.*, appendix A, pp. 208–216.

[2] *Ibid.*, pp. 14 and 16. *Anglo-Saxon Chronicle D* (p. 145) says: ". . . and ravaged all the region that he overran until he reached Berkhamsted."

kingdom had been reduced to little more than a wilderness. Meanwhile, in order to police and hold the land, he built a castle in every important borough. In 1070, he felt himself sufficiently secure to disband his mercenary troops, and two years later he invaded Scotland, and at Abernethy compelled Malcolm Canmore to do homage to him. When, on September 9, 1087, he died from an injury sustained during the siege of Mantes, he was the most powerful potentate in western Europe.

For England, Hastings was not only the most decisive battle ever fought on her soil, but also the most decisive in her history, in fact, there is no other battle which compares with it in importance. In the place of a loosely-knit and undisciplined country was substituted a unified and compact kingdom under a firm and hereditary central authority, a king who knew how to combine feudalism with personal government. William left local institutions as they were and appropriated to himself the entire land, the fiscal value of which he had assessed in his great Domesday Book survey.

Himself a feudal vassal, who had rebelled against his overlord, he understood well the inherent weakness of the Frankish feudal system, and would have none of it in England. As his kingdom was to be indivisible, no man should be to him what he was to the King of France. Although he gave his vassals vast estates on military tenure, they were scattered over different parts of his kingdom, except for the great border earldoms of Chester, Shrewsbury, Durham, Kent, and Cornwall. No man was to swear fealty to anyone but himself, and it was with this object in mind that, in 1086, he held a great assembly at Salisbury, "and there", as we read, "his councillors came to him, and all the people occupying land who were of any account over all England, whosoever's vassals they might be; and they all submitted to him, that they would be loyal to him against all other men".[1]

His external policy was as masterful as his internal. Though a respecter of the institutions of the Church, he refused to admit that the papacy was entitled to impose its policy upon secular rulers. He repudiated Gregory VII's claim to universal dominion and forbade that any pope should be recognized in England without his own consent. When, in 1080, Gregory demanded that he take an oath of fealty to him as his vassal, William repudiated the demand outright.

[1] *Anglo-Saxon Chronicle E*, pp. 161-162.

Second only to the crowning of Charles the Great, William's victory at Hastings, which led to his own crowning – also on Christmas Day – was the greatest event of the Middle Ages. As the former drew the distracted peoples of western and central Europe toward a common secular authority, the latter, as Professor Stenton points out, "drew England from its Scandinavian connection, and united it to the richer world of Western Europe".[1] Therefore it not only put an end to Viking dominance in the West, but by giving the West a new partner, it tended toward consolidating the West at the very moment when eastern Europe was on the point of collapsing before Islam.

[1] *William the Conqueror and the Rule of the Normans*, p. 4.

Some twenty years before the Battle of Hastings, new, persistent and ultimately detrimental enemies appeared on the borders of the Eastern Empire. In the West, kinsmen of the future conquerors of England established themselves in southern Italy. At first these Norman bands were content to hire themselves out to any masters who offered, and from time to time served the Byzantine Emperors as mercenaries. By 1042, however, they had increased in strength and arrogance sufficiently to seize the Byzantine province of Apulia, and by 1071 had expelled the Greeks from Italy.

It was in that year that the new enemy in the East struck the Empire a mortal blow. The Seljuk Turks crossed the Oxus into Khorasan in 1034; in 1049 they attacked the outlying Byzantine province of Armenia; in 1055 they took Baghdad, and made themselves the greatest power in Asia. "It was a day of ill omen for East and West alike," says Professor Tout,[1] "when the capture of Baghdad made the Turkish soldier the type of Mohammedan conquest." The Turks largely ignored the achievements of the Arab civilizations which they overthrew, while adopting their faith. By nature they were cruel and destructive; the terror of their name went before them, and when they arrived they made a desert. Under the Sultan Alp Arslan (1063-72) they completed the conquest of Armenia and attacked the Empire itself.

This strangely resilient organism, despite succession quarrels, the reigns of minors, the rule of women and eunuchs, corruption and decay, yet retained vestiges of the old Roman vitality. The very name itself now brought a brief new hope of greatness: the short reign of the Emperor Romanus Diogenes at least began with honours even against the Turkish invaders. This was chiefly due to the army, and in particular, says Fuller, to "the codification of the art of war by the Emperors Maurice and Leo VI (the Wise)

[1] Professor T. F. Tout, *The Empire and the Papacy*, 1932.

in their manuals the *Strategicon* of 579 and the *Tactica* of 900. It is no exaggeration to say that not until well into the 19th Century were military manuals of such excellence produced in western Europe.

Military stability sprang naturally from the ultra-conservative policy of the Empire. From the days of Justinian onward, the strategy and tactics of the Byzantine army remained fundamentally defensive. The entire realm was divided into themes, or army corps districts, each protected by a number of well-sited fortresses, connected by good roads, and supported by a highly organized and mobile corps of troops. It was this system, rather than the valour of the soldiers or the skill of the generals, which enabled the empire to withstand for centuries the shock of invasion. The invading armies or hordes could seldom storm the fortress, and as they possessed no adequate supply system they were compelled to live by foraging and when so occupied were at the mercy of any organized force. Byzantine strategy, therefore was very similar to that of Marshal Saxe in the 18th Century. A general did not seek battle, usually he avoided it and retired to a fortress when threatened. There he remained in complete safety while the enemy besieged it, and when, through lack of supplies, the besiegers were forced to raise the siege to seek a new 'feeding-ground', he would catch them when foraging and annihilate them. Though, generally speaking, the Byzantine armies were small when compared with those of their enemies, because they were self-contained and based on fortresses (protected supply depôts), time and again they were able to concentrate superiority of force at the point of attack . . .

There can be little doubt that in the year 1071 this organization was nearly as perfect as it had been under Basil II; but the army, though still virile, was rotten, for forty years of court mismanagement and parsimony had undermined it morally. It was not courage, organization, and tactical skill which were lacking, but discipline, morale, and confidence. The army was a highly organized vacuum – the shell of a blown egg.

Nevertheless, even with a "blown egg", Romanus Diogenes successfully defended his empire against sedition and mutiny within and the Turks outside for three years. Then, in 1071, he marched against Alp Arslan, and met him in pitched battle at Manzikert. At first the Byzantines seemed to be winning, and even captured the Turkish camp; then the treachery of mercenaries did its work again, and the day ended in a shattering Turkish victory:

> Romanus's defeat was as overwhelming as that of Crassus at Carrhae in 53 B.C., but tactically it cannot be compared with it; for though the emperor's pursuit had been foolhardy, there is little doubt that, in spite of heavy casualties, he would have regained his camp had it not been for the treason of Andronicus. It was he who was responsible for a defeat which was destined to change the course of history; yet so little was this realized at the time that Gibbon says: 'The Byzantine writers deplore the loss of an inestimable pearl: they forget to mention that, in this fatal day, the Asiatic provinces of Rome were irretrievably sacrificed.'

The loss of Asia Minor, which followed the Battle of Manzikert, in the same year as expulsion from Italy (see above), hastened the break-down of the Eastern Empire. In 1081 Constantinople itself was sacked in the course of another war of succession. Immediately, the victorious contestant, Alexius Commenus, found himself attacked by a Norman baron, Robert Guiscard, Duke of Apulia, who judged the Empire so weak that he might try for the imperial crown. His attempt failed, but it was one more demonstration that strength had left the Eastern part of Christendom, and now lay only in the West.

This is the explanation of the next chain of events. Although Western hostility (not least the hostility of the Roman Church) had played a large part in the collapse of the Eastern Empire, the triumph of the Turks was regarded as a disgrace to all Christians – and a threat which could hardly be ignored. In 1094 Alexius Commenus appealed for Western mercenaries to help him recover his lost provinces. What he got – much to his distaste – was the First Crusade, launched by Pope Urban II in 1095. In 1099 the Crusaders captured Jerusalem, amid un-Christian scenes of massacre and rapine. The Latin kingdom of Jerusalem was created – a fragile, artificial sample of European feudalism which soon became diseased in the climate of the Levant. Its chief support came from the Military Orders (Knights Templars and Hospitallers), the ceaseless flow of pilgrims to the Holy Land, and the Italian merchant cities (Venice, Genoa, Pisa), exploiting a new commercial outlet. Even at its height, the Latin kingdom was little more than a sham; the Christians held their elaborate, magnificent castles, and the main towns, but their hold on the country, as Tout says, was very slight: "Jaffa was their only port, and the road from Jaffa to Jerusalem was beset with Saracen brigands, and marked by ruined villages and unburied bodies."[1]

A succession of able leaders revived the Turkish (Saracen) cause: Imad ed-Din Zangi (1127–46), Nur ed-Din (1146–74) and Saladin (1174–93). A Second Crusade, preached by St Bernard of Clairvaux in 1146, failed miserably. The Latin kingdom struggled for survival ill-supported by Western Europe. And then, in 1176, there occurred an event which, says Fuller, "was so disastrous to the Christian cause that, whatever might subsequently have happened, it doomed the whole crusading movement to ultimate failure." This was the total defeat of the Emperor Manuel at Myriocephalum in Anatolia. Fuller comments:

> The disaster was catastrophic both for the Byzantines and the Franks.[2] For the former it was a second Manzikert, and for the latter it predicted final ruin; for without Byzantine help the Franks had not sufficient men to hold Palestine. Manuel's defeat meant the triumph of Islam.

Eleven years after the Battle of Myriocephalum, riven by internal discords, and beset by the statecraft and generalship of Saladin, the Latin kingdom of Jerusalem collapsed. At the Battle of Hattin, in July 1187, the Christian army under its King, Guy de Lusignan, was utterly destroyed; the True Cross was captured by the Saracens; three months later, Saladin entered Jerusalem, where his merciful conduct was in sharp contrast with that of the victorious Crusaders in 1099. "The Battle of Hattin," says Fuller, "was a catastrophe from which the crusades never recovered."

> Fought as it was under the shadow of the True Cross – the supreme emblem of Christendom – had Guy won it would have been God's victory; as it was, it was Allah's, and in this many Christians must have sensed the triumph of temporal power over spiritual. Thus it was that Saladin's victory struck at the

---

[1] *The Empire and the Papacy.*

[2] The Europeans of the Latin kingdom were generically known as Franks, whatever their country of origin.

foundations of the whole crusading movement and at those of the papacy itself, which hence onward became increasingly secularized because the secular powers would not accept the papal doctrine that they were subject to the divine law as interpreted by the popes. The result was that the secular powers increasingly used the crusades as instruments of their own aggrandizement, and in its turn this reacted on the prestige of the papacy and the popes had to juggle with the different secular powers and to play one off against the other.

A Third Crusade – Fuller calls it "a fiasco of self-seeking kings" – was launched in 1189, and came to nothing. In 1198 Pope Innocent III called a Fourth Crusade which, so far from injuring Islam, developed into a direct attack on the Eastern Empire. In 1204 the "crusaders" stormed Constantinople, and for three days subjected the city to ferocious sack. "Thus," says Fuller,

"after nearly 1,000 years of existence, the Byzantine Empire became a Frankish feudal empire (1204–61), and the colonial empire of Venice was created."

"Nevertheless", he continues,

in every way the fourth crusade was disastrous to the papacy and to the whole crusading movement. Worse still, instead of securing Europe against Asia, the destruction of the Eastern Empire smashed the great eastern bastion which for centuries had held Asia back. The empire never recovered from this fatal blow, politically it ceased to exist.

Yet, in spite of this, for over a century the crusades inspired western Europe with a unity it has never seen since, and has never quite forgotten. They combined its many peoples and stimulated the sense of national unity and of national hostility between them which speeded their growth into nations. Peoples became race-conscious. France emerged as a great power, as England had already done after the conquest. Spain and Portugal won greatness out of their Moorish turmoils and the foundations of Prussia were laid by the crusading enterprises of the Teutonic Knights. Before the coming of the crusades, all the Holy Roman Empire could offer to its distracted subjects was the shadow of unity, during them this shadow was all but dissipated by the substantial glory of the medieval papacy.

Under Innocent III, the papacy reached the zenith of its power; to the western world he was "king of kings". To the ambassadors of Philip Augustus he said: "To princes power is given on earth, but to priests it is attributed also over souls. Whence it follows that by so much as the soul is superior to the body, the priesthood is superior to the kingship. . . . Single rulers have single provinces, and single kings single kingdoms; but Peter, as in the plenitude, so in the extent of his power is pre-eminent over all, since he is the Vicar of Him whose is the earth and the fullness thereof, the whole wide world and all that dwell therein."[1]

The establishment of this spiritual autocracy, as it could not fail to do, led to a conflict over fiscal control; and so we find that out of the first crusade there emerged two financial instruments, indulgences and tithes. Urban II applied the first "to the whole of Christendom by his assurance that 'those who die there in true penitence will without doubt receive indulgence of their sins and the fruits of the reward hereafter' ".[2] Indulgences thus became a source of revenue. In 1184 service was commuted for payment, and, in 1215, a plenary indulgence was promised to all who contributed to the crusade funds. Even more profitable were the clerical tithes: in 1146 Louis VII of France imposed one on all clerics under his jurisdiction, and immediately after the battle of Hattin, Richard I and Philip Augustus established the "Saladin Tithe". Boniface VIII proclaimed that "The Apostolic See" had "absolute power" over ecclesiastical property. "It can exact, as it sees fit, the hundredth, the tenth, or any part of this property."[3]

Thus began to sprout the second great revolution since the decline of Rome, out of which was to emerge the economic and financial civilization of the present day. Demands for money led to the establishment of banks by Jews, Italian merchants, and the military Orders. And because money was kept on the move, and the turbulent spirits went east to leave the burgher classes in peace at home, prosperity was stimulated until many former luxuries became necessities. The Tyrians taught the Sicilians how to refine sugar and weave silk. Damascus steel rose in demand and Damascus potters became the masters of the potters in France. Windmills were introduced, also maize, lemons, apricots, melons, cotton, muslin, damask, brocades, perfumes, carpets—and hot baths.

Prosperity created leisure, and with leisure the intellect

---

[1] *Encyclopaedia Britannica* (eleventh edit.), article Innocent III.
[2] *The Cambridge Medieval History*, vol. v, p. 323.
[3] *The Cambridge Medieval History*, vol. v, pp. 324–325.

reawoke. Many chroniclers appear; Aristotle was brought to the West through Spain and later from Constantinople; the knowledge of medicine and mathematics was advanced, and the astrolabe, gnomon, sextant, and mariner's compass were adopted.

Increased knowledge led to doubt. Thus the crusades witness the beginnings of the age of heresies such as the Waldensian, Paulician, and Albigensian. At Hattin the miracle was exploded; if the True Cross could not conjure forth victory, what could?

Rapidly the social changes, either created or stimulated by the crusades, began to outstep religious conviction and brought the Church into conflict with temporal power, for "the attempt to free the members of the Church from secular control, ended in a more subtle secularization of its very heart–the Papacy itself".[1] In the thirteenth century a steady decline set in, violently hastened by the instrument of the crusade being used to extirpate not the infidel, but the Christian heretic. When, in 1255, Pope Alexander IV preached a crusade against Manfred, son of the emperor, Matthew Paris wrote: "When true Christians heard this announcement, they were astonished that they were promised the same [rewards] for shedding the blood of Christians as they were formerly that of infidels, and the versatility of the preachers excited laughter and derision."[2]

Yet another influence must be mentioned, and possibly the most remarkable of all. The spirit of adventure, released by the crusades, began to trace out the filaments of travel and discovery. Because the sword failed in the Holy Land, greater trust was placed in the word. In 1252 St. Louis sent the Franciscan William of Rubruquis to the Great Khan in central Asia, in the hope that the Mongolian empire, when once converted to Christianity, might descend upon the rear of the Turks and help the Christians in Palestine. Fantastic though the idea may seem,[3] it stimulated the missionary work of the Franciscans and Dominicans and led to traders, notably the Venetian Polos, penetrating as far east as the Great Wall of China. These men, by discovering Asia, fired that economic imagination which eventually led to the discovery of the New World.

[1] *Ibid.*, p. 321.

[2] *Matthew Paris's English History*, trans. J. A. Giles (1854), vol. III, p. 143.

[3] Yet there may have been something in the idea, for in 1256 Hulagu and his Mongols invaded Caucasia and on February 15, 1258, entered and sacked Baghdad and brought to an end the Abbasid caliphate. In 1260 Aleppo was stormed and Damascus surrendered, after which Hulagu meditated the capture of Jerusalem with the intention of restoring it to the Christians, but on hearing of the death of the Khakan Mangu he abandoned the project and returned to Mongolia.

The disruption of the Western Empire and the rise of France and England

The crusades released forces no pope could control and the spiritual impulse of the first of these great adventures was lost in the mercenary impulse of the fourth. This was not due to chance or accident, but largely because the crusades turned war from a private affair of aristocracy into a commercial undertaking, with the consequence that, as internal strife declined, the western peoples were able to devote more of their energies to peaceful occupations—that is, to secular affairs. The result was the growth of commercial cities and towns; of municipal liberties and citizen militias; of commerce and trade; of crafts and guilds and markets; and the introduction of a fixed coinage and common weights and measures. Also, of a host of universities; speculative philosophy (*e.g.* Peter Abelard, 1079–1142, Thomas Aquinas, 1227–1274); empirical sciences (*e.g.* Albertus Magnus, 1206–1280, Roger Bacon 1214–1294); and of heresies, as already mentioned.

Out of these changes and many others the idea of the national state began to oust the conception of the papal satrapy; the end which Gregory VII had set out to gain and Innocent III had all but attained ultimately was defeated by the very means they championed and a new course was set which carried the majestic vessel of the Universal Empire of western Christendom on to the rocks of the Reformation. Nevertheless, three centuries were to separate the death, in 1216, of Innocent III and the nailing of Luther's ninety-five theses on the church door at Wittenberg in 1517, and they were to be centuries of war, during which the theocratic-feudal order passed into the nationalist-monarchical system.

The first of these wars arose out of the position of the Papal States, which were wedged between the two Sicilies and the northern dominions of the empire, and it was the threat to their security which led to a quarrel between Innocent III and the Emperor Otto IV (1198–1218). The former was supported by Philip II (Augustus) of France, and the latter by John (Lackland) of England (1199–1216), and when, in 1208, England was placed under interdict and John excommunicated (1209), Philip prepared to lead a crusade against John. But in 1213, because of John's surrender to the pope, the invasion was not attempted. In the following year John joined Otto against Philip, and on July 27 the Emperor was defeated decisively at Bouvines. For John, now totally discredited, the outcome was that, in 1215, the English barons compelled him to issue the *Magna Carta*, and though Innocent declared it null and void and excommunicated the barons, fortunately for England his and John's death in 1216 ended what might have developed into a devastating civil war.

Two years after Otto's death in 1218, Innocent's ward, Frederick king of Sicily, born in 1194 and son of the Hohenstaufen Emperor Henry VI, was crowned emperor and became Frederick II (1220–1250). A man of unique character and remarkable abilities, he has been called both "The last of the Medieval Emperors" and "The first European". Alone among the Roman emperors he holds the distinction of being consigned by Dante to the pit of Hell (Canto X). Though he had promised Innocent never to unite Sicily and the empire, soon after his guardian's death his activities were directed toward bringing northern and southern Italy completely under his control. In 1227 this brought him into conflict with Gregory IX (1227–1241), who excommunicated him for not starting out on a crusade, as he had promised to do, and in 1228 he excommunicated him again for daring to do so unabsolved. Unsupported by the pope and the Military Orders, Frederick sailed with a small band of knights for the Holy Land, and through astute diplomacy gained possession of Jerusalem, Bethlehem, and Nazareth, and on March 18, 1229, sealed this remarkable achievement by crowning himself king of Jerusalem. Thus, and practically without bloodshed, he accomplished more than any crusader had done since the first crusade.

On his return in 1229 he found that the pope's troops were overrunning his southern kingdom, drove them out, and then came to terms with Gregory at San Germano in 1230. He established his imperial court at Palermo and it soon became the most brilliant in Europe and the greatest cosmopolitan centre of learning in the medieval world.

Peace between the papacy and the empire did not last, and when Frederick set out to subdue Lombardy he was again excommunicated by Gregory. Frederick then proclaimed that his cause was that of all other rulers. "If the pope succeeded in undermining him by aiding rebels", he declared, "it would only be a matter of time before all other rulers would be treated in the same way by the pope." Next, Gregory denounced him as "Antichrist" and "the King of Pestilence" who had openly maintained "that the whole world had been deceived by three imposters, namely Jesus Christ, Moses and Mohammed", and that "all are fools who believe that God, who created all things, could be born of a virgin". These accusations, even if exaggerated, show how times were changing.

Soon after this denunciation Gregory died, and his successor Innocent IV (1243–1254) declared Frederick deposed. Frederick retaliated by urging the rulers to prevent the raising of money on behalf of the papacy, because his battle was equally theirs. Again his appeal was to Europe more than to Christendom.

Frederick died in 1250 and his son Conrad IV in 1254. The latter was succeeded as king of Sicily by his son Conradin (1254–1268); and Pope Alexander IV (1254–1261), who determined never to permit the hated Hohenstaufens to reign again, kept Germany in a furore of civil war unparalleled since the days of the Carolingian *débâcle*. And when, in 1265, Conradin set out to regain his Italian inheritance, Clement IV (1265–1268) called in Charles of Anjou, brother of the king of France, to help him and offered him as a reward both Sicily and Naples. Charles accepted the call, and on August 23, 1268, Conradin was defeated decisively at Tagliacozzo. Eight weeks later he was beheaded at Naples.

Thus perished the last of the Hohenstaufens; nevertheless, the struggle continued until 1273, when Rudolph of Habsburg was recognized as king of Germany and elected emperor of the Holy Roman Empire on condition that he would not interfere in Italy. In 1278, at the battle of the Marchfeld, he wrested Austria from Ottokar of Bohemia and established the power of the house of Habsburg in the Danube valley; it was to last until 1918.

The effects of this long struggle were disastrous. The papacy was discredited by using its spiritual power to gain purely political ends; Italy was lost to the empire and for generations was distracted by the discords of Guelfs and Ghibellines; the splendid civilization of Norman Sicily was largely destroyed by the ruthless rule of Charles of Anjou; and unity in Germany was rendered impossible by her division into a vast congeries of principalities and towns: hence onward for centuries to come she became little more than a geographical expression. The sole beneficiary was France.

When, in 1152, Henry of Anjou married Eleanor of Aquitaine the royal domains of Louis VII of France (1137–1180) covered no more than the middle waters of the Seine and Loire. And when two years later Henry became Henry II of England and Duke of Normandy (1154–1189), Louis was on the one side faced by the Angevin empire stretching from the Cheviots to the Pyrenees, and on the other by the Holy Roman Empire under Barbarossa, and France was at the mercy of both.

Louis's son and successor Philip II (1180–1223)–called "Augustus"–who first secured his home position by adding a number of cities and districts to his domain, set out to rectify his intolerable position. He won Vermandois by diplomacy, then wrested Normandy from King John, and the siege of Château Gaillard, in 1204, decided the fate of that duchy. The conquest of Maine, Touraine, Anjou, and Poitou followed, and in 1206 he occupied Brittany and gave it to Peter of Dreux, as warden of the children of his wife (Constance of Brittany). In 1213 he invaded Flanders, and, as already stated, in the following year defeated the Emperor Otto at Bouvines–the copestone of his many conquests. Languedoc fell to his son Louis VIII in 1226 as the fruit of the Albigensian crusade, and later Champagne, La Marche, and Angoulême were added to the royal domain. The only province left to the English was Gascony.

Because this growth was piecemeal, it followed that in the middle ages France was never so unified as England. Even when annexed to the French crown the great fiefs retained much of their former independence. Nevertheless, under Philip IV, the Fair (1285–1314), in contradistinction to a feudal sovereign, the king became a popular ruler, and again a contest with the papacy was precipitated. Neither he nor Edward I of England (1272–1307) would accept the doctrine that a king was not entitled to tax his own clergy or that it was essential for his salvation to be subject to the pope. The upshot was that when Boniface VIII (1294–1303) set out, like Gregory VII, to enforce "the lordship of the papacy over all the kingdoms of the world", Philip had him arrested, and shortly after he died. Further, to make certain that his successor should not emulate him, in 1305 Philip induced the College of Cardinals to elect a Gascon, Bertrand de Got, pope, who became

Clement V (1305-1314), and who took up his residence at Avignon. Thus began the seventy-year "Babylonian captivity of the Church".

During the above wars, and largely because of the crusades, profound military changes were taking root. On the one hand, the contact of western chivalry with the superb castles and fortified towns of the Eastern Empire and the building of great castles, such as Kerak-in-Moab and Krak des Chevaliers in Palestine, led to castle building throughout western and central Europe, until in the fourteenth century the feudal castle dominated every district and county. On the other hand, the increasing wealth of the towns, due in no small measure to the loans raised by them to finance the crusades, led to the recruitment of city militias, such as fought at Bouvines and Courtrai (1302) and also to the introduction of specialist mercenary soldiers, notably crossbow-men to defend the castle walls. Further, as the feudal knight would neither dig, hew, mine, nor batter, paid specialists to work the siege and other engines came more and more into demand. Another reason for the increasing employment of mercenaries was the introduction of plate armour toward the end of the twelfth century and its full development in the fourteenth. This added enormously to cost, and because the real fighters were the armoured men-at-arms, all who could afford to purchase armour so gained an international commercial value and could auction their services. In contrast with these salaried specialists and superbly armoured mercenaries, war to the rank and file of the feudal levies must have seemed a very unremunerative business.

Another change arose from this. Mercenary soldiers, as long as they were paid, could be maintained indefinitely in the field, but the feudal baron and landed knight could be mustered only for forty days. During the reigns of Philip III (1279-1285) of France and Edward I of England, in order to carry out a prolonged campaign the payment of soldiers became general and whole armies, whatever the source of their recruitment, whether feudal or mercenary, became paid forces. This led to the replacement of feudal by regular service and to the appearance of a class of soldiers, such as the *routiers* in France and the *condottieri* in Italy. These professional fighters raised bands of followers and sold their services to the highest bidder, and as they served only for payment they were anti-feudal, for no code of honour bound them to their masters. A forerunner of this type of soldier was the German mercenary Roger de Flor (de Blum) who, in 1303, with his band of desperadoes, known as the Catalan Grand Company, was hired by the Emperor Andronicus II, to his regret as well as his successor's.

Although at the opening of the Hundred Years War, except for Genoese crossbow-men and galley fighters, the French and English armies and fleets were recruited from the subjects of their respective kings, the employment of hired mercenaries soon became general. When, after the battle of Poitiers, Edward III carried his national forces back to England, many *routiers* were thrown out of employment and as they refused to disband themselves they became brigands in order to live. It was these discharged mercenaries who rendered the Hundred Years War so terrible, for a peace or a truce substituted pillage and massacre for regular warfare. Hence the long, drawn-out struggle, and hence also the paradox that at a time when war was fast becoming national, the soldiers were international: men of all nations, under leaders of every social class, ready to sell their services to whoever paid them best.

Besides these military changes, a political one of fundamental importance also was taking shape. In England, under Edward I, parliament became an established institution, and, because of the development of trade, the merchant class rose in importance, for Edward depended on the merchant community to raise his national revenue, which in its turn demanded the establishment of a less feudal type of government. In the English House of Commons there was close cooperation between the knights of the shires and the representatives of the boroughs, but in France the nobility despised the burgesses, neglected to act with them, and it was only in 1343 that, in the form of local assemblies, the first Estates began to appear to consider grants in aid. Not until 1484 is the name "States General" mentioned.

Thus, by the opening of the fourteenth century, the empire was little more than a name; the papacy was in eclipse; England was becoming a nation in the modern sense of the word, and France a nation in the medieval sense. Throughout western Europe the intellectual awakening, so largely caused by the study of Aristotle, increasingly was leading to the belief in the self-sufficiency of individual intellect and faith. This struck hard at papal policy. For instance, Dante (1265–1321) in his *De Monarchia*, yearns for a universal monarchy with its title held directly from God and in no way subject to the papacy. What would have been the outcome of these changes had they not been interrupted it is impossible to say, for their progress in the most advanced countries of the West was in part arrested and in part accelerated by the Hundred Years War waged between England and France from 1337 to 1453.

CHAPTER 8

The Battles of Sluys, 1340, and Crécy, 1346

Edward III was born at Windsor on November 13, 1312. Son of Edward II, his mother, Isabella of France, was the daughter of Philip IV and sister of Charles IV, who, in 1322, succeeded his brother Philip V as king of France; therefore Edward was Charles's nephew. In 1325, at Isabella's wish, Edward II relinquished the duchy of Aquitaine to his son and Charles IV willingly agreed to the transfer against a conveyance fee of 60,000 *livres*.

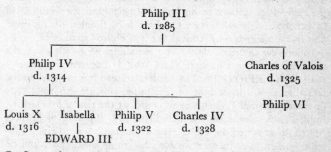

On September 10 that year the young prince performed the same homage to Charles as his father, grandfather, and great-grandfather had in their days done to the king of France. Fifteen months later Edward II was compelled to abdicate, and on January 13, 1327, his son, then in his fifteenth year, was proclaimed Edward III of England and was crowned on January 29.

Almost a year later, Charles IV died and left a daughter and a widow with child. But when, on April 1, 1328, the latter gave birth to a daughter, Philip of Valois, nephew of Philip IV and, therefore, first cousin of Charles IV, on the ground that the succession could only be transmitted through the male line, was recognized by an assembly of the French barons and peers as king of France, and on May 29, at Rheims, was crowned Philip VI.

The news of his election was most unwelcome to his cousin Isabella, who held that, because her son was of the senior branch of the Capetian line, he had the better claim, and to champion it, immediately after Philip's coronation, an embassy was sent from

London to Paris to set forth Edward's claim to the crown of France and to protest against Philip's usurpation. The English court was then in no position to enforce its demands, the protest was not taken seriously, and shortly after Philip took advantage of England's weakness and in retaliation sent an embassy to London to tell Edward that, as he alone of all Philip's vassals had failed to pay homage to him, he must do so. Because the English court temporized and sent back an evasive answer, Philip sent a second embassy to Edward with a thinly disguised ultimatum that, unless he took the oath of fealty due to the king of France, Aquitaine would be confiscated. This threat brought Edward to heel, for he could not defend his duchy by force of arms at the time. On April 14, 1329, he wrote to Philip to say that, as soon as the difficult conditions in his kingdom permitted, he would cross to France and pay homage. On June 6 he fulfilled his promise, and in the cathedral at Amiens became Philip's man.

In this exchange of claims and demands, we touch upon the main cause of the Hundred Years War. It had nothing directly to do with the French royal succession; instead it was based on the fact that Edward, as duke of Aquitaine, was an abnormal type of vassal. Normal French vassals could, at the risk of a brawl, be bullied into submission by their liege lord, the king of France; but to do so with Edward, as king of England, was to risk a full-scale foreign war. In other words, though *de jure*, kings could be vassals of kings, *de facto* they remained kings and therefore equals. Further, as long as Edward was duke of Aquitaine, he held his duchy not merely in fief to the French king, but also as an English bridgehead in France, and unless he was bound in vassalage to the king of France, tied by no moral obligation he could exploit his bridgehead with impunity. Clearly, then, if Philip could not force the English out of Aquitaine, it was to his advantage to insist on Edward's vassalage being as binding as possible; and, as clearly, if Edward could not abrogate it altogether, it was to his advantage to maintain it in its most limited form. When eventually Philip ordered the confiscation of Guienne, which, as Professor Edouard Perroy points out, was his way of declaring war on Edward, the latter forthwith "assumed the position of claimant to the throne of the Capetians" in order to transform "the feudal conflict, in which he was an inferior, into a dynastic struggle, which would make him his adversary's equal".[1]

[1] *The Hundred Years War* (English edit. 1951), pp. 92–93.

Besides this wholly feudal matter, there were others which, by impinging upon it, made a conflict nearly certain. The more important of these were the collapse of the empire in the thirteenth century and the degradation of the papacy by its transference to Avignon, because England and France were left without a counterpoise, either temporal or spiritual, to balance their claims and to distract their quarrels. Another was the question of Scotland. Since 1295, when an alliance between Scotland and France was agreed, it had been exploited by the latter to distract and weaken England. Equally true was this of Flanders, which, after the battle of Cassel, in 1328, had become wholly bound to the French king. Though Edward could not break the alliance, to weaken it he cleverly exploited the dependence of the Flemish weavers on English wool.

Seen in focus, the causes of the Hundred Years War were by no means rooted solely either in the dynastic or in the feudal questions, but rather in the multiple conditions of the age which gave it birth. The authority of the papacy was on the wane; the influence of the empire was all but spent; kingdoms were rising into power; trade was becoming increasingly a cause of contention between kingdoms; the command of the sea was looming over the horizon; the spirit of chivalry, begotten during the crusades, had become blatantly bellicose; and, above all, there was not sufficient room for two would-be dominant powers in western Europe. All these things, under the cloak of Edward's feudal claim to the crown of France, precipitated the Hundred Years War, the greatest tourney of the middle ages, which, in spite of its follies and disasters, sowed the seeds which were to sprout into a greater England and a greater France.

In this long struggle, strictly speaking there were no great decisive battles such as those which so far have been described; yet tactical decisions were not wanting, and more especially at the beginning and toward the end of the war.

With Edward having been compelled to pay homage to Philip at Amiens, the court of France had won the first round and encouraged by England's weakness it set out to win the second. It raised the question of the validity of the oath of fealty Edward had taken, which though not so precise as the one sworn by the great French vassals, was in no important respect different from the oaths of Edward II, Edward I, and Henry III. It was proclaimed "simple" and not "liege" homage, and without further discussion Edward was summoned to appear before Philip's court on July 28, 1330, to declare that his homage implied the latter.

The barons in England were in rebellion against Isabella and her paramour Roger Mortimer at the time, and Edward, tired of his mother's tutelage, sided with the malcontents, banished Isabella and had Mortimer executed at Tyburn. He was, therefore, badly placed to refuse the summons, and on March 30, 1331, he addressed a latter to Philip saying: "We recognize that the homage which we did at Amiens to the King of France was, is, and ought to be accounted liege homage, and promise him faith and loyalty, as Duke of Aquitaine and Peer of France, and Count of Ponthieu and Montreuil."[1] Four days later Edward crossed to France, and during his short visit, as Philip deemed the written engagement sufficient, amicable relations between the two countries were established. The question appeared settled and Philip began preparations for a crusade which was then being preached throughout Europe. Nevertheless, in a little over a year the first spark of the great conflagration was to gleam, not across the Channel, but north of the Tweed.

On the death of Robert Bruce – victor of Bannockburn in 1314 – on June 7, 1329, the crown of Scotland passed to his son David, then a child of five years old, who, in accordance with the treaty of Northampton of May, 1328, was recognized by Edward as king. The treaty also provided that former owners of forfeited lands in Scotland, with three exceptions, were to be reinstated.

In November, 1331, David was crowned at Scone and Edward Baliol,[2] one of the "Disinherited" and *protégé* of Edward, set out to regain his inheritance. On July 31, 1332, at the head of a small body of men-at-arms and archers, he invaded Scotland and, on August 11, at Dupplin Muir, won an astonishing victory over the Regent. Meanwhile Edward learnt that David had been subsidized by Philip, set aside the treaty of Northampton, which he disliked, marched north, laid siege to Berwick and, on July 19, 1333, decisively defeated the Scots at Halidon Hill. David fled to France and was well received by Philip, who refused to discontinue his support of the Scots unless Edward withdrew his troops from Scotland.

---

[1] Froissart's *Chronicles*, trans. Thomas Johnes (1854), vol. i, p. 45.
[2] He was the son of John Baliol who, in 1292, had been forced upon the Scots as their king by Edward I.

As the situation worsened Pope Benedict XII came forward as mediator and, in November, 1335, persuaded Edward and David to agree to a short truce as a preliminary step toward the settlement of their quarrel. Shortly after he informed Philip that until a general peace was established the crusade would have to be postponed. Annoyed by this, Philip, who had set his heart upon leading the venture, in order to bring pressure to bear on Edward, peremptorily ordered his fleet, then assembled at Marseilles, to convey the crusaders to the Holy Land, to move to the Normandy ports, as if he were about to intervene in support of Scotland.

The effect of this on England was immediate. Parliament saw in it a threat of invasion and in September, 1336, voted the subsidies necessary to place the country on a war footing and at the same time ordered the fleet to concentrate in the English Channel. In reply to this counter-challenge Philip sent troops to the borders of Guienne, and on May 24, 1337, he took the decisive plunge and declared Guienne forfeited.

Meanwhile a subsidiary incident had occurred which helped to precipitate hostilities. In 1332, Robert of Artois, Philip's brother-in-law, accused of poisoning his wife, was stripped of his estates and banished. At first he sought refuge in Hainault, but when Philip let it be known that he would take up arms against anyone who harboured him, late in 1336 Robert crossed to England. Royally received by Edward, he incited him against Philip and urged him to reassert his claim to the French crown. Though, as duke of Aquitaine, Edward could not support Robert against his legal sovereign without breaking his oath to Philip, were Philip's accession declared to be illegal he could do so with impunity. The means was at hand – his dynastic claim. Therefore, on November 1, 1337, he sent the Bishop of Lincoln to Paris with an ultimatum in which he addressed Philip as *soi-disant* king of France. Though he did not as yet claim the crown of France, what this form of address conveyed was that his homage at Amiens had been paid to a usurper and so had no binding value. Thus, in the autumn of 1337, Edward won the third round, and the conflict which had been simmering since 1328 reached boiling point.

To conquer France in the present-day sense of the word – that is, by occupation – was out of the question; for not only was the kingdom of France in the fourteenth century a large and prosperous country, but it had a population of some 20,000,000,[1] and in 1377, after the Black Death of 1348–1349, that of England has been reckoned at about 3,700,000.[2] Against this superiority it must be remembered that the feudal system of war, still maintained in France, was based on selected men and not on mass man-power, and though the French chivalry was superior numerically to the English, it was less disciplined, and it still regarded the appearance of infantry on the battlefield as an insult to its class pride.

Compared with France, England was a more united kingdom, and Edward had at his disposal for the recruitment and maintenance of his military forces an incomparably better financial system. To win his battles, all he had to do was to beat the French knights, and whereas French feudal tactics were to dismount one's opponent and to hold him to ransom, Edward's were more definitely out to kill. His tactics were "modern" more than feudal in idea, and the longbow, adopted by his grandfather from the Welsh, enabled him to base them on missile power as well as shock. Therefore, when all is considered, the tactical disparity lay with the French. Nevertheless the size of France prohibited lengthy, let alone permanent, occupation.

Following the plan of his grandfather Edward I in 1297, Edward decided to distract any attempt on the part of Philip to wrest Aquitaine from him by attacking France through the Low Countries–that is, to draw the war northward. And though an alliance with Louis Count of Flanders was out of the question, by grants of money, totalling 300,000 florins, he won over John III Duke of Brittany; Reginald Count Palatine of the Rhine; the Emperor Ludwig of Bavaria; and others. Also he signed conventions with Hainault, Guelders, Limburg, Juliers, and Brabant.

In the meantime Louis of Flanders–French by birth–to give proof of his loyalty to Philip, had posted a strong garrison on the island of Cadsand–below Sluys–expressly to harry English sea communications with the Low Countries. Edward seized upon this as a *casus belli* and sent out an expedition to capture the island, and on November 11, 1337, under cover of a rain of arrows,[3] the

---

[1] *The Cambridge Medieval History*, vol. VII, p. 342. Professor Perroy (*The Hundred Years War*, p. 36) estimates it at "a minimum of 10 to 12 million souls".

[2] *British Medieval Population*, J. C. Russell (1948), pp. 246–260.

[3] Froissart says: "The archers were ordered to draw their bows stiff and strong, and to set up their shouts; upon which those that guarded the haven were forced to retire, whether they would or not, for the first discharge did great mischief, and many were maimed and hurt" (vol. I, p. 44).

Earl of Derby and Walter Manny landed their men on it and destroyed the post. The Hundred Years War had begun and it was to last 116 years.

Next, to disrupt Flanders from within, Edward prohibited the export of English wool. Because of this the Flemings placed themselves under the authority of the celebrated Jacques van Artevelde, a leading member of the Weavers' Guild of Ghent. Artevelde broke away from Count Louis and made a commercial alliance with England. After this success the Emperor Ludwig denounced Philip for withholding homage for certain fiefs held by the empire and demanded that he restore the kingdom of France to its rightful owner – Edward of England. Lastly, the emperor appointed Edward Imperial Vicar for all the provinces west of the Rhine, and homage was rendered to him as such.

While Edward accumulated a heavy debt in his endeavours to enlarge the circle of his allies, Philip waged war in earnest on the English coasts. Squadrons manned by Normans, Spaniards, Bretons, and Genoese swept the Channel, and as early as 1336 English ships trading with Gascony had been ordered to sail in convoy.[1] In 1337 the Channel Islands and the Isle of Wight were ravaged, and in the following year Portsmouth, Portsea, and Southampton were burnt. In May, 1339, most of Hastings was burnt, and late in July a combined fleet of French and Genoese ships not only did great damage at Dover, Sandwich, Winchelsea, and Rye, but so firmly held the Channel "that no vessel could leave England without being plundered, and the crew taken or slain".[2] The most notable of these losses were the *Christopher* and *Edward*, both large ships laden with wool for Flanders. Meanwhile in Guienne, La Penne in the Agenais, which had been besieged since April, 1338, fell in January, 1339.

As a set-off to these mishaps and also to give some assurance for his heavy borrowings, on July 16, 1339, Edward, in a declaration addressed to the pope and cardinals, set out at great length his claim to the crown of France. Next, he met his half-hearted allies, in all 15,000 strong, at Vilvoordun and at Brussels, and in order to reassure them, he renounced his homage to Philip and thereby transformed the feudal conflict into a dynastic war. Then, in true spirit of chivalry, he set out at top speed with forty lances to surprise the castle of Mortagne at the junction of the

---

[1] *A History of the Royal Navy*, Sir Nicholas Harris Nicolas (1857), vol. II, pp. 21–22.
[2] *Ibid.*, vol. II. p. 36.

rivers Scarpe and Scheldt, and when he failed to take it, pressed on and surprised Thun-l'Évêque, near Cambrai.

Unprepared for an autumn campaign, Philip called for a muster of his barons at St. Quentin and Edward advanced into Cambrésis, ravaging as he went. By the time he had reached Marcoing on September 25, Philip had moved his army to Péronne, from where, on October 18, he challenged Edward to meet him in a pitched battle on any "fair field" of his own choice. But Edward fell back to La Flamengerie, near La Capelle, and Philip advanced to Buironfosse. On October 23 both armies prepared for battle. Edward, set upon fighting a defensive action on the lines he had adopted at Halidon Hill, had no intention of attacking, and Philip, counselled by his advisers that the stars were unfavourable, awaited the advance of his rival. The result was that neither side moved, and at vespers Edward retired to Avesnes, and on November 1 was back in Brussels. Thus Edward's first campaign for the crown of France ended in a bloodless and costly fiasco. He had incurred a debt of £300,000 and had forfeited the good will of the pope. Meanwhile in Gascony the French had captured Bourg and Blaye and Bordeaux was threatened directly.

Nevertheless Edward was far from despondent and on January 25, 1340, in order to "legalize" his position with the Flemings, who were still bound by homage to the crown of France, he publicly assumed the double title of king of England and France and quartered the lilies with the lions on the royal coat of arms.[1] The Flemings, relieved of their oath of allegiance to Philip, recognized Edward as king of France, and on February 21 he returned to England.

Once back, Edward's most pressing problem was to raise money to continue the war, and it was not until Parliament had made new grants that he made ready to return to Flanders, where Philip had assumed the offensive against Edward's allies; the armies confronted each other on the Scheldt. Nor had the pope been idle, for at Philip's instigation he had launched a Bull of excommunication against the rebellious Flemings, to appease whom Edward wrote that "the first time he should cross the sea, he would bring priests from his own country, who should say mass for them, whether the pope would or not. . . ."[2]

In order to frustrate his rival's return, Philip assembled a

[1] There the lilies remained until 1801.　　　　[2] Froissart, vol. 1, p. 63.

powerful fleet under Admiral Hue Quieret, Admiral Pierre Béhuchet, and the Genoese sea rover Barbanero, to watch the English coasts, to prevent Edward from recrossing the Channel, and should he attempt to do so, to capture him. When reports of this reached England, Edward was persuaded much against his will to postpone the crossing until an equally powerful fleet had been collected in the Orwell (Harwich).

When all was ready and the west wind blew, at about one o'clock on Thursday, June 22, 1340, Edward embarked in the cog[1] *Thomas* and the fleet got under way. It probably consisted of 147 vessels,[2] and was divided into three squadrons, respectively commanded by Sir Robert Morley, the Earl of Huntingdon, and the Earl of Arundel; Edward held supreme command. With it sailed a convoy of "fair dames and damsels" to reinforce the court of Queen Philippa, who had remained at Ghent.

Toward midday, on Friday, when they neared the Flemish coast, the French fleet was seen in the harbour of Sluys, resembling, according to Froissart, "a forest of masts".[3] In a letter addressed to his son Edward Duke of Cornwall, dated June 28,[4] Edward placed its strength at 190 vessels manned by 35,000 men-at-arms and others. But though the day was still young, because of the tide, instead of sailing to Sluys,[5] which lay some ten miles to the east, the fleet cast anchor off Blankenberg, and a mounted party was sent ashore to reconnoitre the enemy. On its return it reported that nineteen of the enemy vessels were abnormally large and that among them was the *Christopher*.

At daybreak on Saturday, June 24, both fleets prepared for action. Barbanero, a professional sailor, urged attack; but the two French admirals insisted upon passive defence within the harbour. A compromise was agreed upon, by which the French were to move out to the mouth of the harbour by the island of Cadsand,[6] while Barbanero and his squadron of galleys took to the open sea. Once at the harbour mouth, the French admirals, who completely lacked sea-sense, drew up their ships in three divisions or lines with the largest in the van, and as their flanks were secure, in order to make certain that their front would not

[1] A broad ship with bluff bow and stern. The word still survives in "cockboat".
[2] *Genesis of Lancaster*, Sir James Ramsay (1913), vol. i, p. 277.
[3] Froissart, vol. i, p. 72.
[4] For the letter in French and English see Nicolas, vol. i, pp. 502 and 61.
[5] The harbour of Sluys has since been silted up, and Sluis today is an inland town.
[6] Kadzand is now part of the mainland.

be stove in, they linked the ships of the van together with iron chains and cables. In their top castles they placed soldiers provided with stones and other missiles. With the van was the *Christopher*, full of Genoese crossbow-men, and near her were the *Edward*, *Katherine*, and *Rose*, all three recently captured from the English.

Edward's fleet was also ranged in three divisions, with the largest ships, under Sir Robert Morley, in the van. Men-at-arms were posted in every third ship, archers in the two intervening ones, and some ships would appear to have carried primitive cannon[1] as well as catapults. In rear was a reserve squadron, also manned by archers, and 300 men-at-arms were ordered to protect the ships carrying the women.

As the initiative was Edward's, he could afford to wait for wind, tide, and sun, and it was not until after midday[2] that the tide was suitable and the battle of Sluys opened.

To the sound of trumpets, nakers (kettle-drums), viols, tabors, and other instruments, Sir Robert Morley, with the sun to his back, sailed straight for the French van, one side shouting "St. George, Guienne!" and the other "France!" As his ships crashed into the French at their moorings, the English archers poured in volley after volley of arrows to cover the ships bearing the men-at-arms who, when they had grappled an enemy ship, boarded her and cleared her in hand-to-hand fight. Showers of stones, hurled from the fighting tops, crashed on the combatants below. The great cog *Chistopher* and her two sister cogs the *Edward* and *Rose* were speedily captured; their flags were hauled down and the lions and lilies run up. The *Christopher* was manned immediately with archers and sent to attack the Genoese galleys. The French fought with their customary valour and it is said that the entire crew of one English ship was stoned to death; but the decisive weapon was the arrow: it would seem in many cases to have cleared the French decks.

It would appear that some time before the battle Edward had summoned his supporters from Bruges and neighbouring towns to his aid, and, according to Froissart and other chroniclers but not all, they readily answered his call. They crowded out of Sluys in boats and attacked the French in rear. Barbanero considered

---

[1] See Kervyn de Lettenhove's *Froissart* (1863–1877), vol. III, p. 492.
[2] "*Post horam nonam*", see *Chronicon Galfridi le Baker de Swynbroke*, edit. Edward Maude Thompson (1889), p. 68.

the battle lost and with his twenty-four galleys headed for the open sea and escaped the slaughter.

On the defeat of their van, the French abandoned all hope and the crews of their second and third divisions in panic took to their boats, many of which capsized through overcrowding. Nevertheless the struggle lasted until sunset, and according to Edward, late into the night, and ended in the complete annihilation of the three French divisions, 166 ships in all. Admiral Quieret was killed in fair fight; but it would seem that Béhuchet was taken alive, and because he had burnt Portsmouth, in reprisal was hanged from a yard-arm.

Edward remained in the *Thomas* for several days of high carousal, with trumpets blowing and tambours beating in honour of the victory. When he landed he went in procession with the 300 priests he had brought with him to fulfil his promise to the Flemings to the chapel of My Lady of Ardenburg to attend high Mass. Next, he rode on to Ghent to greet Queen Philippa and her newly born son, named after his birthplace John of Gaunt.

Strange as it may seem, the victory, and tactically it was one of the most complete ever won by an English fleet, gave no impulse to the campaign on the Scheldt. Instead of exploiting it strategically, as he could have done, Edward decided to lay siege to Tournai, apparently because it was one of the places he had promised the Flemings as the price for their recognition of him as king of France. On July 23 he established his headquarters between Courtrai and Tournai and invested the latter, while Philip entrenched his army between Aire and Armentières. Philip had no urgency to intervene, for events were moving in his favour: in Gascony his cause was making rapid progress, and in Scotland the Scots had recovered Perth. For nearly two months the siege of Tournai was pressed and cannon were used in its bombardment. Lack of money to keep his motley army together compelled Edward to raise the siege, and on September 25 he agreed reluctantly to the Truce of Esplechin, which was to last until June 22, 1341.

The importance of the Battle of Sluys does not lie in the influence it had on Edward's second Flanders campaign, which ended in as great a fiasco as his first, but on the war as a whole. It was so complete that for the space of a generation it gave to England the command of the Channel, without which it is highly improbable that the war would have continued for long or that the psychologically decisive battle of Crécy would ever have been fought.

Edward returned to England on November 30, and in 1341, when his affairs in Scotland were going badly, an event on the Continent again compelled him to look south. In April, John III, Duke of Brittany and Earl of Richmond in England, died without an heir and a dispute over his succession followed. The claimants were Charles of Blois, a nephew of Philip VI, who married John's niece, and John Count of Montfort, John's half-brother. Philip supported the former, and Edward, who saw in the quarrel the means to counter the Franco-Scottish alliance by an Anglo-Breton one, championed the latter, with the result that a deplorable war began which gave new life to the struggle between England and France and lasted for twenty years. According to Sir James Ramsay it "made the Hundred Years War possible".[1]

Though Philip took no official part in this war, his son, the Duke of Normandy, and his brother, the Count of Alençon, joined de Blois, and on November 21 they forced the surrender of Nantes and were fortunate enough to capture de Montfort. But they had not reckoned with the countess, his wife, who, in the words of Froissart, "possessed the courage of a man, and the heart of a lion".[2] A true forerunner of Joan of Arc,[3] her heroic defence of the castle of Hennebont (north of Lorient) was one of the most remarkable incidents of the Hundred Years War. It roused Edward's chivalrous spirit, and in May, 1342, when the countess was reduced to the last extremity, he sent Sir Walter Manny with 300 lances and 2,000 archers to her relief. Manny raised the siege, but was not strong enough to venture inland, so another army, under the Earl of Northampton and Robert of Artois, was sent out. Robert was mortally wounded at Vannes, and on September 30 Northampton won a desperately fought battle at Morlaix. This success so encouraged Edward that on October 23 he sailed to Brest, resolved that his third campaign should be fought in Brittany. Like his first and second, it proved an all but unqualified fiasco and ended on January 19, 1343, in a three-year truce signed at Malestroit, which included Scotland, Hainault, and Flanders.

Soon after both sides took advantage of the truce to push their respective interests, and Pope Clement VI, who saw that the prospects of a final settlement were rapidly evaporating, persuaded the contending parties to meet in conference at Avignon in October–December, 1344. There Edward first set forth his

[1] *Genesis of Lancaster*, vol. i, p. 297.   [2] Froissart, vol. i, p. 96.
[3] See for her exploits Froissart, vol. i, pp. 105–107.

claim to the French crown, then came down to business. He demanded an enlarged Guienne in full sovereignty—that is, freed from all vassalage. In their turn Philip's councillors contended that although Aquitaine was well and truly confiscated, Philip would nevertheless agree to restore the fief—incidentally Edward was still in occupation—and even to enlarge its frontiers, as long as it was held in vassalage from him.[1]

As neither party would give way, the war was renewed and Edward resolved simultaneously to attack France from Brittany and Guienne. In June, 1345, de Montfort, who by then had escaped from France, and the Earl of Northampton, were sent to Brittany, and a little later the Earl of Derby took ship for Bordeaux. Edward heard that van Artevelde's régime was tottering and on July 5 he sailed for Sluys. There, on July 7, he met van Artevelde, who was assassinated on his return to Ghent. On July 26 Edward was back in England.

In September, de Montfort died in Brittany, and Northampton, who had accomplished little, went into winter quarters. Derby, in the south, was more successful, and in a skilfully fought campaign, the success of which was largely due to his moderation,[2] he took Bergerac, and in a brilliant operation relieved Auberoche. After these successes, Angoulême and many other cities opened their gates to him and he returned to Bordeaux for the winter of 1345–1346.

These many losses roused Philip to action, and toward the end of 1345 he summoned the levies of Normandy, Picardy, Burgundy, Lorraine, Provence, and Languedoc to gather at Toulouse under command of the Duke of Normandy. Early in the spring of 1346 the duke set out, and in April laid siege to the castle of Aiguillon (on the junction of the Garonne and the Lot) then held by Ralph Lord Stafford, Sir Walter Manny, and others. The castle was immensely strong and the siege soon developed into one of the most famous of the whole war. It was pressed until August 20, when the duke suddenly raised it; for that day the alarming news came from the north that Edward had invaded France. Derby—now Earl of Lancaster—had also heard of the king's landing, and now that Aiguillon was safe he set out for Saintonge and Poitou as a diversion in Edward's favour.

---

[1] See *The Hundred Years War*, Edouard Perroy, p. 116.
[2] Froissart (vol. 1, p. 130) records that to the inhabitants of Bergerac Derby said: "He who begs for mercy should have mercy shown him: tell them to open their gates, and let us enter, when we will assure them of safety from us and from our people."

On his return from Sluys, Edward at once began to raise an army to push the war in Gascony, and as he had learnt through experience that feudal levies were unfitted for continental warfare, he decided to recruit a picked force of men by Commissions of Array, a system which on occasions had been used by his father and grandfather.[1] In accordance with this, the sheriffs and commissioners of array first compiled a list of all landlords, next each man who owned land or rents to the value of £5 was ordered by them to find one archer; those rated at £10, one hobeler;[2] and those with holdings worth £25, one man-at arms; and so on upward to the great feudal lords who, according to their means, raised well-organized retinues. Thus, Richard Lord Talbot recruited 14 knights, 60 esquires, and 82 archers, and John de Vere Earl of Oxford, 23 knights, 44 esquires, and 63 archers.[3] Landowners not able to serve in person were allowed to find substitutes, and if they failed to do so were fined at the rate of £1 an archer, £3 6s. 8d. a hobeler, and £6 13s. 4d. a man-at-arms. The archers were recruited from the yeomen,[4] a class completely above villeinage. The French had to resort to hiring Genoese and other crossbow-men to make good their lack of home-trained archers.

Here, a few words must be said on the longbow, a weapon which was to dominate the battlefields of France until Agincourt, after which its decline was rapid. As we have seen, it was adopted from the south Welsh by Edward I. It was made of a six-foot length of elm, from which a three-foot arrow was shot. It was a far more powerful weapon than the short Norman bow and less cumbersome than the crossbow, and its arrows could penetrate two layers of mail armour.[5]

In 1298, Edward I put this weapon to the test against the Scots under Wallace at Falkirk with terrible effect, and because Edward II failed to do so against Bruce at Bannockburn he was

---

[1] See Stubbs's *Constitutional History of England* (1887), vol. II, pp. 284–285.

[2] Hobelers, or hobilars, were mounted infantry, spearmen or archers, first raised in Scotland to operate with cavalry in the Scottish raids.

[3] *A History of the Art of War in the Middle Ages*, Sir Charles Oman, vol. II, p. 128.

[4] As a national sport, archery was encouraged after the conquest. In 1252, according to Henry III's Assize of Arms, all forty-shillings freeholders were required to possess a bow and arrows. The yeomen were, in fact, a standing archer militia.

[5] In a trial made before Edward VI, in 1550. arrows were shot through a one-inch board of well-seasoned timber (*Archery*, Badmington Library, 1894, p. 431). Its range was about 250 yards. Shakespeare mentions as a notable feat 280 to 290 yards (*King Henry IV*, part II, act III, scene 2). In 1798, 1856, 1881, and 1897, ranges of 340, 308, 286, 290, and 310 were attained with the longbow.

defeated decisively and the lesson of the longbow had to be relearned in 1332 at Dupplin Muir.

As already mentioned, this battle was fought between the "Disinherited"–Edward Baliol, Henry Beaumont, and others–and Donald Earl of Mar, the Scottish regent. The former had 500 knights and men-at-arms and between 1,000 and 2,000 archers. The latter commanded, it is said, 2,000 men-at-arms and 20,000 foot–an exaggeration.

Fully aware of the desperate odds against them, the "Disinherited" first attacked Mar by night. But when dawn broke and they discovered their enemy advancing in battle array, they took up position on the slope of a hill. They dismounted all but forty of their cavalry and formed them up in phalangial order, with archers thrown forward on their flanks. Thus their order of battle assumed a crescent formation. Mar paid no attention to the archers, charged down on Baliol's centre and drove it in. At once the flanking archers wheeled inward and opened so devastating a fire that the Scots were driven into a confused mass and all but exterminated. Henry de Beaumont and some of his followers then mounted their horses and chased the fugitives off the field. In 1333, Edward may be said to have patented these tactics at the battle of Halidon Hill, for thence onward for a hundred years they remained the norm of English fighting.

Edward's army mustered at Portsmouth. According to Sir James Ramsay, the forces raised were 3,580 archers from the counties of the Trent, with 100 from the county Palatine of Chester; 3,500 Welshmen, half archers and half spearmen; 2,743 hobelers; and 1,141 men-at-arms, who with miners and supernumeraries, made a total of approximately 10,000 men.[1]

This army d'élite was organized, disciplined, and paid by the king. Tactically, it was superior to the French: in the one missile and shock were combined; in the other shock was all but entirely relied upon. Edward's tactics were defensive, Philip's were offensive; in the former the arrow disorganized and demoralized before the shock set out to annihilate; in the latter, as among the Goths, shock action dominated from start to finish and each subsequent charge became more chaotic than the one before. Because mounted men could seldom play a decisive part during the act

---

[1] *Genesis of Lancaster*, vol. I, p. 319. Oman in *A History of the Art of War*, vol. II, p. 130, says 2,400 horse and 12,000 foot. Ferdinand Lot in *L'art Militaire et les Armées au Moyen Age* (1946). vol. I, p. 346, accepts Ramsay's figures.

of disorganization and demoralization, Edward normally dismounted the bulk of his men-at-arms and formed them up in phalanx, both to withstand the enemy's mounted attack and to protect his own archers. His normal formation was in three battles or divisions, two dismounted in front with an interval between them, and one in rear, either mounted or ready to mount, and held in reserve. The archers were formed up on the flanks of the two forward battles *en herse*[1]–that is, at an angle thrown forward (see diagram), the two inner flanking bodies meeting at an angle,

and the two outer, when possible, resting on an obstacle, such as a wood, stream or village. To protect themselves the archers almost invariably dug *trous de loup* and drove ironshod stakes into the ground in front of their position. Because of these obstacles and the arrows, the French chivalry usually avoided the archers and instead charged the dismounted men-at-arms; when they did so the archers raked their flanks, as we have seen happened at Taginae in 552. There was another reason for attacking the dismounted men-at-arms: according to the code of chivalry it was beneath a knight's dignity to attack infantry because infantry had little or no ransom value. Usually they were indiscriminately slaughtered after a victory to prevent them from turning into brigands, for prisoners' cages were unknown in the fourteenth century.

Simultaneously with his military preparations Edward launched a propaganda campaign against the French in which he denounced "Philip as threatening 'to root out the English tongue'. This document was addressed to the Provincial of the Friars Preachers for circulation through the pulpit."[2] Further, he rejected all interventions on the part of Pope Clement VI to preserve the peace, which made it clear to Philip that a full-scale invasion of France was in prospect. Therefore Philip wrote to King David of Scotland to beg him not to miss an opportunity to strike at England.

On July 11, 1346, when all was ready, the expedition put to sea.

---

[1] See *Battles of English History*, Hereford B. George (1895), p. 62. Though *herse* means "harrow", Mr. George points out that it also means "the stands used in church for seven candles, the centre one forming the apex and those on the sides gradually lower".

[2] *Genesis of Lancaster*, Sir James H. Ramsay, vol. I, p. 320.

According to Froissart its destination was Gascony;[1] but on the way across the Channel, a Norman refugee, Godfrey of Harcourt, convinced Edward "that it would be more for his interest to land in Normandy", because that province was "one of the most fertile in the world" and that "the Normans have not been accustomed to the use of arms; and all the knighthood, that otherwise would have been there", was "with the duke before Aiguillon".[2] Edward changed his mind and ordered the fleet to make for St. Vaast-la-Hogue on the Cotentin Peninsula. What his strategic aim was it is impossible to fathom; but as Sir Charles Oman points out, as Edward's conduct of the campaign of Crécy shows no proof of any rational scheme one can only conclude that the expedition was nothing more than "a chivalrous adventure" or "a great raid of defiance pushed deep into France to provoke its king".[3]

The next day, July 12, Edward put in at La Hogue, and remained there six days to disembark his army. On July 18 he set out for Valognes, advanced by way of Carentan, St. Lô, and Fontenay--le-Pesnel (near Tilly), and arrived at Caen on July 26. Edward left the castle to defend itself, but the city, which was unwalled, was sacked indiscriminately. Edward then ordered that all wounded and booty should be embarked in the fleet, which had put into the mouth of the river Orne, but in the meantime the crews had mutinied and had set sail for England.[4] It would seem that it was this act of indiscipline which settled for Edward his strategic problem. Without a line of communications he could not remain where he was, and because to turn south and to join the Earl of Lancaster would bring him into head-on collision with the superior army of the Duke of Normandy, then moving north, Edward's sole remaining course was to move eastward to establish a base in Flanders.

From Caen he set out on July 31, passed by way of Lisieux and Brionne and reached Elboeuf on August 7. He found the bridge at Rouen broken and ascended the left bank of the Seine to seek

---

[1] Froissart writes: "The King of England, having heard how pressed his people were in the castle of Aiguillon, determined to lead a great army into Gascony" (vol. I, p. 150).

[2] *Ibid.*, vol. I, pp. 151–152.

[3] *A History of the Art of War in the Middle Ages*, vol. II, p. 131.

[4] *Welsh Wars,* John Morris (1901), p. 108. He writes: "In 1346 it is an undoubted fact . . . that Edward III and his army were left stranded in Normandy simply because the fleet disappeared in complete defiance of orders . . . so that the army had to proceed as best it could, and Crécy was as it were an accident."

a crossing. On August 13 he neared Paris. Along the whole of his line of march he devastated the country in a savage way while the French watched him from the right bank of the river. He reached Poissy, repaired the bridge there, forced a crossing on August 16 and pushed on to Grisy. Meanwhile Philip had done nothing to dispute his crossing, and to the consternation of the citizens of Paris had fallen back to St. Denis.

From Grisy Edward set out by forced marches northward, and on the 21st reached Airaines, ten miles south of the river Somme, where his scouts reported to him that all the bridges and fords above Abbeville were either broken or held. Philip was then at Amiens and his army grew stronger day by day.

Unable to cross at Abbeville, Edward pressed on to Acheux and reached it on August 23. There he offered a large reward to any man who could point out to him a ford. A native of the village of Mons-en-Vimeu, Gobin Agache, claimed the reward and offered to guide the king to the ford of Blanque Taque ("The White Spot") ten miles below Abbeville, which could be crossed at low tide. As Philip was now on his enemy's heels, not a moment was to be lost, and at midnight Edward set out and reached the ford early on August 24. There he halted for an hour or two until the tide was out, when, under cover of his archers, he forced a crossing and carried the whole of his army over as Philip came up, but only to be cut off by the rise of the tide. That night Edward rested at Noyelles, where the Countess of Aumale, sister of the late Robert of Artois, was living, and the next morning he resumed his retreat toward the forest and village of Crécy-en-Ponthieu. Meanwhile Philip returned to Abbeville to cross the Somme by its bridge.

When he arrived at Crécy Edward decided to accept battle. The reason given by Froissart is a sufficient one in the age of chivalry—namely, that having reached the inheritance of his grandmother he resolved to defend it; besides he found there a position which fitted his tactics. But to suggest, as some writers have done, that he was compelled to make a stand because further retreat would have demoralized his army, is highly unlikely, for at Crécy he was within three marches of Flanders, and Philip was a day's march in rear of him.

As he suspected that Philip would advance by the Abbeville–Hesdin road—which he did—and as he knew that unless he were to manœuvre round his enemy's left flank, which would have been contrary to chivalrous etiquette, he would be compelled to attack frontally, Edward selected a position which would meet this contingency and fit his tactics and strength. It was a gentle rise of ground between the villages of Crécy and Wadicourt, which still remains much as it was in his day.[1] To the east of them—that is, on Edward's prospective front—lay a dip in the downland called the *Vallée des Clercs*, on the far side of which stood the village of Estrées-les-Crécy, south of which was the village of Fontaine-sur-Maye, a little to the west of the Abbeville–Hesdin road. From Fontaine-sur-Maye, a small stream, the Maye, originates and runs westward through Crécy, south of which the great Forest of Crécy extends. The distance between Crécy and Wadicourt is a little more than 3,000 yards.

Edward's army was marshalled in the usual three battles or divisions, two on the forward slope of the rise east of the Crécy–Wadicourt road with a gap between them, and one in rear, presumably on the road. The right forward battle—the one nearest Crécy—was under the nominal command of the Prince of Wales, then a boy of seventeen; the actual commanders were Warwick the Earl Marshal and the Earls of Oxford and Harcourt. The left battle was commanded by Northampton the Constable and the Earl of Arundel, and was deployed south of Wadicourt. The rearward battle was commanded by Edward, who established his battle headquarters at a windmill on the Crécy end of the rise; the mound upon which it stood can still be seen. To protect his right flank Edward had a series of shallow ditches dug, *trous de loup* were also dug in front of the Prince's battle.

The archers were drawn up *en herse*—as already described—on the flanks of each of the forward battles, the outer detachments at an angle which linked the outer flanks of the battles with the villages of Crécy and Wadicourt, and the inner covered the gap between the battles, forming a V pointing eastward.

According to Froissart, the right battle consisted of about 800 men-at-arms, 2,000 archers and 1,000 Welshmen; the left, 800 men-at-arms and 1,200 archers; and the rearward one, 700 men-at-arms and 2,000 archers; a total of 8,500 men.[2] Though the categories of soldiers may be incorrect, the total number would

---

[1] I visited the battlefield in 1917, and comparing the locality with a copy of a map alleged to have been made in the fifteenth century, I found very little difference in the lay-out of the villages.

[2] Froissart, vol. 1, p. 163. Lot in *L'Art Militaire*, etc., vol. 1, p. 347, says 9,000.

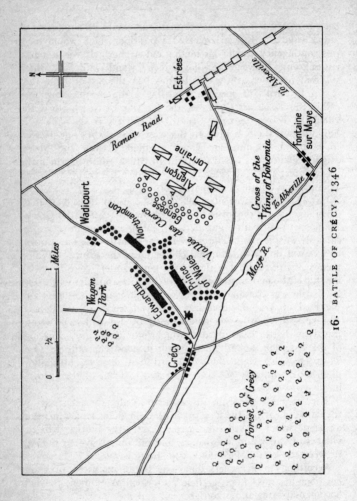

16. BATTLE OF CRÉCY, 1346

seem reasonable as Edward's fighting strength on landing at La Hogue was about 10,000.

In the rear of the battle front Edward "enclosed a large park near a wood" and in it marshalled "all his baggage-wagons and horses".[1] According to Villani in his *History of Florence* and the *Grandes Chroniques de France*, Edward had with him three cannon,[2] which were posted with the archers.

Once deployment was ended, Edward, attended by his two marshals, rode at a foot pace down the ranks encouraging his men. They were then ordered to eat their midday meal and when they had refreshed themselves they again formed battle order and sat on the ground "placing their helmets and bows before them, that they might be the fresher when their enemies should arrive".[3]

Meanwhile Philip had gathered in his army at Abbeville. With him were the blind, or half-blind, King John of Bohemia and his son Charles, King of the Romans; James III King of Majorca; Philip's brother Charles of Alençon; Philip's nephew Louis of Blois; Louis of Flanders; John of Hainault; Rudolf Duke of Lorraine; and most of the chivalry of France. Never before during the middle ages had such a galaxy of knights been seen on one battlefield. According to Lot's estimate, the French men-at-arms numbered 8,000 supported by 4,000 foot,[4] including a body of Genoese crossbow-men under command of Odone Doria and Carlo Grimaldi. The French men-at-arms were also marshalled in three battles, the first commanded by the King of Bohemia and the Counts of Alençon and Flanders; the second by the Duke of Lorraine and the Count of Blois; and the third by King Philip and the King of the Romans.

Not certain where the English were, early on August 26 Philip set out on the Abbeville–Hesdin road and sent forward the Lord Moyne of Bastleberg and three knights to seek them. On their return, Moyne informed the king that Edward was in position at Crécy, and he suggested that the king should halt his army and bivouac for the night, so that the rear might catch up with the van and the whole army attack on the following morning.

---

[1] Froissart, vol. I, p. 163.

[2] See Ramsay's *Genesis of Lancaster*, vol. I, p. 331. Oman, vol. II, p. 142, suggests that they were probably *ribauldequins*, weapons "consisting of several small tubes clamped together and with their touch-holes so arranged that one sweep of the linstock would discharge them simultaneously" (*ibid.*, p. 216).

[3] Froissart, vol. I, p. 163.

[4] *L'Art Militaire et les Armées au Moyen Age*, vol. I, p. 347. But it also suggests that the French army may have been numerically inferior to the English (p. 348).

Philip ordered that this should be done. Then, writes Froissart: "Those that were in front halted; but those behind said they would not halt, until they were as forward as the front. When the front perceived the rear pressing on, they pushed forward; and neither the king nor the marshals could stop them, but they marched on without any order until they came in sight of their enemies. As soon as the foremost rank saw them, they fell back at once in great disorder, which alarmed those in the rear, who thought they had been fighting. . . . All the roads between Abbeville and Crécy were covered with common people, who, when they were come within three leagues of their enemies, drew their swords, bawling out, 'Kill, Kill'. . . . There is no man, unless he had been present, that can imagine, or describe truly, the confusion of that day. . . ."[1]

The hour of vespers (6 p.m.) had passed, when the sky suddenly darkened and "a heavy rain fell, accompanied by thunder and a very terrible eclipse of the sun; and before this rain a great flight of crows hovered in the air over the battalions, making a loud noise". As rapidly as it had come the storm cleared, "and the sun shone very bright, but the Frenchmen had it in their faces, and the English in their backs".[2] Meanwhile the Genoese, who had regained some order, were brought forward, with the Counts of Alençon and of Flanders in their rear, and began descending into the *Vallée des Clercs*. As they approached the English they raised a loud shout "in order to frighten them"; but their enemy remained still. They shouted again, but "the English never moved". A third time they shouted, and began to shoot their quarrels. "The English archers then advanced one step forward, and shot their arrows with such force and quickness, that it seemed as if it snowed. When the Genoese felt these arrows, which pierced their arms, heads, and through their armour, some of them cut the strings of their crossbows, others flung them to the ground and turned about and retreated quite discomfited." Seeing this the King of France cried out: "Kill me those scoundrels; for they stop our road. . . ."[3]

The English archers continued to shoot, and soon their arrows fell among the horsemen and sent their horses plunging among and trampling down the crowds of flying Genoese. Vying with each other to get to the front, the French chivalry pushed their way through the fugitives, hacking at them with their swords.

[1] Froissart, vol. I, p. 164.   [2] *Ibid.*, vol. I, pp. 164–165.
[3] *Ibid.*, vol. I, pp. 165–166.

The English archers next turned their arrows on the French men-at-arms, and this is what we read: "For the bowmen let fly among them at large, and did not lose a single shaft, for every arrow told on horse or man, piercing head, or arm, or leg among the riders and sending the horses mad. For some stood stock still, and others rushed side-ways, and most of all began backing in spite of their masters, and some were rearing and tossing their heads at the arrows, and others when they felt the bit threw themselves down. So the knights in the first French battle fell, slain or sore stricken, almost without seeing the men who slew them."[1]

Once it had been repulsed, no attempt was made by the first French battle to clear the field for the second battle behind it, with the result that before the latter could charge it was thrown into complete confusion, and in its scramble forward the blind king of Bohemia was killed. At times, when the French men-at-arms fell back, the Welshmen in Edward's army, who carried long knives, rushed forward and "falling upon earls, barons, knights and squires, slew many, at which the King of England was afterwards much exasperated";[2] and no wonder, for a dead man brought in no ransom.

It is interesting to read in Froissart that in the assaults made by the Counts of Alençon and Flanders, the French men-at-arms "coasted, as it were, the archers";[3] that is to say, their horses shied away from the enemy arrows, and whether their riders despised the archers or not, they were willy nilly carried toward the dismounted English battles. This happened more particularly on the English right, and the Prince of Wales's battle was so roughly handled that Warwick sent back to the King at the windmill to ask for aid. When he heard that the Prince was unharmed, Edward said to the messenger: ". . . return back to those that sent you, and tell them from me, not to send again for me this day, or expect that I shall come, let what will happen, as long as my son has life: and say, that I command them to let the boy win his spurs. . . ."[4] Nevertheless he sent the Bishop of Durham and thirty knights to strengthen his son's battle.

Probably the reason why he sent no more was that he saw at the time that the left battle, under Northampton, was wheeling to its right to take in flank the French charging the right battle.

---

[1] Quoted by Oman, *A History of the Art of War*, etc., vol. I, p. 143.
[2] Froissart, vol. I, p. 166.   [3] *Ibid.*, vol. I, p. 166.   [4] *Ibid.*, vol. I, p. 167.

And as the French were repulsed, Philip came up with the third French battle, but only to add to the confusion.

From first to last the English counted fifteen separate and successive assaults made against them, the last ones taking place in the night. Throughout the battle the French had no concerted plan; for each band of knights had but one idea, to close with its enemy; hence, from first to last, the inextricable confusion.

There was no question of a pursuit. Edward kept his men under arms on the battlefield and at dawn next day, when the levies of Beauvais and Rouen, unaware that the battle had been lost, came up, he easily routed them. Meanwhile Philip, who had been wounded in the neck by an arrow and had had a horse shot under him, was persuaded by John Count of Hainault to leave the field. He rode to the castle of Broye, where he halted until midnight to refresh himself, and then remounted and rode on to Amiens, where he arrived about daybreak.

When, on the morning of August 27, the last of the French had been driven away, Edward allowed his men to break their ranks and strip the dead. It was then found that among the slain were the King of Bohemia, the Duke of Lorraine and the Counts of Flanders, Alençon, Auxerre, Harcourt, Sancerre, Blois, Grandpré, Salm, Blamont, and Forez, as well as 1,542 knights and esquires. Of the French common soldiery the number of killed varies from 10,000 upwards. The English casualties, as reported, were minute: two knights, one esquire, some forty men-at-arms and archers, and a few dozen Welsh.[1]

On Monday, August 28, Edward advanced from Crécy to Montreuil, and from there by easy stages he moved on Calais, outside the walls of which he arrived on September 4.

Enclosed as the fortress was by a double wall with wet ditches, it could not be stormed; therefore Edward set about to invest it on its landward side, and, as he was master of the Channel, to blockade it on its seaward: hence, unless it could be relieved, its doom was sealed. But Philip, it would appear, was so stunned by his defeat that for six months he did nothing, and to add to his moral collapse, on October 17, 1346, King David of Scotland, who to support him had invaded England and had advanced to Durham, was defeated decisively and captured at Neville's Cross. Not until June, 1347, did the Duke of Normandy appear on the field, and on July 27 he approached Calais. But he found Edward's position

---

[1] These figures are quite unreliable.

too strong to attack; six days later he retired, and on August 4, Jean de Vienne surrendered the fortress. On September 28 a truce between all the allies of both sides was signed to last until July 9, 1348, and on October 12 Edward returned to England.

Calais was the sole strategic gain of the campaign, and as events were to prove, the sole English gain of the whole of the Hundred Years War. It was certainly an important one, as much so as Gibraltar was to be to England in years to come. Edward converted it into an all but impregnable *place d'armes* as well as into a highly profitable commercial centre; for he ordered that no merchandise was to be exported from England to the Continent except by way of Calais. Not only did the fortress provide him and his successors with a bridgehead in France, but as General Wrottesley points out, as long as it was firmly held no invasion of England was possible before the invention of the steamship.[1] For over two hundred years it remained in English hands, and not until it was lost to the Duke of Guise on January 8, 1558, did a serious threat of invasion arise, to materialize thirty years later in the coming of the Spanish Armada.

But the most pronounced influence of Crécy on the war was that it made the English a military nation. Henceforth England's fighting prestige was held so high that it had to be maintained by the English. As Sir Charles Oman says, the English victories over the Welsh and Scots had hardly been noticed on the Continent, and their French wars under Henry III and Edward I "had brought them little glory".[2] But Crécy was a revelation, not only to the French, but to the English also: the former were stunned and the latter inebriated by it. Thus its importance in history is that it morally founded the Hundred Years War, a conflict which was to endure until another moral *débâcle* was to precipitate its close.

[1] "Crecy and Calais", Major-General the Hon. George Wrottesley (*Collections for a History of Staffordshire*, 1897), vol. XVIII, p. 57.
[2] *A History of the Art of War*, etc., vol. II, p. 146.

The dissolution of the Middle Ages

The hundred years which followed the battle of Crécy witnessed the dissolution of the Middle Ages and the emergence of the Renaissance, and of the several causes two of the most important were the Black Death and the discovery of gunpowder.

The former, which was probably bubonic plague, came out of the East in 1347 and recurred at intervals throughout the second half of the fourteenth century. According to Hecker it carried off a quarter of the population of Europe. Its influences on society were catastrophic. Not only were people disorganized and demoralized by death, but barbarized. Witchcraft and sorcery were stimulated; waves of mysticism and doubt swept Europe, and the medieval system of tillage was disrupted by the dearth of labour. This led to an increased demand for hired service and the rapid extinction of the villeinage: the bondage of money replaced the bondage of the soil.

According to Colonel Hime (*The Origin of Artillery*, 1915), the first receipt for the manufacture of gunpowder is to be discovered in Roger Bacon's (1214–1292) *Epistolae de Secretis Operibus Artus et Naturae et de Nullitate Magiae*, written before 1249. But there is nothing in his writings to suggest that he ever contemplated its use in firearms, and who first thought of propelling a ball through a metal tube by exploding gunpowder is unknown.

Apparently the earliest extant document that mentions cannon is one in Arabic, dated 1304. Of others, two belong to the city of Ghent, dated 1313 and 1314 respectively; also in an illuminated MS. of 1326, now in Christ Church, Oxford, there is a picture of the earliest form of cannon, a "dart-throwing vase", also called a "*pot-de-fer*". This primitive weapon appears to have been used in the siege of Metz in 1324, and by Edward III in Scotland in 1327.

According to Sir Charles Oman, in 1339 the first mention is made of another firearm, called *ribauldequin*, a primitive mitrailleuse of several small iron tubes so arranged that they could be fired simultaneously. This weapon was used by Edward III in his war with France, and in 1387 one of 144 barrels was made, the barrels grouped in batteries of twelve apiece, allowing twelve salvoes of twelve balls each.

When one considers the crudeness of fourteenth-century mechanics and the religious restrictions of the age, progress in firearms was rapid. In 1340 we hear of powder mills in Augsburg, and if, in 1346, Edward III did not make use of cannon at Crécy –as some doubt–that year they are known to have been used at the siege of Calais.

By 1391 iron shot are met with, for mention is made of 928 stored in the arsenal of Bologna. Before the century was out progress had so far advanced that it was possible to build bombards of a calibre of twenty-five inches, such as the still existing *Dulle Griete* of Ghent. About this time the hand-gun, first heard of in 1364, was adopted more generally. It resembled a small cannon on a straight stock, which could be carried and fired by a single man. It weighed about ten pounds, was fired by applying a match to a touch-hole, and its bullet was of lead. Usually it was fired from behind defences, and indifferent infantry were armed with it.

Toward the end of the fifteenth century the hand-gun gave way to the match-lock, an iron barrel mounted on a stock which fitted against the chest. It was provided with a cock to hold the match and a trigger to bring it down on to a pan containing the priming. This weapon appears to have been a German invention. It was called *hakenbüsche*, in France *arquebuse*, and in England sometimes "caliver". It was the first true infantry firearm.

With the discovery of gunpowder war passed into its technological phase. Valour gave way to mechanical art: he who could wield the superior weapon was the more formidable foe, irrespective of his social status or his courage. For as Carlyle has said, the genuine use of gunpowder is "that it makes all men alike tall". In short, it democratizes fighting.

Thus, by changing the character of war, gunpowder changed the medieval (Christian) way of life. The search for the perfection of firearms and of defence against them gave birth to a spirit of inquiry which soon embraced all things. It was gunpowder more than contact with Islam during the crusades which gave life to the Renaissance, because it shattered the medieval order physically and morally. War as a trial of moral values by battle, in which the Church refereed for God, gradually gave way to a new certainty: that war is a means toward a political end in which the deciding factor is power. As war was secularized, peace followed suit, idealism gave way to realism, and by the end of the fifteenth century we find such noted soldiers as the condottieri Gian Paolo Vitelli and Prospero Colonna declaring that "wars are won rather by industry and cunning than by the actual clash of arms". Gunpowder blasted the feudal strongholds and the ideals of their owners. As portable firearms multiplied, the medieval contempt for unmounted troops was undermined, until in tactical importance foot soldiers were raised to the level of the mounted men-at-arms.

Though these changes did not begin to take visible shape until the close of the Hundred Years War, those that resulted from the Black Death and its recurrences in no way sobered the rivalries of England and France, and in spite of the efforts of the pope to convert the successive truces which followed the occupation of Calais into a permanent peace, war broke out again in 1355. That year, Edward Prince of Wales, later to be known as the "Black Prince", set out to ravage Languedoc. Meanwhile Philip VI had died on August 22, 1350, and his son and heir, John Duke of Normandy, now John II of France, set out to oppose the Black Prince. On September 17, 1356, at the head of a superior army, he met him near Maupertuis in present-day Vienne, and on the field of Poitiers was defeated decisively and captured, and the Truce of Bordeaux was agreed. Bereft of its king, France was paralysed, and a peasants' revolt, known as the Jacquerie, followed in 1358. Retribution was swift, for within a few weeks of its outbreak the rising was suppressed brutally by the French nobility.

In March, 1359, John, in order to regain his liberty, agreed to abandon to Edward all the west of France from Guienne to Calais, but when nothing came of this war broke out again, and in the spring of 1360 Edward appeared before Paris. As he did not know what next to do, he decided to listen to the papal legate, who was urging him to make peace. The outcome was the Convention of Brétigny and the Treaty of Calais; the latter was signed on October 24. According to its terms Normandy was assigned to France and a vastly enlarged Aquitaine to England, as well as Calais and Ponthieu; John agreed to purchase his liberty at a ransom of 3,000,000 gold crowns, and Edward agreed to renounce the title of king of France.

The relief of the French was immense, but no sooner were the armies disbanded than France became prey to bands of unemployed soldiers, known as "Companies". To rid himself of them, Charles V, who in April, 1364, succeeded John II, gave the task to Bertrand du Guesclin, a rough and stubborn soldier who had gained great renown in Brittany. He collected the Companies and crossed the Pyrenees to support Don Henry of Castile against Don Peter the Cruel, who was being aided by the Black Prince, and in the warring which followed the Companies were largely exterminated.

Once rid of this internal pest, Charles prepared to reverse the Treaty of Calais. First, he established law and order within his kingdom; next he reformed the army, extending the use of the bow, raising artillery, and partly re-walling Paris and other towns. Also he reorganized the royal navy under Jean de Vienne. In diplomacy he took a step which was to have prodigious consequences. In 1369 he arranged the marriage of his brother Philip the Bold, Duke of Burgundy, with Margaret, daughter and heiress of Louis de Male, Count of Flanders, which brought Flanders under the influence of France.

In 1368 tension again grew acute, and when Charles V supported a revolt against the English in Gascony, Edward III resumed the title of king of France. To meet this challenge Charles made du Guesclin Constable of France. He refused to fight pitched battles, relied on attrition to exhaust his enemy, and reconquered Poitou and Brittany. These conquests led to yet another truce in 1375, which was soon followed by the death of the main participants in the war. The Black Prince died in June, 1376, Edward in June, 1377, du Guesclin in July, 1380, and Charles in the September following, by which date the English territories in France had in the north shrunk to Calais, Cherbourg, and Brest, and in the south to Aquitaine, but barely as extensive as it had been in 1336. France, though ravaged, was centrally stronger, and in the struggle national sentiment had become self-conscious.

Nevertheless, largely because of the minorities of Richard II (1377–1400), son of the Black Prince, and of Charles VI (1380–1422), son of Charles V – the one was thirteen and the other twelve years old and of unbalanced mind – both countries became prey to factions and revolts. In June, 1381, in England the peasants revolted under Wat Tyler, and in the following year disturbances occurred in Paris and Flanders. In the latter, Louis de Male called in Philip the Bold of Burgundy, who ruthlessly suppressed the Flemings at Roosebeke on November 27, 1382.

In 1384, Louis de Male died, and Philip the Bold, through his wife, became count of Flanders. At the time, because Charles VI had become insane, Burgundy was the leading power in France, and to put a stop to English intervention in Flanders, in 1395 Philip arranged the marriage of Richard II with Charles VI's daughter Isabella, a child of seven. At the betrothal on March 12, 1396, the truce was prolonged for twenty-eight years. With the end of war in France, regular armies of French knights left for the East to fight the Turks, and John the Fearless, son of the Duke of Burgundy, at the head of one of these armies, was disastrously defeated on September 28, 1395, at Nicopolis (Nicopoli) on the Danube.

Meanwhile the growing rivalry between Philip the Bold and Louis Duke of Orléans, Charles VI's youngest brother, was further stimulated by the Great Schism (1378–1417), which divided the Church into two hostile camps. In 1367, Urban V, to avoid the bands of brigands then roaming southern France, returned to Rome. He died in 1370 and was succeeded by Gregory XI, who, in 1376, abandoned Avignon altogether for Rome. When, in 1378, he was succeeded by Urban VI, under French influence the cardinals objected to him and elected Robert of Geneva as antipope, who assumed the style of Clement VII.[1] France, Scotland, Savoy, Castile, and Aragon were Clementine, and England, Bohemia, Hungary, and Portugal Urbanist. Thus each side had its own pope, which rendered a renewal of the conflict all the more certain.

In 1389, Urban VI died and was succeeded by Boniface IX, and Clement VII, who died in 1394, was followed by a Spaniard under the title of Benedict XIII. Because no means could be found to end the schism, which shocked all Europe, in 1398 the University of Paris and the Burgundian party in France withdrew their obedience from both popes. The Duke of Orléans then championed Benedict and, in 1403, effected the restoration to him of the obedience of the French crown.

During this same period violent changes were occurring in England, where Lollardy, established by John Wycliffe (1324–1384), was ploughing the ground for the Reformation. From England his teaching spread to Bohemia, a country noted for its puritan heresies. Influencing John Huss (1369–1415), it helped to stimulate the ferocious Hussite Wars (1419–1436) in which, under

[1] Not to be confused with Clement VII (Giulio de' Medici), 1523–1534.

Ziska, the *Wagenburg*, or wagon fortress equipped with artillery, played a decisive part in his victory at Deutschbrod in 1422, and after his death, at Aussig in 1426 and Taus in 1431. These wars carried fire and sword into the heart of the empire, already weakened by the wars of emancipation of the Swiss which had started in 1307 with the League of the three Forest Cantons, and which gave rise to the growth of a new and formidable democratic infantry mainly composed of pikemen, who defeated the Habsburg feudal levies at Morgarten in 1315, Sempach in 1385, and Näfels in 1388. "After this achievement", remarks Colonel Lloyd in his *A Review of the History of Infantry*, ". . . it was idle to say that the wearing of armour and the use of weapons was reserved by God and nature for persons of quality."

When in April, 1404, John the Fearless succeeded his father Philip the Bold, France, sunk in corruption, was in the hands of the Duke of Orléans. John denounced the Orleanist government, seized Paris, and though a public reconciliation between the two dukes followed it in no way damped the antagonism of their adherents, and on the night of November 24, 1407, the Duke of Orléans was assassinated. For France it was a fatal blow; it split the French into two violent factions–the Burgundians and the Orleanists, or Armagnacs as they were called. Though fearful excesses at once followed, it was not until 1411 that civil war began in earnest, when, to reinforce their respective sides, each party called in the English to its aid; the Armagnacs in 1412 offered Henry IV, son of John of Gaunt, who had ousted Richard II in 1399, the whole of ancient Aquitaine for his support. Nothing came of this offer because on March 20, 1413, Henry IV died and the crown passed to his son Henry V, born in August, 1387.

Henry V was a man of unlimited ambition, and instead of realizing that peace abroad was needed in order firmly to establish the Lancaster dynasty at home, he forthwith decided to take advantage of the division in France and to revive Edward III's claim to the French throne. In order to accomplish this end, in May, 1413, he entered into an alliance with the Duke of Burgundy, the terms being that, while John remained neutral, he would set out to conquer France and if successful would recompense John with territories for which he would do liege homage to him as king of France.

Henry assembled an army some 6,000 strong at Southampton, and on August 13, 1415, landed it near the mouth of the Seine and besieged Harfleur, which capitulated on September 22. Next he set out for Calais, crossed the Somme, and at Agincourt came face to face with a French army recruited almost exclusively from the Armagnac faction. It was commanded by the Constable Charles d'Albret, the Dukes of Orléans, Bourbon, Alençon and Bar and Marshal Boucicaut. On October 24 the battle of Agincourt was fought, to end, like Crécy and Poitiers, in a total French defeat. Many notable Frenchmen were killed, including the Constable, three dukes, and seven counts, also many, among whom was the Duke of Orléans, were taken prisoner. From Agincourt Henry marched to Calais and from there returned to England.

Though, at the time, the Emperor Sigismund was anxious to unite all Europe against the Turks, and attempted to mediate between Henry and Charles, the former would accept nothing less than the full terms of the treaty of Calais, and when this was refused, in August, 1417, he landed at Trouville. Henry's intention was to make a systematic conquest of the whole of Normandy, and by the end of 1419 he accomplished it with the exception of the island fortress of Mount St. Michael.

Meanwhile Paris was betrayed to the Burgundians, and John began to play fast and loose between Henry and Charles. Negotiations with the latter led to a meeting between John and the dauphin on the bridge of Montereau on September 10, 1419, and in a heated argument, during which the dauphin withdrew, some of his followers fell upon John and assassinated him.

In the ourburst of fury which followed the murder, Philip, the new Duke of Burgundy, opened negotiations with Henry, and on May 21, 1420, a treaty was agreed and signed at Troyes, according to which Henry was to marry Charles VI's daughter Catherine; Charles VI was to disown his son the dauphin (presumably as a bastard) and to declare Henry his heir to the French crown. Meanwhile, during Charles's life, Henry was to retain Normandy and his other conquests and to share the government of France with the Duke of Burgundy.

On June 2, 1420, Henry married Catherine, but her disinherited brother had still to be reckoned with. He rallied Languedoc and in May, 1421, Charles won a success at Beaugé which brought the Duke of Brittany to his side. This brought Henry back to France, but in the spring of the following year he fell seriously ill and died at Bois Vincennes on August 31, leaving as heir a son nine months old – Henry VI. When he was dying, he begged his brother and uncle never to make peace without at least ensuring the retention of Normandy. Charles VI was also approaching his end. In September he came to Paris, fell sick and died there on October 21. The Duke of Bedford, brother of Henry V and regent for Henry VI, was the only prince who accompanied his body to Saint-Denis. There, under the vaulted roof of the old abbey, rang out the cry of the King of Arms: "God grant long life to Henry, by the Grace of God King of France and England, our Sovereign Lord."

CHAPTER 9

The raising of the siege of Orléans, 1429

The iniquity of the Treaty of Troyes roused French patriotism, and when, ten days after his father's death, the dauphin had himself proclaimed Charles VII, King of France, had he possessed but a modicum of courage his court at Bourges would at once have become the centre of a great movement of liberation. Throughout the provinces occupied by the English insecurity reigned, and in Normandy, which was inadequately garrisoned by them, resistance dropped social distinctions and many nobles, monks, townsmen, and peasants merged with the partisans. All that was lacking to detonate a national revolt was the spark of leadership.

But Charles was both a weak king and a degenerate, and unable to count upon the support of anyone except his Armagnac captains, who were little better than brigand chiefs, for his more extended campaigns he had to rely on foreign mercenaries – men equally brutal – notably the Scots under Archibald, Earl of Douglas, and John Stuart, Earl of Buchan who, in 1421, became Constable of France. Incapable of giving a lead, instead of supporting the partisans, Charles allowed military operations to meander on, and with disastrous results. On July 30, 1423, the English and Burgundians, who had joined forces at Auxerre, beat his Scottish and Armagnac supporters at Cravant. Worse was to follow, for on August 17, 1424, the Duke of Bedford inflicted a terrible defeat, as disastrous as Agincourt, on another of his armies, commanded by the Duke of Alençon, Marshal de la Fayette, the Constable Buchan, the Duke of Touraine (Earl of Douglas) and others, at Verneuil, in which the first two leaders were captured. Nevertheless the English losses were heavy, and with his hands full in Normandy, Bedford could ill afford them.

Because of the disaster of Verneuil the Duchess of Anjou, Charles VII's mother-in-law, sought an alliance with John V, Duke of Brittany, which, in 1425, led to the duke's brother Arthur, Earl of Richemont (or Richmond), coming to Bourges, where he was appointed Constable of France. Richemont's aim was to secure Brittany by compelling Charles to come to terms with the

Duke of Burgundy, and as a step in this direction he caused the assassination of two of Charles's favourites and imposed upon Charles one of his own choice, an adventurer named George de la Trémoille, who rapidly set out to usurp his benefactor's powers.

In consequence of the changed attitude of Brittany, in January, 1426, Bedford declared war on John V, and de Richemont hastened to his brother's assistance; but on March 6 he was routed at Saint James (south of Avranches), a defeat which compelled John to come to heel, which he did on July 3 by promising to abide by the Treaty of Troyes. Meanwhile the Earls of Suffolk and Warwick had laid siege to Montargis (east of Orléans), and when they got into difficulties the Earl of Salisbury was sent to England to press for reinforcements. At the same time the quarrel between de Richemont and la Trémoille paralysed the national party in France, and Lord Talbot (later the Earl of Shrewsbury), took Laval in Maine.

Toward the end of 1427 de Richemont was dismissed, and as this made Charles weaker than ever, Salisbury was given 450 men-at-arms and 2,200 archers, and late in January, 1428, he returned to France. After he had recruited further forces he was ordered to lay siege to Angers, because Bedford had decided to conquer Anjou as an appanage for himself. He set out from west of Paris, and when in the neighbourhood of Chartres, much to the annoyance of Bedford, the Anglo-Burgundian Council instructed Salisbury to gain the crossing of the Loire at Orléans, in order to strike at Berry, the heart of Charles's kingdom.

Salisbury, now at the head of between 4,000 and 5,000 men, pressed on from Chartres, first occupied Meung, Beaugency, and Jargeau on the Loire, and, on October 12, took up a position on its left bank immediately south of Orléans. Among his subordinates were the Earl of Suffolk and his brother, Lord de Ros and Lord Scales, Sir Lancelot de Lisle, and Sir William Glasdale.

Orléans was a populous city and one of the strongest fortresses in France. In shape it was a quadrilateral; its western, northern, and eastern sides were strongly walled and moated, and its southern rested on the Loire, which was spanned by a bridge that connected the city with the suburb of Portereau. At the far end of the bridge stood a twin-towered masonry work called the "Bastille des Tourelles", beyond which lay the Monastery of the Augustins, also fortified, and, at the time, between the two the

Orleanists were engaged upon building a work "*faict de fagotz et de terre*",[1] called the "Boulevard (or Boulevart) des Tourelles". This work was linked to the bastille by a drawbridge across a water moat.

The city walls were well defended by numerous catapults and seventy-one large cannon, without counting some small culverins,[2] and before the siege opened all food had been collected to be shared in common. Whoever in the surrounding country was willing to help in the defence was promised free rations, an inducement which made many partisans tender their services. The governor of Orléans was the Sire Raoul de Goncourt, and its defence was entrusted to the Bastard of Orléans, later Count of Dunois, a natural son of Louis the assassinated Duke of Orléans, whose legitimate son, the reigning duke, was at this time a captive in England.

Salisbury's plan was first to gain the Tourelles, in order to cut Orléans off from the south, and next to transfer his army to the right bank of the Loire and to invest the city. On his approach, the Orleanists abandoned the Augustins, set fire to Pontereau and withdrew into the unfinished boulevard which, on October 21, Salisbury attempted to storm, but failed. Next day an arch of the bridge was broken, and the boulevard having been mined, on October 23 the pit props were fired and its defenders withdrew to the bastille. On the following day this was stormed by the English, who at once established a battery in the Tourelles. That same evening Salisbury looked out of one of its windows and was mortally wounded by a splinter of a stone cannon shot, and died on October 27.

The Earl of Suffolk succeeded to the vacant command, and a pause in operations followed, during which the bulk of the army went into winter quarters at Jargeau, Meung, Beaugency, and Paris. On Christmas Day a six-hour truce was agreed,[3] and on December 30 the army returned. On the following day, in order to celebrate the event a tourney was held between two French and two English champions, "*Pour lesquelz regarder avoit assez prez d'eulx plusiers seigneurs, tant de France comme d'Angleterre*".[4]

With the opening of the new year – 1429 – Suffolk carried the

---

[1] *Journal du Siège d'Orléans, 1428–1429*, edit. Paul Charpentier et Charles Cuissard (1896), p. 5.
[2] Throughout the siege cannon played a dominant part, moral more than material, which may be learnt from the *Journal*, see in particular pp. 4, 5, 26, and 29.
[3] *Journal du Siège d'Orléans*, p. 17.　　　　[4] *Ibid.*, p. 21.

bulk of his army over the Loire, and, in order to blockade the city, he built seven forts, or bastilles, on its main northern approaches, four already having been built south of Orléans.[1] But through lack of men, the blockade on the eastern side of the city was never completed, with the result that a trickle of supplies reached Orléans,[2] but it was not sufficient to guarantee its citizens against starvation.

Early in February the defenders became so pinched for food that their sole chance of deliverance lay in Charles's army intercepting Suffolk's supply convoys, and thereby forcing him to raise the siege. An attempt to do so was made on February 12, when a convoy of 300 wagons carrying "herying and lenten stuffe", under command of Sir John Fastolf, was attacked at Rouvray, a few miles north of Orléans. Forthwith Fastolf drew up his wagons in laager, fought a typical Hussite action, and routed the French in what is known as the "Battle of the Herrings".[3]

By now Orléans had become the symbol of French resistance, the one hope of all true Frenchmen; nevertheless, at the time la Trémoille and de Richemont were engaged in a private war of their own, and the situation in the city grew so desperate that an appeal was made to the Duke of Burgundy to take the city over as neutral territory on behalf of its captive duke. But Bedford would not listen to this, and Charles, when he learnt of the failure of the negotiations, was advised by his courtiers to abandon France and to seek refuge in Dauphiné, Castile, or Scotland.[4] But the situation was not as dark as it looked. Everywhere the peasants were rising against the English, whose strength was due almost entirely to the inertia of the French. All that was lacking was a leader, and at this moment, unexpectedly, one was making ready to appear, a girl of seventeen, Jeanne d'Arc.[5]

The story of Joan of Arc is one of the most extraordinary in all history and one of the best documented. Though she did not

---

[1] In *L'Armée Anglaise Vancue par Jeanne D'Arc sous les Murs D'Orléans*, Boucher de Molandon (1892), p. 149, sixty bastilles in all are mentioned, but many were very small works.

[2] See *Journal du Siège d'Orléans*, in particular pp. 22, 25, 27, 53, and 56.

[3] See *L'Art Militaire et les Armées au Moyen Age*, Ferdinand Lot (1946), vol. ii, pp. 47–53.

[4] Lavisse's *Histoire de France* (1902), vol. iv, pt. ii, p. 47.

[5] D'Arc seems to have been a *soubriquet* personal to her father; for at the time of her trial she could give no surname (*Procès*, Quicherat, vol. i, p. 46). "To the world of her own time, English as well as French, she was essentially a mysterious nameless being, La Pucelle de Dieu, *The Maid of God*" (*Lancaster and York*, Sir James H. Ramsay, 1892, vol. i, p. 388).

know her age,[1] the probability is that she was born early in 1412 at Domrémy in the duchy of Bar on the border of Lorraine, near the town of Vaucouleurs, an Armagnac outpost which in 1429 was commanded by Robert of Baudricourt. Her parents were peasant folk.

When Joan was thirteen years old, voices,[2] unheard by others and accompanied by a cloud of brilliant light, bade her go to de Baudricourt, who would provide her with the means to travel to the king's court at Chinon. She was to inform Charles that she had been sent by God to raise the siege of Orléans and to lead him to Rheims to be consecrated king of France. She paid three visits to Vaucouleurs, and on the third de Baudricourt agreed to provide her with a horse and an escort of six soldiers. So she cut her hair short, changed her peasant's gown for male attire,[3] and, on February 13, 1429, set out on a 300 mile ride to Chinon, where she arrived on February 23.

On her arrival, la Trémoille was hostile to her; but in spite of his influence, in a secret conversation she convinced Charles (always to her "*gentil dauphin*" until his consecration) of his legitimacy and of her divine mission.[4] Next, after she had been examined at Poitiers by theologians and the Queen of Sicily, who vouched for her orthodoxy and virginity, she was given the style of *Chef de Guerre*, and on April 27, dressed in full armour and carrying a banner on which was blazoned "*Jhesus Maria*", she set out for Orléans at the head of three to four thousand men and a convoy of supplies. With her rode the Duke of Alençon, recently returned from captivity and to her always "*mon beau duc*"; Etienne de Vignolles (La Hire); Marshal de Sainte-Sévère and Marshal Gilles de Rais; Louis de Culen, Admiral of France; and Ambroise de Loré.

Meanwhile her fame had spread far and wide, her faith in her divine mission inspired the French with faith in victory. Equally important for France, her fame had already begun to terrify the English, to whom, before setting out from Blois, she had addressed a letter saying:

[1] *Procès de Condamnation et de Réhabilitation de Jeanne D'Arc dite La Pucelle*, Jules Quicherat (1849), vol. I, p. 51. (For French translation of the Latin sections, see *Procès de Condamnation de Jeanne d'Arc: Traduction avec Eclaircissements*, Joseph Fabre.)

[2] Soon after, the Archangel Michael, St. Margaret, and St. Catherine appeared to her in bodily form in a cloud of heavenly light and addressed her as "*Jehanne la Pucelle, fille de Dieu*". Clouds, wheels, and flames of light are common phenomena with mystics, and with Yogis are experienced in the state of *Dhyâna*.

[3] This played an important part in her trial. For her reasons for assuming man's attire see "Chronique de la Pucelle", *Procès*, Quicherat, vol. IV, p. 211.

[4] See *Histoire de Charles VII*, G. de Fresne de Beaucourt (1882), vol. II, pp. 208–210.

"*Roy d'Angleterre, et vous duc de Bethfort* (*Bedford*) . . . *rendés a la Pucelle cy envoiee de par Dieu le roy du ciel, les clefs de toutes les bonnes villes que vous avés prises et violées en France* . . . *alés vous an, de par Dieu, en vous païs; et se ainssi ne le faictes, attendés lez nouvelles de la Pucelle qui vous ira veoir briefment a vostre bien grant domaige. Roy d'Angleterre, se ainssi ne le faites, je suis chief de guerre, et en quelque lieu que je attaindré vous gens en France, je lez en feray aller, veulhent ou non veulhent, et se ilz ne veullent obéir, je lez prandray à mercy. Je suis cy venue de par Dieu, le roy du ciel, corps pour corps pour vous bouter hors de toute France. . . .*"[1]

When, on April 27, the convoy and its escort set out from Blois, Joan's "voices" had directed that Orléans was to be entered from the north through the district of la Beauce; therefore it in no way concerned her that an advance in this direction would bring her up against the strongest section of the English defences. But her companions thought differently, and with the concurrence of the Bastard of Orléans, quietly they led the army south of the Loire through the district of Sologne,[2] and seemingly, at the time, Joan was in far too ecstatic a state to notice the change.

That night the army bivouacked in the fields, and when it moved on next morning it encamped opposite the Grande île aux Bœufs. It was only then that Joan became aware that she was on the south bank of the Loire, and growing very angry she accused her companions of having tricked her. Meanwhile the Bastard of Orléans had heard of her approach and had crossed the river to greet her. When he met Joan, who was no respecter of persons (he was first cousin of the king), the following conversation took place:

" 'Are you the Bastard of Orléans?' asked Joan. 'Yes, I replied, and I rejoice at your arrival.' – 'Is it you who advised that I should come here, on this side of the river, and that I was not to go straight on to where Talbot and the other English are?' – 'I told her that I and the wisest among us advised what had been done, believing it to be the best.' – '*En nom Dieu,*' replied Jeanne, 'the advice of the Lord is more certain and wise than yours. You thought to deceive me, but you have deceived yourselves; for I bring you the greatest help that has ever been brought to knight or city, seeing that it is the help of the King of Heaven. . . .' "[3]

Next, Joan demanded that an attack should be made forthwith

---

[1] *Procès*, Quicherat, vol. v, pp. 96–97.

[2] *Journal du Siège d'Orléans*, p. 74.

[3] *Procès*, Quicherat, vol. III, pp. 5–6. In "Chronique de la Pucelle" (*Procès*, Quicherat, vol. IV, p. 218) a slightly differently worded version is given.

on Saint Jean le Blanc, the nearest English bastille on the south side of the river; but her companions protested and the convoy was directed to Pont de Saint Loup, where the Bastard had assembled a flotilla of river craft. With 200 lances Joan boarded the boats while the army stood by. But the wind was blowing from the north-east and it was found impossible to sail. This caused great anxiety, for night was closing in; nevertheless, all Joan said was: *"Attendez un petit, car, en nom Dieu, tout entrera en la ville."*[1] Immediately the wind veered round, the sails filled and the boats stood out up the Loire. This "miracle" sent her followers' confidence in her bounding into the infinite. The attention of the English in the Bastille de Saint Loup had been distracted by a French attack and its garrison prevented from obstructing the unloading of the flotilla on the north bank of the Loire. From there Joan rode on to Reuilly, near Crécy, where she spent the night.

On April 29 the bulk of Joan's army set out on its return march to Blois. It had previously been arranged with her—apparently in order that her divine instructions might be obeyed to the letter—that at Blois the army should cross the river and by moving through la Beauce advance on Orléans from the north, as Joan had intended originally. At eight o'clock that evening, armed *cap à pie*, riding a white horse and with her banner borne before her, Joan entered Orléans and was met by the Bastard and a great gathering of notables, soldiers, and citizens carrying torches *"et faisans autel joye comme se ilz veissent Dieu descentre entre eulx"*.[2] They led her through the city to near the Porte Regnart, where lived Jacquet Boucher, treasurer of the Duke of Orléans, in whose house she lodged.

Though no battle had yet been fought, and the English still held their defences in force, the deliverer of France had arrived. She was there in their midst, and morally everything was changed.

On April 30, when la Hire was engaged in a skirmish outside the Bastille Saint Pouair, Joan, ever eager to avoid bloodshed, addressed a letter to Talbot in which she said: *"Messire (the Lord) vous mande que vous en aliez en vostre pays, car c'est son plaisir, ou sinon je vous feray ung tel hahay. . . ."*[3] She received an insulting reply,

---

[1] "Chronique de la Pucelle", *Procès*, Quicherat, vol. IV, p. 218. Joan, it would seem, possessed second sight; there are so many well-authenticated instances of her power to foresee and foretell coming events that they are unlikely all to be apocryphal.

[2] *Journal du Siège d'Orléans*, p. 77.

[3] *Procès*, Quicherat, vol. III, p. 126. *Hahé* in modern French is a hunting cry meaning "ware there!"—halo!

but that evening, "*fort yrée*", she made another attempt to end hostilities. She went down to the Boulevard de la Belle Croix on the bridge and shouted to William Glasdale, commander of the Tourelles, in the name of God to surrender; to which his men shouted back "*vachère!*" ("cow-girl") and worse, and that they would burn her when they caught her.[1]

The next day the Bastard left Orléans for Blois and Joan and an escort accompanied him part of the way. That these comings and goings were so seldom interfered with was because the English were shut up in their bastilles, which made if difficult for them rapidly to concentrate. So completely were they pinned down in their earth-works that on the following day Joan rode out and reconnoitred them, apparently without any molestation whatever, and, on May 3, the garrisons of Gien and Montargis marched into Orléans. Much the same happened the following day when Joan, at the head of 500 men, rode out, "*à estendart desployé*", to meet the army and the Bastard on their way back from Blois through la Beauce. Triumphantly, at prime (between 6 and 7 a.m.) she rode with him into Orléans under the noses of the English.

Joan had been up early that day, and on her return she lay down to rest; but while she was asleep, the excitement caused by the return of the army would seem to have been too much for the Orleanists, for at noon a party of them issued from the town and attacked the Bastille de Saint Loup, held by Talbot. Suddenly awakening, she sprang from her bed crying out: "*En nom Dé, mon conseil m'a dit que je voise conotre les Anglois.*" Running downstairs, she met her page, Louis de Contes. "*Ha sanglant garsoñ*", she cried, "*vous ne me dysiez pas que le sanc de France feust repandu.*"[2] She ordered him to fetch her horse, was helped into her armour, seized her standard, and mounted and galloped for the Porte de Bourgogne, her horse's hooves striking sparks from the pavement.[3] When near Saint Loup she found that the English had made a sortie from the Bastille Saint Pouair and were attacking in rear the French assaulting Saint Loup. A bloody battle ensued and the Bastille of Saint Loup was stormed and carried; but Talbot effected his escape.

It was an important victory; the capture of Saint Loup opened the road to Jargeau. That evening the bells of Orléans were rung

[1] *Journal du Siège d'Orléans*, p. 79.   [2] *Ibid.*, vol. III, p. 68.
[3] *Ibid.*, vol. III, p. 124.

in celebration of the first success gained over the English since the siege began, a carillon *"que Anglois pouvoient bien ouyr (hear); lesquels furent fort abaissez de puissance par ceste partye, et aussi de courage"*.[1]

May 5 was Ascension Day and Joan decreed that there should be no fighting; but the day was not wasted, for a council of war[2] was held at which the leaders of the army decided, under cover of a feint attack on the Bastille de Saint Laurent, to assault the bastilles on the southern side of the Loire. When this had been arranged, Joan was called in, and, apparently, as they did not trust her to keep a secret, she was told only of the proposed feint attack. To this, angrily she exclaimed: *"Dites ce que vous avez conclut et appointié. Je celeroie bien plus grant chose que cestre-cy"* ("I shall know how to keep a far greater secret than that").[3] The Bastard then told her everything, after which, still wishing to avert blood-shed, Joan dictated another letter to the English, saying: "The King of Heaven commands and orders you, through me the Pucelle, to abandon your bastilles and return to your own country. Should you fail to do so, I will make such a *hahu* that it will eter-nally be remembered. This is what I write to you for the third and last time. . . ."[4] Wrapping the message round an arrow, she went down to the bridge, and there picked up a crossbow and shot the arrow into the Tourelles. The English derisively shouted back: "Here comes news from the Armagnac harlot", which reduced Joan to a flood of tears.

On the following morning, a boat bridge was thrown over the Loire from the island of Saint Aignan; but when the French approached the Bastille of Saint Jean le Blanc its garrison with-drew to the Bastille des Augustins. The French judged it too strong to assault and began to retire. Joan and la Hire then came up and to stop the withdrawal couched their lances and charged the English, who meanwhile had sallied out of the Augustins to pursue their enemy. This bold action put new heart into the retiring French, they again advanced and after a stiff fight drove the English out of the Augustins into the Tourelles.

The Augustins was then occupied and Joan returned to Orléans. There, when at supper, a "noble and valliant captain" came to her room and informed her that the council of war had decided

---

[1] "Chronique de le Pucelle", *Procès*, Quicherat, vol. IV, p. 224.

[2] Joan did not and could not attend a council of war, her council was—through her "voices"—with God alone. All directions came from Him, and what the tactical leaders of the army decided was no concern of hers.

[3] *Procès*, Quicherat, vol. IV, p. 59.   [4] *Ibid.*, vol. III, p. 107.

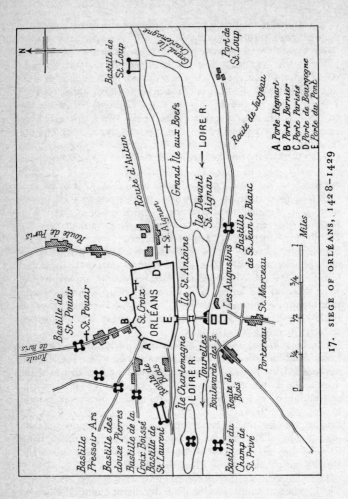

Bastille
Pressoir Ars

Bastille des
douze Pierres

Bastille de la
Croix Boissé

Bastille de
St. Laurent

Route de Paris

Bastille de
St. Pouair

+ St. Pouair

Route de Paris

Bastille de
St. Loup

Grand Île
Charlemagne

Route de Blois

Île Charlemagne

LOIRE R.

Tourelles

Boulevarde des Ts.

Route de Blois

Bastille du
Champ de
St. Privé

Portereau

Porte de
St. Loup

Route de Jargeau

LOIRE R.

Grand Île aux Boefs

Route d'Autun

St. Aignan +

Île Devant
St. Aignan

ORLÉANS

St. Croix +

Île St. Antoine

St. Antoine +

A   E

B   D
C

Les Augustins

Bastille
de St. Jean-le-Blanc

+ St. Marceau

A Porte Regnart
B Porte Bernier
C Porte Parisis
D Porte de Bourgogne
E Porte du Pont

0   ¼   ½   ¾   1
                Miles

17. SIEGE OF ORLÉANS, 1428–1429

not to renew the attack until further reinforcements had arrived, She said to him: "You have been at your council and I have been at mine. Believe me that the council of the Lord will hold good and be accomplished, and that yours will come to nothing." Next, addressing her confessor, Jean Pasquerel, she said to him: "Rise tomorrow at a very early hour . . . and keep near me throughout the day, for I shall have much to do, more than ever before. Blood will flow from my body above my breast."[1]

For the English, May 7 was the most fatal day of the war; for the French it was the "*Journée des Tourelles*", still celebrated yearly.

The *tête de pont*, comprising the Bastille and Boulevard des Tourelles, was held by Sir William Glasdale and some 500 soldiers. To the north of it the bridge was still broken and on its south side the Bastille des Augustins was now in French hands, as also were the bastilles Saint Jean le Blanc and Saint Privée, the latter abandoned by the English the previous night. Completely isolated as the *tête de pont* now was, the Bastard, Marshal de Rais, and other commanders were opposed to a direct attack on it. They preferred a siege, but Joan would have none of this, for rightly she sensed that the psychological moment had come: enthusiasm was at its height and the populace ecstatically supported her: she was not to be gainsaid, and it was she who dominated the situation.

Early on May 7 she left Orléans by the Porte de Bourgogne, crossed the Loire and joined the troops at the Augustins. Meanwhile the Tourelles was bombarded from the island of Saint Antoine, and men were set at work to repair the bridge so that access to the *tête de pont* might be gained from the north.

At seven o'clock, according to Percival de Cagny, Joan ordered her trumpets to be sounded as a signal to make ready to assault, and as the cannon began to thunder, with standard in hand she advanced to the edge of the fosse, or ditch, of the boulevard.[2] From all accounts most of the fighting took place in the ditch itself, which was deep, and each attempt made to storm its far side by means of scaling ladders was beaten back: the struggle is epically described in the *Journal*.[3] In one of the assaults Joan was hit between the neck and shoulder by an arrow, which, according to the Bastard, penetrated her flesh to a depth of six inches.[4] Joan pulled the arrow out and went back to have the wound dressed.[5]

---

[1] *Procès*, Quicherat, vol. IV, p. 109.   [2] *Ibid.*, vol. IV, p. 8.
[3] *Journal du Siège d'Orléans*, p. 85.   [4] *Procès*, Quicherat, vol. III, p. 8.
[5] "Chronique de la Pucelle", *Procès*, Quicherat, vol. IV, p. 228.

At once the energy went out of the attack and the Bastard and others suggested to her that it would be as well to abandon further assault until the morrow. She cried out at this: " '*En nom de Dieu*, you will enter the boulevard very soon; have no doubt of it, for the English have less strength than you. Why not rest a little and drink and eat?' *Ce qui'ilz firent, car à merveilles lui obeissoyent*."[1] Then, says the Bastard, she mounted her horse, and "alone and apart retired to a vineyard to pray for half a quarter of an hour".[2] On her return she found that the soldiers had eaten their hasty meal and ordered them in the name of God to renew the assault; the English, she said, had no longer strength to resist them. This was true, for when they saw her again they "shivered and were seized by a great terror".[3] Rushing forward, the ladders were planted in the fosse, and the boulevard was stormed. When Glasdale and his men sought refuge in the Bastille des Tourelles, Louis le Contes relates, Joan shouted to her companions: "Be of good heart; do not fall back, the bastille will be yours . . . when you see the wind blow the banner toward it."[4] The writer of the *Journal* gives a slightly different version. He says: "Be ready, when the flag-end of my banner touches the boulevard (? bastille)." Soon after a cry arose from the soldiery: "Jehanne, it touches it!" Whereupon she shouted back to them: "All is yours, enter!"[5]

At the same time, the gap in the bridge now repaired, Nicolas de Giresmes, a valiant knight of Rhodes, followed by his men, attacked the Tourelles on its northern side. But the action was brief, for caught between two attacks the English garrison was seized by panic and rushed wildly for the drawbridge connecting the Tourelles with the boulevard. Joan saw Glasdale among the fugitives and cried out: "*Clasdas!* (Glasdale) *Clasdas! rent-ti au Roi des Cieux!* You called me a harlot, but I have pity on your soul and the souls of your men."[6] The bridge gave way at that moment and Glasdale and those following him were precipitated into the river and drowned, "which was a great loss for the valiant French who from their ransoms would have received *grant finance*".[7]

Thus, as night closed, the Tourelles, now on fire, was won, and as the flames shot up, Joan recrossed the Loire to have her wound dressed and to sup on a few slices of bread dipped in wine and

[1] *Journal du Siège d'Orléans*, p. 86.
[2] *Procès*, Quicherat, vol. III, p. 8.
[3] *Ibid.*, vol. III, p. 8.
[4] *Ibid.*, vol. III, pp. 70–71.
[5] *Journal du Siège d'Orléans*, p. 86.
[6] *Procès*, Quicherat, vol. III, p. 110.
[7] *Journal du Siège d'Orléans*, p. 87.

water. The bells of Orléans were ringing out and the people were singing the *Te Deum Laudamus*.

Next morning, Sunday, May 8, the English fired their cantonments on the north side of the Loire, abandoned most of their artillery, and marched away to Meung, Beaugency, and Jargeau.

The news that the siege had been raised thundered through France and across her borders. The English were paralysed; the Duke of Bedford in a letter written some years later to Henry VI, expresses in it the feeling which then prevailed. ". . . there felle, by the hand of God, as it seemeth", he wrote, "a grete strook upon your peuple that was assembled there (at Orléans) in grete numbre, caused in grete partie, as Y trowe, of lakke of sadde beleve (sound faith), and unlevefulle (unbelieving) doubte that thei hadde of a disciple and lyme (limb) of the Feende, called the Pucelle; that used fals enchauntements and sorcerie; the whiche strooke and discomfiture, nought oonly lessed in grete partie the nombre of youre peuple there, but as well withdrowe the courage of the remenant in merveillous wyse; and couraiged youre adverse partie and ennemys to assemble them forthwith in grete nombre".[1]

In spite of this, Charles VII did nothing to exploit Joan's victory; he did not even honour Orléans with a visit, and those around him, especially la Trémoille, feared that the enthusiasm which had stormed the English bastilles might also storm their own positions.

On May 13, Joan met Charles at Tours. Of the two promises she had made to him, the first had now been fulfilled; but as her second had not, she urged Charles at once to proceed to Rheims. But the military leaders rightly saw the danger of plunging into Champagne until the English had been driven from the Loire, and directly the troops had been concentrated, siege was laid to Jargeau and Beaugency. On June 12 the former was taken by Joan and the Duke of Alençon and the Earl of Suffolk and his brother were captured. Immediately after, Joan and her companions marched on Beaugency, which capitulated on June 18.

Meanwhile Lord Talbot and Sir John Fastolf were hurrying south with reinforcements from Paris. When they heard that Jargeau had fallen the latter urged retreat, but Talbot would not, and the army pressed on for Beaugency. When they neared Beaugency and learnt that it was under attack, Talbot marched to Meung to link

---

[1] Quoted from *Lancaster and York*, Sir James H. Ramsay, vol. 1, p. 398. See also *Procès*, Quicherat, vol. v, pp. 136–137.

up with its garrison. When he arrived he was told that Beaugency had surrendered and he ordered a retreat to Patay.

The prestige of the English in the field was still so high that when, on July 19, the French caught up with Talbot, they hesitated to attack, and the Duke of Alençon asked Joan – who was not on the battlefield – what he should do. In a loud voice she answered: "Make use of your spurs!" Those around her were perplexed. "What say you?" they asked. "Are we to turn our backs on the English?" "No!" replied Joan, "it is the English who are going to turn their backs on us. They will be unable to defend themselves, and you will have need of your good spurs to catch them up."[1]

It was as she said. The English were routed, many were killed, and among the captured were Talbot and Lord Scales.[2]

Coming on the heels of the raising of the siege of Orléans, the moral effect of the victory of Patay was electric. Nothing now could stop Joan from realizing her second call – that Charles should be anointed at Rheims.

On June 29, the king and the army set out from Gien. Joan had gone on in advance and town after town opened its gates to her. Troyes alone offered resistance, and though la Trémoille advised retreat, Joan's prestige was irresistible. Threatened with assault, on July 10 the city capitulated. Then Châlons and Rheims submitted and Charles entered the latter on July 16. Two days later he was anointed, while Joan, in full armour and banner in hand, stood by the altar. She had kept her word; her heavenly voices had been obeyed; the anointment of an unworthy king rather than her martyrdom was her apotheosis.

The moral effect of this coronation cannot be exaggerated. It was the decisive moment, not only in Charles's reign, but in the second half of the Hundred Years War. Of it Professor Perroy says: "Now Charles, whom Joan had hitherto persisted in calling only the Dauphin, was King of France, a new Melchisedec sanctified by the sacrament which bestowed upon him the power of a thaumaturge. Henceforth no believer could doubt who was the legitimate sovereign, since there was now a king crowned in circumstances so incredible that they seemed miraculous. . . . So the coronation annulled the deposition illegally pronounced by

[1] *Procès*, Quicherat, vol. III, pp. 10–11.
[2] For a contemporary account of the battle of Patay see "Prise de Meung et de Beaugency. Battaile de Patay", included in Charpentier's edit. of *Journal du Siège d'Orléans*, pp. 137–140.

the Treaty of Troyes and restored to the Valois the legitimacy which had been questioned for the past nine years. . . . How, moreover, could the Burgundians . . . continue their obedience to Bedford without obvious treason?"[1]

To the people, Joan was now *l'Angelique*; of her, chansons, "*moult merveilleuses*", were sung throughout the land; many held her to be a saint, some even a magician who could command the winds, and to the English she was a sorceress: to all, she belonged to the supernatural. Bona Visconti asked for her help to regain the duchy of Milan, and the Count of Armagnac sent to ask her whether it was Clement VIII (Aegidius Muñoz) or Martin V who was the true pope.[2] All the Soissonnais, Valois, Senlisien, Beauvaisis, and part of Parisis submitted to Charles as their rightful king. Paris was at his mercy, and the political importance of Paris was so great that to ring in victory from Notre Dame might, then and there, have decided the war. Joan must have sensed this in a mystical way,. for she urged an immediate advance on the capital. But Charles remained inert, his only wish was to get back to the quietude of the Loire, and la Trémoille encouraged him, for at the time he was intriguing with the duke of Burgundy over a paltry truce.

Meanwhile Bedford, who feared the defection of Paris, was reinforced, and on August 7 he advanced to Montereau, from where he sent a challenge to Charles, and on August 15 both armies came face to face at Montépilloy. But Bedford dared not attack; for he feared that his army would be demoralized at the sight of Joan's banner.[3] Neither would Charles, the creature of la Trémoille, whose one aim was a reconciliation with Burgundy.

While la Trémoille negotiated at Arras, national feeling swept on; yet, in the words of Sir James Ramsay – a most sober historian – "It was admitted on all hands that a bold, prompt advance into the basin of the Somme would have raised all Picardy and brought the English dominion to a speedy close".[4] Without awaiting the issue of the Arras negotiations Joan left Compiègne on August 23 and occupied Saint Denis. There, reluctantly, Charles followed her on September 7, and two days later, though siege material was lacking, she made an impetuous assault on Paris. When engaged in battle in the fosse outside the Porte Saint Honoré she

[1] *The Hundred Years War*, pp. 284–285.
[2] *Procès*, Quicherat, vol. I, p. 245.
[3] *A History of the Art of War in the Middle Ages*, Sir Charles Oman, vol. II, p. 395.
[4] *Lancaster and York*, vol. I, p. 404.

was struck down by a crossbow bolt and borne off the field by the Sire de Goncourt.

Wounded though she was, she ordered a renewal of the assault on the following day; but Charles forbade it, and instead signed a four-month truce with the Duke of Burgundy. Next, she was ordered by Charles to follow him to Berry. So she hung up her armour at Saint Denis, and, on September 21, set out with the army on its return to Gien, "*Et ainssi*", writes Perceval de Cagny, "*fut le vouloir de la Pucelle et l'armée du roy rompue*".[1] At Gien the army was disbanded.

In spite of the truce fighting continued, and Bedford's position became increasingly precarious because his reinforcements shirked service against the *Pucelle de Dieu*. Then, suddenly, the joyous news was received that "the fals wych" had fallen into the hands of the Burgundians.

Unable to bear the inactivity in which la Trémoille sought to keep her, and believing that the only peace possible was one gained at the point of the lance,[2] Joan slipped away from the court of Sully to Melun, and when there, during Easter week 1431, the voices of Saint Catherine and Saint Margaret told her again and again that soon she would be captured; but on what day they did not divulge.[3] In spite of this warning she left Melun for Crépy-en-Valois, and learning that the Duke of Burgundy and the Earl of Arundel were on the north side of the Oise and were about to lay siege to Compiègne, at midnight on May 22–23 she rode to Compiègne, where she arrived at dawn. She rested, then, at about five o'clock in the afternoon of May 23, she rode out to reconnoitre the enemy and in a rearguard action which followed was cut off, unhorsed and captured by soldiers of John of Luxembourg.[4]

Bedford at once saw in her capture a means whereby the moral significance of Charles's coronation could be politically annulled. In order to gain the political initiative – that is, to re-establish the full legality of the boy king Henry VI as king of France – not only was it necessary to crown him king of France, but at the same time to invalidate Charles's crowning. And, as among all Charles's followers, Joan was immeasurably the one responsible for his anointment at Rheims, were she to be condemned by the Inquisition as a heretic and sorceress, in the public eye Charles's corona-

---

[1] *Procès*, Quicherat, vol. IV, p. 29.   [2] *Ibid.*, vol. I, p. 108.
[3] *Ibid.*, vol. I, p. 115.   [4] *Ibid.*, vol. I, pp. 116–117.

tion would be utterly discredited. It was an astute plan, and in its accomplishment the first step taken was to buy Joan from the Duke of Burgundy for 10,000 francs, and the second to bring her to Rouen for trial and there to have her condemned as a harlot, a witch and an envoy of the devil. Then, as Edouard Perroy says, Charles would not only be overwhelmed with ridicule, but "his fleeting successes would be put down to an odious liaison between a criminal bastard and a shameless sorceress".[1]

The preliminaries of the trial opened on January 9, 1431; but it was not until February 21 that for the first time Joan was brought before her judges—Pierre Cauchon, Bishop of Beauvais, and Jean Lemaistre, Inquisitor of France—when every available fact in her life was raked up. "I saw well enough", writes Guillaume Manchon, the court recorder, "that they acted more by hate than by any other sentiment. They intended that Jeanne should die."[2] He should have said, "should be convicted".

The main charges were those of heresy and sorcery, and her chief crime was that she had set her revelations above the judgements of the Church. Thus we read: "If the prelates of the Church do not see to it, subversion of the whole authority of the Church may ensue; men and women may rise on every side, pretending to revelations from God and His angels, sowing lies and errors. . . ."[3] And the University of Paris came to the decision that she had so disseminated her poison that it had infected almost the whole of western Christianity.[4]

On May 24 she was broken down by incessant questioning and induced to place her mark on a recantation, which four days later she revoked; her "voices" had by then renewed her strength of mind. At nine o'clock, on the morning of May 29, she was taken to the Old Market Place at Rouen and burnt, and as the flames and smoke smothered her, John Tressart, secretary to the king of England, cried out: "We are lost, for we have burnt a saint."[5] After the burning, her remains were gathered and thrown into the Seine.[6]

Throughout her trial Charles VII made no attempt to save

---

[1] *The Hundred Years War*, pp. 287–288.
[2] *Procès*, Quicherat, vol. III, p. 138. On the trial Prof. Perroy writes: "These men felt only horror and hatred of the accused. . . . The cruelty of the procedure . . . was simply that of the Inquisition, which was daily applied. . . . There was no vice of form or substance in the trial itself; but, once it had begun, it could end only in conviction" (pp. 288–289).
[3] *Ibid.*, vol. I, p. 317.
[4] *Ibid.*, vol. I, p. 409.
[5] *Ibid.*, vol. II, p. 347.
[6] *Ibid.*, vol. III, p. 182.

her; not even de Beaucourt, his most favourable historian, can find a trace of any such action.[1] Talbot was still in French hands, and had the Duke of Bedford been told that whatever Joan suffered Talbot should suffer, there can be little doubt that she would never have been sent to the stake. For a brief while Joans' death checked the uprising of French nationality and, on December 13, this enabled the English to crown the infant King Henry VI king of France in Notre Dame at Paris.

In 1433 la Trémoille was overthrown, and on September 21, 1435, the twenty-five year feud between the Burgundians and Armagnacs was brought to an end by the Peace of Arras, which caused an explosion of fury in England, for without the support of a continental ally the English dominion in France was doomed. Nevertheless the peace brought few benefits to the French, for when the war with Burgundy ended the country-side was infested with demobilized soldiers, known as *écorcheurs* (flayers), because they stripped their victims to their shirts. The anarchy which now swept France beggars description: murder, pestilence and famine became the order of the day; whole districts were depopulated and the situation grew so desperate that mass migrations from the provinces began to take place.[2] Eventually the exhaustion of both the English and French became such that on April 16, 1444, a truce was agreed at Tours which was to last until 1449.

This breathing space of five years was spent by the French, under the guidance of the Constable de Richemont, in reorganizing the French army with the aim of producing a police force capable of suppressing the *écorcheurs* and *routiers* as well as to provide a standing army ready to engage the English should the truce be broken. It was effected in stages by a series of ordinances, the first of importance being promulgated in 1445. According to this, a general amnesty was granted to all soldiers who had turned brigands, and after the more undesirable had been eliminated,[3] the remainder was formed into fifteen (later twenty) *Compagnies de l'Ordonnance du Roi*, each commanded by a noble chosen for his skill and trustworthiness. The Companies were organized and paid feudal levies, consisting of 100 lances each, each lance comprising one man-at-arms, one *coutilier* to act as squire and,

---

[1] *Histoire de Charles VII*, vol. ii, pp. 240–255.

[2] See Lavisse's *Histoire de France*, vol. iv, pt. ii, chap. iv.

[3] A considerable number had already been sent under the Dauphin Louis to war in Alsace and Switzerland, where many were exterminated, 2,000 perishing in the battle of St. Jacob on the Birs.

normally, three archers, all mounted. The Companies formed the king's cavalry and were lodged in selected towns, paid for by the provinces and kept under strict discipline.

Under the ordinance of 1448, the *Francs-Archers*, so called because they were exempt from taxation, were instituted as an infantry militia; each group of fifty hearths furnished one archer or cross-bow-man. In all 8,000 were raised, the men selected for their fitness and good characters. Simultaneously, the artillery was reorganized by the brothers Gaspard and Jean Bureau, and thanks to them it soon became the most efficient in Europe.[1]

These reforms not only put an end to the terrible anarchy which had hitherto followed each truce, but it placed a powerful instrument in the hands of the king, by means of which he could both control his barons and meet his foreign enemies. They established the foundations of the standing army system, which was the essential ingredient of a national monarchy.

With this reformed army Charles VII brought the long war to an end, for though Henry VI wanted peace, Charles's advisers wanted war, and an infringement of the truce by one of the English captains presented them with the pretext to set it aside on July 17, 1449.

The English still held Normandy and Guienne, and in the former, because of the hostility of the people, precariously held their own in the walled towns. These the French rapidly reduced by cannon. On April 15, 1450, a decision was reached. At Formigny, near Bayeux, an English army under Sir Thomas Kyriel and Sir Matthew Gough, after it had been disordered by two French culverins (long guns of small calibre) was virtually exterminated by the Count of Clermont and the Constable de Richemont.[2] This disaster was followed by the siege of Bayeux and the occupation of Avranches and Caen, the latter entered by Charles VII on July 6. Siege was next laid to Cherbourg, and after a determined defence it fell to the cannon of the brothers Bureau on August 12. English rule in Normandy was at an end – "And we have not now a foote of londe in Normandy".[3]

The conquest of Guienne was more difficult, for it had been

[1] For a full account of these reforms see de Beaucourt's *Histoire de Charles VII*, vol. IV, pp. 387–400.

[2] This disaster was immediately followed by the rising of Jack Cade in England. In vol. VII, pt. 1 of *Histoire du Moyen Age* (*Histoire Générale*, edit. Gustave Glotz), p. 450, M. Déprez calls Formigny "*un véritable Waterloo*".

[3] *Paston Letters*, edit. J. Gardner (1872), vol. I, p. 139; August 17.

occupied by the English for 300 years; their rule had been more tolerant there and commercial ties with England were strong. In the spring of 1451 the Count of Dunois (the Bastard of Orléans) led an army of 6,000 men into the duchy. On June 30 he occupied Bordeaux, and on August 20 took Bayonne. In October, 1452, Talbot, Earl of Shrewsbury, then over seventy years of age yet still full of fire, was sent out to retrieve the situation. He disembarked his 3,000 men at a sandy cove, still known as *l'anse à l'Anglot*, in the mouth of the Garonne, the country rose in his favour, and Bordeaux opened its gates to him. In the summer of 1453, at the head of 8,000 Gascons and English, he set out to raise the siege of Castillon. Confronted by entrenchments and the batteries of Jean Bureau, for a full hour on July 17 he assaulted the French, but only to suffer heavy losses from their cannon fire. Finally, he was attacked in flank, and in the rout which followed was wounded, unhorsed and trampled to death. With him perished the last hope of English dominion in France. Bordeaux fell to the French on October 19.

With the fall of Bordeaux, the struggle between France and England, which opened with the battle of Hastings, ended; France became truly French and England truly English. In France, Louis XI (1461–1483) in his wars with Charles the Bold of Burgundy, which were concluded by the death of the latter at the battle of Nancy on January 5, 1477, established the royal control. In England, the Wars of the Roses (1455–1485) killed many of the English feudal nobility, and with the death of Richard III on Bosworth Field on August 22, 1485, the rule of England passed to the first of the Tudors, Henry VII (1485–1509).

Both Louis and Henry were "bourgeois" kings: the feudal age was at an end, the age of business began, and with its advent western history stepped on to the threshold of the modern epoch. Henceforth, though England and France were to remain antagonistic nations, their jousting days were over.

In the long struggle between the battles of Sluys and Castillon the raising of the siege of Orléans was the grand climacteric. Though in the final lap of the war gunpowder played an increasingly important part in bringing English dominion in France to an end, had it not been for the spiritual enthusiasm of Joan of Arc, the course of history would have been different. Her real achievement was not that she freed Orléans and carried war through Champagne to the gates of Paris; but that she freed the

French from their obsession of inevitable defeat. By making Charles VII the idealized champion of France, she gave voice to the soul of France herself. Miserable creature though he was, through her inspiration the monarchy in France became the symbol of victory around which the people mustered. And had she not been handicapped by his invincible inertia and the self-interest of his councillors, "she might", as Sir Charles Oman has said, "have swept the English out of France in her first impetus".[1] But this was not to be. Nevertheless, though taken and martyred, her spirit lived on unconquerable.

"The heroic peasant girl of Lorraine", writes John Payne, ". . . created the French people. Until her time France had been inhabited by Bretons, Angevins, Bourbonnais, Burgundians, Poitevins, Armagnacs; at last the baptism of fire through which the land had passed and the breath of heroism that emanated from the Maid of Orleans had welded together the conflicting sections and had informed them with that breath of patriotism which is the beginning of national life. France had at length become a nation."[2]

That this passing from medieval manhood into early modern adolescence was realized at the time is improbable; for so many of the great changes in world affairs, like seeds buried in the soil, germinate in darkness, and the flowers which blossom from them are more commonly to be plucked in the light of after events. Nevertheless, no sooner did Charles VII feel that victory was within his grasp than he remembered Joan, not in order to see that justice was done to her memory, but because he did not wish to go down to history as the accomplice of a sorceress. In 1450, when he had regained Rouen and with it come into possession of the documents of her trial, he ordered an investigation into the legality of her condemnation. But Pope Nicolas V would have nothing to do with it, because his aim was to bring about a reconciliation between Henry VI and Charles in order to promote a crusade against the Turks, who were then closing in on Constantinople. In 1455, his successor, Calixtus III, who hoped to persuade Charles to march against the Turks, consented to a revision of the trial, and on July 7, 1456, the proceedings of 1431 were declared irregular in constitution and in procedure. Thus Joan was rehabilitated as the "*Pucelle de Dieu*", a fitting epilogue to the war in which she sacrificed her young life for France.

---

[1] *A History of the Art of War in the Middle Ages*, vol. II, p. 397.
[2] In his Introduction to *The Poems of Master François Villon of Paris* (1892), p. viii.

The rise of the Ottoman Empire

The Latin kingdom, wedged between the Bulgars and Serbs in the west and the Greeks of Nicaea and Seljuks of Rum in the east, distracted within by the quarrellings of the Venetians and Genoese and the contentions of the Latin and Greek Churches, could not be other than impermanent. In 1261 its end came; that year Michael Palaeologus, the Greek emperor of Nicaea, won the support of the Genoese against the Venetians and after slight resistance occupied Constantinople on July 25. Immediately following, he was crowned in St. Sophia as Michael VIII (1261-1282), and in greater part Latin rule ceased in Greece. To secure his position, in 1274 he agreed to a union of the Churches, but this did not last long.

Nevertheless the damage done by the Latin occupation was irreparable, and had it not been that the great Mongol invasion of 1256-1260 under Hugalu, grandson of Genghis Khan, had ruined the Seljuk power in Rum, it is highly improbable that the resuscitated Byzantine empire would have lasted even as long as the Latin kingdom. It was during Hugalu's invasion that a tribe of Turks, recently settled in Mesopotamia under a chieftain named Ertughril, trekked into Anatolia, and for services rendered to the Seljuk sultan, was granted a tract of pasture land in the neighbourhood of Eski-Shehr, under a hundred miles east of the Sea of Marmara. In 1281 Ertughril died, and his son Osman or Othman—after whom his tribe became known as the Osmanli or Ottoman Turks—set out to extend his territory. In this his way was eased by anarchy in the empire, where Andronicus III (1320-1341) struggled against the inroads of Bulgars, Serbs, and Tartars, while his Grand Catalan Company tried to dethrone him. Under cover of this anarchy, in 1326 Osman took Brusa, which became the centre of Ottoman operations against Europe. A few months later he died, and was succeeded by his son Orkhan (1326-1359).

Soon Orkhan decided to occupy Nicaea (Iznik) and Nicomedia (Ismid). The former he captured in 1329 and the latter in 1337. after which he reorganized his army and, at the suggestion of the dervish Hajji Bektash, recruited a regiment of Christians, known as janissaries or "new troops". Meanwhile Thrace had again been overrun by the Tartars, and in 1344 the position of the empire was so desperate that, in order to win the neutrality of Orkhan, the Emperor John V, Cantacuzene (1341–1383), gave him his daughter Theodora in marriage. Three years later, when the Serbs, under Stephen Dushan, threatened the existence of the empire, Orkhan sent 6,000 Ottomans into Europe to assist his father-in-law. The Ottomans defeated the Serbs and withdrew, but only to return in 1349, when 20,000 crossed into Europe to drive the Serbs from before Salonica. In 1352, Suleiman, Orkhan's eldest son, led another expedition into Europe and defeated the Serbs in the vicinity of Demotika.

It would seem that the utter inability of the Greeks to defend themselves roused Orkhan's ambitions. Thus far the Turks had crossed into Europe as plunderers, allies or mercenaries, either to pillage or defend the empire or to make profit out of its frequent civil wars. But in 1356 Orkhan decided to send an army under Suleiman to conquer and occupy European territory. Suleiman ferried 30,000 troops from Sestus and in the following year took Adrianople and Demotika. The former was held permanently, and the date of its occupation marks the beginning of the conquest of European territory by the Ottoman Turks.

On the death of Suleiman in 1359, his brother Murad took possession of Adrianople, and two months later, on Orkhan's death, he succeeded to the sultanate as Murad I (1359–1389). He continued his father's policy of conquest, in 1363 came to an agreement with the Genoese to transport 60,000 troops into Thrace, and three years later defeated an army of 50,000 south Serbs which had set out to capture Adrianople. This victory woke Europe to her danger; but though the pope pressed for a crusade, France and England were too occupied in the Hundred Years War to take an active part against the common enemy of Christendom. Murad continued his conquests and on September 26, 1371, he annihilated an army of 70,000 south Serbs under King Vulkasin, at Harmanli, on the Maritza; a defeat which placed the Greeks in so hopeless a position that soon after the Emperor John V was reduced to recognize the sultan as his suzerain.

Many Ottoman successes followed, but when, in 1386, Murad took Nish from the north Serbs, King Lazar Hrebeljanovich, son of Stephen Dushan, formed a Pan-Serbian league, and in 1387 won a great victory over the Turks on the banks of the river Toplica. This success at once decided the waverers, and Croats, Albanians, Poles, and Hungarians flocked to his standard. To crush the revolt, Murad first turned on the Bulgarians, and once they were subjected he marched on Old Serbia by way of Kustendil and came up with the army of the league on the plain of Kossovo (Plain of the Blackbirds), some 50 miles north of Uskub. There, while arraying himself for battle, he was mortally wounded by a Serb noble named Milos Kobilic who gained access to him by posing as a deserter. Murad's brother Bayazid immediately took over command, and after a fierce battle, the most famous in Serbian history, he routed the allies. Lazar was taken prisoner and slain in the tent in which Murad lay dying. The Ottoman victory was complete; it was the Waterloo of the Serbian empire, and was to remain unavenged until the Battle of Kumanovo in 1912.

Bayazid (1389–1403), known as *Yilderim* ("The Thunderbolt"), who succeeded Murad, was a ferocious warrior who lacked the statecraft of his brother. Between 1392 and 1393 he waged a war of extermination in Thrace, and in 1394 was called to Asia. During his absence the Emperor Manuel II (1391–1425) appealed to the western princes for aid. He was successful, for Pope Boniface IX preached a crusade and a vast army, numbering, it is said, between 50,000 and 100,000 men—mostly Hungarians—was assembled at Nicopolis under Sigismund King of Hungary and the Dukes of Burgundy and Nevers. There they were routed by Bayazid on September 28, 1396, to the dismay of the West.

After this victory Bayazid's one idea was to master Constantinople, where, in 1400, Manuel was reinforced by Marshal Boucicault, who sailed into the Golden Horn with 1,400 men-at-arms in the nick of time to save Galata from the Turks; after which Manuel sailed for France and England to seek aid, and in 1402 set out on his return.

During his absence Constantinople was all but completely isolated by Bayazid. At length, in 1402, he decided to carry it by assault; but no sooner had he invested it than he received a message from the Mongol chieftain Timur the Lame (Tamerlane)—a ferocious monster of destruction—ordering him forthwith to return to the Greeks all cities and territories he had taken from them.

In 1386, Timur, having conquered Persia, had appeared before Tiflis at the head of an immense army of Mongols and Turks, and in 1394, thoroughly alarmed by his western advance, Bayazid had gone to Erzinjan to resist him; but when he found that Timur had no intention to proceed farther west, he returned to Europe. In 1398 Timur conquered northern India and occupied Delhi, and in the following year returned to his capital Samarkand, from where he set out for Aleppo, slaughtering every man, woman, and child on his way. Once Aleppo had been sacked, he headed for Jerusalem *en route* for Egypt, but was forced to turn back by a plague of locusts which deprived his horses of their grazing. Next, he took Damascus and then Baghdad; the heads of the inhabitants of each captured city were piled in pyramids before its gates.

It was when he was at Damascus that Timur sent his message to Bayazid, who forthwith raised the siege of Constantinople and carried his army into Asia. At Angora he was met by Timur who cut him off from his drinking water and so forced him to battle on July 20, 1402. Bayazid's army was routed and he was taken prisoner, to die at Samarkand in the following year. After his victory, Timur moved westward, sacking towns and cities and slaughtering their inhabitants. Brusa, the Ottoman capital, was burnt, Nicaea, Gemlik, and many other towns were sacked, and Smyrna, after a fourteen-day siege, was stormed: its inhabitants as usual were butchered. From Smyrna Timur set out on his return to Samarkand contemplating the invasion of China, and in the midst of his preparations he died in 1405 at the age of sixty-nine.

The advance of the Asiatic hordes had thrown Christendom into consternation, and when the news of Timur's victory was received in the West, it seemed as if Europe were about to be submerged by Asia. But when it was learnt that he had withdrawn eastward, hope revived, and to some, at least, it appeared possible that were the Christian kingdoms to lay aside their quarrels and to form common front against the defeated Ottomans, they might easily be driven out of Europe.

The opportunity was immense and it lingered for ten years; for it was not until 1413 that the war of succession between Bayazid's three elder sons, Suleiman, Musa, and Mahomet, ended when the third re-established the sultanate, by which date its European possessions had shrunk to little more than Adrianople itself. Had the Christians been capable of uniting, as the Greeks had done in the days of Xerxes and Darius, they might have crowned the battle of Angora by taking Adrianople, and had they done so, the power of the Ottomans in Europe would have been annihilated, for Adrianople was its centre of gravity.

Instead of exploiting this heaven-sent opportunity, in the self-same year that Mahomet brought the war of succession to an end, Henry V lay claim to the crown of France and entered into alliance with the Duke of Burgundy to win it. As detrimental, the Hussite Wars were about to deluge central Europe with blood, and worst of all, from 1402 to 1454 the wars of the Milanese, Venetians, and Florentines in Italy paralysed any concerted effort against the Turks. Had Agincourt been fought in the East instead of in the West, the battle of Angora, though it concerned two Moslem powers, would have taken its place in the annals of history as the most decisive battle ever fought for the preservation of Christendom.

The reign of Mahomet I, called Chelebi "the Gentleman" (1413–1421), was spent in establishing order out of chaos. He was a rebuilder and restorer and not a conqueror, as was his successor Murad II (1421–1451) who, because of the ceaseless flood of Turks moving westward, set in motion by Timur's gigantic raids, never lacked recruits, and before his reign ended he was able to carry the Ottoman banner throughout the length of the Balkans.

In 1422, he laid siege to Constantinople, but was compelled to abandon it because of a revolt in Karamania (the region round Konia), and soon after the Emperor John VI (1425–1448)[1] agreed to pay tribute to him. In 1430, Murad regained Salonica, took Uskub, invaded Transylvania, and in 1435 besieged Belgrade. Four years later, in order to gain western aid, at the Council of Florence John agreed to the union of the Churches, which in the following year led the pope to call upon all Christian princes to march against the Turks. Vladislav, King of Hungary, responded to the call, and in 1441 Hunyadi (John Corvinus), the Voivode of Transylvania, drove the Turks out of Serbia. This success was followed, in 1443, by a disastrous Turkish defeat near Kustenitza (45 miles south-east of Sofia), which in 1444 led to a truce between Murad and the king of Hungary. But no sooner

---

[1] John VI was the son of Manuel II, and in 1420 he became associated with his father, after which Manuel became a purely nominal ruler.

had it been agreed than on the suggestion of Cardinal Julian Cesarini – who held that an oath with the infidel might be set aside – it was broken by the Christian allies. Infuriated by this treachery, Murad marched against them and routed them at Varna. In 1446, he destroyed the fortifications of the Isthmus of Corinth, ravaged the Morea, and two years later prepared to invade Albania, then held by the famous George Castriotes, better known as Scanderbeg.

Meanwhile, under the directions of Pope Nicholas V, Hunyadi assembled an army of 24,000 Hungarians, Poles, Wallachs, and Germans on the plains of Kossovo. Murad dropped his Albanian project and, at the head of 100,000 men, marched against him. On October 18, 1448, a battle began, which ended on October 20 in a complete victory for Murad; 8,000 of the flower of the Hungarian nobility were left dead on the field. For Hungary and western Europe the effect of this defeat was catastrophic. For years onward the Turks had nothing to fear from their enemies north of the Danube. Except by sea, Constantinople was isolated and ripe to fall. In 1451 Murad died in Adrianople, and was succeeded by his son Mahomet II (1451–1481), surnamed "the Conqueror".

CHAPTER 10

The siege and fall of Constantinople, 1453

When, on July 6, 1449, the Emperor John VI died and his brother, Constantine XI, surnamed Dragases, succeeded to the imperial throne, the Eastern Empire, which in the days of Constantine I had extended over the whole of the Balkan peninsula (less Illyria), Asia Minor, Syria, Palestine, Egypt, and Cyrenaica, had shrunk to little more than the walls of Constantinople. John had done nothing during his reign except to maintain an abject *status quo*, and to appease his enemy he had even congratulated the sultan on his victory at Varna. Nor were the clergy and nobles less servile, and of the people, Chedomil Mijatovich writes: "The nation became an inert mass, without initiative and without will. Before the Emperor and the Church prelates it grovelled in the dust; behind them it rose up to spit at them and shake its fist. Tyranny and exploitation above, hatred and cowardice beneath; cruelty often, hypocrisy always and everywhere, in the upper and lower strata. Outward polish and dexterity replaced true culture; phraseology hid lack of ideas. Both political and social bodies were alike rotten; the spirit of the nation was languid, devoid of all elasticity. Selfishness placed itself on the throne of public interest, and tried to cover its hideousness with the mantle of false patriotism."[1]

This ignoble state of affairs was largely the product of the centuries old attempt by Rome to unite the Latin and Greek Churches, a question of theology which occupied the critical mind of the Byzantines to the exclusion of nearly everything else, and because in the Age of Faith theology was politics, religious union was the political question which prevented strategic union, the lack of which unbarred the eastern gate of Europe to the Turks.

Though the estrangement between the two Churches dated from the fifth century, it was not until the eleventh that it became acute. In 1073 Pope Gregory VII declared to Ebouly de Rossi: "It is far better for a country to remain under the rule of Islam, than be governed by Christians who refuse to acknowledge the

[1] *Constantine the Last Emperor of the Greeks*, Chedomil Mijatovich (1892), pp. 5–6.

357

rights of the Catholic Church."[1] To such an extent was hatred carried that when, on December 12, 1452, the union which had been agreed at the Council of Florence in 1439 was reaffirmed in Constantinople by Cardinal Isidore, the Grand Duke Lucas Notaras declared that "It is better to see in the city the power of the Turkish turban than that of the Latin tiara".[2] Even during the siege itself, when the situation was desperate, the historian Ducas says: "That even if an angel from heaven descended, and declared that he would save the city from the Turks, if only the people would unite with the Church of Rome, the Greeks would have refused."[3]

In spite of the reaffirmation of the union the assistance given to the Greeks by the western powers was negligible. The Genoese settlement of Galata (Pera), the suburb of Constantinople on the northern side of the Golden Horn, remained neutral throughout the contest, while such help that was offered by others was bargained for material gains. The Emperor Frederick III talked, but did nothing; and Alphonso, king of Aragon, Naples, and Sicily did likewise. Hunyadi demanded for his support Silivria (Silivri) or Mesembria (Misivria), and the king of Catalonia haggled for Lesbos. Only the Venetians, Genoese, and the pope offered some assistance; the first two because their trade was in jeopardy, and the latter because the union had been reaffirmed: this was considered to be worth Cardinal Isidore and 200 soldiers!

Among the Christians we find only disunity and weakness, but among the Turks we see the strength of a young people united under the direction of one of the most remarkable men in Oriental history, the Sultan Mahomet II (1451–1481), son of Murad II and a beautiful Albanian slave. When, early in February, 1451, his father died, he was twenty-one years old, and as soon as the news reached him in Magnesia (western Anatolia), he set out at top speed, crossed the Dardanelles into Gallipoli and thence rode to Adrianople, where he arrived on February 9 and was proclaimed sultan. Typical of the man, his first act was to drown his infant brother;[4] his second to execute the assassin he had hired; and the third to marry the child's mother to a slave.

In appearance he was handsome, of middle height, with a

[1] *Byzantinische Geschichten*, August Friederich Gfrörer (1872–1874), vol. II, p. 459.
[2] *History of the Byzantine Empire*, A. A. Vasiliev (1929), vol. II, p. 349, citing Ducas's *Historia Byzantina*, chap. xxxvii, p. 264.
[3] Cited by J. von Hammer, *Histoire de l'Empire Ottoman* (1835), vol. II, p. 426.
[4] Later he legitimized the slaughter of younger brothers by the sultan.

long aquiline nose which seemed to overhang his thick red lips, partly hidden by long drooping moustaches. Highly strung and nervous, he was too suspicious to make friends and too cruel to make enduring enemies. He loved the grim and the brutal and was known to his followers as "Hunkar", the "Drinker of Blood", a name not undeserved, for after the capture of Constantinople he had the heads of his executed enemies placed on a table before him. He seldom smiled; one of the few occasions would seem to have been when he heard that Drakul, Prince of Wallachia, had nailed the turbans of his envoys on to their heads because they had refused to uncover themselves in his presence. It so tickled his fancy that he at once adopted this form of torture. Again, perhaps, he smiled when Drakul impaled several thousands of his Turkish prisoners; when he heard of it he exclaimed in admiration: "It is impossible to drive out of his country a prince who does such grand things as that."[1] Nevertheless he was a man of high intelligence, which had been sharpened by his stepmother, the cultured Mara Brankovich. Unusual for a Turk, he could speak, write and read five foreign languages—Greek, Latin, Arabic, Chaldean, and Persian, probably also Slavonic. Throughout his life he was a seeker after knowledge and ever anxious to learn. He was a student of philosophy, theology, and astrology and a patron of Persian poetry and the arts. "He united", says Finlay, "the enterprise and valour of youth with the prudence and wisdom of old age",[2] a combination providing an intellectual basis for his generalship and statesmanship which, if not of the highest order, were remarkable. The great men of history were his models, and he greedily studied the lives of Cyrus, Alexander, Julius Caesar, Octavian, Constantine, and Theodosius. " 'He wished', says Tetaldi, 'to conquer the whole world, to see more than Alexander and Caesar or any other valiant man who has ever lived'."[3]

As a general he relied on the force of numbers rather than upon skill. Though time and again he was checked by John Hunyadi and Scanderbeg, and was triumphantly repelled by the Knights of Rhodes and the Persians, his generalship was of no mean order. Unlike many of the sultans, he always commanded his own army; lived and dreamed of war; decided everything for

[1] *Les Sultans Ottomans*, Halil Ganem (1902), vol. I, p. 147.
[2] *A History of Greece, etc.*, George Finlay (1877), vol. III, p. 498.
[3] Quoted by Edwin Pears in *The Destruction of the Greek Empire and the Story of the Capture of Constantinople by the Turks* (1903), pp. 292–293.

himself; brooked no interference and demanded the strictest discipline. As Gibbon writes: "Of a master who never forgives, the orders are seldom disobeyed."[1] He was energetic, painstaking and secretive. Disguised, he would mix with his men and listen to their conversations, and woe to anyone who gave a sign that he recognised him; even a welcome meant instant death. Once he said of his secret preparations: "If a hair of my beard knew, I would pluck it out and burn it."[2] His plans were thorough and meticulously prepared; his movements rapid; he was never discouraged by defeat; and he never let his enemy recoup. He invaded the European provinces twenty times and reduced them to his will. But, above all, as an artillerist he stands supreme: he was the first really great gunner in history.

As a statesman he kept himself in complete isolation and appeared to his subjects as a supernatural power—a god. He was an administrator of the first order, a politic and even a tolerant ruler, also one who knew how to organize his conquests by leaving to his subjects things which were of secondary importance while he held fast to those which were of first.

From early youth his overmastering idea was the capture of Constantinople and from the day of his accession he set out to realize it. First he confirmed the treaty Murad had made with Constantine, and professed to him his peaceful intentions. Next, to obviate an attack in rear by the emir of Karamania, such as had compelled his father to raise the siege of Constantinople in 1422, he brought him to heel. Then he pacified the Venetians, concluded a three-year truce with Hunyadi, and made peace with Hungary, Wallachia, and Bosnia. As Gibbon says: "Peace was on his lips, while war was in his heart."[3] Lastly, remembering that his father in his Varna campaign had to pay the enormous toll of one ducat (about nine shillings) for each soldier ferried across to Gallipoli, he decided to free himself of this inconvenience. Already master of the Asiatic shore of the Bosphorus, where Bayazid had built the castle of Anatolia-Hisar, he determined to become master of the European shore as well and in March, 1452, he landed a force of soldiers and 5,000 workmen a little to the north of Constantinople and began to build the strong fortress of Roumelia-Hisar (Boghasi-Kesen), also called by the Greeks *Laemocopia*

---

[1] *The Decline and Fall*, Edward Gibbon, vol. VII, p. 172.
[2] *Histoire de l'Empire Ottoman*, J. von Hammer, vol. III, p. 68.
[3] *The Decline and Fall*, vol. VII, p. 170.

"Cut-Throat Castle". Nicolò Barbaro writes in his *Journal of the Siege*: "This fortification is exceedingly strong from the sea, so that it is absolutely impossible to capture it, for on the shore and walls are standing bombards in very great numbers; on the land side the fortification is also strong, though less so than from the sea."[1] Six months later, when the work was finished, all communication between Constantinople and the ports of the Black Sea was severed, which meant that the capital was cut off from its main corn supply in the Ukraine. Mahomet then appeared before the land wall at the head of a force, reputed to be 50,000 men strong, reconnoitred it, and on September 6, 1452, he withdrew to Adrianople to complete his preparations.

The Turkish army comprised three bodies of troops, janissaries, bashi-bazouks, and provincial levies. The first was now a standing regular army, between 12,000 and 15,000 strong, of the most formidable soldiers of the fifteenth century: no Christian kingdom, not even France under Charles VII's ordinances, had a body of troops comparable with them. Since the reign of Murad I they had been recruited by means of a blood tax levied on the Christian provinces, each of which was yearly compelled to surrender a quota of boys between the ages of seven and twelve, distinguished for their strength and intelligence. These unfortunates were forcibly converted to Mahommedanism and subjected to the severest discipline and self-denials. They were forbidden to marry, allowed no luxuries, and not permitted to trade or accumulate wealth: they were military monks, and when too old to serve were pensioned.[2] Unlike the janissaries, the bashi-bazouks were little more than an undisciplined rabble of poorly armed Turks and renegade Christians, and the provincial levies, largely recruited in Anatolia, were little better.

The Turkish army and tactics of this period are described by Bertrandon de la Brocquière in his *Travels* of 1432–1433. He informs us that the Ottomans wore coats of mail descending almost half-way down their thighs, and carried on their heads a round white peaked cap ornamented with plates of iron. Their arms were the bow, sword, and mace. The obedience of the Turkish soldier to superiors was boundless, "and it is chiefly owing to this steady

[1] Cited by Vasiliev (*History of the Byzantine Empire*, vol. II, p. 348) from Barbaro's *Giornale dell' assedio di Constantinopli* (1856), p. 2.
[2] For a summary of the rules prescribed for them by Murad I see *Constantine the Last Emperor of the Greeks*, Chedomil Mijatovich, pp. 27–32, and *État Militaire Ottoman depuis la Fondation de l'Empire*, Ahmed Djevad Bey (1882), p. 66.

submission that such great exploits have been performed, and such vast conquests gained". They were adepts at discovering their enemy, keeping him under observation, and then suddenly by a forced march surprising him, as they did at Nicopolis. "Their manner of fighting", he writes, "varies according to circumstances. When they find a favourable opportunity they divide themselves into different detachments, and thus attack many parts of an army at once ... it is in their flight that they are formidable, and it has been almost always then that they have defeated the Christians. ... When the chief, or any one of his officers, perceives the enemy who pursues to be in disorder, he gives three strokes on this instrument [a tabalcan–drum]; the others on hearing it, do the same, and they are instantly formed round their chief like so many hogs round the old one; and then according to circumstances, they either receive the charge of the assailants, or fall on them by troops, and attack them in different places at the same time. In pitched battles they employ another stratagem which consists of throwing fireworks among the cavalry to frighten the horses. They often post in their front a great body of dromedaries and camels, which are bold and vicious; these they drive before them on the enemy's line of horse, and throw it into confusion."[1]

More important even than his janissaries was Mahomet's artillery, the men of which were also mainly Christian: Critobulus says, "it was the canon which did everything".[2] In all, Mahomet had twelve or thirteen great bombards (cannon) and fourteen batteries of lesser pieces; each battery consisted of four guns. His largest bombard was cast in Adrianople by a Hungarian or Wallachian named Urban. Its barrel was twelve *palma* in circumference–that is, twelve span of eight inches each, giving ninety-six inches in all–and it has been calculated that the weight of its stone shot must have been 1,456 lb. avoirdupois.[3] This monstrous weapon required 60 oxen to drag it, 200 men to march alongside to keep it in position, and 200 more to level the ground it passed over.[4] It took two hours to load, and, therefore, could

---

[1] *Early Travels in Palestine*, edit. Thomas Wright (1855), pp. 363–366.

[2] *The Cambridge Medieval History*, vol. IV, p. 698.

[3] Machines throwing larger balls than Mahomet used were in use just before the general adoption of cannon. At the siege of Zara, in 1346, shot of 3,000 lb. were hurled by the Venetians, and, in 1373, the Genoese used some nearly as large at the siege of Cyprus. Mons Meg at Edinburgh was cast in 1455; its granite balls are twenty-one inches in diameter.

[4] See *Le Siège, la Prise et le Sac de Constantinople par les Turcs en 1453*, Gustave Schlumberger (1922), pp. 58–60.

fire only six to eight times a day. According to Phrantzes, eventually it blew up and killed Urban.[1]

When the siege opened, Nicolò Barbaro, who took part in it, states that there were 150,000 men in the besieging army between the Golden Horn and the Sea of Marmara, and Tedaldi, a Florentine soldier, says 200,000, of whom 140,000 were effective soldiers and the rest "thieves, plunderers, hawkers, and others following the army for gain and booty'.[2] Mahomet's fleet was not an efficient one; it is said to have numbered between 145 and 350 warships of various types, mostly small vessels.

To meet this formidable array, outside the walls of Constantinople Constantine had nothing, and within them and in the harbour of the Golden Horn he had only a handful of mercenaries and a few galleys in lamentable condition. Though the city contained some 100,000 inhabitants, when he ordered a census of its fighting men to be made only 4,973 answered the call. In spite of this cowardice Constantine heroically began preparations for the now inevitable death-struggle.

Constantine's first task was to repair the walls, which were in a state of decay. They surrounded the city and, omitting Galata which was in neutral hands, their circumference was about thirteen miles. Topographically they may be divided into three sections:

(1) The land wall of Theodosius II, built in the fifth century, four miles long, stretching from the Sea of Marmara and the Golden Gate in the south to the Xylo Porta (Gate of Wood) and the Blanchern Palace on the Golden Horn in the north.

(2) The sea wall along the Golden Horn from the Xylo Porta to the Acropolis (Seraglio Point), about three and a half miles long.

(3) The continuation of this wall along the Sea of Marmara to the Golden Gate – five and a half miles long.

Though the second and third of these walls were single in construction, the first was triple, consisting of (a) an inner wall forty feet high with 112 towers, each about sixty feet high; (b) an outer wall, twenty-five feet high, also furnished with towers; and (c) a breastwork in front of it, formed by a continuation in height of the inner wall of the water ditch, or fosse, which was some sixty

---

[1] *Histoire de l'Empire Ottoman*, vol. II, p. 398.
[2] *The Cambridge Medieval History*, vol. IV, pp. 695–696. See also Bury's edit. of Gibbon, vol. VII, p. 180. All these figures are suspect.

feet broad and fifteen deep. Between each of the walls was an enclosure about twenty yards broad; the one between the inner and outer walls was called the *Peribolos*, and that between the outer and the breastwork, the *Parateichion*.

For convenience, the land wall may be divided into three tactical sections: (1) From the Golden Gate to the Gate of St. Romanus (Top Capou–Cannon Gate); (2) from the St. Romanus Gate to the Adrianople Gate; and (3) from the Adrianople Gate to the Xylo Porta. Through the second section runs the Lycus stream, and the area immediately west of it was called the *Mesoteichion*.

The main harbour, as to-day, was the Golden Horn, protected on its southern side by the northern sea wall of the city, and on its northern by the sea wall of Galata. Its entrance into the Bosphorus was secured by a great chain–already described in Chapter 12– which was reinforced by immense baulks of wood. Behind it was gathered the imperial fleet which, when the siege began, numbered about twenty-six ships, ten Greek and sixteen Venetian, Genoese, etc.; fifteen of which were allotted to its defence under the command of the Venetian, Gabriel Trevisano, who had offered his services "*per honor de Dio et per honor de tuta la Christianitade*".

Though Constantine could raise no more than 5,000 fighting men out of the 25,000 males of military age in the city, he received small but highly valuable assistance from certain condottieri and others, which brought his total forces to about 8,000. The first reinforcements to arrive were 200 soldiers under the papal legate, Cardinal Isidore, former metropolitan of Kiev and participator in the Council of Florence, who in November, 1452, sailed into the Golden Horn. But his coming only accentuated the ineradicable hatred between the East and the West; for when, on December 12, according to the terms of the Council of Florence, he celebrated a service commemorating the union between the Churches in St. Sophia, the infuriated people, roused by Gennadius (later patriarch), broke into open riot and shouted, "Death to the Azymites (the excommunicated)." Thus, from the very opening of the siege, the Greeks resolutely sacrificed their political independence to their hatred of Rome.[1] Next, in January

---

[1] A factor working strongly in favour of the Turks was that in the provinces they had already occupied, the bishops, nominated by the patriarchs, were fully recognized as the civil and religious heads of the Christian community.

the following year, the Genoese soldier John Giustiniani (Giovanni) arrived with 700 men in two large ships, and with him was Johann Grant, an experienced German artillerist and military engineer.

Giustiniani's arrival was an event of the greatest importance, not only because he brought with him two powerful warships and 700 soldiers, of whom 400 were fully armoured; but because he was one of the most noted soldiers of his age: a skilful leader and a man of outstanding energy, audacity, and courage. When he offered his sword to the emperor, Constantine made him commander-in-chief of the defence forces of the city, and endowed him with all but dictatorial powers. From his arrival a spirit of hope swept Constantinople.

Mahomet, who had reduced two small Byzantine posts at Therapia and Studium on the Bosphorus and impaled their garrisons, and who had used burning sulphur to gas-out the garrison of the castle on the island of Prinkipo, on April 5, 1453, again appeared before the land wall and deployed his army into four corps. They were: (1) Zagan Pasha's to watch Galata and to build a bridge over the western end of the Golden Horn preparatory to an attack on the Xylo Porta. (2) Caraja Pasha's corps to attack the wall between the Xylo Porta and the Adrianople Gate, while (3) Isaac Pasha's neutralized the wall from the St. Romanus Gate and the Sea of Marmara. (4) In the Lycus valley, between the two gates last mentioned, Mahomet drew up his staunchest troops and janissaries under his grand vizier, Halil Pasha, for it was here that he intended to deliver his main attack. To supervise it, he had his red and golden headquarters tent pitched immediately in rear of this corps.

Constantine saw where the main blow was to fall and moved his headquarters behind the land wall in the Lycus valley. He allotted the defence of the central section of the land wall to Giustiniani. North of it he posted the brothers Antony, Paul, and Troilus Bocchiardi, Theodore of Karystos, and Johann Grant; and south of it Catarin Contarini, Andronicus Cantacuzene, and other leaders. The remainder of the walls and the harbours was held by minute bodies of men, many of the towers garrisoned by squads only three or four strong.

On April 12, when the Turkish fleet, under the Bulgarian renegade Baltoglu, was at anchor in the roadstead of Prinkipo, the great cannon, opposite the land wall in the Lycus valley, were advanced to the edge of the fosse, and the first great organized bombardment in history was opened to the beating of drums, accompanied by the shoutings of thousands of excited men. Mijatovitch says: "Since the creation of the world nothing like it had been heard on the shores of the Bosphorus." Nevertheless it was a slow affair; it took two hours to load the great cannon and they could fire only seven to eight times a day.

Though the artillery assault was maintained day in and day out, its effect was slight until an envoy from Hunyadi instructed Mahomet's gunners that they should not disperse their shot, as they were doing, but should concentrate in volleys upon triangular sections of the wall. Phrantzes says that the Hungarians desired Constantinople to fall, because a Serbian hermit had foretold that Christendom would never be rid of the Turks until that seat of heresy was obliterated.[1] Though this Christian aid greatly assisted the Turks, as the wall crumbled it was as rapidly patched up, and, on April 18, Mahomet, impatient, ordered a general assault on the wall and the boom.

The attack was launched to the shouts of *Yagma! Yagma!* ("To the sack! To the sack!"), and with terrifying howls and yells the Turks rushed the ditch. Then, writes the Slavonic Chronicler: "The reports of muskets, the ringing of bells, the clashing of arms, the cries of fighting men, the shrieks of women and the wailing of children, produced such a noise, that it seemed as if the earth trembled. Clouds of smoke fell upon the city and the camp, and the combatants at last could not see each other."[2] But Giustiniani was ready; he opened a terrific fire from hand guns, wall guns,[3] bows, crossbows and catapults and swept the leading ranks of the attackers back into the ditch. Meanwhile the Grand Duke Notaras beat off the naval assault on the boom. So furious was Mahomet at his ill-success that his generals had the greatest difficulty in persuading him not to load his trebuchets with his own dead and to hurl them over the walls of the city.[4]

Two days after this repulse there occurred an incident which led to an astonishing naval battle. In March, three large Genoese

---

[1] *Chronicle of Constantinople*, George Phrantzes (1838), p. 239. (See Mijatovich, p. 155.)

[2] *The Slavonic Chronicler*, p. 27. (See Mijatovich, p. 156.)

[3] These guns were loaded with five to ten lead balls. See E. A. Vlasto, *1453 Les Derniers Jours de Constantinople* (1883), p. 84.

[4] Not a new idea, for at the siege of Carolstein in 1422. 'Coribut caused the bodies of his soldiers whom the besieged had killed to be thrown into the town in addition to 2,000 cartloads of manure." See *The Projectile-Throwing Engines of the Ancients*, Sir Ralph Payne-Gallwey (1907), p. 39.

warships, carrying troops and munitions on their way to Constantinople, had been delayed by contrary winds at the island of Chios. There they remained until March 15, when the wind veered to the south and they set sail again. They fell in with a large imperial grain ship, continued their course with her, and sighted the dome of St. Sophia at ten o'clock on the norning of March 20.[1]

When he heard of their approach, Mahomet at once sent orders to his fleet to put to sea and destroy or capture them, after which with his staff and a large body of troops he hurried to the Bosphorus shore of Galata to watch. He saw 145 Turkish galleys row out, and it seemed to him inevitable that the four Christian ships would be sunk, as it also did to the thousands of spectators who crowded the sea walls of Constantinople and the roofs of its houses.

Howling with joy, Baltoglu rowed straight for his enemy; but the wind was strong and the great Genoese warships and the transport crashed through his fleet, stove in his galleys or carried away their oars. Next, as they rounded Seraglio Point, the wind dropped and they were at once surrounded. A desperate action began. When the Turks attempted to grapple and swarm up their sides, they were cut down with axes. Rocks, pots of Greek fire, darts, and javelins were hurled upon them, and hand-guns and swivel-pieces swept their decks with ball. For two hours the contest continued. Mahomet yelled and threatened and at times galloped his horse into the sea to urge on his admiral. Suddenly a puff of wind returned, the harbour chain was lowered, and the four ships again crashed through their enemy and entered the Golden Horn.[2]

Mahomet, in his rage, ordered Baltoglu to be impaled forthwith, and when his generals prevented this, while four slaves held him stretched upon the ground, he thrashed him with a heavy stick.

Though again checked, Mahomet was far from checkmated. He realized all along how vitally important it was to win control of the Golden Horn, for once in his hands he could threaten the northern sea wall and so compel Constantine still further to disperse his minute garrison. So he decided, probably on the

---

[1] According to Schlumberger (p. 126) the names of the Genoese sea captains were Leonardo of Chios, Maurice Cattaneo, and Domenico of Navarra, with Baptisto of Felliciano. The captain of the transport was Phlantanelas. Their bravery deserves that their names should be remembered.

[2] J. von Hammer quoting Ducas; see *Histoire de l'Empire Ottoman*, vol. II, p. 405.

suggestion of a Genoese in Galata, to transport part of his fleet across the mile of land[1] which separates the Bosphorus from the stream called The Springs, which flows into the Golden Horn west of Galata. With his usual impetuosity he collected thousands of workmen to level the ground, to build a wooden runway and to grease it. Over it some seventy ships with sails unfurled and flags flying were hauled, and under cover of artillery they slid into the Golden Horn. This unexpected manœuvre produced consternation among the Greeks, but when they found that these ships did not attack the boom, they plucked up courage and attempted a night assault on them. This was severely repulsed because it was betrayed to the Turks by the Galata Genoese. Meanwhile, in order to unite the two wings of his army, Mahomet ordered a barrel-bridge 2,000 feet long with a roadway eight feet broad to be built across the Horn: this was done immediately.

The Greeks were now so thoroughly disheartened that a proposal was made to Constantine that he should save himself by escaping from the city. He listened quietly to the suggestion, then replied: "I thank all for the advice which you have given me. . . . How could I leave the churches of our Lord, and His servants the clergy, and the throne, and my people in such a plight? What would the world say about me? I pray you, my friends, in future do not say to me anything else but, 'Nay, Sire, do not leave us!' Never, never will I leave you! I am resolved to die here with you! And saying this the Emperor turned his head aside, because tears filled his eyes; and with him wept the Patriarch and all who were there!"[2]

Constantine's determination infused new life into the defence; nevertheless the situation remained a desperate one, for, unless succour came soon, it was only a matter of time before the city would, if not be stormed, be starved out. Therefore, on May 3, a small, fast brigantine, disguised as a Turkish vessel and manned with a crew of twelve men, slipped out to seek the promised papal fleet, which was supposed to be on its way north. All these days the bombardment continued, and on May 7 and again on May 12 determined assaults of 30,000 and 50,000 Turks were made on the walls about the St. Romanus Gate; in each case they were beaten back by Giustiniani with great slaughter.

---

[1] Again this idea was not an original one. J. von Hammer, vol. II, pp. 405–408, gives a number of past examples.
[2] *The Slavonic Chronicler*, p. 116. (See Mijatovich, p. 174.)

The numerical strength of the Turks, which was steadily increased by the arrival of fresh contingents, now began to tell in favour of the besieged, for Mahomet's problem of supply became so difficult that, unless he could gain the city by the end of the month, he would be forced—as had happened so often on previous occasions—to abandon the siege. When he found that he could not command the shattered walls and so prevent his enemy from repairing them, his next attempt to storm them, on May 18, was

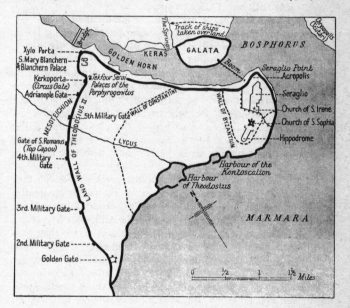

18. SIEGE OF CONSTANTINOPLE, 1453

made under the protection of an immense wooden tower, a *Helepolis* or "city-taker", which was dragged up to the fosse, and from it a deadly fire was poured upon the besieged. Giustiniani blew it up by rolling barrels of powder into the fosse, and the sultan exclaimed: "What would I not give to win that man over to my side!"[1] He attempted to bribe him; but to no avail.

Assault and tower-attack having failed, resort was made to

[1] *Histoire de l'Empire Ottoman*, J. von Hammer, vol. II, p. 417.

mining, more particularly in the neighbourhood of the Adrianople and Kaligaria Gates; the latter was situated close to the Blanchern Palace, where the wall was single. The work was first put in hand on May 15, and from then on to May 25 various attempts were made to undermine the walls;[1] but each was frustrated by Johann Grant, who counter-mined. Either he blew up[2] the Turkish miners or smoked them out, suffocated them by stink-pots or drowned them by letting in water, or else met them underground and fought them with knife, axe and spear.

These repeated failures and the constant rumours that an Hungarian army was approaching Constantinople from the north and the papal fleet from the south, made the Turks lose heart. Even their indomitable leader grew doubtful, and when he failed to induce the emperor to surrender the city on terms, on May 26 or 27 he summoned a council of war to ascertain the opinions of his generals. Halil Pasha, the grand vizier, who throughout had been against the siege, strongly recommended abandoning it. But Zagan Pasha, his rival, scoffed at the idea, reminded the sultan that Alexander the Great had conquered the world with a far smaller army than the one now besieging the city, and said:

"Thou, O Padishah, knowest well the great dissensions that are raging in Italy especially, and in all Frankistan generally. In consequence of these dissensions the Giaours (infidels) are incapable of united action against us. The Christian potentates never will unite together. When after protracted efforts they conclude something like a peace amongst themselves, it never lasts long. Even when they are bound by treaties of alliance, they are not prevented seizing territories from each other. They always stand in fear of each other. No doubt they think much, speak much, and explain much, but after all they do very little. When they decide to do anything, they waste much time before they begin to act. Suppose they have even commenced something, they cannot progress very far with it because they are sure to disagree

[1] At this period the art of mining had little advanced since the days of Philip of Macedon, who made use of this means of attack in his siege of Byzantium in 340 B.C. It consisted in digging out a chamber under the wall, propping up its roof with baulks and then setting fire to them.

[2] *The Slavonic Chronicler*, p. 12 (see Mijatovich, p. 186), says: "It was as if the lightning had struck the place, for the earth shook and with a great crash a greenish whirlwind carried the Turks into the air. Fragments of men and timber fell into the city and into the camp. The besieged ran away from the walls and the besiegers fled back from the ditch." If this is correct, then it is the first recorded case of the use of gunpowder in mining.

amongst themselves how to proceed. . . . Therefore, O Padishah, do not lose hope, but give us the order at once to storm the city!"[1]

The Sultan was overjoyed with this oration and forthwith determined upon a simultaneous assault on the land and sea walls on May 29.

While the bombardment was continued steadily, he decided upon his plan of attack, which was to be a combined one of army and fleet; the object of the latter was, as on the previous occasion, by fire to pin down the defenders of the sea walls and so to prevent them from reinforcing the land wall. He selected three main objectives: (1) the wall between the Tekfour Serai and the Adrianople Gate; (2) the wall in the Lycus valley about the St. Romanus Gate; and (3) the third military gate, half-way between St. Romanus and the Golden Gates. The second of these three objectives was to be the point of decision.

The attack was to be carried out without let or pause, night and day, until the defenders were so exhausted that the final assault would meet with little opposition. Mahomet is reported to have said: "I have decided to engage successively and without halt one body of fresh troops after the other, until harassed and worn out the enemy will be unable further to resist."[2] The plan settled, he issued orders to his fleet to keep the sea walls under fire, and he instructed Zagan Pasha to cross to the south side of the Golden Horn and to engage the northernmost objective. Lastly he arranged for the collection of a vast amount of material: 2,000 scaling ladders, iron hooks to pull down the barricades Giustiniani had built to block the breaches, and a mass of fascines with which to fill in the ditch.

Electrified by his energy, his army at once set to work, and, on the nights of May 27–28 and 28–29, its vast camp was illuminated, a foreboding crescent of fire encircled the city. On the morning of May 28 the sultan inspected his fleet, now commanded by Hamoud (Chamouza), and rode round his entire army, to find all in readiness.

When enthusiasm swept the Turkish ranks, dejection and dissension gripped the life of the doomed city. On May 23 the valiant little brigantine returned, having found no succouring fleet. The news extinguished the last spark of hope in the hearts of the

---

[1] *Phrantzes*, p. 269 (quoted by Mijatovich, pp. 201–202).
[2] See Schlumberger, *op cit.*, p. 259, quoting Critobulus.

inhabitants. Portents of disaster were whispered from mouth to ear: an icon had been seen to sweat; rumbling noises had been heard, and a light had glowed strangely upon the dome of the great cathedral. The garrison now numbered barely 4,000 fighting men, and the rest of the inhabitants, incapable of bearing arms, could do nothing except pray for a miracle. Yet in this pall of gloom one man maintained his dignity and courage: it was Constantine, he who bore the name of the first and the last of the eastern emperors. On the night of May 28–29 he addressed his followers – Greeks, Venetians, and Genoese – saying: "Let us work together, my companions and my brethren, to gain for ourselves liberty, glory and eternal memory! Into your hands I commit now my sceptre. Here it is! Save it! Crowns await you in heaven, and on earth your names will be remembered honourably until the end of time." Thereupon all cried out: "Let us die for faith and fatherland! Let us die for the Church of God and for thee, our Emperor!"[1]

Next, all gathered in St. Sophia, and amid sobs and wailings and cries of *Kyrie eleison* the last Christian service was celebrated in the church of the Holy Wisdom. Based on Byzantine sources, Edwin Pears gives us a striking picture of the ceremony. "The emperor", he writes, "and such of the leaders as could be spared were present and the building was once more and for the last time crowded with Christian worshippers. It requires no great effort of imagination to picture the scene. The interior of the church was the most beautiful which Christian art had produced, and its beauty was enhanced by its still gorgeous and brave Byzantine aristocracy; priests and soldiers intermingled, Constantino-politans, Venetians and Genoese, all were present, all realizing the peril before them, and feeling that in view of the impending danger the rivalries which had occupied them for years were too small to be worthy of thought. The emperor and his followers partook together of the 'the undefiled and divine mysteries', and said farewell to the patriarch. The ceremony was in reality a liturgy of death. The empire was in its agony and it was fitting that the service for its departing spirit should be thus publicly said in its most beautiful church and before its last brave emperor. If the scene so vividly described by Mr. Bryce of the coronation of Charles the Great and the birth of an empire is among the most

[1] The whole address is given by Phrantzes, pp. 271–278, who was present at the time.

picturesque in history, that of the last Christian service in St. Sophia is surely among the most tragic."[1]

After the service Constantine rode out westward toward the setting sun, and with Giustiniani and Don Francis of Toledo he took up his position in rear of the St. Romanus Gate as twilight crept over the city.

Because of the weakness of the garrison, the emperor decided that, because numbers were insufficient to man both the walls, and as the outer wall was not yet completely destroyed, he would hold the *Peribolos*, and, in order to assure that no one should leave it, he ordered that all the military gates leading into it were to be closed and locked. This was done directly the defenders had taken up their posts. Thus it was to be a fight to the finish; either the Turks would be repulsed or the defenders annihilated.

Toward midnight the emperor went the rounds of the walls in the Lycus valley. The night was dark and misty, a few large drops of rain began to fall, when suddenly all the fires in the Turkish camps were extinguished. Until about half-past one in the morning of May 29 all was still, when with equal suddenness there broke forth a cacophony of trumpets, drums and voices: it was the signal for the general assault.

In the Lycus sector, where the principal attack was made, Mahomet had drawn up his troops in three echelons: the bashi-bazouks, the Anatolians, and the janissaries – the worst first and the best last. The first had as their object the exhaustion of the defenders and their ammunition. In wild confusion thousands of them rushed the now half-filled ditch and threw their ladders against the stockade which had replaced the outer wall, but they were met by such discharges of projectiles, Greek fire, and boiling oil that they were driven back in confusion, only to be urged on again by a line of *Chaoushes* (sergeants) armed with iron maces and chain-whips.

At length Mahomet withdrew them and sent forward the Anatolians, and the struggle became fiercer than ever. Some broke into the *Peribolos*, but were driven out by Giustiniani, whose men, being fully armoured, suffered little injury. The attack failed, and lastly 10,000 janissaries, "grand masters and valiant men", says Barbaro, "ran to the walls, not like Turks, but like lions".[2] As they tore at the stockade, "Giustiniani and his

---

[1] *The Destruction of the Greek Empire*, pp. 330–331.
[2] *Ibid.*, p. 340.

little band met the attack with lances, axes, pikes, and swords, and cut down the foremost of their assailants. For a short time the fight became a hand-to-hand encounter, neither party gaining any advantage over the other."[1]

Meanwhile, half a mile to the north of where Giustiniani held his own against the most formidable troops in Europe, a minor incident occurred which led to the fall of the city. At the angle between the triple wall of Theodosius and the single wall which surrounded the palaces of the Porphyrogenitus (Tekfour Serai) and the Blanchern, was a small postern known as the Kerkoporta or Circus Gate.[2] In 1204 it had been blocked up by the Emperor Isaac II, the Angel, but had recently been reopened, and in the attack now made, the Turks having crowded into the ditch and gained possession of the outer enclosure, a party of janissaries, some fifty strong, noticed that the gate was undefended, rushed it and were rapidly followed by others. They entered the inner enclosure, took its defenders in flank, and so enabled their comrades to storm the wall and enter the city, where at once they hauled down the flag of St. Mark and ran up the Turkish standard. Next, they began to plunder the palaces, and the brothers Bocchiardi regained the enclosure; the incident seemed to be at an end.

But fate decided against the defenders; though the third assault in the Lycus valley was beaten back and the emperor shouted to his followers: "Bear yourselves bravely for God's sake! I see the enemy retires in disorder! If God wills, ours shall be the victory!"[3] suddenly, as he spoke, a projectile struck down Giustiniani.[4] He was hit either in the hand, foot, neck, or breast, and bleeding profusely, in great pain he retired for medical aid. Though the emperor implored him to remain, the agony was so great that he refused, and one of the military gates of the inner wall was opened to allow him to be carried out.[5]

According to the Venetian historians, the fall of the city is

---

[1] *The Destruction of the Greek Empire*, p. 341.

[2] According to Alexander van Millingen (*Byzantine Constantinople, the Walls of the City and the adjoining Historical Sites*, pp. 89–94) its full name was the "*Porta Xylokerkou*". Mr. Pears doubts this, see *op. cit.*, p. 342.

[3] Phrantzes, p. 283. (See Majatovich, p. 215.)

[4] He had already been wounded by a splinter on May 27.

[5] He was carried to his ship and taken to Chios where he died a few days later or on the way there. In the Church of St. Domenico, where he lies buried, may be read the following epitaph on his monument: "Here lies John Giustiniani of illustrious fame, Genoese patrician and Master-Merchant of Chios, who, in the war of Constantinople against Mahomet the Turk, as Generalissimo of his Serene Highness Constantine, last Emperor of the Eastern Christians, died of a mortal wound."

attributed to this incident. They say that panic followed, the wall was stormed and the city entered, and because of their intense hatred for the Genoese it would seem that they threw the blame on Giustiniani. That his withdrawal caused confusion is probably true, a confusion which the experienced eye of Mahomet did not miss; for the janissaries returned to the assault led by a gigantic Turk named Hassan. Nevertheless he was killed and his followers beaten back, which certainly shows that the defenders fought as staunchly as ever. What now apparently happened was this, and here we will follow M. Vlasto.[1] The Turks, who had broken in by the Kerkoporta, found their retreat cut off by the Bocchiardi brothers, worked their way south to the Adrianople Gate, and thence toward the St. Romanus, then took their defenders in flank and so enabled the sultan to launch his fifth and final assault, which carried the *Peribolos*.

When this attack was made, shouts rose in rear that the city was taken, which seemed to be confirmed by a Turkish flag seen flying over a tower near the Adrianople Gate. Though it was not true, a panic resulted and thousands of the enemy rushed the *Peribolos*. At this moment the emperor returned from another part of the wall, and when he discovered what had happened he galloped down the enclosure calling upon his men to follow him. With Don Francis of Toledo on his right and Theophilus Palaeologus on his left, he rushed upon the Turks crying out "God forbid that I should live an Emperor without an Empire! As my city falls, I will fall with it!"[2] A moment later he was cut down.

With his fall fell the city, which was soon entered on all sides. Panic then swept it from end to end. Though the slaughter was terrible, it was less so than it had been in 1204. It would seem that some 4,000 persons of both sexes and all ages were massacred when, at about midday, Mahomet regained control over his men and put a stop to the orgy. The houses were systematically plundered, the churches ransacked, some 50,000 men, women, and children seized as slaves, and innumerable books destroyed or sold.[3]

Once some semblance of order had been restored, the sultan entered St. Sophia, in which the thousands of people who had sought refuge there were herded as captives. He ordered an *Imaum*

---

[1] *1453. Les Derniers Jours de Constantinople*, E. V. Vlasto, p. 126.
[2] *Constantine the Last Emperor of the Greeks*, Chedomil Mijatovich, p. 220.
[3] The public library is supposed to have contained 600,000 volumes (Lebeau, *op. cit.*, p. 294). Gibbon, quoting Cardinal Isodore, says 120,000 books were destroyed.

(priest) to mount the pulpit to dedicate the church to Allah, and then, looking around on the scene of desolation he muttered the words of Firdusi:

> The spider's curtain hangs before the portal of Caesar's palace;
> And the owl stands sentinel on the watch-tower of Afrasiab.

Later, he amused himself by buying from his followers those of the Greek nobles who had not escaped and having them executed before him. Among these were the Grand Duke Notaras and his two young sons.

The desolation of the city was complete, and so few people were left in it that for years after Mahomet sent contingents from other places to repopulate it. Wisely he showed toleration towards the Orthodox Church by appointing Gennadius (George Scholarius) patriarch, and though he uprooted the feudal system he did not interfere with the customs of the people. There was astuteness in this policy; for by supporting the Orthodox Church he irrevocably divided the east from the west of Europe.

The shock which followed the catastrophe was stunning. Hallam says: "A sentiment of consternation, perhaps of self-reproach, thrilled to the heart of Christendom";[1] and there was good reason for this, for the fall of Constantinople opened wide the eastern door of Europe. Overrunning the Illyrian peninsula and the Peloponnese,[2] Mahomet turned upon Serbia, and though defeated by Hunyadi, the death of that hero was full compensation for this misfortune. Next, he retook Simendra and established himself in Bosnia; was defeated by Etienne IV of Moldavia; occupied Croatia; and on Scanderbeg's death, decided to invade Italy and march on Rome. But this was not to be. He failed to take Rhodes in 1480 and died the next year, leaving behind him an empire that stretched from the Danube to the Taurus and from the Black Sea to the Adriatic. These were his material gains, but his moral gains were greater still, because for nearly two centuries and a half, that is, from 1453 to 1683, when John Sobieski relieved Vienna, the one topic of European politics was the Turk. When, as described in Chapter 20, Don John of Austria destroyed the Turkish fleet at Lepanto, in 1571, the Venetians proclaimed that the devil was dead.

---

[1] *View of the State of Europe during the Middle Ages*, Henry Hallam (1858), vol. II, p. 136.
[2] He converted the Parthenon at Athens, then the Church of the Holy Virgin, into a mosque.

The reason for this fear was not only that the Turk had been victorious, but that, after a thousand years of a hectic unity, Christendom was segmented – physically broken and spiritually divided. This is how Aeneas Silvius Piccolomini (later Pope Pius II), at the time secretary of the Emperor Frederick III, looked upon Christendom:

"I do not hope for what I want. Christianity has no longer a head: neither Pope nor Emperor is adequately esteemed or obeyed; they are treated as fictitious names and painted figures. Each city has a king of its own; there are as many princes as houses. How might one persuade the numberless Christian rulers to take up arms? Look upon Christianity! Italy, you say, is pacified. I do not know to what extent. The remains of war still exist between the King of Aragon and the Genoese. The Genoese will not fight the Turks: they are said to pay tribute to them! The Venetians have made a treaty with the Turks. If the Italians do not take part, we cannot hope for maritime war. In Spain, as you know, there are many kings of different power, different policy, different will, and different ideas; but these sovereigns who live in the far West cannot be attracted to the East, especially when they are fighting with the Moors of Granada. The King of France has expelled his enemy from his kingdom; but he is still in trouble, and will not dare to send his knights beyond the borders of his kingdom for fear of sudden landing of the English. As far as the English are concerned, they think only of taking revenge for their expulsion from France. Scots, Danes, Swedes, and Norwegians, who live at the end of the world, seek nothing beyond their countries. The Germans are greatly divided and have nothing to unify them."[1]

First of all Mahomet created Turkey in Europe, and so bequeathed to Europe the Ottoman problem. Secondly, the fall of Constantinople, in 1453, rendered irrevocable the schism between the two Churches; henceforth division and not unity was to be a Christian principle. And thirdly, the Turkish conquest not only destroyed all traces of civilization in the cradle of its birth, but deprived that part of Europe of the benefits of Christian autonomy. The lands of the Eastern Empire were utterly degraded: art, literature and commerce foundered under the dead weight of Turkish ignorance and brutality. Fields were uncultivated, industries lost, family life undermined, the people reduced to cattle, and morality emasculated.

[1] Quoted by G. Voigt in *Enea Silvio Piccolomini* (1862), vol. II, pp. 118-119.

But, as the East sank, the West rose. The Greek dispersion, which both preceded and followed the fall of Constantinople, was as prolific in its intellectual conquests as the Hebrew dispersion, which preceded and followed the fall of Jerusalem in the year 70, had been prolific in its spiritual conquests: and in both commercial greed played its part.

Greek scholars percolated through the West, and while science was resuscitated among the thinking, the old Homeric myths again fascinated the common people. Architecture became classical, Cicero and Virgil the masters of the schoolmen, and Alexander and Caesar the instructors of soldiers, and these changes coincided with the discovery of printing—"the money of the mind". Thus it came about that the profoundest influence in this humanist revival, which is called "The Renaissance",[1] was the increasing substitution of pagan for Christian morality. John Addington Symonds once suggested that Faust is the great symbol of this age, Faust who is "content to sell his soul to the devil, but in return he sees Homer and Alexander and obtains Helen as his bride".[2]

This rational (Greek) light brought into flaming day the dead-lock between the papal and feudal systems, and before it both were shrivelled up; for the spiritual rampart of Rome had fallen with the storming of the land wall of Constantinople, and the feudal system could save neither. Again, their fall threw a dust of doubt over the entire West: hence the Reformation, that economic crisis which, masquerading under a monk's cowl, ended by exalting Mammon above God.

---

[1] Though, as Vasiliev points out, the fall of Constantinople did not call forth the Renaissance, which had embraced all Italy during the first half of the fifteenth century, "by transmitting classical works to the West and thereby saving them from destruction at the hands of the Turks, Byzantium performed great service for the future destinies of mankind" (*History of the Byzantine Empire*, vol. II, pp. 433 and 444).
[2] *The Destruction of the Greek Empire*, Edwin Pears, p. 409.

The reconquest and unification of Spain

C ut off from the rest of Europe by the Pyrenees, and dominated by the Moors, it was not until 1037, when Ferdinand I, surnamed "El Magno" (1028–1065), established the kingdom of Castile, that Spain began to creep back into European history. Assuming the title of "King of the Spains", Ferdinand set out to foster unity between the Christian peoples, and was so far successful that, by marrying the daughter of Alphonso V of Leon, he brought Leon and Galicia under his rule. Next, he initiated what in Spanish history is called the *Reconquista*–the reconquest of the Moorish lands.

His success was considerable, for he advanced to the gates of Seville, and had the other Christian kingdoms supported him, the whole of Spain might well have been rewon. Nevertheless, in spite of their chronic dissensions, his son Alphonso VI (1065–1109) in 1082 carried war as far south as Tarifa, and in 1085 conquered Toledo, a victory of decisive importance. Believing themselves faced by total ruin, the Moors in Andalusia called upon Yusuf ibn Tashfin, emir of the Almoravides (a Berber people) in Morocco, to come to their assistance. Yusuf decided to come as master rather than as ally. He swept into Spain, where he assumed complete ascendancy over the Moors, and on October 23, 1086, routed Alphonso VI's army at Zallaca, in the neighbourhood of Badajoz, but failed to take Toledo.

In the luxurious surroundings of southern Spain, the deterioration of the Almoravides was so rapid that Alphonso I of Aragon, surnamed "the Battler" (1104–1134), who had in 1118 occupied Saragossa, in 1120 marched against them and routed them at Cutanda and again at Arinsol in 1126. Immediately following his death in 1134, Aragon and Catalonia were permanently united, and in 1135 his stepson Alphonso VII (1135–1157) was crowned king of Castile at Leon, and "Emperor in Spain and King of the men of the two religions". In 1144 he captured Cordova and advanced as far south as Almeria in 1147, compelling the Moorish princes to become his vassals. On his death in 1157, Castile and Leon again separated.

Meanwhile, in 1147, French and German knights on their way to the second crusade stormed Lisbon and presented it to Alfonso Henriques, son of Henry Duke of Burgundy, who became the first king of Portugal. Next, in 1148, the Almohades, tribesmen of the Atlas Mountains, who in 1125 had conquered the Almoravides's empire in Africa, burst into Spain, and during the latter part of the twelfth century, after subduing the Almoravides, they rolled back the Christian advance, and on July 18, 1196, routed at enormous loss Alphonso VIII of Castile (1158-1214) at Alarcos, west of Ciudad Réal. Again and again, Pope Innocent III urged the Christian kingdoms of Spain to unite against their common enemy, and his endeavours were so far successful in that a confederacy of Aragon, Navarre, Portugal, and Castile, supported by many foreign knights, under Alphonso VIII, was formed, which on July 16, 1212, routed the Almohades in the battle of Las Nevas de Tolosa. The victory was complete, and the predominance of the Christian cause was secured in Spain.

In 1214, Alphonso VIII died, and, in 1217, the crown of Castile passed to the son of his daughter Berangaria, who became Ferdinand III (1217-1252). He permanently united Castile and Leon and continued the crusade. In 1236 he conquered Cordova, and in 1248, with the help of his vassal the Moorish king of Granada, took Seville. Meanwhile James I of Aragon, the Conqueror (1213-1276), gained possession of the Balearic Islands in 1229; overran Valencia in 1238 and Murcia in 1265. This last conquest brought the *Reconquista* to a close: except for the Moorish kingdom of Granada and a chain of ports stretching westward to Cadiz, the whole of Spain was rewon for the Catholic Church.

The extreme slowness of the Reconquest was due not only to the disunity of Spain, but also to the character of the war waged. It consisted almost entirely of sporadic forays and skirmishes, in which organization, discipline, and any recognizable system of supply were conspicuously lacking. Battles were few and far between and raids constant; their main incentive was not to bring the enemy to battle but to obtain booty and plunder. Because both belligerents were mounted, the inhabitants of the field-lands increasingly sought safety within the walls of the towns and in the innumerable castles, the ruins of which are now dotted over the length and breadth of Spain. The result was a return to city states, each more or less self-sufficient and governed by a primitive democracy.

No attempt at unity, nor even at the formation of a loose confederation of Christian states, followed the great victory of Las Neves de Toloso. In fact, under Peter III of Aragon (1276–1286), son of James the Conqueror, division became further stressed. Through his marriage with Constance, daughter of Manfred of Beneventum, he came forward as representative of the claims of the Hohenstaufens in Naples and Sicily against Charles of Anjou, who, as we have seen, in 1268 overwhelmed Conradin at Tagliacozzo. In 1282, taking advantage of the Sicilian Vespers—a popular rising which doomed Charles's hold on Sicily—Peter III was offered the Sicilian crown by the pope, landed in Sicily, raised the siege of Messina and drove the remnants of Charles's army into Calabria. Thus was started the long struggle between the Aragonese and Angevin parties in southern Italy.

The position within Spain at the time was as follows: Castile was assimilating its conquests and was torn by civil wars; Aragon was more concerned with Sicily, Sardinia, and Naples than with Spain; Navarre had its heart in France; and Portugal was beginning hopefully to gaze out over the Atlantic. Castile and Leon had been united, and so had Aragon and Catalonia: such was the sum of the gains towards unity won in 200 years of war.

From now on for nearly a century, no attempt toward a consolidation of Castile and Aragon was made. The former was crippled by a succession of short-lived kings and many long minorities, and the latter was distracted by its Italian ambitions. In Castile, up to the end of the reign of Peter the Cruel (1349–1369) there were constant turmoils and civil wars; order was not restored until the accession of Henry II of Trastamara (1369–1379).

The next event of outstanding importance occurred in 1406; that year John II (1406–1454) succeeded to the throne of Castile, and, as he was still a child, his uncle Ferdinand of Antequera, son of John I of Castile by his wife Eleanor, daughter of Peter IV of Aragon, was appointed regent. The importance of his appointment lay in that, in 1410, Martin I of Aragon (1395–1410) died without issue, and a lengthy dispute over his successor followed, which, in 1412, was decided by the Cortes of Caspe, which offered the crown of Aragon to Ferdinand. By right the Cortes should have offered it to his nephew John II of Castile, for he was the son of Ferdinand's elder brother; but Aragon and Castile were not yet ripe for union. Nevertheless the choice of

Ferdinand, who now became Ferdinand I of Aragon (1412–1416), was a definite step toward its accomplishment.

On the death of John II of Castile the crown passed to his son Henry IV, the Impotent (1454–1474), and when he died in 1474 the legitimacy of his alleged daughter Joanna (La Beltraneja) was disputed by his sister Isabella, who claimed the succession, and who in 1469 had married her cousin Ferdinand, son of John II of Aragon (1458–1479) and grandson of Ferdinand of Antequera. On his death, in 1479, John transmitted his kingdom to his son Ferdinand, whose wife Isabella had been proclaimed queen of Castile and Leon on December 13, 1474.

Thus were the kingdoms of Castile and Aragon united under a dual monarchy, and, except for Navarre and Granada, the whole of Spain was unified. But it is improbable that the union would have proved permanent had not Isabella been compelled to revive the *Reconquista*. Strictly speaking, it had never lapsed completely, but had smouldered on since the days of James the Conqueror. In 1410 Antequera had been wrested from the Moors by Ferdinand I when regent; in 1431 Granada had been invaded and the battle of Higueruela won, and in 1462, after numerous sieges, the rock of Gibraltar was ceded to Castile. From then to 1476 disorders within Castile had halted further progress; but when, during that year, Isabella demanded of Ali Abul Hassan, who had succeeded to the throne of Granada in 1466, the payment of the annual tribute exacted from his father Ismail III, his reply was that "the mints of Granda coined no longer gold, but steel". This meant war, a war which was destined to introduce the Atlantic period of western history. The whole outlook of Europe was about to be changed.

CHAPTER II

The siege of Málaga, 1487, and the conquest of Granada, 1492

When, in 1479, Ferdinand and Isabella assumed their joint rule of Aragon and Castile, the union of the two kingdoms was wholly nominal, and although, in accordance with their marriage contract, all royal charters were signed by both and the heads of both appeared on the coinage, the administration of Castile was reserved to Isabella in her own right and that of Aragon to Ferdinand in his. Therefore Castile and Aragon remained politically apart, and in order to consummate their union some great adventure was required, which in its singleness of purpose would draw away the attention of both Castilians and Aragonese from their internal interests as well as from their mutual jealousies and focus it on a goal of outstanding importance to all Spaniards.

Though in the accomplishment of this quest religion was to play a dominant part, of itself it was insufficient. Other things were needed: a leader, a unifying instrument, and a cause based on a common fear, for fear, like a magnet, brings men together. The first was found in Queen Isabella herself, a fervent Catholic and a practical woman; the second in the establishment of the Spanish Inquisition by Pope Sixtus IV in 1478,[1] and the third in the dread of another great Moslem invasion; for Africa was never lacking in fighting men.

The personality of Isabella not only dominated Spain, but was its oriflamme, its *étendard vivant* which, synchronizing with a chivalrous age, gave *élan* to a quixotically minded people in a way which no male leadership could have done.[2] Of the many and

---

[1] The Inquisition was the sole common instrument to both kingdoms, and there was but a single Inquisitor General for all Spain. Unlike in other countries, the Inquisition was completely under royal control; its officers were paid servants of the Crown. As far as it was concerned, internal political divisions ceased to exist. "It tended to reduce all men—irrespective of their wealth and rank—to a common level before the law, as well as to a common subjection to the Crown" (*The Golden Century of Spain, 1501-1621*, T. Trevor Davies (1937), p. 13).

[2] Walsh calls her "a woman crusader who changed the course of civilization and the aspect of the entire world" (*Isabella of Spain* (1931), **p.** 15).

frequently exaggerated panegyrics which have been pronounced on her, one which rings true is that of de Maulde la Clavière:

"She was a wonderful mixture of different kinds of heroism", he writes. "She was brave and resolute without a touch of the virago. After a night spent in dictating orders, she would tranquilly resume a piece of church embroidery, or, like Anne of France, the practical education of her daughters. In her own private affairs she was plain and simple, in public she was all ostentation. She was a conversationalist of the first order and loved to attack high philosophical questions, here and there dropping into a discussion some original phrase, some bold and clear-cut thought, while her deep blue eyes lit up and darted upon her company a certain glance of warmth and loyalty the renown of which still clings to her name. A strange woman! ardent like Anne of France, guileless, straightforward, somewhat starched perhaps, but all heart for her friends, so fond a mother that she died of the loss of her children, so thorough a woman that she declared she knew only four fine sights in the world: 'a soldier in the field, a priest at the altar, a beautiful woman in bed, a thief on the gibbet'."[1]

As regards the second, though eventually the Inquisition became an instrument of persecution, "It was", writes Mr. R. Trevor Davies, "the offspring of that fierce desire for racial purity that bursts out from time to time like a devouring flame in many parts of the world"; for in Spain "racial purity and religious orthodoxy had become mutually dependent". Further, he says: "The value of the Inquisition as a royal instrument for strengthening the monarchy and unifying the country would be difficult to exaggerate."[2] This is easily understandable when it is recognized that, generally speaking, the greatness of a nation is in direct proportion to the intolerance of its rulers, as long as intolerance has a mystical origin and an heroic goal. These two requirements were to be found in Spain: the former produced St. Ignatius Loyola (1491–1556), founder of the Society of Jesus, and the latter that spirit of knight-errantry which is parodied in *Don Quixote*.

The third—the copestone—fitted the moment, not for Spain alone, but for the whole of western Christendom, because the expansion of the Ottoman empire had awakened the distant memories

---

[1] *The Woman of the Renaissance* (English edit., 1901), p. 323.
[2] *The Golden Century of Spain, 1501–1621*, pp. 11–12.

of 711 and the many invasions since. Checked for the time being on the Danube and in the Adriatic, there was no saying that Islam would not again flow westward through Africa, and Málaga was but a day's sail from Morocco. This possibility had for centuries terrified Christian Spain, and because Spain was as much the bridge-head of western Europe as Byzantium was of eastern, it now terrified Europe as a whole. Then, suddenly, on December 26, 1481, the unexpected happened, and all these ingredients of Spanish unification crystallized. That day Abul Hassan, king of Granada, misreading the internal conditions of Castile, under cover of night and of a howling gale surprised the fortified town of Zahara, north-west of Ronda, slaughtered its Castilian garrison and swept its inhabitants into slavery. Many such raids had occurred during the last 700 years, but this was to be the last one the Moors were destined to make, and it was to lead, not only to their final ruin, but to the unification of Spain and the outburst of yet another imperialism.

Although, at the time, Ferdinand and Isabella were far from ready to face up to the affront, on his own initiative—so it would seem—Don Rodrigo Ponce de Leon, Marquis of Cadiz, did so, and in retaliation, on February 28, 1482, he surprised and captured the town of Alhama, which lies twenty-five miles south-west of Granada. When they heard of this success, the king and queen, then at Medina del Campo, not far from Valladolid, realized that the whole strength of Granada would be turned against the marquis and forthwith determined to support him.

It was well that they did so, for on March 5 Abul Hassan, at the head of a powerful army, appeared before the town, but such was his haste to take the field that he had left his siege train in Granada. Once before Alhama, he found it so strongly defended that it could only be starved out. Next, while he invested it he heard that a relieving force was on its way and on March 29 he raised the siege and returned to Granada to fetch up his train. Barely had he returned to Alhama and planted his batteries than Ferdinand approached, and fearing to be caught between him and the Marquis of Cadiz, he raised the siege and withdrew. On May 14 Ferdinand entered the town.

Ferdinand mustered his army there and on July 1, at the head of 4,000 horse and 12,000 foot, he set out to seize Loja, on the Antequera–Granada road. He ran into an ambush and was so severely routed that the war might there and then have ended, had it not been for a harem intrigue within Granada which led to a *coup d'état*. Abul Hassan was dethroned by his son Boabdil, known as "el Chico" ("the Little"), and to save his life he sought refuge at the court of his brother Abdullah, surnamed "el Zagal" ("the Valiant"), at Málaga.[1]

Meanwhile the war, as on former occasions, had degenerated into a series of fitful forays and skirmishes, when suddenly another disaster befell the dual monarchy. In the spring of 1483, the Marquis of Cadiz, accompanied by the Grand Master of Santiago, set out from Antequera to raid the environs of Málaga, and as they traversed a sierra, called the Axarquia, they were caught in its defiles by el Zagal and routed even more completely than Ferdinand had been at Loja. Nevertheless the ultimate result of this victory was so unfavourable for the Moorish cause that, had it not occurred, the probability is the war would have meandered on indefinitely as so often had happened in the past. The result was that Boabdil in Granada, envious and fearful of his uncle's renown, decided to emulate him. He assembled 9,000 foot and 700 horse and set out to seize the town of Lucena, north-west of Loja, but when about to invest it, was fallen upon by the Count of Cabra and defeated and captured.

When the count discovered who his prisoner was, he sent an urgent message to the king and queen, then at Vitoria. Ferdinand hurried south and assembled a council of war at Cordova. After a hot debate it was decided to release Boabdil and to send him back to Granada on terms which would bind him to the Spanish cause and simultaneously ensure a continuance of the internal Moorish quarrels. The more important of the terms were that: a truce of two years would be granted to Boabdil on the stipulation that he paid 12,000 gold doubloons yearly to the Spanish sovereigns; suffered their troops to pass freely through his territories for the purpose of carrying on the war against his father and uncle; attended the Cortes when summoned to do so; and surrendered his son as hostage. These ignominious terms were accepted. They meant that hence onward the kingdom of Granada would be split in two and, therefore, that each half could be destroyed in turn.

Strategically, this division of their enemy's power presented

---

[1] Abul Hassan reigned between 1462–1482 and 1483–1485; el Zagal (as Mohammed XII) between 1485–1487, and Boabdil (as Mohammed XI) between 1482–1483 and 1487–1492. These changes of dates are illustrative of the chaotic conditions the Moors were in.

Ferdinand and Isabella with so propitious an opportunity to eliminate Moorish dominion in Spain that it could not well be missed. All now depended on the tactical means at their disposal, and as they stood they were far from adequate. Their fighting forces were little more than a gathering of feudal bands–brave, chivalrous, undisciplined, and quixotic. Orders were communicated by the ringing of bells, as monks were wont to be called to prayer in their churches, and before fighting the opposing generals would, as in their tourneys, settle the day of battle in advance, and when it took place it was a mêlée in which luck or courage was the deciding factor.[1] If Admiral Jurien de la Gravière is right when he says *"L'histoire des nations, c'est l'histoire de leurs armées"*,[2] then, as we shall see, the changes wrought in the Spanish army during the Moorish war are a measure of the national changes effected by Ferdinand and Isabella during this period. When it ended, the Spanish soldier had become the most noted in the world, and he remained so until the day of Rocroi (1643), in which battle, the army which had been created by men like the "Great Captain", Gonsalvo of Cordova (1453–1515), went down before the Great Condé (1621–1686).

Isabella's first problem was to find some common factor which would enable her to weld her forces into a single instrument, and there being as yet no true political unity, there was no national spirit to build on. Therefore, a magnetic idea had to be created before the local patriotisms could be united. This she and Ferdinand achieved by basing the war on a religious motive–that is, by substituting the idea of a crusade for that of a war of political liberation. In this they were helped by the recent Ottoman successes in eastern Europe. Only the year before the Alhama was stormed, to the consternation of all Christendom, Mahomet II had occupied Otranto, and when in the following year Pope Sixtus IV learnt of the fall of Alhama, so overjoyed was he that he sent to the Spanish king and queen, by way of a standard, a massive silver cross, which was borne by Ferdinand in each of his campaigns. It was invariably raised on the topmost pinnacle of each conquered town and adored by the assembled host. Further, during the war unity was stimulated by the constant presence of Ferdinand and Isabella in the midst of their advancing armies.

[1] See *Histoire d'Espagne*, Rosseeuw St. Hilaire (1844), vol. v, p. 438.
[2] *La guerre de Chypre et la bataille de Lépante*, Vice-Admiral Jurien de la Gravière (1888), vol. i, p. xlii.

As Merriman points out: "It was the surest possible way of keeping the factious nobles from deserting, of maintaining order and discipline in the ranks, of convincing the soldiers that there was no duty they were called upon to perform in which their sovereigns were too proud to bear a part."[1]

Correctly it may be said that, from 1483 onward, Isabella became the soul of the entire enterprise, until from a crusade it evolved into a vast pan-Spanish movement, which under her grandson, the Emperor Charles V, led to the establishment of an empire unequalled since the days of Charlemagne. While she prepared, Ferdinand fought, and during the long war she proved herself to be one of the ablest quartermaster-generals in history.

Though in extent the kingdom of Granada was not large—two hundred miles from east to west and sixty from north to south—because of its mountainous nature, which rendered supply in the field most difficult, the task of conquest was formidable. Roads were few and castles many, and as for the most part they were built on hill-tops or the brinks of precipices, they were virtually impregnable until the advent of the cannon which, at this early stage in their development, were so heavy and cumbersome that they demanded good roads. It was castles and supply difficulties which in the past had forced field operations into the groove of the *cavalgada*, or cavalry foray, which seldom led to permanent gain: hence the excessive slowness of the Reconquest. Therefore, because cavalry was of little use in siege warfare, which was the essence of the problem, Isabella turned her attention to artillery, engineers, and infantry.

She made use of three means of recruitment: first, feudal levies; but as their independence and lack of discipline rendered them unreliable, secondly she turned to the recently created *hermandad* (constabulary), and converted it into the beginnings of a national army; thirdly, she hired Swiss mercenaries who, at the time, were the most noted infantry in western Europe.[2] Besides these troops, many volunteers flocked from Germany, England, and France to join her crusade, and prominent among them was Sir Edward Woodville, brother-in-law of Edward IV, who assumed the title of his elder brother Lord Scales.

---

[1] *The Rise of the Spanish Empire in the Old World and in the New* (1918), vol. II, p. 66.
[2] In Prescott's opinion (*History of the Reign of Ferdinand and Isabella* (1842), vol. I, p. 452): "Their example no doubt contributed to the formation of that invincible Spanish infantry, which, under the Great Captain and his successors, may be said to have decided the fate of Christendom for more than half a century."

Her three main problems were: (1) the reduction of castles; (2) the supply of the besieging forces; and (3) the devastation of the land adjacent to the town or castle attacked. The first demanded an artillery train, the second a supply train, and the third a body of devastators. In order to raise the first, she invited into Spain gunfounders from France, Germany, and Italy. Forges were built, powder manufactured, and cannon balls made as well as imported from Sicily, Flanders, and Portugal. Don Francisco Ramirez was placed in command of the artillery, and under him was assembled a train "such as was probably not possessed at that time by any other European potentate".[1]

The largest lombards (or bombards) were twelve feet long and of fourteen inch calibre. They were built of iron bars two inches in breadth, held together by rings and bolts, and they threw iron and marble cannon balls, and at times also fire-balls "which", says an eye-witness, "scattering long trains of light in their passage through the air, filled the beholders with dismay, and descending on the roofs of the edifices, frequently occasioned extensive conflagration".[2] These large pieces could neither be elevated nor traversed; they were bedded in wooden carriages without wheels,[3] and as they had to be dragged by oxen over the roughest country, special roads had to be built for them. For this work immense bodies of pioneers were employed, and we are told that at the siege of Cambil 6,000 were needed to build a single causeway.

The supply train consisted mainly of pack mules, of which the enormous number of 80,000 is said to have been collected. The work carried out by the corps of devastators was appalling. According to Prescott: "From the second year of the war, thirty thousand foragers were reserved for this service, which they effected by demolishing farm-houses, granaries, and mills (which last were exceedingly numerous in a land watered by many small streams), by eradicating the vines, and laying waste the olive-gardens and plantations of oranges, almonds, mulberries, and all the rich varieties that grew luxuriant in this highly favoured region."[4]

Besides these preparations, Isabella introduced two novel organizations, a corps of field messengers and a medical service. Many tents were equipped for the wounded, and as Merriman

[1] *History of the reign of Ferdinand and Isabella*, vol. i, p. 442.
[2] *Ibid.*, vol. i, pp. 433–444.
[3] For light pieces, the wheeled gun-carriage began to appear about 1470.
[4] *Ibid.*, vol. i, p. 440.

notes, "It is the earliest recorded case of anything resembling a modern field hospital."[1]

The army was assembled at Cordova, and in all it is said to have numbered 80,000 troops and as many pack animals. The former were made up of from ten to twelve thousand horse, between twenty and forty thousand infantry, and an unknown number of gunners, miners, pioneers and foragers. When one considers the difficulties of the terrain and the thoroughness of the projected operation, even if the total of 80,000 men is an exaggerated one, the forces required must have been large.

Besides the army, the Castilian fleet played an important part in the war; its main task was to cut off the Moors in Africa from their blood relations in Granada. On the fall of Alhama, Abdul Hassan's first action was to solicit aid from the Merinites in Morocco. In answer to this call Isabella had ordered the Castilian fleet south, but as yet it lacked a suitable naval base from which to operate.

Taken as a whole, the Spanish strategy was one of increasing attrition based on: (1) establishing naval bases on the southern coast of Granada; (2) on blockading that coast line and cutting it off from contact with Morocco; and (3) meanwhile devastating Granada itself.[2] Under cover of this attrition a methodical series of sieges was to be carried out, in which Ferdinand, who was commander-in-chief of the army, resorted to the policy of treating each town or castle which surrendered at call with moderation, and each which did not, when taken, with rigour. In the case of Benemaquez, which first surrendered and subsequently revolted, when he retook it he had one hundred and ten of the principal inhabitants hanged above its walls; the remainder he sold as slaves, and the town itself he razed to the ground. Commenting on this piece of frightfulness, Prescott writes: "The humane policy usually pursued by Ferdinand seems to have had more favourable effect on his enemies, who were exasperated, rather than intimidated, by this ferocious act of vengeance."[3]

When, in 1485, all was ready, Ferdinand set out on his initial campaign of conquest. Adhering to his strategy of attrition, his first two aims were to occupy Málaga and Almeria, in order to cut off Granada from Africa. The occupation of Málaga demanded

[1] *The Rise of the Spanish Empire*, vol. II, p. 69.
[2] See *Isabella the Catholic*, Baron de Nervo (English edit., 1897), p. 155.
[3] *Ferdinand and Isabella*, vol. I, p. 446.

two distinct operations, the occupation of Marbella, to gain a base for his fleet, and the occupation of Loja and Velez-Málaga, so that, should he be compelled to lay siege to Málaga, his rear and left flank would be secure; for Loja commanded the Málaga–Granada road and Velez the coastal road linking Málaga with Almeria.

To gain Marbella, in May, 1485, he laid siege to Ronda, and reduced it by his cannon. Next, in 1486, he occupied Alora, and from there he advanced by way of Cartarma and Coin, pinched out Marbella and forced its surrender. He based his fleet on that town and next laid siege to Loja. After he took it, on April 7, 1487, he set out from Antequera, advanced through most difficult country and appeared before the walls of Velez-Málaga on April 17.

El Zagal, then at Guadix, fully realized the strategical importance of that town and made a desperate effort to relieve it, but he was repulsed by the Marquis of Cadiz and fell back on Granada. He found its gates closed to him by Boabadil and withdrew to Guadix, which with Almeria and Baza still remained faithful to his cause. On April 27, Velez-Málaga capitulated to Ferdinand, and following its fall Málaga was encircled by land and sea.

Both in size and importance, Málaga was second only to Granada, and with the exception of Almeria it was the only port left to the Moors from which contact could precariously be maintained with Africa. It was inhabited by eleven to fifteen thousand people, without counting its garrison which numbered several thousands, mostly staunch African troops. It was surrounded by strong walls which were commanded by a citadel, known as the Castle of the Genoese, which by a fortified way was connected with the Castle of Gebelfaro. The town was prepared to stand a siege and was commanded by Hamet Ez Zegri, a faithful follower of el Zagal.

Ferdinand learnt that the inhabitants of Málaga were eager to capitulate and instructed the Marquis of Cadiz to open negotiations with Ez Zegri. But when the latter refused to consider a surrender, on May 7 Ferdinand ordered the camp at Velez to be struck, and after a successful advanced guard action on the coastal road, he arrived before Málaga.

He enclosed Málaga and its suburb with works of contravallation and completed the investment by blockading its harbour with his fleet, then he stormed the suburbs, and next ordered up his heavy siege pieces which were still at Antequera. While roads were built to facilitate their approach, he sent to Algeciras to bring forward supplies of marble cannon shot which had lain there ever since its capture by Alphonso XI in the preceding century. More important still, he sent for the queen, whose presence, much like that of Joan of Arc, inspired the soldiers with the highest heroism. At this time, St. Hilaire writes that "An unbelievable spirit of courage and devotion was shown throughout the land. The whole of Spain was exalted, as Europe had been in the age of the Crusades. From every pulpit the cry of the holy war went forth, and from every corner of the realm reinforcements marched towards the scene of action."[1]

When the siege pieces arrived, wishing to spare the town, Ferdinand again summoned its citizens to surrender and offered liberal terms in the event of immediate compliance. If they refused, then when he captured the town he would reduce the whole of its inhabitants to slavery. Though the people were willing enough to comply, Ez Zegri's answer was a series of vigorous sallies which kept the Spanish camp in constant alarm. Meanwhile el Zagal was not idle. He knew the importance of Málaga and sent two relieving forces from Guadix. On its way, the first was cut to pieces by Boabdil, who at the same time sent an embassy with a present of Arab horses and costly silks to Ferdinand and Isabella, as tokens of his friendship. The second, in part succeeded in penetrating the Spanish lines and in gaining Málaga, but in the attempt many of its men were cut down, and among the prisoners taken there was one who informed the Marquis of Cadiz that he could make important disclosures to the king. Cadiz believed him and had him taken to the royal tent, where, mistaking Don Alvaro, son of the Duke of Braganza, for the king, and Dona Beatrice of Bobadilla for the queen, he suddenly drew a dagger from beneath the folds of his mantle and wounded both. Before he could repeat his attack he was cut down. His remains were shot by a trebuchet over the walls of Málaga.[2]

The position within Málaga rapidly worsened and the city became straitened for supplies, largely because of the numbers of refugees who had flocked into it. Meanwhile the bombardment continued, and when the supply of cannon shot—a crucial problem

[1] *Histoire d'Espagne*, Rosseeuw St. Hilaire, vol. v, p. 483.
[2] A similar incident, but with a live instead of a dead man, is recorded to have taken place, in 1345, at the siege of Auberoche (*Chroniques de J. Froissart*, edit. Simeon Luce, 1872, vol. III, p. 65).

in sieges of this period – grew short, Ferdinand resolved to storm the city. To assist in this he had a number of large wooden towers, moved on rollers, built and equipped with swing-bridges and ladders. Mining was also resorted to under the supervision of Francisco Ramirez. Anticipating what was in progress, in desperation the Moors countermined, attacked the Spanish fleet and continued their sorties, but to no avail. At length a mine was sprung[1] under one of the towers and a possible entrance into the city was gained.

Terrified by this disaster, the citizens of Málaga, many dying of starvation and not a few of whom deserted to the Spaniards, urged Ez Zegri to capitulate, and so critical grew the situation that he withdrew the garrison to Gebelfaro, leaving it to the Malagueños to make the best terms they could with the enemy. At once they sent a deputation of the leading citizens to Ferdinand. But he refused to receive it, saying that because his offer of surrender on terms had twice been rejected, nothing would now satisfy him except an unconditional capitulation. Two further deputations failed to change his decision and on August 18, 1487, the gates of Málaga were opened and the besiegers entered the city.

Pillage was strictly prohibited and Ferdinand's first act was to cleanse the city by the removal of all dead bodies and filth. Next, he had the principal mosque consecrated to the service of Santa Maria de la Encarnacion, and in it mass was held and a *Te Deum* sung. Lastly, he pronounced its doom. It was that all Christian renegades should be executed, all relapsed Jews burnt, and that the rest of the population should be sold as slaves. One third was transported to Africa in exchange for an equal number of Christian captives; one third was sold to pay toward the cost of the war; and the rest distributed as presents – 100 picked Moorish soldiers went to the pope, 50 of the best-looking Moorish girls to the Queen of Naples, and 30 to the queen of Portugal.

On the day following the occupation of Málaga the fortress of Gebelfaro surrendered, and well pleased with his success, shortly after Ferdinand led his army back to Cordova and dispersed it for the winter.

Although the fall of Málaga rendered the conquest of Granada inevitable, because it was the port from which the latter received

---

[1] Prescott (vol. II, p. 29) considers that this is the first authenticated employment of gunpowder in mining. As we have seen, if correctly reported, the first is to be credited to the siege of Constantinople in 1453.

the bulk of its reinforcements and supplies, in order completely to cut off the Moorish kingdom from its potential base—Africa—in June, 1488, Ferdinand advanced against Almeria. He failed to carry it by a *coup de main*, and withdrew to Jaén, from where, toward the end of May, 1489, at the head of 15,000 horse and 80,000 foot,[1] he laid siege to Baza. Six thousand men were employed for two months encircling the town with continuous line of contravallation. The siege proved a long one,[2] and when autumn set in, instead of withdrawing into winter quarters, Ferdinand ordered a hutted camp to be built in which his troops were so well supplied by Isabella that, though plague raged throughout Andalusia, they remained unaffected. Reduced to extremities, Baza capitulated on December 4 and Ferdinand showed great moderation. The terms agreed were that all mercenaries were allowed to march out with the honours of war and that the inhabitants could either remain in the suburbs of the town, or, should they wish, freely go elsewhere.

The fall of Baza was at once followed by the submission of el Zagal, who agreed to surrender the whole of his domains, including Almeria and Guadix. The former of these cities was immediately occupied by Ferdinand, and el Zagal, who some years before is supposed to have assassinated his brother Abul Hassan, was offered the puppet kingship of Andaraz in fief to the Castilian crown. He refused to accept it, withdrew to Africa, and is reported to have ended his days there in indigence.

With the disappearance of Abul Hassan and the submission of el Zagal, all that remained for Ferdinand to do was to occupy Granada. From Almeria, therefore, he sent an embassy to Boabdil to demand its surrender in accordance with the terms of the treaty of Loja, which stipulated that this should be done on the capitulation of Baza, Guadix, and Almeria. But either Boabdil was unwilling, or what would seem more probable, he was now no longer a free agent but the prisoner of the ruined and desperate men of the *routier* class who now thronged Granada.[3] They, it would appear, decided to hold fast to the city, for war was their sole means of livelihood and the city was strongly fortified.

[1] There is something stereotyped about the figures 15,000 and 80,000, which constantly are quoted during this war. They would appear to represent the total establishments rather than the actual field forces. Circourt, *Histoire des Mores, etc.* (1846), vol. I, p. 321, gives Ferdinand's strength as "12,000 horse and 50,000 foot".

[2] Circourt, (*op. cit.* vol. I, p. 323) states that el Zagal had accumulated fifteen months' supplies in Baza.

[3] See Circourt's *Histoire des Mores, etc.*, vol. I, pp. 328–329.

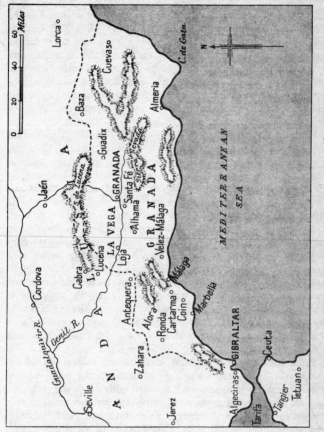

19. CONQUEST OF GRANADA, 1481–1492

It was built at the foot of the Sierra Nevada upon two hills, below which flowed the small rivers Genil and Darro. On the summits of the hills rose two fortresses, the Alhambra and the Albaycin. The town was surrounded by a brick wall, strengthened by a vast number of towers, and at the foot of the Alhambra and beyond the city wall stretched an extensive *vega* (plain) covered with vineyards, gardens, orchards, and fields of wheat, which were irrigated from the Genil. The population of the city is said to have numbered 200,000 at the time, though this figure is probably exaggerated.

Ferdinand's summons rejected, while Isabella prepared for the siege of Granada, in the spring of 1490 he began to devastate the fertile *vega* west of the city. He continued this in the autumn, when he destroyed twenty-four towns and castles, burnt many villages, and swept the country-side clear of all food stocks and cattle. With Granada thus deprived of its sources of supply, in April, 1491, he appeared before its walls at the head of 80,000 men, determined that however long the siege might last, he would carry on with it until the city capitulated. He had learnt during the siege of Baza the economy of sheltering his troops, and he built a new town for them six miles west of Granada, which, symbolically, he named Santa Fé. It was laid out in the form of a Roman camp, and was to be, in the words of a Castilian writer, "the only city in Spain that has never been contaminated by the Moslem heresy".[1] Its building profoundly discouraged the Moors in Granada; it was proof that the king would never cease his efforts until their city was his.

From then on, in spite of its formidable fortifications, its innumerable towers and its two great castles of the Albaycin and the Alhambra, Granada was doomed either by starvation or assault. Again the appearance of Isabella raised the enthusiasm of the besiegers to the highest pitch of devotion, and "with her order and abundance reigned in the Castilian camp. Night and day on horseback she inspected the works, saw everything, not a detail escaping her eye. She distributed the rations, allotted the billets, arranged the routes of the convoys, and by her wit stimulated the good will and courage of her men."[2]

In September the town of Santa Fé was finished, and its building so terrified Boabdil, who by now it would appear had

---

[1] Quoted by Prescott in *Ferdinand and Isabella*, vol. II, p. 83.
[2] *Histoire d'Espagne*, Rosseeuw St. Hilaire, vol. V, p. 502.

regained some of his former authority, that he asked for a suspension of arms in order to treat for peace. Nothing could have suited Ferdinand and Isabella better, and on October 5 they agreed upon a truce of seventy days, during which the royal secretary, Hernando de Zafra, and Gonsalvo de Cordova were entrusted by Ferdinand to negotiate. On November 25 a final settlement was reached, the terms of which were exceedingly liberal. The city was to be surrendered within sixty days; all artillery and fortifications were to be handed over; the Moors were permitted to retain their property, dress, customs, laws and religion, and to be ruled by their own magistrates under a governor appointed by the Spanish king, and those who wished to migrate to Africa were to be given free transport. The surrender took place on January 2, 1492, when Boabdil handed the keys of Alhambra to Ferdinand saying: "They are thine, O King, since Allah so Decrees it; use thy success with clemency and moderation."[1] Then the gates were thrown open, and to the chanting of the *Te Deum* the great silver cross, borne by Ferdinand throughout his crusade, was carried into the city.[2]

Thus, after seven hundred years of conflict, was the Reconquest finally accomplished, and, with the exception of Navarre, Spain was united into one great Christian kingdom ideally placed to establish a new order. Not only was she wedged between the Mediterranean and the Atlantic, and, therefore, could exploit both; but she was protected against invasion in the north by the long rampart of the Pyrenees, and in the south was linked to Africa by the narrow Strait of Gibraltar. Therefore she stood sentinel between the two western continents of the Old World. Potentially she was the strategic hub of a new world system, ready to replace the hub of the old which had been lost in 1453. No other kingdom in Europe was so well placed at the time to expand into a great empire, and expansion now coursed through the veins of her people, and its outburst was immediate.

Because, in the idealistic sense, Spain was now a nation, the tolerance which Ferdinand and Isabella had shown to the conquered Moors acted as an irritant to the rising spirit of nationalism. This may be judged from an event which immediately followed the fall of Granada: the Jews in Spain were offered the alternative

---

[1] *Ferdinand and Isabella*, William H. Prescott, vol. II, p. 87.
[2] Like his uncle, el Zagal, Boabdil was given a puppet kingdom; but he soon abandoned it and passing over to Africa fell in battle in service of an African prince, his kinsman.

of Christian baptism or exile, and many thousands quitted Spain.[1]

Nothing now could divert the spirit of intolerance, begotten by victorious nationalism, from its course. It demanded not only one God and one monarchy, but also one race. Had it not been for the Ottoman threat, which haunted all Christendom, and that after the conquest many Moors withdrew to Morocco to stimulate the Barbaresque pirates, persecution might have been kept within bounds. But this was not to be; the increasing Algerian slave raids and plunderings kept intolerance alive. The Moors in Spain, conquered or unconquered, were, as Louis Bertrand points out, a standing danger. Had they remained, he writes, "The Peninsula, with its unassimilable Moors and Jews, would have been nothing more than a transit territory, as the countries of the Levant still are to-day; a hybrid country, without unity, without character. Europe would have had its 'Levantines' like Asia. Spain would have become one of those bastard countries which live only by letting themselves be shared and exploited by foreigners, and have no art, or thought or civilisation proper to themselves."[2] However cruel the final expulsion of the Moors may have been, it was inevitable; it was a cry of the blood, of the race, of the soul of the Spanish peoples – an all-compelling urge.

Machiavelli (1467–1527), a contemporary of these events, calls Ferdinand "a new prince", adding that "in the beginning of his reign he attacked Granada, and this enterprise was the foundation of his dominions".[3] Yet far greater things than the consolidation of his power emanated from the war. It did not mark the ending of an epoch, rather, as Mr. Merriman says, "it was not so much an end as a beginning".[4] Militarily and politically it ushered in a new age. Militarily, in that it was a school of war in which was trained the finest army in Europe. Politically, in that, "since the conquest of the Holy City, Europe had not experienced a joy equal to what she experienced on the news of the taking of Granada".[5] "The fall of Granada", writes Prescott, "excited general sensation throughout Christendom, where it was received as counterbalancing, in a manner, the loss of Constantinople, nearly half a century before."[6] But what made it so overwhelmingly impor-

[1] On this question see *Isabella of Spain*, William Thomas Walsh, chap. xxv.
[2] *The History of Spain*, Louis Bertrand and Sir Charles Petrie (1934), p. 228.
[3] *The Prince* (Everyman's Library, 1914), p. 177.
[4] *The Rise of the Spanish Empire*, vol. ii, p. 74.
[5] *Histoire d'Espagne*, Rosseeuw St. Hilaire, vol. v, p. 507.
[6] *Ferdinand and Isabella*, William H. Prescott, vol. ii, p. 91.

tant was that in the same year – 1492 – in which Spain became a united country and took her place among the great nations of Europe, under the auspices of and with the assistance of Isabella, Christopher Columbus (1451–1506) discovered for Spain a new world.

This was the most fruitful event in western history since in 334 B.C. Alexander crossed the Hellespont, and both were no accident, but part and parcel of the urge to expand which throughout history has sprung to life in every virile people on attaining nationhood. Therefore the key to the understanding of the world's greatest drama – the discovery of the New World – is to be sought in the extension of the idea behind the Conquest of Granada – the coming of age of Spain. It was the ultimate crusade against Islam.

The times were ripe for this, the greatest of all geographical discoveries, and the two things which assured it were both related to the crusades. The one was the restriction of trade between Asia and Europe through the interposition of the Turks, and the other was the old belief of St. Louis that were the Great Khan of the Indies reached he might be persuaded to attack Islam in rear. The two dovetailed, and no sooner had a solution of the former been ushered in by the Portuguese voyages of discovery, initiated by Dom Henry of Portugal, the Navigator (1433–1460),[1] than Pope Nicholas V (1447–1455) suggested to him that, if he could only render the Oceanic Sea – that is, the Atlantic – navigable as far as the Indies, which were said to be subject to Christ, then by entering into relations with their inhabitants he might be able to persuade them to come to the help of Christendom against the Turks. Thus, in idea, the strategic problem was shifted from the eastern Mediterranean to the Atlantic, in order to continue the crusades as well as to reopen the Asiatic trade routes.

The idea of reaching the Indies by sailing westward instead of eastward had for long intrigued the geographers, for as yet no one imagined that between the western shores of Europe and the eastern shores of Asia there lay a vast continent. Further, Roger Bacon's assumption that the distance between Spain and Asia could not be very great,[2] had been adopted by Cardinal Pierre d'Ailly in his *Imago Mundi*, published in 1410,[3] and also

---

[1] Henry's first ventures down the African coast were in pursuance of a vague plan to unite with the legendary Christian monarch Prester John, whose realm was supposed to be located in Abyssinia, in a campaign against the Turks.
[2] In his *Opus Majus* of 1267 (edit. Jebb, 1733), p. 183, quoted by Fiske in his *The Discovery of America*, vol. I, pp. 371–372 and 378–379.
[3] Probably printed in 1486 or 1487; see Vignaud's *Études critiques sur la vie de Colomb* (1905), p. 298.

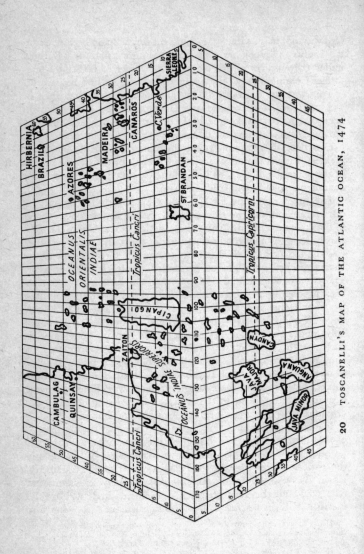

20 TOSCANELLI'S MAP OF THE ATLANTIC OCEAN, 1474

by Paul Toscanelli, the noted astonomer and cosmographer of Florence, who, in 1474 sent to Alfonso V of Portugal a map illustrating the possibilities of the western sea route.[1] Although Toscanelli correctly estimated the equatorial distance round the globe, he so exaggerated the extent of Asia and Europe as to reduce the distance between them by an Atlantic voyage to about 6,500 geographical miles. This put the eastern coast of China in the longitude of Oregon, and Japan, the Cipango of Marco Polo, at about 3,250 miles due west of the Canaries.

Such was the background of the great discovery, which owed its accomplishment to the vision, pertinacity and overwhelming presumption of Christopher Columbus, one of the most enigmatic personalities in history, and whose character and achievements have been as much confused as clarified by modern scholarship.

Until the last quarter of the nineteenth century, when Henry Harisse searched through the archives of Genoa, Savona, Seville and other places,[2] the traditional view held of Columbus was that he was one of the greatest heroes of history. Since then, by several of his biographers, notably Justin Winsor,[3] Henry Vignaud,[4] and Marius André,[5] because of the fantastic stories he invented about his family and his early life, he has been written down as one of the greatest of charlatans. Because these stories have been proved to be pure fabrications, Vignaud goes so far as to hold suspect practically everything he said or wrote. Yet there would appear to be a very sound reason for these fictions – namely, to impress his personal importance upon those he hoped to interest in his grand idea.

Instead of coming from a noble family, as he asserted, he was son of a weaver of Quinto al Mare, near Genoa, and was born in 1451.[6] He followed his father's trade, and in 1476 sailed from Genoa with four merchantmen for England, which, when off St. Vincent, were attacked by a French squadron. Two of the ships were sunk, but Columbus, although wounded, reached the

---

[1] Vignaud, *op. cit.*, p. 23, doubts whether this letter was ever sent. The copy of the map is taken from Fiske (*op. cit.*, vol. I, p. 357). It was used by Columbus in his first voyage across the Atlantic. Each longitudinal space represents 250 geographical miles. This map was the source of the western part of Martin Behaim's globe of 1492.

[2] See his *Christophe Colomb*, 1884.

[3] *Christopher Columbus*, 1891.

[4] *Op. cit.* and *Histoire critique de la grande entreprise de Christophe Colomb*, 1911.

[5] *La véridique adventure de Christophe Colomb*, 1927.

[6] This date is favoured by Vignaud; see his *A Critical Study of the Various Dates Assigned to the Birth of Christopher Columbus* (1903). Other dates vary between 1430 and 1456. That he was a Galician of Jewish parentage, as some suggest, is unlikely.

shore and proceeded to Lisbon. From there, in one of the remaining ships, he journeyed to England, and in 1477 returned to Lisbon, where he remained for seven years.

It would seem probable that during his stay in Lisbon the idea of exploring the far side of the Atlantic took definite form in his mind, and of all places Lisbon was the most likely to foster it, for it was the port of departure and return of the Portuguese expeditions of discovery. Lisbon, accordingly, was the centre of maritime gossip and of sailors' yarns about enchanted islands and the wonders of rumoured lands. These stories must have appealed to Columbus's vivid, romantic and uncritical imagination, which must have been further stimulated and exaggerated by his readings of the *Travels* of Marco Polo, the *Marvellous Adventures* of Sir John Mandeville, and the *Imago Mundi* of Pierre d'Ailly, all of which he accepted at face value.

From these books he cannot have failed to have become acquainted with the prevailing idea of the comparative proximity of eastern Asia to western Europe, and to have been fascinated by the stories of Prester John, the Great Khan, and the amazing wealth of Cipango,[1] until the idea of navigating the Atlantic became so overwhelming an obsession that it shaped itself into a divine destiny.

When at Lisbon, probably in 1483, he placed his proposal before King John II, and when it was rejected, in 1484 he left Portugal for Spain. Two years later we find him at Cordova, where the Spanish court was then assembled. There he submitted his scheme to Queen Isabella, but with no result. In 1488 he revisited Lisbon to meet his brother Bartholomew who, in the previous December, had returned with the Diaz expedition which had discovered the Cape of Good Hope. Fired by this remarkable voyage of 13,000 miles, he persuaded his brother to journey to England to interest King Henry VII in his project, and should he fail to do so, to place it before Charles VIII of France.

Nothing came of this mission, and in May, 1489, Columbus returned to Spain; was present at the siege of Baza, and when, in 1491, he was at Santa Fé, he convinced the duke of Medina-Celi that his scheme was practical. Queen Isabella promised to consider it once Granada had surrendered. That she did so shows that she must have had considerable belief in it, because Columbus's demands were extravagant in the extreme. They were, that

[1] See *The Travels of Marco Polo*, bk. III, chap. II.

he should be appointed Admiral of the Ocean and viceroy of all heathen lands he might discover, and that he should receive one eighth of all revenue and profits which might accrue from the expedition.

It would appear that it was now that the crusading idea took precedence in his mind; for, according to his *Journal*, soon after the fall of Granada he wrote to Ferdinand and Isabella as follows:

"And immediately afterwards, in this same month (January, 1492), in consequence of information which I had given Your Highnesses on the subject of India and of the Prince who is called the 'Great Khan', which, in our Roman, means 'the King of Kings'—namely, that many times he and his predecessors had sent ambassadors to Rome to seek doctors of our holy faith, to the end that they should teach it in India. . . . Your Highnesses, as good Christian and Catholic princes, devout and propagators of the Christian faith, as well as enemies of the sect of Mahomet and of all idolatries and heresies, conceived the plan of sending me, Christopher Columbus, to this country of the Indies, there to see the princes, the peoples, the territory, their disposition and all things else, and the way in which one might proceed to convert these regions to our holy faith."[1]

Success crowned his endeavours. His terms were accepted and an agreement signed on April 17, 1492, and a letter in Latin (the universal language) given to him to hand to the Great Khan, which reads:

"To the Most Serene Prince, our very dear friend. . . . According to reports which have been made to us by many of our subjects, and also other travellers come from your kingdom and the neighbouring regions, we have had the satisfaction of learning of your good disposition and your excellent intentions towards us and towards our State, and at the same time of your keen desire to be informed of our recent success (the conquest of Granada). . . . In consequence whereof we have decided to send you as ambassador our Captain, the noble Christopher Columbus, bearer of these presents, from whom you may learn of our good health and our fortunate estate, as of other matters which we have ordered him to report to you on our behalf."[2]

Thus it came about that, on the morning of Friday, August 3,

[1] Quoted from *The History of Spain*, Louis Bertrand and Sir Charles Petrie, p. 238.
[2] Quoted *ibid.*, p. 247.

1492, Columbus set sail from Palos in three small caravels: the *Santa Maria*, 100 tons; the *Pinta*, 50 tons; and the *Niña*, 40 tons. Their crews numbered ninety men, besides whom there were thirty others, including the brothers Martin Alonzo and Vicente Yañez Pinzon, both noted navigators, and Louis de Torres, a Jew who could speak Hebrew, Greek, Latin, Arabic, Coptic, and Armenian, to act as interpreter should Cipango or the realm of the Great Khan be discovered. On August 9 the Canaries were reached, and a halt was made until September 9, when the little fleet stood out again, this time into the unknown. At two o'clock on the morning of Friday October 12 (new style, October 21) land was sighted, and at dawn a landing was made, probably on Watling Island, which Columbus named San Salvador, and significantly he called the natives who greeted him "Indians".

He sailed on, and on October 28 he struck Cuba, which he thought part of the mainland of China and, therefore, in the realm of the Great Khan. Forthwith he sent two of his followers to seek out the court of that potentate and to present to him the compliments of Queen Isabella and King Ferdinand. Thence he sailed south-east to Haiti, which he imagined was Cipango, and he christened it Hispaniola.

On January 4, 1493, he set out on his return, and on March 15 was back at Palos. From Seville he was summoned to the court at Barcelona, where he was received with triumphal honours. There, without question, it was assumed that his theory had been proved correct; that Cuba was the eastern extremity of China and Haiti the northern extremity of Cipango—therefore, a far shorter sea route to Asia than the one the Portuguese were seeking had been discovered to those lands of illimitable wealth described by Marco Polo. "The sovereigns", writes Fiske, "wept for joy as they thought that such untold riches were vouchsafed them by the special decree of Heaven as a reward for having overcome the Moor at Granada. . . ."[1]

Whether Columbus was a hero or a charlatan, a seer or a driveller, matters little, for the fact remains, as Fiske says, that his discovery was "a unique event in the history of mankind", and that "nothing like it was ever done before, and nothing like it can ever be done again".[2] The old Mediterranean world collapsed. "Millenary barriers", writes Louis Bertrand, "were broken. That world was no longer blockaded by Islam at the two outlets

[1] *The Discovery of America*, vol. 1, p. 445.   [2] *Ibid.*, vol. 1, p. 446.

from the Mediterranean. The horizon expanded, and new ways were opened to human activity, and to human thought. The world escaped at last from that little inland sea where there had been so much scuffling and struggling among European peoples for centuries. Men felt themselves liberated and, at the same time, increased in strength. The power of man had grown, coincidently with the extension of his dominion over new seas and lands. It was, in short, a New Man who was born."[1]

From that moment imperialism began to assume its modern colonial complexion. Trade, rather than pillage and exaction, grew to be its governing principle, and in order to enrich Castile, Queen Isabella restricted the trade of the newly discovered lands to one port – Seville – which became the Alexandria of the Atlantic. On May 4, 1493, Pope Alexander VI traced his famous line of demarcation on a map of the world, a straight line running a hundred leagues west of the Azores from north to south. East of it was to be Portuguese, west of it Castilian, the Indies were given to the one, the Americas to the other – surely the most remarkable gifts in history.

Though for long now the reconnaissances of the navigators had been in progress, the moment had arrived when the Age of Discovery was to engulf the Old World. On March 5, 1496, John Cabot, a citizen of Venice, received letters patent from King Henry VII of England to seek Vineland (the land discovered by the Vikings). So it came about that, early in May, he and eighteen men stood out from Bristol in the *Mathew*, and on June 24 struck the shore of Cape Breton Island,[2] where was laid the foundation stone of the British Empire. Twenty-eight years later, Francis I commissioned Giovanni da Verrazano to reconnoitre the Atlantic shore from Florida to Newfoundland, and when he did so he called that stretch of land "New France". Meanwhile the eastern route was yearly explored, and, in 1498, conquered by Vasco da Gama. He left the Tagus on July 9, 1497, sailed round the Cape of Good Hope, past the Island of the Moon (Madagascar), and in ten months and twelve days arrived at Calicut in India. Thence he and his men returned to Lisbon with a sixty-fold profit, and "with pumps in their hands and the Virgin Mary in their mouths". Twelve years later, on March 4, 1510, Albuquerque entered the

[1] *The History of Spain*, p. 306.
[2] Significantly, it was thought to be the Chinese coast "in the territory of the Grand Cham".

roadstead of Goa, received the keys of the fortress and initiated the European conquest of India and incidentally of the greater part of the Moslem world. The counter-attack had begun.

But of all these great navigators the Portuguese sailor Fernão da Magalhães (Magellan) was the most daring. On September 20, 1519, he set out from San Lucar in five ships manned by 280 men, rounded South America, lost four of his ships, and was killed at Zebu in the Philippine Islands. Nevertheless, his will accomplished its end; for, on September 6, 1522, the sole ship surviving, the *Victoria*, limped home to Portugal "with tackle worn and weather-beaten yards". Eighteen men were left to tell the tale that the world had been circumnavigated.

Meanwhile the Conquistadores were at work. They came mainly from Andalusia and Estremadura, where their ancestors had for centuries struggled with the Moors, and they embarked upon their conquests with a fanatical zeal. Cortés (1485–1547) with 508 soldiers, 109 mariners, and 16 horses set out to conquer Mexico, and Pizarro (1475–1541) with a single shipload of followers, horses and war-dogs, set out to conquer Peru. A religious frenzy seems to have possessed these men and to have driven them through and athwart the most unimaginable difficulties. Cruel though they were, they civilized as they conquered; they brought with them the horse, gunpowder, and steel; also wheat, the vine and the olive. They created a new world and in doing so they transformed the old.

"What a strange thing it is!" writes Louis Bertrand, "–the American enterprise, the last Crusade against Islam, thus presents itself to us as the final flowering of the thought of the Middle Ages, as the liquidation of the whole, long past. It was out of this religious idea that was born the modern world, sceptical and rational."[1] And all this came suddenly to life, like a gale of wind, out of the *Mirabilis Navigatio* of Columbus. The silent thoughts of illimitable ocean awaking in the mind of man the thunderous thoughts of illimitable power. And this would not have happened in the way in which it did happen had it not been for the Conquest of Granada.

[1] *The History of Spain*, Louis Bertrand and Sir Charles Petrie, p. 308.

The 16th Century witnessed Spain's rise to imperial greatness, and the beginning of her decline. It also witnessed the zenith of the Ottoman Empire, under the Sultan Suleiman the Magnificent (1520–66), and the inevitable conflict between these two powers.

Charles I of Spain became the Emperor Charles V in 1520. Already, besides Spain, he ruled the Netherlands and Franche Comté; now he added the broad domains of Austria. Cortes had taken Mexico; Pizarro was planning the conquest of Peru. Spain's empire thus extended to both hemispheres. But in the meantime the Turks had taken Belgrade and Rhodes; in 1526 they conquered Hungary, and in 1529 even attacked Vienna.

The extent of the Ottoman empire was now vast indeed; it stretched from Baghdad in the east to the Atlas mountains in the west, and from Aden in the south to Buda in the north; and 'from the headlands of Istria to the cliffs of Kent', writes Sir William Stirling-Maxwell, the Turkish cruisers 'levied a tax on the coasts of Christendom and the commerce of the world.'

Charles V began the counter-attack after his crowning by the Pope in 1530, but he did not see its climax. In 1556 he abdicated, leaving the Spanish crown to his son Philip II while the Empire passed to Charles's younger brother Ferdinand.

On the accession of Philip II (1556–1598) his rule extended over Spain, the Netherlands, Franche Comté, Sardinia, Sicily, the Balearic Islands, the greater part of Italy, and most of the then discovered New World. Later, after the battle of Alcantara (1580), he added Portugal and the Portuguese colonies to his empire, and also, all but in name, controlled the Holy Roman empire. To hold together so vast a conglomeration of lands, nations and peoples demanded a common factor, and this he found in religion. Therefore, as Defender of the Faith, he set out to establish his hegemony, and as an absolute sovereign became the example of a new system of rule, which was copied by other European monarchs and which only ended with the French Revolution.

Because this hegemony ran counter to the spirit of the Reformation, war was inevitable, and as wars are costly undertakings, more especially those that aim at religious compulsion instead of material gains, war meant money—gold, silver, and credit. It is now that, suddenly, the wealth of the New World impinged upon the poverty of the Old and set up a violent fermentation. In 1493 the stock of gold and silver in Europe has been estimated at £33,400,000, but from the opening of the sixteenth century bullion began to trickle in from Africa and the Americas until, in 1536, it developed into a steady stream, next into a torrent, and lastly into an inundation, so mighty that between then and 1636, Mr. Trevor Davies calculates that well over £250,000,000 of bullion entered Europe.

Because of the Reformation, which challenged Philip's principle of religious unity and, therefore, his hegemony, this vast increase of bullion was spent mainly on war. It flowed through Spain, and instead of fertilizing it laid it waste and left sharper dearth behind. Not only did it destroy the Spanish export trade, but it demoralised the Spanish people. Further, it stimulated the growth of a new civilization, the modern capitalist way of life, much as the release of Persian gold by Alexander the Great had paved the way for Hellenistic and Roman capitalism. Because of war, this stream of bullion flowed into the hands of the money-lenders of Genoa, Antwerp and Augsburg. Gold and silver spent in the Netherlands financed the Baltic States and became the magnetic centre of the reformed religion which, by equating God and Mammon, ripened into a comfortable creed for bankers, traders and merchants—the props of bourgeois civilization.

Spain's part in resisting the expansion of the Turks was at first equivocal and reluctant. Though Spanish force was predominant in saving Malta during the Great Siege in 1565, the revolt of the Netherlands two years later resulted in a serious diversion of strength to north-west Europe. However, the rebellion of the Moriscos[1] in 1568, and their appeal to the Sultan for help, recalled Spanish attention to the Mediterranean, with decisive results. The Turkish attack on Cyprus in 1570, and the cruelties which accompanied it, provided the final goad to action. This was

[1] Moors who remained in Spain after the conquest of Granada.

largely inspired by the determination of Pope Pius V, who set up a Christian League on the lines of the Crusades of earlier centuries, but better organised.

Spain dominated the League; when its forces assembled at Messina in 1571, their commander was Don John of Austria, half-brother of Philip II. His armada consisted of some 300 ships, chiefly Spanish and Venetian, but with contingents from Genoa (under the famous Admiral Andrea Doria), the Papal States, Sicily and Malta (the Knights of St John). About 80,000 men were carried in this fleet, 30,000 of them soldiers, the rest seamen and rowers (both freemen and slaves) to propel the galleys which were still the standard weapons of naval war in the Mediterranean. In the Christian fleet, however, there were also galleons (wholly propelled by sail) and galleasses (part sail, part oars), both of which carried large numbers of cannon. Yet, until this date, as Fuller says,

Naval tactics in the Mediterranean consisted in manoeuvring for position, followed by head-on assault in line abreast, outflanking and boarding, much as they had been at Salamis, Actium, and other ancient naval battles. To all intents and purposes battles at sea were land battles fought on water.

The battle which now ensued, on 7 October 1571, was significantly different, and Don John of Austria ought to be remembered as one of the important innovators of sea-warfare. Two decisions above all should entitle him to this: first, before the battle, he ordered the removal of the metal beaks fitted to all galleys in order to ram the enemy; secondly, he placed his six large galleasses in pairs ahead of his line in order to break up the Turkish onset. Both these dispositions dispay his determination to trust to firepower, rather than the old-fashioned methods of ramming and boarding. The success of the new style makes the Battle of Lepanto a turning-point. As Fuller says, the use of the galleasses was

masterly, and though they were too cumbersome to manoeuvre against galleys, the deadly effect of their gunfire showed that the age-old supremacy of the oar-propelled warship was at an end. Lepanto was the last of the great galley battles, which, tactically, remained much as they had been in classical and pre-classical times. Henceforth sail and broadside fire were to replace oar and head-on attack. Thus, from the point of view of naval history, Lepanto ended an epoch. Further, success was also due to Don John's decision to mix the galleys of the squabbling members of the League, and had he not done so, it is probable that the battle would never have been fought.

Nevertheless, the battle was not cheaply won. Fuller quotes Sir William Stirling-Maxwell[1] to show how fierce the fighting was when the combatants came fairly to grips:

In the *Florence,* a Papal galley, not only many knights of St Stephen were killed, but also every soldier and slave; and the captain, Tommaso de Medici, himself severely wounded, found himself at the head of only seventeen unwounded seamen. In the *San Giovanni,* another vessel of the Pope, the soldiers were also killed to a man, the rowing-benches occupied by corpses, and the captain laid for dead with two musket-balls in his neck. The *Piamontesa* of Savoy had likewise lost her commander and all her soldiers and rowers.

Casualties were heavy on both sides, as might be expected from such scenes: 15,000 Christians, well over 30,000 Turks, with another 8,000 taken prisoner, and 15,000 Christian galley-slaves freed. It is estimated that 113 Turkish galleys were wrecked or sunk, and 117 captured. Yet it was not the material loss to the Ottoman Empire that gave the battle its significance:

The battle of Lepanto did not break the back of Ottoman naval power, it did not recover Cyprus, and it did not lead to the policing of the Mediterranean by Spain. Though a tactical victory of the first order, because of the dissolution of the League,[2] strategically it left the sultan the victor. But morally it was decisive, for by lifting the pall of terror which had shrouded eastern and central Europe since 1453, it blazoned throughout Christendom the startling fact that the Turk was no longer invincible. Hence onward to the Battle of Zenta, in 1697, when Eugene, Prince of Savoy, drove in rout the army of Sultan Mustafa II into the river Theiss, and thereby finally exorcized the Turkish threat to Europe, though there were to be many ups and downs, never was the full prestige of Suleiman the Magnificent to be revived. His reign marks the summit of

[1] *Don John of Austria,* Vol. I.

[2] Pope Pius V died in 1572, whereupon the League disintegrated.

Turkish power, and it was the day of Lepanto which broke the charm upon which it rested.

The rivalry between England and Spain

The commercial centre of gravity of Europe moved westward with the discovery of the New World and of the Cape route to the East Indies. Henceforth it was steadily to be drawn from the Mediterranean lands toward those bordering the Atlantic. Because of this, Spain, Portugal, and England, and later the United Provinces and France, were to become the rivals for world trade and the possession of the newly discovered countries. Henceforth, until recent times, the urge of imperialism moved toward oversea colonization and empires increasingly tended to become maritime in form.

The first phase of the struggle, between England and Spain, opened peacefully enough. When, on November 17, 1558, Elizabeth I (1558–1603) succeeded her half-sister Queen Mary, wife of Philip II, England and Spain were in alliance against France. The next year so firm appeared their friendship that during the negotiations preceding the signing of the Treaty of Cateau Cambrésis, Philip tried on Elizabeth's behalf to recover Calais, which on January 6, 1558, had been wrested from Mary by the Duke of Guise. Next, he offered to marry Elizabeth, but was refused.

Philip's eagerness to support England was wholly self-interested, and his policy pivoted on Mary Queen of Scots (1542–1587), great grand-daughter of Henry VII of England and daughter of James V of Scotland and Mary of Guise. In Catholic eyes she was the legitimate heir to the English throne, and on April 24, 1558, she had been married to Francis II (1559–1560) of France. At the time, her uncle, the Duke of Guise, was all powerful in France, and by means of Mary he aimed to unite France, England, Scotland, and Ireland into a great Guise empire. As this would be fatal for Spain, for 12 years from 1558 Philip tried at all costs to maintain Elizabeth on the throne as a counterpoise to Mary. To Spain the importance of a friendly England was vital, because England flanked the Spanish sea communications with the Netherlands, and since the loss of Calais, England's command of her home waters was insecure as long as the Netherlands were Spanish.

These two strategical questions dominated Spanish and English policy throughout the reigns of Philip and Elizabeth.

In spite of Philip's support, Elizabeth's position was precarious. She did not want a foreign war, for England, divided between Catholics and Protestants, was politically unstable. But the aim of the Calvinists in England was to support Calvinism anywhere on the Continent, and added to this, because England had become a naval power and was a rising commercial one, the anti-Spanish party in England saw in the fleet a means of challenging the Spanish monopoly of the New World. "Military and seafaring men all over England," writes Camden, "fretted and desired war with Spain. But the Queen shut her ears against them." Nevertheless Elizabeth was not strong enough to hold them completely in check.

Soon after her accession a sudden change took place when on December 5, 1560, Francis II died, and was succeeded by his brother, Charles IX (1560–1574), under the regency of his mother, Catherine de' Medici. In August, 1561, Mary returned to Scotland. There, after the murder of her second husband, Lord Darnley, in 1567, she was forced to abdicate, and in 1568 sought refuge in England, where she was imprisoned by Elizabeth for the rest of her life. These events and the growing ascendency of the anti-Spanish party in England caused a change in Philip's policy toward Mary. As she was no longer the direct tool of the Guises, instead of protecting Elizabeth against her, he began to use Mary as the fulcrum of conspiracy and intrigue against Elizabeth, and in this he was supported by Pope Pius V who, in 1570, excommunicated the English queen.

Besides these political changes, an economic cause of friction was antagonizing Spain: it was the poaching of the African slave trade, a Spanish royal monopoly, by John Hawkins of Plymouth. So lucrative was this illicit business that in 1567 the Queen went into partnership with Hawkins and lent him one of her own ships, the *Jesus*. He set sail in her from Plymouth on October 2, and accompanied by the *Minion* and *Judith*–the latter commanded by Francis Drake–Hawkins first made for the Guinea coast. There he either captured or bought some 500 negroes and sailed for the West Indies where surreptitiously he sold them to the Spanish colonists. On his way he put into San Juan de Ulua for water and shelter, fortified the harbour at its entrance, and denied entry to the Spanish. The Plate fleet arrived with the incoming Viceroy of New Spain, Don Martin Enriques, who feared shipwreck because of a storm, and he made a compact with Hawkins that if he were allowed in he would not molest the English in any way but let them water, reprovision, and depart. A few days later Enriques suddenly opened fire on Hawkins's ships. A battle followed in which the *Jesus* had to be abandoned, but the *Minion* and *Judith* cleared the roadstead and after a perilous voyage returned to Plymouth in January, 1569.

When Hawkins was homeward bound, another incident occurred and a more serious one. For years past Huguenot privateers had plundered Spanish ships on their way from Spain to Flanders, and many of them belonged to John Hawkins's brother William, mayor of Plymouth, whose vessels, in order not to implicate the Queen, sailed under letters of marque from Condé or William of Orange. In 1568, 50 were working under Condé's flag and no fewer than 30 of them were alleged to be English. In December, a group of these privateers chased a Spanish squadron into Fowey, Plymouth, and Southampton, and when the bullion it carried was found to belong to Genoese bankers, payable at Antwerp to the Duke of Alva – Philip's general in the Netherlands – Elizabeth impounded it and with Genoese consent borrowed it for her own use. In retaliation Alva seized English ships and goods in the Netherlands and Elizabeth then did the same with Spanish ships and goods in England. On top of this came the news of the loss of the *Jesus* to add fuel to the glowing antagonisms. Thus England and Spain drifted apart, Philip supported the English Catholics and Elizabeth opened England as a refuge to the Dutch Protestant rebels.

Meanwhile William of Orange (1559–1584) built a fleet, and, in 1569, 18 of his ships took to the seas – the beginning of that sea power which during the following century was to cover the oceans with Dutch fleets and to plant colonies in many lands. Their influence on the situation was immediate; for, in 1570, his sailors, known as *gueux de mer* (sea beggars), captured 300 vessels, and to make good their lack of ports of refuge, Elizabeth winked at their use of English harbours until, in 1572, they surprised Brill and turned it into an impregnable base of their own. Henceforth, and in spite of her inborn aversion to rebels, Elizabeth's policy was increasingly directed toward keeping the insurrection alive, not only in order to exhaust Spain, but also to prevent the Dutch in despair offering the sovereignty of their country to the king of

France. So acute grew the crisis that, although Alva was against an open declaration of war, Philip was so incensed that he gave encouragement to the Ridolfi conspiracy of 1571, the aim of which was to foment a Catholic rebellion in England supported by 6,000 of Alva's men; to assassinate Elizabeth; and to place Mary on the throne and restore the Catholic faith in England. The plot was discovered and quashed, and its sole result was to heighten antagonisms.

In order to strengthen her position, in April, 1572, Elizabeth concluded with Catherine de' Medici a defensive alliance against Spain. But it failed in its object, for immediately afterward the French Huguenots won Charles IX to their side, and Elizabeth, who feared that France would occupy the Low Countries, turned toward Spain; Catherine, who feared that the Huguenots would draw France into war with Spain, on August 24 engineered the massacre of St. Bartholomew. It has been estimated that during it 50,000 people perished in France. As it brought the House of Guise back into power Elizabeth opened negotiations with Philip and trade relations, which had ceased in 1568, were in the spring of 1573 restored between the two countries.

A year later Charles IX died and was succeeded by his brother Henry III (1574–1589), and in March, 1576, Don John of Austria, the victor of Lepanto, was appointed Governor of the Netherlands. On his arrival he found that the Spanish army was in mutiny and that its excesses had reawakened the revolt. When he learnt that Elizabeth was financing the rebels he urged upon Philip the invasion of England. But Philip's finances were in chaos and instead he sent Bernadino de Mendoza to placate Elizabeth and to reopen the Spanish embassy in London, which had remained closed since 1572.

Soon after Mendoza's arrival in England, Don John died and the suppression of the rebellion in the Netherlands was entrusted to Alexander Farnese, Duke of Parma, the ablest soldier of his age and a veteran of Lepanto. In a series of brilliant campaigns he regained Bruges, Ghent, Antwerp, and most of the southern Netherlands, and in desperation the rebels offered the sovereignty of their country to Henry III's brother, the Duke of Alençon.

Although Philip continued to hold back from an open declaration of war on England, Pope Gregory XIII (1572–1585) nearly forced him into action by preparing two expeditions against Ireland. One, in 1578, completely miscarried; the other, in 1580, in which a few Spaniards were involved, landed in Ireland, but its members were soon slaughtered. In 1577, Drake, with five ships, had set out on the voyage which was to lead to his circumnavigation of the world. On his way he raided Valparaiso; looted Tarapaca; captured the great treasure ship *Cacafuego*; and sailed into San Francisco Bay where he took possession of the land in the name of Queen Elizabeth and called it "New Albion." He returned in September, 1580, with an immense booty and was knighted by Elizabeth on the quarter-deck of his flagship, the *Golden Hind*.

When Drake sailed round the world, another event took place which was to have a profound influence on the Anglo-Spanish quarrel. In 1578, in a fit of antiquated chivalry, the young King Sebastian of Portugal invaded North Africa and on August 4, at Alcazar Kebir, he was killed and his army annihilated. He left no children and was succeeded by his great uncle Cardinal Henry, childless and 77 years old, after whom came a host of claimants. Among these Philip had the strongest legal claim, and Don Antonio, an illegitimate son of Louis Duke of Béja (son of King Emanuel of Portugal) was the most popular. It was this question of succession which, in 1579, induced Philip to go gently with England so that he might be free to occupy Portugal on Henry's death. He did not have long to wait. Henry died on January 31, 1580, and soon after Philip sent the Duke of Alva and an army into Portugal. Don Antonio was routed at Alcantara on August 25 and Philip then annexed Portugal and the Portuguese empire. Not only did he gain vast territories in which there was no religious barrier, but also the shipping and seamen of an intensely maritime people.

Don Antonio fled to France after his defeat and later sought refuge in England. As he styled himself King of Portugal, it was open to Elizabeth to recognize him as such and to permit her subjects to act upon his commissions.

This change in the balance of power threw both Elizabeth and Catherine de' Medici, the French queen-mother, into panic. The latter fitted out a fleet under Filippo Strozzi and in 1582 sent it with Don Antonio to seize the Azores, the focal point of the Spanish communications with the New World. There, off the island of Terceira, it was scattered by the Marquis of Santa Cruz, who had commanded the reserve squadron at Lepanto. The following year the French Admiral Aymard de Chaste, accompanied by Don Antonio, was disastrously defeated by the Marquis of Santa Cruz, again off Terceira. The effects of these two victories were great indeed; they confirmed the impression gained at Lepanto that the Spanish fleet was invincible, and they secured the Portuguese Atlantic bases, which were essential to Philip in order to strike at England.

Shortly after the second of these battles, when still at Terceira, the Marquis of Santa Cruz wrote to Philip to urge that only by an invasion of England could the Netherlands be regained. The idea was by no means new, for in 1569 the Duke of Alva had suggested it, and after Lepanto Don John of Austria had considered the task an easy one. Philip demurred; but soon after two events persuaded him to accept it.

First, in January, 1584, because of his complicity in the Throckmorton plot, Elizabeth ordered Bernadino de Mendoza, Spanish Ambassador in England, to leave the country. In reply, Philip laid an embargo on all English shipping in Spanish ports, to which Elizabeth retaliated in kind. She also ordered Drake to ravage the West Indies. On September 14, 1585, he set out with Martin Frobisher, sacked Porto da Praia in the Cape Verde Islands; ravaged San Domingo; plundered Cartagena (in Colombia); threatened Havana and destroyed St. Augustine in Florida.

Meanwhile Parma consolidated his gains, a task in which he was greatly aided by the assassination of William of Orange on July 10, 1584. After his death the situation in the Netherlands grew so critical that Elizabeth, who regarded the rebels as "an ungrateful multitude, a true mob," in August, 1585, reluctantly made a treaty with them and sent the Earl of Leicester and 5,000 soldiers to the Netherlands to hold the breach until William's son, Maurice of Nassau (1584–1625) could establish himself. This was the second event: at length, after 27 years of peace, Elizabeth embarked on war, all but in name.

Philip at last was brought to see that in order to re-establish his authority in the Low Countries there was no alternative to the invasion of England. All along he had avoided so desperate an undertaking, but the intervention of Leicester brought him to recognise that it was imperative. So it came about that on March 12, 1586, Santa Cruz resubmitted his project; but as he now asked for 510 ships and 94,222 men, and estimated the cost of the expedition at 3,800,000 ducats,[1] Philip substituted for it a less ambitious scheme. It was that instead of conveying an army of

[1] A ducat in English money was then worth 9s. 4½d.

invasion from Portugal to England, Santa Cruz's task should be limited to gaining command of the English Channel, after which Parma's army in the Netherlands would be ferried across it.

At this moment, most opportunely for England, Elizabeth was able to secure her kingdom from internal revolt before the storm broke. In the spring of 1586 the English adherents of the captive Mary Stuart, who believed that no invasion could succeed as long as Elizabeth lived, entered into a conspiracy–known as the Babington Plot–to assassinate her. Mendoza, then ambassador at the court of France, and Mary Stuart were involved. The outcome was that Elizabeth's chief ministers, Lord Burghley, Lord High Treasurer, and Sir Francis Walsingham, Principal Secretary of State, much against the Queen's wishes, persuaded her to bring Mary to trial. On February 1, 1587, she was condemned to death and seven days later was beheaded at Fotheringhay.

CHAPTER 12

The defeat of the Spanish Armada, 1588

Before Calais was lost in 1558 the security of England depended theoretically on defending her shores by fighting battles on the Continent, which was looked upon as the counterscarp of England's defences. After the loss of Calais this dependence had to be replaced by the command of the English Channel; yet, when the crisis of 1586 occurred, although Queen Elizabeth possessed a private fleet of 34 warships, which in time of war could be augmented by many armed merchantmen, no national navy existed, and so things stood until the days of the Commonwealth. Added to this, there was no standing army – the feudal levies had long disappeared – and though, as in the days of the Saxon *fyrd*, her Majesty's Lieutenants were still authorized to call out levies of armed men, except for those in London they were little more than undisciplined bodies of soldiers which, at their best, would have been unable to meet in the field the highly organized soldiers of Spain.

The trouble was that, as Fortescue says of Elizabeth, "she hated straight dealing for its simplicity, she hated conviction for its certainty, and above all she hated war for its expense."[1] These three idiosyncrasies, particularly the last, persuaded her to rely on diplomacy, and because she lacked the force necessary to make it effective she was outwitted consistently by the Duke of Parma who, until the Armada sailed, covered his preparations in the Netherlands by constant proposals of peace, which Elizabeth largely accepted at face value.

Nevertheless, because of the Babington Plot it became apparent that a crisis had been reached, and on December 25, 1586, Elizabeth was persuaded to order the mobilization of her fleet at Portsmouth and to hold a squadron in the Channel during the winter of 1586–1587 to frustrate any possible attempt by the Guises to rescue Mary Queen of Scots. In March, 1587, Mary was dead, and while the main fleet was mobilized at Portsmouth,

[1] *A History of the British Army*, the Hon. J. W. Fortescue (1910), vol. 1, p. 130. Regarding the expense of war, Queen Elizabeth's yearly income did not permit her to indulge in war without aid from Parliament.

Sir Francis Drake was making ready at Plymouth 23 sail "to impeach the joining together of the King of Spain's fleets out of their several ports, to keep victuals from them, to follow them in case they should be come forward towards England or Ireland and to cut off as many of them as he could and impeach their landing. . . ."[1] As usual, as soon as these orders were issued Elizabeth feared that they might precipitate a war and greatly modified them;[2] but Drake, who knew what to expect, put to sea on April 2, before he could receive her counter-order and arrived at Cadiz on April 19. "We stayed there," he writes, "until the 21st, in which meantime we sank a Biscayan of 1,200 tons, burnt a ship of the Marquess of Santa Cruz of 1,500 tons, and 31 ships more of 1,000, 800, 600, 400 to 200 tons the piece; carried away four with us laden with provisions, and departed thence at our pleasure. . . ."[3] Next, being "furnished with necessary provisions," he made for Lisbon, from where on April 27 he writes: "There was never heard of so great a preparation [as] the King of Spain hath and doth continually prepare for an invasion. . . ."[4]

Lisbon was where the ships of the Armada were being assembled, and though Santa Cruz had established his headquarters there, as yet he had not mustered a man. It was a powerfully defended port. Outside the bar and to the north was an anchorage commanded by Cascaes Castle, and close to it lay the strong fortress of St. Julian. On May 10 Drake cast anchor in Cascaes Bay. The port was thrown into consternation, every vessel cut her cables and sped for the nearest refuge. Thousands of tons of shipping and a vast quantity of stores were then destroyed; the Spanish return puts the loss at 24 ships with cargoes valued at 172,000 ducats.[5] Drake, who had no land forces with him, could not hold the port, so he made for Cape St. Vincent—the strategic point between Lisbon and the Mediterranean. "We hold this Cape," writes Thomas Fenner—Drake's Flag-Captain—"so greatly to our benefit and so much to their disadvantage as a great blessing [is] the

---

[1] *Camden Society Misc.*, "Sir Francis Drake's Memorable Service, etc.," (1843), vol. v, p. 29.

[2] Elizabeth's counter-order reads: ". . . that her express will and pleasure is you shall forbear to enter forcibly into any of the said King's ports or havens, or to offer violence to any of his towns or shipping within harbouring, or to do any act of hostility upon the land . . ." (*Papers Relating to the Navy during the Spanish War*, 1585–1587, edited by Julian S. Corbett, Navy Record Soc., 1898, p. 101).

[3] *Ibid.*, pp. 107–108.

[4] *Ibid.*, p. 111.

[5] *La Armada Invencible*, Captain Cesaero Fernandez Duro (1884), doc. 15 bis, vol. I, p. 335.

attaining thereof. For the rendezvous is at Lisbon, where we understand of some 25 ships and 7 galleys. The rest, we lie between home and them, so as the body is without the members; and they cannot come together by reason that they are unfurnished of their provisions in every degree, in that they are not united together."[1]

Near St. Vincent immense damage was done to the Portuguese Algarve fisheries and thousands of tons of hoops and pipe-staves for casks were destroyed.[2] Could Drake have remained there he might well have prevented altogether the assembly of the Armada, but this was not possible unless he were reinforced. On May 17 he wrote to Sir Francis Walsingham: "If there were here 6 or more of her Majesty's good ships of the second sort, we should be the better able to keep the forces from joining and haply take or impeach his fleet from all places in the next month and so after, which is the chiefest times of their return home, which I judge, in my poor opinion, will bring this great monarchy to those conditions which are meet."[3]

This was not to be and he set out for the Azores. Sixteen days out from St. Vincent, on June 8, he sighted a large vessel off St. Michael's and took her the next day. She was the *San Felipe*, the King of Spain's own East Indiaman, with a cargo valued at £114,000 and papers which revealed the long-kept secrets of the East India trade.[4] On June 26 Drake was back in Plymouth. He had wrecked all possibility of the Armada sailing that year. This was most fortunate for England, for had the Armada been able to put to sea before the end of September, as Philip intended, Parma might have crossed the Channel. As he writes in a letter to the King: "Had the Marquis come when I was first told to look for him, the landing could have been effected without difficulty. Neither the English nor the Dutch were then in a condition to resist your fleet."[5]

Meanwhile Santa Cruz hastened to make good the damage done and to be ready by the end of February, 1588; but he died suddenly on January 30. Again the expedition was delayed. His

---

[1] *Papers Relating to the Navy during the Spanish War*, 1585–1587, p. 139.
[2] See *ibid.*, pp. 131 and 137. As all salt provisions, wines and water, etc., had to be carried in casks, the importance of this loss may readily be understood.
[3] *Ibid.*, p. 133.
[4] *Ibid.*, p. xlii. These papers so stirred the London merchants that later they formed the East India Company, the foundations of the British Empire of India.
[5] Quoted from *History of England from the Fall of Wolsey to the Defeat of the Spanish Armada*, James Anthony Froude (n.d.), vol. xii, p. 324.

death proved to be as great a calamity to the Spaniards as Drake's raid, for he was the ablest sailor in Spain. In his stead Philip appointed Don Alonzo Perez de Guzman, Duke of Medina Sidonia, who, though a grandee of highest rank, had never seen service either with the fleet or with the army. He wrote to the King asking to be excused,[1] but Philip appointed a competent seaman, Don Diego de Valdez to be his naval adviser and nominated the Duke of Parma commander-in-chief of the entire expedition once Medina Sidonia had sailed up the Channel and joined him.

While Medina Sidonia made ready, the main preparations of the Duke of Parma were the cutting of a ship canal from Antwerp and Ghent to Bruges; the building of 70 landing-craft on Waten River, each to carry 30 horses and equipped with embarking and disembarking gangways; the building of 200 flat-bottomed boats at Nieuport; the assembly of 28 warships at Dunkirk; the recruiting of mariners in Hamburg, Bremen, Emden, and other ports; the construction of 20,000 casks at Gravelines; and near Nieuport and Dixmude the building of camps for 20,600 foot, and at Courtrai and Waten for 4,900 horse.[2]

The operations which were soon to follow are better understood by examination of the naval developments of this period.[3]

The factor which differentiated the warship of the sixteenth century from what she had been in previous centuries was the heavy cannon; for though man-killing ordnance began to be mounted in ships in the fourteenth, it was not until the fifteenth century that a heavy enough gun to smash a ship came into existence. This weapon was of two distinct types, a breech-loader and a muzzle-loader. In its original form the former was what is called a "built-up gun"—that is, a piece fashioned by welding together bars of iron, as already described. Its powder chamber was separate from the barrel, and before discharge was screwed into it by means of an uninterrupted thread. Of this type belong *Dulle Griette* of Ghent and *Mons Meg* of Edinburgh; the latter a cast piece of bell-metal with barrel and chamber in one, and equipped with trunnions.

---

[1] See Duro, vol. i, doc. 53, pp. 414–415.

[2] Emanuel Van Meteren's Account of the Armada, *Hakluyt Voyages* (Everyman's Library), vol. ii, pp. 375–376.

[3] Most of the following is based on Professor Michael Lewis's "Armada Guns: A Comparative Study of English and Spanish Armaments," in *The Mariner's Mirror* vols. 28 and 29 (1942–1943), and his *The Navy of Britain* (1948).

There were two main types of muzzle-loading pieces—the cannon and the culverin, both mounted on trucks. The former was a true battering-piece that threw a heavy iron shot at medium range, and the latter a longer piece from which was fired a lighter shot over greater distance. The characteristics of these two pieces were as follows:

Type	Bore	Weight of shot	Calibres	Point blank range[1]	Random range
Cannon ..	7¼ in.	50 lb..(about)	18	340 paces	2,000 paces
Culverin ..	5¼ in.	17 lb.	32	400 paces	2,500 paces

Besides these there was a demi-cannon, which fired a shot of 32 lb., and a demi-culverin—a nine- to ten-pdr. There were many smaller members of the culverin class, the more important were the Saker, a five-pdr.; the Minion, a four-pdr., and the Falcon, a two and a half to three-pdr.;[2] but these pieces were wholly man-killers. Another piece, which at this period was falling into obsolesence, was the Perier, a gun of comparatively short range that threw a 24-lb. stone ball.

Up to the opening of the sixteenth century two main types of vessels sailed the seas—namely, the hulk or round ship, and the galley or long ship. The former was used to carry merchandise, and the latter was *par excellence* the warship. But ocean voyaging and improvement in cannon soon began to change ship construction; sails became more important on the ocean than oars, and the sailing ship could better be adapted to broadside fire.

The first transition set in with the introduction of small man-killing naval ordnance in the fifteenth century. They were mounted in two castles,[3] one built over the bow (forecastle), and the other over the stern (rear castle) of the ship, and were pointed to sweep the waist to destroy boarders. Henry VII's Great Ship, the *Regent*, housed 225 of these man-killing guns—mainly swivel-pieces.

The next transition came with Henry VIII, who adopted the

[1] "Point-blank" range was the distance at which the shot began to fall appreciably, and "Random" was the maximum range.
[2] For these and many other pieces of this period see *Papers Relating to the Navy during the Spanish War*, appendix A.
[3] Previously, elevated platforms had been built for archers.

muzzle-loading, ship-smashing cannon. As this weapon was too heavy to be housed in the castles and was unsuitable as an anti-boarding weapon, it had to be mounted on the upper-deck, or better still the main-deck, with port-holes cut in the sides of the ship. The first of these heavy-gunned ships was the *Mary Rose*, built in 1513.

The last transition was that with this type of ship the castles became less necessary, and that as the weight of broadside fire demanded increased deck space, the round ship was developed into what was to become the ship of the line, a vessel the length of which was three beams or more, instead of the average round ship's two beams. In the sixteenth century the most renowned of these ships was Francis Drake's *Revenge*, a ship wholly of English design. This type of ship was "race-built," or what Monson calls "flush-decked"—that is to say, though her poop and forecastle were not flush with the waist, they were from 25 per cent. to 45 per cent. lower than the great Spanish ships and galleasses. This made many of the English ships of war appear smaller than the Spanish; but the largest ships of the two navies were approximately of the same tonnage. The galleon, which was not peculiar to Spain, was "a sailing-ship—usually four-masted—with the ordinary ship-rig of the time, but with the hull built to some extent on galley lines, long for its beam, rather straight and flat, and with a beak low down, like a galley's, instead of the overhanging forecastle of the ship."[1] The crew of the English warship at this time was approximately two men a ton burden; in the Spanish ships it was three or more.

The influence of the gun on naval tactics was even more radical than on naval construction. In the days of the galley the primary weapon was the beak protruding from the bow and the main tactical operation was ramming. Though the approach might be made in column of galleys, the attack formation was that of line abreast, and, as in land warfare, the battle culminated in an assault or charge. In the gun-ship, the bulk of the primary weapons—the heavy ship-smashing cannon—were not in the bow but along the sides. When the gun-ship neared an enemy, in order to bring a broadside to bear she had to wear or wheel to port or starboard—virtually suicide for the galley. In consequence, with the gun-ship the attack had to be made at right-angles to her line of advance, and in order to carry out this manœuvre methodically

[1] *The Sailing-Ship: Six Thousand Years of History*, Romola and R. C. Anderson (1926), p. 126.

and so to concentrate the maximum hitting power on the enemy, the approach had to be made in line ahead.

This radical change was not yet recognized, fleets went into action in coveys or swarms of ships and the main aim was to board each other's ships. But during the various engagements of the Armada in the Channel line ahead began to take form, and the reason is to be sought in the differences between the armaments of the contending fleets, which Professor Lewis gives as follows:[1]

Fleet	No. of ships	Cannon	Periers	Culverins	Total
English	172	55	43	1,874	1,972
Spanish	124	163	326	635	1,124

The English then, had three times as many long-range pieces as the Spaniards and the Spaniards had three times as many heavy-shotted medium-range pieces as the English. These differences in range and smashing-power dictated the respective tactical policies: the English concentrated on long-range fighting and the Spaniards on medium- and short-range action. Whereas the Spanish tactical aim was to reduce a hostile ship to impotence and then to board her, the English was to sink the enemy or to force her to strike her flag. Although the English culverin had the greater range, it was not powerful enough decisively to batter a ship at long range. Equally important, the inaccuracy of its fire was such that at long range few shots hit their target. Inaccuracy of fire dogged naval warfare, as it also did that on land, until the introduction of the rifled gun and musket. Theoretically therefore, the Spanish, who relied on close-range battering power, were in advance of their enemy as artillerists.

Philip realized clearly the type of tactics the English would adopt and, before Medina Sidonia sailed, he gave him this warning: "You are especially to take notice that the enemy's object will be to engage at a distance, on account of the advantage which they have from their artillery and the offensive fireworks with which they will be provided; and on the other hand, the object of our side should be to close and grapple and engage hand to

[1] *The Mariner's Mirror*, vol. 29, p. 100. Besides the 1,124 heavy ordnance, the Spanish ships carried 1,307 lighter man-killing pieces, mainly in the castles.

hand."[1] But apparently he did not realize so fully that the true advantage of the English lay not in their longer range ordnance, but in their superior seamanship and in the fact that their ships were handier than the Spanish. The Spaniard was a fair weather sailor, the Englishman was not; the Spanish ships were looked upon more as fortresses than vessels and were crowded with soldiers and undermanned with sailors, who were considered little better than galley slaves. In the English ships their crews not only manned but fought them, and though pressed into service received fourpence a day. The greatest difference and advantage of all was that the Spaniard continued to make use of the galley tactics of line abreast in groups, whereas Drake or Howard introduced a rough formation of line ahead in groups and so began to revolutionize naval fighting. ,

For the English admirals, the greatest difficulty during the months immediately preceding the sailing of the Armada was Elizabeth. Though a woman of pronounced personality and force of character, she was one of the most parsimonious sovereigns who ever sat on the English throne. She was genuinely afraid of Spain, and with reason–it was the greatest military and naval power in the world. Rightly she wanted peace, yet she could not understand that so long as she encouraged privateering and supported the Netherlands peace was not possible.

During the autumn a small English squadron under Sir Henry Palmer, in conjunction with a Dutch squadron, in all some 90 warships of small burden "meete to saile upon their rivers and shallow seas,"[2] blockaded the havens of Flanders; but it was not until November 27[3] that the Queen assembled a council of war to discuss such problems as likely landing places; the employment of land forces; the weapons to be used; and internal security. On December 21 she appointed Lord Howard of Effingham "lieutenant-general, commander-in-chief, and governor of the whole fleet and army at sea."[4] She selected him instead of Drake–her most able admiral–not only to enhance the prestige of her fleet,

[1] Duro, doc. 94, vol. II, p. 9.

[2] *Voyages*, Richard Hakluyt, vol. II, p. 379.

[3] *The Naval Tracts of Sir William Monson*, edit. by M. Oppenheim (1902), vol. II, pp. 267–286.

[4] *State Papers, Relating to the Defeat of the Spanish Armada*, edit. John Knox Laughton (1894), vol. I, p. 19. She denotes him as "knight of our illustrious order of the Garter, High Admiral of England, Ireland, Wales, and of the dominions and islands thereof, of the town of Calais and the marches of the same, of Normandy, Gascony and Aquitaine, and Captain General of the Navy and marines of our said Kingdoms of England and Ireland. . . ."

but because it was essential to have in command a man of so high a rank that he could command obedience. Drake was later appointed vice-admiral to reinforce Howard on the technical side. Of Howard, Thomas Fuller says: "True it is he was no deep seaman; but he had skill enough to know those who had more skill than himself and to follow their instructions, and would not starve the Queen's service by feeding his own sturdy wilfulness, but was ruled by the experienced in sea matters; the Queen having a navy of oak and an Admiral of osier."[1]

Ever since his return from Cadiz and Lisbon, Drake had pressed for a repetition of his audacious raid.—an attack on the Spanish fleet in its ports of departure—and had he been allowed to repeat it, the high probability is that the Armada would never have sailed. At length, two days after Howard's appointment, he received a commission to proceed with 30 ships to the Spanish coast. But as soon as this commission had been given the Queen, fearful of antagonizing Spain, cancelled it and ordered that the crews of the fleet be reduced to half their strength.[2] This wavering brought forth a strongly worded letter from John Hawkins to Walsingham on February 15, 1588.

"We have to choose," he wrote, "either a dishonourable and uncertain peace, or to put on virtuous and valiant minds, to make a way through with such a settled war as may bring forth and command a quiet peace. . . . Therefore, in my mind, our profit and best assurance is to seek our peace by a determined and resolute war, which no doubt would be both less charge, more assurance of safety, and would best discern our friends from our foes both abroad and at home, and satisfy the people generally throughout the whole realm."[3]

Hawkins's idea was, like Drake's, that the offensive is the surest defensive. But soon after he had written this letter, the Queen learnt of the death of the Marquis of Santa Cruz. She believed that the Armada could not now sail, and as she also knew that the Duke of Parma was in a difficult situation[4] she fell into the trap the latter had set and sent peace commissioners[5] to the Netherlands.

[1] Quoted in *Drake and the Tudor Navy*, Julian S. Corbett (1898), vol. II, p. 186.

[2] *State Papers*, vol. I, p. 33.   [3] *Ibid.*, vol. I, pp. 59–60.

[4] On March 20, 1588 – that is, about a month later – Parma informed Philip that he had but 17,000 effectives left out of some 30,000 men. Also he writes: "It may be that God desires to punish us for our sins by some heavy disaster." (See Oppenheim's Introduction to the *Monson Tracts*, 1902, vol. I, p. 167.)

[5] They were Henry, Earl of Derby; William, Lord Cobham; Sir James à Crofts, and Doctor Valentine Dale and Doctor John Rogers.

Concerning this, Howard wrote to Walsingham on March 10: "I pray God that her Majesty take good care of herself, for these enemies are become devils, and care not how to kill. . . . I pray to God her Majesty do not repent this slack dealings."[1] Meanwhile, report after report came in that the Armada was soon to sail.[2]

Had Elizabeth been less diplomatically inclined she would have realized that Parma's peace proposals were a blind and that war was inevitable because Philip believed himself to be the instrument of the Almighty. He saw the whole undertaking as a crusade to return England to the fold of the Catholic Church. Day by day, in 50,000 churches, Masses were said; Philip's ships bore the names of saints and apostles; their crews were forbidden to swear, quarrel, gamble, or consort with loose women, and above them floated the imperial banner, on which were embroidered the figures of Christ and the Virgin and the motto: *Exurge Deus et vindica causam tuam.*

Philip wrote to Medina Sidonia: "When you have received my orders, you will put to sea with the whole Armada, and proceed direct for the English Channel, up which you will sail as far as the point of Margate, then open communication with the Duke of Parma, and ensure him a passage across."[3] He warned him to avoid the English fleet, and said that should Drake appear in the Channel, except for rearguard actions he was to ignore him. He also gave Medina Sidonia a sealed letter for Parma in which he informed the duke what to do should the expedition fail.[4]

Philip placed at Medina Sidonia's disposal 130 ships: 20 galleons; 44 armed merchantmen; 23 *urcas*, or hulks; 22 *pataches*, or dispatch-vessels; 13 *zabras*, or pinnaces; four galleasses, and four galleys.[5] These ships aggregated 57,868 tons burden, were armed with 2,431 guns, were manned by 8,050 seamen, and carried 18,973 soldiers. With galley slaves and others the total number of men was 30,493.[6]

The whole fleet was divided into 10 squadrons as follows:

(1) The squadron of Portugal, Medina Sidonia, 10 galleons and two pinnaces.

(2) The squadron of Castile, Diego Flores de Valdez,[7] 10 galleons, four armed merchantmen, and two pinnaces.

[1] *State Papers*, vol. I, pp. 106–107.   [2] *Ibid.*, vol. I, pp. 84, 90–92, 107, 122.
[3] Duro, doc. 94, vol. II, pp. 5–13.   [4] Duro, doc. 96, vol. II, p. 17.
[5] The actual number of warships may be taken as between 60 and 70.
[6] For supplies carried, see *The Royal Navy*, Wm. Laird Clowes (1897), vol. I, p. 560, following Duro, doc. 110, vol. II, pp. 82–84.
[7] de Valdez accompanied Medina Sidonia in his flag-ship the *San Martin*.

(3) The squadron of Andalusia, Pedro de Valdez, 10 armed merchantmen and one pinnace.

(4) The squadron of Biscay, Juan Martinez de Recalde, 10 armed merchantmen and four pinnaces.

(5) The squadron of Guipuzcoa, Miguel de Oquendo, 10 armed merchantmen and two pinnaces.

(6) The squadron of Italy, Martin de Bertendora, 10 armed merchantmen and two pinnaces.

(7) The squadron of *Urcas*, Juan Gomez de Medina, 23 ships.

(8) The squadron of *Pataches*, Antonio Hurtado de Mendoza, 22 ships.

(9) The squadron of four galleasses, Hugo de Monçada.

(10) The squadron of four galleys, Diego de Medrado.[1]

While the Spaniards made ready and Elizabeth dallied with Parma, Drake fretted at Plymouth. On March 30, unable to endure further delay, he wrote a strongly worded letter to the Queen's Council in which, Corbett states, he enunciated "the root ideas of the New English school that Nelson brought to perfection."[2]

"If her Majesty and your Lordships," he wrote, "think that the King of Spain meaneth any invasion in England, then doubtless his force is and will be great in Spain: and thereon he will make his groundwork or foundation, whereby the Prince of Parma may have the better entrance, which, in mine own judgment, is most to be feared. But if there may be such a stay or stop made by any means of this fleet in Spain, that they may not come through the seas as conquerors—which, I assure myself, they think to do—then shall the Prince of Parma have such a check thereby as were meet.

"My very good Lords, next under God's mighty protection, the advantage and gain of time and place will be the only and chief means for our good; wherein I most humbly beseech your good Lordships to persevere as you have begun, for that with fifty sail of shipping we shall do more good upon their own coast, than a great many more will do here at home; and the sooner we are gone, the better we shall be able to impeach them."[3]

Again, on April 13, he wrote in similar strains to the Queen, and added: "The advantage of time and place in all martial actions is half a victory; which being lost is irrecoverable."[4] And again on April 28 he wrote:

---

[1] This squadron did not sail. [2] *Drake and the Tudor Navy*, vol. II, p. 139.
[3] *State Papers*, vol. I, pp. 124–125. [4] *Ibid.*, vol. I, p. 148.

"Most renowned Prince, I beseech you to pardon my boldness in the discharge of my conscience, being burdened to signify unto your Highness the imminent dangers that in my simple opinion do hang over us; that if a good peace for your Majesty be not forthwith concluded–which I as much as any man desireth–then these great preparations of the Spaniard may be speedily prevented as much as in your Majesty lieth, by sending your forces to encounter them somewhat far off, and more near their own coasts, which will be the better cheap [the more advantageous] for your Majesty and people, and much the dearer for the enemy."[1]

The outcome was that Howard was ordered to carry the bulk of his fleet to Plymouth, after he had detached a squadron under Lord Henry Seymour to watch the Channel.[2] He set out from the Downs on May 21 and joined Drake two days later. He then took over supreme command and appointed Drake his vice-admiral; as such he became President of the Council of War.[3] After this, Howard wrote to Burghley: "I mean to stay these two days to water our fleet, and afterwards, God willing, to take the opportunity of the first wind serving for the coast of Spain, with the intention to lie on and off betwixt England and that coast, to watch the coming of the Spanish forces. . . ."[4]

Meanwhile rumours and reports arrived from Spain and the high seas. In April it was rumoured that the Armada would make for Scotland,[5] and on May 16 it was reported that 300 sail had assembled at Lisbon, and "that they stand greatly upon their guard hearing but of the name of Drake to approach them."[6] On May 28 it was reported that the Armada was ready to sail.[7] Howard accordingly put to sea on May 30 and Drake's daring project seemed about to be attempted, but on June 6 the fleet was forced back into the Sound by contrary winds. A few days later a dispatch from Walsingham was received which showed that timidity had again crippled the Council; Howard was ordered not to take his fleet to Spain, but instead "to ply up and down in some indifferent place between the coast of Spain and this realm. . . ."[8] Howard, on June 15, answered:

---

[1] *Ibid.*, vol. 1, p. 166.

[2] At this time Justinian of Nassau (a natural son of Prince William I) and Jan Gerbrandtzoom with two Dutch squadrons were cruising off Dunkirk and the coast of the United Provinces.

[3] Under Drake came Lord Thomas Howard, Lord Sheffield, Sir Roger Williams, John Hawkins, Martin Frobisher, and Thomas Fenner.

[4] *Ibid.*, vol. 1, p. 179.   [5] *Ibid.*, vol. 1, p. 170.   [6] *Ibid.*, vol. 1, p. 173

[7] *Ibid.*, vol. 1, p. 183.   [8] *Ibid.*, vol. 1, p. 193

"Sir, for the meaning we had to go on the coast of Spain, it was deeply debated by those which I think [the] world doth judge to be men of greatest experience that this realm hath.

"And if her Majesty do think that she is able to detract time with the King of Spain, she is greatly deceived which may breed her great peril. For this abusing [of] the treaty of peace doth plainly show how the King of Spain will have all things perfect, [as] his plot is laid, before he will proceed to execute. . . .

"The seas are broad; but if we had been [on] their coast, they durst not have put off, to have left us [on] their backs. . . ."[1]

Even more disastrous than this faulty strategy of Elizabeth and her Council was their administration. Again and again we find complaints by Howard of lack of victuals, a lack due partly to contrary winds, partly to the inefficiency of the period, but mainly to the parsimony of the Queen and her Councillors. Already, on May 28, Howard had written to Burghley: "My good Lord, there is here the gallantest company of captains, soldiers, and mariners that I think ever was seen in England. It were pity they should lack meat when they are so desirous to spend their lives in her Majesty's service."[2] Again he appealed, this time to Walsingham, on June 15, and from then on much of Howard's and Drake's correspondence falls under two headings: "let us attack," and "in heaven's name send us food." Thus, on June 15, Howard wrote to Walsingham:

"The opinion of Sir Francis Drake, Mr. Hawkyns, Mr. Frobisher, and others that be men of greatest judgment [and] experience, as also my own concurring with them in the same, is that [the] surest way to meet with the Spanish fleet is upon their own [coast], or in any harbour of their own, and there to defeat them. . . .

"Sir, our victuals be not come yet unto us; and if this weather hold, I know not when they will come."[3]

At length, on June 17, the Council gave way on the first point and authorized Howard to do what he "shall think fittest."[4] On June 23 the victuals had arrived and Howard informed the Queen that he was about to sail. He added: "For the love of Jesus Christ, Madam, awake thoroughly, and see the villainous treasons round about you, against your Majesty and your realm, and draw your forces round about you, like a mighty prince, to defend you.

[1] Ibid., vol. i, pp. 202–204.   [2] Ibid., vol. i, p. 190.
[3] Ibid., vol. i, pp. 200–201.   [4] Ibid., vol. i, p. 217.

Truly, Madam, if you do so, there is no cause to fear. If you do not, there will be danger."[1]

Directly the ships were provisioned—probably on June 24—Howard, Drake, and Hawkins put to sea. Howard kept the body of the fleet together in mid-Channel while Drake, with a squadron of 20 ships, stood out toward Ushant, and Hawkins, with an equal number, lay toward Scilly. Soon afterward the wind shifted into the south-west and the fleet had to return to Plymouth, from where, on July 16, Howard informed Walsingham: "We have at this time four pinnaces on the coast of Spain; but, Sir, you may see what [may co]me of the sending me out with so little victuals, and the [evil of the same]";[2] which suggests that it was not the wind alone which forced him back. Lastly, on July 17, we find him writing to the same Minister: "I never saw nobler minds that be here [in our] forces; but I cannot stir out but I have an inf[inite number] hanging on my shoulders for money."[3]

Such was the condition of the English fleet, which in four days was to face the Armada. It consisted of the Royal Navy, 34 ships with *The Ark Royal* (800 tons) as flagship; the London squadron, 30 ships; Drake's squadron, 34 ships; Lord Thomas Howard's squadron (merchant ships and coasters), 38 ships; 15 victuallers and 23 voluntary ships, and Lord Henry Seymour's squadron—off the Downs—which numbered 23 ships.[4]

On May 20, while the English fleet gathered at Plymouth, the Armada dropped down the Tagus and put to sea,[5] but was so buffeted in the Atlantic that, on June 9, Medina Sidonia sought refuge in Coruña, where to his consternation he found that much of the provisions was putrid and much water had leaked out of the newly-made casks. He also found that so many ships needed repair and so many men were sick, that on the advice of a council of war he sent a message to the King recommending a postponement of the expedition until the following year. This Philip refused to consider, so after fresh supplies had been requisitioned, on July 12, in spite of the stormy weather, the Armada sailed again. On July 19 the Lizard was

---

[1] *Ibid.*, vol. I, p. 217. [2] *Ibid.*, vol. I, p. 245.
[3] *Ibid.*, vol. I, p. 273.
[4] See *ibid.*, vol. I, p. 167; vol. II, pp. 323–331. Many of these ships did not take part in the fighting. In battle, both sides relied on only a small proportion of their total strength, the English on the Queen's ships and a few others, and the Spaniards on their galleons, great ships (armed merchantmen) and galleasses.
[5] Duro, doc. 115, vol. II, p. 106, and doc. 118, vol. II. p. 113. All dates are Old Style, for New Style add 10 days.

sighted, and there Medina Sidonia rested for a few hours until all his ships had come up. The following day he sailed eastward and shortly before midnight learnt from a captured English fishing boat that the Admiral of England and Drake had put to sea that afternoon.[1] This was untrue.

As soon as the Armada sighted the Lizard, Captain Thomas Fleming—who commanded one of the four pinnaces Howard had left in the Channel—reported its approach. The surprise was complete and Howard and Drake found themselves in the very position they had intended for their enemy—namely, "to meet the Spanish fleet upon their own coast, or in any harbour of their own, and there to defeat them." Nevertheless, on this Saturday, July 20, "his Lordship, accompanied with 54 sail of his fleet . . . plied out of the Sound; and being gotten out scarce so far as Eddystone, the Spanish army was discovered, and were apparently seen of the whole fleet to the westwards as far as Fowey "[2] Howard then struck sail and lay under bare poles.

Because no fighting instructions are known to have been issued during the reign of Elizabeth[3] it is impossible to say what order of battle Howard adopted. There was probably no order, other than "follow my leader," since, as yet, his fleet was not even organized into squadrons. And although the formation the Spanish fleet was found in was described as that of a crescent, no records support this. All that is known for certain is that it was divided into the usual main battle, vanguard (right wing) and rear guard (left wing). Corbett suggests that to meet the assumed strategical situation these three groups of ships were probably formed into two divisions or quasi-independent fleets:[4] the main battle, under Medina Sidonia in advance, to hold off Howard, who was supposed to be at Dartmouth, and the van and rear guards, in rear, to hold off Drake, who was known to be at Plymouth. The diagram illustrates his suggested distribution, which if viewed from the rear might well appear to look like a crescent.

As Drake had not been met with in the Channel, Medina Sidonia concluded that he had been caught napping and was still at Plymouth. The opportunity to destroy him was so apparent that Don Alonzo de Leyva, Captain-General of the Armada, and

[1] *Ibid.*, vol. II, pp. 222, 229.
[2] *State Papers* (Howard's Relation of Proceedings), vol. I, p. 7.
[3] *Fighting Instructions 1530–1816*, edit. Julian S. Corbett (1895, Navy Record Soc.), p. 27.
[4] *Drake and the Tudor Navy*, vol. II, pp. 210–219.

others urged Medina Sidonia to attack him before he could get out of the Sound. This was common sense, because in order to carry out their broadside tactics the English required sea-room to manœuvre in and the Spaniards, dependent on boarding, required a fight in narrow waters. Had de Leyva's suggestion immediately been adopted, it is possible that the English fleet might

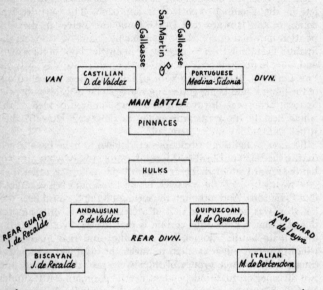

have suffered as disastrous a defeat as the Turkish fleet did at Lepanto. But the King's orders stood in the way, and Medina Sidonia refused to listen to de Leyva.[1]

Strangely enough, so it would appear, during the whole of July 20 the English fleet was unseen by the Spaniards, and it was not until one o'clock the following morning that they discovered from some prisoners that both Drake and Howard were out of Plymouth. Medina Sidonia at once anchored and ordered his squadron leaders to form order of battle.

[1] Duro, doc. 109, vol. i, p. 67.

While they did this, the moon rose and revealed their position to the English. Next, when the attention of the Spaniards was riveted on a small squadron of eight English ships beating out from Plymouth to windward between the shore and the port side of the Armada, which was erroneously assumed to be the van of the English main fleet, Howard and his 50 odd ships "recovered the wind of the Spaniards two leagues to the westward of Eddystone. . . ."[1] and at daybreak Medina Sidonia was dumbfounded to discover a large enemy fleet to windward of him, bearing down to the attack. He realized that he could not avoid battle and ran up the royal standard – the signal for a general engagement.

The English got the weather gauge[2] and drew up in a single long line – *en ala* as the Spaniards called it.[3] Then, writes Corbett, they passed the Spanish vanguard "which formed the starboard and leeward wing of the rear division, firing upon it at long range as they went, and fell on the rearguard, a manœuvre they can only have executed close-hauled in line-ahead. . . . The effect was immediate . . . a number of rearguard captains began crowding in a disgraceful panic upon Sidonia's division."[4] To check the rout, Recalde came up with the *Gran Grin*, and was at once surrounded by Drake, Hawkins, and Frobisher, who poured into his ship a murderous fire "such as never before had been seen at sea." Next, Pedro de Valdez in the *Nuestra Señora del Rosario*, was also engaged, and a little later Medina Sidonia in the *San Martin* came into action. But it was not until Recalde's vessel was completely disabled that Medina Sidonia could collect sufficient ships to relieve him. Howard then broke off the engagement, and soon after this the *San Salvador*, carrying the Paymaster-General of the Armada and his chests, blew up and dropped out of the fleet in flames. Howard signalled to his ships to make sail for the burning wreck, which resulted in a fresh fight, after which he again signalled the retreat.

This engagement, the first between the two fleets, was of outstanding moral importance. It showed that the English ships and gunners were vastly superior to the Spanish. The latter were

---

[1] *State Papers*, vol. I, p. 7.

[2] The weather gauge is the position of a ship to the windward of another, giving the possessor the initiative and advantage in manœuvring. It facilitates bringing an enemy to action and massing on part of his fleet. Also, the cannon smoke drifting to leeward blinds the enemy.

[3] Duro, vol. II, p. 154, and *Drake and the Tudor Navy*, vol. II, pp. 208 and 221. Whether this line was fortuitous or concerted it is impossible to say.

[4] *Ibid.*, vol. II, pp. 222 and 223.

greatly depressed by their failure to board, and also by the abandonment of the *San Salvador*. As Medina Sidonia says: "the enemy's ships were so fast and handy that there was nothing which could be done with them."[1]

That night, "his Lordship appointed Sir Francis Drake to set the Watch. . . ."[2] and then assembled a council of war in the *Ark Royal*, at which the general opinion held was that the Spaniards would make for the Isle of Wight—obviously the correct thing to do—in order to establish a base on English soil and to gain an anchorage for the fleet. This was the course the Spanish captains persuaded Medina Sidonia to adopt; for the English tactics had led to so excessive an expenditure of Spanish ammunition that they considered it essential for Medina Sidonia to occupy a port or roadstead on the south coast of England—actually the Isle of Wight—whence the Armada could cover the necessary flow of munitions from Spain and stand fast until action had been concerted with Parma.[3] To prevent such a contingency, the English war council decided to give chase to the enemy: Drake lit the great poop lantern of the *Revenge* and set out to lead the fleet through the night.

As the night wore on, suddenly his light disappeared, and immediately many of the ships astern of him hove to, while others held on their course. The result was confusion, and when the sun rose on July 22 the *Revenge* was nowhere to be seen.

What had happened was that when he heard that Don Pedro de Valdez's ship lay helpless, Drake extinguished his lantern and put about, for he had been told that she contained much treasure. In the morning he captured her,[4] sent her into Torbay, and rejoined the Lord Admiral. Apparently his privateering spirit had got the upper hand, which so incensed Frobisher that he exclaimed: "He thinketh to cozen us of our shares of fifteen thousand ducats; but we will have our shares, or I will make him spend the best blood in his belly. . . ."[5]

---

[1] *Ibid.*, doc. 165, vol. II, p. 230.   [2] *State Papers*, vol. I, p. 8.

[3] Duro, doc. 160, vol. II, p. 221.

[4] Drake embraced Don Pedro and gave him very honourable entertainment, feeding him at his own table and lodging him in his cabin.

[5] *State Papers*, vol. II, p. 102. Drake's explanation is, that "in the growing light" of the early morning of July 22 he saw three or four strange craft stealing past him. Thereupon he put out his light and tacked toward them. On discovering that they were German merchantmen, he proceeded to take station and fell in with Don Pedro's ship (*Drake and the Tudor Navy*, vol. II, p. 231). This is not very convincing because if dawn were breaking, there should have been little resultant confusion after the lantern was extinguished.

The respite granted to Medina Sidonia by the confusion in his enemy's fleet enabled him to reorganize his rear division. He now placed it under the command of de Leyva, but continued to maintain the van division as it was, because Seymour's squadron was still unaccounted for; then he set sail again. But the English fleet could not be got together until the evening of July 22, when the wind died away and both fleets were becalmed within cannon shot of each other between Portland and St. Alban's Head.

At dawn the following day the wind rose from the north-east, and as this gave the weather gauge to the Spaniards, Medina Sidonia signalled a general engagement, and fighting was resumed. Soon Frobisher's ship, the *Triumph* (1,100 tons and the largest English ship) and five others got into trouble, and when he saw this ". . . the Duke of Medina Sidonia . . . came out with 16 of his best galleons to impeach his Lordship [Howard] and to stop him from assisting the *Triumph*. At which assault, after wonderful sharp conflict, the Spaniards were forced to give way and to flock together like sheep." Howard's account continues: "This fight was very nobly continued from morning until evening, the Lord Admiral being always in the hottest of the encounter, and it may well be said that for the time there was never seen a more terrible value of great shot, nor more hot fight than this was; for although the musketeers and harquebusiers of crock [a rest or swivel] were then infinite, yet could they not be discerned nor heard for the great ordnance came so thick that a man would have judged it to have been a hot skirmish of small shot, being all the fight long within half musket shot of the enemy."[1]

The next day, Howard informs us, "there was little done," as much ammunition had been spent; therefore he sent "divers barks and pinnaces unto the shore for a new supply of such provisions", and divided his fleet into four squadrons, respectively commanded by himself, Drake, Hawkins, and Frobisher. Here for the first time we find a clear attempt to bring order out of disorder. Hitherto, with the possible exception of their first engagement, the English had fought their ships in swarms, in which the ships of their most noted captains had done the bulk of the fighting. Now these captains were to lead their own squadrons, and although this did not mean that Howard and Drake had decided henceforth to fight in line ahead, because each squadron had its own leader it was a definite step in that direction. Further, to facilitate his

[1] *Ibid.*, vol. 1, p. 12.

attack, Howard arranged that during the night six armed merchantmen from each squadron should keep the Spaniards in constant alarm.

Unfortunately, the wind fell and these distracting attacks had to be abandoned. Meanwhile Medina Sidonia told off 40 ships as a rearguard to protect his rear and then continued on his way, but soon after he was becalmed a few miles to the south of the Isle of Wight.

The following morning–Thursday, July 25–Howard noticed that Recalde's flagship, the *Santa Ana*, was "short of her company to the southwards" and ordered Sir John Hawkins to lower some boats and attack her. Immediately three galleasses rowed toward the boats, and were "fought a long time and much damaged" by "the Lord Admiral in the Ark, and the Lord Thomas Howard in the Golden Lion." The wind then rose, the fleets clinched, and for several hours the fighting was intense. This is noted by Sir George Carey, who writes: ". . . with so great expense of powder and bullet, that during the said time the shot continued so thick together that it might rather have been judged a skirmish with small shot on land than a fight with great shot on sea. In which conflict, thanks be to God, there hath not been two of our men hurt"[1]–somewhat of an anti-climax to so desperate a struggle.

Medina Sidonia had hoped much of this day–St. Dominic's, his patron-saint–but when he found his ships again outclassed he abandoned all idea of seizing the Isle of Wight, sent ahead a dispatch boat to warn Parma of his arrival, and stood out for Calais. Howard then made for Dover to link up with Lord Henry Seymour and Sir William Wynter.

This day's fighting really decided the fate of the whole enterprise. The Spaniards had not yet been beaten, for so far their losses were insignificant, but the English tactics of refusal to close –that is, refusal to be pounded by the Spanish heavy cannon–had exhausted the ammunition of both sides,[2] and whereas Howard could replenish his from coastal ports near by, Medina Sidonia could not do so until he had reached Flanders.

[1] *Ibid.*, vol. I, p. 324.

[2] The English ran out of both powder and shot, the Spaniards of shot only. Before starting out, the provision of powder for the Armada was, according to Duro (vol. II, p. 83) 517,000 lb., and according to Meteren (Hakluyt, vol. II, p. 373) 560,000 lb., and of shot 123,790 (Duro, doc. 110, vol. II, p. 83). Though not exactly known, the English supplies were much less. Of this day's fighting, Meteren says that the two fleets were at times engaged "within one hundred, or an hundred and twentie yards one of another" (Hakluyt, vol. II, p. 387), which suggests that both sides were out of heavy shot, and which, when read in context with Carey's statement, points to the extreme inaccuracy of the lesser ordnance.

When Friday, July 26 dawned, "The Spaniards," says Howard, "went away before the English army like sheep," not out of fear, but for want of round shot. On Saturday evening, when he was near Calais, Medina Sidonia cast anchor between the town and Cape Gris-Nez and the English fleet anchored "within culverin shot of the enemy."[1] Howard had been joined by Seymour's and Wynter's squadrons and had in all under his command 136 ships, 46 of which were "great ships," whereas the ships of the Armada had been reduced to 124.

The tactical situation was changed completely, for Howard, who had been able, in part at least, to replenish his powder and shot, whereas Sidonia had been unable to do so, could, whenever he wished, close in to small arms range and use his culverins a true ship-battering pieces. The crisis had been reached – the Armada was cornered. But to board the Spanish ships would clearly be both a desperate and a costly operation, for their soldiers were trained and armed to meet this type of attack.

This situation had been foreseen, and some days before the Armada put into Calais Roads Walsingham had sent orders to Dover to collect some fishing craft, pitch, and faggots, to make fire-ships. This suggestion must have come from Howard and Drake, who could not have failed to see that if their enemy could not hold the Channel he would be compelled to put into some roadstead or port.

Early on Sunday, July 28, a council of war was assembled in the main cabin of the *Ark Royal*,[2] at which it was decided that so urgent was it to attack there would not be sufficient time to bring the fire-craft from Dover. Instead eight ships of 200 tons or under were selected from the fleet and prepared so hastily that not even their guns were removed.

Immediately he reached Calais, Medina Sidonia sent his secretary to Parma to urge haste; but no sooner had he gone than another messenger, who had been sent by boat sometime before, returned to say that Parma was at Bruges and that so far no men had been embarked. Then the secretary returned to say that it was impossible for Parma to get his army on board under a fortnight.

The truth would appear to be not that Parma's embarkation was delayed, but that, because of the Dutch fleet under Justinian

---

[1] *Ibid.*, vol. I, p. 15. See also Duro, doc. 165, vol. II, p. 238.
[2] *Ibid.*, vol. I, p. 15, and vol. II, p. 1.

of Nassau, Parma could not get out of port. It was useless to embark his men before Justinian's ships were driven away. Had it not been for the Dutch blockading fleet, which played a vitally important part in the campaign, in spite of Lord Henry Seymour's squadron, Parma might have chanced a crossing to Margate when the Armada was off the Isle of Wight. Emanuel van Meteren is definite on the effectiveness of the Dutch blockading fleet. "The shippes of Holland and Zeeland," he says, "stood continually in their sight [in the sight of Parma's ships] threatening shot and powder, and many inconveniences unto them: for feare of which shippes, the Mariners and Sea-men secretly withdrew themselves both day and night, least that the duke of Parma his souldiers should compell them by maine force to goe on board, and to breake through the Hollanders Fleete, which all of them judged to bee impossible by reason of the straightnesse of the Haven."[1]

On board the Armada there was discouragement because the Governor of Calais had warned Medina Sidonia that the road-stead was highly dangerous, and because of the bad news received from Parma. "We rode there," writes Don Luis de Miranda, "all night at anchor, with the enemy half a league from us likewise anchored, being resolved to wait, since there was nothing else to be done, and with a great presentiment of evil from that devilish people and their arts. So too in a great watching we continued on Sunday all day long."[2] This is not altogether correct, because the opportunity for an attack by fire-ships was so obvious that Medina Sidonia had ordered out a flotilla of patrol boats to intercept them, should they be launched.

Midnight struck and passed, when early on Monday, as all lay still, the Spanish sentries saw several shadowy ships approach them and then burst into flames. The memory of the "hell-burners" of Antwerp, which three years before had destroyed a thousand of Parma's men, flashed across the minds of the terrified Spaniards. Medina Sidonia gave the fatal order for cables to be cut. He meant to reoccupy the anchorage once the fire-ships had passed by, but a panic followed and in confusion many of his ships crashed into each other in the dark and were borne out to sea. "Fortune," wrote a Spanish officer, "so favoured them [the English] that there grew from this piece of industry just what they counted on, for they dislodged us with eight vessels, an exploit

---

[1] *Voyages*, Hakluyt, vol. II, p. 389.   [2] Duro, doc. 169, vol. II, p. 269.

which with one hundred and thirty they had not been able to do nor dared to attempt."[1]

As soon as the fire-ships had drifted clear – they did no damage – Medina Sidonia ordered a signal gun to be fired for the fleet to regroup at Calais. The *San Marcos* (a Portuguese galleon) and one or two others obeyed the signal, but most of the ships, with two anchors lost and unable to get at their spare ones, drifted north-eastward along the coast. When at last he realized that because the wind blew from the south-south-west it would be impossible for these ships to close in on the *San Martin*, Medina Sidonia weighed anchor and stood out to sea to follow the rest.

When morning broke, a triumphant sight greeted the eyes of Howard's men: right along the coast toward Dunkirk the Armada lay scattered, with no possibility of regaining Calais Road, where, stranded on the sand, close under the guns of the town, lay the *Capitana* galleasse with Don Hugo de Monçada and 800 men on board. Now was Howard's chance to attack and overwhelm his enemy, and he set out to seize it, but when he saw the great galleasse, she proved too tempting a bait. Instead of following the fleeing enemy, he made for the galleasse and took her after a stiff fight, in which Monçada was killed.

Drake, Hawkins, and Frobisher crowded on all sail and set out after the Armada. As they were short of powder and shot they closed in on their enemy so that every shot should tell. This they could do at little risk because the Spanish cannon shot had been exhausted. In this running fight their aim was to cut off the weathermost of the Spanish ships and to drive the rest to leeward on to the banks of Zeeland. Meteren writes of this action:

"Wherefore the English shippes using their prerogative of nimble stirrage, whereby they could turne and wield themselves with the winde which way they listed, came often times very neere upon the Spaniards, and charged them so sore, that now and then they were but a pike's length asunder: and so continually giving them one broadside after another, they discharged all their shot both great and small upon them. . . ."[2]

The battle was continued along the coast toward Dunkirk, and at about nine o'clock the two fleets were engaged off Gravelines. The fight lasted until six in the evening.[3] On the Spanish side

---

[1] *Ibid.*, doc. 171, vol. II, p. 283. See also Pedro Estrade's account in *Monson* (vol. II, appendix A, p. 306) and Wynter to Walsingham (*State Papers*, vol. II, p. 9).
[2] Hakluyt, vol. II, p. 392.
[3] Wynter's account, *State Papers*, vol. II, pp. 10–11.

Estrade's account is interesting, because it describes the severity of the English fire:

"So we bare out of the north and north-east," he writes, "with great disorder investing one with another and separated; and the English in the wind of us discharging their cannons marvellously well, and discharged not one piece but it was well employed by reason we were on so nigh another and they a good space asunder one from the other. The Vice-Admiral St. Martin went before, shooting her artillery. This day was slain Don Philip de Cordova, with a bullet that struck off his head and struck with his brains the greatest friend that he had there, and 24 men that were with us trimming our foresail. And whereas I and other four where, there came a bullet and from one struck away his shoe without doing any other harm, for they came and plied so very well with shot."[1]

This praise of English gunnery is corroborated by Sir William Wynter who, on August 1, wrote to Walsingham: "I deliver it unto your Honour upon the credit of a poor gentleman, that out of my ship there was shot 500 shot of demi-cannon, culverin, and demi-culverin; and when I was furtherest off in discharging any of my pieces, I was not out of the shot of their harquebus, and most times within speech one of another. And surely every man did well; and, as I have said, no doubt the slaughter and hurt they received was great, as time will discover it; and when every man was weary with labour, and our cartridges spent, and munitions wasted [expended] – I think in some altogether – we ceased firing and followed the enemy, he bearing hence still in the course as I have said before [*i.e.* NNE and N by E]."[2]

As the crisis of the battle approached – it was six o'clock in the evening – it seemed that the Armada was doomed to inevitable destruction, when, to the relief of its sorely tried men, a squall of wind swept down upon the contending fleets. Then Howard and Drake broke off the fight,[3] and the *Maria Juan* of 665 tons – one of Recalde's ships – foundered. With the squall the battle ended, and as Medina Sidonia had been forced out of the Channel and to leeward of Dunkirk the possibility of joining hands with Parma grew more and more remote.

As night closed in the wind freshened to a half-gale and the *San Mateo*, the *San Felipe*, and a third ship were driven on to the Zeeland coast. When Tuesday, July 30, dawned, Medina Sidonia

---

[1] Monson, vol. ii, appendix A, pp. 307–308.   [2] *State Papers*, vol. ii, p. 11.
[3] They were now out of shot and in any case could no longer continue it.

looked from his flagship to see 109 English sail little more than half a league astern of his scattered fleet. In his *Relation* we read:

"The Duke fired two guns to collect his Armada, and sent a pinnace with a pilot to order his ships to keep a close luff, seeing that they were very near the banks of Zeeland. For the same cause, the enemy remained aloof, understanding that the Armada must be lost, for the pilots on board the flagship, men of experience on that coast, told the Duke at the time that it would not be possible to save a single ship of the Armada, and that with the wind at N.W., as it was, every one must needs go on to the banks of Zeeland, God alone being able to prevent it. The fleet being in this danger, with no kind of way of escape, and in six and a half fathoms of water, God was pleased to change the wind to W.S.W., and with it the fleet stood to the northward, without damage to any vessel, the duke having sent orders to every ship to follow the motions of the flagship at peril of driving on the banks of Zeeland."[1]

Throughout the entire week's fighting, and in spite of "upwards of 100,000 rounds of great shot" expended by the Spaniards, no English ship was seriously damaged and only one captain and a score or two of seamen were killed.[2] On the other hand, in the battle of Gravelines alone the Spaniards lost 600 killed and 800 wounded.

On the evening of July 29 Medina Sidonia summoned a council of war, which decided that if the wind changed the Armada would regain the Channel, in spite of the fact that his ships were short of provisions and out of great shot. But, should it not regain the Channel, the sole course open was to return to Spain by way of the North Sea. As the wind did not change the latter course was adopted.

It was a desperate venture, for not only were many of the ships now unseaworthy, but they were not provisioned for so long a voyage. Nevertheless, though driven northward by an evil wind and pursued by Drake, to whom had been allotted the post of honour in the chase, it was still possible for Medina Sidonia in part to redeem the disaster. This he could have done if he had landed in the Forth and raised Scotland against the Queen. But his one thought was to get back to Spain; he sailed past the mouth

---

[1] Duro, doc. 165, vol. II, pp. 244–246.
[2] *The Navy of Britain*, Michael Lewis (1948), p. 443.

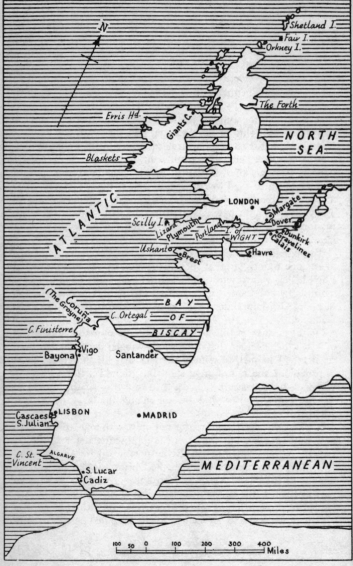

21   THE ARMADA CAMPAIGN, 1588

of the Forth on August 2, and in a single body the Armada stood out for the Orkneys. The next day Howard abandoned the chase, and, on August 7, his ships recovered the Downs, Harwich, and Yarmouth.[1]

From Margate Road, on August 8, he wrote to Walsingham: "I pray to God we may hear of victuals, for we are generally in great want." To guard against an enemy return, he urged Walsingham to look to the country's defences, and then added: "Some made little account of the Spanish force by sea; but I do warrant you, all the world never saw such a force as theirs was; and some Spaniards that we have taken, that were in the fight at Lepanto, do say that the worst of our four fights that we have had with them did exceed far the fight they had there; and they say that at some of our fights we had 20 times as much great shot as they had there . . . Sir, in your next letters to my brother Stafford [Ambassador at Paris] I pray write to him that he will let Mendoza [Spanish Ambassador in Paris] know that her Majesty's rotten ships dare meet with his master's sound ships; and in buffeting with them, though they were three great ships to one of us, yet we have shortened them 16 or 17: whereof there is three of them a-fishing in the bottom of the seas." To this letter he added the postscript—"Sir, if I hear nothing of my victuals and munition this night here, I will gallop to Dover to see what may be got there, or else we shall starve."[2]

The rest of the story, a dramatic one, is soon told, for during the Armada's dreadful voyage home, the galleasse *Girona* went to pieces near Giant's Causeway, and carried to their deaths her crew and Don Alonso de Leyva; the *El Gran Grifon* sank off Fair Island; the *Rata Coronada* was wrecked on the coast of Erris; the *Duquesa Santa Ana* was lost in Glennagiveny Bay; and the *Nuestra Señora de la Rosa* was beaten to pieces on the Blaskets. The *San Marcos, San Juan, Triniada, Valencera,* and *Falcon Blanco Mediano* were lost off the coast of Ireland, and the *San Pedro Mayor,* blown off course, was wrecked in Bigbury Bay, near Plymouth.

Of the 130 sail which stood out from Lisbon in May, 63 are believed to have been lost. Two were abandoned to the enemy; three were lost off the French coast; two were lost off Holland; two were sunk off Gravelines; 19 were wrecked off Scotland or Ireland; and the fate of 35 is unknown. The English did not lose a ship.

[1] *State Papers*, vol. I, p. 18.   [2] *Ibid.*, vol. II, p. 59–61.

Even more horrible than the fate of the castaways on the Irish coast, most of whom were butchered, was that of the crews who were not shipwrecked; thousands of men died of untended wounds, of fever, of hunger, and of thirst—some ships were without water for 14 days. At length, in the middle of September, a messenger arrived post-haste at the Escorial from Santander with the news that Medina Sidonia had returned to that port on September 12. When the messenger gave the King this fatal news, Philip was sitting at his desk. Without change of countenance he observed: "Great thanks do I render Almighty God, by whose generous hand I am gifted with such power, that I could easily, if I chose, place another fleet upon the sea. Nor is it of very great importance that a running stream should be sometimes intercepted, so long as the fountain from which it flows remains inexhaustible."[1]

It was God's will, and so he accepted his defeat. Yet he was not unconscious of the sufferings of the brave men who had risked and undergone so much in this disastrous crusade. He did all in his power to alleviate their ills, and instead of blaming Medina Sidonia, he ordered him to return to Cadiz, there to resume his former governorship.

Very different was the behaviour of Queen Elizabeth, whose first consideration was to cut expense. Unlike Philip, there was nothing either chivalrous or generous in her character, and though Professor Laughton goes out of his way to exonerate her meanness,[2] there is no shadow of doubt that, had she been a woman of heart as well as of head, it would have been impossible for her to have left her gallant seamen to die by scores of want and disease immediately after the victory was won.

The correspondence of Howard proves this conclusively. On August 10—that is, three days after his return from the pursuit—he wrote to Burghley: "Sickness and mortality begins wonderfully to grow amongst us; and it is a most pitiful sight to see, here at Margate, how the men, having no place to receive them into here, die in the streets."[3] Again, on August 29, he wrote to him: "It were too pitiful to have men starve after such a service. . . . Therefore I had rather open the Queen Majesty's purse something

---

[1] Quoted from Motley's *History of the United Netherlands* (1860), vol. II, p. 535. Shortly after the battle of Gravelines a report was received by Philip that the Armada had been triumphant; next, that it had been defeated, but to what extent was uncertain. Not until Medina Sidonia's return did he receive the full news.
[2] See *State Papers*, vol. I, XLIV, XLVI–XLIX.   [3] *Ibid.*, vol. II, p. 96.

to relieve them, than they should be in that extremity for we are to look to have more of their services; and if men should not be cared for better than to let them starve and die miserably, we should very hardly get men to serve."[1]

Although little realized at the time, the influences of this campaign on naval strategy and tactics were profound, and out of them gradually emerged many of the principles which were to govern warfare at sea until the advent of the steamship.

First, the campaign showed the vital importance of bases in relation to command of the sea. Drake's 1587 attack on Cadiz and Lisbon was in idea a more certain method of protecting England against invasion than to meet and beat the Armada in the Channel, and had it been repeated in 1588, as it readily could have been, the high probability is that the Armada would never have sailed. Conversely, the lack of a Spanish naval base near England was the fundamental reason why the Armada was unable to carry out its task. Hence onward, because it is seldom possible to compel an enemy to accept battle at sea, to bottle-up his fleet in its home ports and simultaneously to deny him naval bases near her shores, became the foundations of England's naval policy.

Secondly, the campaign had shown clearly the futility of reliance on armed merchantmen in battle. They took next to no part in the Channel fighting, and the best that can be said of them is that they added grandeur and with it, possibly, terror, to the respective fleets. As raiders, they were of use, but as ships of the line, an impediment rather than a support. Had the English done without them much money could have been saved without in any way jeopardizing the issue.

Thirdly, as artillerists both sides had failed to achieve their respective ends. The English culverins were neither powerful enough nor sufficiently accurate to hit and smash a ship except at close range, and though the Spanish cannon could do so, their ships were not nimble enough nor their seamen sufficiently skilful to bring their superior armament within close range of their enemy. Hence the indecisive nature of the fighting and the tendency for cannon increasingly to become the primary naval weapon in battle.

[1] *Ibid.*, vol. II, p. 183. Professor J. E. Neale excuses this parsimony thus: "It is a sad thought that while battle slew a mere hundred during the fight with the Armada, epidemic disease afterwards raged in the fleet and slew its thousands. But once again there was no novelty in the fact: disease also decimated the Spaniards" (*Queen Elizabeth, 1934*, p. 299).

Historically, the importance of the defeat of the Armada was, as Merriman says, that it constituted "the supreme disaster of Philip's reign."[1] Nevertheless the war meandered on until 1604, to end in a peace of exhaustion which was neither creditable nor profitable to England, nor of any great consequence to Spain. It did not add an acre to Spanish territory, nor subtract an acre from English. It did not change the dynasties of England or Spain, nor did it modify the policies of the contending parties or influence their respective religions. Wherein, then, lay the decisiveness of the battle?

To answer that it spared England from invasion is true, but only conditionally so, for the part played by Justinian of Nassau was as important in gaining the victory as that played by Howard and Drake. Even had these two never put to sea, it is improbable that the Armada could have dislodged the Sea Beggars of Brill, because their nimble, light draught ships could sail the shallow coastal waters of Flanders and Zeeland and the cumbersome and larger Spanish ships could not. Yet, even should this hypothesis be set aside, the defeat of the Armada is to be reckoned the most decisive English battle fought since Hastings – it saved England and it mortally wounded Spanish prestige. It showed to the world at large that the colossus had feet of clay; that the edifice of Spanish power was built upon sand, and that the security of her empire was largely a mirage. It was this illusion which for nearly a century had imposed itself upon the credulity of the world to an extent unwarranted either by the resources, the wealth, or the population of Spain.

Since the conquest of Granada in 1492, Spain had accomplished extraordinary things. Suddenly her sons had stretched out their hands and seized the limits of the known world. They conquered Mexico and Peru, planted colonies in southern, central, and northern America, spanned the Indian Ocean, and established the myth of their invincibility. They accomplished these marvellous things because they believed themselves to be the chosen instruments of God. The defeat of their Armada shattered this faith and destroyed the illusion that had fortified their fanaticism. Thirty years later Spain became decadent, not because the war with England had been long and exhausting, but because the loss of faith in her destiny was catastrophic.

There was another reason for this moral collapse: it was that, before the Armada sailed, the Spaniards had failed to grasp the

[1] *The Rise of the Spanish Empire* (1934), vol. IV, p. 552.

true meaning of sea power. Had they done so they would have sought command of the sea before they attempted to gain full command of their scattered lands. Command of the sea was vital to them if they were to prevent the interruption of their trade with the New World and the Indies and to secure their hold over the Netherlands. It was lack of this command which enabled Hawkins, Drake, and others with impunity to sail the Spanish Main; to pillage Spanish treasure ships; to plunder Spanish colonial towns; and to sail into the ports of Cadiz and Lisbon and insult the Spanish flag. It was lack of command of the sea which lost the United Provinces and which led directly to the defeat of the Armada; for power to command the sea was not Spain's, and least of all when the Armada sailed up the Channel to gain it. Though more clearly seen today than in 1588, the Armada was doomed from the start, not only because it was outclassed in navigation and tactics, but because its commanders had little sea sense.[1]

Strange though it may seem at first, the only two peoples who were not spellbound by the Spanish myth were the English and the Dutch, both small nations. But it appears less strange when it is recognized that both were sea powers who could, even if precariously, command their home waters. It was because they could do this that they were able to defeat the fleets of Spain and so set out on their imperial courses which, in less than a century, made them rivals.

What these two peoples learned was that small nations with limited resources and little native power, so long as they command the sea, can win and hold great oversea dominions; whereas great nations, though they may gain vast oversea territories, unless they command the sea, cannot hold them once they are challenged seriously.

The defeat of the Armada whispered the imperial secret into England's ear; that in a commercial age the winning of the sea is more profitable than the winning of the land, and though this may not have been clearly understood in 1588, during the following century the whisper grew louder and louder until it became the voice of every Englishman.

[1] Only after his supreme disaster did Philip set out to build an ocean-going navy and begin to establish Spanish command of the sea. In order to secure the treasure he drew from the Indies, he abandoned carrying it in great fleets—and brought it to Spain in fast, armed vessels of 200 tons, called *gallizabras*, which could sail without escort. Although, as ships of war, they could not help him to win his war against England, by denying to the English raiders their former booty, they did prevent England winning the trade war—actually the real war.

In the "Epistle Dedicatorie" to the first edition of his *Voyages*, published in 1589, and addressed to Sir Francis Walsingham, Richard Hakluyt voices this imperial spirit in the following panegyric:

"So in this most famous and peerlesse government of her most excellent Majesty, her subjects through the speciall assistance, and blessing of God, in searching the most opposite corners and quarters of the world . . . have excelled all the nations and people of the earth. For, which of the kings of this land before her Majesty, had theyr banners ever seene in the Caspian sea? which of them hath ever dealt with the Emporor of Persia, as her Majesty hath done, and obteined for her merchants large and loving privileges? who ever saw before this regiment, an English Ligier in the stately porch of the Grand Signor at Constantinople? who ever found English Consuls and Agents at Tripolis in Syria, at Aleppo, at Babylon, at Balsara, and which is more, who ever heard of Englishman at Goa before now? what English shippes did heeretofore ever anker in the mighty river of Plate? passe and repasse the unpassable (in former opinion) straight at Magellan, range along the coast of Chili, Peru, and all the backside of Nova Hispania, further than any Christian ever passed, travers the mighty bredth of the South sea, land upon the Luzones in despight of the enemy, enter into alliance, amity, and traffike with the princes of the Moluccaes, and the Isle of Java, double the famous Cape of Bona Speranza, arive at the Isle of Santa Helena, and last of al returne home most richly laden with the commodities of China, as the subjects of this now flourishing monarchy have done?"[1]

The historical importance of the defeat of the Armada is this: it laid the cornerstone of the British Empire by endowing England with the prestige Spain lost. And it was this prestige, this faith in her destiny, that urged the English along their imperial way, until their flag floated over the greatest empire the world has so far seen: the empire of the oceans and the seas, which from rise to fall was to endure for over 300 years.

[1] Vol. 1, pp. 3–4.

The disruption of Christendom

The passing of feudal Europe into the Renaissance; the decay of scholasticism and the rise of humanism; the over-secularization of the papacy and the steady emasculation of the Empire; the budding forth of rationalism and absolute monarchies; the introduction of the printing press and the development of firearms; the discovery of the New World and the sea route to India, coupled with the growth of city life, of wealth, luxury and poverty, of commerce, trading monopolies and usury, reached flash-point in what is called the Reformation–the religious expression of the general ferment.

The two great detonators were Luther (1483–1546) and Zwingli (1484–1531), to be followed by a still greater, Calvin (1509–1564). In order to reinstate, as they conceived it, the pristine purity of religion, these men turned to the doctrine of predestination: that man is irredeemably evil, and however he may live and whatever he may do, from all eternity God has destined a chosen few for paradise and the vast majority for hell. This doctrine, which shifted the centre of gravity from God to the devil, together with the dogma that the Bible was to be the rule of all doctrine and worship, became the two great abutments of the reformers' cult.

Of these three men, the most portentous was Calvin, a fanatical organizer. He looked upon himself as the Oracle of God, whose orders carried with them divine sanction. At Geneva, where he established himself and his police-state, he assumed the infallibility he denied to the Catholic Church, and created a new type of man, the "Puritan", and a new régime, which aptly has been called "Bibliocracy."

"The Reformation," writes Oswald Spengler, "abolished the whole bright and consoling side of the Gothic myth–the cult of Mary, the veneration of the saints, the relics, the pilgrimages, the Mass. But the myth of devildom and witchcraft remained, for it was the embodiment and cause of the inner torture, and now that torture at last rose to its supreme horror."[1] The law of love was

---

[1] *The Decline of the West*, English edit. (1928), vol. II, p. 299.

rejected for the law of hate. Soon there grew up an immense Protestant literature on the devil which polluted true religion.

Today, it is difficult to grasp how such a creed offered any attraction. Nevertheless men of conviction were carried away by the thunderous theology of Luther and the cold logic of Calvin. The challenge was so immense and the propaganda so vitriolic that they appealed to all who were discontented. Swarms of monks and degenerate priests saw in the new creed an opportunity to rid themselves of obligations which had become irksome; princes found in it a means to fortify themselves against the Empire and to increase their domains by plundering the Church; the rising money-power discovered in it a sanction which favoured usury and the new economic conditions, and the oppressed masses a doctrine offering liberty and licence to all.

The turmoil which resulted cannot be discussed here, but in order to end it, on September 25, 1555, a compromise was reached at Augsburg, mainly between Ferdinand, who represented his brother, the Emperor Charles V, and Augustus, Lutheran Elector of Saxony. According to its terms, all Lutheran princes were granted freedom from episcopal jurisdiction and were permitted to retain ecclesiastical property secularized before the Treaty of Passau in 1552. Each secular prince had the right to decide, according to the principle of *cujus regio ejus religio*, which religion should be binding on his people, which meant that the faith of the German people was determined for them by their territorial princes instead of by the Church. And though a clause, known as the "ecclesiastical reservation", imposed forfeiture of land and dignities of Catholic bishops who forsook their faith, the Lutherans declared that they did not consider themselves bound by it.

The Calvinists were not included in this compact, nor was any allowance made for the growth of the Protestant religion, which rapidly spread over the Empire. All that the Peace of Augsburg accomplished was to establish a truce, it left Germany divided into two omnipresent factions, and as Lord Bryce says: "Two mutually repugnant systems could not exist side by side without striving to destroy one another." This destruction was made inevitable by the rising power of Calvinism and the newly constituted Society of Jesus, the one aim of which was the extirpation of Protestantism.

The storm centre became Prague, where Calvinism had strongly entrenched itself. In 1526 Bohemia had passed to the House of Habsburg, and in 1575 Maximilian II's eldest son Rudolf was crowned king. He succeeded his father as emperor in 1576, made Prague his imperial capital, and in 1609 was compelled by his Protestant subjects to grant them the so-called "Letter of Majesty", by which their religion was guaranteed and safeguarded by a body of men known as the Defenders. In 1611, Rudolf was deposed by his brother Matthias, who in May was crowned king of Bohemia and a year later elected emperor.

Meanwhile, after the Treaty of Augsburg, two champions had come forward to personify the elements of strife; Maximilian Duke of Bavaria, the Catholic, and Prince Christian of Anhalt, the Calvinist. The former regarded the treaty as a legal settlement to which all question should be referred; the latter believed that Protestantism had to get rid of the House of Austria, or the House of Austria would get rid of Protestantism. Incident followed incident, until, in 1607, Maximilian occupied the free city of Donau-wörth. This led to the creation of the Evangelical Union under Christian of Anhalt the following year. Challenged by this show of force, Maximilian formed the Holy Catholic League. A conflict was nearly certain, because Matthias was childless and his successor to both the Empire and Bohemia was likely to be the Archduke Ferdinand of Styria, the grandson of Ferdinand I, a fanatical Catholic. Matthias feared trouble and postponed his election until 1617, when a decision became imperative. When Spain agreed to support Ferdinand's candidature, on the understanding that when he became emperor he would surrender the Habsburg fiefs in Alsace to the Spanish crown, on June 17 the king's councillors, all of whom were fervent Catholics, elected Ferdinand heir to the Bohemian throne. At once the Bohemian Protestants, headed by Count Thurn, refused to recognize Ferdinand, and in December, when the Archbishop of Prague, in violation of the Letter of Majesty, ordered the suppression of Protestant services in the churches which had been built on his domains, the Defenders summoned a Diet to meet at Prague. It assembled there on May 21, 1618, and the following day, after a violent altercation, the king's most trusted councillors, Martinitz and Slawata, and their secretary Fabricius, were hurled out of a window of the Hradcany Palace, an event to become known as the Defenestration of Prague. Immediately after this the Bohemians established a provisional government and proceeded to raise an army under Count Thurn. Hostilities with Austria opened in July and, little thought of at the time, they were destined to develop into the first of the great European wars and to last for 30 years.

On March 20, 1619, the death of Matthias accelerated events. The Confederate States, Bohemia, Lusatia, Silesia, and Moravia, declared the election of Ferdinand invalid, and on August 26 they elected as their king Frederick V Elector Palatine, a fervent Calvinist, whose wife, Elizabeth, was the daughter of James I of England.

Two days later the Electoral College met at Frankfort to decide who should succeed Matthias. It was the controlling organ of the Empire, and without its consent the Emperor could not call a Diet, impose a tax, make an alliance, or declare war. It had been created by the Golden Bull of 1356 and consisted of three spiritual, and four temporal princes. The former were the Catholic Electors of Mainz, Cologne, and Trèves, and the latter, the King of Bohemia, the Elector Palatine and the Elector of Brandenburg, both Calvinists, and the Elector of Saxony, a Lutheran. Therefore, as long as the King of Bohemia was a Catholic, the Catholic princes dominated; but should he be replaced by a non-Catholic, they would be in a minority. In this balance within the Electoral College where lay the root trouble of the Thirty Years War.

At Frankfort, only the three spiritual princes attended in person, the other four members of the College were represented by ambassadors, among whom Frederick's was instructed in the first instance to vote for Maximilian Duke of Bavaria (a Catholic), but should the other Electors vote for Ferdinand, he was to agree. As they did so, Ferdinand was elected Emperor under the title of Ferdinand II (1619–1637). No sooner had the decision been made than the news was received that he had been deposed from the Bohemian throne. As this was a challenge, not only to Ferdinand, but to the whole imperial system, the crisis at once became a European problem.

Because Ferdinand had no army wherewith to eject Frederick, he turned to Maximilian, the only prince in Germany who possessed a standing army, and on October 8, 1619, Maximilian agreed to support Ferdinand on the understanding that he had complete control of operations in Bohemia, and on the defeat of Frederick would be given his electoral titles. Also, at the price of Lusatia, Ferdinand gained the support of John George of Saxony, who detested the Calvinists. Further, Philip III (1598–1621) of Spain, promptly granted Ferdinand a subsidy to raise 10,000

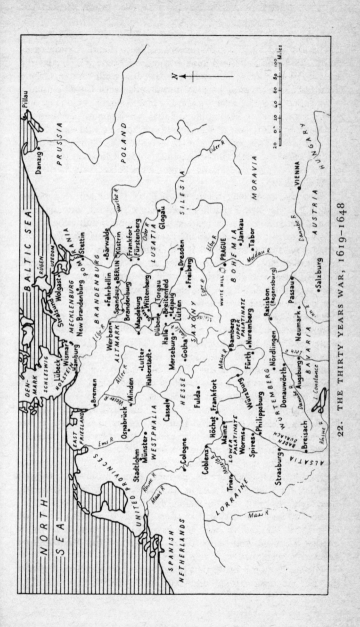

22. THE THIRTY YEARS WAR, 1619–1648

troops and lent him 8,000 more from the Netherlands. On the other hand, the princes of the Union recognized Frederick, as also did the United Provinces, Denmark, and Sweden, while Bethlen Gabor, Prince of Transylvania, entered into alliance with the Bohemians.

In July, 1620, the army of the Catholic League, 25,000 strong, under command of Maximilian, Tilly, and Bucquoy, crossed the Austrian frontier, and at the same time Spinola and 24,000 men set out from Flanders for the Palatinate. On November 8 the former came up with the Bohemians, under Christian of Anhalt, at the White Hill, near Prague, and routed them; Spinola overran the Palatinate.

These disasters broke up the Evangelical Union and might have ended the war had Ferdinand been more tolerant. But his principle, "Better to rule over a desert than a country full of heretics," urged him on; his persecutions exasperated the Calvinists. The result was that the fragments of the Bohemian army, reinforced by numbers of desperate men, rallied round the Calvinist general Count Ernest von Mansfeld, an able mercenary, soon to become known as the "Attila of Christendom", who carried the war into the Upper Palatinate. In the spring of 1622 he was joined by Christian Duke of Brunswick and George Frederick Margrave of Baden Durlach. A series of engagements followed, which in June was ended by a decisive defeat of the Calvinists at Höchst; whereupon Mansfeld and Christian retired into Alsace and later quartered themselves in east Friesland. Lastly, in August, 1623, Christian of Brunswick was crushed at Stadtlohn, and the conquest of the Palatinate was completed.

Ferdinand had, in January, 1621, unconstitutionally placed Frederick under the imperial ban, and in January, 1623, in fulfilment of his promise to Maximilian, he decided to transfer Frederick's electorship to him. As he could not call a Diet on his own authority, he assembled a general Electoral Meeting at Regensburg to sanction the transfer. Apart from Maximilian's brother, the Elector of Cologne, almost every important prince in Germany, as well as the King of Spain, was opposed to it. Nevertheless Frederick was deposed on February 23 and two days later Maximilian was invested with his titles. A storm of protest followed and the Electors of Saxony and Brandenburg refused to recognize their new colleague.

The alarm of the Protestant princes was fully justified. Not only did the unconstitutional deposition of Frederick threaten their individual securities, but, because of the change in the balance of power made by the investiture of Maximilian, they feared that they would be deprived of the ecclesiastical property they had seized since 1555, which included two archbishoprics and 120 abbacies. To prevent this they turned to Christian IV (1588–1648) of Denmark, a Lutheran prince, who, in May, 1624, accepted their cause. The war now entered its second phase; from a European problem it became a European conflict.

Compared with the Danish army, the army of the Catholic League was weak, and Ferdinand consequently was placed in a quandary; he did not wish to barter further territory for allied support. Suddenly the difficulty was overcome by Count Albrecht von Wallenstein (1583–1634), a Czech adventurer of great wealth, who offered to raise for the Emperor an army of 40,000 men free of charge so long as the appointment of its officers remained in his hands. Ferdinand at once accepted the offer and conferred upon Wallenstein the title of Duke of Friedland. Thus, at length, the Empire obtained an army of its own, which cost nothing and which could be maintained indefinitely in the field as long as it was engaged in war, because Wallenstein's maxim was that "war should feed war".

While Ferdinand was thus engaged, James I, at length had espoused the cause of his son-in-law and had quarrelled with Spain. At the same time Cardinal Richelieu (1585–1642), first minister of Louis XIII (1610–1643) of France, whose policy was to break the Habsburg circle which had surrounded France ever since the days of Charles V, concluded an alliance with England, the United Provinces, and Denmark. Thus the French policy of intervention in German affairs was inaugurated, a policy which has agitated central Europe ever since. Because Richelieu was paralysed by a Huguenot rising and James was afraid to summon Parliament, intervention was left to Christian IV, who was eager to extend his influence over the North Sea ports, and in 1626 he took the field.

In April, Wallenstein also set out. He moved against Mansfeld and defeated him at the Bridge of Dessau, then he overran Mecklenburg and Pomerania and increased his army as he went until it numbered some 80,000. On August 27, Christian IV was routed by Tilly at Lutter by the Barenberg and Brunswick was overrun

As the occupation of the Palatinate had freed the middle Rhine and thereby reopened it as the main line of communication between Italy and the Spanish Netherlands, which was of vital importance to Spain, Wallenstein set out to establish Ferdinand's authority over the Baltic principalities. He flooded the Danish mainland with his troops and in March, 1628, was rewarded when the Emperor conferred upon him the duchies of Mecklenburg. This high-handed act, even more than the raising of Maximilian to an Electorate, showed the Protestant princes that none of them was safe, and that the time was approaching rapidly when the whole of Germany would become an Austrian province. So they concerted on the overthrow of Wallenstein, but how to effect it in face of his 80,000 men was beyond their grasp.

The subjection of the Baltic lands was pushed steadily, and when Hamburg and Lübeck rejected Ferdinand's offer of alliances Wallenstein set out to bring the Hanseatic League to heel by an advance on Stralsund. An army of 25,000 men, under his lieutenant, Arnim, appeared before the town in April, but its councillors were not taken unawares. They had already entered into relations with Christian IV and Gustavus Adolphus of Sweden (1611–1632), and Munro's regiment of 900 Scots–then in the Danish service–400 Danes, and 600 Swedes, were sent by sea to the town. On June 23 a 20-year alliance was signed by Gustavus's agent and the municipality. That same day Wallenstein assumed the conduct of the siege, but after two vain assaults he learnt that Christian and an expeditionary force were off the island of Rügen and on July 24 he raised it.

Christian landed his army to the south-east of Stralsund and occupied Wolgast as the first step toward an invasion of Mecklenburg. There, on August 12, he was intercepted by Wallenstein and routed. Early in 1629 peace negotiations were opened and on June 7 they were concluded by the Treaty of Lübeck. Nearly all the European powers were affected.

Wallenstein now had 125,000 troops under arms, and after Christian's defeat, as there was no enemy left in sight, he indiscriminately billeted them on friend and foe. Certain detachments were quartered in Saxony, and as this was done without the Elector's permission, John George, supported by Maximilian, appealed to the Emperor. Both feared the growing power of Wallenstein, and so also did Ferdinand, who was becoming little more than his puppet. But before the latter tackled this knotty problem, now that his power was supreme, he decided to carry out his long cherished wish–the return of the Church lands wrongfully usurped since 1555. Because he knew that no Diet would sanction this, he decided to effect it by imperial decree, and, on March 6, 1629, he promulgated his Edict of Restitution to a defenceless Germany.

But how to get rid of Wallenstein remained a problem, and although Ferdinand did not set out to solve it, his next act precipitated the solution. At the instigation of Spain he became involved in a war against the French duke of Mantua when he agreed to send troops to Italy, a decision that antagonized the Pope and divided the Catholic Church. This prompted Richelieu to arrange a truce between Sweden and Poland in order to release Gustavus as a Protestant champion against the Empire, and as the Swedish occupation of Stralsund and Pillau[1] would enable Gustavus to wage war on Poland with dangerous effect, Sigismund III of Poland agreed to a six-year truce, which was signed at Altmark on September 26, 1629.

Wallenstein, who was violently opposed to the Edict of Restitution because he saw that a quiescent Germany was essential in order to face Europe's hereditary foe, the Turks, began still further to increase his army, so that he might meet Gustavus should he intervene. But because of Ferdinand's Spanish agreement, in May, 1630, he was instructed to send 30,000 men to Italy. Next, Spain demanded Ferdinand's help to subdue the Dutch, and led by Maximilian the Electors refused to discuss the question as long as Wallenstein remained in power; John George further demanded the withdrawal of the Edict of Restitution.

By abandoning Wallenstein, Ferdinand might pacify the Catholic Electors, and by withdrawing the Edict he might bring Saxony and Brandenburg to heel. He decided on the former course, and on August 17, when at Regensburg, he discussed with his councillors how best he could dismiss his formidable general. Surprisingly enough, when Wallenstein was informed of the Emperor's wish he made no complaint, and on August 24 he tendered his resignation. Rid of Wallenstein, Ferdinand set aside all thoughts of revoking the Edict of Restitution, handed over the imperial army to Maximilian and Tilly, and reverted to the position he had been in at the opening of the war. This was the very moment when Gustavus, who on July 6 had landed his army at Peenemünde on the Island of Usedom, was consolidating his base in Pomerania.

[1] Pillau had been ceded by the Elector of Brandenburg to Gustavus in 1627.

CHAPTER 13

The Battles of Breitenfeld and Lützen, 1631 and 1632

The military importance of the two great battles fought by Gustavus Adolphus in Germany lies in that they stemmed from an improvement in tactics and leadership which was profoundly to influence the art of war. Therefore, before inquiring into the events out of which they arose, first it is as well briefly to review the development in land warfare which preceded them; next to take stock of Gustavus's generalship; and then to consider the tactical modifications he introduced.

Although there had been no lack of military inventions since the latter half of the Hundred Years War,[1] and men like Leonardo da Vinci (1452–1519) had even speculated on what were to become submarines, tanks, and aircraft, the main tactical problem before the introduction of cannon was not so much how to defeat an enemy in the field, but how to winkle him out of his fortifications. Not until the castle had been mastered during the second half of the fifteenth century, did the problem of how best to use firearms on the battlefield arise.

Its solution was indicated at the bloody battle of Ravenna, won by Gaston de Foix over the army of the Holy League in 1512, for in it artillery began to play a decisive part. But it was not until the introduction of the improved Spanish matchlock musket, first used at the siege of Parma in 1521, that musketeers set out to prove their worth. This new weapon was six feet long, weighed 15 lb., and was fired from a fork-shaped rest. Its tactical use was developed rapidly by the Marquis of Pescara. In 1522, at the battle of Bicocca, he demonstrated on a large scale the value of musketeers acting independently in the open, and for the first time

---

[1] The ollowing list gives some indication: Hand-grenades, 1382; smoke-balls, 1405; time match, 1405; case shot, 1410; corned gunpowder, 1429; fire balls, 1400–1450; matchlock or arquebus, 1450; bronze explosive shell, 1463; explosive bombs,1470; wheeled gun-carriage, about 1470; pistols, 1483; incendiary shell, 1487; rifling, 1520; wheellock and Spanish musket, 1521; improved hand-grenade, 1536; wheellock pistol, 1543; paper cartridges, 1560; a type of shrapnel shell, 1573; hot shot, 1575; common shell, 1588; fixed cartridges (powder and ball in one), 1590; rifled pistols, about 1592; and percussion fuze, 1596.

pikemen became no more than their auxiliaries. The year following, at Pavia, the steady shooting and manœuvring of Pescara's musketeers won for the Imperialists the most decisive battle of that generation; a battle which founded modern infantry fire tactics. Until the introduction of the bayonet, the musket and pike remained the dominant arms. In all this, it was the Spaniards who led the way, which to a large extent was because they had raised out of the veterans of the conquest of Granada professional bodies of soldiers known as *tercios*. Usually, these Spanish "battles" consisted of 2,000 to 3,000 foot soldiers, one-third musketeers and two-thirds pikemen, and as some of the *tercios* had for their honorary colonels princes of the royal house – the *Infantas* – the new foot soldiers became known as *infantaria* – infantry. In the sixteenth century these heavy "battles" were marshalled in oblongs of men 30 ranks deep with squares of musketeers at their corners, but by the opening of the seventeenth century, because of the progress made in artillery, their depth had frequently been reduced to 10 ranks.

Because of the increasing reliance on the pike, in order to protect the musketeers, cavalry charges became more and more restricted, with the result that the Spanish troopers were trained to rely more on the newly introduced wheellock pistol than on sword or lance. They were heavily armoured against musket fire and marshalled in deep squadrons which, rank by rank, rode up to the enemy pikemen and methodically fired their pistols *dans le tas*; each rank after firing wheeled and filed to the rear to reload.

The foot usually were massed in the centre with the field artillery in front covered by skirmishers, and the cavalry drawn up in rear or on the wings. Battles were almost invariably fought in parallel order, open ground was sought with, when possible, the sun and wind behind. Pursuit was seldom attempted and the Spanish baggage trains were usually enormous, accompanied by numerous non-combatants and women. All told, the Spanish tactics were slow, methodical, and cumbersome, yet nearly invincible against a less well-trained enemy.

At this date most other armies still largely relied upon mercenaries. In peacetime their leaders, who were professional soldiers, would keep in hand a small staff of experts in recruiting and training, and when they received a war contract would rapidly fill their ranks with men, regardless of race or religion. Switzerland and northern Italy were always ready to supply large numbers. The men took an oath to their personal leaders, and when captured or on termination of their contract, frequently changed sides. In winter these mercenary forces were usually disbanded, to be recruited again in the following spring for the next summer campaign. Compared with the well-trained and equipped *tercios*, they were often little more than an armed rabble.

Equally important was the influence of firearms on politics. Not only did they proletarianize war by enabling, as Cervantes (1547–1616) says: "a base cowardly hand to take the life of the bravest gentleman," but they centralized power in the hands of the monarchy. The cost of artillery and the expense entailed in equipping large numbers of arquebusiers soon became too great to be borne by any individual, and in consequence had to be met by the State. Further, this concentration of power in secular hands raised the monarchy above the Church; war became a political instrument and ceased to be a moral trial. The seventeenth century saw the rise of standing armies, the development of competitive armaments, and the introduction of the balance of power as a policy. Military service ceased to be the perquisite of a class and began to be a national profession. The development of massfighting, if not of mass armies, was a characteristic of the age, and it became manifest in the Thirty Years War.

Because the Spanish military system was universally copied by the European powers, it was the Spanish type of army that Gustavus was called upon to meet.

Gustavus was the eldest son of Charles IX of Sweden (1604–1611) and was born at Stockholm on December 19, 1594. His grandfather was the great Gustavus I, who founded the Vasa dynasty, a commercially-minded man who had favoured the middle class against the nobles and had introduced the Protestant religion into Sweden. Gustavus Adolphus succeeded his father in 1611. That same year he experienced his first taste of war against the Danes. Like Alexander the Great, he set out on his military career when still a boy. In many ways, as more than one writer has noted,[1] he bore a resemblance to the great Macedonian; he

---

[1] Gindely (*History of the Thirty Years' War*, 1884, vol. II, p. 41) says: "When we look around us for a historical person with whom he can be compared, we find but one – Alexander the Great." And Dodge (*Gustavus Adolphus*, 1890, vol. I, pp. 73 and 401) writes: "Few young monarchs have ever been so harassed on taking up the reins of government. Gustavus's situation recalls forcibly that of Alexander" . . . "Except Alexander, no great captain showed the true love of battle as it burned in the breast of Gustavus Adolphus. Such was his own contempt of death that his army could not but fight."

largely created an epoch, blazing the trail for France, as Alexander had done for Rome, and he also resembled him in character. Though reserved in small things, he was passionate in great. A fine horseman and athlete, he possessed a brilliant imagination, a restless temperament and a love for perilous adventures; in battle he was always in the van. Of quick temper, he was nevertheless forgiving: "I bear my subjects' errors with patience," he once said, "but they too must put up with my quick speech."[1] Faithful to his friends, he was merciful to his enemies; a man of high convictions he never sacrificed principle for advantage. Wise in his choice of subordinates, he was also wise in the selection of his heroes, among whom Maurice of Nassau was his special favourite. A student of his opponents, he was also a student of history and his favourite books were the *De Jure Belli ac Pacis* of Hugo Grotius and the *Anabasis* of Xenophon. In his studies he was helped by his remarkable gift of languages; for, besides his mother tongue, he understood Latin, Greek, German, Dutch, Italian, Polish, and Russian. In religion he was firmly Protestant, and in politics passionately Swedish; he never lost sight of his dominant aspiration—the *Dominium Maris Baltici*.

As a general, Gustavus is among the few great Captains, and Napoleon says of him: "*Gustave-Adolphe était animé des principes d'Alexandre, d'Annibal, de César.*"[2] His greatness lay in the novelty of his ideas and the courage with which he applied them. Since the age of 17 he had constant experience of war, and was always learning, inventing, improving, and daring to do. For him it was possible to achieve so many things in war precisely because the generality of men supposed them impracticable. His main contribution to his art was that he was the first general during the modern age who realized that mobility is founded upon discipline, and discipline upon efficient administration and leadership. Most of his officers were young men—he did not like generals of 60 and over—and they were compelled to look after their men. Gindely says: "As he provided food, so did he also clothing for his men. He furnished them with fur-lined coats, he kept tents in readiness to protect them against the inclement weather, and secure them a more humane existence. Low and slanderous speech, drunkenness and gaming were banished by rigid penalties from the camp-life. Nor did he tolerate loose women; he insisted that those girls who

---

[1] Quoted from *Gustavus Adolphus*, Theodore Ayrault Dodge, vol. 1, p. 400.
[2] *Correspondance*, vol. XXXI, p. 354.

followed the army should each be connected with some soldier by marriage."[1] Furthermore, he was one of the first since the classical age to base tactics upon weapon-power instead of on convention. As a general, Chemnitz sums him up as follows:

"No one ever equalled Gustavus Adolphus in leading his army against an enemy, or conducting a retreat so as to prevent loss, nor in encamping his troops, or strengthening his camp with field works. No one knew fortification, attack, and defence so well as he did. No one could divine the intention of his enemy, or take advantage of the chances of war, more ably than he did. He took in at a glance the whole position, and drew up his army so as to profit by every opportunity. The three points that he exceeded all others in were tactics, organisation, and arms."[2]

Another contemporary estimate of him reads:

"He did animate his soldiers rather by fighting, than exhorting; nor did he challenge to himself any advantage above the meanest of them, but honour and command. . . . He well understood that faith and loyalty are not to be expected where we impose thraldom and servitude, and therefore at times he would be familiar, as well with the common soldier, as the commander. His invention and execution of all military stratagems were ever twins; for in all his conquests he owed as much to his celerity, as valour. When his foes were in their tents securely discoursing of him, as afar off, he, like a wolf, broke into their fable, to their irrecoverable astonishment. They could not withstand the force of his fame, much less that of his arms. One feather more I must add, without which his victories had not been fully plumed, nor could have soared so high, and that was this: he never persuaded any man to an enterprise, in which he would not himself make one. He taught them as well by hand, as tongue. I may add, that neither antiquity can, nor posterity ever shall produce a prince so patient, of all military wants, as of meat, drink, warmth, sleep, etc. . . . All his great achievements were ever attended by devotion within, and circumspection without. He first praised God, and then provided for man, at once having an eye on his enemies' next designs, and his soldiers' present necessities. The greatest of his glories, purchased with blood and sweat, could neither change the estate of his mind, or copy of his countenance. The true greatness of his spirit was such, that in all his actions he placed ostentation behind,

---

[1] *History of the Thirty Years' War*, vol. II, p. 435.
[2] Quoted from *A Précis of Modern Tactics*, Colonel Robert Home (1892), p. 226.

and conscience before him, and sought not the reward of a good deed from fame, but from the deed itself. . . ."[1]

Though others equalled him in tactical ability and strategical foresight, probably no single soldier, with the exception of Philip of Macedon, excelled him as a military organizer, and so all-embracing were his reforms that he created the epoch of modern warfare. Not only did he reorganize each arm and combine their tactics, but he founded his whole system on interior economy and an efficient service of supply. He realized that the military methods of his day were out of date, for every army had copied the Spanish system without change, and by the opening of the Thirty Years War it had become extremely cumbersome.

Gustavus reviewed military organization as he found it and saw clearly that the superior weapon was the musket. Accordingly, he decreased the number of pikemen, shortened their pikes from 16 to 11 ft., lightened their armour, and combined them with the musketeers to form companies, exclusive of officers, of 72 musketeers and 54 pikemen, which, with the pikes in the centre, stood in line in files six deep. Four companies formed a battalion, eight a regiment, and two to four regiments a brigade. In each of these formations the right and left wings were composed of musketeers and the centre of pikemen. The musket he lightened in order to dispense with the crutch or rest. By degrees he substituted the wheellock for the matchlock, introduced paper cartridges, and provided his men with bandoliers to carry them.

He employed two types of cavalry, cuirassiers and dragoons; the former were partially armoured and the latter were mounted infantry. The former were formed into squadrons of three instead of 10 ranks deep, and were trained to charge at the gallop instead of the trot, with their pistols used only in the mêlée. They rode in lines of squadrons, one behind the other, or else chequerwise, the last line was the reserve. Though Gustavus marshalled his cavalry on the wings of his infantry, which was the usual procedure, he also placed them behind each infantry line and frequently mixed parties of "commanded musketeers" with them. Generally his cavalry charged under cover of the smoke of the artillery bombardment, and once they had driven back the enemy skirmishers, they retired to allow the infantry to advance. Next, under cover of another bombardment, they charged again, this time on the

---

[1] *The Great and Famous Battle of Lützen* . . . translated from the French, printed in 1633 and published in *The Harleian Miscellany* (1809), vol. IV, pp. 197–209.

enemy's flanks to drive them in on the centre and to create confusion; for the maintenance of an ordered and unbroken front was
essential to success.

Yet, in spite of the excellence of his infantry and cavalry, it
was on the power of artillery[1] that his battles were founded. As
Mahomet II was the first great siege gunner, Gustavus was the
first great field gunner. In order to render the gun mobile, he
shortened it, lightened its carriage, and reduced the number of
calibres. He adopted three main types—siege, field, and regimental. The first two consisted of 24-, 12- and six-pounders, the
siege pieces weighed 60-, 30- and 15-cwt., and the field pieces
27-, 18- and 12-cwt. The regimental pieces were light four-pounder
guns, two to a regiment, and were provided with fixed ammunition in wooden cases which enabled them to fire eight rounds to
every six shots of a musketeer. They replaced his famous leather
guns, which he had used in his Polish campaign of 1628–1629.[2]
The projectiles usually fired were grape and canister by field and
regimental guns, and round shot by siege.

For supply Gustavus depended upon well-found and fortified
magazines, to which were attached a regular staff of commissaries.
The baggage wagons he reduced in number and allowed 10 to a
squadron and eight to a company. Promotion was by seniority;
punishments were humane and no flogging was permitted. His
Chief of Staff was General Kniphausen, and his General of
Artillery, Torstensson, a remarkable soldier, who, in 1630, was
only 30 years of age.

Wallenstein's advance along the Baltic brought Gustavus Adolphus into the war, the nature of which he clearly grasped, for at
about that time he wrote to his Chancellor, Axel Oxenstierna
(1583–1654): "All the wars that are on foot in Europe have been
fused together, and have become a single war."

Four years earlier, in 1624, James I and Louis XIII had approached him; but as his terms were no divided command, an
advance of payment for his troops, and the occupation of two
ports, one on the Baltic and the other on the North Sea, the two
kings found them too onerous and turned to Denmark. Charles I,
who succeeded to the throne of England on March 27, 1625,

---

[1] His cavalry and artillery were mainly Swedish, and his infantry consisted of a
nucleus of Swedes, the rest were Scots, Germans, and other soldiers of fortune.
[2] They were invented by Colonel Wurmbrant, and consisted of a copper tube
bound with iron rings and rope and covered with leather. Without its carriage, the
gun weighed 90 lb.

agreed to support the war, which was the beginning of his undoing. But when Wallenstein overran Schleswig and Jutland, gained Mecklenburg and laid siege to Stralsund, Gustavus saw that the design of the House of Habsburg was to master the Baltic and the Sound. Therefore, at Altmark, on September 26, 1629, he had patched up a six-year truce with Poland and had written to Oxenstierna: "If we await our enemy in Sweden, all might be lost by a defeat. By a fortunate commencement of a war in Germany everything is to be gained. We must carry the war abroad. Sweden must not be doomed to behold a hostile banner upon her soil."[1] It was for this reason that he sent a Swedish garrison to Stralsund, so that he might secure a landing on the Pomeranian coast.

France also was perturbed. Soon after La Rochelle surrendered, in October, 1628, and the Huguenot rising was at an end, Richelieu sent an ambassador to Sweden to gain Gustavus's help. His plan was to make Gustavus the tool of French aggrandizement: the war was not to be carried into the interior of Germany, but instead was to be waged in the area of the Emperor's hereditary possessions, that is to say up the Oder into Silesia, Bohemia, Moravia, and Austria, and Gustavus was to be subsidized by the French, English, and Dutch. But the Swedish king had no intention of playing the part of stalking-horse to France. He was free of his Polish war, he realized that because of the severity of his rule Wallenstein's stock was falling, and he knew that the Edict of Restitution had terrified the Protestant Electors. He speedily prepared for war. Thus it came about that, on July 6, 1630, he landed on the island of Usedom at the head of 13,000 men, later to be reinforced to 40,000. From Usedom he advanced on Stettin and compelled Bogislav Duke of Pomerania to surrender the city to him. Thence he marched into Mecklenburg, reinstated its deposed dukes and, early in August, sent a detachment of Swedes under Colonel Falkenberg to help to hold Magdeburg.

Once established in Pomerania, Gustavus was faced by a stupendous task. His resources were insignificant compared with his enemy's[2] and no powerful allies welcomed him. John George of Saxony held aloof and throughout was his secret enemy, for he stood for the solidarity of Germany and looked upon Gustavus as a foreign conqueror, and the Elector of Brandenburg offered him

---

[1] Quoted from *Lives of the Warriors of The Thirty Years' War*, Lieut.-Gen. the Hon. Sir Edward Cust (1865), part I, pp. 142–143.

[2] In 1630 the population of Sweden and Finland was about 1,500,000; that of the Empire some 17,000,000.

no support. Had Ferdinand withdrawn the Edict of Restitution at this moment, he would have won over both and have rendered Gustavus's task impossible. Further, Denmark, though neutral, was hostile; France shifty; Holland jealous; England untrustworthy; and Poland as "bitter as gall". This situation should be borne in mind, for out of it was developed the strategy of the next two years. This was governed by three factors.

Firstly, it must be realized that one of the reasons why Germany was divided into so many small princedoms was the original lack of Roman roads east of the Rhine. Secondly, because Gustavus's main base was in Sweden, before he could move inland it was essential for him to gain control of the Baltic coast in order to secure his advanced base in Pomerania as well as his sea communications. Thirdly, the main Catholic power lay west of the Rhine and south of the Danube–that is, in the old Roman territory–the communications of which enabled Spain and Austria to join hands about the middle Rhine. In part to compensate for this advantage, the main reaches of the great rivers, the Oder, Elbe, and Weser–the thoroughfares of the day–ran through Protestant lands and into a sea which was surrounded by Protestant powers.

Gustavus understood this clearly enough, but it was impracticable for him to move south until his base was secure. Winter now intervened, and though the Electors continued to remain obdurate, France came to terms with Sweden and a treaty between the two countries was signed at Bärwalde on January 23, 1631, by which Gustavus was to provide an army of 30,000 foot and 6,000 horse in return for a lump sum of 12,000 thalers and an annual subsidy of 400,000 thalers for the following five years. Gustavus was to guarantee freedom of worship for Catholics and to leave unmolested the lands of Maximilian.

The spring campaign of 1631 was opened by Tilly, who stormed New Brandenburg while his fiery lieutenant, Count Pappenheim, besieged Magdeburg. In order to draw off the former, Gustavus moved on Frankfort-on-the-Oder, which he occupied on April 13; but the crafty Walloon did not follow him but marched on Magdeburg and joined Pappenheim.

Frankfort occupied, Gustavus's one idea was to succour Magdeburg; but he could not set out on an unauthorized march through Brandenburg and Saxony lest either, or both their Electors should fall upon his rear. After much argument he obtained George William's permission to occupy Küstrin and then was forced to spend the next three weeks in haggling before he could gain his permission to enter Spandau. Meanwhile John George of Saxony was not to be moved, and as he commanded an army 40,000 strong Gustavus was compelled to leave Magdeburg to its fate.

Tilly, at the head of 25,000 men, arrived at Magdeburg, and with Pappenheim pressed the siege. On May 20 the city was stormed, sacked and set on fire; 30,000 people died in the flames.[1] At once, as Professor Gardiner writes, "A great fear fell upon the minds of all Protestant men," and Gustavus used terror to counter-act terror. He marched on Berlin and at the mouth of his cannon compelled George William of Brandenburg to renounce his neutrality. Joined by William of Hesse-Cassel and Prince Bernhard of Saxe-Weimar, Gustavus entrenched himself at Werben and repulsed an attack of Tilly's, when unexpectedly fortune played into his hands. Cut off on all sides and with his army starving, Tilly invaded Saxony at the head of 40,000 men, threatened to deal with Leipzig as he had with Magdeburg, and compelled its surrender. At once John George abandoned his neutrality and entered into alliance with Gustavus. The two allies met at Düben on the Mulde on September 15. Their combined armies numbered about 47,000 men and the following day they set out for Leipzig to offer battle.

As Düben was only 25 miles to the north of Leipzig, retreat for Tilly was out of the question, and as his troops, now in a land of plenty after months of starvation, were out of hand, his best course would have been to hold fast to Leipzig, to stand a siege, and to await reinforcements. But Pappenheim, who considered him senile, thought differently. On September 16 he set out on a reconnaissance during which, to force Tilly's hand, he sent back a message that he had sighted the enemy moving south from Düben, and that, as it was not possible for him to return without great risk, he must immediately be supported. Thus he engineered the fateful battle of Breitenfeld.

Tilly moved out of Leipzig and took up a position some five miles north of it, on a slight rise with the village of Breitenfeld on his left and that of Stenberg on his right. The field was known as "God's acre," because in former times other battles had been fought there. According to an old topographical work it was a "pleasant and fruitful plain, abounding with all necessaries and pleasures, constantly mowed twice, and sometimes thrice a year,

---

[1] It was not destroyed deliberately; Tilly needed it badly to supply his troops.

besides having pleasant woods, and many fine orchards, with all sorts of fruit."[1]

Tilly, an old general, born in 1559, was a sound and conventional soldier. Quoting Marshal de Grammont's memoirs, James Grant describes him as: "Short in stature, he was meagre and terrible in aspect; his cheeks were sunken, his nose long and pointed, his eyes fierce and dark. When not sheathed in gilded armour, he usually wore a slashed doublet of green silk, a preposterously broad-brimmed and conical hat, adorned by a red ostrich feather; a long beard, a long dagger and mighty Toledo. . . ."[2] A past master in the Spanish tactics, Tilly set up his battle order in one or possibly two lines of *tercios*; 17 great squares of foot of 1,500 to 2,000 men each with heavy columns of cavalry on their right and left. His army probably numbered 40,000 men, of which a quarter was cavalry. He commanded the infantry and allotted the left wing cavalry to Pappenheim and the right wing to Fürstenberg and Isolani. He had only 26 guns. The heavy guns he placed between his centre and right, and the light in front of his centre. Monro says he had advantage "of Ground, Wind and Sunne."[3]

On September 16, Gustavus, at the head of his army, came upon Tilly from the north and bivouacked one mile from the Imperialist position. He spent the night in his travelling coach discussing the forthcoming battle with Sir John Hepburn, Field-Marshal Horn, Field-Marshal Baner, and General Teuffel, all sheathed in complete mail.

The following morning, "As the Larke begunne to peepe,"[4] the trumpets in the Swedish bivouac sounded to horse and the drums called a march. The entire plain was covered with a haze through which the Swedes could see the line of red fires which marked Tilly's position. Prayers were said, then Gustavus drew out his order of battle in parallel order to his enemy's; but instead of making use of heavy battles, he marshalled his infantry in brigades or half brigades in such a way that the musketeers were covered by the pikemen and could file between the ranks of the latter, deliver their volley and retire. Thus, instead of an immovable square castle, says an old writer, "each brigade was like a little movable

---

[1] Quoted from *Memoirs and Adventures of Sir John Hepburn*, James Grant (1851), p. 95.
[2] *Ibid.*, p. 71.
[3] *Monro His Expedition*, etc., Colonel Robert Monro (1637), part II, p. 64.
[4] *Ibid.*, part II, p. 63.

fortress with its curtains and ravelins, and each part would be able to come to the assistance of the other."[1]

He drew up his army with the Swedes in the centre and on the right, the Saxons held the left. Of the Saxon formation nothing is known; the Swedish was as follows: In the centre were drawn up four brigades of foot in first line, supported by a cavalry regiment and Monro's and Ramsay's infantry brigades; in second line were three infantry brigades, including Hepburn's Scots,[2] supported by one cavalry regiment; the whole under Teuffel and Hall. In reserve behind the centre were two regiments of cavalry. The right wing, under Baner, consisted of six cavalry regiments in first line with bodies of musketeers between them; in support there was one regiment, and in second line four regiments. To the left wing, under Horn, were allotted three regiments of cavalry in first line with musketeers, and two regiments in second line. The regimental pieces were drawn up in front of the regiments and brigades, and the heavy artillery, under Torstensson, was massed in front of the centre. On the left of Field-Marshal Horn stood the Saxons. The whole array, probably 47,000 men, pinned green branches in their hats; the Imperialists wore white ribands. The Swedish battle-cry was *Godt mit us*, and their enemy's, *Sancta Maria*.

Monro states that Gustavus "ordered his Armie, and directed every supreame Officer of the Field, on their particular charge and stations committed unto them, for that day: as also he acquainted them severally, of the forme he was to fight unto, and he appointed Plottons of Musketiers, by fifties, which were commanded by sufficient officers to attend on several Regiments of horse, and he instructed the Officers how to behave themselves in discharging their duties on service. Likewise he directed the Officers belonging to the Artillery, how to carry themselves. . . ."[3]

"With Trumpets sounding, Drummes beating, and Colours advanced and flying," the battle opened, and soon, as Monro says, ". . . the enemy was thundering amongst us, with the noise and roaring whistling of Cannon-Bullets; where you may imagine the hurt was great; the sound of such musick being scarce worth hearing . . . then our Cannon begun to roare, great and small, paying the enemy with the like coyne, which thundering continued alike on both sides for two hours and a half, during which

[1] Quoted from *Gustavus Adolphus*, C. R. L. Fletcher (1923), p. 190.
[2] There were many Scots in the Swedish Army, including an "Anthony Haig o ⌐ Bemerside"—a spirited young cavalier.
[3] *Monro His Expedition*, part II, p. 64.

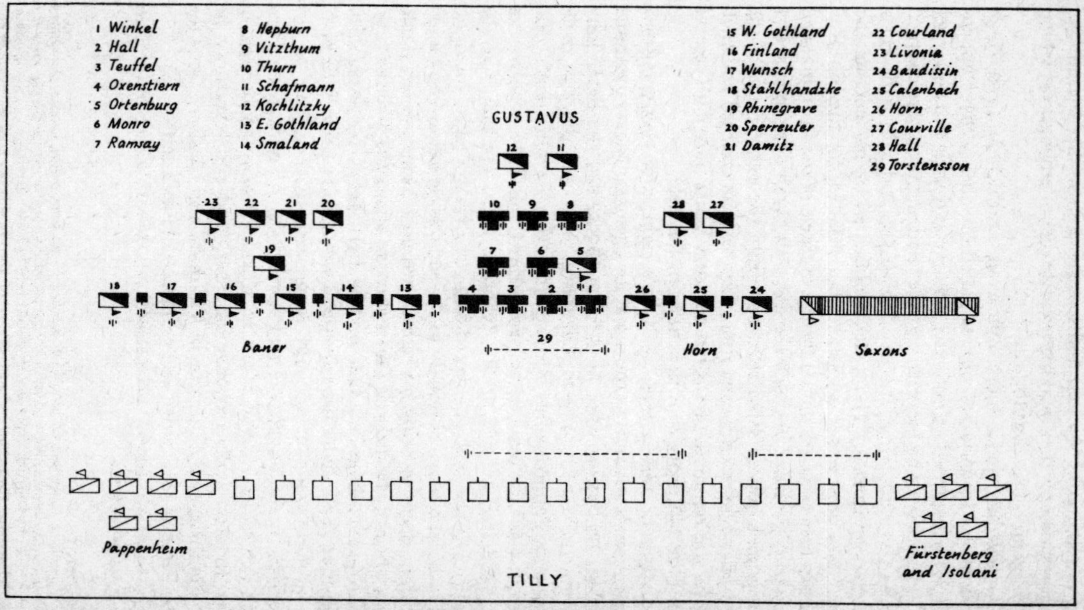

23. BATTLE OF BREITENFELD, 1631

time, our Battailes of horse and foot stood firme like a wall, the Cannon now and then making great breaches amongst us, which was diligently looked unto. . . ."[1]

The Swedish guns, more numerous and which fired three rounds to the Imperialists' one, so galled the enemy that Pappenheim, a high-spirited commander, could stand their fire no longer and, without waiting for orders, at the head of 5,000 horse charged the Swedish right wing. It was a foolish act, and Tilly, who knew it, exclaimed in rage: "They have robbed me of my honour and glory." Not only was it a mistake, but it failed, for the pistols of the horsemen were no match for the muskets of the "commanded musketeers"[2] placed between the Swedish cavalry regiments, and these groups poured salvo after salvo into the dense ranks of the Imperialist horsemen. Seven times Pappenheim charged and each time he was repulsed; on the last occasion Baner hurled his reserve upon him and drove him in rout from the field.

Fürstenberg and Isolani, on Tilly's right, apparently mistook Pappenheim's advance as the signal for a general engagement and charged the Saxons who, at the first shock, fled the field. John George spurred his way to Eilenburg. Not only did this compensate for Pappenheim's mistaken initiative, for Gustavus's total strength was now reduced by over a third, but Tilly, who was an able tactician, at once took advantage of it. He saw that the Swedish left was now uncovered and was overlapped by his right, and ordered a move obliquely to the right to be followed by a left wheel, in order to bring his right down on his enemy's left flank. Simultaneously he ordered Fürstenberg to attack the Swedish rear.

The probabilities are that had he been faced by antagonists other than the Swedes the movement would have proved decisive. But as Gustavus's men could manœuvre twice as fast as the Imperialists, the advantage was not Tilly's. At once King Gustavus Adolphus ordered Horn to wheel his wing to the left in order to meet Tilly's change of front, and simultaneously he brought forward the brigades of Vitzthum and Hepburn from the second line of the centre and reinforced Horn's left.

The Scots advanced in dense column. Monro's account of their action is as follows.

---

[1] *Ibid.*, part II, p. 65.

[2] It should be remembered that, in accordance with the Spanish tactics, the charge was carried out at the trot and with the pistol, the sword being used only after the enemy's ranks had been disorganized by pistol fire. The Swedish charge was the opposite; it was delivered at the gallop and with the sword, the pistol being used for the mêlée.

"The enemies Battaile standing firm, looking on us at a neere distance, and seeing the other Briggads and ours wheeling about, making front unto them, they were prepared with a firm resolution to receive us with a salvo of Cannon and Muskets; but our small Ordinance [regimental pieces] being twice discharged amongst them, and before we stirred, we charged them with a salvo of muskets, which was repaied, and incontinent our Briggad advancing unto them with push of pike, putting one of their battailes in disorder, fell on the execution, so that they were put to the route.

"I having commanded the right wing of our musketiers, being my Lord of *Rhees* [Reay's] and *Lumsdells* [Lumsden's], we advanced on the other body of the enemies, which defended their Cannon, and beating them from their Cannon, we were masters of their Cannon, and consequently of the field, but the smoake being great, the dust being raised, we were as in a darke cloud, not seeing the halfe of our actions, much less discerning, either the way of our enemies, or yet the rest of our Briggads: whereupon, having a drummer by me, I caused him to beate the *Scots* march, till it cleared up, which recollected our friends unto us, and dispersed our enemies being overcome; so that the Briggad coming together, such as were alive missed their dead and hurt Camerades."[1]

While this action was fought, Gustavus seized the opportunity to deliver the decisive blow. He rode over to the right and ordered Baner to send the West Gothland Horse down the Swedish front to charge the left flank of Tilly's battles. Then Gustavus placed himself at the head of four regiments and bore up the slope where the enemy's guns still stood. He swept through them, fell upon the left flank of Tilly's line, and pounded the Imperialists with their own cannon. Simultaneously Torstensson wheeled round the reserve artillery and poured its shot into the dense Spanish squares. A desperate fight ensued; but its end was certain. Soon the Imperialists lost all order and stampeded. They lost 7,000 killed, 6,000 wounded and captured, all their artillery, 90 flags, and the whole of their train. Gustavus's losses, including the Saxons's, "did not exceed three thousand men," most "killed by the enemies Cannon."[2]

The bulk of the Swedish army then bivouacked: "Our bonefiers," writes Monro, "were made of the enemies Ammunition waggons, and Pikes left, for want of good fellowes to use them; and all this night our brave Camerades, the *Saxons*, were making use of

[1] *Ibid.*, part II, p. 66. [2] *Ibid.*, part II, p. 67.

their heeles in flying, thinking all was lost, they made booty of our waggons and goods [the Swedish supply and baggage column], too good a recompence for Cullions that had left their Duke. . . ." But 1,500 Swedish horsemen did not halt, and Gustavus at their head pursued Tilly's fugitives; captured 3,000 at Merseburg on September 19, and on September 21 abandoned the pursuit at Halle.

Thus the battle ended, epoch-making not only because it was the first great test and trial of the new tactics against the old, and therefore the first great land battle of the modern age, a victory of mobility and fire-power over numbers and push of pike, but because, for good or for evil, it shattered the reviving forces of the League and decided that Germany was not to become a Catholic power under the House of Austria. It was, as Professor Gardiner says: "the grave of the Edict of Restitution" and "the Naseby of Germany."[1] Perhaps also, as Lord Bryce writes, it "saved Europe from an impending reign of the Jesuits."[2]

From September 17, 1631, until his death, Gustavus became the hero of the Protestant world and the "common men" in the north of Germany looked up to him "as a redeemer, and as such deified him."[3] He gave spirit and direction to the war, without which the Protestant cause would have collapsed and the history of the western world would have been different. With insight Professor Gardiner writes:

"Those tactics were, after all, but the military expression of the religious and political system in defence of which they were used. Those solid columns just defeated were the types of what human nature was to become under the Jesuit organisation. The individual was swallowed up in the mass. As Tilly had borne down by sheer weight of his veterans, adventurers like Mansfeld and Christian of Brunswick, so the renewed Catholic discipline had borne down the wrangling theologians who had stepped into the places of Luther and Melanchthon. But now an army had arisen to prove that order and obedience were weak unless they were supported by individual intelligence. The success of the principle upon which its operations were based could not be confined to mere fighting. It would make its way in morals and politics, in literature and science."[4]

Breitenfeld fought and won, the question has often been asked:

---

[1] *The Thirty Years' War*, pp. 139–140.
[2] *The Holy Roman Empire*, James Viscount Bryce (1928), p. 383.
[3] *The Thirty Years' War* Anton Gindely, vol. II, p. 85.
[4] *The Thirty Years' War*, p. 140.

"Why did not Gustavus march on Vienna and impose his will upon Ferdinand?" Several historians consider that he should have done so, and Folard compares him with Hannibal after Cannae. But the comparison is inapt, for circumstances were entirely different. Firstly, the road which ran to Vienna was bad; it passed through the forests of the Erzgebirge and the devastated lands of Bohemia, and winter was near. Secondly, Vienna was not the capital of a united nation, but the residence of a shadow emperor, therefore it possessed even less political significance than Madrid did during the Peninsula War (1808–1814). Thirdly, Gustavus, hundreds of miles from his base, could not afford to risk a rising behind him; the loyalty of the Electors of Brandenburg and Saxony was suspect and Bavaria would hug his flank. Fourthly, by moving to the Rhine, as eventually he did, though he would upset Richelieu by carrying war into Catholic territories, he would be able to base himself on the Protestant Palatinate and also to supply his army, for "the Priests Lane," as it was called – Würzburg, Bamberg, Fulda, Cologne, Mainz, Worms, and Spires – included the richest districts in Germany, and they had furnished many men and much money to the armies of the League. Lastly, and not least in importance, by occupying the Palatinate he would cut the Spanish connexion between the Netherlands and Italy. Therefore he decided to advance on the Rhine, while the Elector of Saxony carried war into Bohemia.

Gustavus occupied Würzburg on October 18, pushed on to Frankfort-on-Main, and thence to Mainz which, after a two-day siege, surrendered. Within three months of his great victory he had subdued the whole of the Rhineland; had formed alliances and appointed governments; had forced neutrality on all the Catholic princes of the Rhine; had driven the Spanish troops back to the Netherlands; and was firmly established on both banks of the middle Rhine, in Alsatia, the Lower Palatinate, and Cologne, much to the annoyance of Richelieu, who was alarmed by this prodigiously rapid and thorough conquest. "Means must be devised", he said, "to check this impetuous Visigoth, since his successes will be fatal to France as to the Emperor." Nor were his alarms unfounded, for Gustavus turned definitely toward the formation of a *Corpus Evangelicorum*, a federation of Protestant princes under his leadership. This meant the destruction of the Imperial system, which Richelieu did not want destroyed, but made impotent.

Set upon this idea, in the spring of 1632 Gustavus advanced against Tilly, who had recruited another army since Breitenfeld and, joined by the Duke of Lorraine with 12,000 men, headed some 40,000 men in all. Gustavus crossed the Danube at Donau-wörth and caught up with the enemy on the river Lech. There, under cover of a smoke cloud and an artillery bombardment, he bridged the river and defeated Tilly on April 16. Tilly was severely wounded and died a fortnight later.

Ever since he had dismissed Wallenstein, Ferdinand had regretted the act, and no sooner had it taken effect than he contemplated his recall, in spite of the fact that he feared this formidable man who, though typical of his age, could see beyond it. Wallenstein's aim apparently was to consolidate the Empire under a *fainéant* monarch with himself as Mayor of the Palace. To accomplish this end, Wallenstein saw that the religious disputes must cease; that tolerance must be established, and that, in order to govern a tolerant State, money was the instrument which alone could bit and bridle the greeds of men. He based everything on calculation. Astrologer, man of business, utterly without morals and mercenary, he accumulated enormous wealth. Silent, reserved, mysterious, no man dared question him. He was the typical product of the power-age then dawning, and the kind of man who in days to come was to be venerated and honoured as a captain of industry or a banker prince.[1]

In desperation, Ferdinand turned to him again and Wallenstein imposed the most drastic terms:[2] absolute and unconditional control of the army; complete subservience of the Emperor, who was to issue no orders without his consent; control of all confiscated territories; the speedy revocation of the Edict of Restitution; and probably also an Elector's hat. These terms were accepted, and the Czech came back as the "General of the Baltic and Oceanic Seas" to deliver Ferdinand from the hands of the king of the Baltic and the Protestant territories.

Wallenstein's first action was an attempt to win over John

[1] When, in January, 1622, Ferdinand II debased the coinage by 75 per cent. of its value, Hans de Witte and others carried out a gigantic fraud by reducing it by a further one-tenth of its value. Wallenstein at once took advantage of this. "He was not fastidious about his means; they consisted in the robbing of an unfortunate female cousin, and in the purchase of a great share of the confiscated lands which he paid for chiefly in debased coin." (See Gindely's *The Thirty Years' War*, vol. i, pp. 289–290 and 380.)
[2] The full terms are not known; see *The Thirty Years' War*, C. V. Wedgwood (1938), p. 315.

George of Saxony, and his second to shake the faith of George William of Brandenburg in the Swedish cause. But he did not succeed and in April, 1632, he marched into Bohemia, then occupied by the Saxons. He seized Prague and forced the Saxons to retire, and, on June 27, united his army with the forces of Maximilian of Bavaria and so raised his total strength to 60,000. He moved on Amberg and came into collision with a Swedish force at Neumark; whereon Gustavus withdrew to Nuremberg. He was followed by Wallenstein who, on July 16, arrived at Fürth, in its immediate vicinity, and there entrenched.

For weeks the two armies faced each other, while "all Germany and all Europe," as Gindely writes, "waited with anxiety and hope for news."[1] On September 4, supplies were short and Gustavus assaulted his opponent's position to be repulsed at a loss of some 3,000 men. Fourteen days later, when sickness had claimed thousands of his troops, Gustavus abandoned the siege and decided to march on Vienna in order to draw Wallenstein away from Saxony. But the latter saw through his enemy's plan, and instead of following him he set out for Saxony, while Maximilian retired with the remnants of his forces to defend Bavaria. Next, Wallenstein sent word to Holk and Pappenheim, then on the Weser, to join him with the intention to effect a general concentration against Saxony and to drive John George out of the war.

Directly this became apparent, John George frantically appealed to Gustavus to come to his aid. The king was already on his way, and on October 22 was back in Nuremberg. On November 2 he was joined by Berhnard of Saxe-Weimar at Arnstadt, and on November 8 he occupied the Kösen defile at Naumburg, from where he urged John George, whose army was at Torgau, to join him with all available forces.

In the meantime Leipzig had been occupied by Holk, and with winter imminent Wallenstein, who assumed that Gustavus would call off the campaign and go into winter quarters, entrenched his army around Lützen. To prevent overcrowding, he sent Pappenheim and his cavalry to occupy Halle.

Though, thus far, Wallenstein's defensive strategy had got the better of his adversary, in face of so astute a general as Gustavus this division of his army was a risky decision. When, on November 14, Gustavus learnt of it, he decided to bring his enemy to battle and in spite of his own numerical inferiority.

[1] *The Thirty Years' War*, vol. II, p. 135.

At one o'clock on the morning of November 15 he set out for Pegau to unite with the Saxons. There he halted for four hours, but as nothing was heard of them he marched for Lützen in the hope that he would surprise his enemy while still divided, but the road was so bad that he was much delayed. At Rippach he fell in with a body of Croats and scattered them after a tough fight. That night he lodged "in the playne feildes, about an English mile from Litzen, where the enimies randavow was,"[1] and there held a council of war. Though Kniphausen was for manœuvre and Bernhard of Saxe-Weimar for attack, Gustavus had already made up his mind. He said that "the die was now cast; that he could not bear to have Wallenstein under his beard and not make a swoop upon him," because, as he explained: "I long to unearth him, and see how he can acquit himself in a campaign country."[2]

In his enemy's camp Wallenstein, afflicted with an attack of gout which necessitated his being carried in a sedan chair, "spent that whole night in digging and intrenching, in embattling his army, and planting his artillery. . . ." for he "was infinitely desirous to avoid the combat."[3] When he learnt of Gustavus's proximity, at 2 a.m., on November 16, he sent an urgent message to Pappenheim. "The enemy is advancing," he wrote. "Sir, let everything else be, and hurry with all your forces and artillery back to me. You must be here by tomorrow morning—he is already over the pass [of Rippach]."[4]

The plain of Lützen, upon which the two armies now lay bivouacked, is low and flat, and across it from south-west to north-east runs the Leipzig Road, built on a raised causeway, and flanked on each side with a ditch; and about two miles east of Lützen runs the Flossgraben, a small, sluggish stream, fordable in most places. Wallenstein, who intended to fight a purely defensive battle as he had done at Nuremberg, marshalled his order of battle in one line, a little north of the Leipzig Road; his right flank rested on a slight rise of ground immediately north of Lützen, upon which were some windmills, and his left rested upon the Flossgraben. The ditches along the Leipzig Road he dug into trenches and lined with musketeers. His exact strength is not

[1] "George Fleetwood's Letter to His Father," *The Camden Miscellany* (1847), vol. I, p. 6.

[2] Quoted by Cust in *Lives of the Warriors of the Thirty Years' War*, part I, p. 211.

[3] "The Great and Famous Battle of Lützen. . . ." *The Harleian Miscellany*, vol. IV, p. 201.

[4] Quoted from *Gustavus Adolphus*, C. R. L. Fletcher, p. 277. This letter, drenched in Pappenheim's blood, is to be seen in Vienna.

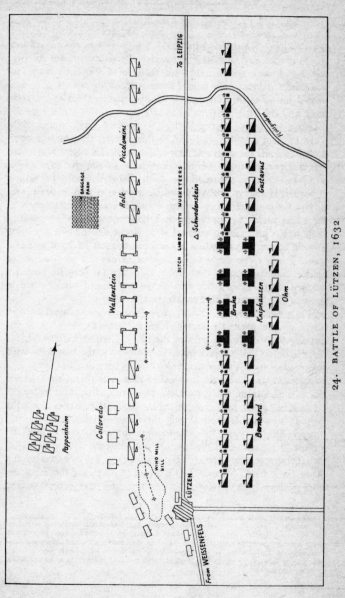

24. BATTLE OF LÜTZEN, 1632

known, it probably was 25,000 men without counting Pappen-heim's 8,000. He divided his army into a centre, right, and left; the first consisted of four great *tercios* of infantry under his own command, and the second and third of Colloredo's and Piccolomini's cavalry. He held Lützen, which he set on fire, and posted his 60 to 66 guns in two groups, one in front of the right wing and the other in front of the right centre.

Gustavus moved forward "by the peep of day"—about eight o'clock; "but so thick and dark a mist arose" that he was compelled to halt. He then addressed his men.[1] His object was to cut off Wallenstein from Leipzig, not only to deprive him of his base, but to free the road for John George, whom he hourly expected. His army probably numbered 18,000, and he drew it up in two lines as follows: four and a half brigades in the centre of each line under Count Brahe and Kniphausen, and on each of their flanks his cavalry ordered as at Breitenfeld. The right wing he held under his immediate command, the left he gave to Bernhard. Further, he drew up a reserve of cavalry in rear of the centre under Colonel Ohm. In front of the infantry he posted a battery of 26 heavy guns, and his 40 regimental pieces stood in front of the "commanded musketeers."

When the mist began to drift away "the cannons played a while, but we were presently under ffavour of their canons. And the battaile ioyned aboute tenn of the clock," writes Fleetwood. He continues: "it being then a faire day; but just as the battaile ioyned there fell so great a miste that wee could not see one another. . . ."[2] It was during this short interval of clearness that Gustavus led forward the right wing cavalry, and, according to Fleetwood, "The King at the first charging of the graft [the ditches along the Leipzig Road] was shott throug the arme and his horses neck," but refusing to retire, "he leaped over the graft and charged the enimie."[3] He scattered Wallenstein's musketeers, routed a body of Croatish horse, and then charged Piccolomini's heavy cavalry and drove them back. Meanwhile Bernhard led forward the left wing, and pushed back Colloredo's cavalry, and the centre moved

---

[1] See *The Harleian Miscellany*, vol. IV, p. 200.

[2] *The Camden Miscellany*, "Fleetwood's Letter," vol. I, p. 7.

[3] *Ibid.*, p. 7. There is no doubt that time and again Gustavus needlessly risked his life; yet many leaders did the same. Hand-to-hand encounters between generals-in-chief were frequent during this war, such as the battle duel between Archduke Leopold and Piccolomini at the second battle of Breitenfeld, November 2, 1642. Marshal de Rantzau, who died in 1650, lost in the course of his service, an eye, a leg, an arm, and an ear.

forward and captured Wallenstein's central battery, but soon lost it.

Because of the mist, no two accounts of this phase of the battle tally. Apparently Gustavus, when he heard that his centre was in retreat, headed a regiment of horse and rode toward it. Separated from his men in the fog, he and three companions rode into a party of enemy cavalry, and he was shot through the head and body and killed; two of his companions were cut down, but the third escaped.

His death, instead of disheartening his men, filled them with a fanatical fury, and as Saxe-Weimar, who took over command, led them forward, Pappenheim came on the field. He fell on the Swedish right wing and drove it back to its original position. At this juncture he was killed and the battle became a frantic mêlée. The King's body was recovered, Wallenstein's guns were retaken, then lost and captured again, but after this the Swedes carried all before them and the imperial army broke up and scattered as night crept over the field. "Thus", writes Fleetwood, "concluded our famous battaile, farr exceeding that of Lypsick [Breitenfeld], for had not our foote stoode like a wall, there had not a man of us come of alyve, they being certen twyce our number."[1] There was no pursuit, and the losses are uncertain. Fleetwood says the Imperialists lost between three and four thousand killed and the Swedes about fifteen hundred. Also he writes: "And I am confident, had it pleased God that he [Gustavus] survived this day, he had putt a period to all the warrs in Germany. . . ."[2]

This is probable, for as Gindely writes: "It lies not beyond the range of possibility that he would have gained his purpose . . . of founding a dominion in Germany, and thus hastening by more than a hundred years the political and mercantile evolution of the country's resources."[3] And Bryce writes: "In four campaigns he destroyed the armies and the prestige of the Emperor; devastated his lands, emptied his treasury, and left him at last so enfeebled that no subsequent successes could make him again formidable."[4] Like Alexander, Gustavus died before his work was accomplished, and like him, he left behind a task too grand in idea for those who followed him.

[1] *Ibid.*, p. 9.　　　　　　　　　　[2] *Ibid.*, p. 9.
[3] *History of the Thirty Years' War*, vol. III, p. 147.
[4] *The Holy Roman Empire*, pp. 383–384.

The war would have ended had it not been for Richelieu. The Empire was in collapse, Wallenstein discredited, turned traitor and was assassinated in 1634. But as French control of the left bank of the Rhine had not been gained the war went on and Richelieu treated "the old German frontierland as having no rights against the King of France."[1] "His will", writes Mr. Stanley Leathes, "fanned the flames of war from the Oder to the Ebro. Dangling before his deluded allies the prospects of a general peace, in which all interests should be secured, ceaselessly impressing on all concerned that a separate arrangement could be neither profitable nor trustworthy, he gradually wore down the strength of the Habsburgs and recovered the ground lost in twenty years of irresolution or of impotence."[2]

Nevertheless Richelieu was not a success as a strategist; though a statesman of the first order, he never understood war as an art.

The next turning point came with the battle of Nördlingen on September 6, 1634, in which Bernhard of Saxe-Weimar was beaten decisively by the Emperor's son Ferdinand of Hungary, Matthias de Gallas, and the Cardinal Infante. By the spring of the following year the whole of southern Germany was again in the Emperor's hands. The treaty of Prague (May 30, 1635) followed, and by it peace was signed between the Emperor and John George of Saxony, and the League was dissolved.

Because Sweden, backed by France, refused to accept this peace, the war entered its final stage of invasion and conquest; in which France and Sweden were ranged against Austria and Spain. The aim of the former, as always, was to break the Habsburg circle. Ferocity now took control. All ideals vanished; that of Ferdinand; that of Gustavus; and that of Wallenstein. The war became a conflict of Bourbon against Habsburg–a gladiatorial encounter for power. The peasants revolted, soldiers alone could live, and soon hordes of starving women and children, like packs of jackals, followed the armies.[3] Werth raided almost up to the gates of Paris and threw its inhabitants into panic. Battles were won and lost and entire regions depopulated, until, slowly out of the agony, the desire for peace gathered Protestants and Catholics about the Emperor and a semblance of national unity began to appear.

Ferdinand II died on February 15, 1637. By his will he directed

---

[1] *The Thirty Years' War*, Samuel Rawson Gardiner, p. 167.
[2] *The Cambridge Modern History*, vol. IV, p. 141.
[3] Gindely (vol. II, p. 334) quotes a case of an army of 38,000 fighting men being followed by 127,000 women, children and followers.

that all his hereditary kingdoms and principalities should remain for ever undivided, and so founded the Austrian monarchy. Richelieu died on December 5, 1642, the creator of monarchial France. Louis XIII died on May 4, 1643, to be succeeded by his son Louis XIV, born in 1638. Fourteen days later the battle of Rocroi was fought, in which the Great Condé put an end to the Spanish military system. Torstensson, one of the most remarkable of the many remarkable generals of the war, won the decisive battle of Jankau on March 6, 1645, which led to peace between Saxony and Sweden, and the war ended in the autumn of 1648 where it began, with the Swedish siege of Prague.

Thus the conflict collapsed, for Ferdinand III (1637–1657) could no longer resist the pressure of France, and as his empire was now a wilderness he was unable to feed his armies. Peace had for long been discussed, and on October 24, 1648, it was signed by the Empire and France at Münster, and by the Empire and Sweden at Osnabrück. The treaty, known as the Peace of Westphalia, for a century and a half remained the norm in the relations between the States of the new Europe created by it, which with slight variations retained its form until 1789.

By the Treaty of Westphalia Calvinism was placed on an equal footing with Lutheranism, and New Year's Day, 1624, was fixed upon as the date on which all religious disputes were to be tested. Thus an epoch was wound up and the Reformation established by law.[1] The sovereignty of Rome was abrogated and the disruption of Christendom sealed. So despiritualized had western Europe become that, when, on November 26, Innocent X denounced the treaty in his bull *Zelo domus Dei*, Europe laughed.

The map of Europe was redrawn according to the treaty. The Upper Palatinate went to Bavaria; the Lower to Charles Louis, son of Frederick, the unfortunate "Winter King". Brandenburg received the bishoprics of Halberstadt, Minden, Cammin, and part of that of Magdeburg; Sweden, Upper Pomerania, Bremen, Verden, Mecklenburg, Stettin, and the island of Rügen; and Saxony retained Lusatia and part of the bishopric of Magdeburg. The Swiss republic was declared a sovereign state, as were the United Provinces, and France, now the enemy of the repose of Europe, received Upper and Lower Alsace, Metz, Toul, Verdun,

---

[1] But it was a very different Reformation from the one contended for by Luther and Calvin, for the Protestant piety was dealt a blow from which it never recovered. It all but ceased to be a religion, and became instead a political programme.

Breisach, and Pignerol, with the right to garrison Philippsburg. Germany was split into some 300 petty, autocratic states in which serfdom was reintroduced and superstition became rampant.[1] With the schools destroyed, there was a lack of education and literature and art suffered accordingly. Long before 1648 the whole country had been barbarized and brutalized, the orderly and prosperous life of the German burgher had perished, as had that of the housewife, dragged about as she had been at the tail of mercenary armies, "half a prostitute and half a gipsy".

In 1880, Prince Hatzfeldt, German Ambassador in London, told Lord Granville that "Germany had not yet recovered from the effects of the Thirty and the Seven Years Wars; and that a determination to prevent the recurrence of similar disasters ought still to be the keynote of German policy"[2]—and no wonder. The entire country had been ruined more completely than on any previous occasion in history, not excepting the Hun and Mongol invasions. Eight million people are said to have perished, besides 350,000 killed in battle. In a district in Thuringia where, in 1618, 1,717 houses had stood in 19 villages, only 627 remained in 1649, and of the 1,773 families which inhabited them, only 316 could be found to occupy the 627 houses. In the same district 244 oxen remained out of 1,402, and of 4,616 sheep—not one. In Bohemia, of 35,000 villages only 6,000 are said to have survived, the population sank from about 2,000,000 to 700,000, and in the County of Henneburg 75 per cent. of the people and 80 per cent. of the livestock perished, and 66 per cent. of the houses were destroyed.[3] And the worst was that the richest areas suffered most.

The peace of Westphalia was one of the great landmarks in history. The Habsburgs turned toward the east, and when a generation later the Ottoman empire began to crumble, they sought on the Danube compensation for their losses on the Rhine. Sweden, until the battle of Poltava, in 1709, became a great power; the leadership of Germany passed into the hands of the Hohenzollerns; and France, her security strengthened by the disruption of Germany, continued her war with Spain. Meanwhile two new powers rose in the north, the United Pro-

---

[1] In 1625 and 1628, the bishop of Würzburg is said to have burnt 9,000 persons for witchcraft, and in 1640–1641 1,000 were burnt in the Silesian principality of Neisse.

[2] Quoted from *The Cambridge Modern History*, vol. IV, p. vi.

[3] None of these figures is very reliable. On this question see *The Thirty Years' War*, C. V. Wedgwood, pp. 510–516.

vinces, a growing commercial empire, and England under Cromwell. As the future *roi soleil* played in his nursery and the signatures of the Treaty of Westphalia were barely dry, the head of Charles I of England rolled into the executioner's basket at Westminster, the challenge of emerging plutocracy to the divine right of kings.

The English Civil War is an admirable example of the manner in which military affairs may determine constitutional and social development. Fuller sees the "root cause" of the Civil War in the substitution, during the Hundred Years' War, of paid armies for feudal levies:

> Until then the sword had been the symbol of authority, henceforth, more and more, the purse was to challenge the sword, and those who held its strings were not the feudal barons, but the moneyed and trading classes from whom the early parliaments were largely recruited.

With the advent of standing armies in the late 15th and early 16th Centuries another change set in. Because no continental nation could feel secure without a permanent army, in all countries which could afford them they became an essential instrument of the king's government. Further, because they endowed the king with power to enforce his will both in peace and in war, continental sovereigns soon began to dispense with their parliaments. Thus, in Spain, they practically disappeared and in France the Estates General ceased to be summoned between 1614 and 1789.

It was because of her insular position that England remained unaffected by this change, and when, on the accession of James I in 1603, her sole land frontier disappeared, the only possible reason for raising a standing army vanished with it.

By the 17th Century, the power of the purse had acquired new significance, for a reason scarcely to be foreseen by those who had, during the previous century, set out on hazardous journeys to find riches, and thus increase the wealth of nations: "ever since the discovery of the New World the enormous influx of bullion had caused a fall in the value of money, and this not only led to social unrest, but decreased the purchasing power of the king's revenue and so rendered it increasingly difficult for him to pay his way." The special failure of James I's successor, Charles I, was in allowing his favourites to entangle him in a costly foreign policy which compelled him to appeal for money to hostile Parliaments. The conflict between King and Parliament mounted steadily, until war broke out between them in August 1642. Fuller writes:

> The Wars of the Roses were a conflict between two royal houses, the Great Rebellion was a clash between two social classes, one representing the dying feudal world, the other the emerging capitalist. Neither side was prepared for war, hence its chaotic character. Armies rose, struggled and faded away, and each county may be said to have had its own war, in which sieges abounded.

Chaos remained the characteristic of the Civil War until first a man, then an institution, curbed it. The man was Oliver Cromwell (1599–1658), who very soon perceived that the rabbles which constituted the armies of that time were utterly defective instruments. "Do you think," he asked, "that the spirits of such mean base fellows will ever be able to encounter gentlemen, that have honour and courage and resolution in them? . . . You must get men of spirit . . . of a spirit that is likely to go on as far as gentlemen will go – or else I am sure you will be beaten still."

This was his grand idea, that leadership is useless without disciplined followership, and that discipline demands not only that officers and men know what they are fighting for, but 'love what they know', for without affection discipline is sterile. He, therefore, sought out men who had the fear of God before them, 'and made some conscience of what they did.'

In his troops of Eastern Counties' Horse, Cromwell worked on this principle. In September 1643 he was able to write: "I have a lovely company; you would respect them, did you know them. They are no Anabaptists, they are honest, sober Christians: they expect to be used as men!" Fuller comments: "In these last seven words lies the secret of the whole system of Cromwell's discipline."

The following year (11 January 1644) the House of Commons passed the New Model Ordinance, which created a national professional army which would be disciplined "in accordance with Cromwell's grand idea".

This idea carried with it more than a military revolution; for, as Frederic Harrison writes: 'To organise the New Model on the frame of the Ironsides[1] was to put the sword of the State into the hands of Independency and of radical reform'; for the New Model was much more than an army, it was a body of Bible warriors. 'It was itself a Parliament – a Parliament larger, more resolute, and far more closely knit together in spirit and will than the Parliament which continued to sit officially at Westminster. From this hour the motive power of the Revolution passed from the House of Commons to the army.'[2]

It was this army, well organised and equipped, soundly drilled, and clad in the red coats which would remain the British Army's standard dress until 1914, which won the Civil War. The decisive victory was Naseby, on 14 June 1645, a Royalist defeat even more shattering than that at Marston Moor the year before. But Fuller makes an even more significant comparison:

The battle of Naseby differs from Marston Moor in that, whereas the latter, had it been followed up with vigour, would have led to the triumph of Parliament over the King, the former led to the triumph of the Independents over Parliament. It saved England from the paralysing autocracy of the Kirk and imposed upon that country the stimulating autocracy of Cromwell. During the years of the Interregnum are to be sought the influences of the battle of Naseby on history.

The irony of the Civil War, Great Rebellion, or English Revolution (it is known by all these names) is that what had begun as a resistance to tyranny ended in a tyranny even greater than that which had been overthrown – a not uncommon result. Charles I was executed on 30 January 1649. Cromwell then became, under the title of Lord Protector, a dictator, and as such

---

[1] Originally a nickname for Cromwell himself, "Ironsides" became the name of the Eastern Counties Horse.

[2] Frederic Harrison, *Oliver Cromwell*, 1898, pp. 85, 86.

was forced, like many others, soon to undertake adventures abroad in order to divert attention from the defects of his regime at home. In order to carry out these policies, he needed a powerful navy. It was Charles I who laid the foundations of a professional British Navy, but it was the Commonwealth which gave it its permanent form; no less than 207 new ships were added to the Navy's strength in the eleven years of Cromwellian rule. "This," says Fuller, "and not his suppression of the monarchy, was the true and permanent dividend of the battle of Naseby."

The outstanding figure of the Commonwealth Navy was Admiral Robert Blake, who, says Fuller, "had a profound and enduring influence on naval command and tactics." The First Dutch War (1652–4) gave Blake his opportunity for action, against a redoubtable opponent, Admiral Tromp. As in the second war, fighting the Dutch taught the Navy much in a hard school. Battle honours were roughly even in 1654, but England had the advantage of size and population, and was thus better able to stand the "attrition" of these tough combats. Cromwell's second foreign adventure – war against Spain in alliance with France (1654–9) – gained England the island of Jamaica, but little else.

Although the Dutch war had some economic justification for England, the Spanish war was a disaster. It left France supreme on the Continent; it ruined English trade to the benefit of the Dutch; it caused a deep economic depression throughout England and raised the public debt to over £2,500,000. 'The political instability of the Interregnum,' writes Margaret James, 'had been paralleled by its economic instability, and it is not surprising that London, which had been the backbone of resistance to Charles I, should have welcomed his successor with open arms.'

Nevertheless, says Fuller, although both his foreign policy and his system of rule at home were failures, "Cromwell left his country a supremely great legacy."

As Margaret James comments on the problems of this period: At home, the doctrine of an active faith helped to sanctify a growing industrialism. Abroad it helped to sanctify the shadowy beginnings of imperialism. In the same way as chosen individuals were held to glorify God by rising to a higher position than their fellows, so a chosen nation was thought to exalt Him by dominating its neighbours. Nations, said one writer, should always be on the alert to attack and acquire fresh provinces as well as to defend existing possessions, "for as Christian saith to him that hath (using it well) shall be given. This riches is your strong tower."[1]

Thus industrialism and imperialism crept out of the religious mists of Puritanism to become the abutments of English civilization. And though it was not the civilization Cromwell and his Major-Generals had dreamed of, it was the civilization woken by their power-politics since Naseby. The sacrifices had been burned, the oracles were propitious, a new age had opened in which England was soon to play the part of ancient Rome, and for 250 years to cast her imperial net over the seven seas.

[1] *European Civilisation, its Origins and Development*, 1937, Vol. V.

The ascension of France

Although the Peace of the Pyrenees extinguished the last sparks of the Thirty Years War, it did not settle the problem France had set out to solve; for by leaving Lille, Besançon, the two Sicilies, and the Milanese in the hands of Spain, in case of need Spain could still effect a junction with the Empire, and together they could encircle France. The consequence was that, when Mazarin died in 1661 and Louis XIV, a young man of 25, burning to emulate Charlemagne and make France supreme and glorious, assumed full powers, the problem of how to break the Habsburg ring became his political inheritance.

In its solution he was greatly assisted by his two great ministers –Louvois and Colbert. The former centralized the administration of the army, and by eliminating the power of the nobles made the King's authority paramount. Besides enforcing honesty, he improved equipment, introduced the bayonet, replaced the matchlock by the flintlock (*fusil*), raised the status of infantry and engineers, and brought the artillery into line with the other arms. Further, he established well organized magazines and made provision for disabled soldiers by building the *Hôtel des Invalides*. But his greatest influence upon Louis was that he dangled before him as the objects of his reign, war, glory and dominion, toward which Louis by nature was only too well inclined. Colbert reorganized the navy and raised it from the 20 warships he found in 1661 to 196 effective vessels in 1671 and to 270 in 1677. He renovated the old harbours and arsenals, modernized Toulon, Rochefort, Brest, Le Havre, and Dunkirk (bought from Charles II in 1662), and, helped by Vauban, laboured to make impregnable the fortresses of France.

Louis had not long to wait for an opportunity to initiate his aggressive policy. On September 17, 1665, Philip IV of Spain died and was succeeded by his half-witted son, Charles II, a boy of four years old. But as Charles was Philip's son by his second marriage, and Maria Theresa the only surviving child of his first, on the strength of a local custom in Brabant and Hainault, the so-called *jus devolutionis*, according to which children of a first marriage had precedence over those of a subsequent one, Louis, in the name of his wife, claimed the whole of the Spanish Netherlands.

England was at war with the United Provinces (Second Dutch War), and because by treaty Louis was engaged to aid the Dutch, in January, 1666, he declared war on England. But Charles II, who was in no way prepared to add to his enemies, in March, 1667, came to a secret understanding with him not to oppose his projected invasion of the Netherlands if, in his turn, Louis withheld all assistance from the Dutch. Shortly after this agreement, the French crossed the Netherland's frontier and seized Lille. Next, in order to prevent the Spaniards, who held Franche-Comté, from reinforcing the Netherlands from Italy, on February 4, 1668, Louis invaded Franche-Comté and overran it in a fortnight.

Before he carried out this aggression, in order that he might assure himself of the Emperor Leopold I's neutrality, in January Louis had induced him to agree to a treaty of partition of the Spanish empire should Charles II, as seemed probable, die without issue. The arrangement was that Spain, the Americas, and the Milanese were to go to Leopold, and Louis was to receive the Two Sicilies, the Spanish Netherlands, Franche-Comté, Spanish Navarre, the Philippines, and the Spanish possessions in Africa.

The immediate results of Louis's aggressions were that on July 31, 1667, Charles II came to terms with the Dutch and agreed to the Peace of Breda, and on February 13, 1668, Spain made peace with Portugal and recognized her independence. At the same time—January to April, 1668—a triple alliance between England, the United Provinces, and Sweden was formed to resist Louis, and he, feeling that he had gone far enough for the present, decided on peace, which, on May 2, was signed at Aix-la-Chapelle. According to its terms, he received Charleroi, Binch, Ath, Douai, Tournai, Oudenarde, Lille, Armentières, Courtrai, Bergues, and Furnes, and gave up Franche-Comté, Cambrai, St. Omer, and Aire. These surrenders he could well afford, because by the terms of the secret agreement with Leopold it had been arranged that, on Charles's death, these places should go to France.

Still bent upon gaining the Spanish Netherlands, Louis set out to disrupt the Triple Alliance, and as a first step toward this, in June, 1670, he entered into a secret agreement, known as the Treaty of Dover, with Charles of England, by which the latter agreed to support France in a war against the Dutch. With his left flank thus secured, he set out to secure his right flank by occupying Lorraine and entering into treaty with the Elector of Bavaria, which established a friendship between the two countries that was to last until 1813. Lastly, in April, 1672, the Triple Alliance vanished altogether when Sweden was won over by a large sum of money.

Meanwhile, on March 17, Charles had declared war on the Dutch, and in May Louis followed suit. At first the French advance, under Condé and Turenne, was rapid, but soon after it was checked when the Dutch cut their dykes. Next, William of Orange was proclaimed Stadtholder of Holland and Zeeland, and thoroughly alarmed, both the Emperor and Frederick William of Brandenburg (the Great Elector), as well as Spain, entered the contest against France.

At sea, in what in English history is known as the Third Dutch War, de Ruyter defeated the English and French in two battles, and had rather the better of them in two more. At length, in 1674, the general fear of the rising power of France, as well as hatred of the French navy, whose barefaced defection in action had led to the loss of the above battles, caused the English Parliament to compel Charles to make peace with the Dutch, which, on February 19, was sealed by the Treaty of London. On land the war continued until 1678, and to the advantage of France, but all the belligerents grew weary and it was ended by a series of separate treaties, which together became known as the Peace of Nymegen (August, 1678, to February, 1679).

This peace placed France in a far stronger position than the one she had gained by the Treaty of Westphalia; for by it she acquired a large slice of the Spanish Netherlands, Alsace, Lorraine, Freiburg, Breisach, and Franche-Comté. Nevertheless England was the real gainer, for during the war, quite unwittingly, France had expended her blood and treasure to no other end than that England should become her most formidable colonial and maritime rival. As part of her spoil, England obtained New Amsterdam (New York)[1] and New Jersey, which enabled her to link together her northern and southern American colonies; also she obtained St. Helena[2] as a base for her East Indian merchantmen. But more important, after her peace with the United Provinces in 1674, because of the continuance of the war, the bulk of the Dutch carrying trade passed to the English flag. Thus, when the Peace of Nymegen was signed, England was left the leading naval and

---

[1] In September, 1664, the Duke of York had obtained New Amsterdam from the Dutch, and had renamed it New York. In 1673 the Dutch reoccupied it, and in 1674 it was restored to England.

[2] Occupied by the British East India Company in 1651. Taken by the Dutch in 1673, and soon after reoccupied by the Company.

commercial power in the world. As such, her homeland was secure, and because of this and her command of the sea, the colonies of all other nations were at her mercy.

In these wars, Louis was not only aided by Charles II, but also by the Turks, who throughout this period were engaged in their final struggle with the Empire, which impeded the Emperor's intervention in strength in the west. Happily for Europe, during the Thirty Years War the Ottoman empire was in one of its periodical states of anarchy, but in 1656, under Mahomet IV (1648-1687) order was restored. In 1663, war was declared on the Empire; but the following year, on August 1, the Turks were routed by Montecuccoli, the Imperialist general, at the battle of St. Gothard. The next Turkish move was made against Poland, where, after several campaigns, on November 11, 1673, a great Turkish army under Ahmad Kiuprili was destroyed by John Sobieski at Khoczim. Ten years later, in order to cripple Leopold, Louis persuaded the Sultan again to march against the Empire. Louis's idea was that were Austria overthrown, Germany would be forced to appeal to him, when, as champion of the Cross, he would restore to France the imperial crown of Charlemagne. Mahomet fell in with Louis's suggestion and assembled an army, reputed to be 250,000 strong, under Kara Mustafa, which crossed the Drave and laid siege to Vienna. At once, Sobieski, now John III of Poland, and Charles of Lorraine, at the head of 70,000 Poles, Bavarians, Saxons, and Germans, marched to its relief, and on September 12, 1683, routed the Turks. Nevertheless the war continued; the Turks suffered a crushing defeat at Har-Kány, near the field of Mohács, on August 12, 1687, and another at Zenta on the river Theiss, at the hands of Prince Eugene, on September 11, 1697. Two years later, on January 26, 1699, this crowning victory led to the Peace of Carlowitz, by which all Hungary and Transylvania were ceded to Austria, and Podolia and the Ukraine to Poland. Thus ended the Turkish peril, which had terrorized eastern Europe since the battle of Manzikert: it was the final echo of the Crusades.

The rout of the Turks before Vienna in 1683 and the accession of James II (1685-1688) to the throne of England on February 16, 1685, placed Louis in a difficult position. The former meant the strengthening of Austria and the latter that, should James, a bigoted Catholic, be unable to retain his throne, the only alternative to him was William of Orange, who had married James's daughter Mary in 1677. Therefore, policy demanded that James's position should be stabilized; but Louis played his cards so badly that the very thing he was most anxious to prevent occurred. Shortly after James's accession he withdrew all toleration from the French Huguenots by revoking the Edict of Nantes, and to make matters worse, James set out to emulate him by attempting by unconstitutional means to force the Catholic religion on his subjects. The result was the "Glorious Revolution" of 1688, by which James was compelled to fly the kingdom and to make way for his son-in-law and daughter, who became joint rulers of England in his stead. "Thus for the divine right of kings", writes Lord Acton, "was established the divine right of freeholders:" government by one of two parties of gentry, the Whigs and the Tories, the one representing the great landowners, merchants and tradesmen, and the other the smaller landowners and country clergy. Power was thus finally transferred from the Crown to Parliament, the former became a constitutional monarchy; freedom of the Press was established; and in 1694 the Bank of England was founded, whereby the English banking system was instituted, which in years to come was to make money all-powerful.

The revolution of 1688 initiated the long duel between England and France for colonial domination, which was to last for over a century, and because at this time France possessed the most powerful army in the world and a formidable navy, when, in 1688, Louis invaded the Palatinate, all the princes of Germany began to rally against him. In order to consolidate this resistance, in 1689 William of Orange, now William III of England (1688–1702), formed the Grand Alliance of England, the United Provinces, and the Empire, and war against France was placed on a more equal footing. On June 30, 1690, the same day that James II in Ireland was defeated at the battle of the Boyne, the allied fleets were severely beaten by Admiral Tourville off Beachy Head; and on May 19–24, 1692, Tourville was defeated decisively by the English and Dutch fleets, under Admiral Edward Russell (later Earl of Orford) at the battle of Barfleur-La Hogue. The importance of this victory cannot be overestimated; there were but few troops in England, and had the battle been lost, 30,000 men under Marshal de Bellefonds were waiting to cross the Channel to invade England and to restore James to his throne.

Although this victory enabled William to devote the whole of his attention to the war in the Netherlands; nevertheless he was nearly uniformly unfortunate. In 1692 he lost Namur and was defeated at Steinkirk, and the following year defeated at Neerwinden. In 1697, largely because of English naval successes in the Mediterranean, Louis expressed his willingness to surrender all conquests made during the war. This, on September 20, led to the Peace of Ryswick, by which William III was recognized by Louis as King of Great Britain and Ireland, and the Princess Anne, second daughter of James II, heiress to his throne. The Grand Alliance was then dissolved, and France was left the strongest power in Europe.

It would seem probable that one reason for the Peace of Ryswick was that Louis, expecting the early demise of Charles II of Spain, wished to conserve the strength of France in order to push the claim of his House to the Spanish throne when that event occurred and, as Mignet says, the Spanish succession was "the hinge on which the whole reign of Louis XIV turned."

Unfortunately for Europe, the hinge was a three-fold one, for on Charles II's death there would be three claimants to his throne. Besides Philip Duke of Anjou, the grandson of Louis XIV, there was the Archduke Charles of Austria, son of the Emperor Leopold, and Joseph Ferdinand, the Electoral Prince of Bavaria, son of the Bavarian Elector Maximilian Emanuel, who had married Leopold's daughter Maria Antonia. Both Louis and Leopold were grandsons of Philip III, and both had married their first cousins, the daughters of Philip IV.

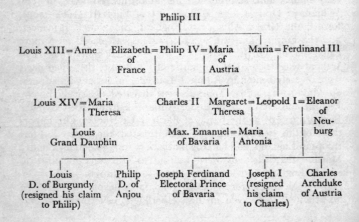

Because Louis would not agree to the whole of the Spanish empire going to the House of Austria, and because Leopold would not agree to it going to France, in order to avert war the sole solution was that on Charles II's death he should be succeeded by Joseph Ferdinand, for under him the Spanish empire would remain independent of both France and Austria. This solution, as Professor Trevelyan points out, would suit England well, because from the reigns of William and Anne to that of George V, it was commercial rivalry and the maintenance of the balance of power on the Continent which constrained England to take part in all continental wars which threatened her in either of these directions. In the present case, the Spaniards, because of their incapacity to conduct their industry and commerce for themselves, during recent years had allowed English and Dutch merchants, disguised under Spanish names, to do it for them and to carry on trade between Spain and her colonies. Therefore, were the Spanish empire to go to France, not only would this very profitable trade be lost, but the Mediterranean would be closed to their ships and both England and the United Provinces would be threatened by the French in the Netherlands.

Neither Louis nor Leopold would, without compensation to themselves, agree that Joseph Ferdinand should succeed Charles, and in October, 1698, in order to overcome these objections, a half-measure, known as the First Partition Treaty, was resolved upon by France, England, and the United Provinces. By this, most of the Spanish empire was to go to Joseph Ferdinand, Milan to the Archduke Charles, and France was to receive Naples and Sicily. Although this was advantageous for Austria, Leopold refused to abandon the whole of the Spanish inheritance for his son, and Spain—which is more understandable—violently opposed partition in any form whatsoever.

Thus things stood until February, 1699, when the whole situation was changed by the unexpected death of Joseph Ferdinand. Louis and William then drew up the Second Partition Treaty. This time the Archduke was to become king of Spain and the Indies and ruler of the Netherlands; France was to receive Naples and Sicily, and the Duke of Lorraine was to surrender Lorraine—already practically a French possession—to France, and in compensation be given Milan.

With incredible folly Leopold again refused to agree. Also the English merchants strongly objected to Naples and Sicily going to

France, because they considered that this would lead to the closing of the Mediterranean to English shipping, and the Spaniards, still opposed to partition, decided to offer the Spanish crown to Philip in preference to Charles, because Louis was better placed than the Emperor to defend the Spanish empire.

At length the crisis boiled over. On November 1, 1700, Charles II died, and by his will he left his undivided empire to Philip, but on the proviso that should Louis not accept it in his name, it was to go to the Archduke Charles. Since this meant that, were Louis to refuse the offer, France would be as fully encircled as she was in the days of Charles V, in spite of his treaty obligations he had no choice but to accept the will and to send Philip to Madrid. Next, in February, 1701, under pretext of protecting them, Louis invaded the Spanish Netherlands and also occupied the Milanese. Then he committed an act which made war inevitable; he seized the Dutch Barrier fortresses,[1] which were guaranteed by treaty. If this were not sufficient aggravation, he excluded English merchants from the American trade, which meant that England had either to fight or abandon her commercial prosperity to France.

The answer to these aggressions was the revival of the Grand Alliance of 1689, and on September 7, 1701, the treaty was signed at The Hague by England, Austria, and the United Provinces. In its original form, the allies accepted the rule of Philip over Spain and the Indies, on condition that the crowns of France and Spain should never be united, and they bound themselves to obtain Milan, Naples, Sicily, and the Netherlands, for Austria. Further, they demanded that the commercial privileges they had enjoyed under Charles II should be guaranteed to them by Philip. Other treaties were made with the King of Prussia, the Elector of Hanover, and other German princes, to raise troops at the expense of England and the United Provinces.

Ten days after the Grand Alliance was formed, James II died at St. Germain-en-Laye, and in defiance of the Treaty of Ryswick Louis acknowledged his son as James III of England. If this were not cause enough to stir England to the core, he added economic injury to dynastic outrage by prohibiting the importation of British goods into France. Retaliation was immediate. In October the House of Commons, which two years before had disbanded most of the army, voted supplies to raise 40,000 English sailors and

---

[1] A line of fortresses in the Netherlands which, according to the Treaty of Ryswick was garrisoned by Dutch troops.

40,000 soldiers, of whom 18,000 were to be British and the remainder foreigners in English pay. Preparations for war were then put in hand. As they proceeded, William III was thrown by his horse and sustained injuries from which, on March 8, 1702, he died. He was succeeded by his sister-in-law, Princess Anne (1702-1714), daughter of James II.

CHAPTER 14

The Battle of Blenheim, 1704

To all outward appearances the death of William III left France supreme and her hoped-for hegemony assured. England was ruled by a woman of no marked ability; the United Provinces were thrown into consternation, and the Empire was in its usual state of decrepitude. Yet again the unexpected happened: fate brought forth the man of destiny, John Churchill, first Duke of Marlborough (1650–1722).[1] Further, fate provided him with an able helpmate, his wife, born Sarah Jennings, who as confidante of the Queen played a dominant part in the direction of affairs.

Son of Sir Winston Churchill, John Churchill was born at Ash, near Axminster, on June 6, 1650, and between 1667, the year he was gazetted an ensign in the King's Regiment of Foot Guards (now the Grenadier Guards), and August 8, 1701, when William III appointed him Ambassador Extraordinary to the United Provinces and Captain-General of the Confederate Armies, he saw much service both on land and sea:[2] at Tangier in 1668; with the Duke of York and Marshal Turenne between the years 1672 and 1674; in the Monmouth Rebellion of 1685; and in Ireland in 1690. These experiences stood him in good stead, for they brought him into touch with the realities of war and, being a man of insight, they enabled him to plumb the French character and to measure up many of his future adversaries.

Soon to prove himself one of the greatest military geniuses his country has known, it was only natural that he was unmercifully traduced by the smaller men of his age. Nevertheless he was far from impeccable in character, and had he been so probably he would never have risen to the position he attained, for in his day, more often than not, intrigue was an ingredient of success. Therefore, in order to judge him as a man, he must be judged by the standards of his age. He was accused of avarice, peculation, and treason, and though it is true that he corresponded with the Jacobites at the Court of St. Germain-en-Laye, for which, in 1692,

---

[1] Created a duke in December, 1702.
[2] At the battle of Solebay, May 28, 1672, in the Second Dutch War.

he was incarcerated in the Tower of London; yet, in 1701, he was the man whom the aggrieved party, William III, appointed as his military successor. The appointment was a wise one, for it demanded above all things tact, an essential of intrigue and diplomacy.

Whatever may have been his failings as a man, as a general and a statesman Marlborough stands high above his contemporaries. Courteous and patient, he possessed what so few men of genius are endowed with—ability to tolerate fools gladly. Though his courage was of the highest, his imagination vivid, and his common sense profound, his master characteristic was his self-control. Nothing unbalanced him, whether it was the stupidity of his allies, the duplicity of the politicians, or the ability of his enemies. As a general he possessed the rare virtue of seeing a war as a whole, and of being able to relate sea power with land power and strategy with politics. Nothing escaped his observation, and no detail, tactical or administrative, was too minute to be overlooked. A master of stratagems, he consistently mystified his enemy; a master of detail, his men were never left in want. In the planning of a campaign he took infinite pains, and in its execution infinite trouble. In an age which believed that the defensive was the stronger form of war, he invariably sought to bring his enemy to battle, and proved conclusively that a vigorous offensive is usually the soundest defence. A contemporary says of him:

"Kirke has fire, Lanier thought, Mackay skill and Colchester bravery, but there is something inexpressible in the Earl of Marlborough. All their virtues seem to be united in his single person. I have lost my wonted skill in physiognomy if any subject of your Majesty can ever attain such a height of military glory as that to which this combination of sublime perfections must raise him."[1]

And Captain Robert Parker, who served under Marlborough in the 18th Royal Irish Regiment, writes:

"As to the Duke of *Marlborough* . . . it was allowed by all men, nay even by *France* itself, that he was more than a match for all the Generals of that Nation. This he made appear beyond contradiction, in the ten Campaigns he made against them; during all which time it cannot be said that he ever slipped an oppor-

---

[1] The Prince of Vaudemont to William III, quoted by C. T. Atkinson in *Marlborough and the Rise of the British Army* (1921), p. 130.

tunity of fighting, when there was any probability of his coming at his Enemy: And upon all occasions he concerted matters with so much judgment and forecast, that he never fought a Battle which he did not gain, nor laid seige to a Town which he did not take. . . . He was peculiarly happy in an invincible calmness of temper and serenity of mind; and had a surprising readiness of thought, even in the heat of Battle."[1]

Such was "Corporal John", as his men affectionately called him, and it is remarkable that 100 years later even a greater than he was called by his men *Le Petit Corporal*. The one was the forerunner of the other, as well as heir of Gustavus Adolphus; for by breaking down the formalities of late seventeenth-century warfare and returning to the ways of the great Swede, Marlborough opened the road for Frederick and Napoleon. To understand this, it is necessary to appreciate the changes in the art of war which had taken place since 1648.

During this period, communications remained primitive, armies were still of moderate size, and as cavalry remained the decisive arm, strategy was largely circumscribed by forage. Water transport and grass were all-important, also the establishment of magazines, which in its turn led to the predominance of siege warfare over field battles, and the general acceptance that the defensive was more important than attack. This led to the avoidance of battles by means of what may be called the "strategy of evasion," which consisted in manœuvring rather than fighting. The great Turenne (1611–1676) was a past-master in such operations, though never a slave to them;[2] but his most noted opponent, Montecuccoli (1609–1650), laid it down that "The secret of success is to have a solid body so firm and impenetrable that wherever it is or wherever it may go, it shall bring the enemy to a stand like a mobile bastion, and shall be self-defensive."[3]

Marlborough broke away from this type of warfare and returned to the offensive strategy of Gustavus and the attack tactics of Condé and Cromwell. He did so because he was imaginative enough to see into the military changes of his day and appreciate their meaning. Since 1648 there were two supremely important changes—the universal adoption of the flintlock and the replace-

[1] *Memoirs of the most remarkable Military Transactions from the Year 1683 to 1718* Captain Robert Parker (1747), pp. 214–215.
[2] See Jules Roy's *Turenne sa vie et les institutions militaires de son temps* (1884), pp. 449–450.
[3] *Mémoires, ou principes de l'art militaire*, R. de Montecuccoli (1712), p. 223.

ment of the pike by the bayonet.[1] Besides fusiliers, in 1667 grenadiers were introduced, who later were formed into companies, each battalion being provided with one. Therefore, between 1650 and 1700, we find four kinds of infantry—pikemen, musketeers, fusiliers, and grenadiers—which, by 1703, had been reduced to one main type armed with the flintlock and socket bayonet.

This reduction in the number of weapons led to a simplification in formation and tactics, the firing-line of four, and often of three ranks, replaced the column and six rank lines. Battalions, usually 800 strong, were organized into right and left wings, each divided into divisions, platoons, and sections; a platoon in the English service was 50 strong, and in the French 100 strong. Firing, which hitherto had been by successive ranks, was usually delivered by divisions or platoons at close range—30 to 50 paces—and under cover of the smoke of the discharges the assault was driven home with the bayonet.

Marlborough realized that these changes favoured the attack; therefore both his strategy and tactics were offensive. By persistent infantry attacks, he pinned his enemy down and then broke him by the shock action of his cavalry, the squadrons of which were marshalled in three lines and, like Cromwell's, with sword in hand charged at a brisk trot. At Blenheim, Parker tells us that the cavalry were ordered "to advance gently, until they came pretty near [their enemy] and then ride in a full trot up to them."[2] And Kane informs us that Marlborough "would allow the Horse but three Charges of Powder and Ball to each Man for a Campaign, and that only for guarding their Horses when at Grass, and not to be made use of on Action."[3] Further, for the infantry, great emphasis was laid on fire-drill and musketry.

[1] The word "bayonet" is supposed to have been derived from the *bayonette*, a short dagger made in Bayonne toward the end of the fifteenth century. The plug-bayonet, which was fixed into the muzzle of the musket, and therefore prevented it from being fired, is mentioned in 1647, was carried by English soldiers at Tangier in 1663, and was issued to French fusilier regiments in 1671 and to the English Royal Fusiliers in 1685. In 1678 a ring-bayonet, which, though it did not block the muzzle easily fell off it, was introduced, also a socket-bayonet, which could be more solidly fixed, is mentioned. In 1687 Vauban proposed to Louvois the use of the latter, and two years later it was adopted by the French army and after 1697 by the English and German. By 1703 the pike was entirely abandoned by the French and nearly so by the English. According to Colonel Home: "The introduction of the bayonet marks the end of the medieval and the beginning of modern war. . . . Tactics were revolutionized by a dagger some 12 ins. long" (*Stray Military Papers*, 1897, p. 23).
[2] Parker, p. 108.
[3] *Campaigns of King William and the Duke of Marlborough*, Genera R. Kane (1747), p. 110

It must be remembered that the armies Marlborough commanded were composed of national contingents—Dutch, German, and English—which considerably added to his difficulties. When hostilities opened, the English soldier, unlike the English seaman, was not compulsorily recruited. Each colonel enlisted his own men and was given a grant to pay and clothe them. This led to widespread corruption and to the wholesale drafting of criminals into the ranks. Discipline was, therefore, rigorous. Trevelyan mentions a guardsman in 1712 who was ordered 12,600 lashes and who nearly died after he had received the first 1,800.[1] In 1703–1704 this system of raising troops gave way to a series of recruiting Acts which within certain limits rendered compulsory enlistment legal. Usually the summer months were given over to campaigning and the winter to recruiting and teaching the men the elaborate drill of the day.

When, on May 15, 1702, war was declared, the situation that confronted Marlborough was as perplexing as any general has ever been faced with. France and Spain formed a united block, but the Grand Alliance was split into two groups, England and the United Provinces on the one hand, and Austria on the other. To the west of Austria lay Bavaria, still neutral though doubtful, separated from France by Baden, whose ruler, the Margrave Louis, had thrown in his lot with Leopold. To the east of Austria lay Hungary, seething with revolt, and to the south were the Spaniards in Italy. Therefore Austria was threatened from three sides, and because Victor Amadeus II of Savoy was in alliance with France, with his connivance the French had already occupied the valley of the Upper Po and, therefore, could reinforce the Spaniards in the Milanese. While France could operate on interior lines, either against the United Provinces or Austria, Spain could either directly support France or operate against Austria from Italy.

Marlborough's strategical task was first to prevent the United Provinces being overrun by the French, and secondly to prevent Austria being overwhelmed by the French and Spaniards. The former demanded the defeat of France in the north, with the United Provinces as the base of operations, and the latter the defeat of Spain in the south. As regards the latter, Spain's position had been greatly strengthened by the alliance Portugal had made with her and France in June, 1701, and as this had closed the

[1] *England under Queen Anne, Blenheim*, George Macaulay Trevelyan (1930), p. 227.

Portuguese ports to both the English and Dutch, before an attack could be made on Spain, either in the Iberian Peninsula or Italy, to gain a naval base within, or near the Mediterranean, was the first essential.

To fit the strategical situation, Marlborough decided on a two-fold plan. Firstly, while Louis of Baden blocked the defiles of the Black Forest, he would strike at Marshal Boufflers who, at the head of 90,000 men, held all the fortresses on the Maas except Maestricht, and who had occupied the Electorate of Cologne and so had blocked the communications between the United Provinces and Austria. Secondly and simultaneously, Admiral Rooke and an Anglo-Dutch expeditionary force would seize Cadiz and establish there a base for the fleet, from which it could set out to gain command of the Mediterranean, cut the sea communications between Spain and Italy, and threaten France from the south.

The campaign of 1702 opened in Italy, where Prince Eugene of Savoy (1663–1736) in command of the Imperial forces, found himself outnumbered by the French and Spaniards under Marshal Vendôme and was hard put to it to maintain himself in the Modenese. Next, in July, at the head of 40,000 men, Marlborough took the field, and on four separate occasions was prevented from bringing his enemy to book by the timidity and obstruction of the Dutch deputies attached to his headquarters. Nevertheless the French were expelled from the valleys of the Maas and Lower Rhine, and the navigation of the Maas from Liège downward was gained, without which the march to the Danube in 1704 could never have been attempted.

In August, Rooke appeared before Cadiz with 14,000 troops under the Duke of Ormonde, and through faulty planning, lack of initiative, and the disgraceful behaviour of the men, the attempt to seize the port ended in fiasco. On the way home, in October, in order to cover the disgrace, an impromptu attack was made on Vigo. Not only was the Plate fleet, then in harbour, destroyed, but 15 French ships of the line were either taken or burnt and an immense booty captured. Though Vigo was not held as a base, this astonishing *coup de main* accomplished all that the capture of Cadiz could possibly have done, but this success was more than offset by an event which had immediately preceded it. In September Bavaria joined France on the understanding that Maximilian Emanuel's territories would be greatly extended, and that, once the Emperor had been defeated, he would succeed to the Imperial throne, the House of Wittelsbach replacing the House of Habsburg. This alliance permitted Louis XIV to pass from the defensive to the offensive and to advance on Vienna.

Marlborough, in control of the Maas and Lower Rhine, invaded the Electorate of Cologne in 1703, and, on May 18, captured Bonn. Called back to the Netherlands, his well-conceived scheme to occupy Antwerp was ruined by the insubordination of the Dutch general Cohorn.[1] In the meantime Villars, the ablest of the French marshals, who had defeated Louis of Baden at Friedlingen on October 14, 1702, in the spring of 1703 seized Kehl—opposite Strasbourg—crossed the Black Forest and in May linked up with the Elector of Bavaria near Ulm. He at once urged a march on Vienna, but the Elector refused and instead carried his army into the Tyrol, in order to add it to Bavaria, to collect reinforcements, and to establish a link between Bavaria and Italy. Meanwhile Villars was left to cover this operation by watching Louis, who had come up from Stolhofen and had been joined by Field-Marshal Styrum and 19,000 Austrians. At the same time Vendôme, on the Po, was ordered by Louis XIV to join hands with the Elector by way of the Brenner, and to "finish the war by carrying it into the heart of the Empire." But Vendôme wasted so much time that in August the Bavarian garrisons Maximilian Emanuel had established in Tyrol were driven out, and when he found his road to the Brenner blocked by the Tyrolese mountaineers, Vendôme was unable to effect a union.

Had Louis of Baden and Styrum remained together during the Elector's absence Villars might have been overwhelmed; but foolishly they separated their forces. Villars parried the Margrave's attack on Augsburg, fell upon Styrum, and on September 20 decisively defeated him at Höchstädt. At once Louis abandoned Augsburg and retired into winter quarters, and although the season was late for campaigning, Villars again urged the Elector to attempt a dash on Vienna, then seriously menaced by the Hungarian insurgents. But the Elector refused and, after a violent quarrel, Villars was recalled to France and replaced by Marshal Marsin, a far less able soldier. At the same time Marshal Tallard

---

[1] See *The Correspondence, 1701–1711,*[1] of *John Churchill, First Duke of Marlborough and Anthonie Heinsius Grand Pensionary of Holland*, edit. B. Van 'T Hoff (1951), 136, p. 85. Marlborough's annoyance is sharply expressed in a letter to Heinsius on September 3. He writes: "The difference of opinions I am afraid will incorage the enemy, for it is most certaine thay know all that passes here; so that if I might have millions given mee to serve another yeare and be obliged to doe nothing but by the unanimous consent of the Generals, I would much sooner dye. . . ." (*Ibid.*, 142, p. 90).

captured Old Breisach and in November occupied Landau, thereby greatly improving the communications between France and the 40,000 French troops wintering in Bavaria. By the close of 1703, the situation of Austria was so desperate that Leopold recalled Eugene from Italy and entrusted him with the fate of the empire.

This series of disasters was in part offset by two events advantageous to the allied powers. The first was the defection of Portugal from France, and the second the abandonment of France by Savoy. The former was largely due to the skilful diplomacy of the Methuens—father and son—successive British envoys to the court at Lisbon, coupled with the news of the attack on Vigo, which swung Peter II of Portugal over to the allies, and in May led to the signing of the Methuen Treaty. By its terms Portugal agreed to accept English cloth in exchange for her wine, which was to be imported into England at a rate one-third less than was charged on French wine—thus port ousted claret. In their turn the allies agreed to send an Anglo-Dutch force to Lisbon and to proclaim the Archduke Charles king of Spain.

As regards Savoy, Victor Amadeus had always been distrustful of French sincerity and felt that the stronger they grew the less sincere they would become. When Vendôme demanded that Turin should be handed over to him, he threw in his lot with the allies, and, on October 25, entered into treaty with the Emperor. The importance of this defection was that, for the time being at least, Austria would be secure on her southern flank.

Yet, in spite of these important gains, in the autumn of 1703 the situation was so critical that Marlborough threatened to relinquish his command unless his subordinates obeyed his orders. On October 12 he wrote to Herr Guildermalsen, the Field Deputy: "I consider it my duty, as well as in the interests of the public . . . to inform you that I am more and more convinced both by the experiences of this campaign and the last one, that the little success we have gained is due to the want of discipline in the army, and until this is remedied I see no prospect of improvement."[1] He then returned to England to think out his plan for the following year.

By now it was obvious to Marlborough that, in the forthcoming campaign, the French would attempt to drive the Emperor out of

[1] *The Letters and Dispatches of John Churchill, First Duke of Marlborough* (1845), vol. 1, p. 198.

the war. This done, they would be in a position to concentrate most of their troops in the Netherlands.

To prevent this, Marlborough's task was to devise a plan which simultaneously would succour the Emperor and be acceptable to the Dutch, or failing this, to be hidden from them. His last two campaigns had convinced him that, because of the formidable French lines and fortresses, a rapid decision in the Netherlands was not to be gained, and he decided that the sole course open to him was to transfer his army to the Upper Danube and to prevent the French and Bavarians forcing their way to Vienna. He clearly saw where the decisive area of operations lay, and as clearly he realized that the Dutch would never agree to his proceeding there. Even were they to do so, the manœuvre was an exceedingly dangerous one. Not only was the distance considerable for a large army to traverse rapidly, but the manœuvre involved a flank march across the French centre, and the sole force Marlborough had to cover it was Louis of Baden's small army, now at Stolhofen, which was quite inadequate for the task. Therefore, it was essential that the ultimate aim of the march should be concealed from the French on the Moselle and in Alsace as well as from the Dutch who, were they to learn of it, would fall into panic. Further, in accordance with the Methuen Treaty, he decided that Admiral Rooke should escort the Archduke Charles and an expeditionary force to Lisbon, and after they had been disembarked, Rooke was next to proceed to the Riviera, and with land forces supplied by Savoy, and helped by the Camisards (Huguenot rebels) of the Cevennes, to carry out a combined attack on Toulon to destroy the fleet in harbour there and to draw the French south.[1]

Who first suggested that the main blow should be struck on the Danube is not known. Coxe says that this decision was arrived at "through the agency of Prince Eugene", with whom Marlborough "had secretly arranged the whole plan of campaign."[2] This is

[1] Rooke and the expeditionary force reached Lisbon toward the end of February, 1704, and once the soldiers had been disembarked and the Archduke proclaimed Charles III of Spain—which started an eight-year war in the Peninsula—Rooke carried the fleet to Toulon; but he found that the Duke of Savoy was unable to spare any troops for the joint enterprise and he returned to the Straits, where strong reinforcements brought his fleet to over 50 sail. He then decided to carry out an enterprise which had been for some time contemplated—the capture of Gibraltar. This was effected with little difficulty on August 4; the Rock was weakly held and indifferently fortified. Three weeks later he severely repulsed a French relieving fleet of 50 sail, under Admiral Toulouse, off Velez Malaga; a battle which gained for England control of the Mediterranean, for during the remainder of the war the French made no serious effort to challenge her supremacy in those waters.

[2] *Memoirs of the Duke of Marlborough*, W. C. Coxe (1820), vol. 1, p. 316.

unlikely, because at the time Marlborough and Eugene were un-acquainted, and no correspondence is known which supports this contention. What is known is that in August, 1703, Marlborough's plan for 1704 was to invade France by way of the Moselle, and that during the autumn he received numerous communications from Count Wratislaw, the Imperial Envoy, pointing out that, if unaided, Vienna was as good as lost. Nevertheless it would appear that until March 1704, Marlborough held fast to the Moselle plan.[1] In January he crossed over to The Hague and discussed it with the Dutch States-General who, fearful that it would uncover the United Provinces, strongly objected to it. On his return home in February he received further urgent appeals from Wratislaw. Finally, in April, Wratislaw presented "a memorial" to Queen Anne, in which he represented to her "the extraordinary Calamity, and imminent Danger, the Empire was exposed to since the Elector of Bavaria had received a Numerous Army of French," and implored that she "would be pleas'd to Order the Duke of *Marlborough* (Her Captain-General) . . . to conduct part of the Troops in Her Majesty's Pay beyond-Sea, to preserve *Germany* from a total Subversion. . . ."[2] Shortly after this appeal, Marlborough made mention of the idea. On May 1 he informed Godolphin, the Lord Treasurer, "When I come to Philipsburg, if the french shall have joined any more troops to the elector of Bavaria, I shall make no difficulty of marching to the Danube."[3] And again, on May 15, he wrote to him: "If they [the French] send no more [than 15,000 troops] and there is no misfortune in Germany before I go to the Danube, I hope we may have success. . . ."[4] Thus, at length, a campaign on the Danube was substituted for one on the Moselle, and part of the new plan was that Eugene should replace Styrum and be ordered by the Emperor to take the field in Germany alongside Marlborough and Louis of Baden.

Marlborough had decided on his plan in the greatest secrecy, and returned to the United Provinces on April 21, 1704. He

[1] See *Heinsius Correspondence*, 165, p. 101.

[2] *A Compleat History of the Late War in the Netherlands*. Thomas Broderick (1713), pp. 93–94. See also *Heinsius Correspondence*, 168, p. 103.

[3] *Memoirs of the Duke of Marlborough*, W. C. Coxe, vol. I, p. 320. On May 2, writing to his wife he said: "But I shall not continue in this country [the Moselle region] long, for I intend to go higher up into Germany, which I am forced as yet to keep here a secret, for fear these people [the Dutch] would be apprehensive of letting their troops go so far." *Marlborough: his Life and Times*, Winston S. Churchill (1934), vol. II, p. 308.

[4] Quoted from *Marlborough: his Life and Times*, vol. II, p. 319.

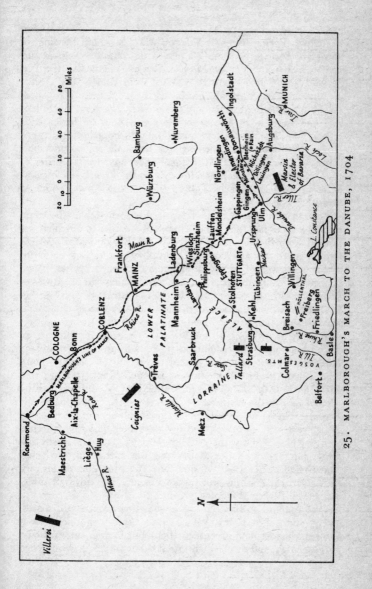

25. MARLBOROUGH'S MARCH TO THE DANUBE, 1704

arrived at Maestricht on May 10 and there he found the situation as follows: Facing him was Villeroi, who lay within the lines of Mehaigne (Antwerp–Diest–Namur) with Count de Coignies and 10,000 men watching the Moselle. Round Vienna lay the Imperialist army, 30,000 strong, watched from Ulm by the Elector of Bavaria and Marshal Marsin with 45,000 men. In April, 10,000 more had crossed the Black Forest by the gorge of Höllenthal and were on their way to join them. Louis of Baden with 30,000 was at Stolhofen and did nothing to impede the advance of these reinforcements; Eugene, who had only 10,000 under his command, was too weak to hamper their advance. In order to cover these reinforcements and to protect the French line of communications with Bavaria, Tallard with an army of 30,000 lay at Strasburg and Kehl.

Though this distribution of forces was formidable, the main difficulty remained the Dutch. Therefore, in order to disembarrass himself from their control, before he left England Marlborough had arranged that all troops in English pay should come under his direct command. This was a fortunate decision, for when he informed the Dutch deputies that the forthcoming campaign was to be on the Moselle, they at once began to obstruct him. Nevertheless, handing over the defence of the United Provinces to General Auverquerque and 70,000 men, he fixed the first *rendezvous* of his own army at Bedburg, 20 miles west of Cologne, for May 16. In all he had under his command 90 squadrons of horse and 51 battalions of foot, of which 19 and 14 respectively, with 38 guns, constituted the British contingent. From Bedburg he wrote to Mr. Stepney, the English representative at Vienna, requesting him to inform the Emperor of his intention of marching to the Danube, but on no account to let the Dutch hear of it.[1] On May 18, he reviewed his troops, and two days later the army marched for the Rhine. Bonn was entered on May 23. There he learnt that Villeroi had crossed the Meuse and was menacing Huy; that Marsin had been reinforced, and that Auverquerque, on his own initiative, was sending him reinforcements. The advance is described by Parker as follows:

"We frequently marched three, sometimes four days, successively, and halted a day. We generally began our march about three in the morning, proceeded about four leagues, or four and a half each day, and reached our ground about nine. As we marched

[1] *Marlborough Dispatches*, vol. 1, pp. 258–259.

through the Countries of our Allies, Commissaries were appointed to furnish us with all manner of necessaries for man and horse; these were brought to the ground before we arrived, and the soldiers had nothing to do, but to pitch their tents, boil their kettles, and lie down to rest. Surely never was such a march carried on with more order and regularity, and with less fatigue both to man and horse.''[1]

On May 25 Marlborough and the cavalry reached Coblenz, and four days later, when the infantry had come up, instead of marching up the Moselle, the army crossed two boat bridges and headed for Mainz. All were dumbfounded, as Parker[2] relates, and not least the French, who now conjectured that their enemy was making for Philippsburg, because bridges had recently been constructed there. On June 3 the cavalry, reinforced by various German contingents, crossed the Neckar at Ladenburg, and on June 7, instead of moving on Philippsburg, from Wiesloch the army turned toward Sinzheim. No longer able to keep his final move secret, Marlborough informed the States-General of his true destination, and Tallard, who was waiting at Landau to confront him once he had crossed the Rhine at Philippsburg, was thrown into consternation by his change of direction, as was the Court directly the news was received in Paris. With his right flank protected by the Black Forest, Marlborough headed for Lauffen.

On June 10 Mondelsheim was reached, and there Prince Eugene and Louis of Baden joined the army. At Gingen, which was entered on June 27, the tasks were distributed. It was decided that Louis of Baden and Marlborough were to work in conjunction, while Eugene was to command on the Rhine and prevent Villeroi and Tallard reinforcing the Bavarians. At length, having marched 250 miles, at the head of 200 squadrons, 96 battalions, and 48 guns, in all about 70,000 men, Marlborough came into contact with Marsin and the Elector entrenched about Dillingen with 60,000 men, 25 miles north-east of Ulm. Eugene, with 30,000 men in the Stolhofen lines, faced Villeroi at Strasburg at the head of 60,000 men.

On June 30 Marlborough moved to Balmershofen, and, on July 1, to Amerdingen, which lies some 15 miles west of the important fortress of Donauwörth, a stronghold it was essential that

---

[1] *Memoirs of the most remarkable Military Transactions from 1638–1718* etc., Captain Robert Parker, pp. 94–95.
[2] *Ibid.*, p. 94.

he should occupy with the least possible delay, for once in his hands he would gain the road to Nördlingen and thus be able to open a new line of communications, as well as to seize the Danube bridge and open the road to Augsburg and Munich. To lay siege to Donauwörth was out of the question because its reduction would have taken several weeks. Further, were Marlborough to attempt it, not only was Tallard well placed to cut his communications, but by advancing he could fall upon Marlborough's rear while Marsin and the Elector attacked his front. Already, on June 30, the Elector hurriedly had sent Marshal Count D'Arco and 14,000 men to Donauwörth, where they had at once begun to entrench the Schellenberg, an oval-shaped hill which dominated the fortress.

As a siege was out of the question, Marlborough decided on a *coup de main*, and in spite of the objections of his generals that after a 15-mile march the troops would be tired, he ordered that on July 2 the Schellenberg was to be stormed. He saw that it was vital not only to deprive D'Arco of 24 working hours, but that during this time Marsin and the Elector would be able to reinforce the Schellenberg by crossing the Danube at Dillingen and moving up its northern bank. Strategically, the whole problem hinged on the fact that Marlborough was 10 miles closer to Donauwörth than Marsin and the Elector. It was this advantage of half a long day's march that decided him not to postpone the attack until July 3, as his generals suggested.

Therefore, early on July 2, the British advanced guard moved out of Amerdingen, and "the way being very bad, long and tedious," it was not until noon that it reached the Wörnitz River immediately west of Donauwörth,[1] where a three-hour halt was made in order to bridge it. Here, apparently, in order to mislead D'Arco into supposing that no attack would be launched until July 3, the allied quartermasters began to pitch camp. Meanwhile Marsin and the Elector moved to the support of Donauwörth, and D'Arco was busily entrenching.

Marlborough's plan of attack was as simple as it was audacious. He decided to assault the Schellenberg on its western and strongest flank; not only because it was the nearest to him, but because, protected as it was by Donauwörth, the attack would be least expected. To do so he assembled two columns, the left one, mainly

---

[1] *A Compendious Journal of all the Marches, famous Battles and Sieges of the Confederate Allies in the late War.* John Millner (1733), p. 95.

English infantry, was to assault on the north-western extremity of the works, and either to carry them, or if that proved impossible, by furious attacks to draw in D'Arco's reserves and pin them down, and so pave the way for the right column. This column, under the command of the Margrave, was to move be-

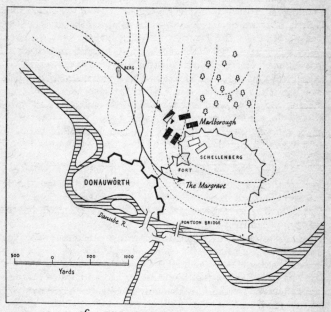

26. THE SCHELLENBERG, 1704

tween Donauwörth and the south-western extremity of the Schellenberg and assault the position in the rear.

At 5 p.m. Marlborough's artillery opened fire; but it was not until an hour and a quarter later that Lieutenant-General Goor led forward the left column, 6,000 men in three lines, with eight battalions in support, eight in reserve and 35 squadrons of cavalry. What followed, is described by an eye-witness:

"So steep was the slope in front of us that as soon almost as the enemy's column began its advance it was lost to view, and it came into sight again only two hundred paces from our entrenchments. . . . The rapidity of their movements, together with their loud yells, were truly alarming, and as soon as I heard them I ordered the drums to beat the 'charge' so as to drown them with their noise, lest they should have a bad effect upon our people. . . . The English infantry led this attack with the greatest intrepidity, right up to our parapet, but there they were opposed with a courage at least equal to their own. . . . It would be impossible to describe in words strong enough the details of the carnage that took place during this first attack, which lasted a good hour or more. We were all fighting hand to hand, hurling them back as they clutched at the parapet; men were slaying or tearing at the muzzles of guns and the bayonets which pierced their entrails; crushing under their feet their wounded comrades, and even gouging out their opponents' eyes with their nails, when the grip was so close that neither could make use of their weapons. I verily believe that it would have been quite impossible to find a more terrible representation of Hell itself than was shown in the savagery of both sides on this occasion."[1]

The assault was repulsed and the men fell back into the dip north of the hill. A similar fate lay in store for the second assault and also the third; nevertheless, at great cost these attacks accomplished their object; they fixed D'Arco's reserves, and in consequence opened the way for the right column.

According to de la Colonie, the town commandant of Donauwörth, instead of lining the "covered way", which linked the fortress to the Old Fort—built by Gustavus Adolphus—on the south-western flank of the Schellenberg, had withdrawn his men into the main works. This not only facilitated the Margrave's advance; but, because of the formation of the ground, the garrison of the Schellenberg was prevented from noticing the movement. Besides, D'Arco considered the day already his, because strong reinforcements would arrive from Augsburg by nightfall. "It was now nearly seven in the evening", and only one regiment, that of Nectancourt, "was strung out in single rank" along the southern face of the hill. Next, writes de la Colonie:

"They arrived within gunshot of our flank, about 7.30 in the evening, without our being at all aware of the possibility of such a thing," when "I noticed all at once an extraordinary movement on the part of our infantry, who were rising up and ceasing fire

[1] *The Chronicles of an Old Campaigner*, M. de la Colonie, *1692-7171* (1904), pp. 183-185.

withal. I glanced around on all sides to see what had caused this behaviour, and then became aware of several lines of infantry in greyish-white uniforms on our left flank. From lack of movement on their part, their dress and bearing, I verily believed that reinforcements had arrived for us, and anybody else would have believed the same."[1]

At this moment Marlborough drove home his final assault, and caught between two fires the enemy broke. At once the 35 squadrons were launched in pursuit "and a terrible slaughter ensued, no quarter being given for a long time."[2] Thus ended this quite extraordinarily audacious battle; an operation of tremendous risks, yet a sure proof of Napoleon's saying that in war *qui ne risque rien, n'attrape rien*. It had lasted a little over an hour and a half, and as it ended the Elector's reinforcements arrived, but only to witness D'Arco's annihilation, for out of his total force he lost some 10,000 men. Marlborough's casualties were heavy—1,400 killed and 3,800 wounded.

The results of the battle were commensurate with the audacity of its conception and execution. Donauwörth fell, and both the road to Nördlingen and the bridge over the Danube were won. Thus, simultaneously, a line of retreat was opened and a line of advance into Bavaria gained. When he heard of the defeat, the Elector at once broke down the bridge over the Lech and entrenched himself at Augsburg. Marsin appealed for assistance to Tallard who, on July 1, had crossed the Rhine, and, on July 16, when about to lay siege to Villingen, received the first full news of the disaster. On July 22 he raised the siege and marched to Ulm, where he arrived on July 29. This move at once placed Eugene in a difficult position, for obviously he would have to follow Tallard, yet simultaneously he had to watch Villeroi. Ostentatiously he marched northward to Tübingen, where he arrived on July 27, and misled Villeroi into believing that he was not following Tallard. Next he vanished among the Swabian hills and headed his army for Donauwörth.

The vital bridge gained, the second act in this amazing campaign opened. With Tallard approaching—and so perfect was Marlborough's intelligence that two days after the French had crossed the Rhine news of their advance had been received by him —it was of the utmost importance to bring the Elector to book. As he refused battle, and because Marlborough could not risk a siege

[1] *Ibid.*, p. 191.   [2] *Memoirs, etc.*, Robert Parker, p. 97.

as long as Tallard was in the field, on July 8 he crossed the Lech and began devastating Bavaria[1] and the terrified inhabitants appealed to their prince for protection or peace. On July 13, under persuasion of the Electress, daughter of John Sobieski, the Elector was on the point of coming to terms when he heard of Tallard's approach. In consequence he continued the struggle and foolishly dispersed most of his army in order to protect his estates. This was a definite gain for the Allies; but as Tallard was now drawing near, autumn approaching, and Parliament would again assemble in November, a victory became a necessity, and to win one it was essential for Marlborough to disembarrass himself of the Margrave, a slow-witted man whom he did not trust; therefore he fell in with his request to lay siege to Ingolstadt. On July 31 he wrote to Eugene outlining his plan, which was: while a detachment of his troops was to join the Margrave at Ingolstadt, Eugene and the remainder were to unite with Marlborough's army, not only in order to cover the siege, but also to bring the combined forces of Tallard, Marsin, and the Elector to battle.

On Saturday, August 10, Tallard and his allies set out north-ward to cross the Danube at Dillingen, and the next day, from his camp at Münster—two hours' march from Donauwörth—Eugene wrote to Marlborough saying: "The enemy have marched. It is almost certain that the whole army is passing the Danube at Lauingen. . . . The plain of Dillingen is crowded with troops. . . . I am therefore marching the infantry and part of the cavalry this night to a camp I have marked out before Donauwörth. Every-thing, milord, consists in speed [*diligence*] and that you put your-self forward in movement to join me tomorrow, without which I fear it will be too late."[2] At once Marlborough set out to support his colleague.

Meanwhile Tallard moved forward to Höchstädt, some five miles down the Danube from Dillingen, where he learnt that Marlborough was joining Eugene. Presupposing that, as the Margrave was absent, Marlborough would fall back on Nörd-lingen, the Elector (in nominal command) urged an attack. Tallard doubted the wisdom of this and a half-measure was agreed

---

[1] Mr. Churchill exonerates this attack on the civil population and writes: "It was not senseless spite or brutality, but a war measure deemed vital to success and even safety. . . . Its military usefulness cannot be disputed." (*Marlborough: his Life and Times*, vol. II, pp. 409–410.) And Marlborough gives his reasons for it to Heinsius in a letter dated July 31, 1704 (*Heinsius Correspondence*, 200, p. 121).

[2] Quoted from *Marlborough: his Life and Times*, Winston S. Churchill, vol. II, pp. 426–427.

upon–to advance three miles downstream to a position a little west of the village of Blenheim (Blindheim); this they did on August 12. There they flattered themselves they had victory in their hands, imagining that Marlborough would be compelled to retire. As Taylor points out, they were incapable of believing that Eugene and Marlborough could be so neglectful of the rules of war as to deliver a frontal attack upon a numerically superior force occupying a strong position.[1] "That night," Count de Mérode-Westerloo[2] informs us, "spirits were at their highest in the Franco-Bavarian camp, for no one doubted that Marlborough and Eugene would be forced to withdraw."

The Franco-Bavarian camp was pitched on the top of a gentle rise about a mile west of a shallow marshy brook called the Nebel. Its right rested on Blenheim, close to the Danube, where Tallard established his headquarters. Through it ran a boggy brook, the Maulweyer, and about one and a half miles up the Nebel, on its left bank, was situated the village of Unterglau, and a mile and a half farther up Oberglau, where Marsin pitched his headquarters. A mile and a half to the west of Oberglau lay the village of Lutzingen in broken country, here was the Elector's headquarters. The camps were, therefore, protected by these four villages or bastions and the Nebel formed a moat in front of the first and third. Defensively it was, therefore, a strong position, flanked on the right by the Danube and on the left by woodland and hills.

At daybreak on August 12 Marlborough reconnoitred his enemy's position by means of his "prospective-glass", and, as Serjeant Millner informs us, at "About One in the Afternoon we saw their Quarter-Master General set up their Camp Standard, and mark out the Camp from Blenheim to Lutzing."[3] What the strengths of the opposing armies were is not known exactly; Millner[4] computes the Allies at 52,000 and the Franco-Bavarians, at 60,000, and Mr. Churchill[5] writes that the former consisted of 66 battalions, 160 squadrons, and 66 cannon[6]–56,000 men in all; whereas the latter numbered 84 battalions, 147 squadrons, and 90 cannon, or about 60,000 fighting men.

When the Franco-Bavarian camps were wrapped in sleep, all

[1] *The Wars of Marlborough, 1702–1709*, Frank Taylor (1921), vol. i, p. 204.
[2] *Mémoires de Mérode-Westerloo* (1840), p. 298.
[3] *A Compendious Journal*, etc., p. 110.
[4] *Ibid.*, pp. 124–128.
[5] *Marlborough: his Life and Times*, vol. ii, p. 442.
[6] Marlborough's own figures, as given to Heinsius on August 16, are 160 squadrons and 65 battalions (*Heinsius Correspondence*, 204, p. 123).

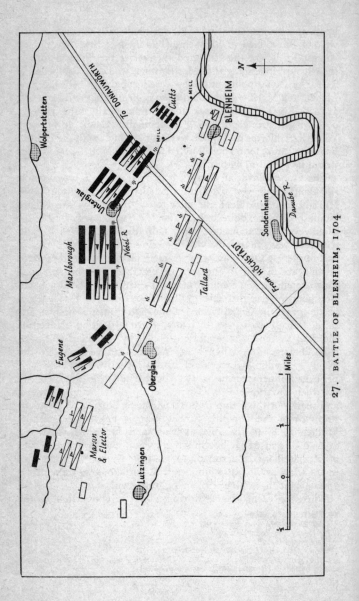

27. BATTLE OF BLENHEIM, 1704

was alive in those of Marlborough and Eugene, and at two o'clock, on the morning of August 13, the joint armies each formed up in four columns and, preceded by 40 squadrons, advanced westward along marked tracks, and an hour later crossed the Kessel Stream by prepared bridges. The morning was dark and misty; Eugene's army marched on the right, Marlborough's on the left, the artillery and pontoons followed the main road to Höchstädt. On the Reichen Stream, a little west of the village of Tapfheim, a halt was made in order to call in the outposts, in all 20 battalions and 15 squadrons, including three brigades of British infantry. These were formed into a ninth column to march on the left, and were placed under the command of Lord Cutts, known as "Salamander". The advance was next continued to Schwenningen, where another halt was made. Marlborough and Eugene with the above 40 squadrons rode forward to the high ground north of Wolpertstetten to reconnoitre the enemy's position. It was now six o'clock, and when an hour later the mist rose, the enemy took alarm and fired two pieces of cannon.

Though the surprise was complete, even now the two French marshals and the Elector were still so obsessed by the idea that their enemy could do nothing other than retire, that at first they judged the advance to be a covering operation to protect the withdrawal of the main body. Even at this moment, about seven o'clock, Tallard wrote to Louis XIV to notify him of his enemy's withdrawal.[1] Next, as the columns came steadily on, Tallard, suddenly realised the truth, ordered the drums to beat and the trumpets to sound, and all was pandemonium in the Franco-Bavarian camps. Although not present at this battle, M. de la Colonie, from the reports of eye-witnesses, gives the following instructive account of this surprise:

"Signal guns", he says, "were fired to bring back the foragers and their escorts; the 'Alarm' and the 'Assembly' were beaten hurriedly, and, without attempting to strike the tents, every effort was devoted to forming line of battle in front of the camp. The hurry and precipitation of all this brought confusion and fear in its train, whilst the foraging parties and their escorts, alarmed by the unexpected signals, returned one by one, rather a prey to misgivings than animated with any desire to fight. The difficulty of having to think of many things at once in the actual presence of the enemy reacted upon the nerves of those in command, and,

[1] *Campagne de monsieur le maréchal de Tallard en Allemagne 1704* (1763), vol. II, p. 140.

above all, upon those who had their carriages packed with the valuables accumulated during their period of winter quarters; such a state of unreadiness is a serious disadvantage in the case of a battle of these dimensions, the preparation for which should have been made much earlier.''[1]

At about half-past eight the allied army came under cannon shot, to which the English batteries replied. Meanwhile Tallard hastily decided on his plan, and as time was too short to do otherwise, he assumed the defensive. Besides, his two flanks were well protected by the Danube and the wooded hills, and his four miles of front by the swampy Nebel. That the two armies, his and Marsin's and the Elector's, took up position as two separate forces instead of one, was a matter of custom, and in any case it was too late to do anything else.

Tallard decided that, while he held the right from the Danube to Oberglau (exclusive), Marsin should hold the centre and the Elector the left. He also decided that the left and centre should take up position close to the right bank of the Nebel and dispute all attempts to cross it, whereas the right would hold back 1,000 yards from that stream, in order that the enemy's left, once it had crossed it, would be caught between the fire of Blenheim and Oberglau, when it could be counter-attacked in front by the French cavalry and driven back into the swamps. Though this plan has been much criticized, when one takes into consideration the shortage of time it was a sound one against any ordinary enemy.

In accordance with this plan, Tallard distributed his forces as follows: (1) To Blenheim he allotted nine battalions as garrison, with seven in support and 11 in reserve in rear of the village; (2) between Blenheim and Oberglau he drew up 44 squadrons (5,500 strong) in two lines supported by nine battalions and four squadrons of dismounted dragoons; (3) on their left he posted 32 squadrons of Marsin's cavalry with 14 battalions in Oberglau; (4) to their left 32 squadrons and 17 battalions—also Marsin's; (5) and on their left, under the Elector, 51 squadrons with 12 battalions in Lutzingen, of which a number was thrown back *en potence*.[2]

From their reconnaissance Marlborough and Eugene saw that the enemy's right was stronger than his left; therefore, as at the

---

[1] *The Chronicles of an Old Campaigner*, pp. 225–226.
[2] The totals of infantry and cavalry are impossible to ascertain, as each account of this battle varies as regards numbers.

Schellenberg, they decided that he would least expect an attack in that direction, and accordingly they arrived at the following general idea; that Eugene should vigorously attack the enemy left, in order to distract the Franco-Bavarian command, and that the decisive blow was to be delivered by Marlborough against the right.

Marlborough saw that Tallard's distribution defensively was an able one, hinged as it was on the villages of Blenheim and Oberglau. If their garrisons were not contained, the risks to his advance would be great; therefore he decided to attack these two villages in such strength that their infantry would be too busy defending themselves to counter-attack in flank his central advance between the villages.[1] If either was carried, so much the better; if not, in any case they would be held and their teeth drawn. Further, as he did not know whether he would be allowed to cross the Nebel unmolested, he drew up his order of battle in an unconventional way. He formed it in four lines; the first consisted of 17 battalions of infantry to gain the right bank; the second and third of 36 and 35 squadrons for the main assault; and the fourth of 11 battalions to hold the ground beyond the Nebel and to cover the withdrawal of the cavalry should the assault fail. On the left of this distribution he drew up Cutts's column; its task was to assault Blenheim. Lastly, he ordered up his engineers to build five bridges across the stream and to repair one which had been broken.

While Eugene's columns toiled over the hilly and wooded ground west of Wolpertstetten, Cutts cleared the left bank of the Nebel immediately east of Blenheim; drove the French out of the water mills, and gained the right bank of the stream. Next, he posted his column in a bottom close to the village, where for several hours his men "with wonderful Resolution . . . stood the Fire of six Pieces of Cannon" planted on the rise beyond it.[2] For four hours the artillery duel was kept up, during which, in order to sustain the *morale* of his troops, Marlborough ordered the chaplains to conduct a service. Also, in full view of the French gunners, he cantered down the line to set an example to his men. A round-shot struck the ground beneath his horse, and to the horror of those watching him, for a moment he was lost to sight in a cloud of dust.

It was now eleven o'clock, and, perturbed because he had heard

[1] See *Memoirs, etc.*, Robert Parker, p. 104.
[2] *A Compendious Journal*, etc., John Millner, p. 115.

nothing from Eugene, Marlborough sent galloper after galloper to the right to ascertain the reason. About this time the situation is vividly described by Taylor: "The sun shone brilliantly on acres of yellow grain, slashed with long, glittering lines of scarlet, blue and steel. The music of both armies rose and fell in challenging paeans. And always the cannon boomed across the marshy stream, and men and horses were cut down, now singly, and now in swathes, and the dismal procession of wounded trailed slowly to the rear. The heat became intense, for it was now high noon. The day was half spent, and already the casualties of the allies amounted to 2,000, when an aide-de-camp of Eugene's came racing from the distant right. The moment had arrived."[1]

It was now half past twelve o'clock, and Marlborough, turning to his generals, said: "Gentlemen, to your posts." Fifteen minutes later Cutts ordered his leading British brigade, commanded by General Rowe, to assault Blenheim, under cover of which the troops on Rowe's right were to move toward the Nebel. Rowe ordered that not a man was to fire until he had struck with his sword the pales of the palisades the French had erected, and then advanced to within 30 paces of the enemy before a withering volley struck him down and a third of his men. The brigade pressed on, and in blinding smoke so uncertain seemed the contest that Lieutenant-General the Marquis de Cléambault, who commanded the troops in Blenheim, called in his seven supporting battalions, and shortly after apparently lost his head, and called the 11 battalions in reserve as well. Thus, 12,000 additional men were jammed into the village, many of whom were not able to move. Parker writes: ". . . we mowed them down with our platoons . . . and it was not possible for them to rush out upon us . . . without running upon the very points of our Bayonets. This great body of Troops therefore was of no further use to *Tallard*, being obliged to keep on the defensive, in expectation that he might come to relieve them."[2]

Nevertheless the assault failed, and a second was delivered and beaten back. Next, the French Gendarmerie, the finest cavalry of France, moved forward on both flanks of Blenheim, and were soon driven back. On the northern flank they were met by Colonel Palmes, who with five squadrons scattered eight by simultaneously charging them in front and on both flanks. A third assault was in preparation, but Marlborough called it off, for he saw that his

[1] *The Wars of Marlborough, 1702–1709*, vol. I, p. 213.
[2] *Memoirs, etc.*, p. 105.

object had been attained, because the French were fixed in the village. Further, his leading infantry were now over the Nebel and the main body of his cavalry was crossing it.

While the battle rolled around Blenheim, a dangerous crisis arose at Oberglau. There 10 battalions, under the Prince of Holstein-Beck, had advanced on that village and had been severely repulsed by the Marquis de Blainville at the head of nine battalions, which included the Irish brigade, known as the "Wild Geese". Driven pell-mell back on the Nebel, the right of Marlborough's centre was left open to attack; whereupon Marsin marshalled a large force of cavalry in rear of Oberglau preparatory to a charge through the gap on the right of his enemy's centre. The situation was critical in the extreme. Marlborough realized it, galloped to the scene, and at once sent an aide-de-camp to Eugene to request him to detach Fugger's cavalry brigade and order it to protect the gap. Though Eugene was fighting a desperate battle in most difficult ground and was also in a critical position, he at once complied, and as Marsin's horsemen charged down toward the Nebel, Fugger struck them on their left flank and drove them back. The charge saved Holstein-Beck, who again advanced and this time drove de Blainville's infantry back into Oberglau, where he "kept those within it besieged", so that, as Campbell says, the allies could now "march before it and attack the cavalry of the enemy with great liberty."[1]

Though Marlborough saw this clearly, for, at three o'clock in the afternoon, the two bastions of Blenheim and Oberglau had been deprived of their offensive power, to the common eye victory was going to the French. The day was advancing; Eugene was at death grips with the Elector, but was making little headway, and if the allies could not advance they would be forced to retire, and to fall back before the French cavalry, as yet little used, meant a rout. But Marlborough knew that victory was his as long as Eugene held on, because so much of the French infantry was locked up in its now purely defensive bastions of Blenheim and Oberglau. There they lay besieged, and between them yawned the gateway to Tallard's doom.

Although Eugene knew that on his front no decision could be gained; Marlborough knew that one was certain on his, as long as Eugene held fast to his enemy. Thus the cooperation between the two generals was complete, and by four o'clock, when the

[1] *The Military History of Eugene and Marlborough*, John Campbell (1736), vol. 1, p. 159.

whole of Marlborough's centre had crossed the marshes, he changed his order of attack and formed his cavalry into two lines in front with two lines of infantry behind them. He had at his disposal an overwhelmingly superior force at the decisive point, for against Tallard's 50 to 60 squadrons and nine battalions he marshalled 90 and 23 respectively. He waited until 4.30 p.m., when he heard that Eugene was working round Lutzingen, and then set the whole of his centre in motion. Only then did Tallard realize what was in his enemy's mind; he ordered up his nine reserve battalions and drew them up to the south of Oberglau to impede the advance. At once Marlborough ordered up three Hanoverian battalions and some cannon, and a desperate fight took place: the Hanoverians were driven back and the whole of Marlborough's line of cavalry recoiled. Now was Tallard's last fleeting chance, but his cavalry hung fire.

At about 5.30 p.m., the Duke ordered his cannon to pour grape on to the nine heroic battalions, and under cover of their fire he ordered a general advance. "With trumpets blaring and kettle-drums crashing and standards tossing proudly above the plumage and the steel," writes Taylor, "the two long lines, perfectly timed from end to end, swung into a trot, that quickened ever as they closed upon the French."[1]

Panic struck most of the enemy horse, who did not wait to receive the shock. Wildly firing their carbines and pistols, the French troopers, including the famous Maison du Roi, swung their horses about and galloped from the field. Some made for Höch-städt and others for the Danube, where some 30 squadrons plunged headlong over its steep bank near Sondenheim into the marshes and river below. Meanwhile the nine battalions were cut down to a man. "I rode through them next morning", writes Parker, "as they lay dead, in Rank and File."[2]

The Franco-Bavarian armies were now rent asunder. In vain did Tallard appeal to Marsin; for at this moment Eugene was storming round the village of Lutzingen. His appeal only pressed home the sense of the general danger, and Marsin and the Elector ordered a withdrawal before their right flank could be overlapped. It was now seven o'clock, and the Duke drew rein and hastily scribbled on the back of a tavern bill this pencil note to his wife: "I have not time to say more, but to beg you will give my duty to

---

[1] *The Wars of Marlborough, 1702–1709*, vol. I, p. 215.
[2] *Memoirs, etc.*, p. 110.

the Queen, and let her know Her Army has had a Glorious Victory. Mons. Tallard and two other Generals are in my coach and I am following the rest: the bearer, my Aide-de-Camp Col. Parke will give Her and (*sic*) account of what has pass'd. I shall doe it in a day or two by another more att large."[1] Within 10 days this message was delivered at Windsor.

After he had scribbled this note and while his cavalry pursued the beaten French and Eugene pressed after Marsin and the Elector, Marlborough turned his attention to Blenheim, where 27 battalions were still held by Cutts, now reinforced by Lord Orkney. Cléambault had galloped for the Danube, had plunged into its stream, and was drowned. At nine o'clock his leaderless men surrendered and the battle ended.

What were its costs? The allies had lost 4,500 killed and 7,500 wounded, including 2,000 British, that is, about 20 per cent. of their original strength. Their enemies, according to Millner, lost 38,609 in killed, drowned, wounded and prisoners, including deserters.[2] That there was no sustained pursuit of Marsin and the Elector is no slur on Marlborough, for he had no fresh reserves at hand, night was falling, and he was encumbered with 15,000 prisoners as well as an immense booty.[3]

Marlborough was elated by his overwhelming victory, and well he might be. Writing to his "dearest soul" on August 14, he called it "as great a victory as has ever been known," and so it was, for Blenheim put an end to the grand design of Louis XIV. It decided the fate of Europe, and as Mr. Churchill writes, "it changed the political axis of the world."[4] Had Marlborough been defeated, the Elector of Bavaria would have replaced the House of Habsburg on the Imperial throne; Munich would have ousted Vienna; and the Empire itself would have become a satrapy of France. Instead, the Elector was chased from his dominions, which were annexed to Austria. Equally important, Blenheim at one stroke cancelled the designs of the House of Stuart; for, had

[1] *Memoirs of the Duke of Marlborough*, William Coxe, vol. I, p. 413.
[2] On August 28 Marlborough informed Heinsius that the enemy acknowledged a loss of 40,000 men (*Heinsius Correspondence*, 210, p. 128).
[3] "100 pieces of cannon, great and small, 24 mortars, 129 colours, 171 standards, 17 pair of kettle-drums, 3,600 tents, 34 coaches, 300 laden mules, 2 bridges of boats, 15 pontoons, 24 barrels and 8 casks of silver." (*History of the Reign of Queen Anne digested into Annals*, Abel Boyer, 1703-1713, vol. III, p. 87.) Regarding the prisoners, Marlborough wrote: "We can't march from hence til we can find some way of disposing all the prisoners . . . for we have noe garrisons to send them to" (*Heinsius Correspondence*, 206, p. 125).
[4] *Marlborough: His Life and Times*, vol. II, p. 478.

France gained a hegemony over the entire west and centre of Europe, there can be little doubt that single-handed England would have had to fight her because of the Pretender's claims.

For England, Blenheim was the greatest battle won on foreign soil since Agincourt. It broke the prestige of the French armies and plunged them into disgrace and ridicule. From 1704 onward Louis XIV sought peace with honour, and though the war continued for another eight years, adding the victories of Ramilles (1706), Oudenarde (1708), and Malplaquet (1709), to Marlborough's fame, Louis's one object was to end it. At length, in 1711, England yearned for peace wherein to reinstate her trade.[1] So it came about that negotiations were opened on January 29, 1712, and at Utrecht a series of peace treaties was signed on April 11, 1713. France retained her hold on the left bank of the upper Rhine, and, on the understanding that the crowns of France and Spain should never be united, Philip of Anjou was recognized as Philip V of Spain and the Indies. Thus Louis broke the Habsburg ring, completed the work of Richelieu and Mazarin, and gave France security until 1792. Further, he recognized the Protestant succession in England. Austria was given the Spanish Netherlands, henceforth to be known as the Austrian Netherlands, as well as Naples and Milan, which she retained until 1866. The United Provinces were allotted certain Barrier fortresses, and Savoy, raised to a kingdom, received Nice and Sicily, which island, in 1720, was exchanged for Sardinia. Of all the booty hunters England obtained what eventually was to prove the lion's share: from France, Acadia (Nova Scotia), Newfoundland and the region around the Hudson–thus the expulsion of the French from North America began–and from Spain, Gibraltar and Minorca, which guaranteed her naval power in the western Mediterranean. Further, an advantageous commercial treaty was signed between England and Spain, in which the most profitable clause was the grant to the former of the sole right to import negro slaves into Spanish America for 30 years.[2]

With the signing of the Treaty of Utrecht, England was left

---

[1] "In 1710 the number of vessels cleared from English ports is quoted as 3,550; in 1711 as 3,759; in 1712 as 4,267; in 1713 as 5,807; in 1714 as 6,614. The shipping in London is stated to have increased in these five years from 806 to 1,550" (*The Cambridge Modern History*, vol. v, p. 439).

[2] The *Asiento* or "Contract" for supplying Spanish America with African slaves, which permitted the slave traders to carry on the smuggling of other goods. "This *Asiento* contract was one of the most coveted things that England won for herself in the war and pocketed at the Peace of Utrecht." (*Blenheim*, G. M. Trevelyan, p. 139.)

supreme at sea and in the markets of the world, and as Admiral Mahan says, "not only in fact, but also in her own consciousness." "This great but noiseless revolution in sea-power", writes Professor Trevelyan, "was accomplished by the victories of Marlborough's arms and diplomacy on land . . . it was because Marlborough regarded the naval war as an integral part of the whole allied effort against Louis, that English sea power was fixed between 1702 and 1712 on a basis whence no enemy has since been able to dislodge it."[1]

But the revolution went deeper still; for it was the machinery of the Bank of England and the National Debt which enabled England to fight wars with gold as well as iron. William's war had lasted for nine years and had cost over £30,000,000, and the War of the Spanish Succession dragged on for 12 years and cost about £50,000,000. Only half this vast sum of £80,000,000 was met out of taxation, the remainder was borrowed and added to the National Debt. Thus a system was devised whereby the prosperity of the future was underwritten in order to ease the poverty of the present, and war was henceforth founded on unpayable debt. The banker merchants of London steadily gained in political power over the landed interests, and, therefore, increasingly into their hands went the destinies of the nation and the Empire, whose frontiers had become the oceans and the seas.

[1] *Blenheim*, p. 248.

The century which saw the first large expansion of the British overseas was also the century of the rise of a new power within Europe, and another on her eastern flank. Under Peter the Great (1682–1725) Russia, hitherto chiefly preoccupied with her struggles against the Tartars and the Turks, began at last to look westward, and to play a part in the European political complex. At the time of his accession, says Fuller,

> Russia was still a barbaric country: its tsar owned the land and the people. Of liberty there was none; justice was bought and sold; taxation was on the level of brigandage; corruption, drunkenness and violence abounded; unspeakable forms of vice were universal, as were the grossest superstitions, and the West was held to be the land of the damned. Kotoshikhin, who . . . sought refuge in Sweden, informs us that 'The Russians are arrogant and incapable, because they get no education except in pride, shamelessness, and lying. They will not send their children abroad to learn, fearing that if they came to know the mode of life and the religion of other folks and the blessing of freedom, they would forget to return home. It was indeed one of the *arcana imperii* of the tsars to hinder their subjects from travelling, lest they should behold the spectacle of liberty elsewhere . . .'

But Peter himself did travel – to Germany, Austria, France, Holland and England, acquiring, *en route,* a technological education which he put to remarkable use when he returned to Russia.

He learnt the use of the mariner's compass, the sword, the plane, axe and saw, and even of dental forceps, and seldom failed to put his knowledge into immediate practice. He built a frigate with his own hands, drilled his soldiers, at times did his own cooking, made his own bed and extracted the teeth of his subjects. He frequented low company and rarely passed a day without being the worse for drink. In his orgies his greatest joy was to make his female companions drunk, and in the torture chamber he would lash his victims with the knout. Yet, all in all, he was the greatest of the Russian tsars, for through sheer force of will and intolerant brutality he forced his reluctant subjects to westernize themselves. And had he not been what he was, a ferocious organizer, remembering what his subjects were like, he would certainly have failed. Brutes by nature, they demanded a super-brute as master.

The high peak of Peter's extraordinary reign came in 1709: his defeat of the Swedish King Charles XII at the Battle of Poltava. Charles was a military genius, but unquestionably mad; as Fuller says, "a knight errant and berserker in one". All his genius was for war: his tactical eye was brilliant, his sense of timing superb, his leadership utterly inspiring to his soldiers. These qualities brought him victory after victory; but too often it was victory for its own sake alone; the sense of a deeper purpose than military triumph itself was lacking. The Battle of Poltava, fought in the depths of southern Russia against great odds, was simply the fruit of this demented energy; despite prodigies of valour, the Swedes were beaten, and their small army practically destroyed. Yet the battle represents more than the calamity of a madman; it was, says Fuller,

a trial of strength between two civilizations, that of Europe and of Asia, and because this was so, though little noticed at the time, the Russian victory on the Vorskla was destined to be one of the most portentous events in the modern history of the western world. By wresting the hegemony of the north from Sweden; by putting an end to Ukranian independence, and by ruining the cause of Stanislaus[1] in Poland, Russia, essentially an Asiatic power, gained a foothold on the counterscarp of eastern Europe. But at the time, the importance of Poltava lay more in what it established than in what it overthrew. It showed Peter that his principal task was to create a regular army and a Baltic fleet, in order to maintain his position *vis a vis* Europe. Further, it showed him that the upkeep of these forces demanded financial reforms, and that these reforms demanded the substitution of European for Oriental administration.

[1] Stanislaus Leszcznski, Charles's nominee for the Polish throne.

By the end of his reign, says Fuller, thanks to his reforms of the Russian system of government, Peter had created a regular army of 210,000 men, supported by 109,000 irregulars, and had built a fleet of forty-eight ships of the line and 787 galleys and lesser vessesls. "Like the hordes of Xerxes, this vast host gloomed over the eastern horizon of the west, a portent of yet another Asiatic invasion. In shadowy form Poltava was Marathon in reverse."

The rise and expansion of Prussia

Better described as the Brandenburg-Prussian State, Prussia was the second of the new powers which emerged during the seventeenth century; yet her origins, like those of Russia, dated from the tenth century, and also like Russia, her expansion was caused by military necessity, for she was a land-locked country surrounded by hostile powers.

In the year 919 (see Chronicle 12 (Vol. I) the Saxon Duke Henry the Fowler founded the Mark of Brandenburg (Brennibor) as a bulwark against the Slavs, and a great colonizing movement began, which in three centuries added all the lands between the Elbe and the Oder to Germany and Christendom. In 1226 the region of the Spree was acquired and Berlin was founded. During the same year the Polish Duke of Masonia appealed to Hermann von Salza, Grand Master of the Order of the Teutonic Knights, to convert the pagan Prussians, a Slavonic tribe inhabiting the region between the mouths of the Vistula and the Niemen. The result was that, between 1231 and 1310, the land–later to become known as East Prussia–was conquered; the towns of Elbing, Königsberg and Danzig were founded, and the Prussians were largely exterminated and replaced by German settlers. In 1313, the headquarters of the Order was permanently established at Marienburg.

With its missionary task ended, coupled with the decline of the Hanseatic League, the union between the Scandinavian States, and the rise of Poland under the Jagello dynasty, the Order fell into a decline, and, in 1410, on the field of Tannenberg, its knights sustained a crushing defeat at the hands of the Poles, from which they never recovered. Seven years later the margravate of Brandenburg passed to Frederick Hohenzollen, Burgrave of Nuremberg, and, in 1466, in accordance with the Perpetual Peace of Thorn, Prussia was divided into two parts. West Prussia, re-named Royal Prussia, including Danzig, became part of Poland, and East, or Ducal Prussia, was restored to the Order as a Polish fief. Lastly, in 1618, on the outbreak of the Thirty Years War, Ducal Prussia was permanently united with Brandenburg and seventeenth-century Prussia was born.

The Thirty Years War was both the death-bed of German medieval civilization and the cradle of Franco-German rivalry, which was to distract Europe for 300 years. When the war ended in 1648, France was powerful and centralized, Germany disrupted and exhausted, and though Brandenburg lost nearly half its population and all its industry and trade, Prussia was untouched. Balked from expansion northward by the English Channel and southward by the Pyrenees, French aggrandizement flowed eastward into Germany, and between the Peace of Westphalia, in 1648, and 1704, when the French were decisively defeated at Blenheim, western Germany was invaded repeatedly. "Louis XIV," writes the Duc de Broglie[1] in his *Frédéric II et Maria Theresa*, "sent his armies so many times across the Rhine needlessly and without a pretext that at length patriotism awoke from its slumber. There are certain faults which Providence punishes by denying them oblivion. The soldiers of Turenne little knew to what an undying hatred on the part of Germany they devoted the very name of their country, when they inscribed it with letters of blood and fire on all the hills of the Palatinate." Thus was German nationalism fostered, as French nationalism had been during the Hundred Years War, and in Brandenburg it began to take form when in December, 1640, Frederick William succeeded to the margravate of Brandenburg.

First he set out to colonize his devastated territories, and by offering complete religious toleration to all comers, thousands of Dutch, French, and other peoples migrated to Brandenburg to become the "true-born Prussians" of later days. Next, he realized that the power of a State is to be measured by its fighting forces, and he improved upon the small standing army created by his father in 1637, and raised it to 25,000 strong. He used it both as a diplomatic and strategical weapon, prevented Ducal Prussia from falling into the hands of the Poles and Swedes, and in 1675 he routed the latter at Fehrbellin, after which he became known to history as the "Great Elector". On his death, in 1688, he was succeeded by his son Frederick, who at Königsberg, on January 18, 1701, crowned himself Frederick I King of Prussia. In May, 1702, as a member of the Grand Alliance against France, Frederick put 14,000 men into the field, a contingent eventually raised to 40,000 strong, which played a notable part at Blenheim,

---

[1] Jacques Duc de Broglie (1821–1901) was the great-grandson of Frederick the Great's opponent at Rossbach.

Ramillies, Oudenarde, and Malplaquet. Though Prussia gained little from the Peace of Utrecht, the part played by Frederick's army in the War of the Spanish Succession was so considerable that when it ended in 1713 the peoples of Brandenburg-Prussia emerged as the Prussian nation–a standing challenge to France.

Frederick I died two months before the Peace of Utrecht was signed, and was succeeded by his son Frederick William (1713-1740), then aged 24 and a figure of great historical importance. Like his contemporary, Peter the Great, he was a man of enormous industry, violent, brutal, and possessed of the manners of a drill sergeant. He instituted rigid economies in every department of state; put the finances of his kingdom in order, and settled 40,000 south Germans in East Prussia and Pomerania. His parsimony, which was remarkable for an absolute monarch, enabled him to raise the strength of his army from 50,000 to 80,000 officers and men; the latter he either impressed or kidnapped in slave-hunts, and the former he conscripted, all nobles of military age were compelled to serve after training in *Cadettenhaüser* (Military Schools). The strength of his army lay not so much in its size as in its discipline and training, which were so brutal that under his son active service was considered a relief from barrack life. His one hobby was his regiment of giant grenadiers, for which he kidnapped men in every country, including Ireland. No abnormally tall man was safe; even the Abbé Bastiani was sand-bagged and collared while celebrating Mass in an Italian church, and any girl who in inches matched his grenadiers was seized in order to mate with them.

Vigorous in everything he did, his queen presented him with 14 children; the fourth, born on January 24, 1713, was christened Karl Frédéric, and is known to history as Frederick II and the Great. His behaviour toward him was nearly as abominable as was that of Peter the Great toward Alexis. He spat in his food to prevent him eating too much; in 1730 he attempted to strangle him with a curtain cord; later he had him condemned to death, and when his councillors refused to be party to his son's murder, he beheaded his friend Katte before his son's eyes. On May 31, 1740, Frederick William I died, and when those around him sang the hymn, "Naked I came into the world and naked I shall go," he had just sufficient strength to mutter, "No, not quite naked; I shall have my uniform on."

Frederick II found himself at the head of a highly efficient

State, with a well filled treasury and the best trained army in Europe. But Prussia was strategically weak, for she had no natural land frontiers and was surrounded by aggressive neighbours. These circumstances demanded that, in order to remain strong, she must expand; but to do so demanded a pretext, however flimsy, and this Frederick found ready-made for him in the question of the Austrian Succession.

When the Emperor Joseph died without male issue in 1711, his brother Charles succeeded him as the Emperor Charles VI. As Charles also had no son, a family compact, known as the "Pragmatic Sanction", was agreed upon. According to this, Charles's daughter, Maria Theresa, was given priority of succession to the Habsburg dominions over Joseph's daughter, Maria Amalia, who in 1722, became the wife of Charles Albert of Bavaria. After prolonged negotiations, this compact was recognized by every important court in Europe, except the Bavarian. Thus matters stood, when on October 20, 1740, Charles VI died.

Realizing that the compact was fragile, that the States of Europe were at sixes and sevens, and knowing that Austria was unprepared for war, Frederick mobilized his army and sent Count Gotter to Vienna with a letter in which he recognized Maria Theresa's (1740-1780) succession and offered her military assistance in case of need, in return for which he proposed to occupy Silesia, pending the settlement of his claim to it, which he based on the long annulled *Erbverbrüderung* (Heritage-Brother-hood) of 1537 between the Margrave of Brandenburg and the Duke of Liegnitz. Frederick received an emphatic denial of his claim and on December 16 he ordered his army to cross the Silesian frontier and march on Breslau. Thus was precipitated the War of the Austrian Succession.

At once Maria Theresa appealed to the guarantors of the Pragmatic Sanction for assistance; but their standard of honour was no higher than Frederick's, and it was not until the Austrians were badly defeated by Field-Marshal Schwerin at Mollwitz on April 10, 1741, that the conflict became general. Charles Albert of Bavaria set out to gain the Imperial Crown by an invasion of Bohemia; the French, who wanted predominance in Europe, crossed the Rhine as Bavaria's ally; and the Saxons and Savoyards joined in the attack on Maria Theresa while the English and Dutch hastened to support her indirectly by preparing to attack

France. Frederick again defeated the Austrians at Chotusitz on May 17, and entered into alliance with France, when, on the promptings of England, Maria Theresa came to terms with him and ceded to him Lower Silesia, so that she might concentrate against the French and Bavarians. Then Frederick withdrew from the war and Saxony followed suit.

Freed from Prussia and Saxony, Maria Theresa set out to annex Bavaria in compensation for Silesia. In the depths of winter she forced the French out of Prague, and on the Rhine, on June 27, 1743, to add to this reverse, the French were defeated by the English and Hanoverians at Dettingen. Alarmed by these events, and as he realized that an Austrian triumph might lead to the ruin of Prussia, in September, 1744, Frederick re-entered the war and invaded Austria, but was outmanœuvred by Marshal Traun. Slowly the tide turned in favour of the French, Marshal de Saxe beat the English at Fontenoy on May 11, 1745, and again at Lauffeld on July 2, 1746. Meanwhile Frederick, who had been forced out of Austria, was followed by the Austrians and Saxons, who advanced into Silesia and were, on June 4, 1745, defeated at Hohenfriedberg. Next, on December 15, 1745, at the hands of Leopold of Anhalt-Dessau, the "Old Dessauer", who had fought at Blenheim, came the Austro-Saxon defeat at Kesselsdorf, which was sufficiently decisive to compel Maria Theresa again to come to terms with Prussia. This suited Frederick well, for in order not to be left at the mercy of France, he did not seek too complete a victory over the Austrians.

Peace was signed between Austria and Prussia at Dresden on Christmas Day, 1745. By its terms, Silesia and Glatz were ceded to Frederick, and in return he guaranteed the Pragmatic Sanction. Thus he added 16,000 square miles and 1,000,000 new subjects to his realm, and on his return to Berlin was acclaimed "the Great".

Although the war dragged on for another three years, Frederick took no further part in it. At length all belligerents, except Austria, were weary of the conflict, and a general peace was signed at Aix-la-Chapelle in October-November, 1748. By its terms, Frederick's acquisitions were guaranteed, a few small territorial adjustments were made; and a return to the situation prevailing before the outbreak of the war was agreed to. Though Frederick was well pleased with the results of his aggression, the Peace of Aix-la-Chapelle was to be no more than an armistice.

CHAPTER 15

The Battles of Rossbach and Leuthen, 1757

Though Carlyle calls him "the last of the Kings", Frederick the Great was a new type of monarch, representative rather of the Classical tyrants and the princes of the Italian Renaissance than akin to the declining absolute and rising constitutional kings of his age.

A man of culture as well as a soldier, he mixed philosophy with war, and is both so self-revealing and contradictory in his voluminous writings that it is most difficult, if not impossible, to discover what he really was like, not only to his contemporaries but in himself. For instance, few great soldiers have been so callous in provoking wars; yet, throughout, he seems to have realized the futility of attempts to achieve permanent worth by their means. In his *Military Instructions* he writes: "With troops like these [his soldiers] the *world itself* might be subdued, if conquests were not as fatal to the victors as to the vanquished."[1] Again, in one of his many poems he alludes to war as "this brazen-headed monster, the War Demon athirst for blood and for destruction", and he terms Bellona "that woeful, wild woman, beloved of ancient Chaos".[2] Yet he insists that "we must not satirize war, but get rid of it, as a doctor gets rid of fever"; and he writes to Voltaire, for years his companion:—

"How can a prince, whose troops are dressed in coarse blue cloth and whose hats are trimmed with white braid, after having made them turn to the right and to the left, lead them to glory without deserving the honourable title of a brigand-chief, since he is only followed by a heap of idlers obliged by necessity to become mercenary executioners in order to carry on under him the honest occupation of highwayman? Have you forgotten that war is a scourge which, collecting them all together, adds to them all possible crimes? You see that after having read these wise maxims, a man who cares even a little for his reputation, should avoid the epithets which are only given to the vilest scoundrels."[3]

[1] *Military Instructions from the late King of Prussia, etc.*, fifth English edit. (1818), p. 6.
[2] *L'ode de la guerre.*
[3] *Letters of Voltaire and Frederick the Great*, trans. Richard Aldington (1927), Letter CXCII, October 9, 1773, p. 343.

In spite of this wholehearted condemnation of war, his outlook on peace was profoundly cynical. When discussing with Voltaire the Abbé de Saint-Pierre's *Project de Paix Perpétuelle*, he declared: "The thing is most practicable, for its success all that is lacking is the consent of Europe and a few similar trifles."[1] From these and other sayings one is brought to the conclusion that the sole thing he really believed in was "original sin", and this is borne out in a conversation he once had with his inspector of education, Sulzer. When the latter remarked that in former times it was held that man was naturally inclined to evil, but now that his inborn inclination was toward good, the reply he received from Frederick was: "Ah, my dear Sulzer, you don't know this damned race!"

As a king he was broad-minded and liberal. He said: "I and my people have come to a satisfactory understanding. They say what they like and I do what I like." He tolerated all religious sects, because he considered that everyone must "get to heaven in his own way". He freed the Press, abolished torture, developed scientific study, fed free the poor and opened almshouses for thousands of old women; but with characteristic economy made them spin. Nevertheless he could be exceedingly brutal. In one place he explains that a way of gaining intelligence is to seize a rich man, to dress him poorly and to send him into the enemy's country, with the threat that if he does not return within a certain time "his houses shall be burned, and his wife and children hacked to pieces".[2] Also, "If we are in a Protestant country," he writes, "we wear the mask of protector of the Lutheran religion, and endeavour to make fanatics of the lower order of people, whose simplicity is not proof against our artifice. In a Catholic country, we preach up toleration and moderation, constantly abusing the priests as the cause of all the animosity that exists between the different sectaries, although, in spite of their disputes, they all agree upon material points of faith."[3]

He would seem to have been a mixture of Puck and Machiavelli welded together on the anvil of Vulcan by the hammer of Thor.

Except for Alexander the Great and, possibly, Charles XII, Frederick was the most offensively-minded of all the Great Captains. Colin says of him: "Frederick II breathes nothing but the offensive – the offensive always, in every situation, in the operations as a whole as on the field of battle, even if he is in the

---

[1] *Ibid.*, Letter LXVI, April 12, 1742, p. 161.
[2] *Military Instruction, etc.,* p. 61. [3] *Ibid.*, p. 66.

presence of a superior army. He is activity itself. . . ."[1] On one occasion Frederick said he would cashier any officer who waited to be attacked, instead of attacking: he always attacked and nearly always struck first. "The whole strength of our troops lies in attack," he said, "and we act foolishly if we renounce it without good cause".[2]

He disliked long wars, not only because of their cost, but because soldiers deteriorate during them, and be it remembered that in the eighteenth century offensives largely depended upon drill (skill in moving). Further, he was aware that, as "battles determine the fate of nations",[3] and as "the first object in the establishment of an army ought to be making provision for the belly, that being the basis and foundation of all operations",[4] the longer a war lasts the more difficult becomes supply. Nevertheless, by always attacking, like Charles XII, he suffered more than one disastrous defeat.

Napoleon's estimate of him is interesting. He says:

"He was above all great in the most critical moments, this is the highest praise which one can make regarding him."[5]

* * * * *

"What distinguishes Frederick the most, is not his skill in manœuvring, but his audacity. He carried out things I never dared to do. He abandoned his line of operations, and often acted as if he had no knowledge whatever of the art of war."[6]

* * * * *

"It is not the Prussian army which for seven years defended Prussia against the three most powerful nations in Europe, but Frederick the Great."[7]

When his campaigns are examined, we find that it was not only his audacious spirit but also his ability to grasp the tactical conditions of his day and to learn from his own mistakes that made him so great a general. He realized how artificially slow

---

[1] *The Transformations of War*, Commandant J. Colin (1912), p. 195.
[2] Quoted from *A Review of the History of Infantry*, Colonel E. M. Lloyd (1908), pp. 160–161.
[3] *Military Instruction, etc.*, p. 125.
[4] *Ibid.*, p. 7. Frederick provided hand-mills for each company, p. 11.
[5] *Correspondance de Napoléon 1er*, vol. XXXII, p. 238.
[6] *Sainte-Hélène, Journal inédit (1815–1818)*, Général Gourgaud (edition 1899), vol. II, pp. 33, 34.
[7] *Recits de la captivité de l'Empereur Napoléon a Sainte-Hélène*, Comte de Montholon (1847), vol. II, p. 90.

and heavy were the tactics of his age, and from the outset of his career he determined to base his system of war on what these tactics lacked – mobility and rapidity of fire. He states: "A Prussian battalion is a moving battery . . . the rapidity in loading is such that it can triple the fire of all other troops. This gives to the Prussians a superiority of three to one."[1] Nevertheless, in his earlier campaigns, he relied more on the bayonet than the bullet, but soon discovered his mistake; for in his later battles he did his utmost to develop the power of both his muskets and cannon. He was a great artillerist and the creator of the first true horse artillery ever formed, a weapon so little thought of that, from 1759 onward for 30 years, the Prussian was the only horse artillery in Europe. Also, because the Austrians, who acted usually on the defensive, were prone to hold their reserves behind the ridges occupied by their firing lines, he was a great believer in the howitzer. Yet, strange to say, he never fully grasped the value of a trained light infantry, and this is all the more surprising because at the battle of Kolin the Austrian light troops – Croats and Pandours – were largely responsible for his defeat.[2]

From his minor tactics, Frederick developed his major, or grand tactics. Hitherto extreme slowness of deployment usually led to a frontal engagement, hence the head-on battles of the seventeenth and eighteenth centuries. But what Frederick grasped was that, should the mobility of one side greatly exceed that of the other, once the slower had deployed, it would be possible to march against one of its flanks, deploy, and attack it before it could change front. This was the essence of his grand tactics, which were so simple that, though they could easily be copied, they were unlikely to succeed unless the attacker possessed superior mobility. It was for this reason that Napoleon said: "His (Frederick's) Oblique Order could only prove successful against an army which was unable to manœuvre."[3]

Frederick explains this order as follows: "You refuse one wing to the enemy and strengthen the one which is to attack. With the latter you do your utmost against one wing of the enemy which you take in flank. An army of 100,000 men taken in flank

[1] *Histoire de mon temps*, Frédéric le Grand (1879), p. 201.
[2] For more information on this subject and for the rising value of light infantry, see my *British Light Infantry in the Eighteenth Century* (1925), pp. 66–72; also Frederick's *Military Instruction*, etc., pp. 80–82.
[3] Quoted from *Préceptes et Jugements de Napoléon*, Lieut.-Colonel Ernest Picard (1913), p. 125.

may be beaten by 30,000 in a very short time. . . . The advantages of this arrangement are (1) a small force can engage one much stronger than itself; (2) it attacks an enemy at a decisive point; (3) if you are beaten, it is only part of your army, and you have the other three-fourths which are still fresh to cover your retreat."[1]

In order to attain the maximum of mobility and rapidity of fire, Frederick relied upon drill, about which much nonsense has been written. It is true that it was severe and even brutal; yet it is quite untrue that Frederick looked upon it as anything other than a means to an end. Also, it is true that he had no very high opinion of the soldiers of his age. In his *Military Instruction* he writes: "An army is composed for the most part of idle and inactive men, and unless the general has a constant eye upon them . . . this artificial machine . . . will very soon fall to pieces, and nothing but the *bare idea* of a disciplined army will remain."[2] Also: "If my soldiers began to think, not one would remain in the ranks."[3] Further, "All that can be done with the soldier is to give him *esprit de corps*, i.e. a higher opinion of his own regiment than of all the other troops of the country, and since the officers have sometimes to lead him into the greatest danger (and he cannot be influenced by a sense of honour) he must be more afraid of his officers than of the dangers to which he is exposed."[4]

Although he wrote like this, toward his men he was by no means unkindly, at times he could be friendly and familiar. On one occasion a deserter was brought before him. " 'Why did you leave me?' said the King to him. 'Indeed, your Majesty,' replied the grenadier, ' . . . things are going very badly with us.' 'Come, come,' rejoined Frederick, 'let us fight another battle to-day: if I am beaten, we will desert together to-morrow;' and with these words he sent him back to his colours."[5]

Though, later on, the Prussian drill came to be taken for the art of war, Frederick never so interpreted it. He "laughed in his sleeve," says Napoleon, "at the parades of Potsdam, when he perceived young officers, French, English and Austrian, so infatuated with the manœuvre of the oblique order, which was fit for nothing but to gain a few adjutant-majors a reputation."[6]

---

[1] Quoted from *A Review of the History of Infantry*, Colonel E. M. Lloyd, p. 162.
[2] *Military Instruction, etc.*, p. 5.
[3] Quoted from *The Biology of War*, Dr. G. F. Nicolai (1919), p. 65.
[4] Quoted from a *Review of the History of Infantry*, Colonel E. M. Lloyd, p. 153.
[5] *Frederick the Great: His Court and Times*, edited by Thomas Campbell (1843), vol. III, p. 138.
[6] *Correspondance de Napoléon 1er*, vol. XXXII, p. 243.

The truth is, that unless Frederick's drill was animated by Frederick's spirit, it was a delusion.

A few extracts from his *Instructions* will show that he was far from being solely a drill-master:

"The army of the enemy should be the chief object of our attention" (p. 49).

"In war the skin of a fox is at times as necessary as that of a lion, for cunning may succeed when force fails" (p. 52).

"It is an invariable axiom of war to secure your own flanks and rear, and endeavour to turn those of your enemy" (p. 101).

"The conquering wing of your cavalry must not allow the enemy's cavalry to rally, but pursue them in good order" (p. 118).

"To shed the blood of soldiers, when there is no occasion for it, is to lead them inhumanly to the slaughter" (p. 120).

"Though our wounded are to be the first objects of our attention, we are not to forget our duty to the enemy" (p. 121).

"You are never to imagine that *every* thing is done as long as *any* thing remains undone" (p. 122).

"My officers ... are expected to profit by my mistakes, and they may be assured, that I shall apply myself with all diligence to correct them" (p. 126).

"Those battles are the best into which we force the enemy, for it is an established maxim, to oblige him to do that for which he has no sort of inclination, and as your interest and his are diametrically opposite, it cannot be supposed that you are both wishing for the same event" (p. 126).

Though Frederick wanted peace, and after the Peace of Aix-la-Chapelle had exclaimed: "Henceforth I would not attack a cat except to defend myself," it would appear that he failed to appreciate the implications of his successful aggression. It had rendered Austria resentful and France fearful; in fact it had provided both with a common grievance which, were they only willing to sink their traditional enmity, could be developed into a common cause. Unfortunately for Frederick, this was what Prince von Kaunitz, Maria Theresa's Chancellor of State, realized. He saw that Frederick's aggression had rendered the traditional rivalry between France and Austria obsolete and suggested to the Queen that France should be approached with a view to obtain her aid in regaining Silesia, in exchange for which she should be offered the Austrian Netherlands. As she loathed Frederick and had been stung by his gibes, Maria

Theresa favoured the suggestion and Kaunitz approached the French Court. Firstly, he pointed out that Frederick alone could gain from a continuance of the rivalry between France and Austria; secondly that, as the Tsarina Elizabeth, whom Frederick had insulted by calling "the Apostolic Hag", was eager to acquire East Prussia; as Saxony could be bought over by an offer of Magdeburg; and Sweden by a promise of Pomerania; if, in exchange for the Austrian Netherlands, France would agree to support Austria, a coalition of 70,000,000 people could be formed which would wipe Prussia and her 4,500,000 inhabitants off the map.

Although this proposal ran counter to French traditional policy, Madame de Pompadour, then the real power at the French Court, whom Frederick had also insulted by calling her "Mlle. Poisson"–her mother was reputed to be a fishwife– readily gave her support. But before a final agreement could be reached, England took a step which precipitated a crisis.

Concerned over the security of Hanover while occupied in their undeclared colonial wars with France, the English Government bought with a large subsidy the Tsarina's guarantee to protect Hanover by concentrating her army on her western frontier.

Frederick's suspicions were aroused, and when he got wind of Kaunitz's negotiations, in his turn he approached England and offered to guarantee the integrity of Hanover. His offer was accepted, and the agreement with the Tsarina, which had not been ratified, was cancelled by the English Government. Next, in January, 1756, according to the terms of the Convention of Westminster, an alliance was entered upon between England and Prussia, and as it was wholly a defensive one, it did not violate Frederick's obligations with France. Nevertheless, as Frederick was well aware, the invasion of Hanover would of necessity in another war become part of the French plan. Lastly, in the following May, in order to offset this Convention, France concluded a defensive alliance, known as the Treaty of Versailles, with Austria. Thus, by the summer of 1756, Europe was divided into two hostile camps–England and Prussia, and France and Austria, supported by Russia, Sweden, and Saxony.

Though for Austria, Kaunitz's scheme was a triumph, for France it was a disaster in disguise. The War of the Austrian Succession had shown how vulnerable the French colonies were, and as already in Ohio and in India an undeclared colonial war was in progress between France and England, the high probability was that a new war in Europe, in which France could not help but play a prominent rôle, would lead to the extinction of most of the French oversea empire. And this is what did happen.

Frederick learnt from his spies that the Tsarina was urging Maria Theresa to hasten her military preparations and saw that to wait until she was ready would be fatal for Prussia. He decided to strike first. "After all," he wrote, "it was of small importance whether my enemies called me an aggressor or not as all Europe had already united against me."[1]

Though the geographical position of Prussia enabled Frederick to operate on interior lines, which in the circumstances was an enormous advantage, Prussia had no defensible frontiers and in face of the alliance her army was outnumbered by about three to one. In the south, when the Austrians had joined up with the Saxons, they would be 40 miles from Berlin; in the north, the Swedes, when they had concentrated at Stralsund, would be within 130 miles; in the east, when the Russians had crossed the Oder, they would be but 50 miles; and in the west, on entering Prussian territory near Halle, the French would be 100 miles from Berlin. Yet there was a saving clause: all these armies were in various stages of preparation; the Austrian had not yet joined the Saxon; the Russian had still to cross the roadless wastes of Poland; the Swedes the Baltic; and the French the Rhine.

In July, Frederick demanded an assurance from Vienna that the Austrian troop concentrations in Bohemia were not directed against Prussia, and received an evasive answer. He waited no longer, but detached 11,000 men to watch the Swedes; 26,000 to watch the Russians; left 37,000 to defend Silesia, and on August 29, 1756, with 70,000 men, suddenly and without a declaration of war invaded Saxony. On September 10 he occupied Dresden. Frederick then blockaded Pirna, and in October came up with the Austrians at Lobositz and defeated them.

Frederick's invasion of Saxony was the signal for a violent outburst of moral indignation which stirred the Imperial Diet, which believed that Frederick would be overwhelmed, to place him under its ban, an action tantamount to outlawing him. More to the purpose, the Coalition determined to put 500,000 troops into the field and crush the aggressor.

[1] Quoted from *Frederick the Great*, F. J. P. Veale (1935), p. 181.

Frederick waited until the passes were free from snow, then advanced on Prague, and when he came up with the Austrians there, on May 6, 1757, he again defeated them. He blockaded the city, and advanced southward, and, on June 18, at Kolin, recklessly attacked an Austrian army, under Marshal Daun, nearly twice the size of his own. He suffered a crushing defeat, in which he lost 13,000 men out of 33,000, and was compelled to raise the siege of Prague and to withdraw into Saxony.

Encouraged by Daun's victory, the allies determined to enclose Frederick in a ring of fire. Their plan was as follows: Prince Joseph of Saxe-Hildburghausen, in command of the Reich Army, 33,000 strong, was to unite with Marshal Soubise and his 30,000 men and reconquer Saxony; Marshal d'Éstrées and the Duke of Richelieu and 100,000 men were to advance against the Duke of Cumberland in Hanover; 17,000 Russians, who had taken Memel, were to invade Prussia; 17,000 Swedes, under Baron Ungern Sternberg, were to land in Pomerania; and 100,000 Austrians, under Prince Charles of Lorraine and Field-Marshal Daun, were to operate against the remnants of Frederick's Kolin army. Thus, nearly 390,000 men were to be concentrated against Frederick who, undaunted, withdrew 25,000 men from before Daun and marched 170 miles to Erfurt, then threatened by Soubise.

On May 1, 1757, Louis XV concluded the Second Treaty of Versailles with Maria Theresa, which granted her a yearly subsidy of 30,000,000 livres to pay for her Russian support. In June d'Éstrées began to move, and, on July 26, by accident he defeated Cumberland at Hastenbeck, near Hamelin. Both generals had ordered a retreat, but the unauthorized intervention of a small detachment gave the French the victory. D'Éstrées was superseded by the Duke of Richelieu, who concluded with Cumberland the ignominious Convention of Klosterzeven, according to the terms of which the Anglo-Hanoverian army was to pack up and go home. Though a few weeks later the convention was repudiated by both the English and French governments, Richelieu, instead of joining up with Soubise, in traditional French fashion began to plunder the country. Still advancing—and plundering—Soubise moved on Magdeburg, an important Prussian arsenal, after which he intended to make for Berlin.

Meanwhile the Russians advanced into Prussia, where they

perpetrated unheard-of barbarities.[1] To halt them Frederick ordered Field-Marshal Lehwaldt with 25,000 men to attack 40,000 of them at Gross-Jägerndorf. On August 30, he did so and was defeated. Thus the road to Berlin was unbarred, but as so often has happened, the Russian army melted away through lack of supplies. Nevertheless, by October Frederick's position was so desperate that it seemed to him the war was irretrievably lost.

Though he realized how slight his chances were, because he could not stand still he decided to move against the French. He left the Duke of Bevern with 41,000 men in Lusatia to oppose Prince Charles of Lorraine's 112,000, and on August 25 he set out for Dresden to assemble his army. From there he marched to Erfurt, where he arrived on September 13; whereupon Soubise retired to Eisenach. Frederick then paid Richelieu a bribe of 100,000 thalers to remain inactive, followed up Soubise, cleared Gotha, and left General Seydlitz there to watch him. On September 19 Soubise and Hildburghausen advanced on Gotha, but were met by Seydlitz and hastily withdrew.[2]

With Frederick thus engaged, Bevern was pushed back on Breslau, and Count Hadik, with 3,500 Austrians, advanced on Berlin. On October 16 Hadik entered the Prussian capital and was paid a ransom of 300,000 thalers to depart. When he heard of Hadik's raid, Frederick left 7,000 men under Marshal Keith to guard the Saale, and set out to save his capital; but, on October 20 he learnt that he was too late and decided to return. During his absence, Soubise, who had been reinforced by 15,000 men under Marshal de Broglie, invaded Saxony, and, on October 27, reached Weissenfels, from where he summoned Keith at Leipzig to surrender the city, but was met by a blank refusal.

[1] "They hung innocent inhabitants from trees, ripped open their bodies, tore out their hearts and their intestines, cut off their noses and ears, broke their legs, fired villages and hamlets, formed a circle round the burning houses, and drove back their fleeing inmates into the flames. Their wanton brutality was especially wreaked on the nobles and the clergy: these they tied to the tails of their horses, and dragged them after them, or stripped them naked, and laid them upon blazing fires. . . . Their senseless revenge was exercised even on the dead; they opened the graves, and scattered abroad the mutilated corpses." (*Frederick the Great: His Court and Times*, edited by Thomas Campbell, vol. III, p. 102.)

[2] At this time the French Army was in a shocking state of discipline. This may in part be gauged by the booty they left behind them in this retreat: "Pommades, perfumes, powdering and dressing-gowns, bag-wigs, umbrellas, parrots: while a host of whining lacquays, cooks, friseurs, players and prostitutes, were chased from the town to follow their pampered masters to Eisenach." (*Frederick the Great: His Court and Times*, edited by Thomas Campbell, vol. III, p. 109. See also *Histoire Critique et Militaire des Guerres de Frédéric, II*, Lieutenant-General Jomini (1818), vol. I, p. 198.

On his return, Frederick rejoined Keith, and so brought his army up to about 22,000, and when he learnt this Soubise fell back to the Saale. Frederick left Leipzig on October 30, entered Weissenfels the following day, and instantly attacked the French outposts, but found the bridge broken. Keith also found the bridges at Merseburg and Halle destroyed. Although Frederick's position was now dangerous, Soubise foolishly abandoned the Saale, and fell back to Mücheln. Frederick repaired the three bridges, crossed the river on November 3, and encamped at Braunsdorf, near Mücheln. He at once advanced 1,500 cavalry under Seydlitz, raided his enemy's camp, and decided to attack it in force on the following day. But this surprise raid persuaded Soubise to move during the night to a securer position, and as Frederick found it too strong to attack, on November 4 he moved his camp to Rossbach.

Soubise's timidity had much exasperated his officers, among whom was Pierre de Bourcet, who had gained great fame in the campaigns of 1744-1747 in the Cottian and Maritime Alps. He realized that Frederick's position was precarious and suggested to Soubise that he should swing round Frederick's left flank and cut his line of retreat. Further, as Lloyd points out, because Soubise and Hildburghausen outnumbered Frederick by nearly two to one,[1] they were so elated "that they resolved to attack him the next morning, and so finish the campaign; the fatigues of which their troops seemed no longer able or willing to endure."[2]

Once decided upon, no preparations for Bourcet's manœuvre were put in hand until the morning of November 5, when, with some of the allied troops out foraging, Soubise received the following message from Hildburghausen: "Not a moment is to be lost in attacking the enemy. From his manœuvre of yesterday it is obvious that he will not attack us, but instead is more likely to cut our communications with Freibourg. Therefore I am of opinion we should advance, gain the heights of Schevenroda and attack him from that side."[3] Not till then did Soubise make ready.

The field upon which the battle was about to be fought was

---

[1] Tempelhoff gives Frederick's strength at 24,360: infantry 18,800; cavalry 5,160; and artillery 400. (*The History of the Seven Years' War in Germany by Generals Lloyd and Tempelhoff* (1783), vol. i, p. 265.)

[2] *The History of the Late War in Germany, etc.*, Major-General Lloyd (1781), Part I, p. 95.

[3] Quoted from *La Guerre de Sept Ans*, Richard Waddington (1899), vol. i, p. 618.

a wide open plain destitute of trees and hedges, with the village of Rossbach on a low eminence from which the allied camp could be seen clearly. Between Rossbach and Merseburg ran a small stream, south of which gently rose the Janus and Pölzen Hills, which Carlyle describes as "sensible to waggon-horses in those bad loose tracks of sandy mud, but unimpressive on the Tourist, who has to admit that there seldom was so flat a hill."[1] To the south of the plain flowed the Saale and the small town of Weissenfels lay a few miles distant and south-east of Rossbach.

When he received Hildburghausen's message, Soubise sent out a body of French cavalry, under the Count of St. Germain, to Gröst, three miles west of Rossbach, to observe the enemy's camp and also to protect the left flank of the manœuvre. Soubise ordered his camp to be struck at 11 a.m. and moved off in three columns. The advanced guard was of Austrian and Imperial cavalry, followed by French and Imperial infantry, with the French horse in rear. At Pettstädt the advanced guard halted and was joined by the French horse, and after a conference of generals the advance was continued and a half-left wheel made in the direction of Reichartswerben. The march was exceedingly slow and "*tout ce qu'ils avaient de musiciens et de trompettes faisaient des fanfares; leurs tambours et leurs fifres faisaient des rejouissances, comme s'ils avaient gagné une victoire*".[2]

These various movements were watched closely by Frederick. He posted on the roof of the Herrenhaus at Rossbach an officer, Captain Gaudi, and sent out patrols, several of which penetrated the abandoned French camp and learned from the peasants that Soubise had taken the Weissenfels Road. Yet he was not certain whether his enemy was making for Freiburg, because he was short of supplies; or for Weissenfels, which was not likely, because the bridge there was still broken; or for Merseburg, in order to cut him off from the Saale.

When the king was at dinner, at two o'clock Gaudi rushed into the room and reported that the enemy had reached Pettstädt and was wheeling toward the Prussian left. Frederick mounted to the roof, from where a moment's gaze revealed to him his enemy's intention to attack him in flank and rear and drive him away from his communications. At 2.30 p.m. he issued his orders, which were so rapidly carried out that a French officer declared

---

[1] *History of Frederick II of Prussia*, Thomas Carlyle (1888 edit.), vol. VII, p. 333.
[2] *Oeuvres de Frédéric le Grand* (1847), vol. IV, p. 151.

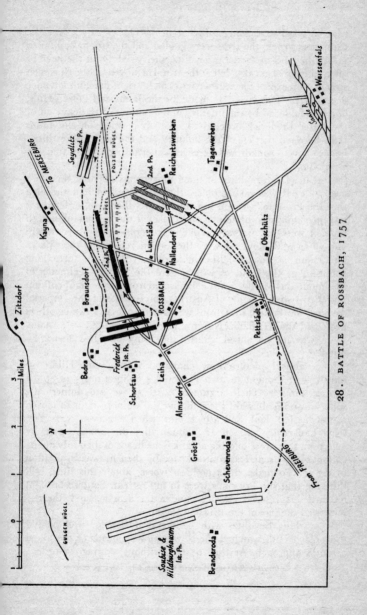

28. BATTLE OF ROSSBACH, 1757

567

that "it was like a change of scene in the Opéra". By 3 p.m. the camp was struck, the tents were loaded and the troops had fallen in. As they did so, General Seydlitz, then aged 33, at the head of 38 squadrons of cavalry, left at the trot. He moved up the Rossbach stream, and except for a few vedettes on his right flank his advance was covered from view. He made for the Janus and Pölzen Hills, and was followed by the infantry and a battery of 18 heavy guns; the latter Frederick ordered to take up position on the Janus Hill, between the left of the infantry and the right of Seydlitz's horse. Seven squadrons were left at Rossbach to watch St. Germain.

Instead of the rapidity of these movements opening Soubise's eyes to what was taking place, they conveyed to him the idea that the Prussians were in full retreat. He, therefore, ordered his advanced guard to hasten on and make for the Janus Hill, and so hurried were his orders that no instructions were issued where and when to deploy, nor were the soldiers relieved of their packs and camp kettles. So "the infantry moved off in three long columns, at the head of which were the French regiments of Piedmont and Mailly. On the flanks and front of the right column marched two regiments of Austrian cuirassiers and the Imperial cavalry; ten French squadrons were in reserve, and twelve others protected the left flank. No ground reconnaissances were made, there was no advanced guard; the army marched forward–blind".[1]

The tactical picture now changes: Soubise and Hildburg-hausen had thought to turn Frederick's oblique order of attack against himself. Their argument was: as we are numerically superior and he has lost the initiative, all we need do is to march round his left flank and attack him, when victory is ours. Yet, what had really happened? Though they did not grasp it, by 3.30 p.m. they were offering a flank—the heads of their advancing columns—to Frederick to attack; for by then he was in position to do so. To make their position worse, about this time, still thinking that the Prussians were in full retreat, Soubise brought forward his reserve cavalry, under de Broglie, and thereby increased the size of the Prussian target.

Meanwhile, Seydlitz, with his 4,000 horsemen, well behind the Pölzen Hill, watched the slowly moving heads of the allied columns approach. As they neared, without waiting for orders,

---

[1] *La Guerre de Sept Ans*, Richard Waddington, vol. I, p. 622.

he led his men forward at the trot. A few minutes later he cantered into sight, and as signal for the attack he flung his tobacco-pipe into the air. "Then," says M. de Castries, a French cavalry officer, "barely had we formed up, when the whole of the Prussian cavalry advanced compact like a wall and at an incredible speed. With its right it attacked the Austrian cavalry, which was in column and was unable to place in battle more than three or four squadrons. With its left it charged us."[1] In a blaze of rapid steel four times the Prussian horsemen cut their way through the undeployed mass, and drove their enemy in rout toward Freiburg. At length, Seydlitz steadied his men and re-formed them in the dip of Tagewerben.

When this action was fought, the battery on the Janus Hill opened on the allied infantry, still in columns of route, and, under cover of its fire, Prince Henry of Prussia advanced seven infantry battalions[2] at the double to support the cavalry by an attack on the leading enemy regiments. His attack proved decisive, for in the words of a Württemberg dragoon: "The artillery tore down whole ranks of us; the Prussian musketry did terrible execution."[3] Thrown back in confusion on their supporting battalions, the allied infantry found it impossible to deploy; when Seydlitz seized the opportunity, advanced from the Tagewerben hollow and burst "terribly compact and furious" upon their rear and drove them in rout across the field. Of the part played by the Prussian artillery, Decker writes: "we may say, with all assurance, that the success of the day belonged to the Artillery. If, as at Kolin, it had remained inactive, the enemy's infantry could have formed and advanced; its defeat would not have been so complete, and the success of the cavalry would have been less brilliant."[4]

At 4.30 p.m. the action was decided. Frederick's right was then at Lundstädt, and his left, at Reichartswerben, was "advancing with cannon in the van on the turmoil into which the combined army had been reduced".[5] The retreat became a rout, and "the country for forty miles round", writes St. Germain, "was covered with our soldiers: they plundered, murdered, violated women,

---

[1] Quoted from Waddington, vol. I, p. 623.
[2] These were the sole Prussian battalions used during the entire battle. See: *Oeuvres de Frédéric le Grand*, vol. I, p. 154.
[3] *Frederick the Great*, Colonel C. B. Brakenbury (1884), p. 171.
[4] *Ibid.*, p. 173, quoting Decker's *Seven Years' War* (French Edition, 1839), p. 115.
[5] *La Guerre de Sept Ans*, Richard Waddington, vol. I, p. 626.

robbed and committed all possible abominations".[1] The truth is that throughout the campaign the French showed a grievous lack of discipline; and though there was no pursuit, not only because night was approaching, but because Frederick had to hasten to Silesia, this lack of discipline submerged the French and Imperialists and reduced them to panic-stricken rabble.

The Prussian losses were 165 killed and 376 wounded, but those of the allies were 3,000 killed and wounded, 5,000 prisoners, including eight generals and 300 officers, 67 cannon, seven pairs of colours, 15 standards, and much baggage.

Politically, few battles have led to greater consequences. For well over 100 years, ever since Cardinal Richelieu embroiled France in the Thirty Years War, eastwardly expansion into Germany had been the French aim. Time and again had the Palatinate been invaded, pillaged and burnt, and, like a phoenix from out of its ashes, had emerged the spirit of German nationalism, which found its focal point in the person of Frederick on the field of Rossbach.

Though Europe could not foresee the future that Rossbach held in store, all European nations were suddenly brought to realize that the French army was rotten to the core; that its invincibility was a myth and its grandeur—tinsel. "No battle, during the whole course of the war," writes General Tempelhoff, "caused such a particular impression as that of Rossbach. Friends and foes laughed at the Generals of the combined armies," and they laughed still more heartily, when shortly after his defeat Soubise was made a Marshal of France by Louis XV.[2]

When the news of Frederick's victory was received in England, bonfires were set ablaze throughout the land, and Parliament, which in 1757 had reluctantly voted Frederick £164,000, in 1758 granted him £1,200,000, which in terms of money is evidence of what the English thought. Nevertheless, the immediate consequences of the battle were restricted, for with the rout of Soubise and Hildburghausen, Frederick's task was but half accomplished, and the situation in Silesia was critical in the extreme.

After a week's pause to refit his army, on November 13, with 13,000 men, Frederick marched from Leipzig and arrived at Parchwitz, 170 miles distant, on November 28. Meanwhile, on

[1] Quoted from *Frederick the Great: His Court and Times*, Thomas Campbell, vol. III, p. 122.
[2] *The History of the Seven Years' War in Germany*, Generals Lloyd and Tempelhoff, vol. I, p. 271.

November 14, Schweidnitz had capitulated to the Austrians, and, on November 22, Bevern had been defeated at Breslau and had abandoned the town. At Parchwitz, Frederick put General Ziethen in command of Bevern's beaten army and ordered a concentration on Parchwitz for December 3. On the same day Frederick advanced on Neumarkt, and captured it by a light cavalry *coup de main*. At Neumarkt, he obtained positive information that Prince Charles and Marshal Daun had left their camp at Lohe and had advanced to Lissa, where their right rested on the village of Nippern and their left on that of Sagschütz. Frederick's rapid advance had surprised them, for they had considered that after Rossbach he would go into winter quarters.

On December 4, their heavy guns left at Breslau, Charles and Daun hurriedly crossed the Schweidnitz stream and took up a position on the west of that river. Their army consisted of 84 battalions, 144 squadrons, and 210 guns; in all between 60,000 to 80,000 men drawn up in two lines. Its right, under Lucchessi, was covered by the bogs of Nippern; its centre was at Leuthen; and its left, under Nadasti, behind Sagschütz, thrown back *en potence* and protected by abattis. The right wing cavalry was at Guckerwitz and the left at Leuthen. Defensively the position was strong, though over-extended, for from flank to flank it measured five and a half miles. To this formidable array Frederick could only oppose 36,000 men; 24,000 infantry in 48 battalions and 12,000 cavalry in 128 squadrons. He had with him 167 guns, of which 61 were heavy and 10 super-heavy pieces. The field of battle was open plain land, over which Frederick had manœuvred during peace time, therefore he knew it well.

On December 5, at 5 a.m. the Prussian army advanced from Neumarkt, with Frederick in the van. About halfway between that town and Leuthen he halted the army, assembled his generals by a birch tree and gave out his orders. "I should think that I had done nothing", he said, "if I were to leave the Austrians in possession of Silesia. Let me then apprise you that I shall attack, against all the rules of the art, the army of Prince Charles, nearly thrice as strong as our own, wherever I find it. . . . I must venture upon this step, or all is lost: we must beat the enemy, or all perish before his batteries. So I think—so will I act. . . . Now go . . . and repeat to the regiments what I have said to you."[1]

[1] *Frederick the Great his Court and Times*, edited by Thomas Campbell, vol. III, pp. 134–136

Frederick's plan was to advance straight up the Breslau road, to feint at the Austrian right, and then to take advantage of his enemy's extended position, march across his front, attack his left flank and drive him off his communications. In his own words, he resolved "to place his whole army on the left flank of the Imperialists, to strike the hardest with his right and to refuse his left, with such precautions that there should be no fear of mistakes like those which had been made in the battle of Prague, and which had caused the loss of that of Kolin."[1]

After his troops had rested, Frederick ordered the advance to continue direct on to the village of Borne. The advanced guard consisted of 10 battalions and 60 squadrons—Frederick in the van—and the main body followed in four columns with regimental bands playing. As the men began to sing the hymn—

> Grant that I do whate'er I ought to do,
>   What for my station is by Thee decreed;
> And cheerfully and promptly do it too,
>   And when I do it, grant that it succeed!

an officer asked the King whether he should stop them. Frederick replied: "Not on any account, with such men God will certainly give me the victory to-day."[2]

At Borne, contact was made with the enemy. Dawn was breaking and a haze covered the ground. Through it a long line of cavalry was seen stretched across the high road, its left disappearing in the mist. At first it was thought to be the Austrian right wing; but to make certain, it was charged in front and flank, when it was discovered to be General Nostitz and five regiments. They were at once scattered and 800 were taken prisoners[3] including Nostitz, who was mortally wounded. Next a halt was made, and shortly after the mist cleared and the whole Austrian army was seen stretched from Nippern to Sagschütz, so distinctly "that one could have counted it man by man".[4]

The loss of the village of Borne was an important factor in the Austrian defeat, not only because Frederick could examine the whole of his enemy's dispositions from it, but also because a rise in the ground hid from view the Prussians who advanced

---

[1] *Oeuvres Posthumes de Frédéric II* (1788), vol. III, p. 238.
[2] *Frederick the Great his Court and Times*, edited by Thomas Campbell vol. III, p. 138. See also Thomas Carlyle, *History of Frederick the Great.*
[3] *Oeuvres Posthumes de Frédéric II*, vol. III, pp. 235–236.
[4] *Ibid.*, p. 236.

toward Borne in four columns. As they approached, Frederick sent forward his advanced guard cavalry in pursuit of Nostitz, that is, toward the Austrian right wing, commanded by Count Lucchessi, who watched their advance, imagined that he was about to be attacked in force, and called for aid so urgently that Marshal Daun sent to his support the reserve cavalry and part of the cavalry of the left wing. While this took place, the four Prussian columns were formed into two, and when they reached Borne they were wheeled to the right under cover of the rise, and advanced southward. Tempelhoff writes: "It was impossible to witness a more beautiful sight; all the heads of the columns were parallel to each other, and in exact distances to form line, and the divisions marched with such precision, that they seemed to be at a review, ready to wheel into line in a moment."[1] The order of march was as follows: Right wing in advance, Ziethen with 43 squadrons and six battalions under Prince Maurice of Dessau, preceded by an advanced guard of three battalions under General Wedel. The left wing, following under General Retzow, consisted of the rest of the infantry, flanked by 40 squadrons under General Driesen. Each body of cavalry was supported by 10 squadrons of hussars, and the rearguard, under Prince Eugene of Würtemberg, consisted of 25 squadrons.

As Frederick's army vanished from sight, Prince Charles and Marshal Daun, who were standing on the mill of Frobelwitz, imagined that it was in full retreat. "The Prussians are off," said the latter, "don't disturb them!" Then a little after noon their head was seen advancing between Lobetinz and Sagschütz, from where it threatened the Austrian weakened left wing.

Suddenly confronted by an overwhelmingly superior force, Nadasti sent galloper after galloper to Charles for reinforcements. But it was too late; at about 1 p.m., Wedel, supported by a battery of six guns and followed by Prince Maurice, advanced and stormed the defences of Sagschütz; and at the same time Nadasti charged Ziethen's leading squadrons and drove them southward upon the six supporting battalions, and while their fire held back the Austrian horse, Ziethen disentangled his men from the difficult ground, turned about, charged Nadasti and drove him and his men into the Rathener Wood.

By 1.30 Nadasti's wing was routed, and the entire field between

[1] *The History of the Seven Years' War in Germany*, Generals Lloyd and Tempelhoff, vol. 1, p. 341.

Sagschütz and Leuthen covered with fugitives pursued by the
Prussian hussars, behind whom the infantry advanced in double
line. On the right was Wedel, in the centre Maurice, and on the
left Retzow, the whole supported by the heavy artillery, which
took the flying Austrians in enfilade.

While this advance was made, Charles, taken by surprise,

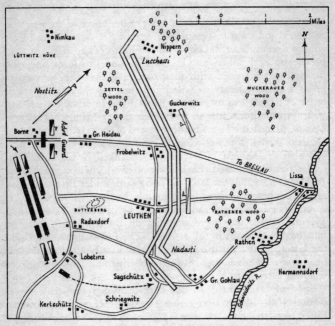

29. BATTLE OF LEUTHEN, 1757

hastily recalled the cavalry which had reinforced Lucchessi, and
while awaiting its arrival, sent forward his infantry piecemeal.
Nevertheless, though Leuthen was weakly garrisoned, a determined stand was made there, in part thus described by the
Prince de Ligne, then a captain in an Austrian regiment of foot:

"We ran what we could run. Our Lieutenant-Colonel fell
killed almost at the first; beyond this we lost our Major, and indeed
all the Officers but three. . . . We had crossed two successive

ditches, which lay in an orchard to the left of the first houses in Leuthen; and were beginning to form in front of the village. But there was no standing of it. Besides a general cannonade such as can hardly be imagined, there was a rain of case-shot upon this Battalion, of which I, as there was no Colonel left, had to take command. . . . Two officers of the Grenadiers brought me what they still had. Some Hungarians, too, were luckily got together. But at last, as, with all helps and the remnants of my own brave Battalion, I had come down to at most 200, I drew back to the Height where the Windmill is."[1]

The overcrowding in Leuthen was as bad as it had been in Blenheim; so jammed together were the troops that in places they stood 30 to 100 ranks deep. Nevertheless, as Tempelhoff writes, "A murderous conflict ensued; the enemy made the resistance of despair; one battalion followed upon another against it without success, till the King was obliged to bring his left wing, which, according to his orders, had kept out of musket-shot, into action. At length the guards, led by their senior Captain, now General Möllendorf, pushed forward with irresistible valour, and after a further resistance of half an hour, forced the enemy to abandon his post."[2]

The problem now was how to debouch from the village, for the Austrians had advanced a battery on to the ridge north of it, under the fire of which their infantry deployed at right angles to their original front. To do so, Frederick ordered the remainder of his left wing to advance; but, as it was driven back by the fire of these guns, he established a battery, including his super-heavy cannon, on the Butterberg and swept the Austrians back. In his *Memoirs*, Horace St. Paul says that it was this formidable artillery, more so than the Prussian infantry, which won the battle.[3]

It was four o'clock when the Austrians were swept back, and as twilight fell Lucchessi, who had assembled the Austrian right wing cavalry at Frobelwitz, saw Retzow's infantry held up and moved forward to charge them in flank. Unfortunately for Lucchessi, behind the village of Radaxdorf Driesen's 40 squadrons were hidden from his sight. Suddenly, under cover of the Butter-

---

[1] Quoted from Carlyle's *Frederick the Great*, Book XVIII, chap. x.
[2] *The History of the Seven Years' War in Germany*, Generals Lloyd and Tempelhoff, vol. I, p. 343.
[3] *A Journal of the First Two Campaigns of the Seven Years' War*, Horace St. Paul (1914), p. 394.

berg battery, they rode into the open, and while 30 squadrons charged Lucchessi in front, the Bayreuth Dragoons struck him in flank and the Puttkammer Hussars galloped round his rear. The result was decisive, Lucchessi was killed and his troopers scattered. Next, Driesen wheeled to his right and charged the Austrian infantry in rear, while Wedel attacked them in flank from near Leuthen. As night closed in the Austrians broke and their retreat rapidly became a *sauve qui peut*.

Frederick followed up the rout and pushed on to Lissa. There he found the small town crowded with fugitives, and as he rode into the courtyard of the château he was met by several Austrian officers with candles in their hands. He dismounted and turned to them and said: "Good evening, Gentlemen, I dare say you did not expect me here. Can one get a night's lodging along with you?"[1]

On December 6 he ordered a day of rest, and the following day advanced on Breslau, sending Ziethen and half the cavalry with nine battalions and the light troops in pursuit of Charles. They followed him until December 9, and captured more than 2,000 prisoners. Breslau surrendered on December 19 with 17,000 men and 81 guns.

As with nearly all battles, the losses at Leuthen are variously given, but probably the Prussians lost 6,000 men killed and wounded, and the Austrians 10,000 as well as 21,000 prisoners, 116 guns, 51 colours, and some 4,000 wagons. According to the *Oeuvres de Frédéric* their total losses during the campaign were 41,442 men, and according to Tempelhoff, 56,446. In either case the loss was annihilating, and not only was the whole of Silesia, except for the fortress of Schweidnitz, rewon, but Prussia emerged as the most formidable military power in Europe. Of the battle Tempelhoff writes:—

"Ancient history scarcely furnishes a single instance, and modern times none, that can be compared, either in the execution or consequences, with the battle of Leuthen. It forms an epoch in military science, and exhibits not only the theory, but also the practice of a system of which the King was the sole inventor."[2]

Napoleon writes:—

"The battle of Leuthen is a masterpiece of movements, manœuvres, and resolution. Alone it is sufficient to immortalize

[1] *Frederick the Great his Court and Times*, edited by Thomas Campbell, vol. III, p. 149.
[2] *The History of the Seven Years' War in Germany*, Generals Lloyd and Templehoff, vol. I, p. 346.

Frederick, and place him in the rank of the greatest generals. All his manœuvres at this battle are in conformity with the principles of war. He made no flank march in sight of his enemy, for his columns were not in sight. The Austrians expected him, after the combat at Borne, to take position on the heights in front of them, and while they thus waited for him, covered by rising grounds and fogs, and masked by his advanced guard, he continued his march and attacked the extreme left.''[1]

It is of interest to compare the two battles which have been discussed in this chapter, for they represent the oblique order of attack at its worst and at its best. At Rossbach there was no generalship; the combined commanders had no plan, and instead of holding the line of the Saale and continuing on the defensive, which must have ended in Frederick's ruin, they abandoned it and did exactly what he wanted – offered him battle. They were novices at manœuvre, and mere copyists of a system they did not understand. They advanced in full sight of their enemy, across his flank and without an advanced guard; there was no co-operation between the three arms, and St. Germain never tried to discover what his enemy was doing. At Leuthen, Frederick moved, concentrated, surprised and hit. Co-operation was perfect, and so were the dispositions of the three arms. Nevertheless, above all, what gave Frederick the victory was that his men had confidence in him as a general.

Though after this superb victory the war continued for five years, in spite of the disasters Frederick suffered during them he emerged from the seven-year conflict the greatest general of his age, to take his place among the few Great Captains of all ages. In 1758, on August 25, he overthrew the Russians at Zorndorf, but on October 14, was surprised and defeated by the Austrians at Hochkirchen; nevertheless, he drove them out of Saxony and Silesia. The following year, on August 12, he suffered an overwhelming defeat at the hands of the Russians at Kunersdorf, and though Berlin was occupied by them, he held back the French. In 1760, undefeatable as he always was in spirit, on August 15, he beat the Austrians at Liegnitz, and, again, on November 3, at Torgau.[2] In 1761 misfortune returned, and in

[1] *Correspondance de Napoléon 1er*, vol. xxxii, p. 184.
[2] In estimating Frederick's generalship in these battles, it should always be remembered that numerically he was vastly inferior to his opponent. At Zorndorf, 36,000 to 52,000; at Hochkirchen, 37,000 to 90,000; at Kunersdorf, 26,000 to 70,000; at Liegnitz, 30,000 to 90,000; and at Torgau, 44,000 to 65,000.

1762 England abandoned him and sought a separate peace with France, a defection which 13 years later left England unable to find a single ally in Europe when her American Colonies rebelled. This in itself, though a momentous result of the war, cannot be credited to Frederick.

But what can be is that, not only did the battles of Rossbach and Leuthen in all probability save Prussia from extinction, but that the memories of them have ever since they were fought dominated German history and through history the German mind. Out of them arose that sense of national unity and superiority which enabled the German peoples to survive the Napoleonic Wars, and out of that, step by step, emerged a united Germany which replaced France as the most formidable continental power, terminated the Anglo-French rivalry of 600 years, and thereby opened a new epoch in world history.